CONTEMPORARY NEW TESTAMENT STUDIES

# CONTEMPORARY
# NEW TESTAMENT STUDIES

*Edited by*

SISTER M. ROSALIE RYAN, C.S.J.

**THE LITURGICAL PRESS**
COLLEGEVILLE, MINNESOTA

*Nihil obstat*: John Eidenschink, O.S.B., J.C.D., *Censor deputatus. Imprimatur*:
✠ Peter W. Bartholome, D.D., Bishop of St. Cloud. July 31, 1965.
Copyright 1965 *by* The Order of St. Benedict, Inc., Collegeville, Minnesota.
Printed by the North Central Publishing Company, St. Paul, Minnesota.

## DEDICATION

To Mary, Mother of Wisdom,
who "kept all these things, pondering them in her heart"
Luke 2:19

# FOREWORD

Periods of transition may be stimulating, but they produce their own brand of difficulties. An obvious one is the need to be conversant in so many areas. Despite the variety of the fields in which activity is going on, they are so organically connected that the one who wishes to practice his *aggiornamento* adequately must do so on a wide scale. The liturgist must be aware of what the biblicist is saying if he wishes to continue making progress in his own field. The clergy and religious, too, can ill afford to neglect entirely any one field because of the role of leadership they are expected to play. Above all, the educated Christian layman, into whose hands is being committed ever greater responsibility, must see to the continued broadening of his education if his newly stressed mission is to be an effective one. All of these need to be eclectic in their reading. And they frequently need books like the present one where someone has already practiced their eclecticism for them. All they now need do is read.

Moreover, activity begets activity. Even in just one area alone it is almost impossible to be aware of all that is being done. No one is reminded more forcefully of this than the biblical student, for whom books are now being published at a pace that will surely cause future generations to dub this, "the age that found the Bible." The greatly increased number of publications will, of course, contribute to compounding the increase in future years by stimulating further study. And again, the answer is not the throwing up of hands but the editing of more books like the present.

One more difficulty we mention here is the new terminology. Complaints are heard at times that expressions are being used for the sake of novelty, or as a status symbol, but that no one seems to know what they really mean. It is difficult for the biblical scholar to imagine that this last complaint could be made by anyone who has done any serious reading. For him, terms like *kerygma, parousia*, witness, mission and so on have such rich biblical connotations that no other words can do the same job. Why not enrich our vocabulary with them? We deplore the looseness with which some have used this new terminology or the false reasons that may have motivated them, but let's not cut off the head to cure the headache. Also, in an age when greater stress is being placed on personalism and existentialism (both rightly understood, of course) there is bound to be an increase in terms that express more clearly these elements, words like "encounter" instead of "meeting," "dialogue" instead of "conversation," "meaningful" instead of "significant." There no doubt will always be those who challenge the changes and opt for the old instead of the new. Can you imagine the challenge when "transubstantiation" was introduced into the ecclesiastical language? The challenge is welcome; it cautions the innovator against an unbridled innovation.

What has this to do with the foreword to this book? At least this much, that a good deal of the change in terminology was sparked by the biblical revival. It is there that the words we mentioned above, like *kerygma* and witness, found their first expression. A greater acquaintance, therefore, with the kind of biblical studies that Sister M. Rosalie Ryan has gathered here will show the depth of study which has gone into the biblical movement. Those who would like to see some of its high points will find an opportunity here. Those who challenge the worth of the biblical movement may read and be converted. But let's not convert all of them too quickly. We still need the challenge!

                                                            Eugene H. Maly

Mount Saint Mary's of the West
Norwood, Ohio

# PREFACE

The purpose of this collection of essays is to bring together significant recent articles which reflect current trends in New Testament studies. Since the collection is intended for the adult non-specialist, some of the more technical problems — such as the synoptic problem, "demythologizing," the "sensus plenior," and similar aspects — have not been stressed, but important formative influences, such as those coming from the Essenes, from the primitive Christian communities and from oral tradition have been included.

In such a selection it is difficult, if not impossible, to bridge the difference in level between some important, but very scholarly, studies and others of a general nature. Examples of both kinds are included so that the various types of research which are going on may be represented. Since the collection is directed especially to the general reader — to individuals and study groups, college and university students — the articles have been arranged under the heading of the chief books of the New Testament, rather than by topics. Necessarily there is some overlapping where an article treats of more than one New Testament book, but each article has been placed where its main emphasis seemed to lie.

It is the hope of the editor that the present collection may assist the reader who would like to reap the benefit of contemporary New Testament scholarship in order to know and meditate more fruitfully on the sacred pages and draw closer to Christ, the source of salvation. Pius XII requested in *Divino Afflante Spiritu*, "that today, as in the past, the Church may have at her disposal learned doctors for the expounding of Divine Letters; and through their assiduous labors, the faithful may comprehend all the splendor, stimulating language and joy contained in the Holy Scriptures" (#61). In these articles, chosen from the many available, we see that his desire has been richly fulfilled.

It is my great pleasure to acknowledge the assistance and encouragement which many people have given to this project — first of all to the authors and publishers who allowed copyright materials to be reprinted, especially to those publishers who did not charge a royalty. Without their generosity this collection could never have been made.

I owe a great debt also to the sisters and superiors of the College of St. Catherine, and especially to the librarians for their indefatigable labors; to Monsignor Thomas J. Shanahan of the St. Paul Seminary; to Mr. Alfred Muellerleile of the North Central Publishing Company; and especially to Sister Richardine, C.S.J., my generous and enthusiastic assistant. To all of these and to many unnamed helpers, I am very grateful.

Sister M. Rosalie Ryan, C.S.J.
The College of Saint Catherine

# CONTENTS

# ABBREVIATIONS

| | |
|---|---|
| A A S | *Acta Apostolicae Sedis* |
| B Z | *Biblische Zeitschrift* |
| C B Q | *The Catholic Biblical Quarterly* |
| E B | *Enchiridion Biblicum* |
| J T S | *Journal of Theological Studies* |
| N R T | *Nouvelle Revue Theologique* |
| P G | *Patrologia Graeca* (Migne) |
| P L | *Patrologia Latina* (Migne) |
| R B | *Revue Biblique* |
| R H PHIL REL | *Revue d'Hist. et de Phil. Religieuses* |
| R S R | *Revue des Sciences Religieuses* |
| Th W N T | *Theologisches Wörterbuch zum N.T.* |
| Z K T | *Zeitschrift für Katolische Theologie* |

CONTEMPORARY NEW TESTAMENT STUDIES

# 1 THE STUDY OF HOLY SCRIPTURE

The flowering of Biblical study in the last twenty-five years is a phenomenon so striking and so widespread that it can only be regarded as a mark of the Holy Spirit's guidance of the Church. Aided by the painstaking efforts of archaeologists, specialists in ancient languages, historians, and many other scientific workers, the Biblical exegete today has at hand a wealth of factual knowledge about the ancient Near East and a knowledge of Semitic literary modes and ways of thought, which were never available before.

Although Biblical studies have been at times conducted by rationalistic critics, whose faulty premises have vitiated the results of their scholarship, other scholars, guided by sound principles of reason and by many insights from the learned and wise men of past centuries as well as the tradition of the Church, have prudently examined the results of many types of scholarship and have conducted their own research. In this way the findings of scientists have been focused on a better understanding and interpretation of Holy Scripture.

The problem of making the findings of scholars available to educated adults who are not Scripture specialists is not a small one. Fortunately Biblical scholars have begun to write books and to publish for non-specialists in periodicals such as The Bible Today, The Biblical Archaeologist, Current Scripture Notes, Worship and others. The eagerness of Christians everywhere for a better understanding of the new Biblical scholarship and what it has to tell them about the word of God is shown by the unceasing stream of Biblical works which are coming each day from the presses.

3

The study of Holy Scripture is scientific, historical and theological, but it is also the source of prayerful meditation and spiritual nourishment. The articles of this section give some indication of how a knowledge of scientific scholarship, under the guidance of the Holy Spirit in the Church, can lead to a more fruitful participation in the liturgy and to a renewal of Christian living.

# BREAD FOR THE FAITHFUL

R. A. F. Mackenzie, S.J.

The great development and flowering of theology which exists in the Church today, so far has been seeping down only in trickles from the higher levels of the dogmatic theologian, professional liturgist, and so on. However, in view of the great importance it has, the possibilities that it opens up for catechetical work at all levels, it is by all means desirable that we should hasten the diffusion of modern twentieth-century theological knowledge to all the faithful in the Church. This bread should be broken for the little ones, and in those "little ones" we can include all those who come to us to acquire an education in Catholic schools.

My purpose here will not be to draw pedagogical conclusions. Remaining rather in my own particular field, I will attempt to give some survey of the situation in Scripture studies as they exist at present in the Catholic Church. Many of you are aware that there is here a very great treasure of truth and insight which needs to be more widespread and more generally communicated. Much of what I will say will not be new to many of you; but putting it together and presenting it on one occasion in a general survey may provide a useful basis for more detailed discussion and application.

I will divide my matter under three headings, three general aspects of Scripture studies. The first one will be the *background of the Bible*, the greatly improved knowledge that we have nowadays of the civilization, the culture, the general human condition against which the books of the Bible must be situated. The second topic is the literary aspect, or, let us say, the *improved literary understanding* of the formation of the books of the Bible — the much better insight we have today into the process by which these books were actually written by human authors. The third topic is that to which the other two are meant to lead, and to which in fact they have led; it is the product of those two factors. I mean our advance in *religious understanding of the Bible*, both Old and New Testaments. We can now have a certain grasp of the message of the two Testaments such as was, humanly speaking, not really possible a hundred years ago. Actually, it was not really prevalent even twenty years ago. This deeper religious understanding has developed, somewhat paradoxically, from our deeper penetration into the human background and human origins of the Bible.

## Background of the Bible

Let us begin, then, with our concrete knowledge of the background of the Bible. A hundred years ago, if a Bible history had to be written, especially in the sense of a history of the Old Testament, it was quite narrowly limited

Published originally in *Perspectives*, 5 (1959), 4-11. Reprinted by permission of the publisher.

to interpretation of the data provided by the sacred books themselves. There was scarcely anything in the way of comparison, of outside checking, of other sources of information, by which the process of the history of the people of Israel could be situated against a larger background. Certainly, it was located against the general history of humanity in the period in which it took place. However, until one came down to the history of Greece, let us say, beginning about the sixth century, B.C., there was really very little comparative material against which to set off the historical narration of the Bible. Even the Greek, Hellenistic, or Roman background was in its details considerably less fully known that it is today.

A most noticeable contrast to this picture has developed in the past hundred years. We have now a quite detailed, satisfactorily full and clear history of the Near East in what archaeologists call the Middle and Late Bronze Ages and the Iron Age, roughly the second and first millennia B.C. It is this Near East that is the geographical theater of the history of Israel. We have a knowledge of the politics, of the successive reigns of kings, the campaigns, the wars, the rising of one nation and the fall of another, comparable to our knowledge, let us say, of sections of European history in the Christian era. The history of the Dark Ages in Europe, sixth to tenth centuries A.D., is not much better known to us than is the history of the Assyrian kingdom in the tenth to seventh centuries B.C. That makes for a vastly improved concretization of our knowledge of the history of Israel.

As a result, the picture presented in the book of Exodus, or in the books of Kings, is no longer a sort of fairy-book picture of events taking place in a "never-never land," something outside of the world of space and time which we know, but something that we can pin down and insert and locate accurately and satisfactorily on a broader canvas, against the broader picture of human development and human history. Immediately, therefore, we have a better contact with, a sense of the immediacy of, sacred history itself.

Most of the increase of knowledge I am speaking of stems directly or indirectly from the science of archaeology, from the actual physical excavation of the remains of those ancient peoples, the careful uncovering of different strata on sites of ancient Eastern cities. It is revealed to us either immediately through the architecture, through the building plans, through the material remains found, or else mediately through the literature thus recovered. All this information about those ancient civilizations, from Egypt eastward through the land of Chanaan and Syria to the northern part of Mesopotamia, down through Mesopotamia itself to the eastern end of the Fertile Crescent, still in the East in Elam, on the north in Armenia, then westward through what is now Asia Minor, the Aegean area, and the western portions of the Mediterranean basin — all this information has been gathered by archaeologists.

Patiently excavating many hundreds of sites, they have pieced together the evidence from these sites themselves, and by comparisons they have arrived at this enormous development of ancient history of which we have spoken. We know, for example, the development of the New Kingdom in Egypt, the glorious and high civilization of the Pharaohs; we know of the Hyksos invading

Egypt in the first half of the second millennium B.C., and the high international civilization that reigned in the Middle Bronze Age; and we know of the Hittite kingdom, totally unknown sixty years ago, ruling from the central area of what is now Turkey. We know of the kingdom of the Mitannians on the upper Euphrates in the fourteenth and thirteenth centuries B.C. We know also of the first dynasty of Babylon; and, coming down into the first millennium, the great and flourishing development of the Assyrian Empire, the first real world empire (as the world was then known); the break-up and collapse of that empire at the hands of the Medes and Persians, its disruption at the overwhelming advance of Alexander; the irruption of Greece into the world of the Near East, the Hellenistic Age marked by that tremendous flowering of Greek civilization throughout the countries bordering on the eastern Mediterranean. Then the steady penetration eastward of Rome, the power that enveloped the civil frontier province of Palestine, of Judea, and, through mismanagement and oppression, that led in the year 68 A.D. to the explosion which was the final Jewish revolt, terminating in the destruction of the nation with all its sacred places and Temple in the year 70.

All that history gives us a magnificent sweep and is in itself, of course, a very valuable and precious extension of human knowledge into the things of the past. However, from our present point of view, it is vastly more precious, because against that great sweep of international history we can now situate the development, the experiences, the travails, the reactions, the positive errors, the repeated falls and repeated returns to their God of the nation of Israel — a history in itself more appealing, more mysterious, more fascinating than the history of any of the other nations, and, to the eyes of faith, a marvelous example of the patient education by God of His chosen human creatures. The experience of Israel, of which I will speak, is the experience of all of us in a sense: there is a vocation; there is a response to the vocation; there is infidelity; and there are repeated calls by God; and, let us hope, in the case of Israel, as in our individual cases, there is a happy ending, a final reconciliation and final rejoicing.

We can fill out that outline of history now because of our better knowledge of the *thought-world* that went with it. By that I mean the ideas, the culture, the outlook on life, the customs and conventions, all the group psychology of those mysterious peoples, both Semitic and non-Semitic, who inhabited those lands and who experienced that tumultuous and complex history. Here we come still closer to the history of the people of God: the rest of the history of which we have spoken is only a background; the history of Babylon is not the history of Israel. But the thought-world of Babylon is in part the thought-world of Israel; and therefore it is of great importance to the student of the Old Testament who wishes to penetrate the ways of thinking, the presuppositions, the conventions of language, the things taken for granted by the chroniclers and prophets and wise men of Israel. To do this, he must understand them against the setting of the presuppositions, etc., of the wise men of Babylonia, of Syria, of Egypt, perhaps most of all of Chanaan.

Fortunately, as we said, archaeologists have uncovered not merely the physical remains, the artifacts, the construction of buildings, fortifications and weapons, and so on. They have rediscovered for us and deciphered the literatures of those peoples, the literature of ancient Egypt, the literature of Babylonia, the literature of Chanaan, a large representation of the literature of the Hittites, and many partial and fragmentary remains of other peoples like the Mitannians. All that is immensely precious because it gives a direct insight from contemporary documents into the way those people lived and thought and worked and conceived their world. Their myths, their accounts as to how the gods originated, how the gods worked, how the gods created this world, how the gods created man — all of these have a certain bearing on corresponding accounts in the Old Testament. Their technique of chronicle writing, their selectiveness, their organization of the records of their own past, have close connections with the oldest historical forms of writing in the Old Testament. Their omen literature, that is to say, their oracles given to guide men in their future behavior, lucky and unlucky days, lucky and unlucky behavior, how to ensnare the good will of their gods and how to avoid their curse, has certain parallels in the prophetic literature of Israel. More than that, there have been found, at Mari on the middle Euphrates, reports from soothsayers (dating from about the seventeenth century B.C.) which are strikingly similar in style to some of the oracles of the prophets of Israel. Later I will come to speak about the distinctive and unique marks of Israelite civilization, but right now I am emphasizing the resemblances. We see, for example, that the oracle style "Thus said Yahweh . . ." is not specific to Israel except for the name of the god for whom it is used. Again, the rituals, the liturgy, the cult, the organization of worship offered by these peoples to their gods are parallel to the ritual and cult of Israel, and in many cases they preceded the cult of Israel.

Much else could be added in connection with their law codes, the position of the king, their civilization, and so on. For the moment, let us speak only of the literary connections. A great deal of light has been shed, particularly on the forms of literature, by finding the origins of ancestors or parallels of Israelite forms in the early Near Eastern literature. More than that, more than just the literature, the religion itself of Israel is greatly illuminated by that Eastern background. In their worship of this strange, unique God who had called them through Moses, the Israelites spontaneously and naturally adopted the whole vocabulary, the whole complexus of rites, actions, and techniques by which the gods of that area and that age were worshipped. There is animal sacrifice; there is sacred dance and procession; there is the composition of sacred song, psalms of lament, of petition, of glorification, of expiation, of cursing, and so on. The concept of a special sacred place or of a temple is not something original with Israel; and, as we well know, the concept of priesthood was taken over from other peoples by Israel. One can go through most of the external forms of religion in Israel and show that they have analogues in those other religions; therefore there existed between Israel and those other religions a certain likeness of mentality. For that reason, we understand Israel better by seeing how those other peoples conceived their forms of worship, what they thought they accomplished by them, what they intended them to be.

Other points of similarity exist in the areas of sociology and law. There are parallels to the tribal system of Israel, this strange religious federation of originally separate tribes who were united simply by their service of one unique god, whose connection was primarily religious, whose social unity consisted precisely in meeting periodically at a given place of worship to renew collectively their allegiance to their god. The Israelite idea of family organization, the subordination of the individual to the head of the family, the real "survival" of the family head in his descendants — all these are part of the common thought-world of the Near East. Common to Israel and to her neighbors is the idea of salvation, what they expected from their god. The semi-nomadic condition of the people at the time of Moses, their gradual transition to sedentary living, the movement from simple encampment to village life and then to life in towns, the transition of a good portion of the people to commercial practice, to the middle-man status, instead of their previous life as simple herdsmen — this is all vividly reflected in the books of the Old Testament, in the images used, in the forms in which God presented Himself to the people, in their experiences; and all those factors are better understood by us in proportion as we understand the ancient Eastern sociology.

The position of the king in Israelite society as seen by the group of prophets around David is the foundation for the doctrine of royal messianism, which becomes so important in later Jewish thinking; and its importance extends into the New Testament, especially in St. John's Gospel, and has remained in the Church. The figure of the king behind this messianism depends ultimately upon the Near Eastern concept of the king as we find it in the second millennium B.C. We notice, in the Bible, how important it was for the Israelites of the eleventh century B.C. to have a king. The king was himself the representative of the whole people, in a sense so real that we can hardly grasp it. He summed up the people; what happened to him happened to them; bad luck befalling him, bad health, weakness, affected everyone else in the commonwealth. And if the king became incompetent and helpless in the performance of his duties he must be removed and another more effective substituted. It was not a matter of punishment or vengeance; it was simply a matter of public safety.

It was only after a period of struggle that the king took such a place of importance in Israel, because within the Israelite commonwealth the king could not be the religious figure he was in other countries. He was not provided for in the charter of Mosaic religion, and hence there is an ambiguous and two-sided attitude towards the kingship. The king was necessary, and yet he was an intruder; this was a problem that Israel never really solved. Eventually, the kingship was abandoned and Israel continued its life, but in the four centuries when the kingship was used by them it gave origin to that tremendous doctrine of messianism.

Just as comparative studies draw our attention to the importance attached to the figure of the king, so, too, they have highlighted the importance of the law. As we know, there were many ancient codes of law: the famous code of Hammurabi, the Assyrian code of the fourteenth century B.C., the laws of the Hittites, as well as the pre-Hammurabi codes. All of these throw light on the pride of the Israelites in the possession of their own code of laws. One of the greatest benefits that Yahweh had given the Israelites in their Exodus from Egypt and the revelation at Sinai was His granting to them a constitution of their own. He had created Israel, He had made them into a people, He had formed them into a united society, and to mark that action He had granted to them a code of laws. Law is not seen as something restrictive: it is a great boon, a blessing. Their law makes them grow up, permits them to hold up their heads among the other societies of the time.

Again, the fact and the idea of a covenant, so central to the Old Testament, are greatly clarified by recent investigations of Hittite covenant treaties. Even more than the idea of royalty, the idea of covenant is important as a theme in the Old Testament. Actually, it corresponds to the Church's doctrine of sanctifying grace, of supernatural love. It was under that formality that the special supernatural relationship of men to God was presented to this chosen people called out of Egypt: namely, an arbitrary, freely-chosen, freely-willed adoption of these people, a raising of them into a special friendship with God. Yet, the idea of covenant, chosen to embody the tremendous concept and truth of grace, was drawn from the sociological situation of the times, modeled upon the action of the Hittite kings, in particular, in making covenants with subordinate princes and with their vassals. Covenant was a freely-bestowed relationship that established a certain bond between the great king and his subordinates, a bond based upon his beneficence towards them. In gratitude for that, the subordinate is bound to be loyal always to the great king, never to deal with his enemies, never to rebel against him, to pay him regular tribute, and to acknowledge no other overlord. To match these fourteenth century treaties with the provisions of the Mosaic covenant which date from the thirteenth century, throws a great deal of light on the understanding the Israelites had of this latter.

## Literary origins of the Bible

My second main area of discussion is that of the literary origins, or rather the better understanding we now possess regarding the literary forms and the origins of the Old Testament books. If you are familiar with the encyclical *Divino Afflante Spiritu* of fifteen years ago (on the progress of biblical studies), you will know that one of the things stressed in that encyclical is the analysis of the literary forms of different sections of the Old and New Testaments. Such analysis, says the Pope equivalently, is the key to our correct understanding of what the human authors, and through them the divine author, are trying to say. The great advance of non-Catholic scholars and of Catholic scholars, too, in this literary analysis is one of the outstanding characteristics of the modern biblical revival. Of our two great sources, or criteria, for determining and interpreting these *genera literaria* (literary forms), one is external: the comparison with the other literatures of which I have just spoken. The other is internal: from literary analysis itself, from the techniques of determining an author's meaning from the context, from the whole bearing of his writing.

We have come to see very clearly that we are dealing with literary forms that are specific to those periods of the world's history, specific to those cultures and civilizations. They are in great part more or less alien to our contemporary ideas; alien, that is, to the literary forms used by us today, classified by our librarians, represented in our newspapers or in the books we read. Of our forms, none quite correspond to any one of the biblical forms, and, on the other hand, no one of the biblical forms perfectly corresponds to a form that we use today. Those forms of writing are fixed, conventional means of expression. The author who wanted to convey, let us say, the truth of something that happened in the past, had a set and conventional way of doing so, a set stock of expressions to indicate what he was talking about, a set stock of images, of constructions, of symbols, by which to convey his meaning.

Let us just take the wisdom literature as an example. Many important parts of the Old Testament are wisdom literature: the book of Proverbs, Ecclesiastes, the book of Job, Ecclesiasticus, many of the Psalms, the book of Baruch (at least in part), and some other smaller sections. Such wisdom literature is a highly developed genre in the literature of the ancient Near East. In these writings we find a conventionalized attribution of such wisdom to the ruler; so also among the Jews: the regular expression for any wisdom writing is "book of Solomon," because the convention was to put such wisdom writing in the mouth of a former king. Wisdom was part of God's gift to the king, and therefore the king was the final exponent of wisdom. Such conventional usages no more deceived or bothered readers of those days than do our modern conventions of novel writing, for example, our "historical fiction" written in the first person.

We have already spoken of parallels to many of the kinds of Psalms and of the similarity of prophetic oracles within and outside the Israelite people. Now I can mention briefly the question that is perhaps most interesting in this regard: the possibility — and for present-day scholarship it is a certainty — that there are different literary genres within the historical writings of the Bible. For some sixty years or so this has been the subject of quite strenuous, and at times bitter, controversy in the Church. Today, it is peaceably settled and agreed upon; but the specific applications to be drawn from these literary insights are still being worked out.

One of these points is, that not all narrative is *ipso facto* historic. I hope that that sounds perfectly obvious, but you would be surprised to find how often in older books *truthful* and *historical* are equated; if a thing isn't historical, it isn't true. Probably the best starting point in discussing this matter is a consideration of the parables of the Gospels. We all know that the parables are stories related by Our Lord. They are fiction; they never happened. And if Our Lord could use that form of literature, why could not the authors of the Old Testament do so? — as some of them, in fact, did.

Even here it is helpful to distinguish two types of parables. There is a type of parable that is completely timeless, and there is a type that is historical in a certain way, in that it treats of God's dealings with Israel. An example of the first type is the parable of the Prodigal Son; its teaching is the truth of the mercy of God. This parable is most unfortunately named: the central figure is really the father, and the parable would be better called the parable of the Loving

Father. However, my principal point in its regard is that this parable is not a presentation of one instance in history or one historical period or situation rather than another.

On the other hand, consider the parable of the unjust caretakers of the vine-yard, the parable of those left in charge of the vineyard, to whom the owner sent messengers to collect the rent, and who, refusing to pay the rent, reject and punish these messengers. Finally the owner sends his own son; he is not only rejected but killed by the caretakers. That parable really is an historical parable, because under the symbol of the vineyard, of the rent, of the landowner and tenants, you have symbolized the history of the Jewish people up to and includ-ing the time of Christ. It is symbolic history.

Besides parables, there are, of course, many other genera, many other liter-ary forms; these require their own kind of interpretation, often quite different from that to which we are accustomed. There are chronicles and genealogies, lists of names and places, legends of ancient heroes, sagas about the history of ancient peoples; and for all of these one can find parallels in the other ancient literatures of which I have spoken. One of the most interesting of these parallels is that of the type we might call edifying or religious fiction; this we can find, for example, in Egypt, and in biblical books like Jonas or Tobias. In all such writings, when we wish to interpret them, it is the intention of the human author that is of primary importance. We must not treat such books as if they had been written by our contemporaries; we must not assume that a biblical author means by his writings what we would have meant in writing them today. We must ask what the author meant *then*, what he intended to convey.

A parallel that I sometimes find helpful, in explaining this to people who raise the question of the degree of historicity in Old Testament narrative, is that of Shakespeare's plays. There is, first of all, the distinction between Shake-speare's tragedies and his histories. As an example of the first, take *King Lear*. I have no doubt that there was some ancient legend from early British history which concerned a King Lear who was badly treated by his daughters; but Shakespeare in writing his play is not the least bit concerned about the histo-ricity of this man's existence or the reality of his daughters. All he is concerned about is the use he can make of this in writing a play; he has taken the name and possibly the outline of the plot from a dubiously historical story. This might be paralleled to something like the book of Job. There is no sense in wasting time or breath in discussing whether there ever was an historical Job; we have no idea, and it is extremely unimportant. What is important in the book of Job is what the author does with his hero, his Job.

Take another Shakespearean play, *Hamlet* or *Macbeth*. There was a king named Macbeth; if I am not mistaken, he lived in the eleventh century, killed his predecessor, and was killed by his predecessor's son. To that extent, the play gives an outline of genuine Scottish history. Yet, even here, where Shake-speare has taken his story of Macbeth from history, it is what Shakespeare has made of Macbeth that is important. It would be ridiculous if one writing Scottish history should say "Fortunately, we have full information about Macbeth and his queen, because Shakespeare wrote a play about them." No, the Macbeth in his play is Shakespeare's creation. There is an historical nucleus to the play, if you wish, but Shakespeare has used it only to present one of his wonderful studies of human nature, of guilt, temptation, and tragedy.

We can come, then, to a third form: Shakespeare's histories, his chronicle plays — *Richard II, Richard III, Henry IV, Henry V*, etc. First of all, the events in these plays are closer in time to the Elizabethan period; Shakespeare has taken them mainly from Holinshed's *Chronicles*, a fairly detailed book of history; and he is at pains to preserve in general, and even in some particulars, the original history. But he still has added a great deal of his own to the story. There is something analogous to these differing levels of historicity in Shakespeare in the Bible — for example, the books of Samuel might correspond somewhat to the last-named type of Shakespearean usage of history. However, I would not want to stress these comparisons too much, because Shakespeare's plays are still non-Hebraic in literary form.

Much more could be said about literary forms in the Bible; we might add just a word about the New Testament. In the New Testament we are not helped by comparison with other literatures as we are with regard to the Old. The New Testament is unique, even in a literary way, in its literary form, to an extent that the Old is not. But this much at least we can say: there has been a tendency to impose upon the Gospels a historicity which their authors did not aim at or care about. Most of the lives of Christ written in the last hundred years or so have tended to impose such historicity; for example, to try to work out a strict sequence of events in Christ's public life, for which we have no real basis. The Gospels are recordings of the preaching of the early Church at a time when the original generation of witnesses began to die out, thirty, forty, or fifty years after the events of Christ's life. They record, therefore, in fixed form, with a certain leeway left to each Evangelist, already determined groups and sequences of teachings about the birth, earthly life, and death of Our Lord. One can see the general outline of this early teaching in each of the Gospel narratives: Baptism, public life, Passion and Resurrection accounts. That is the framework common to all the Gospels; but within this framework the different Evangelists enjoyed great freedom, and they have grouped their matter according to certain pedagogical intentions of their own. Matthew, Mark, Luke, and John arranged their matter, not because this event came after that event, rather than before it, but because this sequence served the pedagogical intentions of which we just spoke.

Although the Gospels are definitely historical, they are historical in this particular way; and they do not have the concern about chronological sequence that we would expect in modern biography. Actually, they are not biographies; in the true sense it is impossible to try to write the life of Our Lord, and the Evangelists did not attempt it. What they did attempt to convey was a better understanding of the work of Christ, and this for Christians who already believed.

## Religious understanding of the Bible

Now, somewhat belatedly, I come to my third point: the improved religious understanding of the Bible. This, of course, is that towards which the previous two aspects of biblical studies are aimed, for it gives them their importance and meaning. In *Divino Afflante Spiritu*, the Pope speaks of our first point, improved knowledge of the background and setting of the Bible, as something already quite well achieved. The second point, study of the Bible according to its different literary forms, is something that the Pope recommends — one might almost say imposes — as something necessary and urgent in the work of the exegete. This third point, improved religious understanding of the Bible, is rather a pious hope to which the Pope looks forward. He expresses his confidence that this will be the result of the other two; and we may say that within the last fifteen years the Pope's expectation has been most consolingly fulfilled. The flood of writings on the Bible among European Catholics, especially in the last fifteen years, has been concerned very largely with the exploitation of its religious values, as we can see them and apply them to ourselves.

There is no longer question merely of picking out separate or isolated stories from the Bible, and drawing moralistic lessons from them of virtues to be practiced and vices to be avoided. Nor is there question of isolating texts, to be interpreted as one would interpret a definition by a Church Council or a sentence from Canon Law. That tended to be the treatment a hundred years ago, the treatment of the Old Testament in our Bible History books, a chopped-up treatment that did not seem to value the Old Testament for its own sake. Now, in our modern approach, Christ is the center of the Old Testament, just as He is of the New. The message of the two parts in the Bible is one, and the Old Testament by itself is a magnificent testimony to the one salvation history. The Old Testament is not primarily a history of Israel or of human events as such; it is a history of God. It is a history of the things that God has worked through and in Israel, recorded by witnesses, testified to by the collective experience of the people, transmitted to posterity precisely because such is the duty and obligation of the sacred writers — a history that possesses from beginning to end, despite all the varieties of expression and differences of outlook and of thought, a unity that is unmistakable, a unity that is due, not to human psychology or to human authorship, but to the action of God which is recorded in the Bible. For that reason, the salvation history is one story from beginning to end.

The history of Israel as such begins only with the book of Exodus, with the constitution of the people of God out of a group of fugitives from Egypt, to whom God had sent the one man Moses. Israel as a people did not exist until they had crossed the Red Sea and begun their wandering in the desert. But from that point, the salvation history, with the great destiny attributed to this people, follows its course for centuries. All the prophets, all the wise men, all the chroniclers and historians of Israel deal with that one situation, with that one theme; what God intends to make of Israel and the difficult time He has in accomplishing this. The literature of Israel is an extraordinary example of national humility — one of the many ways in which it is unique. I know of absolutely no other national literature in the world's history in which the nation is not glorified; the theme of Israel's literature is that of Psalm 113 — "Non nobis, Domine, non nobis, sed nomine tuo da gloriam." It is Yahweh, their God, whom their literature intends to glorify from beginning to end. With astounding humility, Israel makes of its own history one long act of self-accusation and of contrition.

Thus, the Old Testament, just as the New, is testimony to a connected history of God; and that connected history is the working out in practice of what God is: a salvation God, a Being of overwhelming goodness who intends to have mankind with Him for eternity, who wishes them to be happy, who offers them salvation such as no earthly power can offer. These stories of the Old Testament can stand in their own right as the history of Israel, but actually they are part of a pulsating divine activity that is repeated again and again in history. Here it is that we come to that great connection between the Old and the New Testament of which the Fathers of the Church made so much, which they saw so clearly. This connection has always been preserved in the Church's liturgy, but it has not been much exploited until very recent times. What I am referring to is what is known as typology, by which I mean the expressly willed similarity between the way God treated Israel and Israel responded to God, and the way God the Father dealt with Christ and Christ's response to His Father. To carry it still further, there is the similarity between the way the Father dealt with Christ and the way God deals with the members of the Church.

This typology, on which patristic literature laid so much stress, is obviously of great catechetical importance. In the early Church, as we know, before the theology of the sacraments was elaborated speculatively as it came to be by the late Middle Ages, the meaning of the sacraments was largely explained to the people in terms of typology. If you want to know what that typology was — let us say of Baptism — read the early chapters of Exodus and see what happens in the "baptism" of the Israelites: how they were led through water and delivered from the servitude of a pagan power, led from an anti-god power into the service of God. So, too, in Baptism: the passing down into the baptismal font and coming out of the water was to the early Christians a symbolic re-enactment of the passage of the Israelites through the Red Sea. It was a similar salvation of God effected upon them and effected upon Israel, with the difference that this Christian salvation is a salvation through Christ and into Christ; nevertheless there was the fundamental sameness of Exodus and Baptism. Again, with respect to the Eucharist, the figure of the manna in the desert was a particularly favored reference in the early Church; the Eucharist is the support and nourishment provided by God to His people during their pilgrimage through the desert of this world, heavenly food, bread of angels, containing virtue and power and energy that no earthly food could possess; a food, therefore, to be received with utmost reverence, utmost purity, utmost gratitude by God's people. So with the other sacraments; they were explained and interpreted in terms of that typology.

While the typology meaning is secondary and dependent upon the literal historical meaning of an Old Testament passage, it is very important in making the bridge between the Old Testament and ourselves. So, too, is the prophetic role of the Old Testament, which has come to be much better understood. I mentioned earlier the rather unfortunate treatment of the messianic prophecies, by which they are pulled out of their contexts and used as isolated sentences, as examples of God in the Old Testament giving a detailed prophecy about Christ. That is not false, of course, but it is very incomplete, and easily gives a false idea; it prevents us from understanding the full richness, the true development of God's message to His people. In dealing with a prophecy, such as that of the virgin bearing a child whose name shall be called Emmanuel, we must not only ask ourselves how this finds its meaning and fulfillment when the Messiah finally comes, but we must also ask what this prophecy meant to Isaiah and to his contemporaries. It was spoken on a given day about the year 735 B.C., before a given audience that we know quite well. What did these words mean to Isaiah and to his hearers? They had some meaning then, some contemporary reference, which it is worth our while to learn.

Just a few words on the new religious understanding of the New Testament. This lags somewhat behind the development relative to the Old Testament, perhaps because there has been more need for correction in our ideas of the Old Testament. However, there has been some very stimulating and helpful work done on the analysis of New Testament literature. The key book in this recent study is the Acts of the Apostles. Starting from that book rather than from any of the Gospels, a new understanding of the genesis of the Gospels themselves has been given us.

In the first part of the Acts of the Apostles, particularly if we combine what we find there with certain scraps from the Pauline Epistles and from some outside sources, we find an extraordinarily vivid picture of the very first period of the Church. We see the first existence of the Church, the tremendous ferment, the quickening enlightenment that took place in the short span of years from about 30 to 70 A.D. We see the problem arising of finding the relationship of Christianity to Judaism, the need of working out the implications of the tremendous revolution caused by the reception into the Church of Gentile converts, who are not Jews and are not required to become Jewish proselytes before becoming Christians. And in connection with this question of the relation of Jew and Gentile in the Church, we can see the question of central authority in the Church and how it was to be administered. All these events come to life as we read the Acts of the Apostles.

When we turn from Acts to the Gospels, we see these documents as testimony to the faith of the Church in those early years. There was an interval, roughly equivalent to a man's active lifetime — about thirty or forty years — when the Church lived solely by its oral teaching (and the text of the Old Testament). Not only the preaching to unbelievers who were to be converted, but also the instruction of the catechumens and adult converts was all done orally, in the form of accounts of the life and work, the death and resurrection of Christ. Only toward the end of this period did the Gospels come to be written, when the original eyewitnesses were dying off and it became time to recall and record this oral catechesis as closely as possible in its original form. This gave rise to that fourfold presentation, in which a fixed division of the material is discernible; yet within that division great personal freedom and initiative are used by each Evangelist.

As we know from ordinary experience, a witness tells us what he remembers, and as he remembers it, and we expect even the most faithful witnesses to any one event to give somewhat varying accounts of that event. They have seen it from different angles, have experienced it differently; one will lay more stress on this aspect, another on that. The more such witnesses we have, the better picture we can form of the actual event. Now, in this sense it is true to say that we reach Christ in the Gospels only *through* the faith of the early Church, through the faith of Matthew, Mark, Luke, and John. One runs into opposition to such a statement from people who insist that this does not satisfy them; they want to feel that when they pick up their New Testament they are in immediate contact with Christ Himself, without human intermediary, as it were; that what they see on the pages are the very words Christ spoke. However, it simply is not possible to by-pass the very channel of communication that He Himself has chosen — in this case, the faith-illuminated minds of the Evangelists. With all due respect to the people mentioned, their attitude reflects an undervaluing of the incarnational aspect of Christ's revelation, a lack of understanding of the implications of the Incarnation itself, of the fact that Christ chooses to reveal Himself and speak to us through and by means of our fellowmen.

Obviously, one does not have to stress this last point with regard to the Church, Christ's own Body. What I would like to stress is that it is true also in the Church's documents: the record we have of Christ speaking. All they tell us is true, and worthy of divine faith; but, nevertheless, Christ's teaching comes to us through their instrumentality. There are innumerable instances we might cite. For example, St. John, in the great farewell discourse (John 13–18), has obviously included much material that historically must have been communicated by Our Lord after the Resurrection. Again, the missionary discourse in Matthew 10 has two distinct parts: the first refers to the 72 disciples being sent out at that time, during the public life of Our Lord; but the second (from verse 16 on) does not fit into that situation at all — it refers to the experience of the Church after Pentecost. St. Matthew has chosen to add to the record of the original instruction a passage *which expresses Our Lord's will and teaching* for the contemporary Church. Other examples could be given. But the point I wish to make is simply this: that in order to understand the Gospels properly, to take out of them what God wishes us to find there, we must not leave out of account the human authorship, the genuine human activity that entered into their production.

Such, then, are a few ideas about the present state of biblical studies. These I believe should have — and I am confident they will have — considerable impact upon the teaching of the truths of faith to our Catholic children.

# THE STUDY OF HOLY SCRIPTURE

Bernard Cardinal Alfrink

The Editors of *Biblica* have graciously asked me to write a brief preface to this issue in honor of two professors of the Pontifical Biblical Institute [Augustin Cardinal Bea and Father Albert Vaccari], and I am very happy to accede to their request.

It was my privilege for eighteen years to teach Holy Scripture in the service of the Church. During that time I always availed myself, with the deepest gratitude and esteem, of the outstanding knowledge and prudent wisdom of these two professors whose student I had been from 1924 to 1927.

Each in his own way and according to his own characteristics impressed on his students a great desire to engage actively, in their own turn, in the practice of scientific exegesis. This, of course, is the indispensable condition for an exact understanding of the full riches contained in the Word of God. Indeed, the scientific study of Holy Scripture has no other purpose than to help us better understand the message given to us by God through His sacred authors. Therefore all the avenues opened by this science in its effort to attain its end are welcomed by the Church, for the Church wishes to bar no road that leads to a more perfect and complete knowledge of the revelation entrusted to her. The fact that these new avenues involve risks forces the Church to be on her guard. She must even, in some cases, warn her exegetes to be on the alert. But these are stop signals and stop signals are not intended to do more than to regulate traffic in the best interests of all concerned. Our two professors taught us that a good exegete must always watch out for these signals attentively and be thankful for them. Their personal study as well as their teaching were characterized by this absolute fidelity to the directives of the Church. And as their students we too learned to be circumspect in our use of the methods which the continual progress of scientific exegesis put in our hands. However, this circumspection was not the paralyzing fear which prevents all progress. Rather it joined the two cardinal virtues of prudence and fortitude. Indeed, this circumspection had every right to be courageous since it flowed from the Christian attitude which accepts the Scriptures in faith, and which inspires the greatest caution whenever the analogy of faith is endangered.

This truly Christian respect for the data of both science and faith was the attitude which our two professors passed on to their students. I am particularly happy, as I am sure all of their students are, to express my debt to them for having formed this attitude in us. What other attitude may a Christian assume when practicing scientific research in any field?

The Church will always be faced with new discoveries in science and with new research methods. This is equally true in the particular instance of the scientific study of Holy Scripture.

Published originally in *Biblica*, 43 (1962), 255-63. Reprinted by permission of the publisher.

It would be absurd, in my opinion, to reject a new scientific method *a priori* on the pretext that it was first used by non-Catholic exegetes, or even more because it was first developed in such and such a part of the world. It would be no less absurd to reject it because certain non-Catholics have used it to draw conclusions which we Catholics cannot accept. For the question at issue here is precisely whether those conclusions derived from the method itself or whether they flowed from certain preconceptions in the minds of those who used the method. Nor is it right to condemn a method out of hand even if it has led certain Catholic exegetes to unacceptable conclusions. They too, after all, can use their method wrongly, by not being sufficiently attentive, for example, to the analogy of faith or to the limits of the method itself. It is possible also that a method which is valid in the sphere of literary criticism may no longer be so when one passes into the sphere of theology.

Admittedly, some Catholics have not always employed the method of Form Criticism judiciously. But this is no justification, it seems to me, for suspecting or even accusing of disloyalty every Catholic exegete who makes use of the method. As a tool of literary criticism the method may be used in either a legitimate or an illegitimate way. Consequently the results obtained from it may be either acceptable or unacceptable.

Only the ability to make clear distinctions will reveal exactly what can and what cannot be accepted by a Catholic here. The claim that the Annunciation narrative in the Gospel of St. Luke was inspired by certain Old Testament themes is one which is quite acceptable to a Catholic exegete. A comparison of the different Gospels clearly shows that their authors had no intention of composing a stenographer's account or a news report intended to be read as being absolutely literal in every detail. Usually one finds in the Gospels some element due to the Evangelist himself or to the person or persons who furnished him with his source material. There is no theological principle which forbids us searching out and isolating this element so as to penetrate to the oldest stratum of the narrative. But if, for instance, his research were to lead the exegete to consider the Virgin Birth of Our Savior as a fictitious element of later origin, then he would be striking against the faith of the Church.

Similarly, if a scholar were to use the form-critical method to deduce from Matthew 16:13-20 that the primacy of Peter had not been instituted by Christ Himself but only by the primitive community, he would be departing so clearly from the faith of the Church as to make it all but inconceivable that a Catholic exegete could ever arrive at such a conclusion. It is quite a different matter, however, to claim that the formulation used here by the Evangelist does not reproduce totally and literally the words exchanged between Christ and Peter, and that his manner of expression reflects to a certain degree the influence of a later date, provided that one fully maintains divine institution of the primacy of Peter. I do not believe either that the faith is any more endangered if one maintains that one or other verse of this passage (for example, the beatitude of v. 17, "*Beatus es, Simon Bar Jona*") was in fact spoken by Our Lord on another occasion and not at that precise moment. A comparative study of the Gospel texts shows clearly that their authors frequently composed their narratives and discourses with a certain freedom.

Nevertheless we must admit that this method involves a great risk, the risk of minimizing facts, all of which, according to the Gospel narratives, exhibit in one way or another a supernatural character. That is why it must be used with the greatest circumspection. If, for example, this method were to tempt us to cast aside certain narratives which Scripture obviously presents as historical, then we should have to inquire whether such conclusions were justified by our premises, or whether we had not fallen into that minimalism just mentioned, which constitutes the principal danger of the method itself.

Every scientific method of exegesis, as we know, seeks to determine the intention of the sacred writer: that which the instrument wished to convey is also that which the Principal Author wished to express. The fact that the readers of the Bible did not clearly perceive this intention, even over a period of centuries, is not of itself a reason for continuing now to maintain an interpretation which has been shown to have been inexact.[1] In such a case, however, very solid arguments would have to be adduced, and, in addition, these explanations should be proposed *salvo iudicio Ecclesiae, "cuius est iudicare de vero sensu et interpretatione Sacrarum Scripturarum"*. For a Catholic exegete must never forget that *"in rebus fidei et morum, ad aedificationem doctrinae christianae pertinentium, is pro vero sensu Sacrae Scripturae habendus sit, quem tenuit ac tenet Sancta Mater Ecclesia."* [2]

When we consider the unacceptable results of Form Criticism arrived at by those who first applied it to the Gospels, and the conclusions drawn on occasion by Catholic authors, it is not surprising that several members of the Church have become concerned. However, the Monitum of the Holy Office dated June 20, 1961, formulated in prudent terms, did not condemn the method itself. It was simply a serious and justified warning directed against abusive conclusions.

By its very nature every method of scientific exegesis seeks to find the *"germana veritas historica et obiectiva Scripturae Sacrae"*. This is equally true of the method of Form Criticism. But even if we set aside extreme positions, we must admit that it has led several, even of its more moderate exponents, to deny or to cast doubt upon the *"germana veritas historica et obiectiva"* of a number of Gospel episodes, even though these are presented, according to the obvious sense of the text, as historical realities. It is understandable, therefore, that there should be uneasiness, and well-founded uneasiness at that, since occasionally conclusions or hypotheses which are more or less provisory in scientific exegesis are immediately popularized among the general public. Perhaps this is inevitable, considering the widespread diffusion of printed works today. But this only increases the general uneasiness, and should also bring all exegetes to a fuller consciousness of their responsibilities.

In these matters, as we said, we must learn to distinguish clearly. It is one thing to say that the Gospels describe "the Christ of faith" and not "the Jesus

[1] Cf. Pius XII, Encyclical *Divino afflante Spiritu (Enchiridion biblicum, 555)*.
[2] Conc. Vat. I, Sess. 3, cap. 2, *De revelatione (Enchir. bib., 78)*; cf. Conc. Trid., Sess. 4, *Decr. de editione et usu Sacrorum Librorum (Enchir. bib., 62)*; Leo XIII, Encyclical *Providentissimus Deus (Enchir. bib., 108)*.

of history". It is quite another thing to say that faith had its role to play in the description of the historical Jesus of the Gospel. The latter statement does not endanger in any way the inerrancy of the Scriptures. For to search out the role played by faith does not necessarily mean that one intends to eliminate every supernatural element from the historical account. The same method in the hands of a Christian exegete and of a Scripture scholar of rationalist tendencies will yield quite different results. Both scholars may affirm that in presenting the person of Christ the Evangelists saw Him with the eyes of faith. Still, each one means something quite different by that assertion. The concrete results of their research must necessarily — and in fact do — reflect this difference of outlook.

In the practice of this method, the exegete must have, so to speak, the steadiness of hand of a skilful surgeon. Otherwise he runs the risk of cutting away more than he should. By the same token, however, anyone who wishes to judge the exegete's work at its true value must possess a gift of discernment which is equally acute.

Every Catholic exegete, whatever method be employed, must allow himself to be guided in all loyalty by the directives of the Church. The two eminent professors in whose honor these pages are written have always been at pains to instill this principle in their students. It comes as no surprise to us to see them pleading in behalf of a true esteem within the Church for the "sometimes austere, but so important task" [3] assumed by those who are working in all sincerity to bring out more clearly the profound meaning of the Word of God. For the carrying out of this service to the Church, a reciprocal confidence on the part of the Church itself is indispensable. If it should happen that exegetes commit faults or errors, they must accept warnings given because of pastoral care. But let this always be done without offending Christian charity; let it be done as scholars do. I am sure that this sentiment voices the heartfelt wish of the two scholars to whom we are offering today the homage of our gratitude. In recognition of all they have given us, may God's blessing descend upon them in abundance.

# BIBLICAL CRITICISM

P. G. Duncker, O.P.

In the later decades of the last century Criticism began to be applied to the Bible and was used by some authors as a tool and weapon against the divine inspiration and veracity of Sacred Scripture. Hence one can easily understand that the

[3] Message of His Holiness Pius XII to the Catholic Biblical Congress of Brussels-Louvain (August, 1958). See *Sacra Pagina*, vol. I, Paris-Gembloux, 1959, pp. 15-16.

Published originally in *Catholic Biblical Quarterly*, 25 (1963), 22-33. Reprinted by permission of the publisher.

Magisterium of the Church, maintaining and defending the *Depositum Fidei*, watched with alertness and much reserve the efforts of Catholic exegetes to introduce Criticism into their interpretation of the Sacred Books. These scholars were, apart from some exceptions, loyal sons of the Church, and they wanted to show how Criticism, stripped of its rationalistic prejudices, could and should promote a better understanding of Sacred Scripture. However, their applications seemed, on account of the insufficiency of the material of investigation then available, rather conjectural, hazardous and immature. The Magisterium of the Church felt itself forced to step in from time to time in order to keep these applications within well-defined limits. But later on Biblical Criticism came to be applied in a more truly scientific way, less tendentiously and with greater impartiality. Its conclusions also appeared better founded and, when rightly understood, no longer against the divine character of Holy Writ. As a result, Biblical Criticism became less suspect in the eyes of the Magisterium of the Church and eventually the use of its methods — provided the divine character of Sacred Scripture be duly safeguarded — was not only permitted, but encouraged and even prescribed by the Encyclical, *Divino afflante Spiritu*, of 1943.

However, as more and more Catholic scholars with confidence and openness of mind began to apply the principles laid down in the Encyclical, uneasiness and fear arose and spread rapidly. Of this the collaborators of the *Catholic Biblical Quarterly*, who during the 25 years of this journal's existence have themselves in all earnestness endeavored to follow out the papal directives, have surely been aware. Many in the Church were and still are afraid that Biblical Criticism is being pushed too far, so that it oversteps the limits which the same Biblical Encyclical did not fail to set. I will not be far from the truth in stating that some even regret that this Encyclical was ever issued, because of the abuse, as they imagine, made of it. It is no surprise to find that the *Divino afflante Spiritu* is being quoted and adduced not only in favor of Biblical Criticism, but also against it.

In view of this, two things may be remarked. First, no open-minded person who reads and studies the Encyclical without prejudice can possibly deny that the principal object and aim, the whole spirit, of this papal document is to encourage and insist upon an up-to-date scientific approach to the Bible — and of this approach Biblical Criticism forms a real and integral part. Though the term itself is not used in the Encyclical, its subject matter is amply dealt with. It may suffice to note that, after having explained the primary importance of the literal sense of the Holy Scriptures (what the Sacred Authors precisely want to say) and having pointed out that in order to know this, one has to inquire about the various modes of expression or so-called "literary forms" used by the Authors, this severe admonition is given: "Hence, in order to comply adequately with the present needs of Biblical studies, a Catholic exegete in explaining Sacred Scripture and demonstrating and proving its immunity from all error, should also make a prudent use of this means, viz., determine to what extent the mode of expression or literary form ("litterarum genus") adopted by the Sacred Writer may lead to a correct and genuine interpretation; and let him be convinced that this part of his task cannot be neglected without serious detriment to Catholic exegesis." [1] Secondly, in the passage just quoted the Encyclical speaks of a *prudent* use, and this supposes that excesses are to be avoided. It all depends, however — and this must be stressed — on what one means by excesses.

That there have been and still are true and real excesses in Biblical Criticism, must certainly be admitted; and the *Monitum* of the Holy Office, June 20, 1961,[2] is a severe warning against opinions in circulation which compromise the historical and objective veracity of Holy Scripture, both Old and New Testament, and particularly of Christ's words and deeds. It was reported to me that a Catholic had declared we could not be certain of a single word of Our Lord as spoken by himself and that the facts of his life may be considered of little importance as long as one maintains his teaching. Such statements are surely excessive and wrong for the teaching of Our Lord stands or falls with the historical Christ. I can hardly imagine that any true Catholic could seriously ever have uttered such general affirmations, and still less that he wrote them down. One should not too readily believe things that are reported as being said, unless they are verified.

However, quite a number of opinions in Scriptural matters have been called excessive, which do not deserve to be stigmatized as such. One sometimes hears put forward as an example of the alleged excesses of the new scientific trend in Biblical studies the fact that some modern exegetes do not regard the sojourn of Jonah three days and three nights in the belly of the fish as truly miraculous, although Our Lord himself had referred to it as a sign of his own approaching sojourn of three days and three nights in the heart of the earth and had predicted that the men of Nineveh would arise in judgment with the men of his generation and condemn it, for they did penance at the preaching of Jonah. Moreover, all the Fathers of the Church had taken the book of Jonah as historical. But this argumentation is far from being conclusive. That the Fathers considered the story of Jonah to be real history is not surprising. The critical way of looking at a book of the Bible, of trying to get at its precise literary form, is a phenomenon of later times and has only recently become quite common. That is why only the last Biblical Encyclical speaks amply about it, as has already been shown above, urging Catholic exegetes to examine the mode of expression or literary form adopted by the Sacred Writer in order to determine to what extent this may lead to a correct and genuine interpretation. For "quite wrongly," the Encyclical continues, "do some pretend, not rightly understanding the conditions of biblical study, that nothing remains to be added by the Catholic exegete of our time to what Christian antiquity has produced; since, on the contrary, our own times have brought to light much that calls for a fresh investigation and new examination, and stimulates not a little the active study of the present day interpreter." [3] The Fathers' main purpose was to point out the doctrine of Holy

---

[1] *AAS* 35 (1943) 316; *EB*⁴ 560.
[2] *AAS* 42 (1961) 576; *CBQ* 23 (1961) 465.
[3] *AAS* 35 (1943) 313; *EB*⁴ 555.

Scripture, and with regard to the book of Jonah, its doctrine remains the same, whether one considers it historical or a kind of a parable or a midrash. As to Our Lord's words concerning Jonah, he referred to what was written about this prophet in one of the Divine Scriptures and applied it to himself. Again whether the story was real, as very likely Christ's contemporaries believed, or figurative, Our Lord's teaching still holds good. Like Jonah, Melchisedech was also a sign, a prefiguration or type of Christ (Heb. 7:1ff). But in 7:3 Melchisedech is said to have been without father and mother or genealogy and to have had no beginning of days or end of life, only because in Gen. 14:18ff, nothing is written about his parents and birth and death, from which it does not follow that he was not born and did not die. In 1 Cor. 10:4 St. Paul speaks of a rock quenching the Hebrews' thirst in the desert and following them in their journey. This latter and fictitious detail St. Paul derived from a rabbinic legend of his time; yet he declared the marching rock signified Christ. Some of Our Lord's parables are so realistic and vivid, e.g., the good Samaritan, that one could doubt whether the story presented in the parable really happened or was merely invented by Christ; but again in both cases the doctrine is identical. With his reference to Jonah Our Lord does not wish to give any information or teaching about whether the narrative is historical or not, since this has nothing to do with his messianic preaching. The question, one of the very many which have not been answered by the Magisterium of the Church in a decisive way, can only be solved by Biblical Criticism. Hence it is perfectly legitimate to hold that the book of Jonah is a parable or a midrash, as most modern Catholic scholars on very good grounds maintain. Even A. Vaccari, S.J., who recently defended the historicity of the book,[4] admits, as he himself told me, that the other opinion it not against Faith.

Another example of a so-called excessive opinion concerns the famous Petrine text in Matthew 16:13-19 (esp., vv. 16[b]-19), about which there has been much recent discussion. In order to explain the difficulty, we must first consider the two parallel texts in Mark 8:27ff and Luke 9:18ff. Our Lord's question to Peter: "But who do you say that I am?" is answered by the apostle: "You are the Christ" (Mark 8:29); "The Christ of God" (Luke 9:20); after which Our Lord "charged them to tell no one about him" (Mark 8:30), "charged and commanded them to tell this to no one" (Luke 9:21), and then began to speak about the coming sufferings, passion, death, and resurrection of the Son of Man (Mark 8:31; Luke 9:22). According to Mark, who notes that Christ spoke quite plainly about these things, Peter took Our Lord aside and began to reproach him. Whereupon Our Lord rebuked Peter: "Get behind me, Satan, for your ideas are not those of God, but those of men," and next explained to the multitude and his disciples that he who wants to follow him will have to deny himself, take up his cross, etc. (vv. 32-38). From this context in Mark our Lord does not seem to approve Peter's answer: "You are the Christ," because he does not have the right idea of Christ's messiahship. Though a suffering Messiah was

[4] "Il genere letterario del libro di Giona in recenti pubblicazioni," *Divinitas* 5 (1961) 231-256.

announced in various texts of the OT, presenting his Kingdom as a spiritual and not a political one, yet the Jews expected the Messiah as a great king, sub-jugating and dominating all other nations, and into this political picture suffer-ing did not enter at all. At the time of our pericope, which puts the scene in Caesarea Philippi, Peter seems to have shared somewhat the people's idea of the Messiah. Hence his protest, apparently against the idea of a suffering Christ, and Our Lord's very severe rebuke and further explanation of self-denial and suffering for those who want to follow him. In Luke this last paragraph follows immediately on Our Lord's words about the sufferings, etc., of the Son of Man, whereas Peter's protest and Christ's rebuke are omitted.

Turning now to Matthew, we find instead of "You are the Christ" or "The Christ of God," this answer: "You are the Christ, the Son of the living God." Then comes the well known text about Peter's primacy: "Blessed are you, Simon Bar-Jona, because flesh and blood have not revealed this to you, but my Father who is in heaven. And I say to you: You are Peter, and upon this rock I will build my church, and the gates of hell shall not prevail against it. I will give you the keys of the kingdom of heaven, and whatever you bind upon earth, shall be bound in heaven, and whatever you loose on earth, shall be loosed in heaven." Here Our Lord quite evidently approves Peter's magnificent confession.

However, immediately after Christ's exaltation of Peter there follows: "He charged the disciples to tell no one that he was the Christ," the very same remark as after Mark's: "You are the Christ" and Luke's: "The Christ of God." A slight but important difference is to be noted. Matthew did not write as Luke: "to tell this to no one," for "this" would then refer to the two preceding verses, con-taining Christ's praise of Peter; nor did he put it as Mark: "to tell no one about him," because "him" would in Matthew refer to Christ as Messiah and God, whereas in Mark and Luke there is only question of Our Lord's messiahship, and the point of Matthew's remark is apparently the same. Moreover, Matthew has, like Mark, Peter's protest against Christ's sufferings, and in an even stronger form: "No, No, Lord. This shall never happen to you!" and here Our Lord's remark is also more vigorous: "Get behind me Satan! You are a hindrance to me, for your ideas are not those of God, but those of men." Furthermore it is precisely Matthew who introduces Christ's words about his sufferings by saying that he began to speak of these: "from that moment," making us understand that Our Lord had never spoken of them before. Taking account of all this, it seems that Our Lord, apart from the words in which he praises Peter for the confession of faith in his messiahship and divinity, in Matthew just as in Mark (and very likely also in Luke, for, though Luke omits Peter's reproach and Christ's rebuke, yet he has Christ's insistence on self-denial and taking up one's cross, since Christ was going to suffer himself) rather blamed Peter for not having the right idea of his messiahship.

We have now come to the main difficulty about the Petrine text: How is it to be explained that Our Lord, who first praised Peter highly for his splendid con-fession of faith in his messiahship and divinity (attributed to a special revelation from the Father in heaven) and solemnly promised to make him the head of the Church, blamed him immediately afterwards for not thinking rightly about his messiahship? And how could Peter, instructed by the Father in heaven about Christ's messiahship and divinity, shortly afterwards and subsequently right up till Christ's death, show so little insight into Christ's messiahship and divinity? No wonder that some Catholic exegetes who in the above critical way have examined the texts in question — in all good faith searching for a solution of the problem — are inclined to suppose that the Petrine text (Matthew 16:16ᵇ-19) does not stand in its proper place but is an insertion. This sounds rather revolutionary to Catholics and seems to be another excess of Biblical Criticism. Yet the proposed solution is not at all against the inspiration or veracity of this text and Matthew's Gospel. Everybody admits that our Evangelist does not give Christ's sayings and deeds and facts in a strict chronological order; that he puts them together according to certain great themes which succeed each other in a logical order. Hence it is quite possible that the Petrine text originally belonged to another period of Christ's preaching and was inserted, either by Matthew himself or by the Greek translator of his Aramaic text, in its present place, because at Caesarea Philippi Christ certainly questioned his disciples about what they thought of him, as is evident from the agreement on this point of the three Synoptics. But if not at Caesarea Philippi, where and when was the text pronounced by Our Lord? A certain answer cannot be given. But is this not alarming? Has not Peter's primacy now come to hang in the air? Is not this undermining its very foundation? By no means. There are several sayings, deeds, facts of Our Lord, which are given in quite different chronological order and in different places by the four Evangelists, and even by the three Synoptics who for the rest agree in so many points; and it is still very often not easy to find out which Evangelist gives a particular saying or deed or fact in the right place and time. It has been suggested that the Petrine text belongs to the period after Christ's resurrection, during his apparitions. This would not only make it easier to explain Peter's declaration about Christ's divinity, but would set Our Lord's words to Peter in a period during which, according to John (21:15-17), Peter received the task of feeding Christ's lambs and sheep. In any case, whenever and wherever Our Lord spoke these words, the very fact that they belong to an inspired Gospel is an absolute guarantee that they are authentically his words. This raises a last question: does the text in fact contain Christ's precise words? This question brings us to yet another case of seemingly excessive Biblical Criticism.

For several years the "Formgeschichtliche Methode" (usually translated: "Method of Form Criticism") has been applied to Scripture, and particularly to the Gospels. And the way this has been done by its first and principal exponents and advocates (M. Dibelius, K. Schmidt, R. Bultmann, M. Albertz and several others) must be rejected as all Catholics and many non-Catholics plainly admit. To get an idea of what this method, as used by these authors, leads to, a few words may be cited from a very instructive article: *Réflexions sur la "Formgeschichtliche Methode,"* published in 1946[5] but reprinted in

[5] *RB* 53 (1946) 481-512.

1961, by one of the most prominent Catholic Biblical scholars of our day, P. Benoit, O.P.[6] After having shown that these critics, and principally Bultmann, attribute practically the whole Christian tradition as conserved in the Gospels to the creative genius of the primitive community, he asks if anything of historical worth can remain after one has eliminated from tradition all those creations of the community. He answers: "Very little; a quite inoffensive residue: Jesus of Galilee, who thought himself to be a prophet, who must have spoken and acted accordingly, without our being able to say exactly what he spoke and how he acted, who eventually died in a lamentable way. All the rest: his divine origin, his mission of salvation, the proof he gave for these by his word and miracles, finally the resurrection which set a seal on his work, all this is pure fiction, proceeding from faith and cult, and clothed with a legendary tradition, which was formed in the course of the preachings and the disputes of the primitive community." [7]

However, although no Catholic can or will ever approve the above picture of what the Gospels are said to tell us about Christ, presented as the result of Form Criticism by its rationalistic exponents, it does not follow that the method as such is wrong and must be avoided. In the article just mentioned P. Benoit, having objectively exposed the arguments advanced by such authors to prove their statements and having criticized them from the Catholic point of view, comes to the following judicious conclusion: "What separates us from the critics here studied, and prevents us from following them without reserve, is, ultimately, the philosophical and theological principles which govern their research and which, in our eyes, vitiate it. They have those principles, whatever they may sometimes say. Catholic critics are frequently accused of depending on their supernatural faith as on a prejudice; but in the so-called 'independent' criticism which is opposed to us, we see plainly a rationalistic faith which is no less prejudiced, which is only less authorized." [8]

What Form Criticism, as applied to the Gospels, really aims at, is the history of their formation. Before the four Gospels were written, Christ's Apostles and disciples had been preaching the Lord and his doctrine, in association with and based on the great facts of his public life: his baptism, ministry, miracles, passion, death, resurrection, apparitions, glorification (Acts 2:22-36; 3:13-15; 10:37-41; 13:27-37; 18:25). Under the guidance of the Holy Spirit, promised by Christ (John 14:26; 16:13), this preaching was faithfully preserved and transmitted in the primitive Church (Luke 1:2; Acts 1:21-22; 2:42; 6:2-4; 10:41; Heb. 2:3), which, though rapidly expanding outside Jerusalem, took great care to remain in close contact with the Twelve Apostles and its original center (Gal. 2:2; 1 Cor. 11:23; 15:3-11; 1 Tim. 6:20). Out of this common teaching, which we may call the "oral Gospel," the four written Gospels principally arose. Hence their main purpose is not so much to give us an historical sketch of our Lord's life, a biography, as to point out what the facts, sayings and deeds concerning Christ signify for the spiritual life of the faithful. In presenting

[6] *Exégèse et Théologie* (Paris, 1961), I, 25-61.
[7] RB 499; *Exégèse*. . . , 46.
[8] RB 511f.; *Exégèse*. . . , 59f.

the common oral Gospel each Evangelist had his own object and aim, his proper theological viewpoint, his personal information. That is why various details of Christ's life and preaching are not given in the same chronological order, why some elements are found in the one and lacking in the other, why certain aspects of Christ's person and teaching are differently accentuated in the four Gospels. That is also why Our Lord's words are frequently rendered in different fashion by the different Evangelists: a fact which makes it clear that they did not always aim at reproducing his precise words with mechanical exactitude, cf., for instance, the verbally different accounts of the institution of the Eucharist and of the wording of the Lord's Prayer. (Matthew 26:26-29; Mark 14:22-25; Luke 22:15-20; 1 Cor. 11:23-25; and Matthew 6:9-15; Luke 11:1-4). On the other hand the existence of a common oral Gospel (of which various parts certainly had been written down) together with the fact that the Evangelists, and particularly the three Synoptics, somehow depend on each other, explains why the Gospels concur in so many cases and very often agree to the letter. But the four Gospels also reflect that fuller and deeper sense which, under the constant and progressive revelation of the Holy Spirit, had come to be discerned in the facts of Christ's life, as faithfully transmitted in the Apostolic Church. This is specially noticeable in the fourth Gospel, where they are also signs, only plainly to be understood in the light of Our Lord's resurrection and glorification, as is often explicitly stated in this Gospel (John 2:17-22; 12:16; 13:7; 16:4).

That we have come to understand all this so much better, is the result of the method of Form Criticism. Of course, this embraces far more than the mere outline of the history of the formation of the Gospels, given above. According to its original proponents it aims first to discover the various literary forms of the primitive units, out of which, they think, the Gospels arose. In these they distinguish: a) so-called "logia": sapiential, eschatological, apocalyptical sayings, legal or disciplinary prescriptions, Christ's pronouncements about himself ("Ich-Worte"), parables, allegories; and b) "narratives": apophthegms or paradigms, "Novellen," legends, miracle-stories. And from that the method goes on to search for the "Sitz im Leben" of those original literary forms, viz., to determine their precise "situation" and significance in the life of the primitive community; how they originated, why they came to be used, what tendencies they represent, etc. In this respect Form Criticism is often vitiated by a large amount of subjectivism in identifying the primitive units and their various literary forms, by a disregard of the supernatural, and by a scepticism about the reliability of tradition which is supposed to have invented facts, sayings, and deeds concerning Christ, instead of having faithfully handed them down. It is vitiated too by a lack of confidence in the knowledge, capacity, and trustworthiness of writers and eyewitnesses like Matthew and John; it is doubted if they, or Mark and Luke either, had much or anything to do with the composition of the Gospels. However, if Form Criticism is applied not from this rationalistic viewpoint, but from the sound principles of Catholic Faith, and with the necessary prudence and circumspection, it may enable us to get at the proper "Sitz im Leben" of much that the Gospels contain, and will make us understand these better along with the message of salvation they convey. Conclusions can easily be drawn from Form Criticism, and indeed some have been drawn, in a superficial and imprudent way. But this has been done, as generally in all questions concerning Scripture, by those who busy themselves with the popularization of new opinions and recent theories, which they have not personally studied themselves, rather than by real Biblical scholars.

The present state of uneasiness and fear on account of so-called excesses in Biblical Criticism reminds one of a somewhat similar anxious atmosphere some 20 years ago. A certain Dain Cohenel (a pseudonym for an Italian priest Dolindo Ruotulo) began in 1930 an immense biblical commentary: *Holy Scripture, Psychology — Commentary — Meditation.*[9] This work, because of false and erroneous interpretations deriving from the ultra-conservative and anti-critical mentality of the author, after the publication of its thirteenth volume in 1939, was put on the Index with the note "donec corrigatur" by the Holy Office in 1940.[10] The author humbly submitted.[11] But hardly six or seven months later, there appeared an anonymous pamphlet, written, as was ascertained, by the same Dain Cohenel, which was first sent to the Pope, then to the Roman Cardinals, to all the Archbishops and Bishops of Italy and to the Superiors General of the Religious Orders: *A very grave danger for the Church and souls: the critical-scientific system in the study and interpretation of Holy Scripture, its lamentable deviations and aberrations.*[12] In this the study of Holy Scripture, as presented by the then best known Italian exegetes: Vaccari, Ricciotti, Tondelli, Szerbo, and as taught by the Pontifical Biblical Institute and other Pontifical Athenaea of Rome, is described as an astute move and artifice of Satan himself, a hotch-potch of modernism, rationalism, naturalism, scepticism, and atheism. All this the author tries to prove from ecclesiastical documents and mostly from the Encyclical *Pascendi*. Of the Pontifical Biblical Institute, directed by the Jesuits, he writes: "Their school, as one can see from what it has produced and produces, is laden with lethal consequences for souls; for in this case it is painfully verified, that the pupils always surpass the masters and, once set on the slope of Criticism, slide down into its depths and draw ever nearer to rationalistic and Protestant methods."[13] He plainly approves what another anonymous author, cited by him, said, *viz.*, that he would surely not advise the reading of books like *De historia primaeva* (by the late Father F. Ceuppens, O.P., Old Testament Professor at the Angelicum) which appear in the libraries of certain Pontifical theological faculties of Rome, where for some the great master is the late biblicist, Lagrange.[14] Dain Cohenel concludes his pamphlet by appealing to the Supreme Pontiff that he may deign to give his attention to

[9] *La Sacra Scrittura, Psicologia—Commento—Meditazione* (Gravina di Puglia, Seminario Vescovile).

[10] *AAS* 32 (1940) 553.

[11] *Ibid.*, 554.

[12] *Un gravissimo pericolo per la Chiesa e le anime: Il sistema critico-scientifico nello studio e nell'interpretazione della Sacra Scrittura, e sue deviazioni funeste e le sue aberrazioni* (Vale come manoscritto. Riservatissima di coscienza). (Gravina di Puglia) 45.

[13] *Op. cit.*, 21f.

[14] *Op. cit.*, 23.

this embarrassing question of Biblical Criticism and expel the profaners out of the living temple of the Word of God.

Pope Pius XII answered first by authorizing and approving a *Letter* of August 20, 1941, directed by the Pontifical Biblical Commission to the Archbishops and Bishops of Italy, in which the pamphlet was very severely condemned,[15] and then by his own Encyclical *Divino afflante Spiritu*.

Against the similarity indicated above between Dain Cohenel's anxiety and the present state of uneasiness and fear about Biblical Criticism, it may be argued that the difference between the two is greater than the resemblance; for now the cultivation of Biblical Criticism is just as severely censured as Cohenel's rejection of the same, by the recent *Monitum* of the Holy Office (which, moreover, refers to the Encyclical, *Humani Generis*). This grave warning of the Supreme Congregation must certainly be taken seriously and not be undervalued. Yet one has only to read it carefully — and this must always be done with regard to official ecclesiastical documents of which every word and sentence has been pondered — to realize that it speaks in very general terms. And if it does so, it does so on purpose. When the Holy Office thought it necessary to issue this severe *Monitum*, we may rightly suppose that it had concrete modern opinions in view, which compromise the genuine historical and objective truth of the Old and New Testament, particularly of Our Lord's words and deeds; nevertheless it has not even slightly hinted at any particular opinion. And if it has not done so, it has refrained from doing so on purpose. And here, it would seem, lies another lesson which we learn from the *Monitum*: a warning not to be too rash and ready, but to be very prudent and cautious, in signalizing and stigmatizing certain opinions as wrong, erroneous, against Faith, in other words, as excessive. Modernism condemned by the papal Encyclical *Pascendi* was indeed wrong, erroneous, against Faith, but the opinions signalized and stigmatized by Dain Cohenel (the pseudonym means: Judge, priest of God), appealing to *Pascendi*, were not; his own opinions and his very appeal itself were excessive. Modernism itself, in its own day, brought about a counter-movement which became excessive in the opposite sense: Integralism. And the danger is not imaginary, I think, that the search for excessive opinions in biblical matters may lead to a kind of Integralism in our day. And this would be another and grave excess, though in the opposite direction, and it could do much harm. An ultra-conservative and anti-critical attitude in biblical studies, if it were to win through and impose itself, might not only bring those who devote themselves to a truly scientific study of Holy Scripture into a serious crisis of conscience, but would also do great damage to the Church.

The *Divino afflante Spiritu* has greatly encouraged the scientific approach to biblical studies, and it cannot have been the intention of Pope Pius XII to withdraw this encouragement, as one sometimes hears it said, by his grave words in the *Humani Generis*: "Particularly is to be deplored a certain too free interpretation of the historical books of the Old Testament, the supporters of which unjustly appeal to the letter not long ago directed by the Pontifical Biblical

[15] *AAS* 33 (1941) 465-472; *EB*⁴ 522-533.

Commission to the Archbishop of Paris, in order to defend their cause." [16] From the context it is clear that the Pope had principally in mind a too liberal explanation of the first eleven chapters of Genesis, of which alone there is question in the words which then follow; besides, the *Letter* mentioned does speak about those chapters, but contains not a word about the historical books of the Old Testament in general. Yet even with regard to these, there may be and have been excesses. However, by condemning these excesses, the Pope has surely not retracted what with so much emphasis he had recommended and insisted on before. Father, now Cardinal, Augustin Bea, S.J., after having first noted that various opinions, disapproved in the *Humani Generis*, in part do not concern questions directly dealt with in the *Divino afflante Spiritu*, but proceed from the principles of the so-called "New Theology," remarks that there is no contradiction between the two Encyclicals, as some maintained, for "one surely does not retract 'with one hand' what with the other is given in the preceding document. The principles of both Encyclicals are the same; but one must take account of the fact that the so-called 'New Theology' was in 1943 not so developed as in 1950, and that, on the other hand, experience had in the meantime shown certain abuses of the principles exposed in the *Divino afflante Spiritu*." [17] Those who in all sincerity take to heart the admonitions of the *Humani Generis* and the *Monitum* are not dispensed from following up the directives of the *Divino afflante Spiritu*; loyal obedience must be rendered to all the instructions of the Church.

The serious warning Pius XII then gave in the *Divino afflante Spiritu* holds good now also: "Let all the other sons of the Church bear in mind that the efforts of these hard workers in the vineyard of the Lord should be judged not only with equity and justice, but also with the greatest charity; and they should abhor that intemperate zeal which imagines that whatever is new should for that very reason be opposed or suspected." [18]


# THE PASTORAL VALUE OF
# THE WORD OF GOD

Augustin Cardinal Bea


In the school of the word of God were formed the great *lay* apologists of the early centuries, such as Aristides, St. Justin, whose dialogue with Trypho gives

[16] *AAS* 42 (1950) 576; *EB*[4] 618.
[17] "La scienza biblica cattolica da Leone XIII a Pio XII," *Divinitas* 4 (1959) 623, 631f.
[18] *AAS* 35 (1943) 319; *EB* 564.
Published originally in *Worship*, 30 (1956), 637-48. Reprinted by permission of the publisher.

evidence of a marvelous knowledge of holy Scripture, Athenagoras, Minucius Felix, Lactantius and many others.

There is perhaps no more convincing experimental proof of the pastoral value of the word of God in the liturgy than this constant practice of the first centuries of Christianity and its abundant fruit manifested in the holy life of so many of the faithful, in the heroic death of so many martyrs, in the testimony of so many defenders of the faith.

The constancy of the martyrs, the holy life of so many of the faithful in the midst of all the temptations of paganism, their steadfastness in the faith in the face of heretics are certainly primarily a fruit of God's abundant grace, proportioned to the difficulties of the times. But the *doctrinal* basis of this holy, strong, persevering, victorious Christian life was without doubt the instruction drawn from the ever living font of the reading and explanation of the sacred Books. Now it may be asked: *What is the most profound and decisive reason for this marvelous efficacy of the holy Scripture?*

1. Someone might suggest the *literary or intellectual qualities* of the sacred Books or the eloquence of the preachers.

As to these latter, we may be sure that not all were Augustines or Chrysostoms. Most were zealous bishops or worthy priests who explained the sacred texts as best they could, without any pretense at being great orators or learned exegetes.

Nor can the literary and intellectual qualities of the books of the Bible be considered such as to produce particularly notable fruits. To be sure, literary merits and great intellectual values are found in the holy Scripture in more than ordinary measure. Consider St. Paul's flights of thought, St. John's profound meditations, the moving parables proposed by our Lord, the magnificent poetry of Isaiah, the tender accents of Jeremiah, the manifold beauties of the Psalms. All these gems, duly perceived and appreciated by the soul, can certainly make a profound impression.

But it remains true that such gems are not found in all the books of the Bible and that such as there are, are not so easily accessible to all. The simplicity of the style and the limpidity of the doctrine have been an obstacle for a good many persons since ancient times, and are so still. Already in St. Paul's time "the wisdom of the wise" despised the unadorned word of the Apostle, who was preaching Christ crucified (1 Cor. 1:19; 1:23; 1:12), and there were those of the faithful at Corinth who preferred to Paul, with his simple and homely teaching, the learned Apollos who paid more attention to literary form and as a good Alexandrine probably took an interest also in establishing the agreement between the Gospel of Christ and the knowledge of the philosophers.

So also in later times the learned and lettered, "accustomed to smooth, polished discourses and poems, spurned as uncultured the simple common language of the divine Books," [1] saying that they were "written by uneducated and ordinary men" and that "the language is commonplace and of low quality." [2]

---

[1] Lactantius, *Divinae Institutiones*, 6, 21; *P.L.*, 6, 713.

[2] Arnobius, *The Case against the Pagans*, book 1, 58; *P.L.*, 5, 796; translated by George E. McCracken (Westminster, Md.: The Newman Press, 1949), p. 104.

Many had the same impression that the young Augustine experienced: "When I first read those Scriptures, they seemed to me unworthy to be compared with the majesty of Cicero. My conceit was repelled by their simplicity, and I had not the mind to penetrate into their depths."[3]

Again in our days and our environment these ancient Books, expressed in language of another style and with literary genres far from ours, will cause no little difficulty — humanly speaking — to many.

2. And yet these sacred Books have had and still have today an attraction, a persuasive force, a salutary influence exerted by no other literary work, be it Dante Alighieri, William Shakespeare, Homer, Plato or any other. *Where and whence is the secret?* The answer can be given in two words: these sacred Books are *the word of God*.

I say purposely that they *are* the word of God, not that they merely *contain* the word of God, as a catechism or manual of religion might. They *are* the word of God through that singular charism of inspiration by which God, the eternal Truth, subjects to Himself in a manner as unique as it is rare all the faculties of the human writer and, while leaving to him "his own temperament, his own personal features and his own character,"[4] makes him express "all those things and only those things which He Himself should command."[5] Here it is no longer man who speaks; it is the *Holy Spirit* "who spoke through the prophets," "the Spirit of Truth" (John 14:17) who teaches us the truth by means of the sacred Books (cf. John 16:13).

As our late Holy Father Pope Pius XII said in concise words: "This is the reason why the sacred pages inspired by God are in themselves rich with native meaning. Endowed with a divine force, they have value in themselves. Adorned with a splendor from above, they shine resplendent in themselves, provided the interpreter with an accurate and faithful explanation knows how to draw from them all the treasures of wisdom and prudence hidden in them."[6]

When our Lord says of His words uttered in the synagogue of Capernaum: "The words I have spoken to you are spirit and life" (John 6:64), this holds for every sentence, every thought found in holy Scripture. For this reason the Apostle can write of the Scripture: "The word of God is living and effective and sharper than any two-edged sword. It penetrates to the division of soul and spirit, of joints and marrow, and discerns the thoughts and intentions of the heart" (Heb. 4:12).

Although holy Scripture cannot be called, as some have wanted to call it, a "sacrament" in the technical sense of the word (it cannot even be called simply a "sacramental"), as if it produced its effects merely "*ex opere operantis Ecclesiae*," in virtue of the dignity and the powerful intercession of the Church, still there is inherent in the very words of Scripture, read and applied with a

[3] St. Augustine, *Confessions*, book 3, ch. 5; *P.L.*, 32, 686; translated by F. J. Sheed (New York: Sheed & Ward, 1943), p. 46.

[4] Benedict XV, encyclical *Spiritus Paraclitus; A.A.S.* 12 (1920), 390; *E.B.* n. 448 (1st ed.: 461).

[5] Leo XIII, encyclical *Providentissimus Deus*; *A.A.S.* 26 (1893/4), 289; *E.B.* n. 125 (110).

[6] Pius XII, encyclical *Divino Afflante Spiritu*; A.A.S. 35 (1943), 312; *E.B.* n. 553.

devout disposition, a light and a power which surpasses the light and the power of purely human words and gives the words of Scripture a singular, unique authority and strength.

This virtue does not always make itself known so powerfully as it did in the lives of some saints, for example St. Antony, who on hearing the words of the Gospel, "Go and sell all your possessions and give the proceeds to the poor, for which you will have an investment in heaven" (Matthew 19:21), renounced all and became the great hermit admired by his contemporaries and by posterity;[7] or St. Augustine, who, inwardly disturbed for so many years by the most anguishing problems, heard the mysterious "Take and read" and found in the Apostle's words the light and the strength to lead him to a solution;[8] or finally St. Francis, who, right here in Assisi, having heard in the little chapel of the Portiuncula the words of the holy Gospel, "Do not procure pocket money, whether gold or silver or copper; or a traveling bag, or an extra coat, or sandals, or a staff" (Matthew 10:9-10), cast away everything and cried, "This is what I have long been seeking; now my desire is fulfilled!"

But for every man and in every situation the Apostle's word remains true: "All Scripture is inspired by God and useful for teaching, for reproving, for correcting, for instructing in holiness, that the man of God [that is, the preacher with God's mandate] may be perfect, fully equipped for every good deed" (2 Tim. 3:16-17).

3. In these words St. Paul includes all the tasks incumbent on the *shepherd of souls* and shows him where he will find the most efficacious means for satisfying his pastoral duties. This is not the place to set forth in detail the manifold efficacy of the word of God in the pastoral life. Let us note only one thing, the authority which the word of God gives the Christian preacher. "This special and most remarkable virtue of the Scriptures," says Leo XIII, "which arises from the divine breath of the Holy Spirit, is what confers authority on the sacred orator, furnishes him with an apostolic liberty of speech, and bestows on him a powerful and conquering eloquence."[9] How many times the preacher must reprehend defects and vices, call the blinded back to their senses, exhort sinners to repentance, confirm the weak in their good resolutions, comfort the afflicted and raise them up to Christian hope! How could he do all this with more force and authority than by making use of the words of God Himself, pronounced by the Prophets, by the Apostles, by the Lord Himself, and preserved for us in the sacred Books?

4. There can be no doubt, therefore, that a special force and pastoral importance inheres in the holy Scripture, and that for this reason every attempt to have the sacred Books known, read, meditated and used is worthy of high praise and deserves full approval and sincere encouragement. "Let the ministers of the sanctuary be convinced," said our late Holy Father, "that all these efforts, and whatsoever else an apostolic zeal and a sincere love of the divine word may

---

[7] St. Athanasius, *The Life of St. Antony*, ch. 2; *P.G.*, 26, 841; translated by Sister Mary Emily Keenan, S.C.N., in *Early Christian Biographies* (New York: Fathers of the Church, Inc., 1952), pp. 135-136.

[8] St. Augustine, *Confessions*, book 8, ch. 12; *P.L.*, 32, 762.

[9] Leo XIII, encyclical *Providentissimus Deus; A.A.S.* 26 (1893/4), 272; *E.B.* n. 87 (72).

find suitable to this high purpose, will be an efficacious help to the *cure of souls*." [10]

## The Word of God and the Eucharist

1. The singular efficacy inherent in the word of God by virtue of its own nature is increased and given new power, as it were, by its *union with the eucharistic Sacrifice*. The assembly of the faithful who come together to assist at the celebration of the eucharistic Sacrifice is in reality the most propitious setting for the fruitful reading and explanation of the word of God.

Here this reading of the sacred Books is surrounded with the mysterious recollection found in the house of God and the reverent ceremonies with which the Church honors the sacred Book. Here is found that sense of spiritual community which unites the faithful of a parish with one another and with their pastor. Here the attention and devotion of some worshipers transmits itself almost spontaneously to the rest, and there is created an atmosphere of spiritual receptiveness, interior preparation which is hard to come by in another environment.

Here the *shepherd of souls* finds himself facing his entire flock, without distinction of sex or of rank, of intellectual level or of social position. Humanly speaking there may be some disadvantages in this diversity of age, of education, of social stratum; but — setting aside here the possibility of avoiding these disadvantages with suitable organization — in any case the possible disadvantages are largely compensated for by the fruits which the combination of the sacred reading with the sublime eucharistic Sacrifice brings to the faithful, fruits richer and more precious than those of any teaching imparted outside of the liturgical assembly, whether in Bible study clubs or in public conferences or in school rooms or again in magazine articles or pamphlets.

In the liturgical function the shepherd of souls speaks not as president of an association or director of a club or professor in a scholastic chair. Here the priest speaks as a priest, as teacher and guide of the souls entrusted to him, deputy of God, appointed and sent by the bishop, successor of the Apostles. Here, more than in any other place, the priest has recourse with the words of God Himself to the conscience of each one of his flock; without human respect, he sets out for each one authoritatively his sacred duties, promises eternal reward to the good in the name of God and, with the words of God, threatens the disobedient and recalcitrant with eternal punishment in the powerful words of the Prophets and the Apostles. Here the priest carries out in the best way the order given by St. Paul to his beloved Timothy: "Preach the Word of God, be urgent in season, out of season. Convince, rebuke, exhort people with perfect patience and teaching" (2 Tim. 4:2).

2. To all these advantages can be added an element more important and more decisive than any other: *the special divine grace* which comes from the mystical union of the proclamation of the word of God with the eucharistic Sacrifice.

Here, in the majestic frame of the holy Mass, the soul has been carefully

[10] Pius XII, encyclical *Divino Afflante Spiritu*; *A.A.S.* 35 (1943), 321; *E.B.* n. 566.

prepared before listening to the sacred reading: it confesses its faults with the priest, calls on the divine clemency in the *Kyrie*, recites with the Church those prayers full of dignified emotion which the centuries have handed down to us. Thus the seed of the word of God falls not on an uncultivated field but on ground carefully worked, ready to receive it.

Then after the sacred reading and the homily follows the eucharistic Sacrifice, in which the faithful communicant takes part with that happy disposition of soul which has been created through the sacred reading and the exhortation. The word of God has revived the faith in him, raised his mind to filial hope; and, above all, the remembrance of the great divine favors granted to poor humanity, the story of the incarnation of the Son of God, of His holy life and of the death undergone for us and for our sins, has rekindled and nourished the fire of love.

Thus the soul, predisposed and prepared by the word of God, will receive in the eucharistic Sacrifice new and more abundant graces, which will fecundate the seed sown in the holy reading, will make it germinate and grow, that it may bear fruit, here thirtyfold, there sixtyfold, there again a hundredfold (Mark 4:8).

Here we find ourselves face to face with the ultimate and most profound reason why the Church, guided by the Holy Spirit, since the first centuries has united the reading and explanation of the word of God with the offering of the eucharistic Sacrifice in one great liturgical unity and has desired that the same priest be "minister of the word" and "minister of the Sacrament."

3. Moreover, our troubled times present special reasons for taking advantage of this providential union of the sacred reading with the eucharistic Sacrifice. It is a fact that for very many people today the Sunday and feast day Mass is the sole occasion for a religious instruction of any depth. Engaged day after day in long hours of exacting work, whether in industry or in public office or in private enterprises, many of our contemporaries are not in a position to assist at extraordinary sermons or at meetings of religious associations. Unfortunately, they must content themselves, or at least they do in fact content themselves, with assisting at Mass on the festival days to satisfy the Church's precept. Hence this is the *only* occasion offered the priest to speak to these parishioners of his and instruct them in the truths of the faith. In many countries, moreover, atheistic rulers prohibit any meeting for religious purposes outside of the churches, and no longer even admit the priest to the public schools to give religious instruction to the pupils.

It is no wonder, then, that apostolic souls are insisting strongly on the priest's holy duty to make full use of the Sunday Mass, practically the only occasion still left us to instruct great numbers of the Christian people in the truths of the faith in an age when the powers of darkness are doing everything to darken minds with their materialistic and atheistic doctrines and to seduce the younger generation from their very childhood to a licentious and irreligious life.

This situation, in many points similar to that of the Christians in the persecutions and doctrinal struggles of the first centuries, explains also why zealous shepherds of souls ardently desire that the number of "preachable" pericopes, today quite restricted, be increased by some opportune provision, either by introducing a three- or four-year cycle, or in some other manner appropriate to the special needs and particular conditions of our times.

To be sure, subjects extraneous to the biblical pericopes can also be chosen for the sermon; but the homily has always been the sermon preferred by the Church for holy Mass, and the prescription of the *Caeremoniale Episcoporum* is still valid today: "The sermon within the Mass should regularly be on the Gospel of the day." [11]

Many think, therefore, that a greater number of pericopes, well chosen with a view to including all the essential doctrines of the faith, would be a great advantage in our day for the cure of souls. It will be the task of the competent authority of the Holy See to examine the feasibility of such proposals in the light of the entire liturgical reform and to make decisions. The decisions will take account of all the facets of a delicate and complex question which for three or four decades has been the object of study and discussion on the part of liturgists and of zealous shepherds of souls.

4. But perhaps someone will object: Does not all this mean *depriving the sacred liturgy of its sublime dignity* of divine worship and putting it instead at the service of men?

First of all it can be answered: If holy Church, guided by the Holy Spirit, has taken this course from her very first days, certainly the course is not erroneous and is not contrary to the dignity of the liturgy.

Furthermore, the Church's liturgical action comprises not only the eucharistic Sacrifice and the community's prayer, but also a number of "other rites appropriate for the saving of souls and for the honor due to God." Among these liturgical rites our late Holy Father Pius XII in the encyclical *Mediator Dei* enumerates "the reading of the Law, the Prophets, the Gospel and the Apostolic Epistles" and finally "the homily or sermon in which the official head of the congregation recalls and explains the practical bearing of the commandments of the divine Master and the chief events of His life, combining instruction with appropriate exhortation and illustration for the benefit of all his listeners." [12]

And moreover, to listen with reverence to the word of God, to welcome it with readiness and gratitude into the soul, to prepare oneself carefully to follow it out by a truly and solidly Christian life — may not all this be itself a true and valuable worship of God? And may we not say that the holy Eucharist itself, sacrifice of infinite value offered to God, was instituted by our Lord also as a gift, as "communion," nourishment given by God to our souls? Should we be surprised, then, if our Lord in the most sublime act of worship, the holy Mass, wants to reward the veneration we offer Him, not only with the eucharistic Bread of His sacred body but also with the spiritual bread of His holy word?

It is one of the most exquisite delicacies of God's love that this love is at the same time a receiving and a giving in a reciprocity which has no parallel in the natural world. Man, listening to the word of God and welcoming it, prepares and fits his soul to render to God, his Lord and Creator, that sublime worship in spirit and in truth, that most perfect gift, the immeasurable sacrifice of the

---

[11] *Caeremoniale Episcoporum*, book 1, ch. 22, n. 2.
[12] Pius XII, encyclical *Mediator Dei; A.A.S.* 39 (1947), 529.

Man-God, and in return receives from God the precious gift of the grace which flows from the eucharistic Sacrifice and helps the soul to obey ever more perfectly the will of God, made known to him in the word of God. This mystical union of the word of God and the Bread of Life which is wonderfully realized in the sacred liturgy is something peculiar to and characteristic of the Church of Christ, a special gift, rather a unique gift, which the divine Spouse has given His immaculate Bride, the Church.

# THE SACRAMENT OF SCRIPTURE

F. X. Durrwell, C.Ss.R.

In every form, Christ's presence among men has the same purpose. By his very being and in everything he does, Christ is always the Redeemer; his presence is there to create a communion of salvation with men. This Scripture does; it, too, establishes a communion, different from the Eucharist but real none the less, a communion of thought between two people who love each other and talk together, one of whom is Christ.

Whenever we read his Scriptures with faith, Christ speaks. It was long ago that he inspired his Apostles, and centuries have passed since. But though the human writing of the Book was something that happened in the past, the inspired words still live in the moment when they are spoken by Christ. "This was written for us, and preserved for us; it is recited for us and will also be recited for our descendants, right up to the end of time." [1] The redeeming action of Christ in glory knows no succession of time; he speaks to the heart of the Church in eternity. The thoughts formulated by the Apostles and put into writing at a given moment of history are addressed to the Church of all the ages in an eternal present. Men are coming into existence now, are now reading Christ's word with faith, are hearing Christ speaking to them now.

Because Scripture is an everlasting word, always being said, the epistle to the Hebrews introduces all its quotations from Scripture by saying, "The Holy Ghost saith," "The Holy Ghost doth testify" (Heb. 3:7; 10:15) — all in the present tense.

Christ speaks to us at this moment, but not like a friend far away communicating by letter; "God is not far from every one of us" (Acts 17:27) and "Christ dwells in our hearts" (Eph. 3:17). We sit at his feet and listen to him: "We must listen to the Gospel as to Christ amongst us," [2] "the Gospel is the very

Reprinted from *In The Redeeming Christ* (New York: Sheed and Ward, 1963) pp. 41-9. Reprinted by permission of the publisher.
    [1] St. Augustine, *In Jo., tract. 30; PL,* 35 (1632).
    [2] St. Augustine, *In Jo., tract. 30; PL,* 35 (1632).

mouth of Christ," [3] a sacrament of his words to us. There is no human intermediary between his word and our mind; the sound we hear is actually his voice. According to St. Thomas, God has two far from equal ways of teaching us: he speaks through an intermediary in human books or religious instruction, but "he speaks directly to our minds in sacred Scripture." [4] Tired of hearing only a distant echo of Christ's voice from human lips, saints like St. Thérèse of Lisieux resolved to read nothing but Scripture.

This communion with Christ in thought is even closer than that between two people speaking together. When we look for the truth hidden in the text of Scripture, Christ can communicate the meaning of his words directly to our minds. I can read a given human book, and learn a philosophical truth from it. But what I get from its words depends on my perspicacity; I understand it only in proportion to my intelligence. The author may be dead, but even were he alive, he could not communicate to his reader the same understanding of the truth he is expressing that he has himself. The writer's thought comes to me not directly, but through signs, through words which I must interpret. But when we hear the words of Scripture, "the Master is in our hearts" [5] and communicates the same understanding of the truths they express that he himself has; he arouses in us his own sentiments: "Let the word of Christ dwell in our hearts in all its riches" (Col. 3:16). It is a wonderful communion of mind and heart — the communion of Mary of Bethany, of the disciples on the road to Emmaus.

This communion, too, is effective, giving eternal life. Of Scripture as of the Eucharist it can be said, "Pinguis est panis" — it is a substantial bread. For Christ lives now only in his redemptive act, given to God for mankind, immortal in his death for them, and forever an instrument of God's action in raising up to eternal life. Every presence and every action of Christ works redemption. When he appeared in the evening of Easter Day, he sent the Apostles out to forgive sins. In the same way he made them write the pages of the New Testament for the remission of sins and the salvation of men.

By we know not what hidden influence, Scripture bestows a spirit of life on those who read it with faith. "Was our heart not burning within us, whilst he spoke?" (Luke 24:32); "The word of God is living and effectual" (Heb. 4:12); it is the "sword of the spirit" (Eph. 6:17). If ordinary human words, noble or degraded, can transform a man by their psychological dynamism, how much more must the word of God penetrate and pierce to the very depths of the soul, for it is "more piercing than any two-edged sword; and reaching unto the division of the soul and the spirit, of the joints also and the marrow" (Heb. 4:12).

It is not merely that God's word contains the thoughts of Christ, lofty and profound, which can stir up man's heart; but it is spoken for *me* and *my* salvation; it is spoken by my saviour, in the grace of the Holy Spirit which flows from his pierced side. The Gospel is a message of redemption, a sacrament of salvation, in which "the Holy Ghost works in efficacious words." [6]

[3] St. Augustine, *Sermo LXXXV*, 1; *PL*, 38 (520).
[4] *In 2 Tim.*, c. 3. lectio 3.
[5] St. Augustine, *Sermo 85*, 1. *PL*, 38 (520).
[6] Paschasius Radbert, *De Corpore et Sanguine Domini*, 3, 2; *PL*, 120 (1276).

"Attend unto reading" (1 Tim. 4:13). For "the holy scriptures can instruct thee to salvation, by the faith which is in Christ Jesus. All scripture, inspired of God, is profitable to teach, to reprove, to correct, to instruct in justice, that the man of God may be perfect, furnished to every good work" (2 Tim. 3:15-17).

Scripture is the treasure of "the man of God"; it is that rich treasure from which the householder "bringeth forth new things and old" (Matthew 13:32) to accomplish "every good work." That good work is first of all accomplished actually in the heart of the man of God; the word is planted there, grows there and bears fruit there ("the word of truth . . . bringeth forth fruit and groweth" [Col. 1:5-6]); it gives consolation there, too, that joy which glows where there is salvation, whereby we are born to the hope of the Last Day: "For what things soever were written were written for our learning: that through patience and the comfort of the Scriptures, we might have hope" (Rom. 15:4).

The Fathers seem to have been unable to find images strong enough to describe the banquet of redemption offered on the table of Scripture. The Gospel, according to St. Jerome, is true food and true drink;[7] Scripture is an ocean of fulness, says St. Ambrose, a cup from which we drink Christ, a cup that is a river whose waves delight the city of God.[8] It is the cure for all our ills: "Take and drink; all sickness of soul finds its remedy in Scripture."[9] The Eucharist, says St. John Chrysostom, makes us as fierce lions in face of the devil. Also, says St. Athanasius, Scripture puts our adversary to flight, for "in Scripture the Lord is present, and the demons, who cannot bear his presence, cry: I beg you, do not torment us before our time. They burn simply from seeing the Lord present."[10]

Thus the banquet of Scripture feeds and strengthens just as does the eucharistic banquet of Christ's immolated flesh; and like it, it has its joys, "the chaste delights of Scripture" spoken of by St. Augustine,[11] "the comfort of the Scriptures" which gives us hope (Rom. 15:4), that great comfort which made the Maccabees say, "We needed none of these things, nor any one, having for our comfort the holy books that are in our hands" (1 Maccabees 12:9).

Scripture and the Eucharist are the life-force and the joy of the Church, because they are for her a communion in the body given and blood shed for us. Other than that banquet, there exists only what this life can offer us: "We have in this world only this one good thing: to feed upon his flesh and drink his blood, not only in the [eucharistic] sacrament, but in the reading of Scripture."[12]

Despite its own efficaciousness, Scripture does not enter into any kind of competition in our souls with that other sacrament of presence and communion, the Eucharist; it does not supplant it, or make it unnecessary. The central point of Christian worship is the incarnate Word in his eternal sacrifice. Scripture

[7] *In Eccle.*; *PL*, 23 (1039).
[8] St. Ambrose. *In Ps.* 1, 33; *PL*, 14 (940).
[9] St. Augustine, *In Ps.* 36, 1, 3; *PL*, 36 (357).
[10] *Ep. ad Marcellinum*, 33; *PG*, 27 (44ff).
[11] *Conf.*, 11, 2; *PL*, 32 (810).
[12] St. Jerome, *op. cit.*

comes to us from that centre, and must canalize our minds and hearts towards it. It is by the Eucharist that Christ is present to us in the reality of his body, in the reality of his immolation and his glory. So Scripture must collaborate with the Sacrament to unite believers with the redeeming Christ.

In the Mass, the splendour of Scripture comes to surround the sacred body of Christ on all sides, as the royal purple of the incarnate Word in his immolation, as the veil of the Holy of Holies in which the eternal sacrifice is offered — a veil which is not there to hide but to reveal the way into the sanctuary. It was in this way, through the veil of the Scriptures, that the world of the Old Testament was brought to Christ.

Many non-Catholic Christians read Scripture more assiduously than many Catholics, but do not feed on the Eucharist. Among a lot of them there is a profound tendency not to accept the incarnation of the Word in its ultimate reality, but to prefer what seems to be a worship of God's transcendence — to prefer, at least in practice, the spoken Word to the personal Word, to remain in the Old Testament, on the threshold of the fulness of the Incarnation. Many Catholics have a tremendous devotion to the Eucharist, but neglect Scripture. Many of them, perhaps, do not therefore know the personal Word as well as they might, and are not in the best possible dispositions to receive him in the Eucharist. For the secret of opening one's heart to that one Word is contained most fully in Scripture.

## Necessary dispositions for a fruitful reading of Scripture

God allows us to "taste his good word" (Heb. 6:5), but we do not always appreciate its savour. This bread is no more acceptable every day to all tastes than was the manna in the desert, or is the Eucharist. Our soul must be disposed to receive God's word.

### To read in faith

We must have ears to hear the Word of God which are not the ears of the body: "Let him that hath ears, hear what the Spirit saith to the churches" (Apoc. 2:7). The ears to hear are the ears of faith. It is faith which opens the word of God to us. "The word of God worketh in you who have believed" (1 Thess. 2:13).

Like every heavenly reality offered to us during our life on earth, Scripture has two facets — one accessible to the senses, the other visible to faith alone. It was so with Christ, whom his enemies saw with their eyes and nailed to the Cross, but whom his believers adored. It is thus with the Church, whose human face can be seen by all, but whose mystery is hidden for many. It is thus also with the Eucharist which to some is simply bread, and to others the body of the glorified Christ.

There are various ways of approaching Scripture, and not all of them lead to an encounter with Christ. Scholars without faith can make Scripture an object of investigation; but there is no critical apparatus that can bring them to the heart of Scripture, to the point of meeting with Christ. It has been said that

Scripture is a locked house with the key inside. To enter it one must live in it, one must be in Christ, in his house which is the Church. One must be inside faith. This is yet one more sphere in which it is true that "whosoever hath, to him shall be given" (Luke 13:18).

"My sheep hear my voice," said our Lord (John 10:16). Those outside may hear the words, but only the flock hear the voice, the voice which reveals the person. Thus it was on Easter morning that one of Christ's sheep recognized the Lord by the sound of his voice. There are the words, there is the voice; the first express ideas, the second a person. The words of Scripture can be compared with ordinary human words, but the voice is incomparable because the person it reveals is unique. While the believer listens to the succession of words, behind the closed doors of his soul he hears the voice, and the word reveals himself. Only faith has ears to hear the voice; it alone establishes contact with Christ. When he hears the voice, and feels that contact with our Lord, the believer knows that the words are addressed to him. Each sheep is called by his name, the encounter is personal, and becomes a dialogue. "Mary," said Christ, and Mary answered, "Rabboni!"

By the light of faith Scripture is seen to have a dimension that no other book has. It is not invariably the finest of all literature. Not all its lines contain profound ideas, and even the most striking may have had their edges blunted by long use. One can hardly deny that there are human books superior to some parts of Scripture. But to the believer, these words offer a dimension of mystery, a stirring resonance: for it is the Lord who speaks them. One may recall how Mozart once played the clavichord in the house of a rich burgher of Prague. At the end his host, greatly impressed, said, "Would that I were the Emperor! I should give you a pat on the shoulder, and say, 'You really have played well, Mozart!' That would be enough for you. But who am I to be able to reward you?" Similarly, the word which of itself would be but a pebble on the roadway, is a diamond when spoken by the Lord.

## To read in the light of Easter

The Christ whose voice Scripture makes us hear is the Lord of Easter, the Christ of faith. He became the author of that book in the light and fire of the glory of his raising by the Father. The rivers of the Spirit, of all the charismata of the New Testament, the gift of scriptural inspiration, all flow from his pierced side after his return to his Father. The Apostles and Evangelists understood this, and wrote "in that day," in the light of Easter. Even Christ's life on earth was told from the point of view of his resurrection, in faith in the glorified Christ. The thought of his death and resurrection is the golden thread which binds together the separate pages of the Gospel and makes it a book.

Again, it was the risen Christ, source of the Spirit, who opened the minds of his disciples on the road to Emmaus, and interpreted the Scriptures to them.

Just as Magdalene could no longer catch hold of the glorified Lord with her bodily hands, so scholars cannot hear him with their human minds. He is accessible only to faith. He can only be seen, touched and heard by his disciples, those who eat and drink with him after the Resurrection (Acts 10:40).

To him who believes, our Lord's face appears even in the pages of the Old Testament. It is Christ, dead and risen again, who gives the whole Bible its unity and meaning. If it is divorced from the glorified Christ it is a dead letter, a story written in sand, a set of laws which cannot give life. "The letter killeth, but the spirit quickeneth" (2 Cor. 3:6). "The letter" here is the realities of the Old Testament considered in themselves, and all the things of this world. "The spirit" means reality in its fullness, the reality of heaven, of which all other realities are but fleeting shadows. The reality of heaven comes at the end, according to the promise given in the Old Testament; it is none other than the very Spirit of God, in whom all will be consummated, all be made one and living.

Now the risen Christ "is the Spirit" (2 Cor. 3:17). He is the solid body whose shadow was cast right back to the beginning of the world (Col. 2:17). The reality of all things is in him, and without him all is shadow and death. In him all becomes spirit and life. For he has been "enlivened in the Spirit" (1 Peter 3:18), in the total outpouring of the Holy Ghost. He has been so completely transformed in the spirit, that he himself has become a "quickening spirit" (1 Cor. 15:45), and that we may speak of the body of the glorified Christ as in a sense the body of the Holy Ghost.[13] In his redeeming glory, he has become the centre of creation (Col. 1:16). "And I, if I be lifted up, will draw all things to myself" (John 12:32); he draws to himself not only all men, but all things, making himself the centre of nature and history, of the Old Testament and the New, lord of the past and the future; Elijah and Moses, prophecy and the Law, the whole of the Old Covenant, all turn their faces towards the transfigured Christ. He is God's "Amen" (2 Cor. 1:20) to the promise of the Old Testament, and to all the promises contained in the first creation, "because in him it hath well pleased the Father that all the fullness [of the universe] should dwell" (Col.1:19).

The unbeliever looking at the Bible sees only the dead letter, the disparate elements; his eyes are bound. The believer reads with uncovered eyes, and has only to open the Old Testament to find himself face to face with Our Lord in glory; he feels himself "transformed into the same image from glory to glory, as by the action of the Lord who is the Spirit" (2 Cor. 3:14-18).

[13] St. Ambrose, *De Mysteriis,* 9, 58; *PL,* 16(409).

# 2 THE OLD TESTAMENT AND THE NEW

From the early centuries of the Church until our own day there have been widely divergent attitudes among Christians in regard to the Old Testament. Marcion, in the early second century A.D., rejected the entire Old Testament and founded a heretical sect whose main tenet was the complete rejection of Judaism as an influence on Christianity. At the present time certain Biblical critics, notably some of the followers of Rudolf Bultmann, assert a complete discontinuity between the Old Testament and the New. Investigation of the Old Testament to them is not "relevant" since it does not aid man to respond to the Gospel.

Most scholars, both Catholic and Protestant, see rather a continuous historical process of God's divine interventions throughout the Old and New Testaments. The progressive preparation for the coming of the Messiah, the numerous prophecies which link the two testaments as promise and fulfillment, the increasing understanding of God's saving design in history — all mark the realization that God's word is dynamic, that His Spirit guided the formation of Israel as the People of God, and of the New Israel which received the complete revelation of the Word.

In the field of relationships between the two Testaments much work has been done. Scholarly research has clarified aspects of questions like the messianic expectations of Israel, the thinking of devout Jews like the Qumran community and the dynamic character of the prophetic message. We not only have a better insight into the milieu into which Jesus came, but we also understand better many references in the Gospels.

The essential newness of the revelation in Christ is clear, but like the apostles we realize the importance of "all things that are written in the Law of Moses and the Prophets and the Psalms" (Luke 24:44) concerning Jesus.

# THE UNITY OF THE BIBLE

Eamonn O'Doherty

When we speak of the unity of the Bible we are usually referring to the fact that the New Testament is the fulfillment of the Old, so that the two parts of the Bible form a unit. All Christians take this fact for granted. They accept the testimony of the evangelists that the events of the New Testament occurred "so that the Scriptures might be fulfilled." And they express their belief in concrete form by binding the two parts of the Bible into one volume. For a Christian, the two Testaments make one Bible.

Yet most Christians would find it difficult to prove that the Bible is a unit, or to explain exactly how the New Testament fulfills the Old. They know it can be proved, and they leave that to the experts. The average reader is not concerned with proving anything. He is more interested in finding some master-theme which will guide him through the Bible. That is the type of unity we deal with here.

The reader's problem might be compared to that of a music-lover who hears his favorite composition end on one final, harmonious chord. What makes that chord harmonious? Why would any other sound so painfully discordant? A musician might explain it by analyzing the composition, isolating the musical theme, and then showing that this theme can reach its harmonious conclusion on this note, and this note only.

In the same way the Bible can be compared (with many qualifications) to a musical composition. The Old Testament ends on the second-last note. Is the New Testament its harmonious conclusion? If so, there must be some theme which unites all the Old Testament books, and then continues into the New Testament, to find there its perfection and fulfillment.

But what unity is there in the Old Testament? It has such a variety of books! There are books of history, poetry, prophecy, drama; collections of laws, hymns and maxims; books started ten centuries before Christ, and books finished near the end of the pre-Christian era. What have all these books in common? What common theme unites them?

## The common theme

This common theme can be isolated if we recall that Old Testament salvation-history is not a secular history of the Jewish people joined by land, language, and political beliefs, but a religious history of Israel, a group joined by a common faith in God. It is not a political history, describing what Israel did to achieve its political goals. It is a religious history, describing what God did to save His people. In other words, the Old Testament is the first part of the history of salvation.

Published originally in *The Bible Today*, 1 (1962), 53-57. Reprinted by permission of the publisher.

But the Old Testament is, by its own admission, incomplete. It looks forward to something, or Someone, yet to come. It describes God's action in the past only to arouse hope for His definitive act of salvation in the future, an act which is nowhere described in the Old Testament. Even at the end of the Old Testament period, pious Jews like Simeon were still waiting for "the consolation of Israel" (Luke 2:25). In the Old Testament, then, the basic belief expressed is: "God will save Israel!"

To this the New Testament answers: "God has saved Israel!" It presents itself as the Good News of salvation, as the fulfillment of all that Israel hoped for. It introduces something new, the amazing fact of the Incarnation, yet it insists again and again on its continuity with the Old Testament history of salvation. This idea is forcefully expressed in the opening words of Hebrews: "God, in the old days, spoke in many ways to our forefathers through the prophets; but, in these final days, He has spoken to us through His Son" (1:1-2). The New Testament, therefore, is the second and final part of the Bible, that is, of the history of the salvation of Israel.

## Salvation-History

The reader, then, who seeks unity in his Bible must have some idea of what the Bible means by history. We call it "salvation-history" to distinguish it from our modern, secular type of history.

The modern secular historian deals only with what he can see or hear or reason to. When he deals with the life of Christ he must limit his conclusions to the fact that Jesus was born in Bethlehem, raised in Nazareth, and seen publicly for two or three years before His execution in Jerusalem about 30 A.D. He can go no farther. He cannot conclude that Jesus was the Son of God, that He died for our sins, or that He revealed the means by which mankind is saved. All that is out of his department. As a secular historian he can give only a secular explanation of events.

But the evangelists, who are writing salvation-history, describe the life of Jesus as the intervention of God in history, as the act by which men are redeemed, as the "in-carnation" of the pre-existent Son of God. These statements are based on faith, on the acceptance of the revelation which Jesus made about Himself. And they are valid for those who accept with faith the Church's testimony that this is what God has revealed.

In the same way, a secular historian might explain the exodus from Egypt as the migration of Semitic tribes who, for economic reasons, were forced to seek a homeland elsewhere. And this may be true, as far as it goes. But the biblical historian, writing the history of what God did, describes it as the decisive intervention of God in history by which He created for Himself a chosen people. This event forms part of the history of salvation.

The reader seeking unity in his Bible must therefore have some idea of Israel's past and how it was interpreted, not as a series of political events (as it would be in secular history), but as the history of God's intervention in the world.

## The golden age

The best place to begin is with Israel's Golden Age, the period from Moses to Solomon, from about 1250 to 950 B.C. It was the age of the migration under Moses, the conquest under Joshua, the confederation under the Judges, and the rise of the monarchy under Saul, David and Solomon.

It was an age of great literary activity, and the court historians of David and Solomon climaxed this work by assembling the national traditions into the story of how Israel came to be. They based their work on an understanding of history which was unique in the ancient world. For them, history was not (as it was for other nations) a recurring cycle of events which in some way reproduced the primordial acts of the gods. It was the gradual working out of a divine plan, a plan which operated through a promise, an election and a covenant. So they described the religious history of the world from creation to their own time as the history of that promise, election, and covenant.

This history, which forms the backbone of our Pentateuch, describes a divine process of selection from Adam through Noah to Abraham, and from Abraham to Isaac and Jacob, the father of the twelve tribes. At the same time a promise was made and repeatedly confirmed by a covenant. The object of the promise remained unspecified. At times it seemed to be the formation of a powerful nation from the sons of Abraham, or the conquest of the Promised Land. Yet, no matter how often it seemed to be fulfilled, the promise remained.

Because this history was written during the Golden Age, its emphasis was on the idea, "What hath God wrought!" The splendor of the monarchy under David and Solomon was looked on as the sequel to a marvelous chain of divine actions. It was the story of how Israel came to be; later it became the basis of hope for what Israel might be in the future.

## Decline and fall

The next period in Israel's history, from Solomon to the exile, was a period of decline. It began with the division of the kingdom after Solomon's death, continued through the Assyrian destruction of the Northern Kingdom, and reached its climax in the fall of Jerusalem and the Babylonian exile of 587 B.C.

This was the age of the prophets. Amos, Hosea, Micah, Isaiah, Zephaniah, Nahum, Habakkuk, and Jeremiah are among the few whose sayings have been preserved in writing. Their message is primarily one of doom because it was addressed to the corrupt political and religious leaders. They announce the coming of the Day of the Lord, a day which will be a time of invasion, destruction, fire and sword, unless there is total national conversion. And they do not anticipate any conversion.

Yet they foresee the survival of a "remnant," those who are now conscious of their need of God, and who in the future will form the nucleus of a new Israel. At this stage there appear what we call the messianic promises, describing a king-to-come, a Bethlehemite, a prince of peace, and so on. Some are from the Assyrian period (Is. 7:14; 9:1-6; 11:1-9; Mich. 5:1-5), others from the Babylonian period (Jer. 23:1-6; Ez. 17:22-24; 21:32; 32:23-24; 37:24-25).

These promises must be read within their context. The prophets did not use a language which was incomprehensible to themselves and their hearers. Nor were they speaking of something which they knew would happen only centuries later. They were concerned with "the consolation of Israel," something which they hoped would occur within their lifetime, as a sequel to the Day of the Lord.

They foresee a divine intervention in history which will form a new Israel, just as Israel was first formed at the Exodus. The new Israel will emerge from the impulse of the heart. This new testament will no longer be something external, carved on stone; it will, in a sense, be carved on men's hearts. The new Israel will be the establishment and recognition of God's dominion over Israel.

This dominion will be externalized once again in a monarchy. But the king will not be like "the false shepherds" who succeeded Solomon. He will be a fitting heir to the throne of David, an ideal king. Like David, he will be worthy of the title: the Lord's "Anointed" (in Hebrew: "the Messiah"; in Greek: "the Christ").

The prophets recalled the promise made to David (2 Sam. 7:14) and hoped that each succeeding king would be "the shoot from Jesse's stem" (Is. 11:1) or "the righteous branch" (Jer. 23:4), but no king fulfilled that ideal. As a result, the promise of a king-to-come remained unfulfilled even at the Babylonian exile, when the Davidic dynasty seemed to have come to an end.

## The hope of restoration

The final period of Israel's pre-Christian history includes the fifty years of exile and the five centuries of attempted restoration, when the hope for religious and political revival became intense.

From the literature of this period two passages deserve special mention because of their importance in the New Testament. The first is the series of poems on the Servant of the Lord included in the work of a disciple of Isaiah writing during the exile (Is. 42:1-7; 49:1-6; 50:4-9; 52:13–53:12). These poems describe Israel as God's servant, an individual who represents the nation, and who undergoes suffering and reproach, not only for Israel's sake, but for all nations. Emphasis is laid on his innocence and obedience, his role as mediator of the covenant, the universality of his mission, and his final exaltation.

The other passage is the description of the Son of Man in Dan. 7. In this vision of the end, the four great world-powers are represented by four animals. In a divine judgment, power is taken from these kingdoms, and transferred to "one like a son of man," that is, an individual in human form. This individual, as a later verse explains, represents "the saints of the Most High," the community of Israel consecrated to God. The vision, then, represents the promise of an everlasting and universal kingdom to be transferred by God, the Ancient of Days, to Israel, represented by an individual known in Jewish tradition as the Son of Man.

## The fulfillment

If then we are to understand in what sense the New Testament fulfills the Old, we must not think of isolated, enigmatic predictions which are somehow "fulfilled" in Christ. The Old Testament must be read as a whole, so that the hope which it expresses may be understood as a desire for the final and decisive intervention of God in history. There is a consecutive chain of salvation-history which reaches its culmination in Christ.

The Old Testament prepares for the New, but it does not anticipate it in any way; there is no precedent for the Incarnation. The coming of Christ must be understood in two ways. It is joined, as if by a vertical line, directly to God; for, in the Incarnation, the Son of God entered human history and began to exist as man. And it is joined, as if by a horizontal line, to the mediators of salvation-history, from Adam through Abraham to Christ. In other words, Jesus is not only the one through whom God enters history, He is God intervening in history.

It was this double mystery which Jesus sought to reveal gradually to His disciples, and which the inspired writers express in their description of what He revealed. This gradual revelation explains Jesus' reluctance to describe Himself as "the Christ," or to accept the title from others. For, although He was indeed the Messiah, this was a totally inadequate description of His nature and office. For Himself He preferred the mysterious title Son of Man, since He was the individual in whom the kingdom of God was established, and in whom the new Israel was incorporated.

The Old Testament had prepared for the New, at least in this sense, that it provided the language through which this mystery could be revealed. And it prepared for the New by slowly and gradually revealing to men the word of God, until that Word became incarnate.

# "THE END OF DAYS" — MESSIANIC EXPECTATION IN JUDAISM

Joseph J. DeVault, S.J.

At the turning-point of the earliest of the canonical Gospels, our Lord asks the disciples: "Who do people say I am?" Then, hardly attending to their reply that some say John the Baptist, others, Elijah, still others, one of the prophets, Jesus presses further: "But you, who do you say I am?" "The Messiah,"

Published originally in *The Bible Today*, 1 (1962), 181-86. Reprinted by permission of the publisher.

Peter answers, "You are the Messiah" (Mark 8:27-30). With these words the Apostle voices the growing conviction of the group around Jesus of Nazareth that in Him they have found what every Jew yearned to see: the long-awaited Messiah, who would restore the kingdom to Israel.

It is, of course, a commonplace that the terms Messiah, Christ, and Anointed (One) all mean the same thing, reflecting as they do the Hebrew-Aramaic and Greek expressions of the idea conveyed by the English word. What is not so immediately clear, though, and calls, in fact, for some explanation, is the content of the term Messiah, the complex of ideas it summoned up in Jewish minds contemporary with Jesus. For in dealing with this as with many another term we may not simply assume that what modern Christians understand by the Messiah was necessarily the understanding which ancient Jews had of that figure. Such an assumption would be methodologically unsound and would result in a confusion similar to the mistaken identification of classical Greek *barbaroi* and English "barbarian."

Our view of the Messiah is gained from the study of the person and public career of Jesus Christ, clear in its main lines and in many of its details. We know very well what the Messiah should be by seeing what He was. This clear view was not available to most of the contemporaries of Jesus, especially since their expectations differed greatly from what He really was.

## Messianic expectations among the Jews

What, then, was the messianic expectation in Israel at the time of our Lord? Perhaps the first thing to be said of it is that it was eschatological, that is, the coming of the Messiah and of the messianic age was regarded as intimately tied in with the definitive establishment of the kingdom of God on earth in the final age of the world. Messianism at the turn of the era, while varied in detail, as we shall note, was part and parcel of Jewish speculations, ideas, and hopes, which included the restoration of Israel as an independent and even supreme state, together with a soul-satisfying triumph over its enemies.

The messianic expectation must be regarded as composed of two principal elements, closely interrelated, it is true, but nonetheless distinguishable. These are the Messiah as a person and the messianic kingdom. In view of the emphasis in the New Testament on the person of the Messiah, it may come as something of a surprise to us to learn that the contemporaries of Christ, while expecting a personal Messiah, were more concerned with the establishment of the messianic kingdom.

The Messiah, as the agent of Yahweh, had one great work to perform, and that was to establish the kingdom. That He was believed to be sent for this express purpose is often reflected in the New Testament, not least when, after all of Christ's instruction, after His passion, death and resurrection, after the post-resurrection appearances, the apostles, in the last recorded question directed to Jesus, asked: "Lord, will you at this time restore the kingdom to Israel?" (Acts 1:6). Christ had preached a kingdom, of course (see especially Matthew *passim*), but not the sort of kingdom which the Jews expected. It is a measure of the firm grip on the Jewish mind of the idea of national restoration that only with the gift of the Holy Spirit at Pentecost did the disciples of Jesus understand the true nature of His mission.

## Limitations of the Jewish concept of Messiah

The fact of widespread messianic expectation at the time of our Lord, however, should not be taken to mean that there was a clear and systematic doctrine on the subject, particularly as regards the person of the Messiah. That he was to be God's representative, His agent in establishing the messianic kingdom, is clear. From this it is likewise clear that there was no expectation in Judaism of a divine Messiah. However great the person and work of the Anointed One were to be, he was certainly to be a creature, an instrument infinitely separated from the one true God.

We may pause here to remark on the mysterious ways of Providence, which by a millennia-long emphasis in Israel on the unicity of God and by the heavy post-exilic stress on the transcendence of the one God raised considerable psychological barriers in the devout Jewish mind to the acceptance of Jesus the Messiah as true Son of God. Knowledge of His divinity would come only through a New Testament revelation.

It is a curious fact that the canonical Old Testament nowhere applies the title of Messiah to the future redeemer of Israel, except perhaps in Ps. 2:2. Accordingly, when we use the term Messiah to speak of our Lord, we are following a New Testament usage, which in turn is based on the apocryphal writings of the first pre-Christian century. In the Psalms of Solomon, composed probably in the middle half of the first century B.C., we read that he who is to rule the new Jerusalem is the Anointed of Yahweh (Ps. Sol. 17:36; 18:6, 8), whence the expression doubtless passed rapidly into the language both of the ordinary people and of the doctors of the Law.

Christians are accustomed to think of the Messiah as embodying the characteristics of three significant figures in the Old Testament: the Son of David, referred to commonly as the Royal Messiah, the Son of Man, and the Suffering Servant. Our authorization for such an identification is, of course, the best, but we should not allow ourselves to assume that the same identification was made by the Jews in their picture of the expected redeemer. In pursuit of this point we shall take up the Jewish expectations regarding each of these facets of the *de facto* Messiah.

## The Messiah as Son of David

Certainly the most widespread of the ideas about the expected Messiah was that he was to be a king descended from David, the "Son of David" par excellence. The origin and development of the notion of the Royal Messiah cannot be treated here, but there is no doubt that by the time of Christ, "Son of David" had become a messianic title. The acclamations of the Jews on Palm Sunday come readily to mind:

> Hosanna to the Son of David!
> Blessed is he who comes in the name of the Lord!
> Hosanna in the highest!
>
> (Matthew 21:9)

There are many other occasions, too, on which this exact expression is applied to Jesus, as, for example, Matthew 12:23; 15:22; 20:30, and the parallels to these. Earlier we have the following from the Psalms of Solomon, to which we have already referred:

> Behold, O Lord, and raise up unto them their king, the Son of David,
> At the time in which thou seest, O God, that he may reign over Israel,
>     thy servant,
> And gird him with strength, that he may shatter unrighteous rulers,
> And that he may purge Jerusalem from nations that trample her down to
>     destruction (Ps. Sol. 17:21-25).

This passage from the first pre-Christian century serves to bring out the heavily nationalistic tone which characterized the messianic thinking of most of the Jews and sounded the clarion call for their repeated uprisings against foreign domination. Not to mention lesser attempts of which Flavius Josephus tells us, the great revolt of 68-70 A.D., resulting in the destruction of Jerusalem, and the second revolt, led by Simon bar Kokheba in 132-135 A.D., are examples of the very thing which our Lord sought to avoid in His repeated rejection of attempts to make Him the Messiah-King of Jewish expectation.

It cannot be denied that much of the earliest prophetic writing, mightily seconded by the rich apocalyptic descriptions of messianic times, whetted the appetites of patriotic Jews for the national, political and material triumph they hoped for from the leadership of one whose very title, Son of David, recalled his royal dignity and the promises made to his illustrious ancestor. The whole messianic hope was based on the unshakable conviction that Yahweh would make good on His promises to His people, that He would, in fact, establish His rule on earth, confirm Israel in well-being, and bring His and her enemies to their knees.

## The Messiah as Son of Man

Another figure which made its contribution to the messianic fever was that of the "Son of Man." If we are aware only of the New Testament usage of the term as applied by Jesus to Himself, we miss the import it had in the expectations of the Jews. Stemming from the mysterious figure in Daniel, the term, Son of Man, did not originally, perhaps, apply to the expected Davidic Messiah; a glance at the passage (Dan. 7:13-14) will show its great possibilities:

> One like a son of man coming, on the clouds of heaven;
> When he reached the Ancient One and was presented before him,
> He received dominion, glory, and kingship; nations and peoples of every
>     language serve him.
> His dominion is an everlasting dominion that shall not be taken away, his
>     kingship shall not be destroyed (Dan. 7:13-14).

From there it was an easy step for the Book of Henoch (especially in the parables, ch. 46 and 48) and Fourth Esdras in the sixth vision (ch. 13) to identify this Son of Man with the expected Messiah. Indeed, in this line of development the Messiah is a superhuman, pre-existent figure, but not divine:

> And at that hour the Son of Man was named
> In the presence of the Lord of Spirits,
> And his name before the Head of Days.
> Yea, before the sun and the signs were created,
> Before the stars of heaven were made,
> His name was named before the Lord of Spirits (Henoch 48:2-3).

Not only pre-existent, but all-powerful:

> And lo! when he saw the assault of the multitude as they came, he neither lifted his head, nor held spear nor any warlike weapon; but I saw only how he sent out of his mouth as it were a fiery stream, and out of his lips a flaming breath, and out of his tongue he shot forth a storm of sparks. And these were all mingled together — the fiery stream, the flaming breath and the storm — and fell upon the assault of the multitude which was prepared to fight and burned them all up, so that suddenly nothing more was to be seen of the innumerable multitude save only dust of ashes and smell of smoke (Fourth Esdras 13:9-11).

From these and many like passages reflecting the current thought on the Son of Man figure we can readily perceive the impact on high priest and Sanhedrin of Jesus' reply to the question: "Are you the Christ, the Son of the Blessed One?" "I am. And you shall see the Son of Man sitting at the right hand of the Power and coming with the clouds of heaven" (Mark 14:61-62).

## The Messiah as Suffering Servant

But whether the Messiah was to be the pre-existent Son of Man or the richly endowed but purely human Son of David, his work could have but one outcome — victory over the enemies of God and therefore over the enemies of Israel. It is for this reason that the idea of the Suffering Servant as a messianic figure was so alien to Jewish thought in the days of our Lord.

Isaiah (53) and Zechariah (12:10) speak of a servant of Yahweh whose entirely undeserved sufferings and death expiate the sins of his people. Whatever the Jews made out of this figure, they did not regard it as messianic, since his suffering and death in defeat were the exact opposite of what had to characterize the Anointed of the Lord. As is repeatedly the case, the New Testament reflects perfectly both the contemporary attitude in this matter and our Lord's struggle against it. Consider the incident related in Matthew 16:21-23. Peter has just professed his faith in the messiahship of Jesus and is promised the primacy in return (Matthew 16:13-20). Then immediately follows the first prediction of the passion; but Peter emboldened by his recent heady success, takes Jesus aside and begins to remonstrate with Him. The reaction of Jesus is so swift and sharp that we can hear the very accents of His voice: "Get behind me, satan, you are a scandal to me; for you do not mind the things of God, but those of men" (Matthew 16:22-23).

Peter was thinking, in other words, in terms of a triumphant, political Messiah, which was not the divine intention at all. He was not singular in this opinion, as the sequel was to show; he was merely bolder in expressing it. If the disciples had really grasped what Jesus had so often tried to tell them, they would not have been so disheartened by the events of Good Friday, nor so sceptical of the first reports on Easter Sunday. Indeed, it was not until the third Christian century that the rabbis, and after them the Jews in general, admitted a second Messiah, inferior to the Davidic one, who would suffer and be humiliated for his people.

This second Messiah of the rabbis brings to mind the Essene community at Qumran, where we likewise find, according to the common interpretation, a second Messiah. Of the two Messiahs awaited at Qumran, one of Israel and one of Aaron, the former is inferior to the latter, as the secular arm, represented by the house of David, is inferior to the priestly line descended from Aaron. We may agree with specialists in this area that such a conception reflects the sacerdotal character of the sect.

### The messianic kingdom more prominent than the Messiah

The late Père Bonsirven defined the messianic conception as "the conviction that the chosen people of God cannot disappear, that it will attain its peak and reach the fullness of the ideal predestined for it by God only in a future more or less remote, at 'the end of days.' " It will be observed that no mention is made here of a personal Messiah, an omission which reflects the fact that in later Judaism "the figure of the Messiah is not an indispensable part of the future hope or of eschatology. In a whole series of religious writings which speak of the future hope, the Messiah does not appear, e.g., Daniel, 1 and 2 Maccabees, Tobit, the Wisdom of Solomon, Judith, Sirach, Jubilees. In other writings the Messiah appears only occasionally, as a traditional element in the belief about the future, but without playing an important part" (Mowinckel).

What was looked to with eager longing was the definitive establishment of the messianic kingdom, the kingdom of God, and if the Messiah was commonly regarded as initiating the end of days, it was really God in His majesty and power who effectively caused salvation. After a period of tribulation marked by the appearance of Elijah as the precursor (compare Matthew 11:14 and Mark 8:28), and by the Messiah's victory over the forces of evil, the kingdom of God was to be established in Palestine, with a thoroughly restored and glorified Jerusalem at its center. There all enemies would bow the knee, the wicked would be judged, a reunited Israel, purged of all sin, would occupy the land, and a veritable golden age would set in. Such is the vision of the seventeenth of the Psalms of Solomon:

> And he shall gather together a holy people, whom he shall lead in righteousness,
> And he shall judge the tribes of the people that has been sanctified by the Lord his God.

And he shall not suffer unrighteousness to lodge any more in their midst,
Nor shall there dwell with them any man that knoweth wickedness.
For he shall know them, that they are all sons of their God.
And he shall have the heathen nations serve him under his yoke;
And he shall purge Jerusalem, making it holy as of old:
So that nations shall come from the ends of the earth to see his glory,
Bringing as gifts her sons who have fainted,
And to see the glory of the Lord, wherewith God hath glorified her.
And he shall be a righteous king, taught of God, over them,
And there shall be no unrighteousness in his days in their midst.
For all shall be holy and their king the anointed of the Lord.
Blessed be they that shall be in those days,
In that they shall see the good fortune of Israel which God shall bring to
pass in the gathering together of the tribes.

(Ps. Sol. 17:28-30, 32-36, 50)

Blessed, indeed, is the prospect! But how much greater was the reality than
the most extravagant dream! In the days of Jesus of Nazareth the messianic
expectation was rich and strong. But how utterly unexpected that God Himself
should come as Son of David, Suffering Servant, and Son of Man!

# QUMRAN: ITS GEOGRAPHY AND HISTORY

John E. Steinmueller

Qumran lies in the desert of Judah, which played an important role in the
secular as well as in the religious history of the Hebrews. This uncultivated and
thinly populated wilderness comprised the tract of land west of the Dead Sea
and included in early days the city of Engedi (literally, "a fountain of the kid"),
known for its warm spring and vineyards (Cant. 1:14), and five other cities that
were assigned to the tribe of Judah at Gilgal by Joshua (Jos. 15:61f). According
to Josephus Flavius, it may also have included the western bank of the Jordan
River to the north of the Dead Sea.

The earliest biblical mention of a settlement in this desert as well as in the
barren Negeb region, south of Beersheba, was by the Kenites, descendants of
Moses' father-in-law (Judg. 1:16; cf. 1 Sam. 15:6; 27:10). After David's flight
from King Saul's court, the former sought refuge in the strongholds of Engedi,
where he ambushed the king, spared his life and effected a temporary reconciliation (1 Sam. 24; cf. Ps. 62 [63] title). Years later the enemies of King Jehosh-
aphat of Judah assembled at Engedi to march against him (2 Chr. 20:2).

The earliest religious history of this region is uncertain. It seems probable that
the two northern prophets of the ninth century B.C., Elijah and Elisha, visited

Published originally in *The Bible Today*, 1 (1964), 775-79. Reprinted by permission of
the publisher.

this locality. Then, too, it is interesting to observe that the oldest Semitic (palimpset) papyrus (18 x 8 cm.) of the eight century B.C. was found in Wadi Murabba'at. What this document represented and how many original papyri were once in this collection is only a matter of conjecture. Centuries later a group of priests, "sons of Sadoc," settled at Qumran during the Maccabean crisis for the high priesthood in the second century B.C. In this general area John the Baptist preached his penitential message and baptized, and here, according to tradition, Jesus fasted for forty days and was tempted. Even after the destruction of the Jewish state by the Roman army in 70 A.D., this area continued to be settled by Christian monks. Thus at Khirbet Mird (ancient Hyrcania) fragments of biblical codices containing the Old and New Testaments ranging between the fifth and eighth centuries A.D. were discovered in 1952. Even to this day there are Christian monasteries in this region at Mar Saba and St. Theodotion.

## Qumran and its literature (150 B.C.–A.D. 68)

Qumran is situated at the northwest corner of the Dead Sea. From the discovery of the first cave with its literary contents by a Bedouin in 1947 and its subsequent exploration by Pere De Vaux, O.P., and by G. Lankester Harding in 1949, together with the discovery of other Qumran caves in 1952 and excavations of the area in 1951, 1952, and 1954, our knowledge of Hebrew paleography, textual criticism, historical and religious conditions has been richly increased.

The original cave at Qumran (1Q) yielded various leather scrolls and about six hundred fragments, both of which represented about seventy manuscripts containing a variety of canonical and apocryphal books, mostly in Hebrew, and some other books previously unknown. Perhaps the best known of the canonical books found are a complete book of *Isaiah* (IQ Is^a) and the last third of the same book (1Q Is^b). The apocryphal books are represented by fragments from the books of *Jubilees* and *Henoch*, with which scholars have been long acquainted. New materials in the Jewish literature include a commentary on *Habakkuk*; thanksgiving psalms; a *Manual of Discipline* or *Rule of the Community*; a scroll that describes the "War between the Children of Light and Darkness," and others.

The second cave (2Q) contained about a hundred legible fragments that were once part of about forty manuscripts. The canonical books are represented by *Exodus, Leviticus* (in the old Phoenician script), *Numbers, Deuteronomy, Ruth, Psalms, Jeremiah*. There was other non-biblical material, e.g., from the *Book of Jubilees*.

The third cave (3Q) revealed a few fragments from about ten manuscripts and two inscribed copper strips.

Of the three caves (4Q, 5Q, 6Q), the fourth yielded the most materials and its many fragments represent about a hundred scrolls, ninety of which were from Old Testament books (in Hebrew, chiefly according to the Septuagint tradition), comprising all the protocanonical books (except *Esther*) and the deuterocanonical *Tobit*.

## Qumran and the Old Testament

Scholars have now estimated that over one hundred biblical manuscripts (mostly fragmentary) may be identified in the discoveries from the various Qumran caves. All of the protocanonical books, except *Esther*, are represented. There are also fragments from three deuterocanonical books (*Tobit, Sirach, Epistle of Jeremiah*). Besides, there are commentaries (*pešarim*) to *Habakkuk, Micah, Psalms, Nahum*, and *Isaiah*.

The existence of these texts is of importance for the study of the Hebrew prototype underlying the Greek text of the Septuagint translators. A careful comparison of this prototype with the Massoretic text will enable the scholar in many instances to reach the original Hebrew text when textual differences occur.

## Qumran and the apocryphal books of the Old Testament

It is noteworthy that the Qumran library contained various apocryphal books already known to scholars from other sources, such as the books of *Henoch* and *Jubilees* (with proposed calendar reforms) and the *Testaments of the Twelve Patriarchs*. Besides these, the Qumran literature included other short works: a *Genesis Apocryphon* or *Lamech Scroll*, a pseudo-Jeremaic work, *Testimonies Document, Prayer of Nabonidus*, etc. These, as well as the other apocryphal works circulating in circles other than Qumran, whether of Palestinian or Hellenistic origin, were good spiritual reading which inspired, deepened and confirmed the Jewish people in their religion.

## Qumran and sectarian literature

This sectarian literature, in comparison with what is already known from the Jewish writers Josephus Flavius and Philo, the Roman writer Pliny the Elder and the Christian author Eusebius, seems to confirm the fact that these sectarians or monks of Qumran were Essenes. Perhaps the most important document from their viewpoint was the *Rule of the Community* or the *Manual of Discipline*, describing the life of the monks. Then, too, the *Damascus* or *Sadokite Document* (known to us since 1890 when it was discovered in Cairo, Egypt) is also concerned with the practical organization of the New Covenant community and reveals its contacts with the ascetical Therapeutae of Egypt and the Jewish community at Damascus. Based upon the Roman military manual was the *Rule of War* (first published as *The War of the Sons of Light against the Sons of Darkness*), describing the apocalyptic army of the sectaries. The intense spiritual and inner life of these Essene monks may be seen from twenty psalms called *Thanksgiving Hymns* (*Hodayot*). Other literature, both religious and secular, shows the great extent of the Qumran library.

## Qumran and the Essenes

The New Testament mentions three parties as being hostile to our Lord and His teaching. They are the Pharisees, the priestly party of the Sadducees, and the royalist party known as Herodians. The Essenes are never mentioned.

Josephus Flavius, however, regarded these Essenes as one of the three major sects or parties in Palestine. Because of their messianic expectations and deeply spiritual life, many of the Essenes were likely among the early Jewish converts to Christianity. If so, it is understandable that the New Testament writers would have regarded the Essenes sympathetically and not have described them as inimical to Christ.

The name "Essene" is most probably derived from the Aramaic word *chasya* (pl. *chasen, chasayya*), that is, "the pious." There were about four thousand members (Philo, Josephus Flavius) throughout Palestine, near Damascus and perhaps in Egypt. Their principal settlement was near Engedi (Pliny), or the Qumran monastery, and their priest-monks called themselves the "sons of Sadoc."

The monks, numbering about 150 to 200 in each of the six generations living at Qumran, practiced the three monastic vows of poverty, chastity and obedience, set aside special time for private and common prayer as well as for scriptural reading, and were otherwise kept busy through various peaceful occupations such as farming, pottery-making, copying manuscripts, etc. Qumran followed its own calendar and rites of purification. The entire community strictly observed the Sabbath and would send their gifts to the temple rather than offer bloody sacrifices. The protocanonical books were recognized, and some deuterocanonical and apocryphal books, as well as their own literature, were kept in high esteem. Unlike the Sadducees of the New Testament period, the Essenes believed in the immortality of the soul, in reward and punishment after death, and were ardent Messianists, awaiting the imminent coming of two Messiahs. Before becoming a full member of the Qumran community, the candidate had to spend one year as a postulant and another two years as a novice, and bound himself to a strict ethical code.

Because of the Qumran discoveries it is possible to propose an outline of the history of the Essenes. Their beginnings, like those of the Pharisees, can be traced to the religious and political crises during the Maccabean period. Both emerged from the Assideans (*chassidim*, "the pious ones"), the earliest volunteers in the resistance movement to fight against the Hellenization of their country, to punish apostate Jews, and to struggle for independence from a foreign yoke. While the Pharisees represented participation in the movement by the laity, the Essenes were chiefly a priestly organization. Their leaders, the "sons of Sadoc," later broke away from the Maccabean party when Jonathan, a simple priest and not from the Aaron-Eliezer-Zadoc line, accepted the high priesthood (cf. 1 Maccabees 10:15ff) from the Seleucid King Alexander Balas (152 B.C.) They also broke away from their liberal-minded confreres, the Sadducees, when Simon, the brother of Jonathan, together with his descendants, was recognized by the people and by some of the priests to be "high priest forever until a faithful prophet should arise" (1 Maccabees 14:41).

Founded by the Teacher of Righteousness, some of the Essenes established themselves at Qumran, a settlement which lasted for more than two centuries (150 B.C. to 68 A.D.). During this period they retained their ardent desire for redemption that would be accomplished on the arrival of the two Messiahs, an anointed civil ruler and an anointed priest. At the end of this period they participated in the First Jewish Revolt and their monastery was destroyed by the Romans (68 A.D.). The Essenes and the monks of Qumran then disappeared from Jewish history.

### Qumran and Christianity

As noted above, the New Testament does not mention the Essenes or the Qumran settlement. When the Qumran literature was first discovered and translated, some extremists hastily asserted that Christianity owed its origin to the doctrine of the Essenes or monks of Qumran. Because of contemporary conditions we may expect some external points of contact and some similarities between Qumran and Christianity. Thus it is possible that John the Baptist, who "was in the desert until the day of his manifestation to Israel" (Luke 1:80) and "came preaching in the desert of Judea" (Matthew 3:1), was educated by the Qumran monks, was an Essene, or at least had some contact with members of that community. It is very likely that Jesus met some of the pious Essenes in His public ministry throughout Palestine and was aware of their teachings. It also seems probable that some of these Essenes were early converts to the faith. Similarly, there is no difficulty in admitting, as some scholars claim, that the Epistle to the *Hebrews* was addressed to them to prove that there is only one Messiah or Anointed One who is to be identified with the high priest Jesus Christ.

There are, however, so many and such profound differences between the teachings of Christianity and of Qumran that the movements themselves must be considered essentially distinct. The doctrines of the Trinity, the Incarnation, redemptive death and resurrection, sacramental life, the Eucharist, the Mystical Body and others set Christianity completely apart from the movement represented at Qumran. The discoveries in the Dead Sea area add immeasurably to our understanding of the New Testament background, but they do not destroy the unique character of the religion of Jesus Christ.

# QUMRAN AND THE NEW TESTAMENT

Pierre Benoit, O.P.

The detailed picture which the Dead Sea Scrolls give us of the Essene sect of Qumran has raised a question of relationship between the writings of this sect and the New Testament. The following considerations, first proposed at the

Reprinted from *Theology Digest*, 11 (1963), 167-72. Originally published as "Qumrân et le Nouveau Testament," *New Testament Studies*, 7 (1961), 276-296. Reprinted by permission of the publisher.

1960 meeting of the Society for New Testament Studies, do not pretend to probe these relationships in detail but merely to deduce some leading ideas from the accessible data. Numerous doctrinal and literary comparisons have already been made. Some have emphasized similarities and concluded to close relationships between the two literatures; others have insisted on the differences between them. In an effort to deduce some useful conclusions from the general discussion, I here propose three considerations.

*First, we must beware of taking as the immediate contact of direct influence what may be only independent evidence of tendencies common to an era.* There are often striking similarities between the Qumran writings and the New Testament, and it is possible that the latter was the borrower. Again the similarities may be but a reflection of ideas common throughout Palestine toward the beginning of the Christian era. To accept the first possibility to the prejudice of the second is to succumb to the illusion of seeing in the Qumran writings the whole of Judaism contemporary with the New Testament. This is like the error often made recently of regarding rabbinical literature as the typical representative of Judaism at the time of Jesus; everything else, especially the "Apocrypha," is neglected. But these rabbinical writings express only one narrow movement of Judaism, namely the Pharisaism of the Hillel school, which turned to narrow, strict doctrine after the destruction of Jerusalem. We are well aware that such a literature could not be an exact reflection of the Judaism of earlier times.

The Qumran library should not lead us to think we now thoroughly understand all first-century Judaism and how the New Testament borrowed from it, for this would mean attributing to one movement ideas that were surely part of larger streams of thought from which both Qumran and Christianity could equally have drawn. It seems that Judaism, up to the time of the fall of Jerusalem, was as vital as it was varied. Speculation and policies altered with the spirit of each sect; and influences were felt from outside, especially from the Babylonian, the Iranian, and the Graeco-Roman world of the Jewish "Diaspora." These influences affected the religious thinking and hopes of all Palestine, where Qumran was one — but not the only — witness to the cauldron of eschatological and apocalyptic aspiration and more or less esoteric doctrine. These influences must have produced venturesome speculation everywhere, notably among the Pharisees. Therefore, ideas known to us only through Qumran literature may have come to us from Qumran only as through a channel and not as from a source.

## Necessary distinctions

Thus we have the important task of distinguishing between the genuinely original ideas of Qumran and broader tendencies shared in by other movements. The dualistic concept of good and evil, for example, is a part of Essenism. But it may also have been a part of Iranian and Greek thought; in fact, it is found in germ in the Old Testament. Allied doctrines, like angelology, influenced other movements of intertestamentary Judaism, like Pharisaism, and the more traditional teachings of the ordeal of the servant and eschatological purification by the Spirit were developed elsewhere besides Qumran. In short, all speculation about the "mysteries" of the divine order are too characteristic of apocalyptic thought generally to be exclusive to Qumran.

In such areas, agreement between Qumran and the New Testament often means no more than a recourse to common sources, very often to none other than the Old Testament! The history of Qumran itself, however, may at least suggest features which were peculiar to it — its purist, reactionary priesthood, for example, which explains its adherence to the old calendar abandoned by official Jewry; or their doctrine of the second Messiah springing from the line of Aaron; or the plan to build a spiritual temple in the desert where a holier worship than that of the defiled temple in Jerusalem could be cultivated. These specific features, which are reflected in a special literature, make comparison with the New Testament worthwhile in determining relations between the two movements, since it is here that similarities cannot be explained short of some direct influence. They lead us to see a passage like 2 Cor. 6:14; 7:1 as a sort of meteor fallen from the Qumran sky into the middle of a Pauline epistle.

The first point about method, then, tries to set the problem of the relations between Qumran and the New Testament within stricter limits than usual. But even so restricted, the problem persists. Essenism did have a direct influence on Christianity, less than is sometimes stated, but nonetheless real. But, when? how?

*The second consideration about method is: No matter what direct influence of Qumran on the New Testament be proved, it does not necessarily follow that the influence was exerted from the very start, in such a way that Christianity derived from Essenism as from its source. The influence could have been exerted later, helping the new movement to formulate and organize itself, without creating it.* We suggest here that this was rather the case, that the Qumranian influences worked less through John the Baptist and Jesus than through Paul, John, and even second-generation Christians.

The first contact may have been John the Baptist. His message and his proximity to the Qumran desert suggest a connection between him and the Essenes. This connection, however, must not be exaggerated, as if the Baptist had been an Essene who later broke away to carry out a personal mission. Though possible, it has not been proved, and any common characteristics may only be parallel and without direct connection.

## The Baptist and Qumran

The expectation of the messianic era was too widespread to put John in debt solely to Qumran teaching; the idea of the appearance of the Messiah in the desert was a common theme of the time. True, John tried to gain followers and preached a baptism of repentance, which some derive from Qumran. But ritual ablution was common at that time. Further, John's baptism differed from that of Qumran in that it was performed but once and signified the conversion of the heart, whereas the baptism of Qumran was often repeated to maintain or re-establish the ritual purity necessary for a holy life and, especially, for sharing in the common meals. It has not been proved that the Essenes also practiced a baptism of initiation with moral significance. Similarly, John's agreement with

Qumran in preaching purification by the Holy Spirit, chastisement by fire, and the use of the phrase "brood of vipers" is explained by the fact that these are biblical traditions and images. We must not underestimate possible connections between the Precursor and Qumran, but the concern of both for the conversion of men in preparation for the expected eschatological intervention of God does not seem to indicate more than common influences of the same environment.

Even if the Baptist was produced by Essenism, it does not follow that Christianity was. It is with regard to Jesus that the problem becomes more acute, but the connection even less likely. Jesus must have known about Qumran, yet his silence about the Essenes is remarkable. There are a few rare, obscure references to them, as in Matthew 19:12, where the mention of voluntary eunuchs may allude to the celibate Essenes; for the religious ideal of continence is not attested to anywhere else in Israel at the time. The instruction "to hate one's enemy" is found at Qumran; it is nowhere found in the Old Testament. The rules of excommunication in Matthew 18:15-18 recall those in the Manual of Discipline (1QS 5:25–6:1). But these tenuous connections are found only in Matthew's Gospel and could be an expression of the concerns of a less archaic Judeao-Christian milieu.

## Influence on Jesus?

But could not analogous conceptions from Qumran have inspired key ideas about Jesus' person and mission? The theories on this point are unconvincing or are based on mere analogy to be explained by Old Testament and Judaic traditions in general or indicate variations denoting a quite different spirit. True, Jesus mentions the struggle between the kingdoms of God and of Satan. But in this, perhaps only the terminology is peculiar to Qumran. And it is noteworthy that Jesus speaks of Beelzebul, not of the Essene Beliar. The term, "Light-Darkness," characteristic of Qumran, is not used by the synoptic Jesus but by the Johannine Christ. Again, Qumran teaching reveals nothing like Jesus' consciousness of himself as God's envoy, enjoying intimate union with the Father, who has come to die in expiation for sins as Messiah, or, more accurately, as the Son of Man of Daniel, in the sense, at least, of his destiny to become fully so after his triumph over death. At Qumran there are two messiahs, but no mention of the Son of Man; and the messiah is not central to its teaching. Moreover, the messiah's role in the eschatological war is very obscure. There is no unique Messiah playing the essential role of suffering servant in salvation for all men. In the Manual of Discipline (5:6; 8:6; 9:4) the servant theme concerns expiation in the cultic order; the perfect conformity to the Law of the sons of light will atone for sin more efficaciously than material sacrifices, or at least as well. 1QS 4:20ff speaks of no servant or messiah but of man in general, the elect whom God calls to life with the angels. There is no mention whatever of expiation for sinners. In the Hodayoth, the Servant of Yahweh appears more clearly. The application of this image to the author of the hymns, probably the Teacher of Righteousness, bears more on the tribulations peculiar to the eschatological crisis than on the mission of a vicarious, redemptive suffering by substitution which saves others. Isaiah's Suffering Servant is altered to refer to the Teacher of Righteousness struggling to enlighten and lead his disciples to salvation. But there is no notion in the hymns of vicarious atonement for the sins of others (Mark 10:45; 14:24 and parallel passages).

## Teacher not a savior

The Teacher of Righteousness at Qumran is certainly the figure who most reminds us of Jesus. By contrast, however, he actually throws into relief Jesus' transcendence and uniqueness. To say nothing of the absence of an incarnation, a crucifixion, or a resurrection, none of which is attributed in the texts to the Teacher, he is not even the savior who, merely by coming, inaugurates the eschatological era. A creature of flesh and a sinner, he is first to need pardon and purification. He claims only the title of prophet and exegete, a true teacher leading others to self-salvation through perfect observance of the Law. He does not go beyond the categories of Judaic prophetism nor approach the messianic self-awareness of Jesus.

Jesus' practical behavior is even more alien to the Essenes. He definitely and deliberately accepts official Judaism, while criticizing its abuses. But the Teacher belongs to the separated ones who remain in the desert, looking coldly upon the temple at Jerusalem and claiming a monopoly of perfect Mosaic observance. The Last Supper differs essentially from the Essene banquet in the paschal character which gives the Supper its meaning of "passage" from sin to salvific liberation. But what sets Jesus most clearly apart from these sectaries is his liberty with the Law and his love of sinners. These attitudes contradict the Essene exaltation of rigid observance of the Law and jealous separation from sinners, the sons of darkness, who do not belong to God's chosen seed.

## Influence secondary

While Essenism, therefore, did not furnish essential inspiration to Christianity in its origins either through John the Baptist or Jesus, a certain secondary influence, nonetheless, was exerted and reflected in the New Testament, but only after the death of Jesus. The influence can be explained, perhaps, by the presence of Essene converts who brought their ideas into the early Church. The priests in Acts 6:7, for example, and the recipients of the Letter to the Hebrews seem to have been such. Again, young Christianity may have been inspired by the carefully developed structure and doctrine of this sect and borrowed some details from them while rejecting others. Whatever happened, the positive influence of Essenism on Christianity in community organization and theological speculation is evident. But even here we must set limits.

Essene influence on the organizational and cultic life of the Church is more perceptible at a relatively later period than in the beginning of Christianity. Liturgists, for example, suggest that the times for prayer, vigils, and ember days have come to us from Qumran. The historical connection between Christian monasticism and the Essenes will probably be scientifically established someday. Furthermore, the Christian *episcopos* in the Syriac *Didascalia* of the third century very much resembles the Essenian *Mebaqqer*.

But when we go back to the first Christian community of Jerusalem, the traces of Essenism become less obvious. The community of goods among the first Christians shows marked differences from that at Qumran. Nor are the Hellenists in Acts 6 to be identified with the Essenes, since they are too closely allied with the Greeks for Qumran toleration. The early hierarchy, too, in its origins, seem independent of the Essene group. There are Twelve Apostles, as there were twelve men in the council of the Qumran community — a parallel adequately explained by the traditional number of the Jewish tribes. Peter, James, and John have nothing to do with the three *priests* who seem to be *in addition* to the council of twelve laymen at Qumran (1QS 8:1).

Doctrine is the other important sphere where the influence of Qumranian writings on the New Testament can be perceived. But this influence is seen rather in the theological systematization later developed by John and Paul than in the earlier inspiration received from Jesus. J. B. Lightfoot has suggested what has been borne out by the Qumran discoveries, that the Epistle to the Colossians was written against errors strongly tainted with Essenism; and Paul could hardly have been unaware of Essene literature when he wrote Col. 1:12-13. The literary influence of Qumran on Ephesians is even more marked. Both John and Paul encountered Essenism in Asia Minor, where tradition places the composition of the Johannine writings. This may explain the strong Qumranian coloring of the First Letter of John. Such contacts occurred even elsewhere and sooner: 1 Thess. 5:1-11 already speaks of the eschatological struggle between light and darkness, and 2 Thess. 2:6ff presents striking similarities with 1QS 27, 1. Whatever the full explanation of the Essene encounter of Paul and John, it seems that the influence on their thought was at a secondary stage of its growth rather than at its source. This raises the question: Were the borrowed elements major or minor ideas? Were they taught as received, or were they modified? This brings us to our third consideration.

Is not an admission that the ideas of Essenism left their mark on Christian theology, though only in the second generation, the same as conceding that Christianity owes very much to Essenism? There are two reasons for denying this. The ideas borrowed are secondary and in no way essential to the Christian message. Secondly, in its use of these ideas, Christianity profoundly changed them.

## Jesus' death expiates

For John and Paul the essential facts of the Christian faith are the death of Jesus, Son of God-made-man, who expiates by his blood men's sins, and his resurrection, which saves men by bringing them the life of friendship with God. Paul teaches that in Jesus we witness the coming of the Word, who destroyed the old order and recreated a new humanity. John contemplates the revealing Word, which dispels the darkness of sin and enlightens man with the true knowledge of the God of glory. Neither theme goes back to Qumran. Nor do particular themes such as John's Logos or Paul's Heavenly Man find their explanation there. Such similarities as we find in Paul's writings are secondary, like the battle between light and darkness, the revelation of the mystery, and justification by grace alone.

Regarding the struggle between light and darkness, we find many similarities between Paul's texts and those of 1QS and 1QM: Both discuss a battle between two camps and angelic intervention. But there is this difference: In Paul, the battle is over, won singlehandedly by Christ. But Qumran is still in the old order and waiting for the final battle.

## John and Paul vs. Qumran

As for the revelation of the mystery of the divine order, there are similarities between John and Paul and Qumran, suggesting a direct relationship. But there are also great differences concerning the time and the manner of the revelation and its content. Nothing at Qumran corresponds to the eschatological *now* of Paul. There, the revelation to the Teacher of Righteousness is the last step of a very old revelation through time; and his reflections lead him to a plan to restore the force of the ancient prescriptions of the Law. He presents himself as a successor to the prophets, bringing a new revelation of the Old Law. His are revelations in the broad sense only — profound intuitions of a mystic soul who has meditated assiduously on the old revelations. Despite similarities in terminology, Paul sees things in a very different light. He too enjoyed mystical contemplation; but he saw the mystery of God as absolutely new, an unheard of message of salvation attained on Christ's cross and offered to all mankind, a mystery which will be fulfilled in the reassembly of the whole world in Christ.

The last idea common to Paul and Qumran is that of justification by grace alone. The evident analogies here can be explained by common sources. Even then, they show differences in application revealing completely different attitudes.

Paul agrees that gratuitous and merciful pardon is the fruit of God's justice. Both understand a salvific justice which transcends vindictive justice. But the theme of salvific justice is too strongly evident in the Old Testament, especially after the exile, for us to conclude that Paul got this doctrine from Qumran. Paul differs radically from Qumran about the time and the manner of the triumph of God's justice over man's sin. The Teacher sees future pardon after the eschatological crisis. For Paul, this crisis is upon us in Christ; and the Christian possesses Christ's new justice in the degree to which he is incorporated into Christ's new order. The new justice is won by faith in Jesus.

## Cautions

The above considerations are intended to caution us against the frequent error in historical method which interprets a primary stage of development in the light of later advances. A Christian eye tends to discover in the Qumran writings doctrines or attitudes which they simply do not have. We should take heed and try to explain the texts only in the light of earlier and contemporary sources. Thus, we should see at Qumran only a wholly Jewish sect preoccupied with the imminent eschatological crisis, to be prepared for by a deliberate return to the past of the Chosen People. This point is important, because it reveals something of the Jewish mentality in the last stage before Christianity and also gives us a better understanding of primitive Christianity. While there are ideas and expressions in the New Testament analogous to the Qumran writings, they have been profoundly altered by Christianity in a completely new message. It would be regrettable should verbal analogies make us misunderstand the sovereignly new intervention of the divine Word.


# THE SPIRIT OF THE 'ANAWIM

Sister M. Rose Eileen, C.S.C.


The liturgy of Advent is, in the mind of the Church, a liturgy of preparation for the coming of the Savior. The seasonal motifs of humble repentance and of ardent desire together with the overtones of eager anticipation rise to a harmonious crescendo as the feast of Christ's nativity draws near.

This same spirit pulses also through the pages of Scripture where it is most effectively personified in the spirit of the *'anawim*.

This is the name which the Hebrew Bible gives to God's needy and poor, to the little ones of the world of the prophets. Their spirit is born of a profound conviction of utter dependence on Yahweh, the Lord God of Israel. They realize fully that not only is He the primary cause of all that exists, but that He directly presides over the unfolding of the circumstances of daily life, whatever influence may be ascribed to secondary causes by minds accustomed to philosophic patterns of thought.

The Israelite was not prone to distinguish between primary and secondary causes. He sees God at work always and everywhere effecting the good of His chosen ones.

> The needy and the poor (the *'anawim*) seek for waters, and there are none; their tongue hath been dry with thirst. I the Lord will hear them, I the God of Israel will not forsake them. I will open rivers in the high hills, and fountains in the midst of the plains; . . . that they may see and know and consider and understand together that the hand of the Lord has done this, and the Holy One of Israel has created it (Is. 41:17-20).

A concept so profound, so universal in all its implications, was not grasped early in the history of God's chosen people. For us who are predestined to walk our way to eternal beatitude under the clear light of the total revelation of God's love in the person of the God-man, the mystery of that divine action on nothingness to effect goodness runs like a unifying theme from the first page of

Published originally in *Worship*, 35 (1960), 20-25. Reprinted by permission of the publisher.

Genesis through the total record of God's interventions on behalf of His chosen ones. But for the Semites, accustomed to view all in the concrete and particular rather than in the abstract and universal, it was a complex and baffling concept which unfolded in their consciousness only gradually.

The spirit of the *'anawim* was rooted deeply in the Mosaic covenant: "If therefore you will hear my voice, and keep my covenant, you shall be my peculiar possession above all people; for all the earth is mine" (Exod. 19:5-6). The content of this bond was specified for the members of the holy nation in the prescriptions of the Mosaic law which tended to envelop their daily lives with a multiplicity of details. These were to serve as continual reminders of their constant dependence on Yahweh.

He was to become the total object of their thought and desire. The materialities which surrounded their primitive mode of life were to be a succession of sacraments, so to speak, indicative of Yahweh's nearness, His very active presence in their midst. Fertility of soil, rich harvests, abundant progeny, all were to be promised evidences of Yahweh's pleasure with His people living in fidelity to the multiple demands of the Law and growing in conscious awareness of His active presence in the circumstances of their daily lives.

Characteristically, however, the fallibility of the human mind came to center emphasis on material prosperity rather than on the interior spirit of humble reliance upon God. Gradually with David and especially under Solomon a luxurious and materialistic mode of life came to penetrate the former simple nomadic and pastoral life of the Israelites. Royal aggrandizement forged the inevitable chains of oppression and disdain for the poor and needy, and initiated the struggle for alliance with the mighty ones of the earth.

Loudly and insistently the prophets of Israel decried this defection from the spirit of the *'anawim*. But their message was not heard; their teaching on spiritual poverty was not followed.

Divine wisdom, however, decreed the salutary means for mastery of the lesson of lowliness which God inevitably demands of His creature. For it seems that only through personal defeat and humiliation does the rational creature reach the conviction of his utter dependence on his Creator and that abiding sense of need for divine action whereby the spirit of proud self-sufficiency so totally opposed to the realization of the demands of creaturehood is finally and effectively crushed. Only then is God's creature convinced that he needs God not only to be created but likewise to remain alive in the moment by moment struggle for existence.

It is the word *'anawah* which describes this attitude. Translated as spiritual poverty or the spirit of lowliness, it characterizes the reality of all man's relations with God, whether on the natural or the supernatural level of existence. This spirit combines an abiding awareness of man's frail creaturehood with total and absolute dependence on the mighty goodness of the Creator.

The true and adequate penetration of the depths of meaning implicit in this spirit was born in the Israelite mind only after long and bitter experiences, individual and collective. The repeated mysterious interventions of Yahweh in the history of the descendants of Abraham — in their release from the oppressive yoke of the Egyptian Pharaoh, in the ultimately happy ending of their desert wanderings, and in the frequent victories over their enemies consequent upon fidelity in asking Yahweh for deliverance — all this deepened the awareness of their spiritual poverty.

Finally, in the bitterness of the Babylonian exile (586-538 B.C.), separated from their land, their temple, their cult, all of which were pillars of their pre-exilic identity, the Israelites came to learn through endurance of personal and national humiliation the lesson of 'anawah, the demands of the covenanted love uniting the chosen people with the Holy One of Israel. Only then did the full implications of this spirit crystallize in the portrayal so beautifully set forth in Second Isaiah (Is. 40–55).

Noteworthy in the development of the theology of the 'anawim as it unfolds in the pages of the Old Testament and is perfected in the New, is the absence of any condemnation of material prosperity, even when emphasis centers more and more on the importance of spiritual poverty.

External poverty is never the cause of true spiritual poverty. It is merely an occasion. Lowliness of spirit, the humility that looks always to God as cause and source of good, is its essence. While never expressed in the abstract phraseology of future theological treatises, the purpose of the material universe for the Israelite mind is to unite man consciously and abidingly to God in faithful, submissive praise. Should man become lost in material things and forget God, sin inevitably follows (Deut. 6:10-19; 8:11-20).

The riches of the created universe, therefore, are evidence of the continuance of God's creative act conserving that which He has brought from nothingness. It was, however, only through poverty and suffering that the chosen people came to learn the full impact of God's words, "I am Yahweh, the maker of all things" (Is. 44:24).

Later in the history of Israel, just before the time of the messianic fulfilment, there developed among the Qumran Covenanters the compelling desire to renounce voluntarily the pleasures and possessions of material prosperity and to embrace a life of privation and renunciation. This outward renunciation had its vivifying principle in the inward spirit of total loving abandonment to God which is born of deep spiritual poverty. This is the fundamental thesis upon which the theology of the 'anawim is founded.

This spirit was bound to win from God a pledge of His mercy. In Isaiah, the Messiah promises a mission of mercy to the 'anawim: "The spirit of the Lord God is upon me, because the Lord hath anointed me. He hath sent me to preach to the meek (the 'anawim), to heal the contrite of heart . . . to comfort all that mourn" (Is. 61:1-2). It was only in these little ones that God found the nothingness required for His creative act of spiritual regeneration and adoptive sonship: "To whom shall I have respect, but to him that is poor and little and of a contrite heart, and that trembleth at my words" (Is. 66:2).

To the poor in spirit, to those who have levelled the mountains of their own self-sufficiency and filled up the valleys of their nothingness with inward awareness of their total dependence on and submission to Yahweh, and to those who eagerly long for His salvific coming in the divinely ordered circumstances of their daily lives — to these is given the proper name of "the remnant," the Israel of the messianic kingdom, the chosen of the Anointed One.

No longer entangled with the external formalism of the Pharisees, the "remnant" kept the true spirit of interior prayer, making it actual in each day's humble search for God. Along with true repentance they felt an utter confidence in God's abiding and compassionate love. Such is the "remnant" whom He leads into the glorious messianic kingdom.

It is this spirit of the 'anawim which Holy Mother Church presents to her children for inspiration and imitation in the Advent liturgy. It is this spirit which she encourages us to ponder lovingly and to imitate purposefully in these weeks marked by eager longing for His coming in the loving remembrance of the historical event at Bethlehem, in the existential experience of the present reality of grace, and in anticipation of His final coming in the personal and general judgment of every soul before the tribunal of justice.

In the three great characters who dominate the liturgy of Advent — Isaiah, John the Baptist, and the Virgin Mary — the same spirit of 'anawah speak most eloquently. For whether the eyes of the soul rest on Isaiah whose principle of absolute dependence on Yahweh transformed the ancient vocabulary of poverty, or on John of whom Eternal Truth has said, "There is none greater born of woman," or on her who is the lowest and the loveliest of the 'anawim, it is always the same spirit they see personified: "He who is mighty hath done great things to me. . . . He hath put down the mighty from their seats; He hath exalted the humble" (Luke 1:51-52).

The spirit of Mary's *Magnificat* has echoed down the centuries of Christian thought and challenged countless multitudes to follow on the path of perfect surrender in their personal "Fiat" to her Son's call to poverty of spirit whether lived in the religious state or surrounded by the good things of this world. In both, the spirit of 'anawah consists of constant awareness of the presence of God in the needs of daily life wherever and however it may be lived, of absolute surrender to His will as it becomes known through external and internal manifestations, of abiding faith in His love, and of buoyant hope in the fulfilment of His divine promise of peace and joy.

In the 'anawim of God poverty of spirit is never negative. It is always positive, active, dynamic. It is the divesting oneself of all that may impede the divine action; it is the emptying out of all that is not God, in order that divinity may act on nothingness. This spirit is the active dynamism of the soul bound to God in the intimacy of covenanted fidelity. The greater the abyss of true spiritual poverty, the more ardent the soul's longing for the plenitude of divine love; and the greater the buoyancy of hope and expectancy, so much more full will be the Christian's share in the rich graces of Christ's coming at Christmas.

It is this wondrous event of His coming into our midst which brings to fulfilment God's promise:

> I will leave in the midst of you a poor and needy people; and they shall hope in the name of the Lord. . . . In that day it shall be said to Jerusalem: "The Lord thy God in the midst of thee is mighty; he will save; he will rejoice over thee with gladness; he will renew you in his love; he will be joyful over thee with praise" (Soph. 3:12, 17).

# THE MEANING AND USE OF MIDRASH

Brendan McGrath, O.S.B.

*Midrash* is a term frequently heard today in discussions of matters biblical. All too often it is used by people who evidently have not troubled to find out its exact meaning. They insist on making it synonymous with "fable" or "legend," in the sense of stories with little or no foundation in fact. Or else they regard midrash as something so peculiarly oriental as to be quite beyond the comprehension of the Western mind. The truth is that midrash is not a form of fable or legend, nor is it so completely foreign to our way of thinking as to be intelligible only to an expert Orientalist.

## The meaning of "midrash"

*Midrash* is derived from the Hebrew root *darash*, which in the Bible means: to seek, seek out, investigate, ask. It is a very common verb in the Old Testament and is used in many ways, but practically all contain the notion of investigating or striving to learn something. The word itself is found only twice in the Hebrew Bible, both cases occurring in the second book of *Paralipomenon* or *Chronicles* (13:22 and 24:27). There is no general agreement as to the proper way of translating it; some of our modern Bibles are content, in fact, simply to transliterate it (as is done for example in the "Chicago" Bible and in the French "Jerusalem" Bible). Others render it in English as "book," "writings," "record," "story." In at least one instance, however, (2 Chr. 24:27 in the Revised Standard Version) we find "commentary," which suggests more of the later meaning of the word. There is one other biblical passage that helps to point us in the right direction, the Hebrew text of *Sirach* 51:23:

> Come to me, you who need instruction and take your place in my school (*beit midrash*); how long will you be deprived of what you need, how long will your souls remain so sorely parched?

The Hebrew expression *beit midrash* was rendered as *oikos paideias* by the author's grandson in his Greek translation. English versions usually translate this phrase by "school," but Professor Goodspeed in the Chicago Bible prefers the more literal "house of instruction."

All of which leads to an understanding of the word *midrash* as it developed in later Jewish thought and practice and as it is now understood, namely, as a special kind of "commentary" on biblical texts, or even themes, which developed among the Jews. It is the fruit of that "searching the Scriptures" of which our Lord spoke to the Jews (John 5:39).

Midrash, then, can be thought of as a commentary on Scripture, but a commentary of a very special kind. It is the result, not only of study of the sacred text, but of genuinely pious meditation on it. It is true, of course, that not a few

Published originally in *The Bible Today*, 1 (1963), 580-85. Reprinted by permission of the publisher.

of the examples of midrash which have been preserved in writing are characterized by an almost absurd extravagance of imagination run wild, but the same can be said of certain devotional works produced by and for Catholics. At its best, however, midrash exhibits its own special charm and appeal, even to many moderns, manifesting as it does a truly penetrating insight into the deeper and more permanent meaning of the word of God. It is, therefore, eminently fitting that Sirach should describe his "school," wherein the main instruction was to penetrate ever more deeply, by prayer and study, into the true and everlasting meaning of God's word, as a *beit midrash*, "a house of instruction."

That midrash thus understood constitutes a goodly part of traditional Jewish literature no one will deny. But the contention that much of the Bible itself is midrash, or at least manifests definite midrashic tendencies, is not likely to meet with such unanimous acceptance. Some Catholics, for example, seem reluctant to admit the presence of midrash or even definitely midrashic tendencies in the Bible;[1] but others, even of rather conservative stamp, find no difficulty in characterizing certain parts of the Bible, both in the Old and New Testaments, as midrashic in approach and tone.[2] The latter half of the book of *Wisdom*, which was written — almost certainly — only some fifty years or so before the birth of Christ, seems to provide us with an excellent example of a fairly highly developed form of midrash. These ten chapters, with the exception of a long digression (13:1–15:17) on the folly of idolatry, can quite properly be called a midrash, or perhaps, as we would say, a meditation on sacred history, with very special emphasis on the Exodus.

## Prayerful meditation on Israel's past

If we compare the treatment of the events attendant on the Exodus, the ten plagues of Egypt, for example, in *Exodus* itself with that in *Wisdom* — or Pss. 77[3] and 104[4] for that matter — certain rather striking discrepancies cannot escape our notice. At least in a general way, it is not at all difficult to account for these discrepancies in the presentation of factual data. It simply means that the author of *Wisdom* (as well as the poets responsible for the two Psalms mentioned) is primarily interested in showing his readers the great lessons which his prayerful meditation on Israel's past has brought to light. The precise factual details of that history are of little or no concern to him. If he can find data which will assist in the attainment of his purpose in the various traditions preserved among his people, so much the better. It is not that he is serenely contemptuous of the sort of factual historical accuracy which is so important in the eyes of a modern historian — it is just that it would never even occur to him that mere factual accuracy could even remotely compare in importance with the salutary

[1] Cf., for example, Lusseau-Collumb, *Manuel d'Études Bibliques*, I (Paris: Pierre Téqui, 1936), pp. 211, 218.

[2] The article on *Midrash* in the *Supplément au Dictionnaire Biblique, V*, cols. 1263-1281 (Paris: Letouzey et Ané, 1957), by René Bloch, provides a list of midrashic passages in the Bible (cols. 1271-1276; 1279-1280).

[3] The author of Psalm 77 calls his poem a *mashal* (parable) in v. 2, by which he means a sort of moralizing reflection on Israel's past history.

[4] Psalm 104 is a lengthy hymn on God's goodness as exemplified in Israel's history.

lessons which are the precious fruit of diligent searching into the inspired record of God's providential dealings with His people.

What has been said so far is intended to serve as a basis for a better and more complete understanding of the Church's use of a text from the *Wisdom* "midrash" in the Christmas liturgy. It is the Introit antiphon for the Sunday within the octave of Christmas (and, formerly, for the vigil of Epiphany as well), taken from *Wisdom* 18:14-15:

> For when peaceful stillness compassed everything and the night in its swift course was half spent, your all-powerful word from heaven's royal throne bounded, a fierce warrior, into the doomed land. . . .

The passage from which this text is taken treats of the last of the ten plagues of Egypt, the slaughter of the Egyptian first-born. Catholic commentators, in general, call attention to the use of these verses in the Christmas liturgy. The French Jerusalem Bible, for instance, in a note on these verses, remarks that "the liturgy, making use of an accommodated sense, applies this beautiful text to the Incarnation of the Word." [5] And Fr. Cuthbert Lattey, S.J., in *A Catholic Commentary on Holy Scripture* says, "This passage has often been applied to the Incarnation, for which so strong a personification of the Word of God certainly prepared the way, but Christ came to save, not to destroy."

## *The Introit antiphon*

If we consider the liturgical antiphon simply as it stands in the missal, taking no account of the original scriptural context, it raises no questions or difficulties at all. A literal translation of the Latin text would be something like this: "While all things were in the midst of silence, and night was in the middle of its course, your almighty Word, O Lord, came down from heaven from the royal throne." [6] It requires no special insight to see here a sort of poetic statement of the fundamental fact of the Incarnation of the Word of God. Nothing is said about that Word, except the very significant qualification that it is "almighty." [7]

Of course, a good deal of food for meditation can be found in the emphasis placed on the fact that this wonderful event took place in the middle of the night. And it is certainly not going too far to say that the Church is thinking not of the more or less inconsequential detail of the time of day at which the actual physical birth of Christ took place (assuming that we have any way at all of knowing what that was), but is rather concerned about the state of spiritual darkness into

[5] *Le Livre de la Sagesse*, tr. by Chanoine E. Osty, P.S.S. (Paris: Les Editions du Cerf, 1950). In the later one-volume edition of the whole Bible (1956), the mention of the use of "an accommodated sense" is omitted.

[6] The Latin version of *Wisdom* in the Vulgate is not the work of St. Jerome, but rather the Old Latin. It is not an especially careful or accurate translation of this text: "for when peaceful stillness compassed everything and the night in its swift course was half spent, your all-powerful word from heaven's royal throne bounded. . . ." The slight differences here, however, hardly would affect what we are trying to say.

[7] The Greek word thus translated, *pantodýnamos*, is quite unusual. It is found here and twice elsewhere in the book of *Wisdom* (7:23 and 11:17) and nowhere else in the Greek Bible, which ordinarily uses the word *pantokrátōr* to express much the same idea. The word *pantodýnamos* may very well have been coined by the author of *Wisdom*.

which, by the loving-kindness of His Father, Christ, the Light of the World, came.

## A deeper understanding of the text

One could continue, taking as sole point of departure, the *liturgical* text completely divorced from its original *biblical* setting. Providing that imagination and sentiment were kept within reasonable bounds, the result would certainly be a deeper and more immediate appreciation of the great mystery of the Incarnation. But is this all we can derive from a closer and more meditative consideration of this liturgical text? Are we expected to assume that whoever was responsible for the introduction of this text into the Mass liturgy *intended* that we should regard it as something distinct, independent, quite removed from the biblical setting in which it originated? Put thus bluntly, the questions answer themselves. For, certainly, it is unreasonable to assume that the compiler of this Mass formula either was unaware of the biblical background of his Introit antiphon or did not mean that that same biblical background should not significantly contribute to its total understanding in its new context of the Christmas liturgy. In a word, it seems not unreasonable to maintain that a great deal more can be said than that we have here a fairly typical instance of the liturgical "accommodation" of a biblical text.[8] That examples of straightforward and uncomplicated accommodation of scriptural texts are found in the Church's liturgy cannot be denied, but possibly this is not one of those cases. What we have here, it seems to us, is something considerably more subtle and much more meaningful.

In the classic Mass formularies of the Roman rite, it is well known that the Introit is normally, or at least fairly often, intended to state the "theme," as it were, of the day's liturgy. All three of the Masses of Christmas day exemplify this principle to a remarkable degree, and a large number of additional examples could be cited to demonstrate the same principle. Is it borne out by the Mass of the Sunday within the Christmas Octave? We think it is.

Stated very simply, the dominant "theme" of this Mass seems to be the royal dignity of Christ, God's own Son. Psalm 92, the Introit psalm, is also drawn on for the Alleluia verse and the Offertory chant. The Gradual is taken from Psalm 44. Both of these psalms are "royal" psalms, celebrating the majesty of God who is king over all and ultimately the invincible conqueror of all His foes. Psalm 92 does this directly, Psalm 44, indirectly.[9]

The prayers of our Mass formulary are so many protestations of our willing subjection to so mighty and majestic a King; the Epistle (Gal. 4:1-7) tells of the eternal divine Sonship of Christ and our sharing in that Sonship through fellowship with Him, and the Gospel (Luke 2:33-40) sets before us the scene in the

---

[8] "Accommodation" of a biblical text is its use in a sense quite different from that intended by the original author. For examples see any good general introduction to the Bible.

[9] Fr. Robert North, S.J., in the *Paulist Pamphlet Bible Series,* #45 (New York: Paulist Press, 1963) calls Psalm 92 one of a series of "royal eschatological psalms." Significantly, it is the first psalm of festive Lauds — the early morning "sacrifice of praise." Psalm 44 is a royal wedding ode, but even in pre-Christian times it was regarded as having definite messianic significance, the bride and bridegroom being looked upon as "types" of Israel and Israel's God.

Temple where the elderly Simeon proclaims the Child to be "a sign that shall be contradicted."

In other words, the whole Mass formulary under consideration treats not only of the basic fact of the Incarnation, that the Word of God became man, but also intimates that this same Word-made-flesh is the King of Glory precisely because He is the only-begotten Son of God and also because He is to win that eternal glory for Himself by His final and crushing victory over all His enemies. It is in this very light that He is aptly prefigured by God's "almighty Word" coming down from His heavenly throne to destroy the Egyptians as a necessary prelude to the liberation of God's people from their Egyptian bondage.

It is in reference to certain events connected with the Exodus that St. Paul says that "all these things happened to them as a type" (1 Cor. 10:11). In this he is continuing an already firmly established tradition of Israel, which saw in the Exodus and the events surrounding it the most striking manifestation of God's providential intervention in the history of His people. The Exodus is a theme to which the Old Testament writers — prophets, psalmists, sages — constantly return to draw new lessons or reinforce old lessons. The New Testament writers also find this a favorite theme, sublimating the traditional lessons to be learned from the Exodus to the new level of grace in Christ.[10] It is, therefore, not surprising in the least that the Church in her liturgy should continue to mine this extraordinarily rich vein of divine doctrine, adding new developments to the typology of the story of the decisive moment of Israel's history.

## Some Biblical Parallels

Strict biblical parallels to what the Church has done in the liturgy with the text from *Wisdom* 18:14-15 are by no means hard to find. Perhaps one of the most striking is in the series of five "prophetic" texts cited by St. Matthew (1:18-23),[11] of which the most telling, from our present point of view, is the one from *Hosea* 11:1 (Matthew 2:15). The eleventh chapter of *Hosea*, summed up in the simple statement, "Out of Egypt I called my son," unquestionably one of the most moving passages in the whole Bible, is a kind of midrash on the story of the Exodus, in which the prophet sees *the* exemplification of God's love for Israel, His "first-born son" (Exod. 4:22), a love which He will continue to manifest throughout all Israel's vicissitudes and infidelities. The evangelist then carries this midrashic process one step further, showing that Christ is the true "first-born of God," prefigured by Israel.

## The King of Glory

This, it seems, is just what the Church in the liturgy has done with our midrashic text from *Wisdom*. She has simply carried the process one step further, by identifying the descent of "God's almighty Word" to crush the

---

[10] For a fine full-scale treatment of the "Exodus theme" cf. Barnabas M. Ahern, C.P., "The Exodus, Then and Now" in *The Bridge*, I, pp. 53-74.

[11] "There are really only four prophetic texts cited; the last, "He shall be called a Nazarene," (Matthew 2:23) is not to be found in any known prophetic oracle. Its actual source has been the subject of a great deal of discussion and controversy.

Egyptians in order to liberate the Israelites with the Incarnation of the Son of God. "Jesus Christ came into the world to save sinners," as St. Paul emphatically insists (1 Tim. 1:15). But just as in the case of the liberation of the Israelites the crushing of the Egyptians was a necessary preliminary, so also in the more complete salvation wrought by Christ the destruction of those forces which hold sinners in bondage is necessary before they can be set free. The Babe of Bethlehem is our Savior, true; but He is also the great conquering Hero who has vanquished all His enemies and made it possible for us, too, to be victorious in Him.

The Mass of the Sunday in the Christmas Octave emphasizes the fact, as an old carol puts it, that "He came all so still," but it also intimates that He *is* the King of Glory, and His victory, which has set us free, is complete. In response to which, it is certainly no more than right that we should make the Church's sentiments really our own, as expressed in the Collect: "Almighty and everlasting God, direct our acts according to Your good pleasure, that in the name of Your Beloved Son we may deserve to abound in good works." What choice have we but to submit to so great a King?

# THE INCARNATIONAL ASPECTS OF OLD TESTAMENT WISDOM

Roland E. Murphy, O. Carm.

The wisdom literature of the Old Testament is disarmingly simple at first reading. All would admit that mighty problems of God's justice and man's suffering are wrestled with in *Job* and *Qoheleth*. But what about *Proverbs, Sirach,* and *Wisdom*? Here we find the down-to-earth sayings that we meet in every culture; the "no-nonsense" type of saying exemplified by: "Better a dry crust with peace than a house full of feasting with strife" (Prov. 17:1). Besides, in the tidy world of the Israelite sage (cf. *TBT*, pages 31-47), mankind is clearly categorized into fools and wise men, sinners and saints (e.g., Prov. 11:18). The road to success, riches and prosperity seems neatly marked out (Prov. 3:1-4, 13-15). All one has to do is follow the invitation of the sage.

It is no wonder, then, that biblical students are able to point to the humanistic and universal character of the wisdom literature. The Israelites shared these ideas about decency, honesty and homely virtues with their Egyptian and Babylonian neighbors; the wisdom movement was an international one. Perhaps this is the reason why the study of the wisdom books is somewhat glossed over. They are admittedly not as important or distinctive as the historical narratives

Published originally in *The Bible Today*, 1 (1963), 560-63. Reprinted by permission of the publisher.

and prophetical writings which incorporate Israel's great traditions. For some, indeed, there is question as to how the doctrines of the sapiential books fit into Old Testament theology. We hope to show that Israelite wisdom presents some definite characteristics of its own, a certain dynamism that formed an important preparation for Jesus Christ, the "Wisdom of God" (1 Cor. 1:24).

## Wisdom as inaccessible

One of the most surprising aspects of wisdom is her inaccessibility. This sounds paradoxical, in view of the many invitations to acquire wisdom. But it is very clearly and very often stated. Qoheleth admitted defeat in his search for wisdom:

> When I applied my heart to know wisdom. . . .
> However much man toils in searching,
> he does not find it out;
> and even if the wise man says that he knows, he is unable to discover it
>     (8:16-17).

The twentieth chapter of *Job* warns that silver and gold have a place in the earth from which they come, but "whence can wisdom be obtained" (28:12)?

> It is hid from the eyes of any beast; from the birds of the air it is con-
>     cealed. . . .
> Abaddon and Death say,
> "Only by rumor have we heard of it."
> God knows the way to it;
> it is he who is familiar with its place (28:21-23).

The same theme is continued in the wisdom poem contained in the book of *Baruch*:

> Who has found the place of wisdom, who has entered into her treas-
>     uries? . . .
> She has not been heard of in Canaan, nor seen in Teman. . . .
> Yet he who knows all things knows her;
> he has probed her by his knowledge (3:15, 22, 32).

Even Sirach, writing toward the end of the Old Testament period, repeats the old question:

> To whom has wisdom's root been revealed?
>     who knows her subtleties?
> There is but one, wise and truly awe-inspiring,
>     seated upon his throne:
> It is the Lord . . . (1:5-7).

This search for wisdom reveals that she is inaccessible precisely because *she is with God*. He alone knows her. Man's only way to her is through "fear of the Lord," which is "the beginning of wisdom" (Job 28:28; Prov. 1:7; 9:10; Sir. 1:16).

## Wisdom as divine

Wisdom is with God. Even if she invites man to possess her, she is conscious of her divine origins — such is the firm teaching of *Proverbs* 8, *Sirach* 24, *Wisdom* 7:

> The Lord begot me, the first-born of his ways. . . .
> from of old I was poured forth . . . (Prov. 8:22-23).
> From the mouth of the Most High I came forth. . . .
> In the highest heavens did I dwell (Sir. 24:3-4).
> For she is an aura of the might of God and a pure effusion of the glory of the Almighty. . . .
> For she is the refulgence of eternal light,
> the spotless mirror of the power of God,
> the image of his goodness (Wis. 7:25-26).

Especially in the last passage (utilized in the Epistle to the Hebrews, 1:3, and in the prologue of St. John, 1:1-10), the reader feels how the author is struggling for words to express this favored position of wisdom. She reflects the power, the glory, the light, the goodness of God Himself. Pseudo-Solomon describes other characteristics of this personified Wisdom. She is the attendant at God's throne (Wis. 9:4), she is with God and was present when He made the world (Wis. 9:9, and cf. already Prov. 3:19; 8:27ff). But one should keep in mind that Wisdom remains a personification, just like Yahweh's Word (Is. 55:10-11) or His Spirit (Is. 63:10-11) or His Arm (Is. 51:9-11). In fact, in Wisdom 1:4-6 and 7:22-24, wisdom is identified with the spirit of God. Like Wisdom, God's spirit is a gift which leads man to a knowledge of God's will:

> Who ever knew your counsel, except you had given Wisdom and sent your holy spirit from on high (Wis. 9:17)?

We are here confronted with a mystery which, for the Old Testament man, was part of the mystery of God, the "totally Other." Happily, this mystery received a concrete expression, a concrete communication, which could be described: the Law of Moses.

## Wisdom as communicated

The wisdom which originated from God looked about for a resting-place and the Creator commanded her: "In Jacob make your dwelling, in Israel your inheritance" (Sir. 24:8). The book of *Baruch* describes wisdom:

> She is the book of the precepts of God, the Law that endures forever (4:1).

Clearly, wisdom is identified with the Law. This appreciation of God's revelation is also reflected in the exhortations of *Deuteronomy*, for if Israel observes the divine statutes, she will give evidence of her *wisdom* and intelligence to the nations who will say, "This great nation is truly a wise and intelligent people" (Deut. 4:6).

It is well that this equation between wisdom and Law is made for us in the

Old Testament. The Christian reader might leap to the conclusion that the description of the divine origin of wisdom is a revelation of the Christian mystery of the Trinity, or of the origin of the Son from the Father. It is not. In the literal sense it refers to the Torah or Law, but it is a preparation for this Christian mystery. It enunciates a fundamental fact about God: He communicates Himself.

This was an idea that was not foreign to Israel. Man was made in God's image and likeness (Gen. 1:26-27), a communication in creation. And all life, man and beast, depended upon the breath of Yahweh (Ps. 103:29-30). God had revealed Himself to the patriarchs and to Moses. And now the supreme communication of the Old Testament is seen to be the bequest of this mysterious wisdom. A. M. Dubarle, O.P., has well said: "If this transcendent figure prepares in some manner for the Christian dogma of the Trinity, it is not by insinuating a plurality of persons in God, but rather by showing how infinitely close God is to His work, and how He desires to communicate Himself in some way. . . . The role of wisdom is to unite the faithful one to God in an intimate manner. By pouring herself out among holy souls, she makes them friends of God and prophets (Wis. 7:27); those who possess her have a share in divine friendship (7:14). Thanks to her purity she pervades all things (7:24). . . . Thus, for our author (of the book of *Wisdom*) divine perfection does not mean solitude, but on the contrary, communication of self. One can easily understand how such an idea leads to a doctrine which will place in God Himself a giving, a flowering of Himself, which constitutes a new divine person" (*Les Sages d'Israel*, Paris, 1946, p. 204).

Père Boismard, O.P., has pointed out that the same *movement* of thought is found in both the Old Testament descriptions of the origins of wisdom and the prologue to the Gospel of St. John. The key points in this movement are: relation to God and existence before creation; the part played in creation; the mission to earth to dwell with Israel; the benefits brought by wisdom. St. John reproduces this, but of course transposing it to the Word of God: in the beginning the Word was with God and equal to Him, before creation (John 1:1-2); the role of the Logos in creation (1:3); the mission of Logos in the world, among "his own," (1:9-11); the benefits brought by the Word, that men might become the children of God (1:12ff; cf. *Saint John's Prologue*, Westminster, Md., 1957, p. 76).

Are there any currents of thought which might explain this unusual revelation concerning wisdom? No, it appears suddenly. Indeed, early in her history Israel seems to have been chary of predicating wisdom of God Himself. It is true, God "makes wise," or "gives wisdom," much as He "makes rich," or "gives riches," but only very rarely is He said to be "wise." Both wisdom and riches were apparently felt to be on the merely human level. God is not said to be "wise" until relatively late in Old Testament revelation. The reason for this may lie in certain undesirable connotations of wisdom (perhaps with pagan divinities, or perhaps the association with court and court training?) which remain unknown to us.

The incarnational aspect of wisdom is brought out in ways other than merely the fact that she was communicated to Israel. She is a Leader and Savior and Spouse.

## Wisdom as leading to life

Wisdom appears frequently as a Leader, leading man to peace and life:

> Her ways are pleasant ways, and all her paths are peace (Prov. 3:17).
> On the way of wisdom I direct you,
> I lead you on straightforward paths.
> When you walk, your step will not be impeded,
> and should you run, you will not stumble.
> Hold fast to instruction, never let her go;
> keep her, for she is your life (Prov. 4:11-13).

The concept of life is a rich one in any culture, and among the Hebrews it ranged across several values: the very existence of the person, the "breath of life" which was God's (Gen. 2:7), sheer length of days (Prov. 10:27; Sir. 1:18), days spent in health and wealth, success and blessings (Ps. 102:3-5, etc.). We know that the Old Testament man had no concept of a blessed immortality; the future life was the sphere of Sheol and death (e.g., Qoh. 9:10). But the sages made a happy association between wisdom (virtue) and life, on the one hand, and folly (evil-doing) and death on the other. Life and death became pre-eminently a matter of conduct and relationship to God, as the Deuteronomic exhortation puts it:

> Here, then, I have today set before you life and prosperity, death and doom.
> If you obey the commandments of the Lord, your God . . . loving him
> . . . you will live . . . (Deut. 30:15-16).

In the wisdom literature the relationship of life to wisdom (= justice) is a constant. "The fruit of virtue is a tree of life" Prov. 11:30); "The teaching of the wise is a fountain of life" (Prov. 13:14; cf. 14:27). This idea grows into the triumphant assertions of the book of Wisdom that "justice is immortal" (Wis. 1:15), that "there is immortality in kinship with wisdom" (Wis. 8:17). By that time Israel had attained belief in the immortality of a future life, thanks to the association of wisdom and life. It was finally realized that this was *life* in the fullest sense, the life that associated with "the living God" (Ps. 42:3). Wisdom described herself in a very true sense, therefore, in *Proverbs* 8:35:

> For he who finds me finds life,
> and wins favor from the Lord.

## Wisdom as savior

Salvation is another concept with rich overtones, from the prosaic to the sublime. At the very beginning of Israel's (salvation-) history there was the experience of the *magnalia Dei,* the saving acts of the Lord, by which they were freed from Egypt and constituted the People of God. Constantly through Israelite history, it is Yahweh who saves His people; it is not the sword, nor the horse, nor any other earthly agent (Ps. 32:16-19).

Salvation was not merely a national experience; the individual, too, experienced it. In the liturgy he called for it (Ps. 53:1, etc.), and he reminded the Lord that He had saved the "fathers" (Ps. 21:6). The situation usually described in the psalms (of lament) is that of sickness or the opposition of enemies; a personal deliverance is asked for — and received (cf. thanksgiving psalms).

The role of Yahweh as Savior of Israel and of the individual Israelite is taken over by Wisdom in the sapiential literature. The sage instructs his "children":

> Forsake her not, and she will preserve you;
>> love her, and she will safeguard you (Prov. 4:6).

The author of the book of *Wisdom* describes the history of man as a salvation-history — from Adam to the Exodus, Wisdom was at work, saving men:

> Thus were the paths of those on earth made straight,
>> and men learned what was your pleasure,
>> and were saved by Wisdom.
> She preserved the first-formed father of the world. . . .
> When on his (Cain's) account the earth was flooded, Wisdom again saved it. . . .
> She saved the just man (Lot) from among the wicked who were being destroyed. . . .
> She took them across the Red Sea and brought them through the deep waters . . . (Wis. 9:18–10:18).

## Wisdom as spouse

We are not able to determine exactly why wisdom is personified as a woman. It may be due to the feminine gender of the abstract term, *hokmah* ($=$ wisdom). But there can be no question of her feminine characteristics. She is personified as a woman who invites young men to dine with her:

> Wisdom has built her house,
>> she has set up her seven columns;
> she has dressed her meat, mixed her wine,
>> yes, she has spread her table. . . .
> "Come, eat of my food,
>> and drink of the wine I have mixed!
> Forsake foolishness that you may live;
>> advance in the way of understanding" (Prov. 9:1-6).

She is counterbalanced by Dame Folly (also feminine!), who issues an invitation to *her* house: "Stolen water is sweet."

Sirach develops the betrothal idea in metaphors that describe the lover of wisdom as one "who listens at her door . . . who pitches his tent beside her . . . and dwells in her home" (Sir. 14:20-27).

The climax of this marriage relationship appears in the book of *Wisdom*, where the pseudo-Solomon describes his courtship:

> Her I loved and sought after from my youth;
>> I sought to take her for my bride
>> and was enamored of her beauty . . .
> So I determined to draw her into fellowship,
>> knowing that she would be my counselor while all was well,
>> and my comfort in care and grief.
> Within my dwelling, I should take my repose beside her . . . (8:2, 9, 16)

In a similar vein the alphabetic psalm in *Sirach* 51:13ff, describes the pursuit of wisdom, in whom "was my heart's joy":

> When I considered how I might make her mine,
> I strove to do well, lest I should be rebuffed . . . (51:18).

Here the emphasis is clearly placed on the moral cleansing and preparation necessary before finding wisdom (vv. 19-20). But when she is found:

> My whole being was stirred with the sight of her;
> therefore I have made her my prized possession (50:21).

## Wisdom incarnate

In the foregoing considerations we have briefly indicated the rich meaning and varied activities of wisdom in the Old Testament. Our initial observation about the "simple" appearance of the sapiential literature has been justified; wisdom is a very complex and manifold concept. And here perhaps is a lesson for us in evaluating the progressive revelation of the Old Testament. It progresses in several directions at once, developing now one thought and then another. The seeds of future ideas and developments are almost casually strewn across these pages. But these seminal ideals all contribute to the final enrichment, the fufillment and completion and perfection in the New Testament.

Jesus Christ, as the "Wisdom of God" (1 Cor. 1:24), gives the true and profound meaning to the various dynamic aspects of Old Testament wisdom. The wisdom that was inaccessible, because divine, did indeed offer Himself to mankind. "In Jacob make your dwelling" — these words of Sirach (24:8) suggest the Old Testament matrix from which He, the fulfillment of the Law, came. He is the Way and the Truth and the Life (John 14:6), towards which Old Testament wisdom was leading Israel. By His resurrection He was made "Leader and Savior" (Acts 5:31), the "great God and Savior Christ Jesus" (Titus 2:13). He is the Bridegroom, who has invited His Spouse the Church to the "wedding banquet of the Lamb" (Apoc. 19:9).

# THE BIBLICAL THEOLOGY OF PERSON

Bernard Cooke, S.J.

One of the most interesting aspects of Old Testament revelation that emerges as one studies the progression of Old Testament thought is the gradual deepening, under divine guidance, of the understanding of human personality. Revelation is concerned first and foremost with God's unfolding to man of His own

Published originally in *Spiritual Life*, 7 (1961), 11-20. Reprinted by permission of the publisher.

intelligibility; but since man has been supernaturally transformed, much of the revealed message concerns itself with clarifying this second mystery.

At the very beginning of the Mosaic dispensation, the Law given by Yahweh is intended to give a new insight into the nature and meaning of man. While there is a great deal in the legislation of Moses that is derivative from and parallel to other ancient law, still there is an insight into the dignity of each human person that is quite distinctive. At the root of this new vision of the personal greatness of the human being is the fact that Yahweh has manifested an interest in the people of Israel and has brought them into a covenant relationship to Himself. This covenant between God and His people is couched in legal language, but the familiarity of the ensuing relationship is revealed in the fact that the covenant is enacted at Mount Sinai by a ceremony of sharing of blood, i.e., of life, between Yahweh and Israel.

It is due to this covenant, to this choice of Israel by Yahweh, that Israel as a people and each individual Israelite have a new dignity and value; they are the object of divine interest and concern. We must not exaggerate the clarity or the depth of understanding possessed by the early generations of Israelites; they were quite primitive and barbaric, sharing many of the cruel customs and warped attitudes of the peoples who surrounded them. However, the very first commandment of the Law, in revealing that the nature of man oriented him in conscious acceptance toward Yahweh, introduced into Israelitic thinking a germinal insight which worked over the centuries to transform Israel's natural knowledge about man as a person. Each Israelite was bound by the Law; but each Israelite was also to be protected by the Law; no class of Israelitic society was exempt from the responsibilities or the privileges of the Mosaic covenant.

Flowing from this covenant dignity of each Israelite comes the Old Testament emphasis on social justice — not only the privileged classes enjoy the divine favor; as a matter of fact, Yahweh manifests a special interest in the poor and the widow and the orphan. Much of the message of the great prophets concerns itself with a castigation of social ills; and the prophetic oracles make it clear that social justice is not something incidental to God's covenant dispensation. Isaiah, for example, will express Yahweh's displeasure with His people in the beautiful imagery of Israel as Yahweh's chosen vine; and he will point out explicitly that the fruit of the vine which God expected to find, and which He did not find, were actions of social justice. Such an alliance of social reform with religious thought is again unique to Israel among ancient peoples; and this serves to draw attention to the peculiarly personal strain of the Old Testament revelation.

If the prophetic thought of Israel is notable for its insistence on social justice, it is equally important in the thought history of the Old Testament for the role it played in developing the sense of individual responsibility. From the beginning, the thought of Israel is marked by a strong corporate consciousness. This awareness of the social dimension of human existence is not lost, but with the passage of the centuries and with the key contribution of prophetic thinking, the people grew in the awareness of each Israelite's obligation to contribute to the fulfillment of the covenant with Yahweh. Accompanying this insight were the developing ideas of personal culpability and of the need for prayers and sacrifices of expiation. One can see how the movement of Old Testament revelation toward a more profound and more accurate moral consciousness is actually an unfolding of the deeper levels of man as a person.

If the Old Testament understanding of man as personal progressed over the years, so did the Israelites' understanding of their God and of their relationship to him. They were His elect, His chosen ones. While sanctifying grace was not yet revealed in its fullness, there was already the beginnings of this revelation: the sharing of a common life which the ceremony enacted at Sinai symbolized, pointed toward that supernatural participation in divine life which we denominate sanctifying grace.

Yahweh had taken the initiative in calling His people, in sharing His life with them; but the role of human freedom as response to divine calling received increased attention as Old Testament thought progressed. Deuteronomic and prophetic thought lay stress on the conditioned aspect of the Sinai covenant: Yahweh remains faithful, but the covenant can be revoked if Israel proves faithless. Thus, in Israelitic thought man is not a pawn of fates; he is a responsible agent whose free choices play a determining role in history.

New depth and richness comes to the understanding of the relation of Israel to Yahweh with the inspired employment of the husband-wife imagery in the prophets beginning with Hosea (about 750 B.C.). While the view of Yahweh as the loving and faithful husband of Israel did much to reorientate the people's thinking about their God, it also served as a powerful force in deepening the understanding of the human marital relationship. Surrounded as they were by the erotic religions of their neighbors, the Israelites badly needed this revelation about the sacredness of human love. In safeguarding and explaining the dignity of married love, Old Testament revelation contributed most importantly to the gradual refinement of the Hebraic view of man. Man, as we know, is a being who is created to know and love; if a civilization looks upon human love in degrading fashion, this must inevitably reflect itself in the lessened dignity attributed to the human person in that civilization.

Another important influence on the revealed Old Testament notion of person that is exerted by the Yahweh-husband and Israel-wife imagery is this: the very notion of law is transformed, as we can see in the Deuteronomic expression of the Law, an expression that was strongly influenced by the prophetic thought. In *Deuteronomy*, the first commandment reads: "Thou shalt *love* the Lord, thy God . . ." Law becomes in this context, not a restriction upon human behavior in an imposed legalistic way, but a guidance provided for a profound and freely chosen personal commitment. Few things are as deep and important an influence on a people's view of life and of the human person as is that people's law; thus the shift in emphasis, midway through Old Testament history, to a law of love must be considered an important factor in shaping the Israelitic notion of human personality.

Though clarification about the after-life came only toward the end of Old Testament times, and even then in very incomplete form, the Old Testament pages contain many precious insights about the destiny of man. Attention has often been drawn to the "eschatological" character of Old Testament thought, i.e., to the Israelite insight that history was moving toward some fulfillment which Yahweh would effect in "the day of the Lord." In such a world view, men's existence takes on meaning; human history is going somewhere; the human person has a value that cannot be measured ultimately by the happenings of our present temporal context. If, under the guidance of our fuller Christian knowledge of revelation, we put together the elements of God's message to Israel, we can see the Old Testament speaks of the possession of God as the destiny of man. To what extent Israel saw this is highly questionable; it remained for the "fullness of time" to complete the revelation.

## Christian revelation of person

This fullness of time occurs, obviously, with the coming of Christ. It is impossible to overestimate the contribution made by the mystery of the Incarnation to our understanding of the human person. The fact that the infinite God became one of us, walked our earth, shared our human experiences even unto death — this would give mankind an unimagined dignity and worth. But the mystery goes deeper: the Incarnation is redemptive; the Son of God shares our lot, so that we can share His; "God became man, so that we might become gods." With the Incarnation, man is linked with the divine, drawn into the sphere of God's own personal living. One can see, then, that the entire revelation of Christ pertains to our understanding of person; the present article can only single out a few of the more prominent aspects.

We saw earlier that the revelation of the Old Testament Law and its restatement in the Deuteronomic form gave a precious insight into the personal nature of man. Christ, as one of the most profound expressions of His divinity, further transforms the Law by saying, "Come, follow Me." Imitation of Christ is for the Christian a basic precept, the one which epitomizes his Christian vocation. At the same time, it is law given in a heightened personal context; for the path is sketched for human behavior in terms of a concrete, living ideal rather than in verbalized commands. Ordinary law contains only direction for human action; motivation for observance of the law must come from some other source. In the case of Christ, He is both the law and the motivation for living the law.

Excessive legalism can afflict and strangle any religion, as it did the Old Testament religion as explained by the Pharisees of Jesus' day. Christ decried this misunderstanding of revealed law, precisely because it overlooked the primacy and dignity of the person. "The Sabbath was made for man, and not man for the Sabbath." Genuine religion, a most profound relation of the human person to his God, is a dynamic force that always tends to go beyond mere verbal legislation. The force of Christianity resisted constraint by the Old Testament Law, and it won out over the Judaizing tendencies of some in the early Church who did not understand the words, "You cannot put new wine in old wineskins."

This is not to say that New Testament times are without law, that the "freedom of the children of God" is an unguided and unregulated way of action. Christ quite definitely spelled out the behavior that should characterize those who were His followers; but as we examine it we see that His precepts are pro-

COOKE: *The Biblical Theology of Person*                                              87

foundly liberating, because profoundly in accord with human personality. Christ's moral teaching can be distilled to two elements: honesty and love; and these two are the fulfillment of man's orientation to personal activity in knowledge and love. Actually, Christ's teaching could be stated, "Be true to the personal way of being which you possess."

One would miss a most important element of the New Testament revelation, however, if he were to think of Christ's law as being only the following of man's natural personal powers. With Christ comes the final unfolding of the knowledge that man has been raised to the level of God's own way of being. Man's nature is transformed by faith and hope and charity. Thus "raised" to a supernatural way of being and acting, man is introduced into the personal, familial living of the three divine Persons; a whole new world of personal encounter, incomparably richer than what he could experience in the purely natural realm, opens up to him. While not yet vision, faith gives man the ability to turn to the first of the three divine Persons and call Him "Father"; this is not a blind, unintelligent use of a word; it is the expression of the knowledge that the Father is his father. And the same kind of personal knowing can be directed to the Son and the Spirit.

As Christ Himself told His disciples at the Supper, "I will not now call you servants, but friends." Only against the background of the Old Testament can we see the depths of this statement: in the centuries of Israel's existence, the greatest encomium that the sacred writers could pay the spiritual heroes of Israel was to call them "servant of Yahweh." Moses, Samuel, David, the prophets; these merited the title; and when the Messianic Figure who epitomizes the spirituality of the chosen people is described in the second part of the book of Isaias, He is named "Servant." Now, in Christian times, the greatest familiarity granted to man before Christ is far surpassed by the grant of intimate friendship with Christ; the word "servant" no longer suffices; it must give way to "friend."

Actually, the grant of divine friendship to man is such an incredible thing that few people advert to its reality. Revelation, however, is clear and indubitable on the point; man is treated by the three divine Persons as an intimate, and man is meant to deal with them as intimates. "If any man love Me, he will keep My word, and My Father will love him, and We will come to him and make Our abode with him." Nor is this an arbitrary or artificial gesture on the part of God; so that we can associate with Him genuinely and from the resources of our own personal living, the Father associates us with His divine Son and actually communicates to us a share of the divine way of being. What this means for the understanding of the human person is unfathomable. To have our human personal potential so radically transformed that our manner of personal activity becomes comparable to that of God means that we can understand the depths of our own personal being only by probing into the tri-personal life of God Himself. We know things by their actions; if man's supernatural actions carry him so deeply into communion with the divine Persons in their life of mutual knowledge and love, what must man be? We can only join the Psalmist in his cry of amazement "Ah, what is man that Thou should think of him; ah, what is mortal man, that You should care for him!" (Ps. 8.)

Thus, with Christ and His revelation of man's elevation in the mystery of sanctifying grace, there comes the fullness of the vision already contained in the book of Genesis: the human person stands clearly above everything else in the visible creation. All things have been made for him; among the other creatures, even the living and sensible, he can find no one like unto himself; for he alone is created to the image and likeness of God. How much he is made like God and how superior he is to the nonpersonal levels of creation becomes clear with the coming of Christ. What must be the dignity and worth of those for whose salvation God become man did not hesitate to suffer and die?

Christ's properly redemptive actions — stretching from the Last Supper to the Ascension — reiterate and fulfill all previous revelation of God to man; and they clarify as does nothing else in human history the nature, role, and destiny of the human person. The Eucharistic institution, with its central symbolism of feeding a new life with that food which is Christ Himself; the passion and death of Christ, in which a member of the human race triumphs in a supreme exercise of human freedom over the mystery of evil that would have divorced man's personal living from God; the Resurrection and Ascension, containing the victory over evil by subduing death and guaranteeing a glorious destiny for all men who deeply wish to possess it — these are the events that manifest the greatness of personal expression at which a human can aim. No one, obviously, can hope to duplicate Christ's unique actions; yet in the mystery of the Christian Sacraments, the Christian is baptized unto the death and resurrection of Christ; in increasing fashion he is meant to live out those mysteries in his own person and actions, and to do so in union with and dependence upon the risen Christ.

Mentioning this union with Christ brings us to the last point in the New Testament revelation of person which we wish to discuss: the profoundly social nature of man's redeemed personal living. Man, by the very fact of his being a created and limited person, is oriented to life in society; in the Christian picture, Baptism by incorporating man into the mystery of Christ's Mystical Body introduces him into a deeper and richer dimension of social existence. Genuine Christian sanctity can never be individualistic; no Christian is saved and sanctified in isolation; no Christian can absolve himself of the basic obligation of entering into Christ's work of redeeming mankind. Unified by a common vision of faith, linked together by the bond of charity through the operation of the Holy Spirit, the members of Christ's Church are meant to express this vital unity in a sacrificial action, the Mass, whose sacramentalism and effect is that of uniting men to one another by uniting them to the Father in and through Christ. No action in human living can rival the Sacrifice of the Mass as an expression of man's personality; and it is in this act of worship that man can find his greatest mortal fulfillment, both as an individual and as a member of the human race.

### The Trinity and the revelation of person

At the root of all revelation about person lies the incomprehensible mystery of God's own personal life. Human reason can come to the knowledge that there must be in the Infinite Being something analogously corresponding to what we know of person from our human experience; but only supernatural revelation received by faith can tell man of the existence of three coequal, coinfinite, coeternal divine Persons. While the ultimate understanding of the Trinity will always remain far beyond human power, still there is an area of unlimited richness wherein the analogy of being and the analogy of faith can help man to a deeper knowledge of the Father, Son, and Spirit. Trinitarian theology, which exploits this possibility of deeper understanding, is aimed essentially at a fuller knowing of the three divine Persons Themselves; but it provides correlatively some precious insights into personality in general.

One thing that the revelation of the Trinity makes clear is that being at its very source is personal. Philosophical reasoning by way of analogy can tell us that whatever we know of personal perfection in the human situation must be eminently contained in the divine perfection; but of that rich interpersonal living of Father, Son, and Spirit which revelation describes, unaided human reason could have no inkling. To know the Creator in this profoundly personal context is to see all creation in a warmer light: the world about us is not the cold product of an ultimate uncaused cause; it is a prodigal manifestation of the love of a Father, and it is caught up into the redemptive life of Him who is the Son.

But we can learn some things about personality itself, things which we would not know so clearly were it not for the revelation of the triune God. From our knowledge of the trinitarian mystery we can now know that relatedness to another person stands at the core of personality. That very relation which He is distinguishes the Son from the Father and from the Spirit; this relation is not incidental; it is necessary, because it is that which constitutes His personality as Son. This truth which we know about personality in its infinite expression tells us that personality in its created forms is also a question of relatedness; to be a person means to be an "open" being, one related in personal communication to other persons. As one probes this insight, he not only appreciates the potential richness and breadth of his own existence, he also understands much more profoundly the ordering of each man to social unity with his fellow human beings. Then, when this is deepened by the mysteries of the Mystical Body and of sanctifying grace, one begins to be aware of the amazing bond of unity intended for all those who share the name "person."

Finally, there is limitless growth in understanding of personality that can come by reflection upon the revelation that personal living in God means communication of life in thought and love. Though knowing and loving in God, since they are identical with the divine nature, are for the divine Persons an incomparable basis of communion; still, the knowing of the Father communicates the Godhead to the Son, and the love of Father and Son, infinitely unitive and infinitely expressive, terminates in the Holy Spirit. Thinking upon this revelation, one becomes more conscious that in the human context of personality the sharing of knowledge and affectivity are real living. To think and to love, to "open up" to truth and goodness, especially when these are found in other persons, is to exist truly as a human. Not to develop one's thought and love is scarcely to be; to grow in personal awareness and affectivity is to reflect a bit the mystery of God's own inner living.

# ℬ THE APOSTOLIC PREACHING

One of the achievements of contemporary Biblical research has been a more accurate knowledge of the role of the apostolic preaching in the development of the early Christian message, and the singular importance of the kerygma in the formation of the written Gospels.[1] The chief examples of the apostolic preaching are preserved in the Acts of the Apostles (e.g., 2:14-36; 3:12-26; 10:34-43). Although Acts is probably not one of the earliest books of the New Testament in date of composition, forming as it does a complement to St. Luke's Gospel, the examples of the earliest preaching which it preserves seem to record the basic message of the eyewitnesses appointed by Jesus.

The speeches of Peter in the first ten chapters of Acts represent the early preaching of the Church at Jerusalem (2:14-36, 38-39; 3:12-26; 4:8-12; 5:29-32; 10:34-43). The great themes of God's consummation of His saving design in Christ are briefly but forcefully proclaimed: God has fulfilled His promises, made over centuries to the patriarchs and prophets, by raising up His Son Jesus; Jesus, the Holy and Righteous One, had been put to death, but by His Resurrection and exaltation at God's right hand has been established as Messianic head of the new Israel; as a pledge of the inauguration of the Messianic Age the Holy Spirit has been poured out upon chosen witnesses in a visible and extraordinary way. Salvation may be found henceforth only in the name of Jesus, "who has been appointed by God to be Judge of the living and of the dead" (Acts 10:42).

As always in course of God's dealings with Israel, a response to His saving word was required. The offer of God's saving mercy and the receiving of the Holy Spirit

[1] See C. H. Dodd, *The Apostolic Preaching and Its Development* (London: Hodder and Stoughton, 1936). F. X. Durrwell, *The Resurrection* (New York: Sheed and Ward, 1960).

had as a condition: "Repent and be baptized, every one of you, in the name of Jesus Christ, for the forgiveness of your sins; and you will receive the gift of the Holy Spirit" (Acts 2:38).

Most significant in the studies of the primitive preaching is the central importance given to the doctrine of the Resurrection. This is God's seal showing the fulfillment of His plan through the life, death and resurrection of Jesus. Now the final age has been inaugurated. Those who received the apostolic message would be raised up with Jesus.

Other books of the New Testament develop more fully the significance of the Resurrection; the primitive kerygma points only to its decisive importance. From Pentecost on, the course of salvation-history can be fully understood; the faith of the primitive community and its forward-looking eschatology can be seen as the first fruits of the descent of the Holy Spirit.

# THE CONCEPT OF SALVATION-HISTORY IN THE NEW TESTAMENT

David M. Stanley, S.J.

It would appear that in leaving Egypt the Israelites were not really Israelites as we understand the word, but simply a group of runaway Hebrew slaves with no particular ideal in mind. Certainly they had no religious purpose — only a desire to escape from their taskmasters, who had imposed upon them the impossible burden of making bricks without straw. So if we are to discover the purpose, the sense of history, which Israel found upon the mountain in Arabia, we have to begin the reading of the Bible with the book of Exodus.

The first chapter tells us that the Hebrews were "crying out." Undoubtedly, since most of us automatically supply certain things when we read, we tend, as Christians, to take it for granted that these Hebrews were crying out to God. But as a matter of fact, there is no mention of God, and this "crying out," as the Bible puts it, was simply complaining. They would have been perfectly happy to live in the higher culture of Egypt if only they would have been allowed some measure of freedom. The idea of leaving Egypt was entirely God's idea. This is evident from the fact that as soon as they found themselves in the desert, they began to realize that they could no longer enjoy the luxuries and comforts they had once possessed in Egypt.

It was when they came to the mountain of Sinai that, through the mediation of Moses, they had the first experience of their God, the God of their fathers, whom (it would appear also from the book of Exodus) they had for some generations forgotten. It was then that Israel began to see some meaning in those experiences we call the "Exodus." Or perhaps it was still later, when they entered the land of Canaan, which their God had promised they should inherit, that they actually acquired their unique sense of history. Still, this was not yet a fully evolved sacred or religious history, or salvation-history, in the sense in which we commonly accept that term.

Not until after the monarchy came crashing down and the political ambitions and hopes of the northern and southern kingdoms were definitively ended with the Babylonian exile did Israel and Israel's priests and sages begin to compose the full epic of their people, or rather, the history of what God had done for His people. It is the unique characteristic of Israel's sacred history that it was written, not to glorify the nation, but to glorify the nation's God. This long period of maturation lasted about six hundred years, from the time of the Exodus until the sacred books of the Old Testament were finished in the centuries after the Exile. We draw attention to the length of this period because it is helpful to realize its duration, not only to appreciate what the Old Testament ought to

Published originally in *The Bible Today*, 1 (1964), 686-93. Reprinted by permission of the publisher.

mean to us Christians, but also to appreciate the somewhat analogous experience that we find in the composition of the New Testament.

Here, obviously, the time elements are foreshortened considerably. Our Lord comes into the world, grows up, and dies. In the course of His public ministry He assembled the twelve apostles and other disciples about Him and taught them a great deal. Just as Israel learned much from the Exodus, the flight from Pharaoh, the crossing of the Red Sea, the experience of God at Sinai and the subsequent entry into the land of Canaan, so too the disciples learned a great deal from the Sermon on the Mount and from the other instructions the Master had given them during His public life.

Everything takes a certain amount of time to mature; this was true also of the intuition and expression of the data of the Christian faith. Indeed, when it is a matter of faith, it takes more than time — it takes the Holy Spirit. It is to be remembered that the New Testament event which corresponds to the experience of God on Sinai in the Old Testament is the experience of the Holy Spirit which the disciples underwent after the departure of our Lord on the day of His ascension. Just as the term "Exodus" designates the cluster of events that formed the initial experience from which the Israelites derived their conception of sacred history, so in the New Testament the term "Pentecost" designates the complex of the apostolic experiences of the Holy Spirit. At least, in the written account of the event which Luke gives us in chapter 2 of *Acts*, we see more clearly what the coming of the Holy Spirit meant than we do perhaps from the other hints and descriptions of the gift of the Spirit in the Gospel of St. John. St. John insinuates that even with His dying breath, our Lord gave the Holy Spirit to our Lady and to the Beloved Disciple as they stood beneath His Cross. In chapter 20 of his Gospel, John certainly brings out the fact that on Easter Sunday evening, the risen Christ breathed forth the Spirit upon His apostles and disciples in the upper room, effecting a new creation. But it is with Luke's account of Pentecost that we really begin to see how much this experience of the Spirit meant for the formation, not only of the Christian Church, but also of the Christian concept of what sacred history now meant for the new Israel, the new people of God, the Church.

St. Luke introduces chapter 2 of Acts by narrating the election of the twelfth apostle to replace Judas (Acts 1:15-26). We can see from the various sentiments expressed on this occasion that the disciples were still very far from having what we might call a "spiritual" view — we might even say a Christian view — of what the life and teaching, and even the death and resurrection of our Lord meant for them. Without the gift of the Holy Spirit, that is to say, without the gift of Christian faith, no one can have the insight into the meaning of this Christian religious history. And that insight makes all the difference in the world between a Christian and any other sort of religious person.

St. Luke tells us that the Holy Spirit descended at Pentecost in a very tangible way. We have descriptions, particularly in Paul's first letter to the Corinthians (14:6-40), of a similar experience of the Spirit by the early Christians. There, as in Luke's chapter, this is called "speaking with tongues." For a long time indeed, perhaps for centuries, this was considered to have been a God-given ability to speak various foreign languages. But it would appear much more probable, from reflection upon the evidence provided in Acts 2, that it was rather some form of ecstatic or mystical prayer.

As a result of this "noise" which followed the experience of the Spirit, a crowd gathered to hear Peter explain the meaning of this strange phenomenon. From Peter's speech we gather that God's new Chosen People had learned several things. They had completely new insights into the nature of the dramatic experience of the Spirit, and specifically into the nature of those experiences which they had shared with our Lord during His public life. In the first place, it is rather clear from the citation of the prophet Joel that the apostles were aware that they were assisting at a crisis or a turning-point in the history of Israel. Things were never to be the same again. The age of the reality of Israel's messianic hope, of which the prophets had spoken frequently, if somewhat obscurely, had dawned. The messianic age had begun in the absence, or at least without the presence, of the Messiah.

The message which the disciples had received on the day of our Lord's ascension was simply that, just as He had been taken up into heaven, so would He return at some future date. But they discovered on Pentecost that the beginning of the messianic era did not include this promised return. The messianic age was not inaugurated by the presence or the return of the risen and triumphant Christ, but by the presence of a new personality, the third Person of the Blessed Trinity, the Holy Spirit. With this realization, this group of disciples, who up to this point had been held together only by the memory of their departed Master, also became conscious henceforth of their new identity as the Israel of God, "the remnant," the congregation or assembly of which the prophets had spoken. They realized that they were the charter members of this new community or "church" of God, the faithful ones of Israel, those who, as Luke says at the end of the chapter, "are being saved" (Acts 2:47).

They also realized for the first time, through the grace of the Holy Spirit, the great truth — and one not easily assimilated by Jews long instructed in monotheism — that our Lord is truly the Son of God. Thus, this experience of the Holy Spirit, this experience of Pentecost, eclipsed Israel's experience of God upon Sinai. For these Jews were made aware that the Messiah, the Lord Jesus, the Son of God, had returned to be present unseen in the Church, through the operation of the third divine Person, the Holy Spirit. On Sinai God had used the mediation of Moses. Through Moses He had given His Chosen People their initial consciousness of their vocation, the sense of purpose in their history. The New Testament conception of sacred history, on the other hand, owes its existence to the mediation of our Lord and to the operation of the Holy Spirit.

The experience of Sinai had made a group of unruly, freedom-loving tribes conscious of their new existence as a confederacy, or amphictyony, a nation. And the only thing that effectively held them together was their appreciation of a new religious fact — that Yahweh, the one God, had chosen them to be His own People. In the New Testament experience of the Spirit, the apostolic group learned that the Church, the new Israel, was not to be merely a nation. Membership in this new unity was not to be confined to members of any one race. It was open to

all, and that gift of the Spirit which was the gift of "tongues," the truly supranational language of prayer, illustrated, perhaps better than anything else, this important facet of the new Christian concept of the sacred history of the new Israel.

## Christian history after Pentecost

The old Israel had been constituted as a nation; hence Israel's conception of
history was a religious conception of national history. As mentioned above, it is
to the credit of Israel that when the sacred writers wrote down this salvation-
history, their purpose was not to glorify the nation. It was not any sense of nationalism that led to the creation of the sacred books of the Old Testament, but the
religious purpose of glorifying God.

In the New Testament it was the consciousness that the Lord had departed
and that the Spirit had descended upon the community that was at the basis of
the Christian idea of religious history. This notion contrasts with the earlier one
found in Israel because the Christian community had a supranational, not a national, character. Actually, to say this is to foreshorten the story somewhat,
since it was to take the Church some years and a variety of experiences before
it was fully recognized that not every Christian need be a Jewish Christian. Only
gradually did it become clear to the primitive community that there were other
ways of coming into the Church than through the Judaism of their ancestors.
Certain stories in the Acts of the Apostles, and still more the experiences of
Paul, the Apostle of the Gentiles, show us how slowly this idea was assimilated
in some quarters of the Church.

The primitive community undoubtedly recalled that our Lord had hinted, as
is seen in chapter 8 of St. Matthew, that other people besides the Jews were to be
called into the Christian Church. Many were to come from east and west and
were to sit down at the messianic banquet with Abraham, Isaac, and Jacob
(Matthew 8:11). From the four corners of the world the pagans would arrive.
The Church was not meant merely for the Jews, not even for those of the Dispersion.

Yet it had never been entirely clear in our Lord's teaching as to when or how
this was to begin. And so we see in episodes like that of Peter's admission of
Cornelius into the Church (Acts 10:1–11:18) that it took some time, and indeed
considerable persuasion by the Holy Spirit, for the Judaeo-Christian wing to
realize this aspect of the new sacred history, to comprehend that their Christian
fellowship must extend beyond the limits of the disciples of Jesus Christ. Even
after Peter had admitted Cornelius and had defended himself very ably before
the Jewish Christian community (Acts 11:1-18), explaining that such was the
will of God, it would appear that they felt the admission of these pagans was
somewhat by way of exception. For even as Christians they themselves had continued to observe all the precepts, ritual and moral, of the Mosaic Law.

So it was left to the experiences of Paul, as crystallized in his writings (particularly in the letters to the Galatians and to the Romans) to show that, in the
Christian Church and in the Christian conception of the Church's history, these
observances had necessarily a very minor and secondary role to play.

## Creation of New Testament sacred history

While Israel's history was finally written about six hundred years after her experience of her God at Sinai, the creation of the New Testament history and of the inspired Christian library that resulted from the experience of Pentecost did not take near that length of time. But it is important to remind ourselves that the first books of the New Testament to be written were the letters, and not the Gospels. Of the existing and canonical books from the apostolic age the letters of Paul are certainly among the earliest. We tend to think almost subconsciously of the Gospels, perhaps that of Mark particularly, as being the first written books, but as a matter of fact most, if not all, of the Pauline letters were in existence before Mark wrote his book. They were certainly in circulation before Luke, Matthew or John wrote their Gospels.

It took all this time, it would seem, for the Church to reflect upon the experience of Pentecost. It took time also for certain new significant experiences to underline and clarify and sort out the multiple meaning of the disciples' Pentecostal encounter with the Holy Spirit. It was only as a consequence of these meaningful happenings that the sacred writers were able to formulate their insights into the most important part of Christian sacred history: first, the death and resurrection of the Lord, then His public ministry, and finally His conception, birth and early years. We must be on our guard against considering the Gospels as simple, untheological documents. These books only appear "simple" to us because, as Occidentals, we are not familiar with the background and culture of first-century Palestine, with the Semitic point of view and the biblical modes of expression, which are alien to our own Western ways of thinking.

The Gospel of Mark, for instance, so brief and seemingly written with such artless, candid, untheological simplicity, is actually instinct with a great depth of theological insight. As a record of the apostolic preaching, it stands closest of all our Gospels to the official testimony of the apostles regarding a quite well-defined series of events. Recall that in his "election speech" (Acts 1:21-22) Peter outlines the qualities necessary for the candidate for the office of apostle. He states that the candidate must be one "who has been with us," the Twelve, continually "from the baptism of John," that is, from the period of John the Baptist's activity, "until the day when the Lord Jesus was taken up from among us." It is, then, a question of a definite sequence of events within a carefully limited space of time. Note that it begins with the mission of John and the subsequent public ministry of our Lord. Moreover, the happenings must have been a matter of personal experience. This personal experience (we usually call it eyewitness testimony) is only one part — and, in a sense, a less important part — of the apostles' official attestation. For his principal role consists, as Peter states in this same verse, in acting as "a witness with us of Christ's resurrection." In other words, it is the testimony of Christian faith, added to and inspiring such a man's firsthand evidence of the doings and sayings of our Lord, which is of paramount significance. The apostle is not merely to witness to a series of historical events which he has personally experienced in company with the Twelve, but he also has to interpret these events in the light of the gift of the Pentecostal Spirit, which is his Christian faith.

St. Mark's Gospel is written precisely within these limits, from the baptism of John to the ascension of Jesus. This, then, was the object of the official testimony. This was, in consequence, the primary basis of the New Testament notion of salvation-history, to which, in later years, the first two commentators on Mark — Matthew and Luke — added, by way of prelude, certain episodes connected with the infancy of our Lord, and to which the fourth evangelist added his own very beautiful hymn, the prologue to his Gospel, in honor of the Incarnation.

The events which the infancy narratives relate do not therefore form part of the official apostolic testimony in the sense defined by Peter in the first chapter of Acts. This is not to say that these narratives are simply imaginary, whereas the others recount facts. But it is to say that, from the viewpoint of apostolic testimony and so from the viewpoint we call Christian salvation-history, these infancy accounts are of a different order. No apostle witnessed the events narrated in Matthew 1 and 2, any more than he witnessed those related in Luke 1 and 2.

Moreover, we can also see, even within the chronological sequence defined by Peter, certain incidents in the Gospels which did not fall within the personal, collective experience of the Twelve. The basic historical character of these events may not be doubted, but they are interpreted by the evangelists in a somewhat different way than those which the apostles had witnessed as a group. Let us take, for example, the extended descriptions of our Lord's temptation in the desert. St. Mark states merely that the Spirit led, or "drove" Jesus out into the desert to be tempted by the devil (Mark 1:12-13). Matthew and Luke, on the other hand, have employed a sort of classical trilogy (cf. 1 John 2:16) as a framework to elaborate upon our Lord's confrontation with Satan in the desert, which had probably been related to the disciples only in barest detail. Similarly, the prayer of Jesus in the garden could hardly have been heard by the three selected witnesses, since they were asleep. But it could have been reconstructed by the evangelist on the basis of the "Our Father," the Christian prayer *par excellence*.

If we are to grasp the unique character of this New Testament sacred history, we must comprehend first of all the nature and the object of the apostolic testimony which is its basis. We must also be able to evaluate the role, within the apostolic Church, of the Holy Spirit — His work at Pentecost and in the first formative years of the existence of the primitive community, which gave the apostles and the evangelists their insight into the meaning of the happenings to which they bore testimony. Only in this way will we be in a position to appreciate the historical and theological character of those other Gospel narratives concerned with Jesus' infancy, or His temptations, or His struggle in the garden. We can then put all these in their proper perspective. That is to say, we can begin to grasp the character of all this history, both as regards its factual content and its Christian significance.

We cannot emphasize too much the fact that the period between all these events and their formulation as Christian salvation-history was considerably shorter than in the case of the Old Testament. Luke states, as a matter of fact, that he got his information from "the original eye-witnesses" (Luke 1:2). It is also important to recall that, while with respect to the immediacy of information and accuracy of detail, the New Testament history is in many ways superior to the Old, yet both of them have at least this in common, that they took their origin from the supernatural experience of a collectivity — that of the Hebrews at Sinai, on the one hand, and that of the apostolic group at Pentecost on the other.

Accordingly, if we are to understand the message of the Gospels today in the twentieth century, we must do more than regard them as human documents of a rather high quality, as the human testimony of men who are at once reliable and informed regarding the events they attest. For we can never fully understand the New Testament formulation of Christian salvation-history without deeply appreciating the significance of the work of the Holy Spirit. Not only did He govern, direct and dynamically effect the experiences of the apostolic Church, but He guided the expression, directed the selection and interpretation of the New Testament hagiographers.

Finally, it is the same Holy Spirit who remains active today by constantly assuring the efficacy of the word of God in the Gospels, in the letters of Paul and others, or in the Apocalypse. This contemporary reading of the word of God with faith, as well as with intelligence, is the only way in which we can receive the full message of the New Testament. It remains also the only way in which we can appreciate the extraordinary and divine character of the Church's conception of her own history.

# "I AM THE RESURRECTION AND THE LIFE"

J. Terence Forestell, C.S.B.

In the holy city of Jerusalem there is a church in which are venerated the site of Calvary and the nearby tomb of Christ. To Latin Christendom this church is known as the Holy Sepulchre. The Greeks call it quite simply the Resurrection. This terminology may serve to illustrate how Christian thought in the West has often tended to consider that our salvation was fully achieved by the death of Christ upon the Cross. The resurrection of Jesus is sometimes considered to be nothing more than the personal reward of Jesus and the greatest of His miracles. By rising from the dead, He proved His divinity and confirmed the faith of His disciples. In the New Testament, however, the resurrection of

Published originally in *The Bible Today*, 1 (1963), 331-36. Reprinted by permission of the publisher.

Jesus from the dead is *the saving event*, in such a way that salvation, redemption and the kingdom of God are almost synonymous with the resurrection of Jesus.

## The Resurrection in the primitive apostolic preaching

The good news of salvation was first preached by the apostles before being written down in the four Gospels. The oldest summary of Christian faith is furnished by St. Paul in 1 Corinthians 15:3-5: "For I delivered to you first of all, what I also received, that Christ died for our sins according to the Scriptures, and that he was buried, and that he rose again the third day, according to the Scriptures, and that he appeared to Cephas, and after that to the Eleven." The redemptive death of Jesus is certainly the first proposition in this creed, but it is integrally united to the resurrection, as witnessed by the apostles.

If we turn now to the summaries of apostolic preaching which St. Luke has preserved in the Acts of the Apostles, we shall see how the resurrection of Jesus is the very substance of the good news of salvation. In Acts 2:14-36, St. Peter explains the meaning of events to the crowds assembled in Jerusalem on the feast of Pentecost. He asserts that today the Old Testament prophecy of Joel has been fulfilled. He explains that these are the last days and God has intervened to pour out His Spirit on all men; henceforth whoever calls upon the name of the Lord shall be saved (2:21).

St. Peter then turns to the career of Jesus of Nazareth, "a man approved by God among you by miracles and wonders and signs" (2:22). The events of Jesus' career were familiar to this audience up to and including His crucifixion. To these known facts St. Peter adds something new. Jesus died according to "the settled purpose and foreknowledge of God, but God has raised him up and we (that is, the apostles) are all witnesses of it. Therefore, exalted by the right hand of God, and receiving from the Father the promise of the Holy Spirit, he has poured forth this Spirit which you see and hear" (2:23, 24, 32-33). St. Peter concludes his discourse with this solemn affirmation: "Let all the house of Israel know most assuredly that God has made both Lord and Christ this Jesus whom you crucified" (2:36). St. Peter considers the resurrection and ascension of Jesus to be His enthronement as divine, messianic king. The giving of the Holy Spirit is the exercise of that kingship. By recognizing that the title "Lord" belongs properly to Jesus, the Apostle affirms His divinity and equality with Yahweh, the one, true God of Israel. Henceforth whoever calls upon the name of Jesus shall be saved.

It may appear to the modern reader that, according to St. Peter's conclusion, Jesus became God on the day of His resurrection. Such an interpretation would not only be heretical, but would fail to present St. Peter's point of view. He is not concerned here with the nature of Jesus but with His work. He had known Jesus as a man amongst men during the years of the public ministry. In the risen Christ, however, St. Peter had seen the manifestation of His divinity. In the gift of the Holy Spirit, the true meaning of His work as Messiah became evident and the exercise of this office began. Later, at Pisidian Antioch, St.

Paul applied to the day of the resurrection the words of Psalm 2: "Thou art my son, this day have I begotten you" (Acts 13:33).

In other words, the earliest theological reflection of the apostles considered Jesus as a man whose divine nature was hidden throughout the public ministry. Through His passion and death, according to the plan of God, Jesus merited an exaltation which brought Him into the full enjoyment and exercise of His divine prerogatives. Enthroned on high at the right hand of the Father, He then began to exercise His role as king by pouring forth the Holy Spirit.

This primitive theology is beautifully expressed in the hymn of Philippians 2:5-11: "Have this mind in you which was also in Christ Jesus, who though he was by nature God, did not consider being equal to God a thing to be clung to, but emptied himself, taking the nature of a slave and being made like unto men. And appearing in the form of man, he humbled himself, becoming obedient to death, even to death on a Cross. Therefore God also has exalted him and has bestowed upon him the name that is above every name, so that at the name of Jesus every knee should bend of those in heaven, on earth and under the earth, and every tongue should confess that Jesus Christ is Lord to the glory of God the Father."

The other sermons of St. Peter preserved in the Acts of the Apostles all reach their climax in the affirmation of the resurrection and the witness of the apostles (3:15; 4:10; 5:30-32; 10:39-41). This early preaching consistently sees the resurrection of Jesus from the dead as the culmination of His career and constantly attributes it to God the Father. In this way God has intervened in human history for the salvation of men.

Theologically speaking, the resurrection of the human nature of Jesus is the work of all three Persons of the Blessed Trinity. Jesus affirmed His own power to raise Himself from the dead in John 10:18; 2:19. By attributing the resurrection of Jesus to God the Father, the apostles made it clear that the initiative in man's salvation belongs to God the Father. He has accomplished this salvation through His Son, Jesus Christ, by the power of His Holy Spirit.

## The Resurrection in the Gospels

The first three Gospels are chiefly catechetical in character. Consequently, they are content to record the words and deeds of Jesus with a minimum of theological interpretation. Nevertheless, they all make it abundantly clear that the saving work of Jesus was to culminate in His passion, death and resurrection, and that thereby the kingdom of God would be established on earth.

In Matthew and Mark, whenever Jesus foretold His approaching passion, He always included the resurrection (Matthew 16:21; 17:22; 20:19; Mark 8:31; 9:30; 10:34). Moreover, He considered these things to be His divinely appointed destiny: "The Son of Man *must* suffer many things . . . and be put to death, and after three days rise again" (Mark 8:31).

By identifying Himself with the heavenly Son of Man in Daniel 7:13, Jesus indicated to Caiaphas that the kingdom of God would be established on earth through His passion, death and resurrection: "Hereafter you shall see the Son of Man sitting at the right hand of the Power and coming upon the clouds of heaven" (Matthew 26:64). In the book of Daniel, the mysterious apocalyptic figure of the Son of Man comes before the Ancient One to receive an ever-lasting kingship; this vision is there interpreted as the gift of eternal kingship to the holy people of the Most High (Dan. 7:27). Through the resurrection of Jesus Christ, this kingship is established upon earth and is extended to all those who are united to His Body by baptism and the Eucharist.

Before His arrest in the garden, Jesus reassured His disciples that after His resurrection He would go before them into Galilee (Matthew 26:32; Mark 14:28). St. Matthew and St. Mark conclude their Gospels with the fulfillment of this promise: "Go, tell his disciples and Peter that he goes before you into Galilee; there you shall see him, as he told you" (Mark 16:7).

St. Matthew records this meeting in Galilee (28:16-20). It is only now, after His resurrection, that Jesus proclaims, "All power in heaven and earth has been given to me. Go, therefore, and make disciples of all nations, baptizing them in the name of the Father, and of the Son, and of the Holy Spirit, teaching them to observe all that I commanded you; and behold, I am with you all days even unto the consummation of the world." The universal power of Jesus and the universal mission of the apostles are conditioned, in the divine plan, upon the resurrection of Jesus. This fact, which is only implied in Matthew, will become more explicit in Luke and John.

Luke makes the connection between the passion and resurrection of Jesus more explicit than does either Matthew or Mark: "Did not the Christ have to suffer these things before entering into his glory?" (24:26). At the Last Supper, Jesus told His apostles that He would no longer eat and drink with them until the kingdom of God should come (22:16, 18). St. Luke then emphasizes the meals which Jesus took with His disciples *after* His resurrection (Luke 24:30, 41-43; Acts 1:4).

As in Matthew, the universal preaching of repentance and remission of sins is conditioned upon the resurrection of Jesus: "Thus it is written; and thus the Christ should suffer, and should rise again from the dead on the third day; and that repentance and remission of sins should be preached in his name to all nations, beginning from Jerusalem. And you yourselves are witnesses of these things. And I send forth upon you the promise of my Father. But wait here in the city, until you are clothed with power from on high" (Luke 24:46-49).

The joyful news of life from death, of forgiveness and resurrection, is what is meant by the paschal mystery. Just as God passed over the houses of the Israelites in Egypt, saving them from death, and just as the Israelites passed through the waters of the Red Sea to become united to God in the Sinai cove-nant, so Jesus passes through death from this world to the Father in order that men may be united to God. The Gospel of St.John fully exploits the theme of the paschal mystery, already suggested by Luke. Jesus is the Lamb of God (1:29); He is sentenced to death as the Passover sacrifices are being offered in the temple (19:13-14); in the piercing of His side St. John saw the fulfill-ment of a passover ritual: "Not a bone of him shall you break" (19:36; Exod. 12:46).

St. John considered Jesus' career as an exaltation and a glorification. These two words recall the destiny of the Suffering Servant of Yahweh: "See, my servant shall prosper, he shall be raised high and greatly exalted" (Is. 52:13). For St. John, this exaltation of Jesus began with the physical elevation on the Cross: "As Moses lifted up the serpent in the desert, even so must the Son of Man be lifted up" (3:14). " 'And I, if I be lifted up from the earth, will draw all things to myself.' Now he said this signifying by what death he was to die" (12:32-33).

The physical elevation of Jesus upon the Cross was only the beginning of an ascent which would lead Him back to the Father. He had come from God as the incarnate Word. Now he returned to God, glorified in His own human nature. In the glorified Jesus, man was once more united to God. This was Jesus' hour, the hour of His glorification. Through His passion, death and resurrection, He returned as man to the bosom of the Father. From there He would send the Holy Spirit to all who believed in Him. In the plan of God, the gift of the Spirit was conditioned upon the glorification of Jesus: "For the Spirit had not yet been given, seeing that Jesus had not yet been glorified" (John 7:39). St. John has thus succeeded in explaining the true nature of the paschal mystery. It is the passing of God among men in the person of the incarnate Word, Jesus of Nazareth. God passes among us and saves us from death. We pass with Christ through death to the bosom of the Father.

All four Gospels have made it abundantly evident that the passion and death of Jesus are not to be considered apart from His resurrection and ascension to the Father. All these temporally distinct events are part of one divine mystery which makes the gifts of salvation available to men. It remains for St. Paul to tell us how the resurrection of Jesus is in itself the salvation of men.

## The Resurrection in St. Paul

St. Paul never saw Jesus of Nazareth prior to His resurrection. St. Paul's conversion took place on the road to Damascus, when he saw the risen Christ. When Christ appeared to him in risen glory, St. Paul saw that the Christian claim was true: Jesus of Nazareth was no longer dead. Not only was He alive, but the glory of the Son of God was manifest in Him. In the risen Christ, St. Paul saw the destiny of all mankind. He also learned that the risen Christ was mysteriously one with all who believed in him: "I am Jesus, whom thou art persecuting" (Acts 9:5). The crucified and risen Jesus became central to his life and thought: "If Christ has not risen, vain then is our preaching, vain too is your faith . . . for you are still in your sins" (1 Cor. 15:14, 17).

In the Epistle to the Romans especially, St. Paul shows how the resurrection of Jesus in its concrete, historical reality already is the salvation of mankind: "All have sinned and have need of the glory of God" (3:23). All men of Adam's race are born in a state of separation from God and continue to widen this gulf by their personal sins (5:12-14). Only the obedience of Christ is able to restore union and peace between man and God (5:1, 19). God sent His Son in the likeness of sinful flesh (8:3). By freely submitting to the consequences of sin out of love for His heavenly Father and for all mankind, Christ conquered sin and death in His own flesh. This victory was achieved by the resurrection from the dead. "The death that he died, he died to sin once for all, but the life that he lives, he lives unto God" (6:10).

Because of His solidarity with Adam's sinful race, Christ's victory over sin and death is the victory of all mankind. He is the firstborn from the dead (Col 1:18), the first-fruits of a new human race (1 Cor. 15:20, 23). "Since by a man came death, by a man also comes resurrection from the dead" (1 Cor. 15:21). The risen Christ is the first man to live entirely for God. He calls all men to share in His new life by faith and baptism. In the sacrament of baptism the Christian already dies and rises with Christ to a new life (Rom. 6:4; Col. 2:12). Baptism unites the Christian in a mysterious way with the risen Jesus; the life of the risen Jesus is communicated to him through the gift of the Holy Spirit. The Holy Spirit lives and acts within the Christian as the principle of a spiritual resurrection in this world and the pledge of bodily resurrection in the next. St. Paul has fully explained the words of Christ, "I am the resurrection and the life" (John 11:25).

In Philippians 3:10-11, St. Paul wrote of his own spiritual life. He sought to know Christ and the power of His resurrection and the fellowship of His sufferings, so that, becoming like to Him in death, he might attain the resurrection from the dead. St. Paul referred to a conscious experience of the risen Christ, living and active in the world. The power of His resurrection is poured forth in the Church through the sacraments. There we come in contact with the risen Christ, knowing that His resurrection is also ours.

# THE RESURRECTION IN THE PRIMITIVE COMMUNITY

Josef Sint, S.J.

The preaching of the Risen One holds for all time the central position in Christian faith and life. The following reflections concern the theological content of this preaching in the primitive community as presented in the NT. Both the person of the Risen One and his work will be considered after some introductory remarks concerning the historicity of the Resurrection.

The NT clearly testifies to the faith in the Resurrection of Jesus which together with his death forms the core of the preaching of the early community. According to the now widespread view of Rudolph Bultmann, this faith does not concern an objective event, a "real occurrence," but the death and resur-

Reprinted from *Theology Digest*, 12 (1964), 33-39. Originally published as "Die Auferstehung Jesu in der Verkündigung der Urgemeinde: Ein Durchblick," *Zeitschrift Für Katholische Theologie*, 84 (1962), 129-51. Reprinted by permission of the publisher.

rection of Jesus must be understood merely eschatologically. Through faith in the Resurrection of Jesus the believer experiences his death as a saving death and faces final judgment in his death and resurrection. The Resurrection itself serves only as the occasion of insight into the personal experience of salvation.

Without being able to enter more closely into Bultmann's concepts of faith and history, we must at least test whether this interpretation is compatible with the language of the NT and ask how we are to understand the historicity of the Resurrection. We begin with two negative observations. Of the event itself we have no direct eyewitnesses. Even the guards at the tomb could perceive only the earthquake, the apparition of the angel, and the rolling away of the stone. Moreover, could the event of the Resurrection be grasped in space and time at all or be made the subject of proof since it is not a simple return of a dead person to his previous state? But a predominantly positive factor is the manifold evidence of the apparitions of the risen Lord which the Gospels, Acts, and Epistles offer.

## Earliest tradition

The starting point of our consideration will be 1 Cor. 15:3-8 which belongs to the earliest tradition and was probably formulated already in the Palestinian community. Four elements of this report will be singled out to illustrate the historicity of the appearances of Jesus: 1. the *parodosis* (tradition) of which the apostles knew they were witnesses, 2. the expression, *ophthe*, "he was seen," 3. the raising of Jesus *ek nekron*, "from among the dead" in the context of the empty tomb, and 4. the formula, "according to the Scriptures." The first two expressions point to the Resurrection as an objective event, as transsubjective reality; the last two as a salvation-event having a meaningfulness grasped only in faith.

"I passed on to you, as of first importance, the account I had received." Paul introduces a whole chain of witnesses who are publicly cited in the early preaching as guarantors of the Resurrection: Cephas, the twelve, more than five hundred, James, and then the rest of the disciples. Paul speaks in the technical language of the rabbis and with a conscious appreciation of tradition which the early Church took from its Jewish background. From the beginning of the Christian preaching the apostles were called upon to be witnesses to the living tradition, especially with regard to the appearance of the risen Lord. The apostle who was to fill the place of Judas had to be "a witness to his resurrection" (Acts 1:22). Thus Peter professes on Pentecost: "This Jesus God has raised up and we are witnesses of this" (Acts 2:32). Again and again this same assertion occurs in the preaching of Acts. Paul's explicit appeal to tradition through witnesses argues against reducing these testimonies to a mere plea for faith in the risen Lord. Luke makes no distinction between eyewitness testimony for the life of Jesus previous to the Resurrection and testimony to the Resurrection (Acts 1:21). Clearly the event holds the same degree of reality in the minds of the preachers as the life of Jesus before the Resurrection.

## Jesus made visible

"On the third day he was raised . . . and was seen" — *ophthe*. Paul uses this expression four times in succession. The word does not have an intransitive meaning in the sense of *appear*. The Greek means rather that something *becomes* or *is visible* and in the language of the Bible especially in the sense of an emergence from invisibility which is linked with the world of God. As God is the agent with *egegertai*, "he was raised," so God also causes Jesus to be seen. This recalls the archaic and unusual formula of Acts 10:40: "caused him plainly to be seen" — which is nothing else than an early interpretation of *ophthe*.

Thus in the conviction of the early community the activity of God upon Jesus comes clearly to the fore. The concrete "see" stresses the transsubjective character of the apparitions. Behind every critique which considers as secondary and legendary creations of the community the reports of touching Jesus and eating with him, there lies the unacknowledged postulate of a Kantian idealistic theory of knowledge questioning the knowability of any objective reality. The theory of an "objective image" attempts both to acknowledge and not to acknowledge the data. But the frequently stressed *ophthe* seems to be a protest of the first generation of Christians against any explaining away of the Resurrection.

## A salvation-event

The factual character of the Resurrection is not the only element found in the preaching of the early community. The Resurrection is also a salvation-event of the deepest meaningfulness. Its objective character is emphasized not for apologetic reasons but because of the desire to understand this event more profoundly in faith.

The risen Lord is not merely raised up and returned "from the tomb" — an expression never used in connection with the Resurrection — but "from among the dead" — an expression that appears over thirty times in this connection. Is this not a hidden reference to the fact that the Resurrection of Jesus was more than a mere return from the tomb to his earlier earthly life? Acts clearly expresses this point when it applies Psalm 15:10 to Jesus (Acts 2:24). The idea of the "ways of life" is reflected in the later preaching when Jesus is called the "source of life" (Acts 3:15) and "the firstborn from among the dead" (Col 1:18). Thus the Resurrection as part of salvation history begins to unfold in the early preaching.

This meaningfulness for salvation history is also seen in the fact that the Resurrection was considered a fulfilment of the Scriptures. Already in his Pentecost sermon Peter applies the words of the psalmist to the Resurrection (Acts 2:30). In the fourfold expression of 1 Cor. 15:3-5, the first and third clauses emphasize the fact that the saving action of God foretold in the OT is fulfilled in Jesus. The addition "for our sins" underlies this meaningfulness for salvation.

## Resurrection unexpected

During the entire time spent with his apostles before his death Jesus had not succeeded in giving them a profound understanding of the mystery of his person. In spite of all his preparation, all their contact with the power of his deeds and teaching, and all their devotion to him, they could not and would not understand that the way of the Son of Man must pass through suffering and death. The catastrophe of the crucifixion brought complete confusion ending in flight and desertion. The apostles were anything but disposed to expect the Resurrection of their master. In the reports of the Resurrection doubt and uncertainty appear again and again. Only gradually and with effort does the risen Lord succeed in raising up their shattered faith.

But through this trial and the overpowering impressiveness of the apparitions their faith is deepened and brought to an entirely new understanding. The Easter experience illumines all the previous life of their master and deepens their understanding of the plan of salvation. The teaching of the risen Lord discloses to them the meaning of the Scriptures which foretold the path through suffering to glory, and the gift of the Holy Spirit reveals to them the full understanding of their vocation as witnesses to the salvation-event in Jesus.

The Jesus of history was no irrelevant matter to the early preachers of the Resurrection. The Risen One is seen as continuous and identical with the Jesus of history. Through the apparitions the apostles gained a deeper understanding from which a theology of the meaningfulness of Jesus' person and work for salvation begins to develop. For the raising of Jesus is the proof of his true messiahship and lordship (Acts 2:36).

## Messiahship misunderstood

Throughout his entire earthly life Jesus was reluctant to admit that he was the Messiah in order to avoid national and political misunderstanding of his mission. Nonetheless, the messianic consciousness of Jesus is seen clearly in his earthly life, above all in the self-imposed title of Son of Man (Matthew 12:8). As soon as the disciples partially understand his messianic mission, Jesus tries to bring them to a further understanding that his path as Messiah must lead through humiliation to glory (Matthew 16:21f). This effort, however, meets only with misunderstanding and even protest.

## New understanding

The situation is fundamentally changed after the Resurrection. Not only is the notion that Christ must suffer and die no longer a stumbling block, but the passion is now seen as a fulfilment of the prophecies (Acts 3:18). An important moment for the apostles' realization of the Risen One as the Messiah was the pouring out of the Spirit, which is characteristic of the messianic times according to the prophecies which Peter cites (Acts 2:17-20). As Jesus knew that he himself was filled with the Spirit (Luke 4:18) and as the Spirit descended upon him at his baptism (Matthew 4:16), so the apostles now realize that he "has received from his Father the promise of the Holy Spirit and has poured out what you see and hear" (Acts 2:33).

The preaching of the early Church confessed the Risen One as the Messiah and sought in a series of attributes applied to Jesus to construct the first elements of a Christology. These archaic expressions no longer used in the later development of the NT are authentic matter of the first Christological preaching. Moreover, these expressions, at least in part, refer to the life of Jesus before the Resurrection and hence emphasize the continuity between the Jesus of history and the Christ of faith.

### Glory of Messiah

Through the Resurrection Jesus has been "exalted to God's right hand" in fulfilment of Psalm 109 (Acts 2:30-35). "He is the one whom God has appointed to be the judge of the living and the dead" (Acts 10:40). Peter's sermon after the cure of the lame man mentions the glory into which the Messiah has entered (Acts 3:13). The Risen One is also the fulfilment of the prophecy from Isaiah regarding the figure of the servant. Like this servant Jesus has been anointed with the Spirit, has taken upon himself vicariously suffering and insult (Acts 4:25-30), and has been glorified for the salvation of the chosen people (Acts 3:26).

In the sermons of Acts Jesus is often called the Holy One or the Righteous One (Acts 3:14), allusions to OT messianic expectations. For the Messiah will be righteous (Jer. 23:5), a just, humble, and peaceful king (Zach. 9:9). Later Jewish writings further develop this theme to which the early preaching refers. For though Jesus has fulfilled these expectations in his life, the Jews have "disowned the Holy, Righteous One" (Acts 3:14).

Similarly Jesus is the Holy One (Acts 3:14), "the holy servant" (Acts 4:27), for the Messiah is anointed with the holy Spirit of God. Finally in his sermons Peter gives Jesus another title, *archegos*, "prince" (Acts 5:31), "source of life" (Acts 3:15). The Hebrew *nasi'* underlying the Greek recalls Ez. 34:24 where God promises a new covenant of peace with his people and that "my servant David will be prince among them."

### Messianic lordship

These early attempts to express the experience of the Risen One are rooted in the OT atmosphere and yet have transcended their origin under the influence of the Resurrection which gave the disciples a new understanding of Jesus as the Messiah. These Christological attributes at least implicitly indicate the divinity of Christ. Besides the frequent use of the title *lord* as an expression of respect even before the Resurrection, there are clear expressions of a more comprehensive lordship. Drawing upon the common Jewish conceptions of the Messiah, Jesus claimed during his early life an absolute lordship. The question concerning the lordship of the Messiah, the son of David, whom David calls Lord (Matthew 22:44), Jesus clearly applies to himself. He is "Lord of the Sabbath" (Matthew 12:8), and calling Jesus the Lord could merit heaven (Matthew

7:21ff). The sovereign authority of Jesus regarding the Law reveals the power implied in this title (Matthew 5:21f). The power and dignity of Jesus reflects the idea of the messianic lordship of the contemporary literature. With this idea in mind, Jesus' opponents question his authority at the cleansing of the temple, and thus the puzzling expression, "The Lord needs them" (Matthew 21:3), must be understood. The Resurrection clarifies and deepens the meaning of these instances. The Aramaic *maranatha* (1 Cor. 16:22) shows the very early origin of this title. The Hellenistic churches adopted the expression untranslated — a certain sign that it was a familiar formula of faith in the Palestinian community. Hence, the prayer of Stephen, "Lord Jesus, receive my spirit," belongs to the earliest period.

Two passages from Paul show that the connection between the Passion and Resurrection of Jesus and his lordship was clearly grasped in the earliest preaching. Both passages are of pre-Pauline origin and reflect a very ancient view. In Rom. 10:9 the confession, "Jesus is the Lord," is equated with faith that "God has raised him." The hymn to Christ (Phil. 2:6-11) develops in six strophes the entire mystery of Christ from his divine dignity through the incarnation, suffering, and death to glory. The historical experience of the lordship of Jesus finds its continuation, development, and deepening in the Resurrection brought to its fulness especially in Paul's speculations on the cosmic power of the lordship of Jesus (Col. 1:14).

## Jesus' divinity

Two lines of development have had an important influence on the *kurios* title: the OT *Yahweh-Kurios* and the *kurioi* of the Hellenistic cults. Through them the explicit theological declaration of Jesus' divinity emerges more clearly in the consciousness of the Christian preaching.

The application of the prophecy of Joel to Jesus in the sermon of Peter (Acts 2:17-20) is the first suggestion of the application of the *Adonai-Kurios* title to Jesus. The "day of the Lord" (Acts 2:33) immediately refers to Yahweh, but mediately also refers to Jesus. "Everyone who calls upon the name of the Lord will be saved" (Acts 2:21). For in Jesus of Nazareth "is salvation and in no other" (Acts 4:12). As the savior of the end-times, Jesus is unmistakably identified with the OT *Adonai-Kurios*.

A series of further linguistic formulas gradually clarifies the identification of the resurrected Jesus with Yahweh. In Samaria Peter and John preach "the word of the Lord" (Acts 8:25). The Lord is the object of faith (Acts 3:16), and to the Lord fidelity is pledged (Acts 14:23). Similarly one speaks of "fear of the Lord" and of his grace (Acts 9:31, 14:3).

Although the radical thesis that the *kurios* title of Jesus is of purely Hellenistic origin and transferred to Jesus from the ruler cults of the Near East is now proved inadequate, the fact of contact with the ruler cults in the Greek world remains inescapable. This confrontation of the Christian message led to a more conscious realization of Jesus as the only and unique Lord above absolutely every other lordship (1 Cor. 8:5). The Apocalypse reflects this conflict of the lords of this world with the absolute lordship of Christ (1:5, 22:20).

The experience of the risen Lord also casts light upon his work. The salvation-message centers about the reality of our Christian existence in the risen Lord, the salvation both of the individual and of the community of the Church. Peter speaks of the consequences of the Resurrection for his hearers. Through it Jesus has become the "source of life" who has himself shattered the power of death and can also blot out sin for him who believes (Acts 3:19). Faith and baptism are the fundamental requisites for the salvation of the individual.

## Resurrection and faith

In Paul the central meaning of the Resurrection-event for the salvation of the individual stands out more clearly. Faith is essentially faith in God who has raised Jesus Christ from the dead (Rom. 4:24), and upon this faith depends our salvation (Rom. 10:9). So central is the Resurrection in Pauline faith that if Christ is not risen, faith is empty. The content of faith is stated in the short formula, "Jesus is the Lord." Through this faith we attain "the promise of the Spirit" (Gal. 3:14); "Christ dwells in our hearts" (Eph. 3:17); we become "children of God" (Gal. 3:25). Through faith in Jesus we attain "justification . . . to know him and the power of the resurrection" (Phil. 3:9). Thus man becomes a "new creature" (2 Cor. 5:17). We live no longer but "Christ lives in us" (Gal. 2:20). Finally, the Resurrection of Jesus also guarantees the resurrection of each individual (1 Cor. 15; 1 Thess. 4:14).

## Baptismal union

Secondly, baptism is required for salvation as a rite of initiation, as an exterior visible sign of belonging to Christ and of faith in the Resurrection. Paul's theology of baptism views the Christian existence of the individual in his relation with the risen and glorified Lord. Christian existence is a real sharing in death and life with the spiritual Christ, the Lord present in the Church in mystery. The event of baptism symbolizes the mysterious reality of salvation (Rom. 6:3-5). Through baptism our whole life has entered into a new and mysterious union with the risen Lord (Gal. 3:27), a mysterious union of destiny that the risen Lord will bring to the fulness of glory (Col. 3:3).

The salvation of the individual is realized only in the Church, which as a society is more than the mere sum of individuals who share this salvation in the risen Lord. The experience of the Resurrection opened a path toward the apostles' understanding of Jesus' intention in founding his kingdom.

During the forty days he speaks to them of the kingdom of God (Acts 1:3). Before he definitively left them, he told them that after receiving the Spirit, they would be his witnesses even to the ends of the earth (Acts 1:8). On Pentecost Peter announces that the Resurrection of Jesus has fulfilled what David foretold, "that God . . . would put one of his descendants upon his throne" (Acts 2:30). For Jesus has entered into the position of Lord in his kingdom. The fulfilment of the promise to send the Spirit proves that the predicted enthronement has been realized. As the glorified Lord at the right hand of the Father, the risen Jesus rules his kingdom (Acts 13:38f).

This message of salvation is not for the Jews alone, but for "all those far away whom the Lord our God calls to him" (Acts 2:39). Thus "Jesus Christ of Nazareth . . . whom God raised from the dead" has "become the cornerstone" (Acts 4:10). Paul develops this image of a building, the temple of the new Israel founded upon the risen Lord (1 Cor. 3:11-16; Eph. 2:20f). In the image of head and body Pauline ecclesiology reaches its peak (Eph. 1:22). And precisely as the risen Lord, Christ is the head of the body.

## *Risen Christ head of body*

The mystery of the Christian existence of the individual finds its completion in this mysterious membership of all the faithful in the glorified body of the Lord (Eph. 4:4-6). If the risen Christ is the glorified head of his body, then the community of the Church is the mystical glorified body. Thus we "have all — Jews or Greeks, slaves or free men — been baptized in one spirit to form one body; we have all been saturated with one Spirit" (1 Cor. 12:13). As "the firstborn from among the dead" the risen Christ is the new Adam, a life-giving Spirit, and hence the head and beginning of the new humanity. Unlike the first Adam, through whose sin death came into the world, Christ by his obedience unto death destroyed Adam's guilt, conquered sin and death, of which his Resurrection is the proof. If we are one with Christ as one body and share in the glory of his Resurrection, then our home is no longer on earth, but in heaven (Phil. 3:20).

Thus for us the new time of the world has already begun since we are torn from the world of sin through the power of the Resurrection (Eph. 2:7; Rom. 6:3). Christian time and the reality of Christian existence have their beginning with the "now" of the Resurrection in salvation history. As an historical event it is bound to the time and space in which was manifested God's power in Jesus. But this event has for all future time established a new beginning so that this "now" causes a crisis; for through the Resurrection and glory of Jesus, the Messiah and Lord, salvation is given to all who believe in his name. The Resurrection is thus the unending salvation-reality which gives ever-present validity and meaning to the unique event of history.

# JESUS IS LORD

Sister Mary Trinitas, R.D.C.

"Let all Israel, then, accept as certain that God has made this Jesus, whom you crucified, both Lord and Messiah" (Acts 2:36). This ringing challenge

Published originally in *The Bible Today*, 1 (1964), 701-8. Reprinted by permission of the publisher.

of faith held out to the people of God in the apostolic kerygma finds its echo
in Paul's message to the church at Rome: "If on your lips is the confession,
'Jesus is Lord,' and in your heart the faith that God raised him from the dead,
then you will find salvation" (Rom. 10:9). Stephen had crowned his grace-
filled witness to the risen Jesus with the triumphant cry, "Lord Jesus, receive
my spirit" (Acts 7:59). The idea behind the martyr's final testimony was so
often in the hearts and on the tongues of early Christians that it had woven
itself into the fabric of the liturgy. Paul does not even translate it when he
concludes his first letter to the Corinthians. Instead, he reproduces the phrase
in its familiar Aramaic form, *Maranatha* — Come, O Lord! (1 Cor. 16:22).

What is the meaning of the phrases "Jesus is Lord" and, Jesus "is made
Lord"? Why does "Lord" become a favorite form of address for Jesus among
His early followers? The answer to these questions should provide this title of
the Savior with a new and deep significance even for us of the twentieth century. For it is a title still cherished by the Church: we call on the Lord for
mercy in the prayers of the Mass; we profess belief in the Father's "only Son,
our Lord" when we recite the Apostles' Creed; we pray, in union with all children of the Father, the "Lord's Prayer." But a greater awareness of what we
pray should emerge from a study of the origins of this title. To make it a
meaningful confession of faith we must see it in its first environment, that of
the apostolic Church. And, since no aspect of that Church is comprehensible
apart from its Old Testament heritage, we must first search out the meaning
of "Lord" for the people of Israel.

## Old Testament background

The name *Yahweh* was, for the Chosen People, "terrible and holy" (Ps.
98:4). Indeed, the entire atmosphere of reverence and awe surrounding the
presence of Yahweh and His appearances to men extended to the very name
He bore. It was a name so sacred that it could not be pronounced aloud. In
their liturgical reading of the Scriptures the Israelites substituted for it *Adonai*
(in the Hebrew) or *Kyrios* (in the Greek), i.e., "Lord." However, unlike other
ancient peoples who used the term "Lord" as signifying the power, dominion
and sovereignty of their kings, the Israelites made of it a divine title. They did
not dream of using it, as did the Greeks, to indicate one deity among many,
singled out only by the proper name connected with the title *Kyrios*. For Israel,
*Adonai* or *Kyrios* was used alone as a substitute for the divine name *Yahweh,*
and thus amounted, as Dodd has said, to a manifesto of monotheism. This
unique understanding of the title, which has no exact parallel among ancient
peoples, most certainly has a bearing upon its use in the pages of the New
Testament.

In fact, we derive our first real insight into the apostolic call to faith in
Jesus as "Lord" from the practice of the Old Testament. Cullmann points out
that, if the Jews chose "Lord" for the highest function of replacing the unspeakable name *Yahweh* in their worship, they must have considered it (Lord)
the "unsurpassable majestic name." Therefore, when we find Peter and Paul

and the other apostles using the name as that of Jesus Himself, we can come to only one conclusion: they must believe He is divine.

## Divinity of Jesus

To Catholics, whether of the second, fifteenth or twentieth century, the divinity of Christ is an accepted fact. But we must study the very slow growth of this doctrine in the faith of the apostles if we are to absorb the full impact of their post-Pentecost proclamation of it. Post-Pentecost, indeed, for it took the abundant outpouring of the Spirit on that occasion to perfect in them what Jesus Himself had begun. "The Holy Spirit whom the Father will send in my name *will teach you everything, and will call to mind all that I have told you*" (John 14:26). Jesus, it is true, had asserted by word and deed His equality with the Father during His public ministry. But He seems to have aimed at merely planting the seed here, one which would blossom in the hearts of the Twelve only later on, after their baptism with the Spirit. For the present, He was content to receive from them their protestation of belief in His messiahship: "You are the Messiah" (Mark 8:30).

That the apostles were beginning to comprehend Jesus' divinity seems to be indicated for us in Thomas' penetrating expression of faith after his dark night of doubt — penetrating because, confronted by those overwhelming signs of Christ's humanity, His wounds, Thomas sees beyond them to the divinity and exclaims, "My Lord and my God!" (John 20:28). Recall that the exultation of Jesus has, at this time, already taken place, since He has been raised up on the Cross, has risen, and has returned invisibly to the Father. So the sending of the Spirit is now in force, is, in fact, the risen Master's first gift to His disciples (John 20:23), and they begin at last to understand the things which before had been obscured by their own lack of spiritual insight.

As the Spirit becomes more deeply rooted in the souls of the apostles, we find them preaching the lordship of Jesus as a key doctrine. It is, as a matter of fact, in this that their position as apostles consists: "Am I not an apostle? Did I not see *Jesus our Lord?* " (1 Cor. 9:1). They are to preach the good news of Him whom God has made both "Lord and Messiah." And this title on the lips of men who have all their lives applied it to no one but Yahweh, can mean only one thing — that they believe Jesus to be not only their Savior, but also their God!

## Exercise of lordship

However, the divinity of Jesus is not the sole burden of the apostles' message. Presupposing this truth, they preach the *activity* of lordship to which Jesus has been raised by the Father. For in the Septuagint, *Kyrios* never refers solely to the divine nature as such, but rather to the kingly function of this nature. It indicates the absolute and supreme governorship of the Most High God, the mighty King, the God of hosts. So, also, in the New Testament. The fact that Jesus is called "Lord" assures us that the apostles know Him to be God, equal to the Father in all things. But nothing could be more remote from their practical, Semitic mentality than speculation upon the divine essence in the abstract. The entire concentration is, in fact, a functional one, centered upon the concrete manifestations of that divine essence in the operations of the risen Jesus through His glorified humanity. These operations, as the New Testament shows, include those of the Son of God, Judge, Messiah, possessor of the *pleroma*, and Head of the Church.

When Paul tells his "beloved in Rome" that Jesus Christ our Lord was "declared Son of God by a mighty act in that he rose from the dead" (Rom. 1:4), he refers to Christ's entry, by way of His resurrection, into the full possession of kingly powers. From eternity, indeed, in His divine nature Jesus has been the Son of God, but now in His humanity He comes into His regal inheritance. This involves dominion over heaven and earth, over all creation, together with the Father. Or, more precisely, it involves the Father's handing-over of total sovereignty to His Son in, of course, that sacred humanity which, once assumed, is never separated from His divinity.

This is not to deny that Jesus exhibited authority over the world during His public life. He forgave sins, cast out devils, calmed the wind and the waves, multiplied the loaves, and called on men to subject themselves to Him, to follow Him. But it is not until He has risen and invisibly ascended to the Father that He claims total dominion over all creation (Matthew 28:18). Only then does He come into the plenitude of His rule.

Cerfaux, to whom we owe so many insights into the meaning of Christ's lordship, gives this interpretation to Ephesians 1:20. Paul refers to the might and strength of the Father

> which he exerted in Christ when he raised him from the dead, when he enthroned him at his right hand in the heavenly realms, far above all government and authority, all power and dominion, and any title of sovereignty that can be named, not only in this age, but in the age to come.

Here, says Cerfaux, the Father resigns, as it were, His royal powers in favor of the Son, with the consequence that all the homage due to the Father as sovereign Lord now goes to Christ. It is in this respect that the title *Kyrios* signifies in Christ all that it represented in the Old Testament. Now the Son has, in the words of Hebrews 1:2, been made "heir to the whole universe." So, when He has "brought about the purgation of sins" and has taken "his seat at the right hand of Majesty on high," Jesus can be addressed by the Father as Son: "Thou art my Son; today I have begotten thee (Heb. 1:4, 5; cf. Acts 13:33; 2 Peter 1:16f).

Once the Son has, in His manhood, fulfilled the Father's will by suffering, dying and rising again, He returns to the Father to be vested with the powers of governing, judging and saving. This is truly an exaltation for the sacred humanity. It is what He Himself had prayed for before His death:

> Father, the hour is come. Glorify thy Son, that the Son may glorify thee. For thou hast made him sovereign over all mankind, to give eternal life to all whom thou hast given him. . . and now, Father, glorify me in

thine own presence with the glory which I had with thee before the world began (John 17:1, 2, 5).

Lordship and sonship are, indeed, associated in the closest possible union. To say "Jesus is Lord" is to affirm His exercise, as Man, of the powers of God Himself.

## The Lord and the Second Coming

"Lord" has eschatological overtones, too. A purely temporal kingdom was of little interest for a Jew of Christ's time. The prophets had by then accomplished their task of directing men's hopes to the glorious reign of the Anointed One who would usher in the last days and the kingdom that would have no end (2 Sam. 7:12f; Is. 9:1f; Dan. 7:13f, etc.). It is in the context of such hopes that we find the early Christians waiting expectantly for the parousia, the Second Coming of their Lord. It will be a triumphant coming (1 and 2 Peter; 1 and 2 Thess.) and one of great consolation to the faithful. The predominant note of the parousia, however, is that of judgment: "Before God, and before Christ Jesus who is to judge men living and dead, I adjure you by his coming appearance and his reign . . ." (2 Tim. 4:1) ". . . he is the one who has been designated by God as judge of the living and the dead" (Acts 10:42). ". . . he [God] has fixed the day on which he will have the world judged, and justly judged, by a man of his choosing; of this he has given assurance to all by raising him from the dead" (Acts 17:31).

It is not surprising that emphasis is placed on the returning Lord's position as Judge. He Himself had described the parousia in terms of judgment:

> When the Son of Man comes in his glory and all the angels with him, he will sit in state on his throne, with all the nations gathered before him. He will separate men into two groups, as a shepherd separates the sheep from the goats, and he will place the sheep on his right hand and the goats on his left. Then the king will say to those on his right hand, "You have my Father's blessing . . ." (Matthew 25:31f).

We cannot fail to see in such passages the connection between the lordship, sonship and messiahship of Jesus. He comes a second time as Lord of all, the King who is both Son of the Father and Son of Man. He comes as the just Judge to mete out to men the rewards and punishments merited by them through their acceptance or rejection of Him as Lord and Messiah. It is because He has fulfilled His mission as Messiah that Jesus has been "made Lord" by the Father. The Father has glorified Him by calling Him Son, that is, by permitting the powers of Jesus' divine sonship to flow in uninhibited activity through His human nature. To Him the Father has said, in that Old Testament passage most frequently quoted in the New Testament, "Sit at my right hand until I make your enemies your footstool" (Ps. 109:1).

## Lord and the Spirit

Paradoxically, however, while Jesus becomes "Lord" because He has carried out His commission as Messiah, yet He cannot complete His messianic work until He has been made Lord! In other words, His exaltation is not simply the crowning triumph, the grand reward of His redemptive work; it is at the same time the necessary condition for the completion of redemption.

"God loved the world so much that he gave his only Son, that everyone who has faith in him may not die but have eternal life" (John 3:16). Redemption means life, eternal life, life in the kingdom of God. But life cannot come except by way of the Spirit: "In truth I tell you," says Jesus to Nicodemus, "no one can enter the kingdom of God without being born from water and spirit" (John 3:6). Jesus, if He is to be truly the Christ promised of old and effecting man's reconciliation with God, must bestow the gift of the Spirit on mankind.

This explains why there is always, whether in Christ's own words or in those of the New Testament writers, such an insistence upon the resurrection as a necessary element of the messianic work. With but one or two exceptions, the Gospels never refer to the death of Jesus without immediately affirming the fact of the resurrection (Matthew 16:21; Luke 24:6, 26; 9:22; Mark 9:31; John 2:19, etc.). Equally significant is Paul's explicit teaching in Romans 4:25 that Christ "was delivered to death for our misdeeds, and raised to life to justify us." He here expresses what the Council of Trent would later claim to be the two simultaneous aspects of reconciliation or justification: forgiveness of sins and infusion of grace. In the divine plan redemption demands not only the passion and death of Christ, but His resurrection, too. Rising, He returns to the Father, and it is then that He can at last send the Spirit upon the world.

John's recollections of the Master's teaching on this point are blended into his Last Supper account of the legacy of love which was Christ's for His disciples (John 13-17). Jesus must go, or else the Comforter cannot come. Jesus is returning to the Father to ask Him to send the Advocate. He will not leave His children bereft: because He lives, He wants them also to live, and this He will accomplish by sending the Spirit. Once the Spirit has come, they will understand all they have been taught by their Master. Understanding, they will keep His word, i.e., they will love, and Father and Son will live in them even as the Spirit does.

The life-giving activity of Jesus, then, is dependent upon His return to the Father, that one continuous act of rising, ascending and being enthroned which we call simply His "exaltation." True, He had exerted His life-giving powers even before His death. Christ's whole life on earth had been a redemptive incarnation. He went about healing the sick, casting out devils, forgiving sins, and inspiring faith, hope and love. All these are, to a certain extent at least, a bestowal of the Spirit. But for the fullness of the Spirit, for the completion of redemption, man had to wait until Jesus had been glorified. "He was speaking of the Spirit whom believers in him would receive later; for the Spirit had not yet been given, because Jesus had not yet been glorified" (John 7:39).

Why must this be? Because, as we have already seen, it is not until He has been "made Lord" that Jesus' humanity can be so thoroughly divinized that it will no longer exercise any restraint upon His divine powers. On the day that He is "begotten" by the Father, i.e., called "Son" in His human nature, seated at the right hand of the Father while His enemies are made His footstool, then it is that He grants the Spirit complete freedom in that humanity.

Again, it is true that Jesus was Himself filled with the Spirit from the first instant of the incarnation. Conceived in His mother's womb by the power of the Spirit (Luke 1:35), He advanced as He grew up in wisdom and favor with God and men (Luke 2:52), and inaugurated His public ministry under the aegis of the Spirit (Luke 3:22; 4:1f). Jesus testified to the presence of the Holy Spirit in Himself (Luke 4:18f), and all His works bore witness to the same fact. Even His parting instructions to the disciples were given through the Spirit (Acts 1:2). However, as He had held back the fullness of His dominion over all things until His exaltation, so likewise with the activity of the Spirit. This explains, too, His withholding of the gift of the Spirit (in the full sense) to others until He enters into His lordship.

With His redemptive act of dying, rising and returning to the Father completed, Jesus becomes, in Paul's words, "a life-giving spirit" (1 Cor. 15:45). It is of His complete humanity that Paul speaks, for the Semitic mind never separated man's nature into its component parts. His body from now on will be a "pneumatized" body — one completely dominated by the soul. And His soul? It is thoroughly given over to the activity of the Holy Spirit. "Spirit" in the Jewish sense implied, not immateriality, but divine holiness and power. Paul's meaning is, therefore, that Jesus in His *entire being* becomes a source of divine power and sanctity.

The risen Christ is, in body and in soul, filled with divine holiness. He has become so much a "spirit" that Paul tells us, "in him the complete being of God, by God's own choice, came to dwell" (Col. 1:19). The complete being, *pleroma*, of the Godhead dwells embodied in Him (Col. 2:9). This *pleroma* dwells in Christ and is exercised by Him, not for His own sake, but for man's. Having entered once for all into the "real sanctuary" not made by man, He lives always to plead on man's behalf (Heb. 7:25; 8:1f). He has become "spirit" in order to give life, that is, in order to send the Holy Spirit to the world, for which He is now most truly the Messiah.

The Gospel accounts of the resurrection portray a preliminary donation of the Spirit by the newly risen Christ. He breathed on the apostles that first Easter evening, saying, "Receive the Holy Spirit!" (John 20:23). He interpreted His redemptive death and resurrection for the disciples on the way to Emmaus (Luke 24:13f), and the women at the empty tomb recalled His prophecy of the resurrection (Luke 24:8). All this involves the gift of the Spirit (John 2:22) which Christ must, then, have given to some extent. Nevertheless, for the outpouring of the Spirit the visible ascension is needed, and so it is not until Pentecost that we can have Israel witness the fulfillment of the prophecy of Joel: "I will pour out upon everyone a portion of my spirit . . ." (Acts 2:17).

## The Lord and the Church

Thus does the world enter upon the messianic era, and it continues until the end of time to enjoy the redemptive activity of the Lord Jesus through His Body which is the Church. For it is by virtue of His possession of the *pleroma* that Jesus becomes Head of the Church "which is his body and as such holds within it the fullness of him who himself receives the entire fullness of God" (Eph. 1:23). When He pours out the Spirit upon mankind, Christ becomes one with it in a way even more intimate than by the fellowship of the incarnation. For "we were all brought into one body by baptism, in the one Spirit. . . ." (1 Cor. 12:13). The force which supplies the members of the Church with life, energy and direction is none other than the Holy Spirit Himself, the very Breath of Father and Son, who is sent to vivify us only upon the exaltation of our redeeming Lord. Then only, in the plan of divine Wisdom, are we granted a share in the life of Christ, so that we can say in all sincerity with Paul, "The life I live is not my life, but the life which Christ lives in me" (Gal. 2:20). Now, because we live by the one, same Spirit, we are so much at one with Christ that we can be called His Body.

When today we pray with the Church, "through Jesus Christ our *Lord*," when in the rosary we remind our heavenly Mother "the *Lord* is with thee," when we respond at Mass to the celebrant's prayer, "The *Lord* be with you," should not the title have a new and enriched meaning for us? Should it not recall the intoxicating joy of the apostles when, filled with the Spirit on Pentecost, they went out to preach salvation in the name of the Master they now knew (even though their understanding would have further development) to be divine, equal to Yahweh Himself? Should we not acknowledge with them that He exercises supreme dominion over all the universe, and this in His human nature as well as in the divine?

We should not see in this mystery, breathtaking as it is in its full impact, a cause for fear and trembling. Rather, it should inspire us with genuine humility and gratitude. For God is not content with "so loving the world" that He gives His only Son to be one of us; no, He must go further and raise this frail humanity up, even to the heights of the divine! This is so because it is in His humanity that Jesus is made "Lord" and is "declared Son of God." We, his brothers in the flesh, share in this divinization of humanity.

Moreover, now that we have seen the New Testament usage of *Kyrios*, we can profitably meditate on our communal profession of faith in Him who "will come again with glory to judge the living and the dead" and whose "kingdom will have no end." Many a Christian in this year of our Lord neither understands nor adverts to what he proclaims each time he recites the Creed, i.e., the parousia, or Second Coming, of the Lord in majesty.

The full significance of Jesus' messiahship will be present to our minds now as we call upon our "Lord." We will remember that the title is at once the result and the condition of His redemptive mission. He is called "Lord" only after He has suffered, died and risen again. And this resurrection-exaltation becomes the means of His sending the Spirit to apply the fruits of redemption to mankind. Christ's entering upon His lordship makes Him the vivifying Spirit, possessor of the *pleroma* and sharer of that life-impulse with the members of His Body, the Church.

Supreme Ruler, Son, Judge, Messiah, life-giving Spirit, Head of the Church — these are but so many facets of the one name, dear to Christians today as in times past, the name above all names, at which "every knee should bend — in heaven, on earth, and in the depths — and every tongue confess, 'Jesus Christ is Lord' " (Phil. 2:11).

# JESUS' MESSAGE IN THE THOUGHT OF THE APOSTLES

Jean Levie, S.J.

In Acts 1–12, Luke traces the spread of the gospel from Jerusalem to Antioch. The conversion of the Samaritans, the baptism of the Ethiopian eunuch, and especially the conversion of Cornelius made it clear to the apostles that God was calling the gentiles to the faith. Principles are formulated which Paul will later apply to the whole pagan world.

We have no history of the apostles' growth in understanding the whole of Christian doctrine comparable to the account of their gradual understanding of the vocation of the gentiles presented by Luke. Yet the apostles were aware that such a progressive comprehension of Christ's total teaching would occur (John 14:16-17, 20, 26; Acts 1:5-8). Here arises the fundamental problem in the early history of dogma. Was the Master's genuine teaching gradually better understood in the light of events and under the guidance of the Holy Spirit? Or were his person and teaching transfigured, idealized, and finally deformed by the faith and the milieu of the primitive Church, the Christ of history becoming the Christ of faith and the message intended for the Jews becoming a universal doctrine of salvation? Both our Christian faith and a convergence of historical indications make us choose the first alternative. Its proof is the essential task of the exegesis of the whole NT.

## Apostles' thought in synoptics

We can understand Paul's teaching only if we first investigate how the apostles understood the message of Christ. This we can discover historically from the Synoptic Gospels even though they were given their definitive form later than most of Paul's letters and after more than thirty years of Christian

Reprinted from *Theology Digest*, 12 (1964), 27-32. Originally published as "Le message de Jesus dans la pensee des apotres," *Nouvelle Revue Theologique*, 83, (1961), 25-49. Reprinted by permission of the publisher.

thought. Although influenced by the development of the early theology, these Gospels faithfully express the original content of the life and teaching of Jesus Christ. The synoptic message forms the core of the apostles' thought which, illumined by the Resurrection and activated by Pentecost, constitutes the point of departure for the theology of the primitive Church.

When chosen by Christ, the apostles shared Jewish notions of a coming messianic kingdom with worldwide dominion. Several incidents in the Gospels show how resistant to purification were these nationalistic and worldly dreams of the kingdom.

John the Baptist proclaimed the advent of the kingdom (Matthew 3:2). The expressions "kingdom of heaven," "kingdom of God," "kingdom," appear more than one hundred times in the Synoptics. The apostles' first act of faith was belief that with the appearance of Jesus the kingdom was at hand. The Master's initial task was to teach them by means of parables and images a sound, religious concept of the kingdom of God.

## Kingdom is new economy

The kingdom appears in Jesus' teaching as a divine economy of the future, a joyously anticipated banquet at which even justified pagans will be seated along with Abraham, Isaac, and Jacob (Luke 13:28f). Moreover, since the preaching of the Baptist, the kingdom is already present and operative (Luke 17:21), even for those who did not seem to be chosen for it (Matthew 11:12). It is so transcendent that its least member is superior to the Baptist (Matthew 11:11f). The kingdom is a treasure, a jewel of great price, given to those who seek it (Matthew 7:7), especially to the apostles (Luke 12:32). This gift demands a total change of life, a new justice superior to that of the scribes and Pharisees, and to that of the Law (Matthew 5:20-48). The kingdom is bound up with the idea of a community not based on racism or nationalism, but made up of true sons (Matthew 13:38).

The relation of this new economy to traditional Judaism remained unclear to the apostles. Points of Jewish observance to be retained or rejected will be determined by doctrinal developments of the future, formulated by Peter (Acts 10-11) and fully illumined by the apostolate of Paul (Acts 13ff).

Although the apostles lived in humble anticipation, the date of the Lord's return and the definitive establishment of the kingdom remained obscure for them. Christ himself had emphasized the incertitude of its final consummation.

Gradually and patiently Jesus transformed the apostles' idea of the kingdom. Before its eternal phase the kingdom will have a preparatory one on earth characterized by love for God and neighbor, humility, disinterested service, persecution, and the cross. A kingdom beyond space and time replaced the Jewish concept of a purely historical one. The apostolic Church began its march with thoughts directed toward heaven, its treasure and future home, where the Father and the angelic hosts dwell (Matthew 18:10; 6:21).

The apostles conceived the present kingdom, which prepares the future one, under three aspects: its centering around Jesus Christ, its founder, the Messiah,

Lord, and Son of God; its signification of and demand for a totally new justice; its supposition of and call to "the community of the kingdom" which will live this new justice.

The initial step of the apostles in their newly awakened thought was an act of faith: "The kingdom is here because Jesus is here." The triumph of Jesus over Satan proves that the kingdom, long desired by the prophets, has begun (Matthew 12:25-30). Men who fail to profit from the new era sin more gravely than Sodom or Nineveh (Mark 12:41-2). Again, the apostles recognize Jesus' absolute authority over the kingdom. He disposes of it as its master and gives its keys to Peter (Matthew 16:19). Jews and gentiles alike may enter if they become as little children. The touchstone for admittance at the Last Judgment will be whether or not they have treated the lowly as Christ himself (Matthew 25:31-46). Those who follow Jesus will gain entrance (Mark 10:21); those who hesitate are unworthy. The evangelists draw no distinction between "for my (Jesus') sake," "for the gospel's sake," and "for the sake of the kingdom" (Luke 18:29). The "kingdom of God" and the "kingdom of Christ" are identical.

To see this identity is to recognize Jesus as the awaited Messiah. Always in the forefront of the apostles' minds was Peter's decisive confession of Jesus as the Christ, an insight which according to Jesus was owing to light from above (Matthew 16:16-7). The evangelists do not trace the preparation by which Jesus led Peter and the apostles to this conviction, but it is in the light of the Lord's messiahship that they understand more profoundly all his actions and teachings. They are not astonished at the words of the Father after Jesus' baptism (Matthew 3:17), at his power over Satan and the possessed, at the miracles to which he points as signs of his messiahship (Matthew 11:2-6). The apostles understood in messianic terms his solemn entrance into Jerusalem, the expulsion of the sellers from the Temple, and his reply to the High Priest and Sanhedrin in images drawn from Daniel.

## New concept of Messiah

Jesus' teaching, however, transformed the Jewish notion of Messiah for the apostles. Humility, detachment, and service replace human glory and Jewish nationalism as part of the concept. After Peter's profession of faith Jesus warns them that the Messiah must suffer and die (Matthew 16:21-3) and be the ransom for many (Matthew 20:28). One day the apostles will come to realize that the Messiah must also be the suffering servant of Isaiah (53), and the Master turns their thoughts in this direction.

The apostles understand the mission and dignity of Jesus as Messiah in the fact that he is the Son of God in an utterly unique way transcending the sonship attributed to chosen souls by the OT. Peter's confession of Jesus as "the Christ, the Son of the living God," does not join two disparate concepts; rather, the notion of divine sonship enriches the idea of Messiah with all that is implied in the unique bond between Jesus and the Father.

For the apostles Christ was not only the founder of the kingdom but also its object and center. Love for God is love for Jesus. Seeking the kingdom and doing the Father's will are the same as following Christ. The disciple must leave all for Christ (Mark 11:21); he must love Christ more than mother or father (Matthew 8:22), more than life itself (Matthew 10:38-9). Whatever is done in Christ's name will receive an eternal reward (Matthew 9:41). The Father will grant anything asked in his name (Matthew 18:19-20). Men will be judged according to their love for Christ in the present life (Matthew 7:21-4).

## Jesus' special sonship

So many texts agree so consistently and remarkably in exalting Jesus that they cannot be explained as creations of the faith of the primitive Church. Sound history demands as the ultimate source of so many converging texts the explicit testimony of Jesus himself.

The homogeneity of so many texts and the attitude towards himself which Jesus gradually instilled into the apostles indicate that they understood Jesus' sonship in regard to the Father as a sonship which by its nature surpassed and differed essentially from that of mere men. The conceptual expression of this sonship, manifested in the writings of Paul and John, culminated in the metaphysical formulas of Nicaea. The Synoptic Gospels contain the same doctrine but without the same theological depth. The apostles knew that Jesus distinguished the way in which he was Son of God from the way other men were children of God. The parable of the vine dressers (Matthew 21:35-42) taught them the essential difference between the prophets and the Son who is the unique heir of the Father. In explaining the psalm "The Lord has said to my Lord" (Matthew 22:41-6), Jesus suggested to the apostles that besides his Davidic sonship, he was conscious of another which gave him the right to be David's Lord. "No one understands the Son but the Father, nor does anyone understand the Father but the Son and anyone to whom the Son chooses to reveal him" (Matthew 11:27-29) — this text shows better than any other in the synoptics the exclusive and transcendent relation between Jesus and the Father.

The only possible response for the apostles to all these claims of the Master was what he had emphasized so much — faith, a total commitment of their understanding. It became the foundation and center of religion for St. Paul and the early Church.

The Resurrection is the central point of the first two sermons of Peter in Acts. The doctrinal import of the Resurrection for the primitive community cannot be overstressed, for the early Church's thought, life, and prayer centered on the risen Christ in expectation of his second coming. The prospect of life with Christ beyond space and time in the definitive kingdom of God filled the community with a thrill of relief and hope.

## Passion as salvific act

But the primitive Church also recognized the mystery of the passion and cross as a sublime doctrine revealed by God. Christ's own predictions of his death, various texts of the OT, especially those concerning the Suffering Servant (Is.

53), and the sacrifices of the old law formed the background against which the Church, enlightened by God, came to see the meaning of the Passion as salvific redemption. The apostles discerned the Redeemer of mankind in the man of sorrows and the lamb of God. Here in the early Church was a rich Christology, more lived than doctrinally developed.

The kingdom of God demands a new justice, a "salvation" by which Jesus frees the world from the rule of sin and Satan. Its first characteristic is repentance, which both John the Baptist (Mark 1:4-5) and Jesus (Mark 1:15) appeal for in their preaching. The Christian must flee the wrath of God provoked by sin (Matthew 3:7) and escape the power of Satan (Luke 4:6). The universal dominance of sin and its satanic hold on the world constantly appear in the gospel conception of salvation. Christ definitively solves the problem of sin. His victory destroys the power of Satan (Matthew 28-9). Again and again the synoptics repeat that Jesus is our salvation and that the gospel is, first of all, salvation from sin.

The apostles realized that only faith in Christ saves and that we must become like him, bearing the cross after him (Matthew 10:38-9). Jesus gradually revealed to them the lesson of the cross and the redemptive role of his coming death in the divine plan. The Passion itself provided the crowning lesson concerning human sin and salvation through Christ (Mark 14:23-4).

The master idea behind the whole life of the historical Jesus is life everlasting. Only this totally religious ideal, transcending the cares of this life, explains the eight beatitudes (Matthew 5:1-12) and the exclusive concern for the kingdom undergirding the entire Sermon on the Mount. Man's heart should be directed toward heaven, his true treasure. Man must choose between this life and the next; he must lose the present life to gain an eternal one (Matthew 16:24-6).

Another element of the new justice is God's fatherhood toward all men individually (Matthew 5:45; 6:8, 9, 25-32). It should give rise to unbounded confidence in prayer (Luke 11:9-13). When two or three are gathered in the name of Jesus, their prayers will be granted, for Jesus is with them and their prayer is included in his (Matthew 18:19-20).

A second consequence of God's fatherhood is purity of intention. We cannot serve two masters, God and the world; our prayers and fasting must be for God alone (Matthew 6:22-4). This purity of intention rests on the profound convictions that no sacrifice is too great to gain life eternal (Mark 9:43-5) and that no external or ritual purity but only purity of heart can determine our relation with God (Matthew 15:11, 18-20). This deep grasp of the inwardness of religion, of the direct contact of the soul with Jesus and the Father, became for the apostles a living ideal and motive force for their apostolate.

Finally the new justice of the kingdom demands an immense charity. Love for God and for the neighbor are linked together. The second great commandment, love for the neighbor, is like the first which demands that we love God with our whole heart and whole soul (Matthew 22:37-40). The great number of gospel passages which teach charity indicates its primacy. In the golden rule (Matthew 7:12) and in proposing the Father as our model (Matthew 5:48, Luke 6:36), Jesus summarizes his teaching on charity. Paul and John then

stated in theological terms how love has come down to earth with and in Christ
and spread out to all men.

Christ did not conceive of the kingdom of God in a way that excluded the
notion of an earthly kingdom, a society preparing the way for the final kingdom.
His was not to be a purely internal kingdom uniting the souls of men to God
without any social intermediary. Nor was his kingdom only the eschatological
kingdom expected within his own generation. Nor finally was it a kingdom that
would be dependent on and incorporated into Judaism.

## Kingdom is visible society

From his library a nineteenth-century professor could picture primitive Christianity after the pattern of Liberal Protestantism, but in the real milieu of first-
century Judaism only a group religious movement is conceivable. For those who
accepted Jesus as the Messiah, adherence to the group around him was God's
will. Jesus had demanded that his followers leave all and love him above father
and mother. Those who deny him before men will be renounced before the Father (Matthew 10:32-3). In his prophecies and parables Jesus describes a visible society, a city upon a mountain (Matthew 5:13-16), a net filled with good
and bad fish (Matthew 13:47-51). The entire Gospel of Matthew and texts
from the other synoptics create the clear impression that Christ organized a
visible, structured community for the kingdom and that the apostles were thoroughly aware of this.

Jesus solemnly chose twelve of his followers as special companions and
sent them to preach (Mark 3:13-9). After a long instruction he tells them,
"Whoever welcomes you welcomes me, and whoever welcomes me welcomes
him who sent me" (Matthew 10:40). Their privileged place in the kingdom is
beyond doubt. To them is reserved the full explanation of the mysteries of the
kingdom (Luke 8:10) and the predictions of the passion, death, and resurrection. They accompany Jesus, collaborate in his miracles, and witness the Last
Supper, the agony, and the apparitions after the Resurrection.

At first the apostles did not realize the immense authority given them: only
Christ could see in these humble fishermen the future episcopacy of the
Church. They perceived only vaguely their relation to the Jewish hierarchy and
the relation of their community to the chosen people. When the Master judged
opportune, light was given — the vision of Joppa (Acts 10:9-16), the Council
at Jerusalem (Acts 15), the destruction of Jerusalem. The intervention of the
Spirit, external events, and the diffusion of grace clarified previous statements of
the Lord. Faithful to his ideas, the apostles reached the great decisions which determined the Church's future: "For the Holy Spirit and we have decided . . ."
(Acts 15:28).

The primitive Church was convinced that Christ had given the twelve full
authority. Acts 1–12 pictures them as the center of the Church; nothing happens without them, and their decision is always final. Paul claimed the same
power and authority as the twelve.

The predominant authority given to Peter shows the intention of Jesus to form a community. Jesus confers on him the power to bind and loose and proclaims him the bedrock supporting the Church (Matthew 16:18-9). After his conversion Peter will confirm his brethren (Luke 22:32) and feed the flock of Christ (John 21:15-8). The great authority attributed to Peter by the early Church is clear from Acts 1–12, the Epistles of Paul, and the lists of the apostles with Peter always at the head. Here again the future will unfold the richness of Christ's solemn promise of the primacy, though Peter and the apostles were well aware of the promise and knew how to remain faithful to the Master's thought.

## Enduring Church formed

A number of texts show very clearly the intention of Jesus to form an *enduring* Church. These texts, when buttressed by the convergence of all the other indications of the Master's thought that we have reviewed, possess a consistency which places them beyond any serious historical objection that they are creations of the infant Church. The most important text is the promise of the primacy to Peter and of indestructibility to the Church (Matthew 16: 17-19). The current Aramaic style and thought patterns in it confirm its historicity. The only other gospel passage which uses the word *ekklesia* (Matthew 18:17-20) envisions the concrete exercise of disciplinary authority within the Church and again confers the power of binding and loosening.

Hence the Christian historian is not surprised to find that Jesus accentuates the permanent and societal character of the Church in the apparitions after the Resurrection (Matthew 28:18-20). This perspective of the "Church of tomorrow" (John 13:17; 20:23) is not the creation of the evangelist, but a faithful echo of Christ's wishes. Of all this the apostles were conscious from the beginning, as is clear from the very activity of the primitive Church which despite its many problems knew it was under the guiding hand of an all-powerful Master who foresaw its destiny.

Before leaving them, Jesus promised to send to the apostles the Spirit of God (Luke 24:49). The abundant outpouring of the Spirit was an essential characteristic of the messianic age (Joel 3:1-4). A baptism (Acts 1:5) of total purification will transform the apostles into witnesses to Christ even to the utmost limits of the world (Acts 1:8). Christ tells them that the Father promised to send the Spirit (Acts 1:4); thus Father, Son, and Holy Spirit focused their salutary intervention on the apostles. This triple intervention will find expression for the rest of men in their baptismal consecration to the Father, Son, and Holy Spirit (Matthew 28:19).

Even as the Son revealed himself to mankind by his presence and action, so the Holy Spirit is revealed to Christians by his action in the Church. The presence of the Spirit of Christ sent by the Father made the early Christians keenly aware of their adoption in Christ by the Father. An ever intensified perception of the intervention of Father, Son, and Spirit upon its collective and individual life led the Church to penetrate more profoundly into its faith in the Trinity. Personal memories of the Master's words and the experience of the Church helped John to formulate the capital role of the Spirit in the primitive Church (John 14:16-17). In Acts Luke mentions more than forty times the Spirit's intervention in the life of the Church.

In a mysteriously divine yet remarkably human way, the astonishing convergence of all these seemingly unconnected texts indicates God's revelation of himself and of his plan for human salvation. Man must not decide a priori by definitions and syllogisms what revelation must be. Rather, here as everywhere, man must let himself be taught by him who surpasses human minds and hearts (1 John 3:20).

# 4 THE SYNOPTIC GOSPELS

## A. THE GOSPEL TRADITION

The Synoptic Gospels, with their similar and dissimilar methods of narrating events of Jesus' life and ministry, have been the subject of intense study and criticism since the first part of the nineteenth century. Form-criticism early identified and classified units which were used in various ways by the evangelists. Miracle stories, pronouncement stories, formal narratives and liturgical pericopes were seen to be the materials from which a large part of our present gospels were constructed.

The so-called "Synoptic problem" occupied critics for decades in a hunt for the sources of the Synoptic Gospels. It was clear that Luke and Matthew had incorporated most of Mark, but that their Gospels also had common elements which were not in Mark. The search for "Q," or various forms of Q, a document which was supposedly the source or sources of the Synoptic Gospels, did not yield very decisive results. Today scholars look chiefly to oral tradition and early written narratives for the common sources of the Synoptic Gospels.

Another group of scholars studied the content of the primitive apostolic message and the life of Christian community in which the message was transmitted and developed. J. V. Schmitt, as well as Durrwell, recognized that the central theme of apostolic preaching was the proclamation of the Resurrection of Jesus. The apostolic preaching interprets the whole new era of salvation in the light of the risen Christ, who was seen as the fulfillment of Old Testament prophecies and the inaugurator of the messianic era by His gift of the Holy Spirit.

From the apostolic preaching to the written Gospels was neither a short nor a simple development. A generation of preaching and reflection, "many" attempts to write summaries of the sayings and deeds of Jesus, as St. Luke says in his prologue, were to contribute to a body of materials, somewhat standardized by frequent repetition in the oral catechesis, but basically the message of eye-witnesses appointed by Jesus.

Examination of the milieu in which the primitive preaching developed and spread has now shown that in our study of the Gospels we must distinguish three levels of transmission of the message. As the Instruction of the Pontifical Biblical Commission "On Biblical Research" (April 21, 1964) states: "The exegete, in order to affirm the foundation of what the Gospels tell us, should give diligent attention to the three stages which mark the teaching and the life of Jesus before they came down to us."[1]

The Instruction describes the three stages of formation: 1) "Christ our Lord, in setting forth verbally His teaching, followed the forms of thought and expression which were then in use, thus adapting Himself to the mentality of the listeners, in order that what He was teaching should remain firmly impressed in their minds and could be easily remembered by the disciples. . . ."

2) "The Apostles announced first of all the death and resurrection of the Lord, faithfully giving testimony to Jesus. They set forth His life, repeated His words, bearing in mind during their preaching the needs of the various persons who listened to them. After Jesus had risen from the dead and when His divinity had appeared in a clear manner, faith not only did not cause them to forget the memory of the events, but on the contrary, consolidated it, because that faith was founded on what Jesus had done and taught. . . . As Jesus Himself after the Resurrection 'interpreted to them' the words of the Old Testament as well as His own, so they [the Apostles] explained the facts and words according to the needs of their listeners. 'Constant in the mystery of the Word' (Acts 6:4), they preached, stating things in a way suitable for their specific aim and for the mentality of the listeners. . . . In fact, in the preaching which has as its theme Christ, there can be discerned the following: catechesis, narration, testimonies, hymns, doxologies, prayers and other similar literary forms which appear in Sacred Scripture and were in use among men at that time."

3) "This primitive instruction which was done at first orally and then set down in writing — in fact it did happen that many endeavored to 'order the narration of the facts' (Luke 1:1) which concerned Jesus Christ — was gathered by the sacred authors in the four Gospels for the good of the Church, and with a method in keeping with the purpose of each. Some elements they chose; others they expressed in synthesis. They developed some elements, bearing in mind the situation of the various churches, seeking by every means that the readers should know the truthfulness of what they were being taught (Luke 1:4). Indeed, among all the material at their disposal, the sacred writers chose that in particular which was suitable to the various conditions of the faithful and the aims they had set themselves, narrating it in such a way as to meet those conditions and that aim. Now since the meaning of a statement de-

[1] Pontifical Biblical Commission for Biblical Studies, *On Bible Research* (Washington, D.C.: National Catholic Welfare Conference, 1964).

pends on the context, when the evangelists present different contexts in reporting the sayings and the deeds of the Saviour, it is to be thought that they did this for the convenience of the readers. The exegete should therefore seek to find out what the intention of the evangelist was in setting forth a saying or a fact in a certain way or in a certain context."

The whole text of the Instruction of the Biblical Commission should be studied carefully and pondered deeply. It praises the untiring efforts of Catholic Biblical scholars and encourages them to make use of all that has been found to be sound in modern methods of research. In fact, the Instruction admonishes the scholars: "If the exegete does not bear in mind all these things which concern the origin and composition of the Gospels and will not make proper use of all that is good in recent studies, he will not fulfill his task of investigating what the intention of the sacred authors was and what they really said."

Between the technical preoccupations of the exegetes and the prayerful pondering of the faithful there is a wide difference in knowledge, subtlety and depth. But Christians everywhere — in their readiness to hear and to try to understand whatever will make the word of God more meaningful, more dynamic and fruitful for the life of the Church — have shown themselves eager to learn and receive instruction.

A knowledge of the stages of the Gospel tradition makes the incidents of the Gospels more meaningful because of their context.[2] The rich field of the special doctrinal content of each evangelist is being studied. What were the considerations that made the evangelist choose these incidents from the numerous materials which we now know were available to him? What did he mean to convey by the context in which he placed the incidents? The complete meaning may for a long time to come elude us, but we are able now to understand better what the words and saving deeds of Jesus have to say to us.

[2] See David M. Stanley, "New Understanding of the Gospels," in *The Bible in Current Catholic Thought*, ed. John L. McKenzie (New York: Herder and Herder, 1962), pp. 169-83.

# THE GOSPELS IN THE LIGHT
# OF MODERN RESEARCH

Barnabas M. Ahern, C.P.

This study might well carry the subtitle, *Quadragesimo Anno — salva reverentia*. The time is now ripe to measure the impact of the past forty years on the study of the gospels.

In 1920, at the close of the first World War, the German scholars Rudolph Bultmann, Martin Dibelius, Karl Schmidt and others worked concurrently though not in concert to open the gospels to agnostics dominated by Heidegger philosophy. As zealous army chaplains these students of the Bible had come into contact with soldiers whose philosophy denied all divine intervention in the world of men. Working within the same philosophic framework Bultmann and the others devised a means to make the gospels meaningful to men who could not envision the supernatural.

The new approach viewed the gospels as the fabrication of the primitive Christian community. "Community" became the password for full access to the Christian message. Whatever riches the gospels contain derived form and substance from the creative activity of a community which had come to believe that Jesus had risen from the dead. This faith created a message about Christ for the sole purpose of helping man achieve authentic understanding of himself before God. Here the center of gravity was not the past but the present; the point of interest was not the Jesus of history who was almost unknown but the Christ of faith whose words and deeds were created to meet every human need.

This thesis was offered as an emergent of gospel analysis. Following the method which Hermann Gunkel had used in the Old Testament these scholars studied the gospels not as unified works of a literary author but as a mere collection of individual units. One by one these units were subjected to careful analysis on the supposition that the form of each would reveal the sociological factor which brought the unit into being. This method, aptly called Form Criticism, regarded each unit as the product of a need in community life. Preaching, liturgy, controversy — these factors were looked upon as the creative agents of the gospel forms.

## Reaction against form criticism

From the very beginning other scholars like Charles Dodd and T. W. Manson reacted strongly against the postulates of German Form Criticism. While acknowledging that large portions of the gospels were first formulated in the teaching apostolate of the Church, they denied categorically that the community had created these elements. A community creates nothing; it is rather the womb in which the compelling thought of an original genius becomes viable.

Published originally in *Chicago Studies*, 1 (1962), 5-16. Reprinted by permission of the publisher.

They pointed out, moreover, that no one in the community could qualify as the originator of a gospel message which contradicted cardinal tenets of Jewry and ran counter to prevalent Jewish hopes.

Gradually even the disciples of the Form Critics came to share this adverse reaction. They sensed the embarrassment of Bultmann when he was asked to explain the enigma of a nameless community creating within twenty years a fully formed Christianity without basis in fact. The theory of a definitive Christian gospel coming to life in so short a time lacks *raison d'etre* if it rests on the obscure figure of a merely human Jesus and on a life without challenge or meaning. The first Christian community was made up of ignorant and hard-headed Jews who would have been the last ones to turn Jesus into a "Son of God." They themselves had lived through the events of His public life like the others to whom they preached. Eye-witnesses are not duped by a hoax when they have everything to lose.

## Emergence of redaction criticism

Under pressure of this reaction the pendulum has swung away from the thesis of Form Criticism. At the end of the second World War another school arose which shifted attention away from the study of individual units in the gospels (Form Criticism) to concentrate on the gospels as unified compositions of literary authors. This school of Redaction Criticism is represented by scholars like Gunther Bornkamm, Hans Conzelmann, and Willi Marxsen.

It is the evangelist who has now become the focal point of interest. His literary activity, his theological insights and purpose, his background of personal interests have left a distinctive mark on his literary work. Each evangelist contributed so much to his own presentation of the gospel message that Willi Marxsen has written, "There are no Synoptic Gospels." The day of the diatesseron is gone forever; the gospels can no longer be lumped together. Each must be studied as the unique work of a literary artist.

The recognition of a unique literary quality in each gospel is not new. Pere Lagrange, for instance, in the masterful introductions to his commentaries studied carefully the special contribution of each evangelist. He was fully aware that the sacred author has forged a message in the fire of his own spirit. The text inspired by God involved also a full play of human powers.

The recent emphasis on this aspect is blighted by a certain weakness. The school of Redaction Criticism gives the impression at times that it has merely shifted creativity from the "community" of the Form Criticism school to the "evangelist" of its own school. A reader of Hans Conzelmann's *Theology of St. Luke* will find himself asking, "Is so large a part of the gospel merely the creation of Luke?"

Weakness as well as strength characterize the approach both of Form Criticism and Redaction Criticism. Biblists of these schools center attention on factors which must be taken into account if the gospels are to be studied in the spirit in which they were written. Both schools, however, labor under weaknesses which must be eliminated if perspectives are to remain true.

## Gospel study on three levels

These perspectives have been greatly sharpened by the work of the past forty years. Gospel study today occupies a vantage point gained by the positive advances of Form and Redaction Critics. Because of their labors the student of the gospels now has a triple sight.

Previously gospel study was bi-dimensional. The reader moved from his analysis of the text to the lower level of the actual words and deeds of Jesus. This procedure rested on the presumption that the gospels offer a consecutive biography of Christ, a stenographic report of His words and a chronological record of His deeds. Viewing the gospels in this light men wrote lives of Christ in the same style as modern biographies of Chesterton and Belloc.

A certain malaise was inevitable. Authors like Lagrange and Lebreton, Fillion and Prat seemed uncertain in their reconstructions. It had to be so. The conflicting reports of the different evangelists, the notable lacunae in their accounts, the divergent geography and time computation which set one evangelist against another — elements like these called for constant harmonization. The simple fact is that the evangelists never intended to provide material for a biography in the modern sense of the word.

Their story of Christ centers in the words and deeds of Jesus of Nazareth; but this portrait of Him reveals a "likeness" rather than an "image"; it is an inspired interpretation of what He really was rather than a photographic reproduction of what He seemed to be. The evangelists present His life as illumined by the revealing light of the Spirit who, after Pentecost, recalled to the mind of the Church all that He had said and done, in order to make known the profound meaning of His words and the eternal import of His deeds.

This intermediary level of the Church's understanding of Christ is essential for full understanding of the gospel. Something is missing if gospel study is merely bi-dimensional. Between the inspired text and the actual life of Jesus there intervened thirty years of the Church's teaching. All three levels must be kept in mind if we are to glimpse the luminous gospel portrait of the Son of God.

## The first level: the evangelist

The first level is that of the inspired text itself. Each evangelist as a literary artist has drawn his own portrait of Christ. Native gifts of style and personal theological interests formed the mold into which he cast his materials. Even when using common sources each evangelist reshapes the data to accord with his own equipment as writer and thinker.

Mark burned with desire to show that Jesus was the Christ even though men did not receive Him. He reiterates this theme; he heaps up evidence to prove a plus quality in everything Jesus said or did: "Who then is this, that even the wind and the sea obey Him?" (Mark 4:40). Mark achieves this portrayal of the divine Christ by dividing his gospel into two neat parts, each rising climactically to a resounding cry of faith. The first half of his gospel (cc. 1–8) cul-

minates in the confession of Peter the Jew, "Thou are the Christ" (Mark 8:29).
The second half (cc. 8–15) rises to the awe-filled cry of the gentile centurion
on Calvary, "Truly this man was the Son of God" (Mark 15:39).

Mark, however, was hampered by literary shortcomings. His style is pedestrian and repetitious like that of a beginner. He therefore followed the easier
course and incorporated source material without re-touching it. If his gospel is
vital and colorful it is because he has reproduced exactly the memoirs of Peter.
This dependence on his sources brings the gospel of Mark close to the bedrock
of tradition. The Christ of Mark is strikingly human in the play of his emotions,
in the earthy color of His deeds, and in the limitation of even His miraculous
powers.

Christ in Mark is a study in chiaroscuro, truly divine yet wholly human.
This development is only one of many distinctive features in this gospel.
To share the full light of Mark's unique vision we must study the mystery of
Jesus from his perspective. Full familiarity with his style and purpose, clear
knowledge of his plan, painstaking analysis of his gospel as a personal literary
composition — all this is essential if we are to garner full riches on this first
level of gospel study, the inspired text.

Luke, Matthew, and John also present their own distinctive portrait of
Christ. "Mark," writes Pere Lagrange, "works in the warm earthiness of terra
cotta; Luke sculptures from white marble." For Luke, both in the Gospel and in
Acts, geography is theological; his mind is fascinated by the vast sweep of Christianity's universal mission, from humble beginnings in Jerusalem to glorious
consummation in Rome. Matthew's outlook is colored by a strong interest in
ecclesiology; his style is often hieratic and liturgical. John, on the other hand, is
a sacramentalist with a mystic's insight into the mystery of the Word inspiriting
flesh.

## The second level: the community

This interpretative activity of the evangelists has long been recognized. Previously, however, the next move was to proceed from the gospel text to the actual words and deeds of Jesus. Recent form critical studies have now focused
light on an intervening level. This intermediary stage has always been well
known to Catholics. We above all others have constantly affirmed that the gospel
was first lived and preached before it was written. Today we must face the involvements of this thesis.

Whatever the evangelists wrote they had to receive from the Church, for
none except John were eye-witnesses of the ministry of Christ. Mark entered
on the scene only after the resurrection; Luke was a gentile doctor from Antioch; the canonical "Matthew" was an anonymous author of the late first century. These synoptic evangelists had to draw on materials which only the Church
could supply. John, too, was markedly dependent on the full faith of the
Church, for he wrote not a mere reproduction of words and deeds but a profound interpretation of their meaning and mystery.

This dependence of the evangelists upon the Church focuses light on a second level in gospel study. The materials which the evangelists record were already illumined by the full light of the Spirit.

The Church had never locked up her memories of Jesus in a hermetically sealed box to be opened only when someone wanted to write a documented history, with barren references to exact times and places, with sterile photographic reproductions. On the contrary she constantly interpreted and applied the words and deeds of Jesus that they might play a vital and informative role in her own life. The history of the Man-God was never viewed as a mere incident of the past; it was seen rather as a power always operative, ringing a challenge and charting a course in the here and now.

This daily use of His words and deeds was bound to shape their telling and to bring out what was deep and rich in every event. The gospel record, therefore, drawing its material from the Church, will often show an identification tag of community usage.

## A. Miracle stories

The miracle stories, for instance, are drawn from the preaching of the apostles. This *kerygma* involved the recital of how Jesus "went about doing good and healing all who were in the power of the devil" (Acts 10:38). Keeping to the demands of oral style and following the rabbinical pattern the first preachers described the wonders of Christ with careful economy of phrase and with indifference to irrelevant details of time, place, and circumstance. The account was whittled down to brief notes on three phases: (1) the illness and condition of the sufferer; (2) the action of Christ the wonder-worker; (3) the saving effect of His power.

The gospel miracle stories bear the cachet of this community use. They are not a candid photo with background and details but a clean etching of what is strictly essential. The story of the cure of Peter's mother-in-law is typical; it presents only the three points listed above and nothing more: (1) a brief indication of her illness: "Simon's mother-in-law was keeping her bed sick with a fever" (Mark 1:30); (2) a terse action photo of what the miracle worker did: "Drawing near, he took her by the hand and raised her up" (v. 31); (3) a cryptic final statement of the effect: "The fever left her at once" (v. 31).

This crisp brevity is explained by Mark's dependence on a previous oral form which centered all attention on Christ's saving action. Details which would be essential for integrating this incident into a biography of Christ have all been omitted. Such poverty of detail and concentration on what is essential characterize most of the gospel miracle stories.

## B. Liturgical accounts and logia

The community had also a liturgy to prepare for its distinctive rites of baptism and the "breaking of bread." It came natural to incorporate into the liturgy the story of those events in Jesus' life which prepared for the sacraments of the Church or provided a parallel. The recountal of these incidents in the liturgical assembly called for a hieratic style and the rhythm of solemnity.

When incorporated into the written gospels these readings of the liturgical assembly retain the color and tone of their cultic origin. The description of the Last Supper in the Synoptics is typical. The courses of food, the songs, the conversation — all this is omitted. We find nothing but a sharply etched portrayal of Christ's eucharistic action in a style which is solemn and lapidary.

The early Church had also to answer many questions and to solve bristling problems. As each difficulty arose memories of Jesus were rekindled and relevant words of His were recounted. There would have been the question about divorce. Was the Church to use the concession granted by Moses? If so, was she to follow the lenient casuistry of the rabbi Hillel or adopt the stern requirements of the rabbi Shammai? The remembrance of a pointed word of Christ ended the whole discussion: "Whoever puts away his wife and marries another commits adultery" (Mark 10:11). This logion became a directive principle in the community and as such was incorporated into the gospel.

Other problems too called for solution. What was to be done with gentiles who wished to enter the Church (cf. Acts 10:15)? Some urged that they first become Jews. It was helpful to recall how Jesus had dealt with gentiles. In healing the servant of a gentile centurion He offered to enter the gentile's house even though Jews looked upon this as a defilement. What is more, He gave full praise to the man's peerless faith: "Amen, I have not found so great a faith in Israel" (Matthew 8:10). This conduct of Christ directed the Church's attitude towards gentile converts; she accepted them just as they were. This incident lived in the Church's memory; more than likely it was already in writing when the evangelists inserted it into their gospels.

## C. Pronouncement stories

The early Church had its conflicts with a hard core of Jewish Christians who wanted to couple observance of the Law with the service of Christ. It was encouraging to remember that Jesus had faced similar controversies. His solution of these thorny problems provided ammunition in controversies which the Church herself had to conduct. The frequent rehearsal of His conflicts resulted in a clearly defined literary form which we today call the pronouncement story. The pattern is easy to detect in the gospel. Everything in the narrative is pared down to bare essentials in order to place emphasis on the conclusive pronouncement of Jesus.

The story in Luke 5:29-32 provides an apt illustration. First a single sentence describes the situation: "There was a great gathering of publicans and others who were at table with them" (v. 29). Next follows the criticism not only as Jesus heard it from the Pharisees but also as the first Christians heard it from their critics: "Why do you eat and drink with publicans and sinners?" (v. 30). This criticism is met with a memorable pronouncement of Jesus which would serve as a principle of action for the whole Church: "It is not the healthy who need a physician, but they who are sick. I have not come to call the just, but sinners to repentance" (vv. 31-31).

This was the kind of material which the evangelists had to use in their re-countal of Jesus' ministry. The majority of words and events in our gospels are there not only because they figured in the life of Christ but also because they served some vital need in the life of the early Church.

## D. *The Gospels as a portrait of Christ*

It is unwarranted, therefore, to look upon the gospels as a journalist's report of what happened yesterday. They are not a documented biography written in the style of the Mommsen-Von Ranke school. Whatever memories of Christ they contain have lived a fruitful life in the soil of the community. The narratives, therefore, do not follow a chronological succession of events; they do not mention details of place and circumstance; they do not guarantee verbatim quotations of Jesus' words. The very formulae which the gospels should have treasured in exact reproduction (e.g., the Lord's prayer, the words of eucharistic consecration) are found in as many different forms as there are evangelists who recount them.

What the evangelists have preserved for us is not a photographic reproduction of the words and deeds of Jesus but an interpretative portrait as the Church herself prepared it under the light of the Holy Spirit. Jesus Himself had promised, "The Holy Spirit . . . will teach you all things, and bring to your mind whatever I have said to you" (John 14:26). Under the light of this Spirit both the evangelist and the Church came to see not only what Jesus said and did but, far better, what He really meant.

## *The third level: historical life of Jesus*

It is only a study of the gospels from these two levels of the inspired evangelist and the Spirit-guided Church that brings full understanding of the third level on which all else is based. This is the historical level of the earthly life of Jesus, His words and deeds. A casual reader of the gospel text might see in His miracles merely human beneficence restoring health to the body. When seen, however, through the eyes of the Church and of the evangelist these miracles reveal the saving power of the messianic Son of God.

We ourselves know what it means to hear in the rite of baptism the story of the cure of the deaf and dumb man. In the light of the Church's application of this miracle to the transformation of the soul the story comes alive with new meaning. The miracle is now seen as more than mere restoration of speech and hearing. Working as Messiah Jesus changed the whole man giving not only physical hearing but also spiritual power to hear the word of God, bestowing not only physical speech but also spiritual power to speak the praises of God. The Church's use of the miracle story in her liturgy brings us to share her own deep understanding of the full meaning of every messianic miracle.

In the same way the agony in the garden gains new significance when one remembers that it was first recounted in the primitive catechesis. The Greek words which the Church employed and the evangelists repeated bear the cachet of the community, echoing words frequently repeated in early catechetical instruction: "Watch and pray," "Pray lest you enter into temptation." These were the words with which the first preachers urged their converts to bear trial and to endure struggle as a real share in the messianic tribulation (*thlipsis*) which must precede the glorious Parousia.

In the light of the contribution which each Christian must make in "prayer and watchfulness," the Church was able to interpret the true meaning of Jesus' words to His apostles in the garden. His plea, "Watch with me," was not an appeal for human sympathy. It was the heartful cry of a father and shepherd urging His own to be faithful to God in the dread "hour" of messianic struggle with the powers of darkness.

Through this interpretation coming from the first days of the Church and preserved for us in the gospel's Greek translation of Jesus' Aramaic words, the scene in the garden comes alive with deep meaning which rings resonantly in the heart of every reader. The apostle in the garden and the Christian in the struggle of daily life are one. Both hear the same plea to "watch and pray" that they may be found worthy of the "hour" of Christ's supreme glory.

## Conclusion

Gospel study, therefore, means work on three levels. It is only when we view its message from the perspectives of the evangelist's insight and the Church's understanding that we too, under the light of the Holy Spirit, shall come to appreciate the full, rich meaning of Christ's words and deeds during the days of His earthly life.

An example may help to make all this clear. The floor of the ocean is littered with sea shells. Only some of these are swept onto the shore. There wind and rain smooth away sharp edges. The sunlight brings out rich coloring. A man finds them there, gathers them up and forms them into a vase, beautiful in shape and color. To appreciate the exquisite beauty of the vase we not only gaze at its whole contour and color pattern but we study also the graceful turn and delicate tint of every shell.

It is the same with the gospels. Our Lord's life was like an ocean bed filled with words and deeds in such abundance that books could not contain them. Only some of these reached the shore of the primitive community. There the wind and light of the Spirit shaped the telling of each deed and illumined its deep meaning. The evangelists gathered together these living memories and molded them into a gospel under the light of the Spirit. No two gospels are the same; each has its own contour and coloring.

To measure the truth and to appreciate the beauty of the gospel we cannot be content to study merely the formative work of the evangelist and the over-all impression of his literary composition. We must also study each unit in the gosepl, as we would study each shell in a vase, to discover what the Holy Spirit disclosed to the Church — the full meaning of each event and the vital significance of each word in the life of Jesus.

# THE HISTORICAL THEOLOGY
# OF THE GOSPELS

Bruce Vawter, C.M.

## History and Historicism

On August 15, 778 A.D., the army of Charlemagne was retreating into France through the Pyrenees. At a place called Roncevaux a part of the rear-guard was cut off by Basque marauders and annihilated. Among those who fell in the battle that day was a certain Hrodland, Count of the March of Britanny.

These are the somewhat jejune facts of statistical history that lie behind the figure of the Roland or Orlando who fired the imagination of medieval Europe. The *Song of Roland*, which made the names of Roland, Oliver, and Roncevaux houseworld words for ages to come, was composed sometime in the second half of the eleventh century from the prose and poetic legends of chronicler and troubadour. Under various forms, it has entered into the literature of man forever.

In the *Song of Roland*, however, quite a different story is told than appears in the first paragraph above. The minor rear-guard action has become a great national and Christian defeat. The small band of Basque highwaymen has been transformed into a vast army of Saracens. Charlemagne, a young man in 778 A.D. who was never personally involved in the action at Roncevaux, enters to wreak a satisfying vengeance on an enemy that in reality escaped scot-free. Roland and the Twelve Peers, all types of the pure Christian knight, die in testimony to their faith that "Christians are right, pagans are wrong." The Twelve Peers, incidentally, seem to have been intruded into the primitive legend from another story of Charlemagne's having sent twelve chiefs against the Basques — on a quite different occasion with a quite different sequel.

I rather suspect that the uneasiness with which even cultivated and informed Christians sometimes regard the historical criticism of the Gospels can very well be motivated by historical "debunking" of this kind. The memory of what historicism tried to do to the Gospels in the late eighteenth and the nineteenth centuries is still quite fresh. From Hermann Reimarus' caricature of Jesus as a political fanatic through Ferdinand Christian Baur, David Friedrich Strauss, Friedrich Schleiermacher, and into the twentieth century, the higher criticism of the New Testament appears to have been obsessed with the conviction that what had really happened in the life of Jesus must have been as unlike the Gospel story as what had really happened at Roncevaux was unlike the *Song of Roland*. The Christian who cherishes his historical religion might well feel that he has cause to distrust historical criticism in principle.

Historicism, however, was not the product of historical criticism, and the latter has no duty to atone for the sins of the former. The historicism which in

Published originally in *Homiletic and Pastoral Review*, 62 (1962), 681-91. Reprinted by permission of the publisher.

biblical studies manifested itself as a sterile scepticism was rather the product of the age in which historical criticism first appeared, an age that lived to see the blasting of most of its sureties on which historicism had been premised. The historicists made use of historical criticism to atomize biblical history into disintegration, but they were historicists before they became historical critics. Their scepticism with regard to biblical history derived more from their rationalism and their naïve evolutionary theories than it ever did from the historical positivism in which they had been trained. Those who continue their sceptical tradition today, furthermore, have not acquired their working principles from coming to grips with any new historical problem. The contrary has often been suggested. We have been reminded many times that the "de-mythologizing" of the New Testament practised by Rudolf Bultmann and his school began in the Germany of World War II and that many of the school had served, as chaplains or otherwise, in the German army. We have been asked to accept "de-mythologizing" as a critical response to a felt need in a generation that had suffered the attrition of Nazi philosophy and was no longer capable of receiving Christianity on its old terms. I venture the judgment, however, that not a single sceptical attitude of this school cannot be found anticipated as critical dogma in Bultmann's initial work on Jesus that was published in 1926. It was in this that Bultmann wrote:

> I am frankly of the opinion that we can know practically nothing about the life and personality of Jesus, since the Christian sources, fragmentary and overgrown with legend as they are, had no interest in such things, and there are no other sources concerning Jesus. All that has been written for the past century and a half on the life of Jesus, his personality, his interior development, and the like — critical research aside — is fantasy and romance.[1]

There is nothing here that could not have been written by David Friedrich Strauss, who would have had precisely the same reasons for writing it. In their wholly sceptical approach to biblical history, Bultmann and those who share his views are simply the final survivors of nineteenth-century rationalistic liberal Protestantism — a spiritual ancestry that Bultmann has more than once been called upon to acknowledge and which he would prefer to disavow. It must be said to the credit of Bultmann, who is a genuinely religious man, that he is not entirely happy over what he conceives to be his critical duty to preach a de-historicized Gospel, the consequences of which he may perhaps better appreciate than do some orthodox Christians. However this may be, his substitution of the existential moment for historical revelation has not salvaged Christianity from the shambles in which rationalism would have left it. At best, he can be said to have articulated a philosophy of life with a Christian coloration.

## History and historical criticism

The historical criticism that truly represents present-day scholarship in no way resembles the historicism of the nineteenth century. This was made quite clear in 1952 with the appearance of Vincent Taylor's commentary on Mark's

[1] *Jesus* (Berlin: Deutsche Bibliothek, 1926), p. 12.

Gospel, the first full-scale commentary on Mark in English since the preceding half-century. Taylor devoted some twenty pages to a discussion of the Gospel's historical value, concluding that:

> In sum we may say that in Mark we have an authority of first rank for our knowledge of the Story of Jesus. Separated at the time of writing by little more than a generation from the death of Jesus, its contents carry us back farther into the oral period before Mark wrote to the tradition first of the Palestinian community and subsequently that of the Gentile Church at Rome. The historical value of Mark depends on the Evangelist's fidelity to that tradition, including his special advantages as a hearer of Peter's preaching. Whether we judge his work by a consideration of the various influences which affected it, those of defence, worship, teaching, and doctrine, or whether we consider its objective character, we reach the same conclusion that here is a writing of first-rate historical importance . . . Without this Gospel, which is not only invaluable in itself, but is also one of the most important sources upon which all the Gospels depend, it is impossible to account for the history of primitive Christianity, or to imagine the perils from which it was preserved; for it sets at the centre the personality of Jesus Himself and His redemptive work for men.[2]

In 1906, in a book that was later given the English title *The Quest of the Historical Jesus*, Albert Schweitzer proclaimed that the critical research of the past century into the life of Jesus had reached a total and impenetrable impasse. Schweitzer was, of course, quite right in this judgment, which was a judgment on historicism. The quest of the historical Jesus failed because its issue had been prejudiced from the outset. The historical record itself, the only historical record that exists, was first rejected in a gesture of inane self-denial by the historian, who thereupon became a romanticist. The present-day scholar, however, belonging to a time that has successfully weathered the extravagances of the earlier research, can with equal justice proclaim the continuation of the quest. Thus the late T. W. Manson could say of the Gospels that

> the story they tell, in its main outlines and much of its detail, fits with what we otherwise know about contemporary Jewish faith and life in Palestine. It makes sense in the context of Roman Imperial policy in the Near East. It gives an adequate explanation of the genesis of the Church. It does not give a complete biography of Jesus, not even a full chronicle of the Ministry. His life lasted between thirty and forty years, and his public career not less than eighteen months; and all the records we possess can be read in a few hours. The gaps are enormous. But we have some details; and I think it is true to say that these short stories, parables, sayings, poems, and so on, which go to make up the Gospels, themselves epitomize the whole story . . . All this means that we are driven back to the business of treating the Gospels — as wholes and in detail — as historical documents, using all the resources of exact scholarship and strict historical method for the task . . . There is no escape from the historical inquiry. And there is no need to be despondent about its prospects. We may venture to hope that as it prog-

[2] *The Gospel According to St. Mark* (London: Macmillan; New York: St. Martin's Press, 1952), p. 148f.

resses, we shall find that the Ministry of Jesus is a piece of real history in the sense that it is fully relevant to the historical situation of its own time, to the hopes and fears, the passionate convictions and the gnawing needs of our Lord's own contemporaries. And just because it was so relevant to their life, we shall find it relevant to our own.[3]

Affirmations similar to these of Taylor and Manson are to be found generally in the work of today's leading Protestant New Testament scholars, men like Reginald H. Fuller, C. H. Dodd, A. M. Hunter, Joachim Jeremias, Ethelbert Stauffer, Walter Grundmann, Hermann Diem, Oscar Cullmann, Harald Riesenfeld (Sweden's leading New Testament scholar), and others. The degrees and nuances of affirmation are many, of course, but the emergent impression is one: that historical criticism is now in the safe hands of firm believers in historical religion.[4] Study of this kind gives no reasonable cause to fear that historical research can ever again become so unscientific as to treat the story of Jesus, written down within the living memory of its eye and ear witnesses, as if it were a legend of centuries past that had been told by troubadours. With the exceptions that I have already noted, present-day critics accord to the Gospels the serious historical consideration that they deserve.

## The historic and the historical

On the other hand, there is a much more subtle danger that historicism still holds for us than might appear from the relatively few thoroughgoing sceptics who can be encountered in today's world of New Testament scholarship. The danger is that we may have rejected the historicist conclusions without completely rejecting the premises as well. The nineteenth-century criticism had as its working principle, a principle that was as gratuitous as it was arrogant, that no history was worthy of the name that did not conform to the norms of modern scientific historiography, that is, it was not history unless it was a disinterested attempt to reconstruct the past statistically, isolating the bare event *wie es eigentlich gewesen war*, "as it actually was," from any interpretation of the event on the historian's part. Since this was not the conception of history it found in the Bible, it felt free to dispense with biblical history. The apologist for biblical history rightly rejected this conclusion, but not always for the right reasons. At least on the popular level, our apologetics has sometimes tried to sustain the illusion that the biblical authors did write with such a modern historical perspective in view. What is worse, we have to some extent been conditioned to approach the Bible from an historical viewpoint that the biblical authors never shared, with the result that we have seriously misunderstood what biblical history is all about.

What is history, in the sense that we speak of ours as an historical religion?

[3] "The Life of Jesus: Some Tendencies in Present-day Research," in *The Background of the New Testament and Its Eschatology*, ed. by W. D. Davies and D. Daube (Cambridge University Press, 1955), pp. 219–221.
[4] Cf. Béda Rigaux, O.F.M., "L'historicité de Jésus devant l'exégèse récente," *Revue biblique* 65 (1958), pp. 481–522. This article has been summarized in *Theology Digest* 9 (Winter, 1961), pp. 26-32.

History, I am sure we must agree, is the one factor above all that completely sunders revealed religion from the natural religion of paganism. Paganism by its very definition is a static religion which finds its gods in the cyclic and recurring permanence of nature; the explanation of all its rites and myths is the explanation of paganism itself, which, in Bultmann's words, exists "to secure control of the divine."[5] Revealed religion, in contrast, is the result of God's having taken control of affairs in history, the result of His having intervened, of His having altered the normal course of events and of His having manifested Himself in so doing. Revealed religion depends for its existence on God's having done certain things at certain times and under certain circumstances. This fact, that it once was not and now is, that it did not find its God immanent in nature but is instead His creation, that it has in consequence been given a sense of purposed time, of beginnings and of ends — all this has contributed to historical religion a dynamism that is utterly foreign to paganism.

In the biblical view, history is not merely a preliminary to revelation but revelation itself; by the same token, the historical writing of the Bible, its *Heilsgeschichte*, "salvation history," is biblical theology. The God of Israel's election revealed himself in word, certainly, but no less in the events by which he constituted Israel. The law was the spelling out of the *hesed* (mercy, loving-kindness), the *sedeq* (rightdoing, justice), and the *emeth* (fidelity, truth) which Yahweh had revealed in the saving acts of the Exodus and the donation of the promised land, which were in turn the standard of life for an Israel whose duty it was to imitate the holiness of its God. "He has shown you, O man, what is good. What does Yahweh require of you? What else, but to do justice, to love *hesed*, and to walk humbly with your God?" (Micah 6:8). In like manner, in the New Testament the law of Christ is the law of charity, God's ultimate revelation in Christ which has created and animated the Church (John 3:16f; 15:12f, etc.).

History, then, is the very air that we breathe in a religion of revelation. The Church has always, instinctively and inevitably, anathematized every attempt that has been made to withdraw Christianity from its essential historical framework. The heresies that have tried to dispense with history — Docetism, Marcionism, Gnosticism, the Modernist search for "external values" — it has condemned promptly and uncompromisingly, as they must be condemned by every Christian who knows the meaning of his faith. The meaning of Christianity has been missed by anyone who can in practice be a Marcionist, who can treat the Old Testament as an irrelevancy and convert the religion of the New Testament into a de-eschatologized ethical system, confounding sight with faith and dispensing with hope.

Since history is of the very essence of the Judeo-Christian revelation, it is obvious that we cannot count it as significant only with the development of critical methodology and scientific historiography less than two centuries ago. It would be absurd to think that the ancient Israelite, when he heard cultic re-

---

[5] *This World and Beyond. Marburg Sermons,* tr. by Harold Knight (New York: Scribners, 1960) p. 11.

citals of the great deeds of Yahweh of the type preserved, for example, in Psalms 78 and 105, had a grasp of Old Testament history that was any the less for his inability to verify any single fact that had been recorded there. It would be equally absurd to think that the Gospel story was of less significance to the Fathers or to St. Thomas Aquinas than it is to ourselves, who can, as they could not, authenticate much of its detail by the aid of archeology, linguistics, and other means afforded by modern study and research. If these means were lacking to us — as, in point of fact, they are lacking to the average Christian who is no student of history — would the historicalness of our religion be diminished in any way? Obviously not. To come to this conclusion, however, is also to conclude that the biblical authors' concern for history was something quite different from that of the modern historian.

To follow this argument further we need to make a modern distinction that has given separate terms to conceptions that once did not need them. I refer to the distinction that has long been made by German scholars between *Historie* and *Geschichte*, between the *historisch*, therefore, and the *geschichtlich*. Father David Stanley, S.J., has suggested as English equivalents "historic" and "historical" respectively.[6] I shall adopt this terminology in what follows.

What is historic is statistical history, the verifiable past. It is historic, for example, as it is recorded in the *Annales* of Cornelius Tacitus (or in the Gospels, for that matter), that Jesus Christ was put to death by the procurator Pontius Pilate in the reign of Tiberius Caesar. What is historical is an event that lives in its effects, that has transcendent and perennial significance. It is historical that for us men and for our salvation Jesus Christ suffered under Pontius Pilate, was crucified, died, and was buried. Three men were crucified on Golgotha on a Friday afternoon. All three deaths were historic, but only one is historical. Though the events of salvation are, for anyone who accepts the traditional Christian Gospel, both historic and historical, it is evidently with the historical rather than with the historic event that Christianity is primarily engaged. It is here, indeed, as Oscar Cullmann has written, and not in any supposed incompatibility of Christian dogma with modern technology (as Bultmann has thoughtlessly expressed it, after the rationalists), that the real enduring *skandalon* and "foolishness" of Christianity consists: "that historically datable events ('under Pontius Pilate') are supposed to represent the very centre of God's revelation and to be connected with all his revelations."[7] That, Cull-

[6] Cf. "Rudolf Bultmann: a Contemporary Challenge to the Catholic Theologian," *Catholic Biblical Quarterly* 19 (1957), pp. 347-355. See also by the same author, "The Conception of our Gospels as Salvation-History," *Theological Studies* 20 (1959), pp. 561-589. It will be obvious, I think, that "historic" and "historical" are arbitrarily chosen, since the two terms are interchangeable in English. It is true, "historic" is sometimes used by us for that which is momentous or celebrated in history, and therefore would be preferred by some as the equivalent of *geschichtlich*. Actually, however, *geschichtlich* means much more than this. Furthermore, it would be inconvenient to restrict our customary word "historical" to what is, in respect to the historicalness of the Gospels, of purely secondary importance. I have thought it preferable, therefore, to employ this less-used "historic" to refer to this secondary aspect of biblical history.

[7] *The Christology of the New Testament* (London: SCM Press, 1959), p. 327.

mann correctly says, was as difficult of acceptance to the men of the "mythological" world of the first Christian century as it is to the men of the scientific world of the twentieth.

The historical faith of Christianity is the acceptance of the historical rather than of the historic in this sense, that what is really essential to this history can only be believed, it could not and cannot ever be proved. The fact that it does contain in part events that are verifiably historic is secondary as far as religious significance is concerned, however important may be this factor in the realm of apologetics. Ultimately, its acceptance is the response of faith to revelation, and it was to achieve this response to this kind of history that the Gospels were written.[8]

The validity of the distinction between the historic and the historical is not lost simply because it has been employed, by Bultmann and others, to reduce the historic to an irrelevancy, or virtually so. In Catholic eyes, Bultmann's acceptance of historical significance without historic fundament can only succeed in making the act of faith irrational. On the other hand, the neglect of this distinction has contributed to our giving the impression, as we sometimes have, that the act of faith can be a rational conclusion based on the evidence of history.[9] The retraction of faith from all contact with the historic is in obedience to a conception of *fides nuda* which ties the modern existentialist theologian to primitive Protestantism. Between this fideism, however, and the rationalism that would substitute sight for faith, between faith, therefore, as an irrational act and faith that is reduced to a rational conclusion, lies the traditional Catholic idea of faith as assent to historical revelation. In these days of historical criticism, I believe that we shall understand our faith much better by preserving the distinction between the historic and the historical, assigning to each its proper role and significance.

## *The priority of the historical*

The very exaggeration of the existentialist theology in minimizing the importance of the historic has been of real service to us in recalling our attention to the priority of the historical in our faith. In reference to a work by C. H. Dodd, Rudolf Bultmann has written:

> Can we speak of the call of God as an event of the past, or rather only as it is God's call directed to me in my situation? Further, is not the preaching of the Church God's word in the true sense only as it is the word directed to me, the concrete man, in my concrete situation? If God's word is event, it can be such only to the extent that it is occurring, *in actu*. It cannot be

[8] Cf. Cullmann, *Christ and Time. The Primitive Christian Conception of Time and History* (Philadelphia: Westminster, 1950), pp. 97-100.

[9] "Thus in regard to the act of faith, it would seem that the current emphasis on faith as an act of reason, or the end result of an historical or philosophical proof, which has crept even into Catholic literature, is actually the unhappy result of Catholic attempts in the last two centuries to meet the deists and rationalists on their own grounds." This is the conclusion of Father John L. Murphy in his article, "Faith and Reason in the Teaching of Kierkegaard," *American Ecclesiastical Review* 145 (1961), pp. 233-242.

event in the sense of a verifiable fact lying in the past. God's revelation (*Offenbarung*) is not publication (*Offenbartheit*).[10]

Strip this statement of its needless either-or, remove its "only," and it remains a testimony to a truth that has too often been mislaid in Christian thinking. That is to say, the concern of the Gospels and of Christianity itself with history has always been and must be primarily with the historical mystery rather than with the statistical fact.

Must we not confess that the resurrection of Christ, for example, has figured in our thinking rather exclusively as an historic event — as a miracle of apologetical import or simply as a momentous detail in the earthly career of Christ — rather than as a central mystery of faith that is to be believed? Have we not, therefore, tended to obscure the significance attached to the resurrection by the authors of the New Testament, the Fathers of the Church, the greatest of the Scholastic theologians, and the Church's liturgy? In the preface of the Easter Mass the Church bids us to praise our Lord "qui mortem nostram moriendo destruxit *et vitam resurgendo reparavit";* and in the collect we pray: "O God, who *this day* by your only-begotten Son, having conquered death, *have reopened for us the gate to eternity* . . ." These prayers, paraphrases of such passages as Rom. 4:25 and 1 Cor. 15:45, recognize the authentic historical moment of the resurrection in a way that our popular preaching and teaching, and even our post-Reformation theology itself, have not always done.[11] All this we have obviously missed if we have gone to the Gospels seeking only the verification of an historic fact.

Again, how much stress have we been accustomed to lay on the relevance of Christ's ascension to the mystery of salvation? I fear that the ascension has been regarded largely, when it has been regarded at all, as something quite extraneous to the Christian life: a wondrous thing, surely, among so many wondrous things we take for granted in biblical history, but something with which the divine economy could easily have dispensed without loss to man's eternal destiny. Yet that Christ "ascended into heaven" is recalled in the Creed as one of those things done "for us men and for our salvation"; and in the preface of the Ascension Mass the Church says that Christ "was raised up into heaven that he might make us partakers of his divinity."

The ascension of Christ is described in the New Testament as a visible event, we know, only by St. Luke (in Luke 24:50-53 and Acts 1:2-14), since Mark 16:19 is now generally conceded to be dependent on Luke. Outside the New Testament, it is not until the fourth century that the Fathers begin to

[10] " 'The Bible To-day' und die Eschatologie," in *The Background of the New Testament and Its Eschatology*, p. 407.

[11] Cf. D. M. Stanley, S.J., "Ad historiam exegeseos Rom. 4:25," *Verbum Domini* 29 (1951), pp. 257-274; Bruce Vawter, C.M., "Resurrection and Redemption," *Catholic Biblical Quarterly* 15 (1953), pp. 11-23; Edwin G. Kaiser, C.PP.S., "The Theology of the Resurrection of Christ," *Proceedings of the Catholic Theological Society of America*, 1959, pp. 28-53. The renewed interest in the biblical theology of the resurrection is illustrated by the appearance of *The Resurrection. A Biblical Study*, by F. X. Durrwell, C.Ss.R., tr. by Rosemary Sheed (New York: Sheed & Ward, 1960).

treat of a visible ascension, and then only as commenting on Luke's description. On the other hand, an ascension or return of Christ to the Father after the resurrection, independent of the visible description and the forty days' interval of the Lucan account, is a common affirmation of the New Testament. "He who believes in me, the works that I do he also shall do, and greater than these he shall do, because I am going to the Father . . . And I will ask the Father and he will give you another Advocate to dwell with you forever, the Spirit of truth whom the world cannot receive, because it neither sees him nor knows him. But you shall know him, because he will dwell with you and be in you" (John 14:12 16f). In John 20:17, following the resurrection, Jesus tells the Magdalene not to touch Him, as He has not yet ascended to the Father, but to take the message to the disciples that He is ascending to the Father. This ascension is certainly presupposed in the next episode, the giving of the Holy Spirit to the disciples, which occurred "the evening of that same day." It is certain that both Luke and the other New Testament authors refer to the same historical mystery, the article of faith with which the preface of the Ascension Mass is concerned, Christ's exaltation in glory as the condition of his giving us a share of His divine life through grace, His reign as king and head over His Body the Church and giver of the Spirit who sanctifies.

As to the historical event, therefore, the New Testament authors are at one. When we attempt to reconstruct the historic details, however, we evidently find that their testimony is more ambiguous, simply because these details were not their primary concern, any more than it was their primary concern to give us an exact chronology of our Lord's life. This was not their idea of history. At all events, when scholars point out some of the symbolic potentialities of the Lucan account of the ascension — the forty days, for example, and the cloud enveloping our Lord — we should understand that they are not minimizing its historicalness in any way.[12] They are, instead, trying to determine the form in which Luke has communicated the historical event, recognizing the priority that he has given to this over all other interests.

## History and theology

The historical character of the Gospels, we have said, is today accorded the serious respect that is its due. Their historic framework in all of its essentials is, to all but the most sceptical of sceptics, better demonstrated than any other records of comparable antiquity. Modern studies have only strengthened this position. It would hardly have been possible, for example, prior to 1948, when the Qumran literature first began to be published, to maintain critically, as it has now been maintained, that the Gospel of John is the most "Jewish" of all the Gospels. Even though the radical criticism of the nineteenth century had already been abandoned, the Dead Sea Scrolls proved anew that the Johannine Christ was no Gnostic figment of the second century and that the Fourth Gos-

[12] Cf. Pierre Benoit, O.P., "L'Ascension," *Revue biblique* 56 (1949), pp. 161-203; E. Schillebeeckx, O.P., "Ascension and Pentecost," *Worship* 25 (May, 1961), pp. 336-363.

pel faithfully reflects the Palestinian background of John the Baptist and Jesus.[13] The old arguments of the "traditional" apologetics for the authentic coloration of the Gospels, for their notable historical intent and their lack of special pleading, have better confirmation today than they had a generation ago. The present-day emphasis on form criticism, that is, on the role of the primitive Christian Church in the formation of the Gospel materials, likewise has its strong contribution to make. In the Gospels we do not have simply four isolated Christian witnesses writing a generation and more after the death of Jesus, but the accumulated testimony of the Christian Church to what God had done through Christ and the Holy Spirit.[14]

At the same time, we know that we must respect the historical purposes of the Gospels and renounce the temptation to ascribe to them the passion for historic detail that is the characteristic of modern history. In many cases, as a simple comparison of the Gospels with one another will show, we must recognize that we have testimony to historic fact but not to its details, since the historical event has been proclaimed in the terminology of faith and not of statistical history. This, obviously, is not to impair the historicalness of the Gospels, but to enhance it. The reduction of the historical to the merely historic would not only impoverish our theology, it would convert our faith itself into a pious historicism, into a natural religion based on a human rather than a divine word.

We have long since discarded, in favor of what I am sure we all agree are considerations more germane to the Gospel, discussions as to whether one or two blind men were healed by our Lord at Jericho, and whether the restoration of sight took place on the hither or thither side of that city. We have come to realize that the attempt, once made in the best of good faith, to resolve the "apparent inconsistencies" of parallel Gospel accounts was often to miss the very point that one or the other evangelist had intended to make by his use of the story in question. We have, in other words, come to a better understanding of the properties of the Gospel materials we are dealing with, and to realize that the evangelists were biblical historians and not mere chroniclers of facts. We have come to recognize the applicability of the principle of literary forms to the New Testament just as we recognize it in respect to the Old Testament.

The conclusions reached in present-day New Testament study have not been derived from any *a priori* imposition of historical standards on the Gospel texts, as was so often the case in nineteenth-century criticism, but from the study of the Gospels themselves and of the oral and literary processes that produced them. Neither can any literary form be excluded *a priori* from the Gospels simply because such a form is foreign to modern historical norms. Midrash, for example, to the extent that it becomes an ascertainable and definable literary form of the period of the Gospels, could as easily have been em-

[13] Cf. William F. Albright, "The Bible After Twenty Years of Archeology," *Religion In Life* 21 (1952), pp. 547-550. Reprinted by The Biblical Colloquium, Pittsburgh, 1954.

[14] Cf. X. Léon-Dufour, S.J., in Robert-Feuillet, *Introduction à la Bible* (Tournai: Desclée, 1959), II, pp. 321-334.

ployed by the Jewish authors of the Gospels in the first Christian century as it was by the Jewish author of the Book of Wisdom in the first century B.C. Exotic forms such as midrash, the verification of which would cause the revision of some popular ideas concerning supposed historic details in the Gospels, can obviously disturb the minds of those whose studies have not prepared them to understand their spirit. The recent *monitum* of the Holy Office concerning Scripture studies took cognizance of this danger. The prudence and caution enjoined by the Holy Office, however, are conditions for continued study and publication, not for inactivity. The *monitum* did not disapprove, alter, or suppress any existing trend in Catholic biblical interpretation — a fact that seems to have escaped the attention of some who commented on it.

As a matter of fact, while the resolution of such questions as that of the Gospel's literary forms will naturally be of prime interest to theologians, apologists, and all who share in the Church's intellectual life, it is hard to see its immediate relevance outside this circle. Whatever eventual popularization of its assured results needs to be done should, of course, be done with prudence and caution and with the laying of necessary groundwork by those who are qualified to do it — *after* the results have indeed been assured where they can only be assured, in the world of Catholic scholarship that is left free to work within the analogy of the Church's faith. It is difficult to see how, in any case, the results of this study will ever seriously affect the pulpit, which is the forum for the proclamation of the Gospel message, not for historical criticism. The Catholic does not take his faith from historical criticism, but from the Church. In distinction to the Protestant, perhaps, the Catholic does not accept a teaching as Christ's because he thinks that he can prove that Christ ever uttered such a teaching in so many words, but because the Church has told him that this is Christ's teaching. The infallible teaching authority of the Church was not an invention of the Vatican Council; it was also possessed by the Church that produced the Gospels.

Neither is this to take refuge in a dismissal of the relevance of the historic element of the Gospels, or to accede to the position of the early form critics who ascribed to the primitive Church a creative role, in the crassest sense of the term, in the formation of the Gospel materials. As we have seen, the motivation of this critical position was nothing more novel than the principles of nineteenth-century rationalism, completely anachronistic in the present age of scholarship. The first Christians were the heirs of an historical tradition, they were not myth-makers; and there is nothing scientific in ascribing the Gospel to an amorphous *Urgemeinde* that has no continuity with Jesus and his generation on the one hand nor with the historical Christianity of the Fathers on the other, and which would be an affront to all that the Gospel stands for. It is precisely those who have studied the Gospels most deeply, with all the means of study that are at our disposal today, who know best that they are an unshakable part of the world's history, without equivocation and without qualification.

# THE PREACHER AND THE GOSPEL

Francis J. McCool, S.J.

Preachers are needlessly disturbed by scripture scholars' new insistence that
none of our Gospels can be considered "pure" historical sources in the nineteenth century tradition of Ranke, Meyer, and Mommsen. These were the scholars who canonized the precise, detailed, carefully objective diplomatic reports
which Ranke found in the Venetian archives as a kind of ideal historical
source.

Such "pure" historical sources are not the only kind of authentic history.
And the Gospels provide us with a witness to Christ that is truly authentic history. Scholars hold firmly to the divine inspiration and absolute truth of the
gospel message.

What we must understand is the approach of the new exegesis, which, by
scientific methods fully as rigorous as those of Ranke and his school, discovers
in the Gospels a rich and valuable history of Christ as Master — Christ seen
not through the half-opened eyes of dispassionate contemporaries, but Christ
seen in his full dignity, seen by those "who received his words, his nature, and
his will into themselves."

The contemporary historian approaches the Gospels in two stages. First,
a general study of the Synoptics reveals that the Gospel tradition is authentic.
In regard to the Gospel tradition there are three historical notes that the historian will profitably recall. First, Jesus' preaching was eschatological, salvific,
exclusively religious, and challenging. Secondly, Jesus was constantly developing his relationships with the general public, with his enemies, and with his
apostles; these were not static relationships. Thirdly, Jesus' language and style
was Aramaic, Palestinian, and parabolic.

In the second stage the historian examines this authentic New Testament
tradition to determine the exact historical value of the elements in that tradition.
In this investigation one distinguishes between the activity of the early Church
(kerygmatic, catechetical, liturgical) and her motives (conversion, instruction,
exhortation). It is imperative to separate various groups within the early Church
— Jews, converts, pagans — and to consider their developing inter-relationships. One must also be aware of the methods employed by the Christian
community. For example, the community occasionally changed the point of
emphasis in its explanation of a parable.

A scholarly analysis of the Parable of the Sower, embodying these two
hypotheses, will exemplify the approach of an historical scholar and will interest preachers faced with problems of interpretation.

Reprinted from *Theology Digest*, 9 (1961), 145-7. Published originally as "The
Preacher and the Historical Witness of the Gospels," *Theological Studies*, 21 (1960), 517-
43. Reprinted by permission of the publisher.

## Jesus' parable: Mark 4:4-9

And as he sowed, some seed fell by the wayside, and the birds came and ate it up. And other seed fell upon rocky ground, where it had not much earth; and it sprang up at once, because it had no depth of earth; but when the sun rose it was scorched, and because it had no root it withered away. And other seed fell among thorns; and the thorns grew up and choked it, and it yielded no fruit. And other seed fell upon good ground, and yielded fruit that grew up, made increase and produced, one thirty, another sixty, and another a hundredfold.

## Early explanation: Mark 4:14-20

The sower sows the word. And those by the wayside are they in whom the word is sown; as soon as they have heard, Satan at once comes and takes away the word that has been sown in their hearts. And those likewise who are sown on the rocky ground are they who, when they have heard the word, receive it immediately with joy; and they have no root in themselves, but continue only for a time; then, when trouble and persecution come because of the word,they at once fall away. And those who are sown among the thorns are they who listen to the word; but the cares of the world, and the deceitfulness of riches, and the desires about other things, entering in, choke the word, and it is made fruitless. And those who are sown upon good ground are they who hear the word, and welcome it, and yield fruit, one thirty, another sixty, and another a hundredfold.

## Summary of Mark 4:4-9

Just as in the case of the sower, so also Jesus' initial lack of success will not prevent his work being crowned with glory.
1. Pure parable.
2. Stresses unity of the Kingdom, Jesus' ministry.
3. Theme of initial failure, final success.
4. Proclaims the Kingdom, its outcome as a climax.
5. Same vocabulary as Jesus'.
6. Numerous Semitisms.
7. Expertly framed.

## Summary of Mark 4:14-20

The harvest yield depends upon the fertility of the ground in which the seed is placed; so Jesus' word (its effect) is proportioned to the disposition of his hearers.
1. Allegory.
2. Stresses obstacles to the message.
3. Theme of harvest depending upon the soil.
4. A practical application of Jesus' teaching; no climax.

5. Vocabulary of the New Testament Epistles.
6. No Semitisms.
7. Carelessly refers to classes of people as "seeds."

The pure parable (Mark 4:4-9) is a series of concrete pictures that combine to indicate a single lesson. The hearers could discover this lesson by reflecting on the concrete historical situation in which they found themselves. Why, for example, did the early Church change Jesus' parable to an allegory (Mark 4:14-20), change its emphasis (initial failure — final success to fertility of ground — yield of harvest), and shift the focus from Jesus' Kingdom to internal and external obstacles to Jesus' message?

### Preaching and the parable

These differences should not prevent us from preaching the Parable of the Sower, for they can be reconciled if we recall that the synoptics had a double preoccupation. First, they reproduced the manner, contents, and effects of Jesus' preaching in Palestine. Secondly, they explained why Jesus chose this manner of preaching and showed the relevance of that preaching to the Church as she existed after Easter and Pentecost. The significant point is that both of these purposes are *historical*.

What was present in germinal form in Jesus' preaching, that is, the secret presence of the Kingdom of Christ, had become an explicit Christology to the Church. And the audience, no longer the Jewish contemporaries of Christ, were the faithful, who found it difficult to put into practice what the Christian revelation demanded of them. The Church has neither added to, nor subtracted from Jesus' parable; rather, because of a change in audience, she has shifted the accent from the "moment of the Kingdom" to the present trials of Christians.

The Church, therefore, has not changed Jesus' message; rather it has faithfully reproduced it in the exact form in which Jesus spoke it in the last moments of the "old aeon" and applied it for the benefit of her children who must live their lives in the "new age." Keeping in mind that the Scriptures belong to the Church, the preacher may reassure himself that no falsification has taken place.

## B. SAINT MARK

The earliest statement about the Gospel according to St. Mark is that of Papias (ca. 140 A.D.) who calls Mark "the interpreter of Peter." The significance of "interpreter" may be that Mark translated Peter's sermons from Aramaic into Greek, or even that he wrote them down. The reference to the presence of Mark in Rome with Peter in 1 Peter 5:13 seems to substantiate the tradition.

The Gospel opens with the brief prologue: "The beginning of the Gospel (evangelion) of Jesus Christ." The similarity of this prologue to the proclamation with which Mark introduces the public ministry of Jesus: "Jesus came into Galilee proclaiming the good news (evangelion) from God," seems to indicate the beginning of a type of preaching familiar to the early Church, the kerygma. As C. H. Dodd has demonstrated so well,[1] Mark's Gospel is the closest of the Synoptics to the primitive preaching or kerygma. After the prologue and a summary of the testimony of John, Mark begins his narrative of three sections: 1) Jesus' ministry in Galilee (1:14–9:50); 2) Jesus' ministry in Judea and Jerusalem (10:1-13:37); 3) the Passion-Resurrection narrative (14:1—16:20), of which the conclusion (16:19-20) is regarded by many scholars not to be written by Mark.

From qualities within the narrative it seems that Mark's Gospel was written for a church of predominantly Gentile converts. There are fewer citations from the Old Testament than in Matthew and less stress on the Mosaic law. Aramaic words are translated for Greek readers (3:17; 5:41; 7:34) and Jewish customs are explained to them (7:3; 14:12; 15:42).

The unique charm of Mark's Gospel has been re-discovered by recent scholars. A lively style, a frequent use of the present tense puts the reader in contact with things as they happened. Mark's frequent use of "immediately," "at once," "then," gives the impression that the years of Jesus' public ministry came all too quickly to a close.

The special doctrinal message of Mark's Gospel is developed by the articles of this section, and also some debated questions, such as the "messianic secret" and the prominence of the passion narrative. One of the achievements of recent Biblical scholarship is its effectiveness in making us see that the Gospel according to St. Mark puts us into close contact with the message of salvation as it was preached in the early Church.

[1] C. H. Dodd, *The Apostolic Preaching and Its Development,* pp. 46-52. J. M. Robinson, *The Problem of History in Mark.* (London: Allenson, 1957).

# THE GOSPEL ACCORDING TO MARK

Gerard S. Sloyan

These lines are being written in the nation's capitol, which is famous among other things for possessing a manuscript of the Greek gospels known to the world of scholarship as "W" — *Codex Washingtonensis*. Mr. C. L. Freer acquired it in Egypt in 1906 and it reposes in a gallery bearing his name which is part of the Smithsonian Institution. It dates to the late fourth or early fifth century. The text varies, as if it had been copied from several familes of manuscripts: the so-called Byzantine, Alexandrian, Western, and Caesarean.

The notable thing about Codex W is its conclusion, for after verse 14 of the sixteenth and last chapter, where the Eleven are reproved at table by Christ for their lack of faith in the witnesses to His resurrection, the following ending appears:

> And they replied saying, "This age of lawlessness and unbelief is under Satan, who by means of evil spirits does not permit the true power of God to be apprehended; therefore reveal thy righteousness now." They were speaking to Christ, and Christ said to them in reply: "The limit of the years of the authority of Satan has been fulfilled, but other terrible things draw near, even for the sinners on whose behalf I was delivered up to death, that they might turn to the truth and sin no more, in order that they may inherit the spiritual and incorruptible glory of righteousness which is in heaven."

This late second or early third century attempt to soften the condemnation of the Eleven has all the literary grace of a modern collect, in its desire to leave nothing unsaid. It serves, however, to bring attention to the mystery of why Mark stopped at the conclusion of verse 8 as he seemed to do: "And they [three women at the tomb] told naught to any man, for they were afraid."

The last twelve verses of the canonical gospel (9-20), the so-called "longer ending," were almost certainly written by another hand than the evangelist's, though the Church has always venerated them equally as inspired Scripture. They are a compilation of four distinct incidents found in Luke and John: Christ's appearance to Magdalene; Emmaus; His reproach of the Eleven at table; His ascent followed by their dispersion. The commission to "Go forth to every part of the world and proclaim the Good News to the whole creation . . ." (16:15) is an echo of Matthew 28:18.

## Authorship

The text of Mark's gospel underwent less change in transmission than the other three, not simply because of its brevity (only 678 verses, as compared

Quotations from the New Testament in Father Sloyan's articles on the synoptic Gospels are from the New English Bible (Oxford and Cambridge University Presses, 1961), with permission.

Published originally in *Worship*, 32 (1958), 548-57. Reprinted by permission of the publisher.

with 1071 in Matthew) but because, containing far fewer of the Lord's utterances it was quoted less. In fact, the fifth century writer known as Victor of Antioch complains that no commentary on Mark exists, that is to say in Greek.

Parenthetically it may be observed that the Roman Missal employs Mark only 23 times in all, 6 of them for communion verses. The other three gospels are employed many dozens of times each.

Papias of Hierapolis who informs us around the year 125–30 about the authorship of Matthew's gospel tells us of Mark that he was St. Peter's *hermeneutēs* or interpreter, and that he "wrote down accurately all of the things said and done by the Lord, but not however in order (*táxei*)." [1]

This order would have to be the topical or logical order proper to rhetoricians (in Mark's case, one with a theological intent). Surely there is no question of chronological order, for Matthew, who is praised by Papias for having adhered to an order (*synetáo*), has no special interest in a time sequence. Papias says that Mark had neither heard nor followed Jesus, but "recorded things just as he remembered them" as they came from Peter's lips — not by way of a connected account but adapted to the needs of the hearers.

We shall see later that despite its antiquity this view oversimplifies the problem of authorship, or rather mode of composition.

St. Mark is very probably the son of that wealthy Christian, Mary in whose house Peter sought refuge upon his release from prison (Acts 12:12). "John whose other name was Mark" appears again in the fifteenth chapter, not to very good advantage. Paul seems to have had enough of him (vv.37f) for deserting them at Perga in Pamphylia (13:13) and going back to Jerusalem. However, by the time of Paul's imprisonment with Aristarchus (c. 60 A.D.) Paul and Mark, "the cousin of Barnabas," are friends again (Col. 4:10; Philemon 24), and in 2 Tim. 4:11 the reconciliation is complete: "For I find him a useful assistant."

St. Peter in his first epistle sends a greeting from Rome in which he tenderly refers to Mark as "my son" (5:13).

## The Petrine preaching

Every indication is that the speeches of Peter in Acts 10:36ff, where he reviews Christ's saving career for the family of Cornelius the centurion, and the speech of Paul in the synagogue in Pisidian Antioch (Acts 13:16ff), are types of summaries in fixed form which were current in the apostolic Church. They are in no sense "lives of Christ" but examples of *kerygma* or the proclamation that in Christ crucified and risen we are saved, on condition of repentance for our sins.

Yet if the technique of the first preachers of Christ was a bold declaration of His miraculous career as the fulfilment of all hope from Abraham until that day, followed by a summation of His passion and resurrection, surely even those who believed this announcement would require further testimony as to what manner of man He was.

The Petrine preaching outlined above has God first announcing His good

[1] Eusebius, *Ecclesiastical History*, III, 39, 16.

news of peace in Galilee, where, "after the baptism proclaimed by John . . .
Jesus of Nazareth . . . anointed [by God] with the Holy Spirit and with power . . . went about doing good and healing all who were oppressed by the devil,
for God was with him" (Acts 10:38).

All of Jesus' public career is thus summarized, for immediately the reader is
brought to Jerusalem where as reliable onlookers "we" (the disciples) saw
Him "put to death by hanging on a gibbet" (v. 39). He was then raised up by
God's power and manifested to certain foreordained witnesses, who had the
subsequent task of preaching Him as the judge of the living and the dead.
Whoever would believe in Him might have forgiveness of his sins.

It does not take too lively an imagination to recognize in this recital the skeleton of Mark's written gospel. He does not have an infancy narrative, but goes
directly from the Baptist's preaching to eight chapters of almost solid *kerygma*, i.e., divine testimony to the truth of Jesus' claims in the form of exorcisms
and miracles, hence proclamation in deed of the advent of the kingdom. The
events take place entirely in Galilee for all we know.

The ninth chapter serves as a sort of watershed in the Master's career, for
six days after Peter's confession at Caesarea Philippi (a biblical "six days" leading to a particularly noteworthy, i.e. a "Sabbath" happening?) He is transfigured while in the company of Moses and Elijah and binds the three witnesses
to silence until He shall be risen from the dead.

Chapter 10 brings the company "up to Jerusalem" — Jesus "walking in front
of them" and more a teacher on the way than heretofore in Mark; the disciples
bumptious over a share in His glory, two against ten (10:37).

There is considerable teaching (*didachē*) in the next two chapters and
even a parable, that of the wicked vinedressers (12:1-12). Parables are very
few in Mark, there being in all only four which reach the stage of narrative
and five simple comparisons.

The thirteenth chapter is a sermon about the last days — Matthew's long eschatological discourse of chapters 24 and 25 sparsely told. With the concluding three chapters of trial and condemnation events, the gospel is complete.

## Interdependence

There can be little doubt that the oral catechesis of the infant Church is basic
to all four written gospels. Nonetheless, a study of the highly complex interde-
pendence of the first three and of even more subtle relations such as that of
John to Mark and Mark to Paul leads to the necessary conclusion that their human authorship, under divine guidance, was far more than a simple recording
of apostolic sermons.

Mark is so brief (not lacking in detail — for he tells more about less than
any), that the assumption in possession is that he wrote first and was elaborated
on by the others. Mr. E. V. Rieu in his lively introduction to the translation of
the four gospels he has made for the Penguin Classics (1953) bypasses certain
subtleties of the synoptic problem altogether by saying, "In this book I have

abandoned the customary order and put his [Mark's] Gospel first, because he wrote first and should therefore be read first."[2]

He then has Matthew abridging Mark and appending to him by a fairly simple editorial process. Rieu, far from being unaware of the synoptic problem, simply considers it solved in favor of the absolute priority of Mark.

The scholarly hypothesis in possession, for all uncommitted to the force of ecclesiastical tradition, is a fairly uncomplicated version of the "Two-Source theory," in which Mark and a no longer extant Q document (for *Quelle,* in German "source") between them provide most of the material found in Matthew and Luke. In this theory the elusive Q is a "sayings-collection" of some 250 verses, without a passion narrative.

The chapter of introduction to the synoptic Gospels in *La Sainte Bible de Jérusalem,* presumably the work of Père Benoit, refers to a more recent solution, largely put forth by Catholics.

According to it, Mark depends on the first or Aramaic version of Matthew but is in turn used by the author of canonical Matthew, even to the borrowing of certain phrases. The *SBJ* introduction theorizes that Mark had access to the first Palestinian Gospel (of Matthew, i.e.) and a supplementary collection of the words of Jesus, likewise written in Aramaic, but both by now rendered into Greek, and that he wove a Greek gospel of his own from the two. He was able to add all kinds of picturesque touches and colorful details because of his familiarity with the preaching of his master, Peter.

The inspired editor of canonical Matthew went to work aided by this Mark. He enriched and corrected it in many places, but the only narrative portions he was able to add were those of Christ's infancy. Mark's gospel has all the action there is to be found in any of the three synoptic narratives.

Before leaving the question of Markan authorship, it might be mentioned briefly that the Anglican scholar Wilfred L. Knox, brother to Msgr. Ronald, proposes in his *The Sources of the Synoptic Gospels, I: St. Mark* (Cambridge: At the University Press, 1953) that Mark employed numerous written sources, among them a "conflict-stories source," a "Twelve-source," a "parable source" (ch. 4:1-35), and several "books of miracles" (pp. 8-46).

This is surely the swing of the pendulum away from any theory in which all the oral narratives and sayings that were common property in the primitive Church were molded into a single product. The whole community accomplished this, in Bultmann's theory of the "history of [literary] forms," employing legendary tales of hellenistic origin to illustrate Jesus' sayings.

## Literary characteristics

As with each of the four evangelists, there is something about Mark that defies literary dissection. His grammar is bad, but his narrative power is immense. He is extremely brief throughout. The Master is described as passing from one event to another at high speed.

---

[2] E. V. Rieu, *The Four Gospels, A new translation from the Greek* (Baltimore: Penguin Books, 1953), p. xxii.

The net effect on the reader is a sense of urgency, almost breathlessness. If one goes through the book at a single sitting he feels hemmed in by the crowds, wearied by their demands, besieged by the attacks of demons.

Rieu gives a telling example of Mark's genius for brevity and detail within the same narrative. In 15:24 Mark writes: "Then they crucified him, and parcelled out his clothes, casting lots for them to see what each should have." The English scholar remarks the four words devoted to Christ's crucifixion and the fifteen to the men who had nailed Him to the cross, as evidence of this literary strength.

Yet Mark is also characterized by incomplete and interrupted ideas, and much repetition of phrasing. There is also the use of "doublets," little overlapping phrases which indicate he was loath to trim from either of his two sources.

Consequently he is more to be praised as a skillful compiler of all the sources at his disposal than as a journalist reporting vividly on all he has seen, though the touches of an eyewitness are at times unmistakable.

## The person of Jesus

The person of Jesus is central in Mark's gospel; He is seen there as "a Jew who acted like God." He casts out demons and He heals unceasingly so as to sow seeds of faith in Himself. When He calms the winds and raises Jairus' daughter, walks on the water or curses the fig-tree, it is with the sovereign word or gesture proper to divinity.

Vincent Taylor, the leading Markan scholar of our day, somewhat regretfully declares these "nature miracles" legendary because there is no attempt in conjunction with them to demonstrate Jesus' messiahship or convince men of His supernatural claims. Moreover, they are capable of a non-miraculous interpretation, they were acts of exceptional compassion, even for Jesus, and so on. Mostly, however, they are at odds with the true "christology of the Markan tradition," in which Jesus is a "hidden God."

The Christ of the nature miracles embarrasses Dr. Taylor because in them He "throws off all disguise and is not bound by the conditions of human existence." [3] This does not necessarily mean that the Methodist scholar is a rationalist. He says that he is a believer in the possibility of miracles who is facing the "theological question whether they cohere with a true doctrine of the Incarnation." [4] He relies here on critical scholarship rather than the living Church for witness to the truth underlying the written gospels.

Despite the unacceptability of Dr. Taylor's position to the Catholic, it must be admitted that the problem of Jesus' insistence on keeping His identity secret in Mark, while at the same time working endless miracles calculated to disclose it, is not a small one.

Our Lord enjoins silence on the demons many times (1:25, 34 and 3:11f). He charges onlookers not to speak of the cures they see, as in the case of Jairus' daughter (5:43) and the deaf and dumb man of Decapolis (7:36). He insists

[3] Vincent Taylor, *The Gospel according to St. Mark* (London: Macmillan, 1955), pp. 142ff.

[4] *Ibid.*, p. 141.

that the disciples keep silence after Peter has called Him the Messiah at Caesarea Philippi (8:30). Coming down from the transfiguration mount He warns them not to tell what they have seen (9:8). The man of Gerasa who yields up his legion of demons to the swine is unique in being instructed by our Lord to publish the word to his fellow countrymen (5:19).

There is no way around the problem. Mark's account contains the inner tension of a Christ who wishes to prepare hearts for belief yet who is dismayed at the prospect of widespread acceptance. A traditional Catholic solution has been to say that He wanted genuine supernatural faith and not the enthusiasm of those ready to hail Him as a wonder-worker only. Yet the problem remains.

A more fruitful solution is probably to be sought in our Lord's desire to bring about faith in His companions first (though they themselves insist it did not come until the descent of the Spirit), rather than in the crowds at large. Secondly, our Lord knew the kind of faith in His divinity and messiahship He wanted: not a docetism that was sure of His divine nature and doubtful or disinterested in His human, but a faith that accepted Him as He was, His divinity elevating His humanity to heights of holiness and union and accepted by the believer through that humanity.

St. Mark's gospel has been characterized as a "passion narrative with an introduction." The three concluding chapters (14–16) devote 139 verses to the final saving drama — roughly 20% of the whole.

Mark begins his gospel abruptly where the earliest preachers of Christianity had begun: with John's baptizing activity. By verse 9 he is into the baptism and temptation of Jesus, by 14 he has come to the opening of the Galilean ministry (after John's imprisonment) and the call of the disciples.

A series of Capernaum-centered activities follows (1:21 to 2:12 and 3:19-35), though the identity of theme in 2:1 through 3:6 (conflict with the Pharisees, on whom He "looked round in anger and sorrow at their obstinate stupidity," 3:5) probably takes precedence over the locale as a unifying principle.

It is hard to discover any order after that. Chapter 4 is "at the lakeshore" and contains four fully developed parables, of which "the seed growing silently" (vv. 26-29) is unique to Mark. Jesus is roused from sleep "on a cushion in the stern" toward the close of the chapter (v. 38) and calms the storm both in their hearts and on the sea.

Particular days stand out in Mark, notably this one which contains the crossing of Gennesaret in both directions. The Gerasene swine episode takes place at the farther shore and the Jairus'-daughter and hemorrhaging-woman unit (the so-called "miracle within a miracle") on the western or nearer side.

After His rejection in the Nazareth synagogue (6:1-6), Jesus sends out the Twelve on mission. They come back and report to Him (v. 30) all that they had taught (*edidaxan*, a verb usually reserved to Him), and He retires, first with them (6:31) for a little respite from the activity that allowed them no time even to eat, and later alone (7:24) where in "Tyre and Sidon" He tries unsuccessfully to go unrecognized.

## The God of compassion

Mark's gospel is a gospel of compassion. Both multiplications of loaves have a place in it (6:34-44 and 8:1-9). Pity is given as the Lord's motive for the two miracles, though in the first instance it is clearly His concern for their shepherd-less condition that moves Him to instruct and then to feed them.

In Syro-Phoenicia, the Decapolis, and "Dalmanutha" (that textual riddle, possibly a dittograph in Aramaic of the phrase "into the district" which immediately precedes it in Greek, 8:10), He is compassionate too, but the more noteworthy point is that He is retreating from the Jews.

Once He receives from Peter the affirmation of faith that He is the Christ (8:21), He proceeds to insist to His companions His need to suffer and to die (8:31; 9:30; 10:33). The journey to Jerusalem is begun, with the Master *teaching* all the way now. *Kerygma* or miraculous proclamation of His saving role is largely put behind Him. He has a work to do, and Mark wastes little time bringing Him "on the way going up to Jerusalem" to do it (10:32).

Mark wrote his gospel at Rome, dependable tradition tells us, at the urging of the Christian community there. This is easy to believe. Greek was a language proper to Rome so there is no problem on that score; more than that, Mark's Greek has a number of Latin loan-words. What is unmistakable is the Semetic character of his gospel.

It has been said that our age has an affinity for Mark because he is simple and direct. This may be true. It is at least worth noting that when Mark does choose to describe an incident he does not deal with it briefly, rather the contrary. The great feature of his account is not its miraculous element nor even its "picturesqueness," so universally remarked, but that it is a gospel of suffering. Christ for Mark is the Savior victorious precisely in virtue of His humiliations.

This is a matter of no small importance. Mark calls our Lord "the son of Mary" once (6:3 — no other evangelist does this), "the Lord" sparingly, "Rabbi" three times, and "Teacher" eleven.

Jesus is "the son of Man" for Mark, however, fourteen times. All but two of these uses (2:10 and 28) occur after Peter's confession of faith in Him. In each of the latter cases Jesus claims the title Himself. He takes the Aramaic *bar nasha*, son of man, which connotes little more than "weak human," and welds it cleverly into the Old Testament conception of the Lord's "Suffering Servant" (Is. 52:13 to 53:12). This is true in nine of the twelve cases; in the other three the Books of Daniel (chapter 7) and Enoch are echoed: there what is connoted is the triumphant "son of Man" returning at the end.

Mark is just as certain of Christ's divinity as he is of His suffering humanity. He is the "son of God" five times for Mark, notably in the high priest's challenge (14:61) and the centurion's exclamation (15:39); but there is also the divine voice calling Him "Son" in the baptism and transfiguration narratives.

Much more important than the term, however, is the fact. Jesus is described as entertaining every human emotion in Mark, so that the casual reader might think that this pen-portrait of a sensitive man predominates.

Yet the mighty power (*dýnamis*) of God is never absent from His slightest word or work. Messiahship alone will not do to explain the person of Jesus in Mark. In this second gospel He is, quite simply, God's Son come down from heaven.

The Christ of Mark yields nothing to the Christ of John. In both He is the sovereign Lord proclaimed by Catholic faith, truly God and truly man. In Mark he is attractive beyond compare, an evidence of the Spirit's peerless work of inspiration from the earliest days of the Church's preaching.

# THE RESURRECTION IN MARK

## David J. Bowman, S.J.

To understand the importance that the resurrection of Jesus Christ has in the New Testament it is imperative to understand its importance in the lives of the first official witnesses. It was for them an experience that literally changed their world, and ours. Probing deeper, we can better appreciate this apostolic experience the more fully we appreciate their sense of utter loss during the period that intervened between the Master's death and His resurrection. Our own shocked sense of loss on the occasion of the violent, sudden death of our president can give us some gauge to measure that of the Lord's followers.

The deep sorrow of the apostles was, of course, turned into a correspondingly deep joy when they heard the crucial tidings: "He is risen!" These tidings, the good news of victory, became the "gospel," the central message preached by the apostles and their successors to the end of time. It is our intention here to see just how the resurrection has conditioned the composition of the first of the canonical Gospels, that of St. Mark.

### Mark's Gospel in general

This Gospel is Mark's attempt to tell how the good news of Jesus Christ began, and follows the same broad outline as the Gospels of Matthew and Luke, as also of Peter's speeches in the book of *Acts*. In it the kingdom of God is not yet at hand, above all not in any earthly or political institution, but is mainly eschatological even though "the end is not yet" (17:7). Very likely the account is influenced by the expectation of an imminent parousia, and, like the earthly sermons in *Acts*, dwelt on the death and resurrection as the great reassuring fact of belief.

Mark's own post-pentecostal faith in the risen Christ as Son of God (1:1) must underlie the pre-paschal structure of his Gospel. Despite this fact, Jesus of Nazareth in *Mark* is an almost hidden God, seeming only human but mani-

Published originally in *The Bible Today*, 1 (1964), 709-13. Reprinted by permission of the publisher.

festing equality with Yahweh for those with eyes to see and faith to believe. In the daily events of Jesus' life, externally so limited and human (cf. Philemon 2:5f), Mark shows his readers the way to resurrection-glory and the Name given in the added conclusion: Lord. He never has any disciple make an act of divine faith in Jesus; the closest such act is put in the pagan Roman's mouth at the Cross after Jesus' death — a surprising thing for the Roman community to do. Mark's own belief is clear from the first line, which is a title and a proclamation, but we almost never perceive traces of that belief in the account. Like Jesus' Godhead-glory, it remains hidden beneath the rather pedestrian phrases about untheologized events.

## Impact of the resurrection story in Mark

That belief, however, acts as a suffusing light through the Gospel, and finally bursts into full glow in the brief resurrection-account of chapter sixteen. Whatever be the truth about the original ending, the impact of this resurrection story on the believing reader is sharp and decisive: this Jesus who taught and healed, who did works of power in Galilee and predicted His own death as well as his own resurrection . . . this same Jesus is risen and is "Lord" (16:19), or "Son of God" (1:1), for the rising from the tomb manifests the Father's acceptance of Him as an equal. His entire life-passion-death, then, is illumined by the Easter-dawn of faith. The messianic secret is finally revealed by this perfect manifestation of the Father's good will in this His Son, who was equal to Yahweh all along. During mortal life, His messianic character was one of human action, as a Jew and an artisan, as Mary's son and a Nazareth neighbor, as teacher and victor over demons and death. Mark's resurrection story ends the secret and enriches its contents: Jesus was Son of God all the time, showing men the wondrous truth about human life.

## Mark 1:2–8:29

In the first of the two usual large divisions of this Gospel up to chapter sixteen the author describes Jesus' struggle against multiple death (cf. Rom. 5:12f). The man from Nazareth combats and overcomes demonic control of human life. He fights ignorance and illness, diabolic possession and human malice, prejudice and pharisaism. These things belong to the kingdom of death, but the life-giving Christ conquers them and is finally recognized as such by Peter (8:29). This is the Anointed One, the Davidic kingly victor sent by God into the world!

## Mark 8:30–15:47

The second large division contains the threefold prediction of the integral passion-event, including resurrection each time. The Markan community told it this way, and so should we — never omitting the resurrection from any salvation account, for without it the redemption is simply unreal. With each of the predictions the apostle Peter appears closely connected, for the deepening of our faith. In 8:31-34, the apostle's proclamation of Jesus as the Christ is followed immediately by the first prediction of the passion, which draws from Peter a chiding and from Jesus in turn a rebuke. Peter seems to attend only to the idea of suffering and death; he has no amazement at the thought of resurrection. We seem to learn from this how dismal mere death must be without the saving glory of resurrection.

The transfiguration follows, a mysterious event, after which the three apostle-witnesses wonder about the resurrection, asking themselves what "after he shall have risen from the dead" might mean (9:9). No answer is given. The second prediction of the passion occurs soon after (9:29-31), yet "they did not understand the saying and feared to ask him." Such fear is perhaps reflected in the women's fear in 16:8, the present ending of Mark's own Gospel. Until they actually perceived Him risen, they did not understand, and so feared — as do we when we think only of death without the glory of risen life.

The third prediction is made to the Twelve on their way to Jerusalem, to the Temple and Golgotha, to the tomb and glory. Mark's account situates it after Peter's "we have left all and followed thee" (10:28), and again ascribes fear to them, although this time in the verse immediately preceding the prediction. More detailed than the other predictions, this account is perhaps in part *ex eventu*, and ends with the familiar theme: "and on the third day he will rise again" (10:34).

No further reaction of the disciples is mentioned; nowhere does the Gospel mention the strengthening that assurance of resurrection would have given men fearful of death for the king. We seem to be in contact with their worry, with their emptiness of mind and heart in the face of tragic death — and this in spite of the recurrence of the resurrection-theme in the story.

## Two other incidents

In 10:35-45, James and John ask for special honors "in thy glory," so Mark seems to indicate that they thought they understood at last. They soon learn the truth, however: they shall suffer with Him, but glorification remains uncertain for now. The indignation of the others must have humiliated them: Mark has Jesus take the occasion to teach them all the great new truth: "the Son of Man has come not to be served, but to serve, and to give his life. . . ." (10:45). Humble service is the way to glory. This is Mark's way of repeating his theme: the hidden Son of God manifests Himself in ordinary human life, even in lowly service of others, but as the salvation of men.

Another example of what resurrection-faith added to Mark's good tidings occurs in the Eucharistic meal (14:17-31) which contains the institution story in Mark's own way. The liturgical style is familiar from the multiplication stories of chapter eight, "took . . . blessed . . . broke . . . gave . . . ," but the cup is an addition, of course. The only eschatological remark attributed to Jesus in this Gospel occurs here, ". . . . until that day when I shall drink it new in the kingdom of God." The Roman community was drinking the sacrament of His Blood in the realized kingdom of the post-pentecostal Church, and could easily ascribe present salvation to the reception of this New Covenant Blood as the sign of Christ's new kingdom.

This supper-story is followed by another prediction: "But after I have risen, I will go before you into Galilee" (14:28). Liturgical sacrificial meal . . . eschatological kingdom . . . risen Christ leading to Galilee — this Gospel seems to connect these elements deliberately. Christians who told and heard this story at Rome in the first century could hardly miss the significance of this connection: Galilee is the whole world, exemplifying all areas of human life. Liturgical contact with the Body and Blood of the risen Redeemer gives new life to all who see Him in Galilee — in their faith-filled, varied human lives.

This second large division of the Gospel ends in the double climax of 14:62, "I am . . . and you shall see the Son of Man . . . ," and 15:39, "Truly this man was the Son of God." The Roman story left even the faithful women "at a distance." The bleakness of death takes hold of the account. Only Joseph of Arimathea is said to act; the others are gone from the scenes, except two women named Mary — neither of them His mother. Even these were merely "looking on and saw where he was laid" (15:47).

## The Christian reality: Mark 16:1-8

But the Gospel does not and cannot end with a cadaver in a tomb. A "gospel" is Good News, and the heart of the news is: He is risen! (16:6). "Go, tell his disciples and Peter that he goes before you into Galilee. You shall see him there, as he told you."

Again Mark brings Peter into the story, just after the denial; again he indicates the theme: crucifixion, then glory. The women fear and say nothing. If this is the original ending, as is possible but not certain, Mark seems to be saying to us: Jerusalem failed Him, so He returns to the site of His first ministry, Galilee. "Go, tell them . . . " — tell the world outside Zion that Christ is savior not merely of the Jews but of all men. Where He lived and taught and did His wondrous works, there He now appears as risen, as Lord indeed and acknowledged as such in faith. You faithful, wherever you are in Galilee, re-read the gospel now. Go back to Galilee and find Him there, your Lord.

The dignity and restraint of this narrative reassure us who have not seen and have believed. Thirty years after the event, thirty years of prayer and joy and martyrdoms and hope, the Roman Gospel still maintains a simplicity and unadorned truth that makes this account speak to our condition. The "young man in a white robe" is a prophetic figure; scholars conjecture he is an angel, or Christ, or a saint, or just a young man. His prophetic message is the same for the women and for us: "See, he is risen, he is not here." In 14:28 Jesus promised to meet the disciples in Galilee after rising; this is the reminder and the fulfillment. God is faithful, and so is Jesus.

"Trembling and fear" seized the women. They were beside themselves, unable to collect their thoughts. And yet the fear of the women in 16:8 must have been a far different fear from that of Calvary. It was a reverential ecstatic awe, in all likelihood, and a consequent inquietude at the thought of trying to communicate the great news to the rest, even to the other women. Who would listen to them just now? Later perhaps, after they all saw Him in Galilee, but here in Jerusalem, at the death-place, they have only fear.

## The added conclusion: Mark 16:9-20

The inspired conclusion in the last verses of our Gospel seems to be a composite drawn from other scriptural sources. It strongly stresses the resurrection event. "He upbraided them for their lack of faith . . . in that they had not believed those who had seen him after he had risen" (16:14). "So then the Lord, after he had spoken to them, was taken up into heaven, and sits at the right hand of God" (16:19). We glimpse the apostolic and baptismal creed in these verses, and thank God for our faith. This added conclusion stamps in greater detail the impact of the resurrection on the reader: Jesus of Nazareth showed how a divinely human life can be lived, for all the time He was "the Lord," even in undergoing the vagaries and penalties of human existence, even to passion and violent death. So we try to imagine the difference made by the resurrection-story for those re-reading the Gospel as *didache*. Galilee becomes "the whole world"; the events in Galilee become significant for all men, and for us, too.

## Our Christian faith

Of one man and only of Him is that soul-tearing prayer true. "Christ is risen" was at Rome, and is for us, the Christian cry of triumph, joy, and relief. Jesus' body no longer lies in stony silence or beneath green branches. His hopes and fears and great human love have not been stifled on earth, so as to live on only as Camelot-memories. "He has risen. He is the Lord!" remains our Christian proclamation of faith in God's salvation worked in His Son for us. The risen body-soul belongs to God our Savior, the Lord. The teaching therefore is true; the life is love; the glory is gained. "Go, tell everyone!"

And the Lord is still working in us and confirming our preaching by the signs that follow now: sacramental life and Christian love. All our lives we shall thank God for Mark's message and that of our weekly Easter: "The Lord is with you. Go, tell the world!"

# THE PREACHING WITHIN THE PREACHING

William F. J. Ryan, S.J.

In *Hamlet*, while Shakespeare with his hero's aid declares that he "holds the mirror up to nature," the hero of the drama himself holds another mirror up to show the king and queen their unnatural images. The play within the play brings home incisively to Claudius and Gertrude, and thus to the audience as well, the

Published originally in *The Bible Today*, 1 (1963), 457-64. Reprinted by permission of the publisher.

purport of Hamlet's intriguing, and consequently the purport of the whole play.

St. Mark in his Gospel preaches Jesus Christ, and he preaches Him precisely as Jesus-who-preaches. Mark presents the *kerygma* of Jesus as a preaching within a preaching in which Jesus speaks not only to a Jewish audience of 2000 years ago but also to every person who will ever read or hear Mark's Gospel. Mark preaches so that Jesus can preach.

The first words of Mark's Gospel serve as a prologue which proclaims the sum and scope of his Gospel: "The beginning of the good news of Jesus Christ, the Son of God" (1:1). Mark here enunciates the act of faith which he would have his reader also enunciate. The title in these words of proclamation, "Jesus Christ (or the Messiah), the Son of God," recurs twice again in the Gospel, once at Caesarea Philippi when Peter declares Jesus to be the Messiah, and then on Calvary when the Roman centurion confesses Jesus to be the Son of God. Thus the truth that Jesus is the divine Messiah, Mark asserts at the beginning, middle, and end of his Gospel drama. Mark's prologue, "Jesus Christ, the Son of God," and the confessions of Peter and the centurion bracket the Gospel, and stand as its benchmarks to point out how faith can find Jesus.

## Preaching, the identity of Jesus, and faith

The first section, from the prologue to Peter's confession (1:1–8:29), presents Jesus who is preaching and working miracles to win faith in Himself. Up to Peter's profession of faith in Jesus as the Messiah (8:29), there are other episodes in which different men illustrate the preaching and faith theme by acting out their faith or lack of it. But when Peter states that Jesus is the Messiah, one of the main *evangelii personae* has made the perfect response to the preaching of Jesus. Peter is not only the spokesman for the faith of the Twelve, but for that of the reader as well.

The heart of Mark's message is expressed in 7:1–8:33. Its conclusion, Peter's confession, serves both as a climax to what goes before and as a prologue to what follows. In this dramatic part, Mark has arranged three miracles and an insolent challenge of the Pharisees as the *mise en scène* for Peter's act of faith. It contains the three elements which constitute the preaching of Jesus as Mark presents it. They are: the teaching of Jesus; the identity of Jesus, the preacher and wonder-worker; the belief or unbelief of the Jews. Insofar as Peter affirms that Jesus is the Messiah, the confession is the climax to the first section. But insofar as Jesus' preaching and works will demand more professions of faith from Peter and others too, this faith-event is a prologue to the second section of Mark's Gospel which culminates in another faith-event, the Roman centurion's profession of faith.

At the very beginning of his Gospel, Mark sets forth the three elements in the first preaching of Jesus (1:14-15). Then at Capernaum Jesus is preaching the "word" when four men lower a paralytic so that Jesus may cure him. Jesus praises their faith and heals the man (2:3-5). He sends out the Twelve to prepare the countryside for the good news to come (3:14-15). The worst sin a man can commit, he avers, is to resist and slander the faith-giving operation of the Holy Spirit (3:28-29). With the parable of the sower, Jesus illustrates the relation of preaching and faith (4:3-20). Then, after the eerie moment when He calms the tossing lake, the apostles in frightened undertones query, "Why, who is this whom even the wind and the sea obey?" (4:40).

But it is not only mortal men and women who marvel at Jesus. Even the mysterious world of the devils breaks forth with exclamations about Him. The first voice in Mark's Gospel that seems to acknowledge the identity of Jesus is that of a demoniac (1:24). And the legion of devils in the land of the Gerasenes in an unforgettable incident give their testimony to Him (5:1-20).

## Three signs for faith

The act of faith which Peter makes is of such paramount importance that Mark very carefully chooses episodes that foreshadow it and then reveal its full significance when it does occur.

The first episode is the cure of the deaf-mute in the area of the Ten Towns (7:31-37). (One indication that Mark may be employing this miracle for a special purpose is that the man cured seems to have been a Gentile. Mark almost entirely restricts Jesus' work to Israel.) In general, miracles are presented by Mark as examples of Jesus "preaching-in-act." Here, besides leading to belief in Jesus' true identity, this miracle is a sign pointing to a moment of clarification in the future.

The next episode, another sign, is the miraculous feeding of 4000 people (8:1-9). (Whether this miracle is a doublet with that described in 6:34-44 is not important here. However, its significance is important.) Certainly, the reader thinks, such a miracle should compel belief in Jesus. But Mark says that after the miracle, the Pharisees with incredible effrontery demand a sign from Him (8:11-12).

The third sign that a subsequent event must clarify is the cure of the blind man at Bethsaida (8:22-26). Again Jesus performs a ritual, again, perhaps, to point up the blindness of the man that He is at work to heal.

These three signs worked by Jesus and the shameless demand of the Pharisees all contain in various ways the three elements that Mark records in his Gospel: the preaching-in-word and the preaching-in-act of Jesus, His identity, and the belief or unbelief of those present. In order to define and emphasize these three signs and the brazenness of the Pharisees, Mark interjects two recurrent phrases of Jesus, "Can you not hear, can you not see?" This challenge rings out like a prophet's summons to faith.

When He has completed the parable of the sower, Jesus says, "Listen, you that have ears to hear with" (4:9). Then He quotes Isaiah: ". . . for those outsiders, all is parable: 'so they must watch and watch, yet never see, must listen and listen, yet never understand . . .' " (4:11-12). After the parables of the sower and of the lamp, He says, "Listen, all you that have ears to hear with" (4:23).

But these formulas are most effective when Jesus utters them immediately before the cure of the deaf-mute and the cure of the blind man. Just before He heals the deaf-mute, Jesus says, "Listen, you that have ears to hear with" (7: 16). And then, before the cure of the blind man, He says, "Have you eyes that cannot see, and ears that cannot hear?" (8:18). These repeated exclamations of Jesus serve, like the chorus of a song, to frame and punctuate these two miracles. Thus Peter's confession throws light on them, as it also throws light on the feeding of the 4000. And the request of the Pharisees, in its turn enables us to understand Jesus' own words.

## Peter's faith

The apostles in some ways resemble the deaf-mute and the blind man. Just as Jesus has performed a drawn-out ritual to cure the deaf-mute and the blind man, so He has labored painfully to open the eyes and ears of the apostles' minds and to unloosen the knot in their intelligence so that they may articulate their faith in him. The Twelve have not the faith to see and to hear the true mission of Jesus, and He must continually prod them with His vexing questions, "Can you not hear, can you not see?" Then suddenly, in a most dramatic event, Peter hears and sees: "You are the Messiah" (8:29).

But Peter has no time to settle down in the security of his messianic belief. Almost immediately he must make another act of faith, and his old faith, so to speak, is transcended by a new faith-event. Peter, and the other apostles with him, have advanced to a momentous act of faith. Jesus prepares to lead them further.

To His preaching Jesus now adds a new dimension, the concept of the suffering "Son of Man." Mark records after Peter's confession: "And now he began to make it known to them that the Son of Man must be much ill-used, and be rejected by the elders and chief priests and scribes, and be put to death and rise again after three days" (8:31). Jesus begins to concentrate His instruction on His disciples by explicitly teaching them that He must die and rise from the dead.

Once before, in His parable of the bridegroom (2:20), Jesus made a veiled allusion to His death, but here He unequivocally announces His passion and glorification. And though He has also used the title "Son of Man" earlier in His career (2:10 and 28), He now uses it to suggest the glory of His redemptive death and resurrection.

Whenever Jesus employs the expression, "Son of Man," He employs it, not just in its meaning as an Aramaic idiom for "the man," but with the fuller significance of Daniel 7 where it indicates a mysterious figure who symbolizes the Messiah and his people. Jesus probably chooses the title for its evocative power. In general, ". . . Jesus assumes the title when he is teaching his disciples the meaning of his mission and the mystery of his ultimate destiny. Thus, in Mark's eyes, it appears to epitomize that fuller instruction which the Master imparted to his faithful followers" (David M. Stanley, S.J., *The Gospel according to St. Mark*, p. 24, Toronto: Regis College, 1961). Jesus closes in the circle of His preaching so that, generally speaking, it now includes just His disciples. But the preaching and faith-elements are still vitally present. By the title "Son of Man" He enriches His identity for the faith of His hearers to grasp.

The first two times Jesus calls Himself the "Son of Man," He wishes to assert His divine mission. He cures the paralyzed man who is lowered through the roof in order "to convince you that the Son of Man has authority to forgive sins . . ." (2:10). The vicious thoughts of the scribes are a trenchant comment upon His claim: "Who can forgive sins but God, and God only?" (2:7). Then, when the Pharisees rebuke Him because his disciples plucked grain on the Sabbath, Jesus makes an assertion which, as all Jews knew, could be made only by one sent by God who instituted the Sabbath: "Thus it follows that the Son of Man is master, even of the Sabbath" (2:28).

## Son of Man and Suffering Servant

The title "Son of Man" does not appear again in the vocabulary of Jesus until after Peter's confession. Then Jesus resumes the expression, but makes a synthesis of the "Son of Man" concept in *Daniel* 7 with that of the Suffering Servant in *Isaiah* 52:13–53:12. By His modification of the concept of the "Son of Man," therefore, He opens wide a new vista of rich meaning in His messianic work, and sets His preaching in a new direction, and consequently men's faith in Him.

The new turn in Jesus' preaching confuses Peter. He cannot conceive of Jesus' disgraceful death, and with a self-assurance born from his recent pre-eminence at Caesarea Philippi, he confidentially takes Jesus aside to disabuse Him of His disastrous plans. But Jesus ". . . turned about, and seeing his disciples there, rebuked Peter: 'Back, Satan,' he said, 'these thoughts of yours are man's, not God's' " (8:33).

The rebuke is made to Peter, but it is also made for the sake of the other disciples. Peter has acted like Satan by conceiving the Messiah in too selfish terms. He would have the glory without the suffering. Jesus insists that faith in the "Son of Man" must include both. Mark then relates how Jesus summons His disciples and a crowd of people to explain to them the conditions of discipleship. The man who wishes to share in His triumph "when he comes in his Father's glory with the holy angels" (8:38) must be willing to share in His suffering.

## A glimpse at the Son of Man's glory

For the apostles, depressed by Jesus' announcement of His passion, the transfiguration is a stirring foretaste of the glory to come. The Father Himself testifies to Jesus and then commands belief in Jesus: ". . . hear him" (9:7). As Jesus accompanies the favored three down the mountain, He alludes to the glory of His resurrection, but at the same time He returns to the fact that ". . . it has been written of the Son of Man that he must be much ill-used, and despised" (9:9, 12).

After the transfiguration, Mark next records Jesus' encounter with the demoniac boy and his father. Faith again is the central point of Mark's story. The man falters in his belief. "But if you can do anything, have mercy on us and help us." But Jesus answered him, "You say, 'If you can' — everything is possible to the man who believes." At once the father of the boy cried out in tears, "I do believe, help my unbelief" (9:22-24). The transfiguration is thus preceded and followed by two faith-events: Peter's unbelief in the suffering "Son of man" and the heart-wrung cry of belief from the possessed boy's father. These episodes help to point up the significance of the transfiguration, a glimpse of the "Son of Man's" future disgrace and glorification.

As Jesus passes secretly through Galilee, He predicts a second time the imminent death and resurrection of the "Son of Man." Mark notes Jesus' concern as He tries to instruct them about the events to come (9:31). "But they did not understand his meaning and were afraid to ask him" (9:32). Jesus is on the road to Jerusalem and His destiny when for the third time He predicts His death and triumph. ". . . and Jesus was walking on in front of them and they followed him, bewildered and dismayed. And again he took the Twelve and began to tell them what would happen to him: Now, we are going up to Jerusalem and the Son of Man will be given up into the hands of the chief priests and the scribes, and they will condemn him to death . . . and after three days he will rise" (10:32-34). Once more Mark notes Jesus' care as He gathers His disciples to tell them very clearly what is about to happen. But they are filled with dismay as He walks ahead of them, symbolizing, as it were, by his position in front that he will lead and they need only follow, carrying their crosses. Later they will understand better what this means.

The memory of the transfiguration's splendor may still have glowed in the minds of James and John when they requested the places of honor in Jesus' kingdom. If it did, they have remembered only the glory of the transfiguration and have overlooked entirely Jesus' insistence upon His death. Mark has just recounted the third prediction of the passion, but it seems the two brothers have heard nothing, except, perhaps, the part about a resurrection. Jesus informs them: "You do not know what you are asking for" (10:38). If they ask for a share in His glory, they are asking for a share in His ignominy. Whether they know it or not, they are requesting to be like the "Son of Man" who "has not come to be served, but to serve, and to give his life as a ransom for many" (10:45).

When Jesus, to prepare for His entry into Jerusalem, sends two of His disciples to obtain a colt, according to Mark Jesus calls Himself "the Lord" (11: 3). Some scholars think that this is the first time in Mark's Gospel that Jesus, either by Himself or by another, is named "the Lord." At this eventful march into the Holy City, Mark apparently wishes to emphasize by using the solemn title of "Lord" that Jesus is on the threshold of His manifestation as the divine "Son of Man."

Jesus' apocalyptic utterances concerning the destruction of the temple are the next occasion when Jesus speaks of the "Son of Man." The ruin of the Jewish temple, a visitation of God, is one phase in the glorification of the "Son of Man" as the universal Messiah, and Jesus foresees His salvific work for all men pointed up by its destruction: ". . . and then men will behold the Son of Man coming surrounded by clouds with great power and majesty. And then he will send out his angels and will gather his elect from the four winds, from the ends of the earth to the ends of the heavens" (13:26-27).

## The suffering Son of Man

Three times during His passion Jesus uses the title "Son of Man." The first instance is at the Last Supper when He reveals that one of the Twelve has betrayed Him — the betrayal is an aspect of the Son of Man's vocation that He has already foretold (9:31; 10:33). "The Son of Man, it is true, is taking his departure, as it is written about him" (14:21). Jesus, by His reference to Scripture, is thus recalling the Suffering Servant in *Isaiah* and the Son of Man in *Daniel*. The second occasion is in Gethsemane before His capture: ". . . the hour has arrived. See, the Son of Man is being handed over into the power of sinners" (14:41). Thus another part of Jesus' repeated prophecy is fulfilled.

Jesus' final use of the title "Son of Man" occurs in His declaration before the high priest who has adjured Him to tell whether He is the Son of God. "I am, and you will see the Son of Man seated at the right hand of the Power, and coming with the clouds of heaven" (14:62). The response of Jesus is almost entirely a quotation of *Daniel* 7:13 which portrays the majesty of "one like to a Son of Man" advancing through the sky.

As before, in the case of Peter's confession at Caesarea Philippi, Mark employs faith-events to declare Jesus' identity. One is Peter's denial in the courtyard. The other is the Roman centurion's climactic profession on Calvary. The strong contrast between Peter and the centurion heightens the impact of the words of the centurion's act of faith.

## Failure and faith

While Jesus, on trial for His life, is asserting His identity, Peter in the courtyard, before the impertinence of a servant girl, loses his courage and refuses to acknowledge that he even knows Jesus. Peter has heard Jesus preaching and seen His marvels; he has professed his messianic faith in Jesus once before: he has witnessed the transfiguration; he has heard Jesus foretell the death and glorification of the "Son of Man." But it is not Peter who survives the crisis to assert his faith, rather it is a Roman soldier who has seen nothing but the suffering "Son of Man," yet affirms: "It is clear that this man was God's Son" (15:39). Whatever depth of meaning the centurion's words may have held for him, Mark intends his reader to repeat them with the same swift directness, *and* with their full theological significance.

This profession of the centurion is not to be disjoined from the rest of Mark's Gospel, the resurrection narrative. Faith in Jesus includes not only His crucifixion, but also His resurrection and enthronement. Mark therefore proceeds to complete his Gospel by showing the "Son of Man" in the glory of His resurrection which He had predicted to His disciples: ". . . he has risen. . . . He goes before you into Galilee; there you will see him, as he told you" (16:6-7).

## The glorified Son of Man

The epilogue (16:9-20) is written to enable the reader to find faith in Jesus. The writer underlines the importance of faith by exposing the residual core of unbelief in the Eleven. They cannot believe in the "Son of Man" even after the testimony of Mary Magdalene and the two disciples (16:9-13). When Jesus does appear to the eleven apostles, He upbraids them for their "lack of faith" (16:14). He then commissions them to preach the "good news" so that all men may be baptized and saved (16:15-16). The necessity of baptism recalls the "baptism" of the "Son of Man's" passion and glory in which He had once promised a share to James and John (10:38-45). For the sake of the reader, it is recounted that Jesus assured the apostles of signs that will testify to the power of faith in Him. Now at last there can be no doubt that Jesus is called "the Lord," the title of His exaltation. "So then the Lord Jesus, after he had spoken to them, was taken up into heaven, and is seated now at the right hand of God. And they went forth and preached everywhere, while the Lord worked with them and attested his word by the miracles that went with them" (16:10-20). Mark's Gospel then closes with the certainty that the presence of the risen Lord Jesus working in His Church is for all who believe in Him an earnest of His final glory to come.

As Mark's Gospel draws to a finish, the reader is left to reflect upon this story of faith. Certain episodes stand out clearly, especially the two great faith-events: the confession of Peter and that of the centurion. Like points plotted on a map, these two testimonies have indicated the course of faith in this Gospel narrative.

The very obtuseness of the apostles is almost enough to evoke an act of faith from the reader who wonders at their slow understanding. When Peter has his moment of glory, the reader rejoices with him. But if Peter has triumphed, he also immediately falls when he tries to dissuade Jesus from His passion. Peter's act of faith is not sufficient because it is not ultimate. In the remainder of Mark's Gospel, he has still more acts of faith to make, with the possibility of being called a "Satan" whenever he fails.

During Jesus' passion there is another "moment of truth" for Peter in which he could have professed Jesus but failed. Instead, a pagan Roman makes the proper response to the identity of Jesus. Peter does not advance from his faith of Caesarea Philippi to make the act of faith the centurion makes. Just as Peter's confession serves as a benchmark to point out the progression of faith in the first part of Mark's Gospel, so the faith of the Roman serves to show in the second part a new advance in faith from that confession.

When the reader comes to the realization that he, too, must advance from confession to confession as he progresses in his faith, he becomes more sympathetic to Peter and the apostles. Peter's act of faith is not sufficient, because no act of faith is final. A paradoxical aspect of faith appears. Faith, in a sense, exists only to be left behind. It is like walking. In order to advance, one's feet must always immediately leave the place they have just reached.

As St. Thomas says, a man grows in his faith when his intellect understands better what he believes and his will is more prompt and ready to assent (*Sum. Theol.* II-II, q. 5, a. 4c). So the reader also, just as the audience to which Jesus once preached, must awaken his will to hear and move his intellect to see.

Mark leaves his reader with the risen "Son of Man." He has shown him how to believe in Jesus, "the Lord," by presenting how others believed or did not believe in Jesus, who is the same "yesterday, today, and forever." The preaching within the preaching in Mark's Gospel once brought Jesus before the people of Galilee, Judea, Tyre and Sidon; still today it does the same for the reader. As Hamlet's play within the play is performed for a larger audience than Claudius and Gertrude, so the preaching of Jesus is intended for more people than His audience of 2,000 years ago. It is to catch the consciences of men from every era.

# THE EUCHARIST: A COVENANT MEAL

William E. Lynch, C.M.

The Eucharist is a many-sided mystery. Sacrament and sacrifice, it contains the Body, Blood, soul and divinity of Jesus of Nazareth. This the Catholic knows well. What is perhaps known only to the Bible-reading Catholic is that the Eucharist is a covenant meal. As will be made clear, one of the most important effects of a covenant meal is the strengthening of the bond between the participants. It is this bond, or union, that we wish to emphasize here.

## The covenant

A covenant is an agreement between two parties who may be either equal or unequal. It forges a union between two otherwise disparate parties. If two people wish to be more closely united, there is no better means than forming a covenant. Between intimates such as Jonathan and David, the covenant was so strong as to make them one soul (cf. 1 Sam. 20), or one person, as we would say. Surely, the Israelite has captured the notion of taking a foreigner and making him a relative; a stranger comes into the very life of the family or of the friend.

Of the several covenants of the Old Testament, that between Yahweh and Israel was the most influential for the history of Israel (cf. Exod. 19:3-8, 24; Jos. 24). Through it Israel shared, in a sense, the very life of God. ". . . you shall be my special possession, dearer to me than all other people . . . you shall be to me a kingdom of priests, a holy nation" (Exod. 19:5-6). Be-

Published originally in *The Bible Today*, 1 (1963), 319-23. Reprinted by permission of the publisher.

cause of the bond of unity effected by the covenant, Israel shares and must share the holiness of God. "Be holy, for I, the Lord, your God, am holy" (Lev. 19:2).

## The covenant meal

Frequently with the striking of the covenant a meal was given (cf. Gen. 26:28-30; 31:44-54; Exod. 24:11). The meal did not establish the unity between members, but it celebrated and strengthened it. This notion of giving strength is in accord with the facts: food does not *give* life, but it *strengthens* it. Food taken in common has a unifying power.

This eating together and common life brought peace to the members of a covenant. It is unthinkable that the two who had been divided and had now entered into a presumably sincere pact could remain hostile. In fact, the Old Testament looked with horror upon the man who turned against one with whom he had eaten: "Even my friend who had my trust and partook of my bread has raised his heel against me" (Ps. 40:10). Peace was the expected result of the unity achieved by the two who had entered into a covenant. In the psalm quoted above, the word correctly translated as "friend" is, in the literal rendering of the original text, "my man of peace."

The Old Testament covenant meal was an imperfect reality. It symbolized, but did not effect, the union between the two parties. Even the covenant between God and Israel was an imperfect reality inasmuch as it was conditioned. The union between God and people could be broken and the covenant annulled.

The new and perfect covenant, predicted by Jeremias (Jer. 31:31-34) and ratified by Jesus Christ, was a lasting covenant that would never be abrogated. The Eucharist, which is the covenant meal of this new reality, shares in its perfection. It both symbolizes and effects the increase of unity between the Christian and God and between Christian and Christian. It enables the Christian to share in the very life of God, to become a member of God's "family." As a result the Christian is united more closely with his fellow Christian. Rightly, therefore, does the commonsense of the faithful call the Eucharist "Holy Communion." This union leads to peace with God and to peace with all those who are similarly united by the covenant bond.

## The covenant meal in Mark and Matthew

The covenant meal, like so many other theological ideas, is gradually developed in the New Testament. St. Mark and St. Matthew speak of the covenant and allude to the unity that this covenant has effected. St. Paul makes their teaching more explicit in the com-munion of being. And St. John carries the doctrine to its logical conclusion in relating Christ's words about the resurrection to a new life and the mutual indwelling.

Both Mark and Matthew refer to the covenant when they relate the institution of the Eucharist (cf. Mark 14:22-24; Matthew 26:26-28). In both texts we read that the Blood of Jesus is the Blood of the New Covenant which is being shed for the remission of sins. According to the Semitic mentality, a covenant had to be sealed in blood. An animal was slaughtered and its blood sprinkled on the contracting parties. Thus, at Sinai, Moses sprinkled part of the blood of the victims on the altar, representing Yahweh, and part on the people. He then said: "This is the blood of the covenant which the Lord has made with you" (Exod. 24:5-8). The similarity between these words and those of our Lord is apparent. The Last Supper, therefore, was truly a covenant meal.

If a covenant meal, then the Eucharist must, as the evangelists realized, express the bond of union between man and God. Once it is realized that the Eucharist contains the Body and Blood of Jesus Himself, it is easy to conclude that by partaking of it the faithful are united in a real way with their covenant partner. And the union is obviously much closer than that achieved by the old covenant meal. In the latter the union was only symbolized; here it is both symbolized and effected.

The consideration of the Eucharistic Blood leads to a similar conclusion. For a Semite, blood is the carrier or the seat of life. Hence, to receive the Blood of Jesus is to receive His life. Jesus, sharing His Blood, shares His entire being and thereby establishes a bond of fellowship between Himself and the faithful. St. Augustine has placed these words on the lips of our Lord: "You do not change me into you as food of your flesh, but you are changed into me."

All these notions can be deduced from the words of the evangelists recording the event of the Last Supper, for they are based on the fuller understanding of the Old Testament background. Israel of old had become one family with God by the covenant of Sinai. Christians become a new and more perfect family of God by the covenant sealed with the Blood of Christ. Israel celebrated its covenant with a meal (Exod. 24:11); Christians do likewise.

## The covenant meal in Paul

The full meaning of this covenant meal was clear to St. Paul. The Corinthian Christians had asked him a twofold question: "Is it ever licit to eat idol-offered meat? Is it ever licit to attend the sacrificial banquets of the pagans?" Paul deals with these questions in chapters 8–10 of his first letter to the Corinthians. We are chiefly concerned with chapter 10, where Paul makes more explicit what the evangelists had implied: the Eucharist is a true meal effecting our union with Christ and with one another.

That Paul considers the Eucharist a covenant meal is clear from his reference to the covenant in recording the words of its institution (1 Cor. 11:25). The notion, therefore, of a covenant meal is in the background of Paul's thought throughout this section and must be kept in mind in order to appreciate his response to the questions asked of him.

Paul's answer, in brief, is that participation in non-Christian sacrificial banquets is unlawful. One of his arguments is based on the effects symbolized by these meals. Just as the Jewish people of the Old Testament attained a certain union with Yahweh by means of their covenant meal ("Behold Israel according to the flesh, are not they who eat of the sacrifice *in communion with the altar?*" — 1 Cor. 10:18), so, too, the pagan Gentiles attain a union with their gods by their sacrificial banquets. But these gods are false gods and their worship is inspired by the evil spirits, the devils. Consequently, the union achieved by these banquets is a union with devils. Since the Christians are united with God, it is impossible that they be united at the same time with devils (1 Cor. 10:29-30).

But Paul emphasizes that the chief reason for this prohibition is the union already effected by the Eucharist between Christ and the Christian: "The cup of blessing that we bless, is it not the sharing (communion) of the Blood of Christ? And the bread that we break, is it not the partaking (communion) of the Body of the Lord?" (1 Cor. 10:16). These words bring out the full meaning of what Christ had done at the Last Supper and show the basic impossibility of any other union achieved by any other covenant meal.

In this same passage Paul refers to another union that flows from the union with Christ and that is effected by this same covenant meal — the union between all Christians. "Because the bread is one, we, though many, are one body, all of us who partake of the one bread" (1 Cor. 10:17). The many grains that constitute the one bread are referred to in this passage. And just as the many grains make one bread, so we, eating it, become one.

But Paul has placed the greater emphasis on Christ. Since He is the bread and the bread is one, therefore His Body is one. In other words, Paul is saying: "Because we partake of the one Body of Christ, we become one with one another." This is but another way of expressing what he will say later in the same epistle: "Now you are the Body of Christ, member for member" (12:27). Christians become one with Christ and one with each other.

These ideas are similar to those that we have already considered from the Old Testament. The covenant has brought two strangers into friendship and union. The covenant meal has strengthened their individual life, and both symbolized and effected their common life. Paul has simply taken these Old Testament concepts and given them their fullest meaning in the light of the new reality.

We know, of course, that the actual union of Christians is begun in baptism. There we already become one family with Christ, partaking of the divine life. The Eucharist strengthens and increases this life of union. To establish any other union, therefore, would be equivalent to "provoking the Lord to jealousy" (1 Cor. 10:22).

## The covenant meal in John

Unlike Paul or the other evangelists, St. John does not use the word "covenant." That his explanation of the Eucharist, however, refers to the same essential union which the other authors had called a covenant is certain. First of all, the sacrifice that is necessary for the covenant is alluded to in the words, "The bread that I will give is my flesh for the life of the world" (6:52). The Eucharist is the sacrifice by which the covenant is sealed.

The entire passage in 6:51-60 emphasizes the life-giving qualities of the bread that Christ will give. Consider the assertion, "Unless you eat the flesh of the Son of Man and drink his blood, you shall not have life in you" (6:54). Unless man partakes of natural food he cannot live; unless man partakes of this covenant food he cannot live the covenant life. It is the negative form of a concept expressed positively in the next assertion, "He who eats my flesh and drinks my blood has life everlasting and I will raise him up on the last day" (6:55).

In these words of John's Gospel we find the fullest expression of the concept of unity through the covenant meal that was found in the other inspired writers. We find here the logical conclusion to all that had been said before. Since the Eucharist is a genuine meal, it strengthens the life of the partaker. But since the Eucharist is the Body and Blood of Him who lives forever, it gives man the power to live forever. This perfect covenant meal will achieve the resurrection of the whole person, since the whole person is now part of the family of Christ.

An even greater emphasis on the unity achieved is found in the following verses of this same chapter. Christ says: "He who eats my flesh and drinks my blood abides in me and I in him" (6:57). In other words, by reception of the Eucharistic food a mutual indwelling is caused — Christ dwells in the Christian and the Christian in Christ. The nature of this union is even stated to be similar to that between the Father and Son: "As the living Father has sent me, and as I live because of the Father, so he who eats me, he also shall live because of me" (6:58).

In John's Gospel, therefore, we find clearly stated two effects of this covenant meal not expressed by the earlier authors. The one who partakes of the Eucharist shares in the divine life in such a way that it will effect his ultimate resurrection; and the union achieved by the Eucharist is so intimate that it can be compared to that between the Father and the Son. As we have seen, these two basic notions of giving or preserving life and forming a union between the parties of the covenant are inherent in the notion of any covenant meal. But the covenant meal of the New Testament has brought to perfection all the reality that was only dimly implied in its antitype of the Old Testament.

## The liturgy of the covenant meal

We can conclude this study of the Eucharist as a covenant meal by a brief reference to the liturgy of the Roman Mass. There we find expressed time and again the two notions of life and unity that are the proper effects of the Eucharistic banquet and that we have seen present in the covenant meals of old. The reality of the one family, for example, is found beautifully expressed in the *Our Father*, which we pray in union with Christ, the sacrificial Victim. Again, the breaking of the Host symbolizes uniquely and almost paradoxically the oneness that the Eucharist will effect: from this one broken Bread all will partake and become one.

# MARK AND MODERN APOLOGETICS

David M. Stanley, S.J.

After centuries of neglect the Gospel of St. Mark has come into its own in the twentieth century. The early Church preferred St. Matthew. The earliest known commentaries on Mark appear only in the fifth and sixth centuries; in the patristic age it was explained but rarely. As the second evangelist was thought to have abridged Matthew's more complete account, it was sufficient to study the first Gospel.

Mark, however, found favor with the late nineteenth-century critics, who regarded his work as a simple, untheological "Life of Jesus." The early twentieth century discovered the presence in Mark of the "messianic secret," a theme supposedly invented by the evangelist to explain away the inconvenient fact that Jesus was given the title of Messiah only by the primitive Church. Mark sought to justify this by insisting that Jesus' real mission went unsuspected during His earthly life, even by His most intimate disciples. The theory was an exaggeration, of course, but it did point out that Mark was truly aware of the mystery surrounding the Person of Jesus Christ. In recent years the study of the apostolic preaching has increased the popularity of Mark's Gospel and has shown it to be nearest to that teaching in form and content and in the picture it gives of Christ.

## The oral Gospel

We customarily use the term "Gospel" in the plural to signify four New Testament books. But the New Testament writers employ the word in the singular to mean preaching. The message announced a set of facts that had changed the world, giving men a basis of hope in place of despair. This "Good News" the early Church called a Gospel, a key-word in Old Testament prophecy (Is. 52:7-10), where it denoted the proclamation of Yahweh's definitive act of salvation ushering in a new era of salvation. This prophetic announcement had two essential qualities: it ushered in the Kingdom of God, and it was concerned with God's action in history.

Jesus' first disciples had heard Him utter just such a message (Mark 1:14-15); in Mark's words it was "the beginning of the Gospel" (Mark 1:1). After Jesus' death and resurrection the apostles proclaimed in Jerusalem the Good News of salvation which had become a reality through these two events (Mark 13:10; cf. 1 Cor. 15:1-3; Rom. 1:2-4). Only in the second century does the term Gospel come to mean a book. "Luke," says Irenaeus, "made a book of the Gospel preached by Paul."

But in the apostolic age the missionaries who preached the Good News of Christianity were the "evangelists" (Acts 21:8), and the Gospel was the official announcement of a set of facts which began with the work of John the Baptist

Published originally in *The Bible Today*, 1 (1962), 58-64. Reprinted by permission of the publisher.

and ended with Jesus' glorification. Peter tells us this when he defines the qualifications necessary to be an apostle. He must be one "who has been with us
all the time the Lord Jesus moved about among us, beginning from John's baptism until the day he (Jesus) was taken up from among us: to become with us
a witness of his (Jesus') resurrection" (Acts 1:21-22).

Note that it is question here of: (1) a well defined sequence of events, (2)
personal experience of these events in company with the other apostles, and
(3) solemn testimony to events perceptible by the senses and also perceptible
by Christian faith. Peter's sermon to Cornelius (Acts 10:34-43) exemplifies
these points.

## Apologetic aim of the apostolic testimony

We now see why the preaching of the apostles was called Good News or
Gospel. It proclaimed to the world new grounds for hope by providing eyewitness testimony to certain facts about Jesus Christ accompanied by the witness
of Christian faith which explained the redemptive significance of those facts.
Addressed to Jews and Gentiles, the apostolic preaching aimed at conversion
(*metanoia*) to Christ (Acts 2:38; 3:19-21). The Christian convert continued
to deepen his knowledge of Christ by assiduous attendance *within the community* at more complete instructions called the "teaching of the apostles" (Acts
2:42). Thus the apostolic testimony had an apologetic aim in two distinct ways.
It offered the non-believer reasons for accepting the Good News through Christian faith, and it gave the convert a "guarantee," as Luke calls it, of what he
had heard in the apostolic catechesis (Luke 1:4).

We have several samples of Peter's preaching (Acts 2:14-39; 3:12-26; 10:
34-43) which tell us Peter's conception of the oral Gospel. But was Peter's version of the Good News knowledgeable and authoritative? Peter was a disciple
of Jesus from the earliest days (Mark 1:16). Moreover, there is evidence
that he witnessed several episodes at which only some of the apostles were present. He saw the raising of Jairus' daughter (Mark 5:37), Jesus' transfiguration
(Mark 9:2-8), Jesus' agony in Gethsemani (Mark 14:33). He accompanied John to prepare the Last Supper (Luke 22:8) and to witness Jesus' trial
before the Sanhedrin (John 18:16). Finally, the authority of Peter's Gospel is
heightened immeasurably by his position of privilege within the apostolic college. The first half of Acts clearly attests to Peter's primacy in the Church con-
ferred on him by Jesus Himself (Matthew 16:18). Most striking proof of this
is offered by Luke's assertion that, after Christ's ascension, people had recourse
to Peter for cures (Acts 5:15) in the same way they had had to Jesus during
His earthly life (Mark 6:56). This man who had, in the eyes of all, evidently
replaced Christ within the Christian community was certainly a reliable as well
as an informed witness to the Good News.

## Mark records Peter's preaching

Before we can accept Mark's book as an accurate and faithful record of the
events proclaimed in the oral Gospel, we must investigate our evangelist's connection with the apostolic preachers.

Two preliminary indications speak in Mark's favor. The events he records fall within the period of time covered by the apostolic preaching, i.e., from John the Baptist's ministry to Jesus' glorification. In this respect he remains closer to the oral Gospel than Matthew, Luke, or John. In the second place, modern scholars agree that Mark is the earliest of our four *canonical* Gospels, since Matthew's Aramaic Gospel has not been preserved. Mark is dated between 65 and 70 A.D.

Ancient Christian tradition, moreover, connects Mark's Gospel closely with Peter's preaching. Bishop Papias in the early second century asserts that Mark made Peter's preaching the basis of his book, a piece of evidence that is widely accepted today by Gospel critics. St. Irenaeus adds that Mark wrote his Gospel after the deaths of Sts. Peter and Paul. While it would be an over-simplification to conclude that Peter was Mark's only source, it is certain that our evangelist had mastered Peter's authoritative version of the Gospel since he was Peter's disciple and, according to Papias' testimony, accustomed to act as Peter's official "interpreter" for those who knew Greek but not Aramaic.

Our confidence in Mark's fidelity in recording Peter's preaching and other traditions about Jesus received from the apostolic eyewitnesses is further increased by another consideration. Mark wrote in the early Church as a member of the Church with the more or less conscious aim of preserving the Church's official traditions about Jesus for future Christians. That the primitive Christian community exercised constant vigilance to be faithful to the teaching of her Master is illustrated by an interesting episode (Acts 11:1-18) in which Peter must explain an action which appeared to some to be contrary to Christ's known will. He had admitted the pagan Cornelius and his family to the Church, even though they had never embraced Judaism. If the orthodoxy of the head of the apostolic college might thus be called into question, what hope could anyone else have of foisting myths and legends about Jesus on the early Church?

Paul's care in identifying his Gospel with that of the other apostles (1 Cor. 15:1), in appealing to Jesus' sayings to back up his own authority (1 Thess. 4: 15; 1 Cor. 7:10), and in transmitting the apostolic narratives of episodes from Jesus' earthly life (1 Cor. 11:23-25) reveals this same preoccupation with authoritative tradition. As for Mark, we know that his unassuming little book was universally accepted by the Church from the beginning, since both Matthew and Luke are in a very real sense the first commentators on Mark's Gospel.

Before we conclude our reflection's on Mark's reliability in recording the oral Gospel, we must include some valuable internal evidence drawn from two seemingly contradictory features of Markan style. On the one hand, Mark displays little literary competence. His vocabulary is limited and commonplace. His sentence-structure and his method of telling a story reveal no creative imagination. Yet surprisingly Mark's narratives surpass those of Matthew or even Luke in vividness and in wealth of detail. One has only to recall the picture of Jesus asleep in the boat with His head on a cushion (Mark 4:38), of the crowds who looked like "flower-beds" against the green grass (Mark 6:40), of the gleam of Jesus' garments at His transfiguration (Mark 9:3).

Again, Mark's account of the disciples' frenzied search for Jesus (Mark 1:

35-39) demonstrates a lively realism which the Lucan parallel completely lacks (Luke 4:42-44). How explain these qualities in Mark who, as a writer, is not in the same class with Luke or even Matthew? The best answer is that Mark, the man of little artistic skill or imagination, has carefully set down these details or reproduced the atmosphere of a scene noted by the observant eye of Peter.

## The Gospel according to Mark

By calling his story "the Good News of Jesus the Messiah, the Son of God" (Mark 1:1), Mark tells us how he planned his book. He wanted to tell his readers about the victory Jesus won in His earthly life by His death and resurrection, and how in the process He disclosed to us the divine mystery surrounding His mission and His Person.

This manifestation took place in two stages. Jesus revealed Himself during His public ministry as the Messiah, "a man accredited to you by God through acts of power, miracles, and signs" (Acts 2:22). Then by His death and resurrection He showed Himself to be the Son of God, fulfilling "the promise made to our fathers which God made good for us their children by raising Jesus" (Acts 13:32-33). Each of these moments in Christian salvation-history is set in the context of a distinct geographical background. The Galilean ministry ends with Peter's profession of faith in Jesus as Messiah, while in Jerusalem Christ is revealed as Son of God.

It is this twofold aspect of the mystery of Jesus which governs the two major portions of Mark's book. A brief introduction (1:1-13) presents John the Baptist's message as the link between the utterances of the latter prophets (cf. Mark 1:2-3) and the Gospel of Jesus. Jesus' Galilean ministry (1:14–9:1) serves to point up the various facets of the mystery surrounding Jesus. The question inspiring Mark's narrative is expressly posed, "What manner of man is this?" (4:41).

No other evangelist has set so clearly in relief the complete humanity of Jesus. He is represented as displaying the whole gamut of human emotions. He attracts men's unswerving loyalty by the most appealing qualities of human leadership. He learns many things by the ordinary avenues of human experience (5:31; 6:5-6).

But all the while Mark is continually directing his reader's attention to a mysterious dimension in Jesus' personality of which His associates become half-aware at times without ever comprehending it, i.e., His divinity. For the Christian reader, Jesus points to it inescapably by the circumstances of His cure of a paralytic (2:1-12). He announces it unmistakably by asserting His power over the Sabbath, a divine institution that dates from the creation of the world (2:28). He illustrates it dramatically by demonstrating His control of nature in the storm on the lake (4:39).

And yet the reaction of the disciples, especially on this last occasion, underscores the utter impossibility of an act of true Christian faith in the Person of Jesus until the Holy Spirit is given. "What manner of man is this?" Again, Jesus' parabolic method of teaching, the only reference to a discourse in this section of the Gospel (4:1-34), is for Mark another emphasis of the mystery surrounding our Lord.

As a consequence, the reader is almost unprepared for the dramatic avowal which Peter makes at the close of this first half of Mark's book. At Caesarea Philippi, Peter speaks in the name of all Jesus' closest followers, "You are the Messiah!" (8:29). After this remarkable pronouncement, which is the highpoint of the Galilean ministry, the second major section of the Gospel begins.

Jesus at once reveals to His disciples that His life is to end with His death and resurrection (8:31). Peter's automatic reaction informs the reader how imperfect as yet is his knowledge of the Master (8:33). Within a week of this episode the riddle of Jesus' identity is displayed in the transfiguration before the astonished eyes of Peter, James, and John (9:2-8). But this epiphany only leaves them wondering, "What does resurrection from death mean?" (9:10).

The scene shifts to Jerusalem where Jesus is acclaimed as Messiah (11: 1-11). He describes in the apocalyptic style familiar to the disciples from the Old Testament prophets (13:1-37) the future coming in power of God's dominion in the world. He inaugurates the New Covenant at the Last Supper (14:24). All this is simply an introduction to Jesus' final self-revelation in His death and glorification.

The Markan passion is sheer unrelieved tragedy; the disciples' hopes of an earthly kingdom and their too human attachment to their Master must be purged. By His solemn deposition before the supreme tribunal of Judaism, Jesus asserts His real identity, and provokes only horrified incredulity (14:61-62). But upon witnessing His death on Calvary the pagan centurion is moved to make an avowal which, in the light of the resurrection, will become the precious formula of Christian faith, "In very truth this man was God's Son!" (15: 39). The Easter encounter of the disciples with the risen Lord (16:1ff) gave full meaning to this expression by the revelation of Jesus' divinity.

## Mark's "messianic secret"

Here, then, is the way Mark exposes for the Christian reader his famous "messianic secret." More than any other evangelist he insists upon Jesus' desire to hide His true identity during the public life. He shuns publicity from those He cures. He remains an enigma to His closest friends. He forbids the demons to proclaim who He is.

What is the significance of this peculiarly Markan convention? For there can be little doubt that we are dealing with a convention which expresses, without falsifying, one real attitude of Jesus. Our Lord appears in Mark to ask the impossible by demanding that those who benefit from His miracles keep secret the grace they have received (cf. 5:43; 7:36). And in reality they do not keep it secret. The evangelist is simply underscoring the basic lesson of Jesus' whole career; the mystery of Jesus can only be revealed, as indeed it can only be grasped, by that Christian faith which is the immediate result of Christ's death and resurrection. Mark has not only preserved with the utmost fidelity the ocular testimony of the apostolic witnesses to the events of Jesus' life and death; he has also conveyed the genesis of the disciples' Christian faith which gave them the clue to the meaning of this salvation-history. This, we submit, is Mark's significance for modern apologetics.

A deeper, more precisely formulated appreciation of the historical value of our Gospels has been one of the happy results of the recent progress in scriptural studies. To employ these discoveries in the service of Christian apologetics it is not necessary, or desirable, that we renounce the traditional method of approach. To demonstrate the historicity of a Gospel such as Mark's we must still show that the evangelist is worthy of credence and possessed of sufficient information to control, directly or indirectly, the facts he recounts.

Today, however, we recognize, perhaps more clearly than hitherto, the need of showing that it was not merely one individual, Mark, who stands behind the narrative he records. It is above all the testimony of the primitive Church herself. Moreover, we see that an integral part of our apologetics must be the discernment of the *kind of history* Mark intended to write, both in his book as a whole and in the individual narratives. And this discernment will be facilitated by the investigation of the various *literary forms* which Mark has employed. Only by these means can we provide a reasoned basis for the faith of the Christian (*fides quaerens intellectum*) and offer to the open-minded unbeliever the full assistance that human reason can provide as a basis for conversion.

## C. SAINT LUKE

The oldest Christian tradition (Justin, Irenaeus, the Muratorian fragment) attributes the third Gospel to St. Luke. The evangelist seems to have been one of the disciples of Paul, as Paul's reference to "Luke, our most dear physician" (2 Tim. 4:11) would indicate. Also the Pauline account of the institution of the Eucharist (1 Cor. 11:23-26) is much closer to Luke 22:19-20 than it is to the accounts given by Matthew and Mark.

The Gospel is addressed to an otherwise unknown "most excellent Theophilus" (Luke 1:3; Acts 1:1), but the work seems to have been intended for the Gentile Christians in general. There is great stress on the universal call of mankind to salvation in Christ, and on God's redemptive mercy to the Gentiles.

St. Luke's Gospel has a large number of elements which are not in the other Synoptics. These he seems to have found in the sources, both oral and written, to which he refers in the prologue (1:1). The infancy narrative, a number of parables, and the journey narrative (9:51–18:14) are among the elements found only in Luke.

St. Luke, while maintaining to some degree the traditional framework, has altered its perspective. Hans Conzelmann [1] advances the theory that Luke was attempting to solve the dilemma in which the early Church, which expected a speedy coming of the parousia, found herself as she faced its indefinite delay. It is not probable that Luke was adopting an eschatological view very different from that of the rest of the primitive Church. Yet in his Gospel he does show the magnitude of the Church's mission, that of bringing salvation to all men without exception.

Luke shows salvation as God's gift to the poor and lowly of every nation. In his Gospel there is greater stress on renouncement — "leaving all things" (5:11; 12:49-53; 13:1-5), on prayer and the guidance of the Holy Spirit. Above all, Luke's Gospel is the Gospel of mercy and pardon, as several of the articles of this section show.

[1] The Theology of St. Luke (New York: Harper, 1961). Many scholars do not agree with some of the theories advanced by Conzelmann. For a more traditional view see Adrian Hastings, Prophet and Witness in Jerusalem (Baltimore: Helicon, 1958).

# THE GOSPEL ACCORDING TO LUKE

Gerard S. Sloyan

St. Ignatius of Antioch (d. 110) in his letter to the Christians at Ephesus (7, 2) describes Christ as the "one, only Physician . . . first subject to suffering and then incapable of it." The Greek word for physician which he uses is the same one found in Luke's gospel when Jesus quotes the proverb, "Physician, heal thyself." This is the designation by which St. Luke is known to the centuries, for St. Paul — whose companion he was — took the pains to send greetings to Colossae from a number of people, including "Luke the well-loved physician" (Col. 4:14). That usage largely settles the question of the profession of the writer of the third gospel.

Sixth-century legend made an artist of him, but that may have been because an image of our Lady had made its westward passage from Jerusalem to Constantinople. The Empress Eudoxia had found it. Clearly nothing less than an evangelist would do for an empress.

If Luke was a doctor his style should show it, many have reasoned. (But is this really so? With Oliver Wendell Holmes and William Carlos Williams you can deduce nothing.) The most serious attempt at internal criticism was made by a certain W. K. Hobart in the last century. His *The Medical Language of St. Luke* (Dublin: Hodges, 1882) sifted all the evidence and concluded with an affirmative verdict. Carefully, term by term, Hobart built the case for a specialist's vocabulary and delicacy of phrasing. Mary's virgin motherhood, persons afflicted with various diseases, and the bloody sweat of Christ all come into the argument.

The Lucan prologue, brief as it is, is not unlike the opening words of Hippocrates "On Ancient Medicine." The first century physician Pedanius Dioscurides, who was trained in Tarsus, greatly resembles Luke as he launches his *Materia Medica*: "Since many, not only among the ancients but also in recent times, have arranged discourses concerning the preparation and the efficacy and the testing of drugs, O excellent Areus, I shall attempt to show you that I have had for this subject an attitude which is neither vain nor unreasonable."

Yet the safest verdict as to the specifically medical character of Luke's gospel is, "Not proven," for the reason (as Cadbury demonstrated) that Greek writers who were not doctors were even more given to this usage.[1]

## Luke the author

There is no reason whatever to doubt the ancient attribution of the third gospel to the learned companion of Paul, and very little to suppose that a different hand than Luke's composed the Acts of the Apostles. He was probably a gentile,

Published originally in *Worship*, 33 (1959), 633-41. Reprinted by permission of the publisher.
[1] H. J. Cadbury, *The Style and Literary Method of Luke* (Cambridge: Harvard University Press, 1920).

but our best biblical evidence for that is the Pauline letter to the Colossians rather than Luke's prose style in Greek. There (4:12ff) Aristarchus, Mark, and Jesus the Just are described as "of the circumcision" ("one of yourselves," in another translation), while Epaphras, Luke the doctor (v. 14), and Demas are seemingly not.

The brother "whose reputation is high among our congregations everywhere for his services to the Gospel," a companion to Paul and "helper in this beneficent work" for the Jerusalem church (2 Cor. 8:18), is more probably Luke than any other, but this is impossible to prove. Ancient prologues appended to this gospel in the late second century and the historian Eusebius make Luke native to Antioch in Syria.

It is a much easier matter to establish the meticulousness of the third gospel, its special attention to the mercy of Christ, its use of Mark, and its citation of sources which were not accessible to either of the other two synoptic authors or John. The writer's intention is specified from the outset of his gospel. He means to do research and to provide "proof" (better, "authentic knowledge": *aspháleia*), which will strengthen the faith already professed by his reader Theophilus. He will be orderly about it though his meaning seems to be that he will respect the order of his sources.

He will be faithful to the testimony of "original eyewitnesses and servants of the Gospel." The former are the sole authentic testifiers to the Lord's career (Acts 1:21f); the latter are evidently those primitive Christians who had it as their special task to spread the gospel orally.

Who are the "many writers" who tried their hands at such written accounts before him? Doubtless those authors of Aramaic and Greek fragments of gospels whose widespread activity culminated in the canonical four of the New Testament collection.

If Luke is a Greek writing for Greeks (and surely the address to the "noble Theophilus" is only a device to ensure the widest possible circulation for his account), he has a keen ear for Septuagint-like writing when the occasion demands. That Greek rendition of the Hebrew Scriptures colors much of his writing. The possibilities here are two: either he comes upon narratives which have originated in Jewish-Christian circles of Jerusalem and Caesarea and incorporates them unedited, or else he has a fine ear for archaic speech and recasts his materials in "Bible language" just as a modern man might do long familiar with the phrases of the King James or Douay-Rheims version.

Yet Luke is by no means a mere compiler, whatever the case. He can write well whenever he chooses: better Greek than any evangelist, in fact. He improves on Mark's phrasing in those instances where he employs him (or uses some source common to both). He is generally faithful to Mark's order, though at times he will either write at greater length than Mark or omit passages entirely (see, for example, Mark 6:45; 8:26, the stilling of the storm, Christ's declaration on foods and defilement, the Syro-Phoenician interlude, the second miracle of the loaves, and the healing of the blind man by stages, and the parallel places or absence of any parallel account). When Luke finds a passage too Jewish for his readers' taste he will simply omit the need to explain it by de-Hebraizing it. His treatment of the beatitudes and the material from the sermon on the mount, generally, is an example of this.

## Luke's unique contribution

When we try to identify the most interesting section of Luke we must choose either the infancy narratives, which are unique to him and totally unlike Matthew in his treatment of the same period, or else his "Perean section." The latter is that long portion extending from 9:51 to 18:14, when Luke's gospel is not oriented as to place and time in any identifiable way. The more than eight chapters are very little related to the other synoptic accounts. Much of the richness that makes Luke to be Luke is found there: the parables of mercy, the miracles and other teaching of our Lord.

Roughly, the Master is headed for Jerusalem during all that time (9:51; 13: 22; 17:11), but we are given little chronology or topology. Luke's source was evidently ordered exclusively according to events and teachings. He trusts it so completely that he seems to employ it just as he finds it. Yet the Holy Spirit could scarcely have inspired him to a selection better suited to our needs, for without this "massive insertion" there would have been lost to the ages Christ's stories of the Pharisee and the publican, the rich man and the beggar Lazarus, the prodigal son, and the good Samaritan.

So many touches in Luke are proper to him that the mind falters at the prospect of a picture of Christ without his contribution. "You fool, this very night you must surrender your life" (12:20). "Or the eighteen people who were killed when the tower fell on them at Siloan — do you imagine they were more guilty than all the other people living in Jerusalem?" (13:4). "My boy," said the father, "you are always with me, and everything I have is yours. How could we help celebrating this happy day? Your brother here was dead and has come back to life, was lost and is found" (15:31f). "Zaccheaus, be quick and come down; I must come and stay with you today" (19:5).

Despite His mercies in Luke, the Master is far from a mollycoddle savior. In the parable of the talents or pounds in its various tellings the other synoptics have the stern master counseling profitable investment with bankers after the dereliction by the servants. Thrusting the delinquent subjects out into the night is the worst punishment reported. In Luke, however, Christ describes him as the perfect tyrant: "But as for those enemies of mine who did not want me for their king, bring them here and slaughter them in my presence" (19:27). God will never be vindictive as a bloody despot is vindictive — only just as God is just. Yet lest we foolish men fail to note that, we are given the picture of the enraged monarch which our poor imaginations so badly need.

## The infancy narrative

A great question in the authorship of Luke's gospel concerns precisely how much the first two chapters are the work of the evangelist: did he search out all the data and compose them completely anew, did he come upon them in a written source and finding them authentic simply include them, or did he discover their substance in some document and rework them in a vocabulary that is demonstrably his own through the rest of the gospel?

The question is an important one. Most of our knowledge of Mary's response to the mystery that enveloped her, and all of our knowledge of Christ's birth and its antecedents, are found there. Moreover, the three great pieces of New Testament poetry (there are many more, of course) are found in those chapters: the songs of Zechariah, Mary, and Simeon. It is no small matter to know whether Luke the hellenic stylist is equally capable of works of genius in the quite different, Oriental mold. Is he a superb Aramaist (Hebraist?) or merely a *transmitter* of these poems which have bitten so deeply into our lives of prayer and art?

R. Laurentin of the theological faculty of Angers discusses the question in his exhaustive study of Luke 1 and 2. [2] He observes the archaic expressions which none can miss, noting in particular that although universal salvation is to be one of Luke's great themes, in the first two chapters the spirit is completely nationalistic; the messianic joy is for Israel only. Even the phrases, "to shine on those who live in darkness, under the cloud of death" (1:79) and "a light that will be a revelation to the heathen" (2:32) do not outrun the spirit of Isaiah 40–55. Laurentin concludes that Luke has access to a Semitic document which originated in the theological circle of the fourth evangelist.

Uncertain of this type of writing, Luke translates it into Greek with the aid of the Septuagint (Greek) Bible. Yet so skilled is he that he puts his own stamp on it in the transfer. As a result the John-Jesus relation of the infancy narrative becomes the basis of the structure of Luke's succeeding chapter; the boy Christ in the temple foreshadows Him in His public role as teacher; and Simeon's prophecy, followed a dozen years later by the loss and anguish of the "three days" in Jerusalem at Passover time, both hint at the passion.

Luke's preoccupation with certain themes is ever-present, yet he employs his materials with a supreme delicacy. Thus, he is greatly concerned with Davidic sonship, with sonship of God, and with divine judgment, all in common with the fourth gospel. Quite distinctly on his own Luke emphasizes poverty, praise of God, prayer, the outpouring of the Spirit, and the importance of Jerusalem.

His latter interest is perhaps best illustrated by his employment of Mark in the composition of his post-resurrection narrative, which is marked by no violence to the facts of the second gospel but an utter silence on appearances in Galilee (Mark 16:7; see Luke 24:8 also John 21:1ff, which has no parallel in Luke). No, Jesus' triumph must be complete in the city of the Great King. In Israel's temple at the hour of sacrifice Luke opens his account. In the temple where the apostles returned from Olivet praising and blessing God continually he closes it.

[2] René Laurentin, *Structure et Théologie de Luc I-II* (Paris: J. Gabalda, 1957).

*Jesus the prophet*

Each of the evangelists portrays Jesus from a particular viewpoint. If for Matthew He is primarily the new Moses and for Mark a man who acts with the authority of God, then for Luke Jesus is above all else the prophet, that is to say the anointed spokesman and teacher. Moses was "powerful in his words and works," said Stephen before the Council (Acts 7:22). In Luke's gospel, "Jesus of Nazareth . . . was a prophet powerful in speech and action before God and the whole people," according to Cleopas and his fellow disciple at Emmaus (24:19).

On four different occasions in Luke, Jesus is designated a prophet: by His own lips in the Nazareth synagogue after He has read from a scroll Isaiah describing His anointing by the Spirit to proclaim salvation to the poor (4:24); by the crowds at Nain after the widow's son has been raised to life (7:16); by His own disciples who quote others when Jesus challenges them as to His identity (9:19); and again by Himself as He hastens to Jerusalem — where alone it is fitting that a prophet should perish (13:33).

Especially, however, is Jesus the new Elijah for St. Luke. This is a doubly interesting identification for as Vaganay has pointed out in his important book *La question synoptique*, every time Mark identifies Elijah with the Baptist, Luke takes pains to underscore Jesus as *the* prophet. An exception is Luke 1:17, where Gabriel describes Zechariah's son in terms of the "spirit and power of Elijah," but in Mark 1:6 (Matthew 3:4) the Elijah-like dress of John finds no parallel in Luke. When Jesus describes John as the Elijah who is to come in Matthew 11:12ff, Luke does not report it although he has ample opportunity (7:18-35; and see 16:16). After the transfiguration, Luke makes the same omission of Christ's identification of the Baptist with Elijah (9:36; Matthew 17:10-13; Mark 9:11ff). The greatest of the prophets is just as prominent in his account, flanking Christ along with Moses.

No, it suits Luke's literary purpose better to have the Thesbite more perfectly fulfilled in Jesus than in John who is the last prophet but one.

On the positive side, since silence is such a weak argument, there is Luke's account of the widow's son at Nain, which he alone among the synoptics gives (7:11-17). The parallel with Elijah's miraculous raising of the son of the widow of Zarephath is unmistakable (1 Kings 17:8-24). At Nazareth Jesus had likened Himself to both Elijah and Elisha in order to make the point that a prophet is not accepted in his own country (Luke 4:25ff).

When the Master sets out for Jerusalem in Luke's "Perean section," He sets His face steadily for the time of His "taking up" (*análempsis*). That noun of Luke's choice occurs nowhere else in the Greek Bible. It comes from the verb employed in 2 Kings 2:11 to describe Elijah's taking up in a chariot of fire.

Nor do the resemblances end there. I. de la Potterie has scrutinized them all in a recent study of the prophetical anointing of Christ.[3] There is the plea of

[3] "L'onction du Christ: étude de theologie biblique," *Nouvelle Revue Theologique*, 80 (March, 1958), 225-52.

James and John for fire to consume the Samaritan towns (9:54; see 1 Kings 18:37f, where Elijah sees the bullocks consumed in answer to his prayer). Our Lord corrected this intemperate zeal, but it is not long before Luke reports Him claiming to have come to cast fire on the earth (12:49) which He wills to be kindled. Again in this He resembles Elijah that prophet "like fire" whose "word burnt like a torch" (Sir. 48:3).

When a man asks Jesus to take leave of his kin (Luke 9:62), the very question which Elisha ploughing with his twelve yoke of oxen put to Elijah (1 Kings 19:20), the Master responds even more sternly than the ancient prophet, saying that whoever looks back is not fit for the kingdom.

All of these hints at fulfillment are clearly in the service of a great Lucan idea: the anointing of Jesus by the Spirit as prophet *par excellence*. For what is the peace preached by Jesus Christ, the word sent by God to the children of Israel (Acts 10:36), if not the salvation preached to Sion by an anointed one whom the Spirit impels (Is. 61:1; see Acts 10:38), so that God shall reign (Is. 52:7).

This unction is with *power*, Luke insists (4:14) — power over the demons (4:36), over bodily ills (5:17), but most especially to proclaim the good news (4:22). All of this marked the "spirit and power of Elijah": miracles and a total fearlessness in proclaiming the divine word. The greatest hopes of the Jews since the days of wicked Ahab were "this day" fulfilled in their ears (Luke 4:21) by the words of grace, that is, prophetic charism, which proceeded from his mouth (4:22).

"I will give you power of utterance [lit., a mouth] and a wisdom," said Jesus the great prophet (Luke 21:15). None could resist or gainsay this prophetic force, the "mouth of the prophet" of old. Luke takes care to tell us of Jesus' own mouth more than once (4:22; 11:54; 22:71). In the "acceptable year of the Lord" the Lord's Prophet will not be accepted. When violence threatens Him, He passes through their midst (4:30). It is not yet the designated time (4:13).

Throughout Luke's gospel Jesus is seen as "passing" through Samaria, beyond the hospitality of Martha and Mary, out of Herod's clutches — forever passing on to Jerusalem and thence to the Father's side. He enters into His glory because He has suffered thus (lit., "all these things," 24:26) as anointed Prophet and Servant of the Lord.

## Christ's universal kingship

Luke's gospel is in many ways the most satisfying of the four. He claims to be a careful historian and in a sense he is that, but man's salvation in Christ is ever his main concern; Luke's multiplication of place-names and personages is not to be identified with the technique of the modern historian.

He cannot be called exclusively an evangelist to gentiles. It seems true that he is interested in the Samaritans in a special way; it may be that he refers to Philip and Lysanias, ruling respectively in obscure Ituraea and Abilene, because he is addressing an Antioch-centered world (3:1). Yet he directs his attention to the Pharisees and their opposition to Christ as much as the other evangelists do. His concern for Jesus' affinity with Elijah is matched by a concern for Moses' authority and Abraham's fatherhood. The inclusion of the parable of the rich man in torment establishes that. Moreover, salvation comes to Zaccheaus precisely because he is a son of Abraham (19:9); the woman bent double for eighteen years, a "daughter of Abraham," is to be loosed from Satan's bond on the sabbath day (13:16).

Perhaps, then, it is Luke's universal outlook that recommends him to us. He fuses the Jewish and gentile calls with a perfect sense of the loving plan, the "philanthropy" of God.

Yet the third gospel is concerned with Christ's kingship above all — His eschatological kingship. The beloved Son is sent and killed, but like a rejected stone He will fall and crush His opponents; the Son of Man will come in a cloud with power and great glory; high priests and scribes say they have heard from His lips that He is the Son of God; witnesses say He has said He is Christ the King; He declares that Pilate has said it; Luke's inscription over the cross is rhetorically the strongest of the four readings given: *This is the King of the Jews.*

The reign of this King begins with His risen glory. There is only left to His disciples to announce it, starting from the royal city Jerusalem. He blesses them and goes back to the Father's side; they proceed to the work of proclaiming His lordship and kingship until He come.

If there is any danger of fear before so awesome a Master, Luke tempers it: "The Son of Man has come to seek and save what was lost." "Today you shall be with me in Paradise." "And while he was yet a long way off, his father saw him and was moved with compassion." "And drawing near he bound up his wounds." "And when he has found it, he puts it on his shoulders, rejoicing." "He ordered that she should be given something to eat."

There is neither Jew nor Greek, black nor white, rich nor poor, in face of a love like that. We cling to the differences that separate us only in virtue of disregard for the message of the third gospel.

# LUKE: WITNESS AMONG THE GENTILES

James C. Turro

When a man sets out to write a book, as a very general rule, he aims it at a specific audience. If he is not to be wide of the mark, he must have somehow achieved an image of his readership, what its besetting problems are, what

Published originally in *The Bible Today*, 1 (1962), 121-26. Reprinted by permission of the publisher.

ideals it cherishes, and so on. Only then can he effectively communicate with his readers.

St. Luke is the author of the Gospel that goes under his name and also of a book called the Acts of the Apostles. The burden of this article is to show that Luke's racial background and education, coupled with his studied efforts, worked together to qualify him to write for the people he wanted to reach. He was a Gentile writing chiefly for Gentiles. The tactic will be to examine various facets of Luke's life and work and from them to determine

a) how Luke's Gentile background served to advantage in addressing Gentile readers;

b) what steps Luke took to select and deploy his materials for maximum impact on these same Gentile readers.

## Luke's purpose

Perhaps at no point can one better judge of the Gentile quality of Luke's work than at its very center, that is, in its underlying purpose. Why basically did Luke write? Several theories attempt an answer to this question. According to one assessment, Luke wrote a two-volume work. In the first volume, the Gospel, he sought to portray Christ as the turning-point in the history of salvation. Christ is the final stage in the salvation story but the final stage is not the end of everything. It is really the beginning of a new era of salvation-history. This new era is the Church. Having reached this plateau in his argument, Luke was ready to embark on a second volume, the Acts, which should tell the story of the early days of the Church which sprang from Christ. Luke wanted to make clear that the Church did not come into being spontaneously; its roots lie in the past. Its seed was in Christ; it was the outcome of the life of Christ. This life Luke had reported in his first book.

The Church with its origins firmly anchored in Christ was open to all, Gentiles included. Luke is at great pains to emphasize this point. With this in mind he seems almost to minimize the opposition to admitting Gentiles to the Christian community. He gives the impression that the matter was speedily set to rights. Of set purpose, he shows that those who took the lead in evangelizing the Gentiles were men who had been with Christ. He wanted in this way to connect the apostolate to the Gentiles with Christ.

Clearly, the Gentiles loomed large in Luke's goal as outlined above. For that goal was, in part, to persuade the Gentiles that they could be certain of a place in Christ's Church. This in itself goes a long way toward explaining the Gentile orientations of Luke's writings.

## Luke as a Hellenistic historian

A careful scrutiny of Luke's philosophy of history and his method of writing it invites comparison with Hellenistic authors. Polybius, Plutarch and Tacitus among others come to mind as fellows of his, sharing the same view of historiography as he. Luke, it seems, preferred to view history through the screen of personality. For example, the story of the Acts of the Apostles is told in terms of the lives of Peter and Paul. Stephen, James and Philip figure too; they have supporting roles to play. Before Luke, Herodotus, Plutarch and others had indulged in this very practice of writing history by means of biography.

Counterpoised to what has just been asserted is the fact that one can find parallels for Luke's historical method in the Old Testament. This need not, however, be construed as ruling out any part which Hellenistic authors might have played in shaping Luke's mentality on history. Rather it shows that two ingredients went into creating Luke's historical viewpoint — one Jewish and biblical, the other Gentile and profane. The fact remains that in the area of historiography Luke is seen to be actively aware of the prevailing currents in the Gentile world. These he employed with effect in his discourse to the Gentiles.

## Luke and Hellenistic ideals

A dearly-held Greek ideal was the maximum development of human personality. In Christ, Luke saw the person who fully embodied this ideal. Luke tried to show that Christ as man, independent even of His perfection as God, exemplified the ideal of the perfect individual. He depicted Christ as strong, humble, wise, fearless, in brief as excelling in every virtue. Above all, in His relationship with God was Christ exemplary. Luke demonstrates this by his frequent allusions to Christ's life of prayer. More than any other of the Synoptics, Luke concerned himself with the prayer of Christ.

## A key-concept in Luke

Throughout the whole fabric of his Gospel, Luke attempts to show that the coming of Christ was not just an event in the history of Israel but an occurrence of worldwide relevance. Luke insinuates this by linking the events of Christ's life with secular circumstances. The birth of Jesus, for instance, is noted as having taken place during the reign of the Roman Emperor Augustus (Luke 2:1). In giving the genealogy of Jesus, Luke traces His descent not only as far as Abraham, as does Matthew (1:1-16), but beyond Abraham to Adam and even to God Himself (Luke 3:23, 38).

Christ came to achieve a universal redemption. He is for Luke more the Redeemer of mankind than the Messiah of the Old Testament. The evangelist lays stress on the fact that Christ held out redemption to all, irrespective of the privileges of a particular race or generation. There is a place in the Kingdom for everyone: for Samaritans (Luke 9:51-56; 10:30-37), for pagans (Luke 2:32; 3:6; 4:25-27; 7:9; 10:1) as well as for Jews (1:33; 2:10). The significance of Christ is cosmic, touching upon the lives of all for "all flesh shall see the salvation of God" (Luke 3:6). With directness and emphasis he makes clear that Christ sent His seventy disciples to humanity at large (Luke 10:1).

It is significant that Luke should omit the words quoted by Matthew: "These twelve Jesus sent forth having instructed them thus, 'Do not go in the direction of the Gentiles, nor enter the towns of the Samaritans; but go rather to the lost sheep of the house of Israel'" (Matthew 10:5). Gentiles could easily misconstrue this command and take offense at it. To obviate this, Luke passes over these lines in silence. Conversely, the parable of the Good Samaritan might prove comforting to Gentiles, showing as it does a non-Jew in favorable light. Accordingly Luke alone reports this particular parable (Luke 10:25-37).

## Style and structure of Luke's work

The third Gospel opens with a finely balanced sentence couched in refined and flawless Greek. One is prompted to think that the man who could fashion such masterful Greek prose must have behind him the better than average education which was readily available in a large urban center like Antioch or, as has also been suggested, nearby Tarsus. This view is bolstered by the statistic that Luke in his two books exhibits a larger Greek vocabulary than any other New Testament writer. There are about eight hundred words found in Luke which occur nowhere else in the New Testament. Renan referred to Luke's Gospel as "the most literary of the Gospels." Luke is a writer who is at home in the language he is using. He plys it with all the ease and grace of one who is writing in his mother tongue.

This conclusion is reached without losing sight of the fact that Luke's work is not devoid of Semitisms, turns of thought and phrase which are peculiar to the Jewish milieu. But when these occur they are sometimes to be explained on the grounds that Luke at that point is translating a Semitic document and, as it were, the outline of the original shows through in Luke's text. At other times, when a Semitic tinge is discernible, the explanation is that Luke is treating a subject which he found best to handle in Semitic style and idiom. As a master of style, Luke was remarkably versatile. It is also useful to bear in mind that there had developed in the Church by this time a Jewish-Greek vocabulary that was quasi-technical. With this evangelical language Luke would have been familiar, and would naturally have drawn upon it.

Very instructive are the topographical indications found in Luke. They strongly suggest that he is writing for circulation outside Palestine. Towns are located and identified in such a way as would hardly be necessary for Jewish readers. These would be sufficiently well acquainted with Palestine to know without being told the section of the country in which a particular town lay. It was for people unfamiliar with the geography of Palestine that Luke had to specify further the place names he used. The following are examples: *"to a town of Galilee* called Nazareth" (Luke 1:26); *"into Judea to the town of David,* which is called Bethlehem" (Luke 2:4); "He went down to Capharnaum, *a town of Galilee"* (Luke 4:31); "they sailed to the country of the Gerasenes *which is opposite Galilee"*(Luke 8:26); *"Arimathea, a town of Judea"* (Luke 23:51); "to a village named Emmaus, *which is sixty stadia from Jerusalem"*(Luke 24:13).

Luke also felt compelled to clarify for his readers other particulars of Jewish life and custom. For example in Luke 22:1 he writes: "the Feast of the Unleavened Bread which is called the Passover." Where Mark alluded to "the abomination of desolation" (13:14), Luke wrote more forthrightly: "and when you see Jerusalem being surrounded by an army" (Luke 21:20). Mark's expression, "abomination of desolation," would surely have been incomprehensible to Gentile readers.

There are numerous places where Luke substitutes a Greek word for a Hebrew one. In Luke 6:15 and Acts 1:13, Simon is referred to as "the Zealot." Elsewhere in the Synoptics he is called "the Cananean" (Matthew 10:4 and Mark 3:18). This latter term appears to have designated an extreme political faction in Palestine. However, as it stood it would hardly have been clear to one outside the area. The word Luke uses, "Zealot," is Greek and would carry an idea to a Greek mind.

In his narration of the crucifixion, Luke avoids the Aramaic word "Golgotha." Instead he gives its translation: the place of the Skull (Luke 23:33). Luke makes relatively small use of the Hebrew expression "amen." Matthew employs it some thirty times, Luke only seven. He prefers to use in its place such words as "truly" (9:27) or "in truth" (4:25).

Another instance of Luke's accommodating his account to the Gentile mentality is the addition of the specifying adjective "unclean" in the phrase "unclean spirit" (Luke 4:33). This would have been called for since the Gentiles had a lively awareness of good spirits as well as bad. There is a whole list of Hebrew and Aramaic words that turn up in the other Gospels but are wanting in Luke. Abba (Mark), Boanerges (Mark), Gabbatha (John), Emmanuel (Matthew), ephpheta (Mark), Korban (Mark), Messiah (John), hosanna (Matthew, Mark, John); also the phrases "talitha koumi" (Mark), and "Eloi, Eloi . . ." (Matthew and Mark).

Compared with Matthew, Luke employs few Old Testament quotations. Most of those that do occur in Luke are found in the speeches of Christ.

The Mosaic Law, of vast importance to the Jews, is seldom alluded to. After observing that it was obligatory for the Jews, Luke lets the matter rest (Luke 2:21ff, also Luke 17:14). The disquisitions on the Law which are found in Matthew, e.g., 5:17ff, are not encountered in Luke. The topic is ignored as having slight appeal and import for Gentile readers.

## Luke and Paul

Luke was the faithful companion of Paul. Paul makes several references to his association with him. In Col. 4:14 he indicates Luke is at his side; in Philemon 24, he refers to Luke as one of his fellow-workers, and in 2 Tim. 4:11, just before his martyrdom, Paul touchingly writes: "Only Luke is with me."

Luke for his part also hints at his companionship with Paul. This is the implication of the so-called "we-passages" in the Acts of the Apostles (Acts 16:10ff). By a sudden shift from the third person plural to the first person plural, Luke intimates that he began to accompany Paul from that point on. He must therefore have travelled with Paul on his second journey. He was once again with Paul on the trip from Philippi to Jerusalem as Paul returned from his third missionary journey.

One might also take note of the conviction of some of the early Church to the effect that just as Mark's Gospel represents the preaching of Peter, so the Gospel of Luke reflects the preaching of Paul (cf. Irenaeus, *Adv. Haereses* 3, 1; Eusebius, *Hist. Eccl.*, VI, 24, 4). There is a curious confirmation of this in the behavior of the heresiarch Marcion. Marcion appropriated Luke's Gospel to himself. The very fact that he did so presupposes that he considered it to be the work of a disciple of Paul. For Marcion had previously decided in favor of Paul largely because of the "non-Jewishness" of Paul's work.

By and large, contemporary scholarship has endorsed the judgment of antiquity regarding the influence of Paul upon Luke. One modern commentator finds in Luke "a general and indirect influence of Paul not merely in doctrine but also in historical matter" (H. A. W. Meyer, *Critical and Exegetical Commentary*, 269). Another has observed that Luke "exhibits the spirit of Paul" (A. Plummer, *Commentary on Luke*, xliii). Others have assembled a catalogue of Lucan texts that have parallels in the letters of Paul. Studies in the diction of Luke and Paul have brought to light a considerable number of stylistic elements common to both.

The force of this evidence is to reveal Luke as an intimate of Paul and as one who felt the dynamic impact of Paul's spirit and teaching. The link between the two strongly confirms the view that Luke shared in Paul's apostolate to the Gentiles.

## Racial background

In Col. 4:11, 14 Paul lists his fellow-workers. Luke is indeed mentioned but in such a way as to distinguish him from some of the others named. These are designated as "men circumcised," that is, Jews. By indirection, then, Paul testifies to Luke's Gentile stock. The evangelist himself also gives several indications of his Gentile background. This is the inference frequently drawn from Luke's rather extended treatment of Antiochian affairs (see Acts 11:19-27; 13:1; 14:19, 21, 26; 15:22-25; 18:22). The supposition is that Luke devoted so much space and attention to Antioch because he himself was a native of the place and had been a member of the Christian group that flourished there.

This conclusion is perhaps too broad for its premise but it is shored up by the testimony of tradition. The Anti-Marcionite Prologue (dated between 160-180 A.D) says: "Luke was an Antiochian of Syria." St. Jerome (about 400 A.D.) alluded to him as "a medical man from Antioch." Even before Jerome, Eusebius in his *Historia Ecclesiastica* had written: "Luke who was by race an Antiochian. . . ."

From Scripture and tradition testimony has been adduced bearing on the Gentile character of Luke's writings. It is necessary now to assess the accumulated evidence. It seems safe to conclude that (a) Luke was himself a Gentile who had been given an above-average Gentile education; (b) traces of Luke's Gentile upbringing abound in his work; (c) Luke allowed this Gentile background to influence his writing designedly, because he had in mind principally a Gentile reading audience.

The last conclusion must be tempered with some reservation. Admittedly Luke's address to the Gentiles was delicately articulated, that is to say, it was hinted at rather than explicitly stated.

Besides, the possibility remains that Luke did not concern himself exclusively with Gentiles but to a certain extent wanted to communicate with Jews as well. In any case some recent commentators have thought this to be so. Luke 16:19-31 is cited as an instance of the author looking in the direction of Christians nurtured in Judaism. This passage expresses an element which would gratify the sentiments of Jewish Christians. The Law and the Prophets are referred to approvingly through the medium of Abraham.

A final, summarizing statement. When in the life of the nascent Church, the Gentiles were ready to assume a role of increased importance, God provided an evangelist in the Christian community who spoke their language, sympathized with their aspirations, and consummately understood their mentality because he was one of them himself.

# "NOW IT CAME TO PASS IN THOSE DAYS . . ."

Eugene H. Maly

The biblical exegete, by definition, is directly concerned with the inspired text before him. While the theological clarifications of the Church of a later age will guide him in his interpretation, they are not his primary concern. He must determine, as best he can with all the sciences at his disposal, "what the writer intended to express," as Pius XII insisted in his encyclical *Divino Afflante Spiritu*.

For this reason the exegete must try to enter into the background and the mentality of the biblical author. He must divest himself of any merely modern idea about the meaning of a word or expression, about the literary form that is used, or about the meaning of the passage. But the search for the imagery and thought-patterns of the ancient writer is not always easy. This is especially so since the Church has rarely defined the precise sense of Scripture texts and because Christian teachers through the ages have been more concerned with doctrinal instruction and practical applications than with exact scientific exegesis.

Published originally in *The Bible Today*, 1 (1962), 173-78. Reprinted by permission of the publisher.

As one, therefore, who must answer the objections of a new age and furnish new approaches to eternal truths, the exegete must go back to the original sources of those truths. He must study them as they were given by the Church of the early Christian community. He must show how divine revelation provided a firm basis for the later theology of the Christian Church.

## Infancy narratives

In his article on St. Mark's Gospel in the first issue of *The Bible Today*, Father David Stanley showed how the primitive Gospel, or message of "good news," began with the account of John the Baptist preaching in the desert and ended with the glorification of Jesus at the right hand of the Father. In all of Peter's sermons the message is seen to be compressed within these two events (cf. Acts 2:14-36; 3:12-15; 10:34-43). Mark, Peter's "interpreter," has followed the same methodology in the composition of his Gospel. It was in the *public* life of Jesus that they found the material of the "good news."

This *public* nature of the salvation-events is worth noting. All the evangelists are concerned to mention the many witnesses to the teaching, miracles, passion, death and resurrection of our Lord (cf., e.g., Matthew 7:28-29; Mark 2:1-12; Luke 4:14-15; John 2:11). The early Church similarly stressed the importance of these witnesses (cf. Acts 2:32; 3:15; 5:32; 10:39-41). This is understandable in the light of the Old Testament's attitude on witnesses (cf. Num. 35:30; Deut. 17:6). Jesus, too, emphasizes this (Matthew 18:16). Clearly, then, those events that were by their very nature *private* events, such as the annunciation, the visitation, the actual birth of Jesus, could not fulfill, as such, the same role in the Gospel that the public events could. In other words, the infancy narratives present us, not with *kergymatic* events, i.e., proclaimed to produce conversion, but with *didactic* events, i.e., explained to deepen the Christian's faith in salvation-history.

## Luke's infancy accounts

We can suppose, then, that St. Luke had a higher purpose in mind than simply recounting historical incidents. His infancy narratives have an essential relationship to the salvation-history of our Lord's public life. It is not difficult to determine the general relationship. Clearly the central figure is Jesus Himself, with whom John the Baptist is placed in a parallel but subordinate position in the accounts of their annunciation and birth.

Moreover, Luke's frequent and skillful allusions to the Old Testament would have revealed to the practiced eye of the early Church his deliberate intention to emphasize the divinity of Jesus. For example, the child spoken of in Gabriel's annunciation is presented in the words of Zeph. 3:14-17, which, in their original context, refer to God. So, too, John the Baptist is, in Luke's mind, the messenger predicted by Malachi who would come to prepare the way for the Lord (compare Luke 1:16-17 and Mal. 2:6; 3:1, 23-24). Consequently Jesus is implicitly identified with Yahweh who "comes to the temple" (cf. Mal. 3:1). The divinity of our Lord, an early emphasis of the Gospel preachers, is thus more profoundly presented through the medium of these narratives.

Mary, too, has an essential role in salvation-history. Although the primitive oral Gospel had not developed the theology of her role, by the time that Luke wrote several of its aspects must have been thought out. By appropriate scriptural allusions again, Luke has the infancy scenes evoke the divinity of the Child through the emphasis on Mary as the eschatological "daughter of Zion" and the new Ark of the Covenant, where the divinity dwells (compare Luke 1:28ff with Zeph. 3:14-17; Luke 1:35 with Exod. 40:34-38 and 2 Sam. 6:9, 11).

Finally, we can note that the role of Jerusalem in these chapters accords with Luke's concern in the rest of the Gospel to show that in this city, the center of the biblical world, the climax of redemption takes place (this will be shown more clearly later on). But Jerusalem figures strongly also in the infancy narratives, and particularly as the climax of this "hidden" life of Jesus (cf. Luke 2:49). For Luke, these events of the early life foreshadow, and thereby give deeper meaning to, the events of salvation-history strictly so called. While they were not part of the official kerygma, they could throw greater light on that kerygma and so achieve their didactic purpose.

## The composition of Luke 1–2

For a better understanding of the didactic purpose of these chapters a few words will be said about their composition. While no scholar would deny to Luke the authorship of our two chapters as we now have them, there is considerable debate about their pre-Lucan development. Seemingly the best founded opinion is that Luke had before him a Hebrew account which he translated into Greek and arranged in accord with his own plan (for the translation he could have had the help of one more familiar with Hebrew than himself).

There are also some indications that the Hebrew account itself may have been developed over a rather long period. This would plausibly have taken place within the circle of St. John and his disciples. There are certain similarities between Luke's infancy narratives and the fourth Gospel that are striking enough to suppose that Luke was acquainted with the Johannine tradition. Thus both Luke and John share the same attitude toward Mary and John the Baptist; both center attention on "glory," the temple, the priestly element in Christ's vocation, etc. The Johannine tradition, then, would have been the direct source of the material contained in these first two chapters.

Ultimately, of course, the source would have to be Mary. She alone could have borne witness to the annunciation and to her own reactions to other events (cf. Luke 2:19, 51). Moreover, her connection with St. John (cf. John 19:25-27) would accord with the possible Johannine influence already noted. Between Mary's own original memoirs and Luke's composition of them as a prelude to his account of the "good news" we must, therefore, admit the possibility of several stages of development. But this would only emphasize the early Church's concern to draw out the full meaning of these events.

In the remainder of this article we shall consider some of the theological emphases to be found in Luke's account of the nativity of our Lord. We hope thereby to show what the sacred writer intended to express and what the didactic value of this central event in the world's history was.

## Luke 2:1-7, Jesus and John the Baptist

When we compare the account of the birth of the world's Savior with that of the birth of the Baptist, as the sacred writer intended us to do, one difference that immediately strikes us is the chronological setting of each. It is well known that St. Luke, more than any of the other evangelists, is concerned to place the events of salvation-history within the context of secular history. He thereby emphasizes the impact of these events on that history. At the same time, by varying references to secular history, he brings out the varying significance of the events he is describing.

In introducing the account of the annunciation of the Baptist's birth, Luke notes that it took place "in the days of Herod, king of Judea . . ." (Luke 1:5). This birth is of limited importance. John will carry out his mission among the Jewish people alone; his impact will be principally on those who are subject to Herod, king of Judea.

But the birth of Jesus is placed in a larger context of secular history. It occurs during the long reign of Caesar Augustus (30 B.C. to 14 A.D.), ruler of the "whole world" (2:1). It is because of an edict issued by the Emperor that Joseph took Mary from the obscure town of Nazareth to the equally obscure village of Bethlehem. While he doubtless mentions this census to explain Joseph's decision to go to Bethlehem, Luke could not have been unaware of the fuller import of this world-wide census and of the obscure movements of a Nazarean family. An incident that was to mark only one more statistic in the official eyes of the world would give birth to a movement that would turn that world upside down (Acts 17:6).

## Jesus' birth in the theology of Matthew and Luke

In comparing Luke's account with that of Matthew, we can see how the two complement one another in theological significance. It is commonly admitted that the two Gospels are independent of one another in the infancy narratives. Although there are no outright contradictions, there are sufficient differences to conclude that the one evangelist was not acquainted with the other's story.

This mutual independence underscores the agreement of the two in the basic truths. Thus both agree on the virginal conception of Jesus (Matthew 1:18-20; Luke 1:26-38), on the role of Joseph (Matthew 1:18-20; Luke 1:27), on the name to be given to the Child (Matthew 1:21; Luke 1:31), and on the birth in Bethlehem (Matthew 2:1-6; Luke 2:4-7). These and other basic agreements in two otherwise independent documents indicate that the events were firmly fixed in the Church's tradition before the inspired writers made them part of a larger theological context.

In general, the author of the first Gospel shows throughout his infancy narratives how the Old Testament was perfectly fulfilled even in the private life of the Messiah. The role of the Old Testament, as he sees it, was to point forward to a greater reality that becomes the climax of all historical movement. Theological concerns, therefore, dominate his account, as they do Luke's. The events of the hidden life become didactic; they teach a deeper meaning for those who have accepted the kerygmatic pronouncement of the good news of salvation.

But while Matthew's didactic intent is to link all that went before with this appearance of the Child Jesus, Luke is at pains to teach that He is born into a Roman world that will one day know the full impact of that birth. While the one sees the past summed up and fulfilled in the Child, the other sees the future converging on Him. The combined accounts of both evangelists, therefore, fully identify the Babe of Bethlehem as the central figure who directs and dominates all history, past and future.

More particularly, we can note that in the account of the birth in Bethlehem the author of the first Gospel has indicated his theological concern by showing that the Child must be born in the city of David because of the prophecy of Micah (cf. Matthew 2:4-6). Luke, on the other hand, connects the birth in Bethlehem with the reign of Caesar Augustus and the census of Quirinius, thereby making Bethlehem and its newest citizen cast a long shadow over the Roman world. And since the Roman world was *the* world of that day, we can also find here a hint of the universal mission of Jesus, a theme that is stressed by Luke in his Gospel. The salvation-history of the Old Testament, intimately tied to the chosen people of Israel, now branches out to embrace all people.

## Theology of renunciation

We can see in Luke's reference to the swaddling clothes and the manger another element of the author's theology. One of the many titles given to Luke is that of the evangelist of poverty and renunciation. In His public life Jesus is shown to rebuke, with an intransigence that is peculiar to the third Gospel, those who make their life consist in an abundance of possessions (Luke 12:33). Many passages in which the poor are extolled and the wealthy admonished appear only in Luke. Can we not, then, see in the circumstances of Jesus' birth a foreshadowing of what the Master will teach explicitly later on?

In this same light the pregnant phrase, "because there was no room for them in the inn," also takes on fuller meaning. Jesus not only taught His followers to embrace poverty and the renunciation of worldly goods but gave them the supreme example. When a certain scribe (cf. Matthew 8:19) expressed his desire to follow Jesus wherever He would go, our Lord warned him that "the foxes have dens, and the birds of the air have nests, but the Son of Man has nowhere to lay his head" (Luke 9:57-58). This renunciation is already foreshadowed in the scene of Jesus' birth.

*Journey to Jerusalem*

But this saying of our Lord's public life has an even deeper meaning when seen in the light of the context in which it has been placed. In Matthew's Gospel we find the saying at the beginning of Jesus' ministry in Galilee (cf. Matthew 8:19-20). But, as we mentioned earlier, the author of the third Gospel has made a point to show that Jesus' whole mission is ordered to Jerusalem, the center of the biblical world, where salvation would be effected. The latter part of his Gospel presents the long "Journey Narrative" (Luke 9:51–19:28), where St. Luke has grouped sayings and events which would emphasize this mission (cf., e.g., Luke 13:33). He also has composed the piece that his readers might be instinctively drawn to make a similar journey to the Cross and resurrection (cf. Luke 9:53, 57; 10:38; 13:22, 31-33; 14:25; 17:11; 18:31-33; 19:11, 28).

When Luke, therefore, mentions the "homelessness" of our Lord in this journey context, he presents more than a precious teaching on the virtue of poverty. He is also saying that this is the *necessary* condition of Him whose mission takes Him inexorably to that earthly Jerusalem whence He will eventually gain His true home in the heavenly Jerusalem (cf. Luke 24:44-52).

In the light of this overpowering concern of Luke in the presentation of the public life of Jesus Christ, we can well suppose that he also found this "anticipated" theology in the nativity scene. That the Holy Family should have found the inns of Bethlehem full was natural enough, considering the number of Jews who must have been "of the house and family of David." But for Luke, as for all the inspired writers of the Bible, the events of secular history have a higher meaning in God's plan. Even Bethlehem, the city of David, cannot claim its divine Citizen for long. His only abiding-place is with His Father. "Did you not know that I was bound to be in my Father's house?" (Luke 2:49, *New English Bible* translation). Hence He must constantly move on to Jerusalem, where He will leave this earth to be with the Father forever.

# BLESSED ARE THE POOR

Jean Daniélou

Poverty is, with charity and truth, one of the essential traits of the evangelical spirit. And the evangelical spirit is the map of Christian existence. Not to be faithful to it is to betray the Gospel in its essence.

Today, many Christians have the uneasy sense of massive infidelity to the

Published originally in *Cross Currents*, 9 (1959), 379-88. Reprinted by permission of the publisher.

Gospel on the score of poverty. It exists among the middle class, many of whom question themselves concerning the compatibility of the Gospel with wealth: they ask what sacrifices are expected of them. But it exists among the working class as well; militants worry over the legitimacy for them of access to a higher level of life on which they fear they will be cut off from their less privileged comrades.[1]

But when it is a question of stating precisely what this demand of evangelical poverty involves, we find ourselves in the midst of uncertainty. Does it consist in lowering one's standard of living, eliminating all that is superfluous? Does it call for detachment in regard to all possessions and common ownership of goods? Does it, more radically, demand a break with the middle-class world and participation in the workers' fight? Or, quite the reverse, is it a question of a purely interior attitude, which can be accommodated to luxury and comfort? All these solutions have been proposed, and have been tried by restricted groups. But they still leave everyone uneasy.

And so we find ourselves in a paradoxical situation: poverty is a substantial part of the Gospel, but the point at which we should apply it is difficult to determine. It is therefore needful to try to throw a little light on a question that is simultaneously obscure and vital. That is what I hope to do here.

The question is primarily one of disclosing the ambiguities of the term *poverty*: it has different meanings in the Gospel itself; and the exaltation of poverty as one aspect of the royal dignity of the Christian must not be confused with the obligation to charity which directs the Christian to the poor in order that he may rescue them from their poverty. We can ask ourselves what is essential to poverty according to the Gospel. And this will allow us to decide how to resolve some practical problems.

When we ask what Christ meant by numbering the poor among the blessed, two extremes leap to mind. The first underlines the fact that it is a question of the "poor in spirit." One would then say that evangelical poverty is before all else an interior attitude of detachment in regard to material goods, but that this is perfectly compatible with possession of those goods. This solution, which doubtless contains a great deal of truth, seems nevertheless a bit convenient. It can furnish facile, Pharisaic excuses. And it is difficult to have a good conscience while calmly using the goods of this world at the same time that others are in misery. We would come close, there, to the abuses of what has been called the ethic of intention.

Moreover the Gospel itself makes difficult the purely interior interpretation. In fact, it seems that, in the version of St. Luke, at least, the problem of wealth as such was envisaged. To the blessing given the poor corresponds in effect the woe put upon the rich. Thus it has seemed to me from the outset that it is impossible to hold a simplistic solution. A poverty that did not involve effective renunciation would be a mystification. But it would be equally false to raise up privation of material goods as an absolute and supreme

[1] See "Les béatitudes dans la vie d'un militant ouvrier," *Masses ouvrières,* (November 1955), pp. 42-43.

value. This deviation is also quite common today in certain circles. That is why I shall put special emphasis on it.

Let us recall the distinction that Péguy made between destitution (*misère*) and poverty. An initial error in interpretation would be to identify "the poor" of the beatitude with the destitute. It is necessary to understand here by "poor" or "destitute" those who do not have the minimum necessary for realizing a truly human life. Certainly, these poor have a major place in the Christian perspective. It is of the essence of Christianity to go toward him who is abandoned or lost. This continues the gesture of Christ himself, who did not keep his equality with God like an ace in the hole, but took the form of a slave. In a sense the Christian ought to be with the poor, with all the disinherited of this world. But he is with them in order to lift them from their misery. This does not imply any special value in destitution, nor indeed any complicity with it. Mounier put it well: "The Christian tradition is no more one of pauperism than it is one of dolorism." [2]

It is possible in the sense Mouroux gives the term to have a completely ambiguous exaltation of degradation; this is at odds with the Christian attitude. Christ has a horror of misery, as he has a horror of sickness and death. Nothing could be falser to his character than to attribute to him complicity with the forces of destruction. He does not descend into misery only to pull mankind in after him. He does not love destitution but the man who is destitute. Any exaltation of misery which is a revulsion against values similar to that of which Nietzsche accused Christianity is a pure perversion of the Gospel.

But the exaltation of "pauperism" has a more modern form. A controversy at a recent congress of the *Confederation Genéral du Travail* permitted French economists to refute the thesis, which the Communist Party holds, of the absolute pauperization of the laboring class under the capitalist system. Increased production, together with social legislation, tends to raise the general level of life. May this not reduce the militancy of the laboring class? Given the existence of an exploited and miserable proletariat is not revolution a necessary resort? Does not the reduction of pauperism risk reinforcing the capitalist system? We have heard certain Christians utter these doubts. But there is no need to say that, if they would resolve these doubts by employing this otherwise inadmissable political tactic, they do not share the outlook of the Gospel spirit. Evangelical poverty is not the revolutionary means of class war. [3]

This leads us to a second and equally sociological conception of the poor of the Gospel: it identifies the poor not with those who do not have the necessities, but with those who have only the necessities. Here, it is no longer a question of the destitute, of the proletariat, but of the people, the mass of rural and urban semi-skilled and skilled workers. It is noted that Christ was a worker, and this brings forth certain shades of meaning. In the interpretation

[2] Emmanuel Mounier, *De la propriété capitaliste à la propriété humaine*, p. 88.
[3] Thus it is represented in Jean Massin's *Le festin chez Levi*, p. 161.

of the working classes, we recall the statement: "I have come to preach the Gospel to the poor." It is suggested that there is a kind of affinity between the Church and the people and, in contrast, an incompatibility between Christ and the middle class.

There is no denying that confusions of this type have existed throughout the history of Christianity. It is therefore useful to recall that it is false to restrict Christianity to one social class, whatever that class may be. Christianity is not a prerogative of the middle class, but it is not a prerogative of the working class either. There is no need to be a worker in order to be a Christian. Belonging to the middle class is not an original sin. If there are among the working class natural virtues of generosity, solidarity, and simplicity which dispose it to the Gospel, these are not yet Evangelical virtues. It is dangerous to identify the Gospel with the working class. In addition, there exist among the middle class other virtues which, though not those of the Gospel, are also a preparation for the Gospel.

This position, no longer "pauperism" but "workerism," tends to put the question of evangelical poverty in false perspective. It identifies evangelical poverty with a certain way of life. And then, because there is danger of becoming bourgeois, we experience disquiet over improvement in living standards. This fear appears in the statement of the militant Christian worker whom I have cited in *Masses ouvrières*: "The great question posed to militants is that of poverty. They seek a more human life, for more material comfort in their homes. And this is normal under modern conditions. But there is disquiet, nevertheless."[4] Mounier has quite rightly denounced the confusion that is at the bottom of this disquiet. Evangelical poverty does not consist in what he calls "the little life."[5] Quite the contrary, it is a question of raising the general level of life. It is an error to identify poverty with the middle level of the worker's life. A militant notes: "Poverty is not a gimmick for remaining in the labor movement; no more is it an end in itself."[6] St. Thomas' formula is the same: *"Non enim paupertas secundum se bona est."*[7]

The workerist conception locates poverty on the level of the standard of living. The "collectivist" locates poverty on the level of private property. The first is on the plane of use, the second on the plane of possession. The two are not necessarily joined. Indeed they can be dissociated. A man can possess great wealth and live frugally, whether through avarice or through ideals. The latter case provides admirable examples of men who possess many goods yet live in poverty, disposing of what they have to others. And reciprocally, within a system where there is no property, whether it is a question of a religious community or a collectivist society, the use of goods can be more or less developed.

The confusion here would be the identification of evangelical poverty with

[4] *Masses ouvrières, op. cit.*, p. 42.
[5] Mounier, *op. cit.*, p. 89.
[6] *Masses ouvrières, op. cit.*, p. 43.
[7] *Contra Gentiles*, III, 134.

the common sharing of goods. We might recall the passages in the Acts of the Apostles where it said that the first Christians held all in common. Among them, being a property owner was considered incompatible with the spirit of the Gospel. We might then be led to deem intrinsically evil all systems based on private property, and we might be scandalized to see that the Church has not radically condemned them. We might deem this infidelity to the Gospel. Reciprocally, we might feel that there is a natural affinity between Christianity and communism. And we might be astonished that the Church has condemned that system, not only in its metaphysical presuppositions, but indeed by reason of its rejection of the right of private property.

Here again it is clear that the question is complex. It is perfectly true that the common sharing of goods was practiced in the primitive community and is always practiced in the religious communities, in which common sharing is made the object of the vow of poverty. There is, then, a relation between community of goods and evangelical poverty. The error would lie in wishing to make an end that which is only a means and to see in community of goods the essence of evangelical poverty, with the result that where community of goods did not exist evangelical poverty could not be found.

The example of the first Christian community is not at all convincing as it is used in this argument. In fact, far from being a specifically Christian phenomenon, the common sharing of goods seems to be one of the features that were quite certainly received from outside. The Dead Sea Scrolls have shown us that in fact the system was current in fervent Jewish circles of the epoch. And it is found in many other religions. It appears in Christianity as a means of perfection that helps in the practice of, but does not constitute, evangelical poverty.

If we look at the common sharing of goods on the sociological level, this is even more evident. Purely and simply to identify collectivism and Christianity, and to oppose them to property ownership, is gross confusion. In reality, in this sphere, community and property ownership are two equally necessary poles of the economic life; each ought to safeguard the other. The Constitution of '89 was right in making the right of property one of the rights of the human person and in defending it as a legitimate freedom; its only error lay in putting forth an incomplete and partially false notion. And socialism was right to recall that the community has a certain right over the mass of goods produced and cannot permit concentration in the hands of a few what is destined for all. Moreover, the Church has always stressed this double aspect. But this does not in any way resolve the problem of evangelical poverty.

I have tried so far to disengage evangelical poverty from a certain number of confusions which obscure its real meaning. We have seen that it is impossible to identify evangelical poverty with any one form of actual poverty, and that at the same time evangelical poverty is not a pure, interior disposition that implies no effective realization. We must now get to the heart of the question and in a positive way ask ourselves in what evangelical poverty consists. The error lay in wishing to explain evangelical poverty with human perspective as our starting point. If we want to understand it, we must return to Scripture and ask ourselves what the word *poor* means there. As is the case with other notions — justice, for example — the sense in the Bible differs from current usage. If we are not acquainted with the true meanings of the terms, it is hardly surprising that Christians make mistakes in applying them.

Here, as in most instances, if we want to understand the New Testament, we must take as our starting point the Old, especially in the Psalms, where the poor, the *anawim*, are often mentioned. The description given us is initially shocking.

In the first place, the poor man appears as oppressed. He is the object of persecutions by the powerful. He is at once pursued by their calumnies, despoiled of his goods, caught in a web of misfortune. Material poverty is only one aspect of his trials. And it is by no means considered a value. The poor man, on the contrary, hopes for deliverance. But he waits on God alone. He is sure throughout that one day he will see Him.

These texts have been interpreted many times as the expression of the social conflicts that divided the people of Israel. The prophets and the psalmists expressed the protest of the little people against the exactions of the powerful, the rich property owners, and the high-level functionaries. And certainly at least part of the text that concerns the poor alludes to sociological facts: "Victims of social injustices, of provocations by the insolent rich, of mistreatment by unjust judges, the psalmists recount their oppression."[8] But nothing would be falser than to see in the prophets and psalmists champions of class warfare looking for a way to free the proletariat from exploitation by the rich. André Neher has admirably shown that this would have been foreign to their outlook.[9]

Besides, oppression is only a secondary characteristic. In the Bible, the poor are before anything else "the pious," "the just." They are the men faithful to the Law of God. This gives the term *poverty* a fundamental meaning. Poverty is defined essentially in its relation to God and not primarily in relation to material goods or to other men. And this is enough to mark the specific character of biblical poverty. It belongs to a world of thought in which the relation with God is primary, and commands all the rest. The poor man is one who observes God's law, who suffers from not seeing God's law observed in the world. Hunger and thirst for justice consume him; that is, in the Biblical sense, hunger and thirst for the accomplishment of the will of God.

As a result, the poor man is inevitably put in conflict with the powers of this world. These are not those who possess material goods or hold high station. Rather they represent the men who, instead of obeying God's law even at cost to their own interests, serve only their own interests even at the expense of God's law. Conflict between these two cities is inevitable. For "the

[8] A. Gelin, *Les pauvres de Iahweh*, p. 54.
[9] *Amos*, p. 136. See *Sainteté et action temporelle*, p. 44.

rich," "the poor" are a living reproach. Their efforts to bring about the reign of God's law oblige them to war against the selfish interests of others. And from then on they are necessarily wedded to their sarcasm, their service, their persecution. Poverty introduces us, at the very heart of the Bible, to what constitutes its structure: the interior of the conflict between two cities.

We see how far this carries biblical poverty. On the one hand it is not defined by any sociological context whatsoever, but by a relation to God. The poor man is one who puts the will of God above all because he understands that God is preferable to all. We are within the religious perspective that permeates the Bible. But at the same time this fidelity to God will inevitably carry with it certain material consequences. Anyone who takes God seriously will necessarily be led to compromise his reputation, to sacrifice his interests, to lose his tranquility. It is not a question of putting together a little poverty, which will satisfy the conscience at slight cost and provide a shelter under which one can live without difficulty. Evangelical poverty accepts the immense risks that fidelity to the law of God will always bring. There is no need to look for them. They will come of their own accord — and sooner than we might wish. He who takes God seriously may be sure that he will be a poor man.

This conception of poverty, which is that of the Old Testament, is also that of the New. In his recent book devoted to the beatitudes, Dom Jacques Dupont remarks at the outset that their nucleus seems to be made up of the first and last blessings of Christ, those that bear on poverty and on persecution.[10] This happens to confirm in a remarkable way what we noted in the Old Testament. The poor man will necessarily be a persecuted man. And reciprocally it will be disquieting for a Christian to receive too warm a welcome from the world. He may well ask himself whether he owes this excessive benevolence to secret compromises.

In addition, Dom Dupont also remarks, these two beatitudes give us the key to all the others. In reality, they all describe the same attitude. Whether it be a question of "justice," of "kingdom," of "earth," in every case it involves thirst for the accomplishment of God's will. And this is not only on the individual plane, but on the collective as well. It is so primarily on the spiritual plane of the realization of God's design, which is the growth of the Mystical Body; but it is also so on the temporal plane, where fidelity to God demands that the law which rules human societies be made to respect Him. Thus the poor man will be led to wage war on social injustice not by solidarity with a class but by obedience to God.

This attitude, the New Testament repeats after the Old, necessarily leads the poor man to compromise his interests. Said Christ: "You must serve God or money. You cannot serve both" (Luke 16:13). From the point of view of the world, the serious follower of Christ will surely lose himself. We cannot simultaneously look for personal success and for success for the work of God: "The man who tries to save his life shall lose it; it is the man who loses

---

[10] *Les Béatitudes*, pp. 15-26.

his life for my sake that will secure it" (Matthew 17:25). The man who follows Christ is necessarily lost — his reputation, lost; his peace and quiet, lost; his fortune, lost.[11] For the servant cannot be greater than the Master. He, the leader, wished to lose all. He is the Poor Man. Whoever follows him will necessarily be a poor man.

We see the changed perspective that the *données* of Scripture introduce to the consideration of poverty. They substitute for all particular ends the single rule of God's will. For we can, in fact, become attached to poverty if we make it an end. Pascal said that truth can be made an idol. So, too, can poverty be made an idol. It, too, can become a piece of property. That is precisely what we find in the diverse errors I mentioned earlier. They identify poverty with a certain standard of life, with a certain sociological milieu, with a certain method of distributing goods.

Instead, evangelical poverty is free, even in regard to poverty. It consists in being free in regard to everything save the will of God. Privation will be good, when it is willed with God; so will prosperity, when it is willed with God. We attach too much importance to earthly goods when we become attached to their privation. Christ formulated the evangelical law, when he said: "Do not fret over your life, how to support it with food, over your body, how to keep it clothed" (Luke 12:22). Non-use is not more perfect than use. Rather, use is good, if it is willed with God; so is non-use, if it is willed with God.

Such was the conduct of Christ during the greater part of his life. He was not an ascetic; like John the Baptist. He himself said to the Jews: "When John came, he would neither eat nor drink, and they say of him that he is possessed. When the Son of Man came, he ate and drank with them, and of him they say, Here is a glutton; he loves wine" (Matthew 19:19). Christ led the ordinary life. He formulated no dietary prohibitions. He did not attract notice through any ascetic oddness. He saw in the goods of the earth the gifts of his Father. And he made use of them with thanksgiving. But he also knew well that these things pass, when it is the will of his Father. He thirsted at the well of the Samaritan woman. He had not a rock on which to rest his head.

That is evangelical poverty. It does not consist in attachment to deprivation as such, but in readiness to accept deprivation, if God asks it. St. Paul expressed it in a lapidary phrase: "I am capable of living in plenty and I am capable of living in want." That is, what matters is neither want nor abundance, but the service of the kingdom of God and His justice, "now honored, now slighted, now traduced, now flattered. They call us deceivers, and we tell the truth; unknown, and we are fully acknowledged; dying men, and see, we live; punished, yes, but not doomed to die; sad men, that rejoice continually; beggars, that bring riches to many; disinherited, and the world is ours" (2 Cor. 6:7-10).

Thus evangelical poverty appears as the disposition of a heart occupied

---

[11] See my book, *The Lord of History* (Regnery, 1958), pp. 283-296.

solely with the interests of the kingdom of God and free in regard to earthly goods. It is the expression of the dignity of the Son of God. When we are called to share in the Banquet with the Son, it is lacking in dignity to linger over the crumbs that fall from the table; they are for the lap dogs. This is so not because the crumbs are nothing, but because they are not what matters: "Look for your glory where it is," says St. John of the Cross. "Do not linger over the crumbs that fall from the table of your Father. Then you will find what your heart ambitions." We sin against evangelical poverty when attachment to our leisure, our reputation, our interests, prevents us from accomplishing the will of God. The sin against poverty is preoccupation. "Nothing must make you anxious," says St. Paul (Phil. 4:6). And Tauler shows us Christ, "living without any preoccupations, but receiving at each moment all things from the hands of his Father."

I have tried to isolate the essence of evangelical poverty according to what makes up its originality. We have seen that it refers essentially to God, as do all the other Christian dispositions of soul — charity, obedience, humility. It is in working for the primacy of God and His Kingdom that evangelical poverty appears to be a way of choosing and behaving in regard to earthly goods. The primacy of God implies radical liberty in regard to all created things, not that they should be depreciated or rejected, but that their use should always be subordinated to the demands of the divine will. And in fact these demands always imply effective sacrifices. They will make the Christian, as I have said, a man who is lost: lost to himself, lost to the world; freed from the world, freed from himself. That is, a man who is saved.

But this radical disposition must still be realized in concrete fashion. We have seen that evangelical poverty can be identified neither with destitution and the lack of necessities, nor with poverty and the simple life, nor with collectivism and the common sharing of goods. Nevertheless, it remains true that these different realizations of poverty in fact are far from valueless in the eyes of evangelical poverty. If it is not identified with them, it can be brought to make use of them as means. And that is what is left for us to see.

We have said that evangelical poverty consists in being free in regard to earthly goods, capable of using or of not using them. But, concretely, men are not free in regard to these things; they are naturally attached to them. There is, then, a risk that on the day God's will demands a sacrifice, we will not be ready to make it. This liberty — we must take it by storm. To conquer it, it will be necessary to go against man's natural inclination to be attached to his comfort, his reputation, his enjoyments, his money, his ambition. Effective privation of these things will become a necessary ascetic discipline. We have said that this is not a value in itself, nor should it be sought for its own sake. Such a seeking, which is asceticism, in so far as it is only a human technique, is not evangelical poverty. Moreover, it exists in primitive religions everywhere, among the holy men of India and the wise men of Greece. But the Christian will be led to practice this asceticism as necessary discipline for keeping free.

I must add that neither the use of pleasures nor the management of riches is ever without danger. The use of pleasures will always provoke development of the instinctive life which, to repeat, is never bad in itself, but inevitably overgrows the field of the individual's psychology. You cannot simultaneously develop all your senses. Gide was wrong in thinking he could simultaneously cultivate his sensuality and his spirituality. St. Augustine has put it admirably: "If you wish to expand the space of love, you must contract the space of the flesh." Effective poverty, a frugal diet, a simple life, all create a climate favorable to the spiritual life. "Nothing disposes us better to prayer," says Psichari, "than living on a handful of dates and some clear water."

The same is true of wealth. Wealth is a source of countless temptations because of the resources it furnishes. It is also a source of preoccupation, which leaves little time for a man to devote himself to the service of God. That is why, as we have seen, next to the beatitude of Matthew, which considers poverty solely as a spiritual attitude, we meet, in Luke, an interpretation that underlines the advantages of effective poverty and puts us on guard against the dangers of wealth. The woe put upon riches is not in the least a condemnation of wealth as such, but a warning against the obstacle wealth constitutes to the practice of evangelical poverty. It is the snare of which Satan avails himself to enlist us in his ranks.

Thus it is not wealth that is evil. And for certain men it may be the will of God that they have many goods at their disposal. Rather, it is we who are evil. And because we are evil, creatures are dangerous for us. It is not more perfect to have one eye than to have two. Nevertheless it would be better to have one eye and to enter into the Kingdom than to fail to enter while keeping two eyes. "And if thy eye is an occasion for falling to thee, pluck it out and cast it away from thee" (Matthew 18:9). There can be cases where wealth would be such a danger that it would be best to renounce it in order to save one's soul. This has been the origin of many monastic vocations. And in every case there is a constant obligation to guard against the dangers of wealth, and in using it, to practice effective renunciation, without which wealth turns into slavery, destroying spiritual liberty, evangelical poverty.

The same thing can be shown of the common sharing of goods and the renunciation of property. We have said that evangelical poverty does not condemn private property, which is a sociological reality grounded in the nature of man. Yet it poses many problems. Property is in fact essentially bound to responsibility. The problems posed by property are those posed by any assumption of temporal responsibilities. They do not differ substantially from those of the company president, high official, large stockholder, statesman.

Indeed, far from there being an incompatibility for men of this type between their responsibilities and evangelical poverty, I think that their greatest mistake would be not to look for evangelical poverty in their responsibilities. This is precisely what I want to say. We might have instead a somewhat imaginative and poetic conception of evangelical poverty: "the duty to lack foresight." We might term the evangelical spirit a kind of irresponsibility, thus bringing it into the sphere of spiritual infantilism. The outcome is that life is broken into two parts. There is temporal life — professional, social — which is amendable only to selfish cares. And against it is played off a private life scented with evangelism. One might toy with poverty — but only to turn from it with derision.

Evangelical poverty should reach to the heart of our existence. It is no more opposed to the assumption of monetary responsibilities than to any others. A full Christian life is, on the contrary, a life shot through with responsibilities, laden with work. Poverty consists in carrying responsibilities with liberty of spirit, in taking on occupations without preoccupation. Evangelical poverty does not, then, consist in renouncing private property, but in assuming it as a responsibility. Thus evangelical poverty will be placed in service of the common good. It is not private property as an institution that is opposed to evangelical poverty, but the spirit of acquisitiveness, which uses goods solely for the satisfaction of selfish pleasure and ambition, and shuns the duties ownership involves.

From this point of view, evangelical poverty manifests itself primarily as a disposition not to keep goods for oneself but to share them with others. This does not in the least imply that personal acquisition is to be repressed but that greed and the spirit of possessiveness are to be destroyed. The ideal here is an order of things in which persons share what they have, the community is built through the exchange of gifts, and goods are considered common not through the absence of private property but through the free sharing by each of what he has with others. Herein is the ideal of the Christian community, which is an image of the community of the Divine Persons in which each person communicates Himself entirely to the others. One present application of this spirit would rest in the duty of hospitality, and in the wish to cut down on expenses for luxury in order to help those in misery.

There remain cases in which evangelical poverty will involve the common sharing of goods and the renunciation of private property. But this is only a way of managing and does not constitute the essence of poverty. Such is the case of religious orders. Their renunciation of private property is justified by the fact that private property, though exercised in the spirit of poverty, implies an ordinary occupation with earthly cares. God calls certain men to be disengaged from this responsibility in order that they may consecrate themselves totally and exclusively to spiritual goods and to the service of the Kingdom of God. If it is an essential aspect of evangelical poverty that the Kingdom of God be primary, this liberation from earthly cares will appear to be a high form of evangelical poverty. But it is only a high form.

We have delayed until now discussion of that poverty that includes suffering. We said that it is not a constitutive element of evangelical poverty, but it does not follow that suffering poverty is foreign to evangelical poverty. Nevertheless, the reasons why evangelical poverty includes suffering poverty are not practical, as they were in the case of the two preceding forms of evangelical poverty. From the viewpoint of wisdom, suffering poverty is absolutely unjustifiable. It will seem like madness, but a madness supremely desirable to the Christian. For it was from the first embraced by Christ.

Here we enter the mystery of the Cross itself. The Word of God, coming into the world, did not choose as his lot honor, wealth, prosperity. He did not condemn them. But he did not choose them. He picked shame, humiliation, privation. This choice he alone had the right to make. And no one else can make it on his own account. Yet we recognize that across the centuries friends of Christ have desired to share the lot that was his in order to conform more closely to him. Thus Francis of Assisi wed Lady Poverty; thus Ignatius Loyola demanded in the *Spiritual Exercises* imitation of Christ in bearing all injuries and scorn, all poverty, actual as well as spiritual.

Certainly, as I have said evangelical poverty can be accomplished through a good as well as through a bad reputation, through abundance and through privation. Above all, it is liberty in regard to the one or the other. The abjectness of Jesus Christ could itself become an idol. The only proper attitude is holy indifference. But even within this indifference, which is evangelical poverty, a preference is allowed. The friends of Christ will tend to prefer poverty and abjectness, because such was the lot of their Master. Pure indifference would be the law of a world without sin. But in a world immersed in enjoyment and ambition, the madness of the cross must redeem the madness of the world.

Poverty is indeed at the heart of Christian existence. And Christians have reason to know it. The error lies in wishing to establish its role by identifying it with some particular realization. These realizations are not foreign to evangelical poverty. But they are valid only to the extent that they express a deeper attitude. And this attitude, in so far as it takes seriously the kingdom of God and his justice, is Christianity itself. Any attempt to establish poverty outside this perspective falsifies its meaning. In this perspective, on the contrary, all forms of poverty take on their true significance. They are the particular realizations, according to personal vocations, of the universal vocation of all Christians to poverty.

# THE PARABLES OF MERCY

Jean Cantinat, C.M.

The fifteenth chapter of St. Luke's Gospel gives us three of our Lord's most loved parables: the Lost Sheep, the Lost Drachma, and the Prodigal Son. To

Reprinted from *Theology Digest*, 4 (1956),120-23. Originally published as "Les Paraboles de la Miséricorde," *Nouvelle Revue Theologique*, 77 (1955), 246-64. Reprinted by permission of the publisher.

gain a full appreciation of their meaning, we must examine them in their context and in their mutual relations.

The introduction to the chapter is an especially important key to the inner
meaning of the three parables: "Publicans and sinners were pressing close to
Jesus to hear Him. But the Pharisees and scribes murmured within themselves
saying: This man receives sinners and eats with them." The content of the
parables is largely determined by the occasion of their telling. Let us first,
then, examine this occasion more closely.

Drawn by the goodness of Jesus, in spite of the hard things He demanded
of His followers, a number of publicans and sinners are pressing around Jesus one day. Eager for His every word, they do not leave Him even to eat.
The Pharisees show once again their extreme distaste for the kind of company
in which Jesus seems to like to travel. They find it impossible to understand
or accept this man who claims to be sent by God, yet who mingles with sinful
people, with people whose manner of life excludes them from the ritual practices of the ancients. The Pharisees would prefer that Jesus hold Himself aloof
from these impure contacts, as do they themselves, in order to remain pure.

Jesus does not attack the hypocrisy of the Pharisees' position — not this
time. And He does not bother to show — as He has before — that not all
these despised people are necessarily sinners in the eyes of God. Nor does He
point out again the fact that He has come precisely as a physician.

This time He aims at something different. With the help of three parables,
He answers the Pharisees' criticisms. He shows that His attitude towards sinners is the attitude of God and that their attitude is the direct opposite.

### The lost sheep

Jesus first describes a pastoral scene His hearers know quite well. "Who of
you," He asks, "if he has a hundred sheep and has lost one, will not leave the
ninety-nine there in the desert and hurry after the one lost until he has found
it?"

Leaving the group of ninety-nine standing alone is, of course, not to aban-
don them utterly. He mentions it to bring out more fully the shepherd's deep
attachment to each individual sheep. Even when ninety-nine stand contrasted
with one, he still goes after the one. "And when he has found it, he puts it joyfully upon his shoulder, and returning home he calls together his friends and
relatives to tell them: Rejoice with me, for I have found my sheep which was
lost."

The details of this exuberant joy give us the lesson of the parable; they describe under human characteristics the ways of God Himself. They describe
them so strikingly that this picture of the shepherd carrying his lost lamb has
been particularly dear to Christian piety from the days of the catacombs.

## The lesson of the parable

Jesus defends His own solicitude for sinners — God the Father, through His grace, goes out after sinners too. And what a difference the parable shows between the divine attitude and the attitude of the Pharisees. They would remain apart, distant from the sinner, merely waiting, at most, for him to return to them and to justice.

There is a lesson, too, in the tremendous joy of the recovery. In the eyes of the shepherd, all his sheep are of equal value. The loss and recovery of any one of them would cause him to express the same sentiments as those described here. Moreover, common sense forces us to admit that his peaceful possession of the ninety-nine faithful sheep gave him a proportionally greater and deeper satisfaction than the recovery of a mere one-hundredth part of his flock. When he carries that one recovered sheep about on his shoulders and calls together all the neighborhood for its sake, he is showing only an incidental outburst, a sudden explosion, of feelings that he has always. That spectacular emotion, a direct reaction to the fear he felt before, is called joy. The habitual feelings are better described as peace, well being, or tranquillity. But essentially they are the same. This is popular psychology applied to God Himself; analogously, of course, for God, being spirit, has no emotions.

The point is not that the converted sinner is more loved by God or is more worthy of God's love than the just man who has remained faithful. That would be a confusion of joy and love. It is only so stated that we may fully grasp how completely God receives the sinner back into love and friendship.

Finally, let us by no means believe that in speaking of "the ninety-nine just who need not penance," Jesus was using irony. He was not referring to the scribes and Pharisees as though they were only hypocritically just. All that the text calls for and all it really intends is to oppose frankly and honestly the truly faithful to the truly strayed, whether men or sheep.

## The lost drachma

This parable re-enforces and to some extent repeats the preceding — a common Semitic literary technique. The two are, moreover, perfectly parallel in structure:

| | |
|---|---|
| "What man of you | "What woman |
| who has a hundred sheep | who has ten drachmas |
| and if he lose one of them | if she lose one drachma |
| does not leave . . . | does not light . . . |
| until he find it? | until she find it? |
| And when he has found it | And when she has found it |
| he calls together his friends | she calls together her friends |

| | |
|---|---|
| and neighbors | and neighbors |
| saying: | saying: |
| Rejoice with me | Rejoice with me |
| because I have found | because I have found |
| my sheep | my drachma |
| which was lost." | which was lost." |

Since the audience must have contained a certain number of women, Jesus describes this time an interior scene, more familiar, at least to them, than the pastoral scene of the preceding story. Everything in His description is an exact reproduction of what happens in daily life and might well have occurred in the humble house of Nazareth under the eyes of Jesus Himself as a child.

## Doctrinal lesson

The application of this parable is parallel to that of the Lost Sheep:

| | |
|---|---|
| "I say to you | "So I say to you |
| that so there will be | that there will be |
| joy in heaven | joy among the angels of God |
| over one sinner | over one sinner |
| who does penance | who does penance." |
| rather than over ninety- | |
| nine just who need not penance." | |

("Heaven" and "the angels of God" are both typical Jewish ways to signify God Himself without using His sacred name.)

Here again the joy of God over the sinner's return is indicated, and the persevering efforts of God to bring about that return are implied. The image of the lost coin seems to stress a little more the idea of the searching, the seeking out. Thus it brings out still more the attachment God always has to each single man as if that man were the only one in the world.

## The prodigal son

The parable of the Prodigal Son crowns in a marvellous way the trilogy of parables of mercy. Whether Jesus actually spoke it at this time or not, St. Luke has certainly put it in the most suitable place. It is the last strophe of a divine poem of mercy.

Remember that this parable is told in the same circumstances as the two preceding ones. It is referred to in the introduction at the head of the chapter. The point of the parable is to respond adequately to the murmurs of the Pharisees and scribes — to justify Christ's attitude towards sinners. This fact is very important, for it tells us that the parable has the same application as the two preceding. God here will be the father, and the repentant sinner the son.

But there seems to be a difficulty. There enters here a person who does not appear in the other two stories: the elder son, who reproves the father's indulgence towards his repentant younger child. But the introduction at the head of the chapter gives us the key to the meaning of this character too. For St. Luke, who started his gospel with such high literary intentions and who so well lives up to those aims in general, could hardly have intended to leave us here a pure enigma. No, in the elder son, so conscious of justice, and so contrary to the merciful attitude of the father towards the prodigal, he means us to see no other than the scribes and the Pharisees. That is why the introduction called them to our attention in all their hostility towards sinners and in their keen consciousness of their own moral superiority. With St. Jerome and many modern authors, we think this is the only interpretation possible.

## The picture

The situation in the parable did not seem improbable to Christ's Palestinian hearers. Quite the contrary. Every detail — the number of sons, the distribution of the inheritance, the dissolute life, local famine, swineherding, and longing for the "husks" — have all been challenged at one time or another by scholars, and have all been re-established by careful research as completely familiar concepts in the Palestine of those days.

Of course, the description of the father's pardon is the real masterpiece in this story. All the little details, one more human than the next, are found in the perfect place and are drawn to life. Each of them re-enforces powerfully the impression of pardon swallowed up in love. The father rushes to meet the son, covers him with kisses — the affectionate oriental embrace — interrupts the tale of repentance to hurry the restoration of the son to his former high condition. The robe and ring and fatted calf — nothing is too much. The return of the son is to the old man like a resurrection from the dead.

And now the re-entry of the elder son. We should not be surprised at his anger and refusal to join them in the party once he has learned the reason for it. It is only our Christian upbringing which makes us aware of the selfish jealousy in his anger, in his description of his brother's sins, and in his accusation that his father is ungrateful.

Study the father's final answer to this elder son. See how it vibrates with the same love for both sons: the same love which habitually places all things in common — both joys and sorrows; a love which is sorely afflicted at not being followed in its generosity.

## Doctrinal lesson

The lesson of this parable carries us one step beyond the other two. It brings out still more strongly God's solicitude for sinners, for it compares God to a father rather than merely a shepherd or a housekeeper. It stresses the universal and constant salvific will of God — all men, at every moment, have access to the house of their father. But it teaches us also that the sinner must consciously turn back to God.

In the second part of the parable, seen in the light of the chapter's general introduction, we finally are told directly and clearly what has so far been only implicit: that every human creature is bound to applaud the universal salvific will of God. Every man is duty-bound to rejoice at God's all-merciful ways. None can in fairness take it badly — as did the elder son and the scribes and Pharisees — when God receives repentant sinners into His paternal mansions. And no one consequently can have any good grounds for grumbling that Jesus spends His days and nights with sinners in order to win them back to God.

## To imitate God

All three parables point to a significant conclusion for those engaged in apostolic activities. For all three show, by the example of Christ, that it is worthwhile to go out to sinners, mingle with them while they are still lost, in order to bring them to repentance and so eventually to allow God to love them as He desires. And no one can blame such action. It is most praiseworthy. It is to imitate Jesus; it is to imitate God. The opposite attitude of aloofness, of merely sitting and waiting for the sinner's eventual return, deserves only the condemnation of the scribes and Pharisees.

Moreover, every apostle can be encouraged when he remembers that in approaching sinners, even those who have wandered farthest away, he is not beginning work on completely new territory. God has been over this soil before him. God has already worked on it with His grace; and so the soul of every straying sinner is, as a matter of fact, carefully and well prepared for the apostle's message.

# THE CHARITY OF THE GOOD
# SAMARITAN — Luke 10:25-37

Ceslaus Spicq, O.P.

A lawyer put a test question to Jesus. He asked what he should do to obtain eternal life. Jesus had him recite the commandments of the Law as a pupil would. The scribe felt ridiculous and thought he had asked too simple a question. "Anxious to justify it" (Luke 10:29) and show himself no simple man, he

Reprinted from *Agape in the New Testament* (St. Louis: B. Herder Book Company, 1963), I, 108-18. Reprinted by permission of the publisher.

immediately said: "And who is my neighbor?" (v. 29). Jesus answered him by telling the parable of the good Samaritan.

A man was traveling along a deserted road. He was no one in particular, neither his race, nationality, religion, nor any of his circumstances are described. He fell in with robbers who stripped and beat him and left him lying on the road. A priest and a levite passed by, one after the other, but avoided the place where he was lying, apparently not bothering even to glance in his direction. Next a Samaritan came along. He stopped to take care of the wounded man and then brought him to a safe place. Our Lord ended His story with a question of His own: "Which of these three seems to you to have been neighbor to the man who had fallen in with the bandits?" (v. 36).

## The meaning of the law

At first glance, Jesus' question does not seem to correspond to the scribe's, "Who is my neighbor?" He had probably meant, "Who precisely is the object of the charity prescribed by the Law — is it a compatriot, a proselyte, a pagan toward whom I am bound to observe this precept?" However Jesus answered the question, the scribe could object, in the name either of the Law or of oral tradition, that under certain conditions one should ignore and refuse to help the impure, the idolatrous. Not only did Jesus refuse to answer him with a definition of "neighbor," but in His parable and final question He set up a new problem: How does one act as "neighbor"? Which of the three passers-by behaved as a neighbor and drew near the unknown victim to help him?

Because Jesus' parable introduces this new question, many critics believe the dialogue with the scribe (vv. 25-28) originally formed a document separate from that of the parable (vv. 30-37). According to this theory, St. Luke used the dialogue as an introduction to the parable, joining them artificially by the question: "Who is my neighbor?" (v. 29). Others have noticed that the parable responds essentially to the question — a neighbor is every man who is in need. That is true, but it is not the meaning of Jesus' last question: "Which of the travelers showed himself a neighbor to the unfortunate man?"

## A parable?

The apparent contradiction disappears with less attention to the words and more to the living reality of the situation. Rigid logic in Occidental style will not serve in dealing with Oriental mentality, which loves enigmas, parables, and proverbs. Precise definition of a word or notion is no help; it is necessary to perceive what an image suggests and to respond to unspoken meaning.

To begin with, the "parable" of the Samaritan is not, strictly speaking, a comparison, much less an argument designed to persuade. It is rather a paradigm, a "pattern story," a concrete, particular case illustrating a point of doctrine and presenting a model of religious or moral life to be imitated. The scribe had come, perhaps in good faith, perhaps not, to ask what *he* must do to have eternal life. Humiliated at having been forced to answer his own ques-

tion, he tried to involve Jesus in a scholarly debate and escape his embarass-
ment on the speculative plane.

But the Lord, always master of a situation, turned the discussion as He
wished it to go. He had been taking the scribe's questions seriously and is
concerned only with the salvation of souls. Just as when He forgave the sinful
woman He had sought to rouse Simon to the value of the love of gratitude,
here He refused a technical definition to the scribe in order to give the light of
life instead. What is important is not *knowing* who is a neighbor, but *acting*
with charity to all men, whoever they may be. Both the parable and Jesus'
last question are clear answers to the scribe's, "What must I do to obtain a
place in eternal life?"

## Neighborly

It is not even certain that the scribe's second question, as it is phrased in
Greek, means exactly: "Who is my neighbor?," or even that it had only one
meaning for the doctor of Law. The Greek text has the adverb "neighborly,"
without the article preceding as it had in v. 27 ("Love your neighbor"). This
difference in formulation suggests a difference in meaning. If we understand,
"Who is neighbor to me?" or "Who, exactly, is a neighbor to me?," the parable
becomes a perfect answer to this moral problem about a practical action. Only
the Samaritan both felt and behaved as neighbor to the wounded man; charity,
then, makes of a stranger a neighbor. By love we become brothers of all men,
whether or not they are already close to us by blood, nationality, religion, or
any other bond. The dialogue had been extremely rapid. The scribe had put
his question vigorously: "And who is my neighbor?"

The Lord did not let him continue, either because He guessed a trap was
coming or because He wanted to use the occasion to present a new teaching.
He seems to have interrupted the scribe in picking up his last word, "neighbor." The Greek words translated, "Jesus replied" (v. 30), may also mean
"Jesus picked up again" the thought of the dialogue. He returned to its original point. To obtain eternal life one must "love his neighbor as himself"
(v. 27).

The scribe wanted to clarify the notion of "neighbor"; Jesus explained "love"
as He had already done in the Sermon on the Mount. Prophet of the New
Covenant, He authoritatively defined the meaning of the *agape* prescribed by
God. The scribe did not object that his question had not been answered. That
he acquiesced in the Lord's teaching shows that the fundamental question really was about *agape* and that "neighbor" can be defined only in terms of living
love and not according to juridical categories.

## Which of these three . . . ?

It must be recognized, then, not only the story of Luke 10:25-37 is homogeneous, but also that it is one of the Gospel's richest teachings on the love of
charity. Our Lord invited the scribe to reflect: "Which of these three do you

think was neighbor to the man who fell into the hands of the robbers?" (v.36). The question concerned all three men who traveled that road, not just the Samaritan. The priest and the levite represented the hierarchy, the quintessence of Judaism. They were included to signify the opposition between the letter of the Old Covenant and the spirit of the New.

They may have had excellent reasons for avoiding the wounded man. Perhaps there were conditions that justified their refusal to help. The man lying in the road was unknown to them and probably could not even be identified. His misfortune might have been a divine punishment which should not be interfered with. If they went near him, they might contract legal defilement and become incapable of carrying out the ritual ceremonies. Admittedly, their attitudes suggested total indifference more than concern for legal purity, and it is remarkable indeed that the Lord had not one word of blame for them. Jesus practiced the charity He preached; His all-demanding *agape* had nothing sectarian or aggressive in it.

## The Samaritans

The hero of the parable is a Samaritan, a man from whom generosity would never be expected. It is important to remember how the very word "Samaritan" sounded to contemporary ears. Its history began with Sargon's capture of Samaria in 722. The Assyrian monarch massacred part of the population and deported the surviving Samaritan men. He repopulated the country with emigrant Arabs, Babylonians, and others. These newcomers intermarried with the remaining Samaritans. Although they admitted Yahweh to their pantheon, they also kept the cult of their own divinities. The ethnic mixture led to the greatest confusion in religion. When they returned from the Babylonian captivity, the Samaritans, who claimed to be followers of Yahweh, made an official offer to Zerubbabel and Jeshua to assist in the reconstruction of the temple. Their offer was refused because they did not belong to the holy nation. (Ezra 4:3).

After that, hostility between the two groups grew stronger. The Samaritans raised up "the people of the country" against the project of reconstruction and denounced it to Artaxerxes (vv.4-16). Under Alexander the Great, who sent them a whole group of Macedonian colonists, they took in turncoat priests from Jerusalem and every malcontent who decided to leave the Israelite community. They erected a schismatic temple on Gerizim, "the blessed mountain," and rejected the prophets, keeping only the Pentateuch, with modifications, as inspired Scripture.

The best Jerusalemites considered this motley group of emigrants and half-breeds perfect specimens of traitors and apostates. "Two nations with all my heart I loathe; and a third I can name that is not even a nation — the hill tribes of Samaria, and the Philistines, and the miscreant folk that dwell in Shechem" (Sir. 50:25-26). At the time of the Maccabees the Samaritans made common cause with the invaders against the Jews. They went so far as to write to King Antiochus congratulating him for treating the Jews "as their wickedness deserved." They joined themselves entirely to his cause, even to the extent of designating their temple on Gerizim as the temple of Zeus and considering Sabbath observance a superstitious practice.

For a Jew of the first century A.D. a Samaritan was a symbol of a stranger, enemy, and heretic. Racial, political, and religious antagonisms had gradually developed into absolute contempt. It is understandable that the Synagogue considered the Samaritans impure and forbade them access to the Temple. Their religious contributions were refused, and their testimony not accepted in courts of justice. Not only was marrying a Samaritan woman forbidden, but also accepting food or drink from one of them was against the Law. The Samaritans were equally hostile to the Jews. If someone so much as intended to go to Jerusalem, the Samaritan refused him all hospitality. This was the reason the Sons of Thunder wanted to call down fire from heaven upon these impious people (Luke 9:52, 54).

### The true Israelite

Our Lord's choosing a Samaritan to play the hero's role in His parable on fraternal love is significant. This heretical stranger, without the scribe's learning or the priest's and levite's religious dignity, showed himself profoundly human and profoundly religious. He put the two great commandments of the Old Testament into practice in the spirit of the New Covenant. Of the three travelers, he was the true Israelite. In the Sermon on the Mount, Jesus had asked His disciples not to limit their love to those near them who had already shown them affection. Christians were to distinguish themselves from sinners by becoming or showing themselves sons of the Most High in the enormous reach of their charity (Luke 6:32-34).

But here the model of authentic *agape* is a Samaritan who helped a man he knew nothing about. Does this not mean that true children of God existed outside official religion and that Jesus had come to gather them all together (John 11:52)? A Samaritan woman had received the revelation that real worshippers, beyond all distinction of race and ritual, are those who worship the Father in spirit and truth (John 4:23-24). Surely it is charity that makes this worship agreeable to the Father. The parable teaches for the first time that charity obtains eternal life (vv. 25, 28, 37), as St. Paul and St. John later outlined so forcefully.

The Samaritan's conduct revealed a perfect charity and enriched the concept of the verb *agapan* (to love) enormously. Love is characterized by its *spontaneity* and *promptness*. The scribe knew the precept of love of neighbor and wanted to find out how far it extended. He would not love unless he had to, and then only in the required degree. The Samaritan loved without even thinking of the Law or trying to find out who was the object of his care. His goodness welled up spontaneously, as God's does, who cherishes His creatures independently of their lovableness.

## Charity is pure gift

In the Sermon on the Mount our Lord had asked that love be larger than mere response to affection already received. Not only was the Samaritan the first to love, but he also loved *disinterestedly*; his charity was pure gift. Consequently the notion of "neighbor" as someone with whom there was an already-existing relationship, a greater or lesser "proximity," disappears. It is no longer a question of finding among all humanity the persons we can love, but of loving, purely and simply, whether or not the others are lovable.

The Samaritan's charity, in marked contrast to his predecessors' indifference, was singularly *personal, active,* and *effective.* He interrupted his trip, bandaged the man's wounds, and took care of the expenses. He did these things himself. Great as was his generosity with his money, it did not begin to match the value of his personal involvement. His love aroused in him a profound interest in the misery of the wounded man, and he reached out to him directly and personally.

## Charity is compassion and mercy

The supreme revelation of the parable of the Good Samaritan is that charity is composed of *compassion* and *mercy.* It was already known to be a love of adoration and gratitude toward God, strong enough to dominate all bitterness and anger; one was to pray for enemies and even show them respect and help them. A centurion, like the one from Capharnaum, proved his love for strangers by his benefactions. The Samaritan must have suspected that the wounded man lying on the road between Jerusalem and Jericho would be a Jew, a detested enemy. Yet he not only helped him but was deeply moved at seeing him so badly treated.

Our Lord stressed this response; as soon as the Samaritan saw the wounded man, he was moved to pity (v.33). The verb in Greek conveys a great deal. It is proper to the synoptic writers, who use it only when speaking of Christ. Compassion is a feeling deeply suitable to the Savior. It is a physical emotion experienced at the grief, pain, or misery of others. Jesus never resisted it; it explains His miracles.

St. Luke accounts for it as being the result of an encounter with grief; faced with great sorrow, Jesus is filled with pity. "When he was approaching the town of Nain, He met the funeral of a dead man (who) was the only son of his widowed mother," and when He saw her His heart went out to her, and He said: "Weep no more" (Luke 7:12, 13). He seems to remember His feeling then and attributes the same pity to the Samaritan, whose compassion sent him straight to the wounded man to take care of him. The priest and levite were incapable of experiencing this pure and true compassion, but it is the explanation of all the Samaritan did. And compassion is an integral part of charity.

The scribe understood. He knew that to win eternal life he had to love his neighbor. Our Lord had given him a beautiful example of fraternal charity and asked: "Who showed himself a neighbor to the wounded man?" (v.36).

The scribe answered: "The one who showed him mercy" (v. 37). This equivalence of love of neighbor (v. 27) with mercy to him (v. 37) brings a note of tenderness to *agape* in the New Testament analogous to that given in the Old Testament by the spouse of the Canticle. Our Lord's approval, "Go and do as he did," shows that this exegesis is correct.

A good heart, moved to pity by every man's sorrow, is charitable; it will live eternally. Not the least wonderful thing about this scene is that the Samaritan, who acknowledged only the Pentateuch, applies the most elevated teaching of the prophets: "A tender heart wins favor with me, not sacrifice; God's acknowledging, not victim's destroying" (Hosea 6:6).

# THE DRAMA OF THE CITY OF GOD: JERUSALEM IN ST. LUKE'S GOSPEL

P. Simson

> On the holy mount stands the city he founded;
> the Lord loves the gates of Zion
> more than all the dwelling places of Jacob.
> Glorious things are spoken of you, O city of God (Ps 87:1-3).

How strange and wonderful is the history of Jerusalem! The political capital of David's kingdom, it represented in the Old Testament the national unity of God's people. Chosen by God as a dwelling-place for His holy name, it was Israel's spiritual centre and it was destined to become the spiritual centre of the world. These were two vocations which were meant to coincide but which, in fact, were the source of a growing tension; incapable of fulfilling her spiritual mission the political Jerusalem lost her prestige little by little: in 931 B.C. a schism between the Northern and the Southern tribes reduced her to the state of capital of the Southern Kingdom; some three centuries later, in 597 and 587, Nebuchadnezzar destroyed it, and in those days of affliction and bitterness Jerusalem could only remember "all the precious things that were hers from days of old" (Lam. 1:7). But God had not abandoned His city; from the ruins of 587 a new Jerusalem was born; no longer the capital of a kingdom, for there was no longer any kingdom of Israel or Judah; but the religious centre of the Israelite community purified by the exile. It looked as if at last the city of God was about to become what God meant her to be: "the city of righteousness, the faithful city" (Is. 1:26). But as time went on, the reality betrayed more and more hopes and dreams; after a moment of glory at the time of the

Published originally in *Scripture*, 15 (1963), 65-80. Reprinted by permission of the publisher.

Maccabees, Jerusalem fell again into the hands of strangers. In the year 63 B.C. after a three-months' seige, Pompey entered the town, and Jerusalem was reduced to the level of a small provincial city in the Roman empire. The political Jerusalem was dead.

Had God forgotten His promises? Or rather had not the time come when He would carry out His plans and fashion after His own heart the Jerusalem described by the prophets? — "All the promises of God find their Yes in Christ" (2 Cor. 1:20). It belonged to Christ to build the new city; and the New Testament, the gospels in particular, show us God's architect at work. From Mark to John, Jerusalem occupies a more and more important place in the gospels. But it is in Luke that her role is best underlined. In the pages that follow we shall try to decipher the message which Luke intends the theme of Jerusalem to convey.

## At the dawn of the New Testament: Luke's infancy narrative: ch. 1–2

Luke is said to have represented all the events of the life of Christ as "driven by some mystical force towards Jerusalem."[1] This is noticeable from the very first pages of his gospel: the opening and the closing scene of the infancy narrative are staged at Jerusalem, in the temple (1:5-23 and 2:41-50); so is one of the central episodes, the Presentation (2:22-38). These first two chapters, permeated as they are with an Old Testament atmosphere, betray Luke's intention of showing the continuity of God's plan of salvation: the good tidings are proclaimed within the framework of the Mosaic dispensation. In this sense, the annunciation of John the Baptist's birth is typical: just as in the Old Testament, an angel appears bringing a message from God to a Levitical priest at Jerusalem in the temple, during the offering of the daily sacrifice of the lamb. Jerusalem is still truly the city "chosen by God to make his name dwell there" and therefore Israel's spiritual centre.

And yet, somewhat hidden perhaps under this calm fidelity to traditional values but none the less alive, a sense of expectation fills the hearts of many, from Simeon "looking for the consolation of Israel" (2:25) to Anna "looking for the redemption of Jerusalem" (2:38). In fact the fullness of time has come: John the Baptist is "to make ready for the Lord a people prepared" (1:17) and above all, he who is to sit on the throne of David has already been conceived in the womb (1:32).

Jerusalem does not seem to be affected by these great events. Life goes on as usual within her walls, and no notice is taken of Mary and Joseph going up to the temple to present their child to the Lord (2:22f). Yet on this child rests the fate of the city of God, for he is the Servant of Yahweh spoken of by Isaiah, and he will offer salvation to the Gentiles as well as to Israel, but also and perhaps first of all to Jerusalem (2:30-2).[2] The Servant however had been described by the prophet as the "suffering Servant" who would meet with fierce opposition (Is. 50:4-7) and finally suffer a shameful death for the trans-

[1] E. Osty in *Bible de Jérusalem, Saint Luc*, p. 19.
[2] Simeon's canticle is inspired by Is. 42:6; 46:13; 49:6; 52:10.

gression of his people (Is. 53:8). Simeon's mysterious words to Mary (Luke 2:34-35) echo this prophecy and already suggest at what price the redemption of Jerusalem will be paid.

Thus in the first pages of his gospel Luke outlines for our benefit the drama which he is about to describe: the time has come for Jerusalem to make a decisive choice: God is going to "visit" her. Will she consent to rejoice because her king comes to her, even if he is "humble and riding on an ass" (Zach. 9:9, quoted in Luke 19:30f) or will she refuse the message of peace offered to her (Luke 19:42)? On her choice will depend her very existence as the city of God.

## Jerusalem, the city of the greatest temptation (4:1-13)

The beginning of the drama is ominous: Jerusalem appears immediately as the place where Jesus meets with Satan's strongest challenge.

Christ's temptations in the desert are mentioned or narrated by the three synoptic gospels[3] and all three place them in the same context: Jesus goes down to the Jordan to receive John's baptism,[4] he also receives from God his messianic investiture[5] and is thus ready to begin his public ministry. But led by the Spirit, he first goes into the wilderness where he is tempted by the devil. Luke seems to follow the same source as Matthew, but his narrative differs from that of the first gospel by some additions and above all in the order in which he presents the temptations. Whereas according to Matthew the second temptation is staged on the pinnacle of the temple in the holy city, and the third on a very high mountain, in Luke's narrative the temptation at Jerusalem comes third. To Jesus exhausted by a long fast (4:2) Satan has already suggested: "rely on yourself, on the power you possess" (4:3); then, showing him "all the kingdoms of the world in a moment of time" (4:5) he has told him "rely on me and it will all be yours." But the first two temptations having failed, Satan makes a final attempt, an attempt which for Luke will constitute the climax of the trial imposed upon Jesus: "rely on God" says Satan. Jesus is the messiah, and therefore by right king of Jerusalem; why should he not show it immediately by throwing himself down from the pinnacle of the temple? Surely God will protect him, and the Kidron valley, already so rich in memories, will become the scene of the first great triumph by which the messiah conquers the hearts of his people.

This then is the choice offered to Jesus: either the easy way suggested by Satan, of propaganda-miracles which would give Jerusalem a messiah after her own heart; or the humble and hard way of the cross winding through the streets of the city and leading up to Calvary. But the Father's will is clear: Jerusalem will witness the triumph of her king, but not the sort of triumph she expects; to save her from utter ruin, to make her the centre of the world, Jesus will have to die; Jerusalem will be the scene of his Passion.

[3] Matthew 4:1-11; Mark 1:12; Luke 4:1-13
[4] Mark 1:1-11; Matthew 3:13-17; Luke 3:1-22
[5] Mark 1:11; Matthew 3:17; Luke 3:22

But the hour of the Passion is still far away; and Jesus must now begin his mission in Galilee. Satan, having "ended every temptation" (4:13), can only withdraw from the field; he already knows however that Jerusalem will offer him one day another and better opportunity: "he departed from him until an opportune time" (Luke 4:13; cf. Luke 22:3).

## Jerusalem the city of Christ's 'exodus': 9:28-36

While describing Jesus' Galilean ministry, Luke seems to forget Jerusalem: between 4:14 and 9:28 the name of the city appears only once: in 5:27.

Jesus' fame has already spread far and wide (5:15) and it seems to disturb the authorities; the Pharisees side with the teachers of the law to watch him; not only the Pharisees and teachers of Galilee, but also, as Luke points out, those of Judea and Jerusalem (5:17).[6] This is perhaps only a detail which by itself does not mean much; but it certainly suggests that Jerusalem is not particularly well disposed towards the young rabbi. More important however is the way Luke, throughout the Galilean section of his gospel, simplifies Jesus' itinerary: his narrative follows closely that of Mark, but he leaves out Jesus' journey to Tyre and Sidon (Mark 6:45-8:26); he also leaves out the names of Caesarea Philippi in 9:18-21 (see Mark 8:27) and Galilee in 9:43-44 (see Mark 9:30). It looks as if he intentionally omitted any topographical indication which might unduly distract our attention from Jerusalem. And when his description of the Galilean ministry comes to an end, he takes advantage of an important event, the transfiguration, to remind us of the place which Jerusalem is to have in the mission of Christ.

The narrative of the transfiguration appears in Luke in the same context as in Matthew and Mark: Christ who has told his disciples about his coming passion,[7] and has invited them to follow him carrying their cross[8] takes with him Peter, John and James and goes up to the mountain to pray (9:28). While praying he is transfigured before them, and they catch a glimpse of his glory. We can assume that for Luke, just as for Matthew and Mark, the transfiguration is meant as a promise and foretaste of Christ's glorious resurrection, and as such it brings comfort to the disciples whom the first prophecy of the passion has disheartened.

But Luke's narrative contains a special message, for whereas Matthew and Mark are content with mentioning the presence of Moses and Elijah talking with Jesus,[9] Luke explains:

> They spoke of his departure which he was to accomplish at Jerusalem (9:31).

There is, in this sentence, one word particularly worth noticing, the word "departure" which translates the Greek noun *exodos*. Rare in the New Testa-

[6] See Matthew 9:3 and Mark 2:6
[7] Luke 9:22; Matthew 16:21-3; Mark 8:31-3.
[8] Luke 9:23-7; Matthew 16:24-8; Mark 8:34—9:1.
[9] Matthew 17:3; Mark 9:4.

ment,[10] this term occurs fairly frequently in the Old Testament where it often means a "going out" in general,[11] but where it also refers especially to the "exodus" from Egypt. Now in Luke 9:31 this same term could be understood in the sense of death, without any other precision: "They spoke of his death which he was to accomplish at Jerusalem."[12] But the context seems to suggest a more pregnant meaning: the presence of Moses at Jesus' side, the mountain (9:28), the glory (9:32), the cloud (9:34), the voice coming from the cloud (9:35), remind us forcibly of the theophany of Mount Sinai,[13] that is of the central event in Israel's journey from Egypt to the promised land, in a word, of *the* Exodus. The theme of the exodus was already underlying the narrative of the temptations in the desert: just as Israel, after having been chosen by Yahweh as His son, had been led into the desert by a column of fire, that is, according to a consecrated interpretation in Israel, by the holy spirit of Yahweh, in order to be tempted for forty years, so too was Jesus, the well-beloved Son of God, impelled into the desert by the Spirit in order to undergo his temptations.[14] Matthew, Mark and Luke have this same theme in mind when describing the transfiguration, but Luke brings it out more clearly by using the very word "exodus": Jesus is about to go up to Jerusalem; his journey will not be an ordinary pilgrimage; he will remake, on his own account, Israel's spiritual journey, and just as the first exodus had brought Israel to the promised land, so Jesus' exodus will end at Jerusalem where he will "pass over" from this world to the Father, thus fulfilling his mission of Saviour of the world, and Jerusalem will be for him, in some mysterious way, what the promised land had been for Israel.

Thus, in one sentence, Luke gives us the deep meaning of the events that lie ahead, and in particular, of Jesus' journey to Jerusalem.

### Jesus' journey to Jerusalem: 9:51–19:27

To this journey, Luke consecrates the central section of his gospel; a section which is all the more interesting and important for our purpose as it is, for the greater part, proper to the third gospel.

What are Luke's sources for this section? From 9:51 to 18:14 Luke abandons Mark, his usual guide, and within the framework given him by Mark (Mark 10:1) of a journey to Jerusalem, he assembles materials gathered from a tradition also used by Matthew, and from other sources to which he alone has access.[15] Luke had probably at his disposal a number of elements which no historical or thematic thread linked together, and he gave them the

[10] In the NT the term *exodus* appears only twice beside our text: in Heb. 11:22 (where it means exodus) and in 2 Peter 1:15 (where it means death).

[11] Going out of a territory, of a house: Exod. 23:16; Num. 35:26.

[12] This is the translation adopted by Knox; see also Lagrange: *Évangile selon St. Luc*, p. 272.

[13] See Exod. 24:15f.

[14] See J. Guillet: *Themes of the Bible*, p. 15.

[15] The whole section counts 24 pericopes common to Matthew and Luke, 22 proper to Luke, and 4 belonging to the 3 synoptic gospels.

unity they lacked by inserting them into the narrative of a journey taking Jesus from Galilee to Jerusalem. In 18:15, however, Luke picks up Mark's narrative where he had left it (see Mark 10:13) and follows it closely, though some divergences bring him here and there nearer to Matthew.

But what is the exact historical value of Luke's narrative? Is this journey he describes a real journey? Jesus, no doubt, did leave Galilee for Jerusalem where he was to die, and Luke, just as Matthew and Mark, makes this clear. Luke, however, is not so much concerned with geography as with theology, and Jesus' itinerary does not interest him as such; shading off therefore all topographical notations except those of Jerusalem, he shows Jesus heading with great decision towards the holy city. We thus find scattered through his narrative texts which he uses as signposts destined to remind us of Jesus' goal. These texts are purely redactional, in the sense that they allow him to unify his sources; but at the same time, they give us indications of his theological intentions.

## En route towards a hostile city: 9:51

Going up to Jerusalem was always for the Jews a great event; and many psalms echo the joy of the pilgrims making their way over the steep hills of Judea and finally discovering from afar the city and the house of their God:

> How lovely is thy dwelling-place, O Lord of hosts!
> My soul longs, yea, faints for the courts of the Lord;
> my heart and flesh sing for joy to the living God . . .
> Blessed are they whose strength is in thee,
> in whose heart are the highways to Zion (Ps. 84:1-5).

. Jesus too looks forward to going to Jerusalem once again,[16] but he knows that Satan is waiting for him there, and that the joy of the first hours in the city will be followed by a fierce and lonely struggle against the powers of darkness. Indeed, as Luke seems to suggest, the struggle begins at the very moment Jesus leaves Galilee:

> When the days drew near for him to be received up, he set his face to go up to Jerusalem (9:51).

The very tone of the evangelist is solemn: "a verse full of majesty, written in Old Testament style."[17] The expression "to be received up" refers to Christ's death, but also, and perhaps first of all, to his ascension.[18] But the glory to come is overshadowed by the sufferings of the passion, and Jesus appears as the Suffering Servant who, under persecution "set his face like a flint" (Is. 50:7) and held on, knowing that he "who vindicated him was near." Jesus starts on his journey, to face the agony of Gethsemane and the passion.

[16] See Luke 12:50; 22:15.
[17] E. Osty, op. cit. p. 87, note c.
[18] The verb from which the word used by Luke derives, is applied in the OT to Elijah's assumption: 2 Kings 2:9-11; and in the NT to Christ's ascension: Mark 16:19; Acts 2:1, 11, 22.

## Jerusalem, the city that kills the prophets: 13:31-35

The following chapters show Jesus on his way to Jerusalem; he presses on, hardly finding time to stop and speak to those who would like to join the group of his disciples (9:57-61). Many episodes, it is true, give us a completely different impression, and his ministry resembles very closely that of the Galilean period when he travelled from village to village, preaching the gospel and healing the sick. And yet, Luke does not want us to forget that it is "journeying toward Jerusalem" that Jesus goes through towns and villages, teaching (13:22).

He thus reaches Herod's territory, probably Perea (13:31-33). But he is not given much time to rest there, for the Pharisees, as if they were anxious about his security, come and tell him: "Get away from here, for Herod wants to kill you" (13:31). Is it likely that Herod bothered at all about Jesus? Did he really intend to kill him? Perhaps he had heard about Jesus and simply meant to keep him away from his territory so as to forget more easily about John the Baptist (see 9:7-9). Hence his intervention through the Pharisees! Or perhaps the Pharisees themselves invented this trick so as to oblige Jesus to go to Judea and Jerusalem, their stronghold, where they would find it easier to hold him in check?

But whatever be the facts, Jesus' answer plays an important part in Luke's narrative:

> Behold I cast out demons and perform cures today and tomorrow, and the third day I finish my course (13:32).

The expression "today and tomorrow" should not be taken literally; it simply means a short and determined space of time. Whatever be Herod's plans, it is true that Jesus has nearly reached the end of his mission: the day approaches when he "finishes his course," or literally, "when he is achieved," the word being chosen by Luke suggesting both the idea of "end" and the idea of "achievement, fulfillment"; and in fact, Jesus' passion and death will not only put an end to his earthly mission, but will also "make him perfect" (Heb. 2:10; 5:9). The third day has not yet come, however, and in the meantime Jesus must, for such is the Father's will, be on his way casting out demons and performing cures, and it will be in Jerusalem and nowhere else that he will finish his course, for:

> it cannot be that a prophet should perish away from Jerusalem (13:33).

These are ironic words, partly explained by Jesus' lament over Jerusalem, which Luke links up with the episode in Herod's territory.

The text of this lamentation is common to Matthew and Luke,[19] but whereas in Matthew it concludes a long section dealing with the imminent coming of the kingdom (Matthew ch. 19–23) and introduces the long eschatological discourse of ch. 24–25, Luke inserts it in his journey narrative, thus giving the journey itself a specific meaning. Jesus' lament is addressed to Jerusalem, and to Jerusalem considered not only as the symbol of Israel as a whole, but also

[19] Matthew 23:37-39; Luke 13:34-5.

and above all as the city entrusted with a special mission in which she has hopelessly failed, in spite of the efforts made by the prophets in her favour. For God did send in time past many prophets to remind her of her divine vocation; relentlessly, they denounced her sins and invited her to conversion,[20] but to no avail: far from listening to their call, she persecuted them: "This man deserves the sentence of death, because he has prophesied against this city" (Jer. 26:11). And it was actually in Jerusalem, in the court of the house of the Lord, that King Joash had Zechariah stoned to death (2 Chr. 24:20f), just as it was probably also in Jerusalem that King Jehoiakim slew Uriah (Jer. 26:20f). As to King Manasseh's cruelties, they struck, according to Josephus,[21] the prophets above all, and their blood flooded the city (2 Sam. 21:16). Many other similar crimes, not mentioned in the Bible, may have given rise to the tradition echoed by the New Testament [22] and earned the city of God the lament of Christ himself:

> O Jerusalem, Jerusalem, killing the prophets and stoning those who are sent to you! (13:34).

But it was precisely Christ's task to make a final attempt to save Jerusalem:

> How often would I have gathered your children together as a hen gathers her brood under her wings, and you would not! (13:34).

Christ's call has hitherto remained unanswered, just like the call of the prophets; and the catastrophe is now at hand:

> Behold, your house is forsaken (13:35).

And yet, all hope is not forbidden: Jesus' threat ends with a mysterious promise of salvation:

> I tell you, you will not see me until you say, 'Blessed be he who comes in the name of the Lord!' (13:35).

Jerusalem's refusal of her divine vocation will be her ruin, but her Lord will come back, and this time, his reception will be a triumph lasting for ever.

### Jerusalem, the city that rejects her king: 19:11-27

From Herod's territory Jesus must have headed towards Jerusalem, though Luke does not say so. The mention of a dinner offered to Jesus by a Pharisee allows the evangelist to group together several sayings to which the theme of the meal gives unity (14:1-24); and again, abruptly, the theme of the journey reappears: "Now great multitudes accompanied him . . ." (14:25), as if the whole people of Israel took part in Jesus' pilgrimage. On two other occasions, Luke reminds us of Jesus' journey. In 17:11, 'On the way to Jerusalem Jesus was passing between Samaria and Galilee.' This is a purely redactional element: since 9:51, Jesus, starting from Galilee, has been on his

---

[20] See Ez. ch. 8-11.
[21] *Antiq.* X, III, 1.
[22] See Acts 7:51f; Heb. 11:37f.

way to the city; but in 17:11 he has not yet left the border between the two Northern provinces. In 18:15, Luke catches up the Markan narrative which he had left in 9:50; and in 18:31, following Mark (Mark 10: 32-34), he gives us the third prophecy of the passion; but so as not to repeat himself he simplifies Mark's text, and the third prophecy of the passion becomes in his gospel one more signpost making it clear that Jesus *is* going to Jerusalem.

Finally the journey-narrative comes to an end, and summing it all up, so to speak, we find the parable of the pounds (19:11-22). In spite of important divergences this parable is probably to be identified with that of the slothful servant in Matthew (25:14-30), each evangelist having modified and developed in his own way an initial theme. Matthew's parable belongs to the eschatological discourse made by Christ just before his passion (Matthew ch. 24–25): after having foretold in one and the same perspective both the ruin of Jerusalem and the Parousia, Jesus presents several parables destined to show the repercussions of these two events in the life of men: men are servants to whom their master has entrusted a task in the making of the kingdom and who, one day, will have to present their accounts.

In Luke, the setting of the parable of the pounds is different: as already pointed out, it brings to an end the section consecrated to Jesus' journey to Jerusalem, and even if in itself, it is only loosely connected with the preceding texts, it is certainly meant to play an important role where it is.

Luke seems to have grouped together two parables: the parable of the pretender to the throne (19:12, 14, 27) and the parable of the pounds (19:13, 15-26). The first constitutes a severe prophetic warning to all those who within a few days will reject Christ the king and proclaim: "We have no king but Caesar" (John 19:15). In the background we sense the drama of the passion, the conflict between Jewish messianism and divine messianism, between the political city of Jerusalem and the city of God. The second parable, just as the parable of the slothful servant in Matthew, is an invitation to a vigilant activity.

But what has Jerusalem to do with these parables? Luke makes it quite clear:

> As they heard these things, he proceeded to tell a parable, *because he was near to Jerusalem*, and because they supposed that the kingdom of God was to appear immediately (19:11).

We may conclude that Jesus *is* the pretender who is coming to his city to be crowned king; but not the king which the city expects: "We do not want this man to reign over us!" (19:14).

### Jerusalem, the blind city: 19:28–44

> And when he had said these parables, Jesus went on ahead, going up to Jerusalem (19:28).

Jesus' entry into Jerusalem is told by the four gospels, but the structure of Luke's entire gospel gives it a special relief: it is in Jerusalem that Jesus is going to achieve his mission (see 13:32). Moreover, whereas in Matthew and Mark, Jesus travels constantly, after his solemn entry, between Jerusalem and Bethany, and even, according to Matthew and John, goes as far as Galilee after his resurrection, in Luke he never leaves the city. Of Mark's dramatic introduction to the entry into Jerusalem (Mark 11:1) Luke keeps only the essential: "Jesus went on ahead." Since the day he left Galilee (9:51), Jesus has always taken the lead [23] as if he wanted to be the first to meet the danger.

And yet, just now, there is anything but danger ahead: Jerusalem seems to be all joy to receive her king. Luke stresses this note of joy, and instinctively as it were, it reminds him of the first reception ever granted in this world to the Son of God made man: the reception of Bethlehem: "Peace in heaven and glory in the highest" (19:38; see 2:14). But the triumph of this first "Palm Sunday" is only a timid rehearsal of what is to come later, much later, at the wedding-feast of the Lamb in the New Jerusalem. And the enthusiasm of the crowd cannot make Jesus forget the drama the immediate future keeps in store both for himself and his city: "When he drew near and saw the city he wept over it" (19:41). The second lament of Jesus over Jerusalem, which these words introduce (see 13:34-5), is proper to Luke and therefore particularly worth our attention. Only once elsewhere in the gospels is it said that Jesus wept: when he arrived at the tomb of his friend Lazarus (John 11:35). Jesus loved Jerusalem. But it will take more than a word to rescue Jerusalem from the jaws of death, for she refuses the peace which her king brings to her:

> Would that even today you knew the things that make for peace! But now they are hid from your eyes (19:42).

Instead of peace, therefore, there will be war, and utter destruction:

> For the days shall come upon you when your enemies will cast up a bank about you and surround you, and hem you in on every side, and dash you to the ground, you and your children within you, and they will not leave one stone upon another in you; because you did not know the time of your visitation (19:43-4).

Thus will finally be fulfilled the threats already uttered by the prophets against the rebellious city.[24]

Jesus' entry into Jerusalem gives us the impression that once more, but for the last time, the political and the spiritual Jerusalem are identified: in God's name, the Messiah takes possession of his city, the glorious city which he loves; Jerusalem, the city of David, rejoices in the presence of the Lord; her ambitions are fulfilled, she is the royal city, the centre of the world, and her name is "The Lord is there" (Ezra 48:35). But this identification is only provisional; or rather, it is but the last attempt made by the Messiah to gather the children of Jerusalem. Today, just as yesterday, this attempt will fail; Jesus

[23] See 9:55; 10:23; 14:25.
[24] See Is. 29:3; Jer. 52:4; Ez. 4:1-3.

knows it and the rejection of God's last visitation moves him to tears because it will bring about her final rejection.

## The ruin of Jerusalem: 21:5-36

Jesus' second lament over Jerusalem (19:41-44) contained a concrete but brief description of the ruin with which the city was threatened. But Jesus takes up and develops the same theme in a long discourse given us by Luke in 21:5-36. Luke depends here on a catechetical and literary tradition which considered in the same perspective both the ruin of Jerusalem and the glorious return of Christ at the end of time.[25] But as he has already dealt with this second aspect of Christ's Parousia (17:22-37), he only devotes to it a few verses at the end of the discourse (21:25-8, 29-33), and focuses all his attention on the ruin of Jerusalem: the destruction of the city will mark the end of a world, a world chosen by God and called to a very high destiny, but finally rejected because it has not been faithful.

## The passion: Satan's last chance at Jerusalem

The crucial moment has now come. While every day Jesus spends his time teaching in the temple (21:37), the chief priests and the scribes are seeking how to put him to death (22:1). This is the opportune time for Satan (see 4:13), he enters into Judas (22:3) and is ready to tempt Simon (22:31). The passion begins, the hour and the power of darkness (22:53). Luke, just as the three other evangelists, follows scene by scene the development of the drama which takes Jesus from the Mount of Olives to Golgotha. But behind Jesus' passion, the shadow of another passion stands out: the passion of Jerusalem. Jesus himself cannot but see it: to the women who bewail and lament for him while he is led away to be crucified, he says:

> Daughters of Jerusalem, do not weep for me, but weep for yourselves and for your children. For behold the days are coming when they will say, 'Blessed are the barren, and the wombs that never bore, and the breasts that never gave suck!' Then they will begin to say to the mountains, 'Fall on us,' and to the hills, 'Cover us.' For if they do this when the wood is green, what will happen when it is dry? (23:27-31).

There is no longer any hope for the political Jerusalem; she has condemned her king to death; she too will die.

## Jerusalem, a small provincial city in the Roman empire

We might expect not to find even the name of the deicide city in the pages which Luke consecrates to the appearances of the risen Christ. In fact, Jerusalem is everywhere present in these pages. On the day of the resurrection, two disciples disheartened by Jesus' death, decide to leave the town, but while they are making their way to Emmaus, Jesus himself joins them and as soon as they have recognized him "at the breaking of the bread," they return to Jerusalem

[25] See Matthew ch. 24-25; Mark ch. 13.

(24:13-35). Meanwhile Jesus has already appeared to Simon in Jerusalem (24:35); and while the disciples of Emmaus are telling the eleven what has happened to them on the road, Jesus himself stands among them (24:36). This is his last appearance before he goes back to the Father, and in his final message, he entrusts his disciples with a mission:

> Repentance and forgiveness of sins should be preached in his name to all nations, *beginning from Jerusalem* (24:47).

The Acts will explain further:

> You shall be my witnesses in Jerusalem, and in all Judea and Samaria and to the end of the earth (Acts 1:8).

Thus the evangelisation of the world will proceed by stages, and whereas up to the death of Christ, Jerusalem had been the focal point towards which all nations were invited to converge, the day is now near when the apostles "clothed with power from on high" (24:49), will leave Jerusalem and spread the good news to the four corners of the earth; the political Jerusalem will no longer be the spiritual centre of the world.

> Then Jesus led them out as far as Bethany, and lifting up his hands he blessed them. While he blessed them, he parted from them. And they returned to Jerusalem with great joy, and were continually in the temple, blessing God (24:50-52).

Luke's gospel ends as it has begun: in the temple of Jerusalem. As if nothing had happened; as if Jerusalem did not understand, or even did not know that she was now, in all truth, only a small provincial city in the Roman empire.

## Towards the new Jerusalem

Of the four evangelists Luke is the only one to present the life of Christ as a unique, resolute and decisive "going up" to Jerusalem. When Jesus, the Son of God made man, enters the world, Jerusalem is far from having lost her prerogatives: she is still God's city. The life of the Israelites is focused on her and on her temple, and the main feasts of the Jewish calendar bring throngs of pilgrims to her. She is not simply a political, but a religious capital whose hegemony is undisputed. God himself considers her as His city: in preference to all other cities in Palestine, He chooses her as the stage where the messianic times open. It is at Jerusalem, in the temple, that the birth of the precursor is announced in whom Old and New Testament meet. As to Christ himself, he loves Jerusalem because she is God's chosen city and her temple his Father's house (2:49; 19:45-46); even after his resurrection he wants her to enjoy special rights (24:52). There is therefore perfect continuity between Old and New Testament: Jerusalem the political centre of Israel is also the city of God.

But Jesus is also entrusted with a mission on which the very existence of the city depends. He himself calls this mission a "visitation" (19:44), an Old Testament term, already used by Zechariah singing the intervention of the Lord who has "visited and redeemed his people" (1:68). It will be his task to resume the efforts of the prophets and to make a final attempt to gather the children of Jerusalem (13:34). To this mission Christ consecrates himself wholeheartedly: his first visit to the city already provokes a timid but real gathering: Simeon and Anna, led by the Spirit, are the first fruits of the gathering of Pentecost (Acts 2:5-11). On his great journey to Jerusalem he is accompanied by a group of people, a group which increases steadily: the twelve and some disciples (9:51f), a crowd of people (11:14), increasing crowds (11:29), many thousands (12:1); and when he enters Jerusalem, one might think that his mission is over: unity has been achieved. After his resurrection he wants his disciples to stay in Jerusalem and he specifies that their work of evangelisation will have to start from Jerusalem. The Apostles obey him: after the Ascension, they return to the city, and on the day of Pentecost, Jerusalem becomes the scene of an immense gathering, the description of which (Acts 2:5-12) suggests the final gathering of the heavenly Jerusalem (Apoc. 7:9-12). It is as if Christ's mission had sanctioned for ever the religious role of the earthly Jerusalem.

Christ's mission, the final attempt, met with the absolute refusal of the city. God's city and his city, was a battlefield first for him, and after him for his disciples (Acts 4:1-22; 7:55-8; 12:2). The many motives which explain the attitude of Jerusalem all spring from the same source: her messianic dreams; she expected a political messiah who would make her the political centre of the world. She did not therefore and she could not understand the attitude of Christ, the friend of the poor, the enemy of the rich and the powerful; in her eyes, he was mistaken, and dangerously so. Her disappointment changed little by little into open hostility, and finally led her to condemn him to the fate she had already meted out to so many prophets. And as a consequence, he whom God had chosen to be the cornerstone of His city, was for Jerusalem who rejected him the stone on which she fell and was broken into pieces (30:17-18).

Christ's last discourse foretold the utter ruin of Jerusalem. Did this mean that God had altered His plan of salvation? If, after his resurrection, Christ did ask his apostles to remain in the city until the Spirit was sent to them, he also told them to go, after Pentecost, and preach the good news to the whole world. There was no hint, in his parting message, of a future gathering of all nations in the city. And in fact, the history of primitive Christianity shows how little by little the Church severed the ties which held her bound to Jerusalem and Judaism: the first Christians gathered frequently in Solomon's portico (Acts 5:12), and the apostles may have at first hesitated to start on their missionary journeys; but persecution soon obliged them to go abroad (Acts 8:1), and the Lord lent them a helping hand. He commissioned Philip, one of the deacons, to go and baptise a pagan "on the road that goes down from Jerusalem to Gaza" (Acts 8:26), and invited Peter himself to go and baptise a Roman centurion at Cesarea (Acts ch. 10). A Christian community developed in Syria, and Antioch became an active Christian centre which rapidly took precedence over Jerusalem (Acts 11:19f). And above all Saul of Tarsus, chosen by Christ to carry his name "before the Gentiles and Kings" (Acts 9:15) began his missionary expeditions which took him through Asia Minor and Greece to Rome, the capital of the world. Thus when Luke brought to an end his history of the primitive Church, not only had Jerusalem ceased to be the city of God, but she was approaching her last hour, and the churches of God were scattered throughout the Roman empire. The image of unity so clearly brought out by the third gospel was replaced in the Acts by an image of dispersion.

"The gifts and the call of God, however, are irrevocable" (Rom. 11:29). There was no longer, it is true, any earthly, political city which could lay claim to the title of "city of God." But God was nevertheless building a new city which would inherit the privileges of the ancient Jerusalem. Luke's message must be completed here by that of Paul and John. Paul was the first to stress that the ancient Jerusalem "in slavery with her children" was being superseded by a new Jerusalem from above (Gal. 4:24-31). The Letter to the Hebrews resumes the same image and speaks of Mount Zion and of the city of the living God, the heavenly Jerusalem to which Christians have already come through baptism (Heb. 12:21f). But it belonged to the Johannine tradition to offer us the description of this New Jerusalem, the Church, the Spouse of the Lamb. For the Apocalypse, the Church here on earth is already this city, trampled, it is true, by the nations (Apoc. 11:2). But the day will come when God manifests her full glory:

> And I saw the holy city, new Jerusalem, coming out of heaven from God, prepared as a bride adorned for her husband . . ., having the glory of God, its radiance like a most rare jewel, like a jasper, clear as crystal. . . . And I saw no temple in the city, for its temple is the Lord God the Almighty and the Lamb. And the city has no need of sun or moon to shine upon it for the glory of God is its light, and its lamp is the Lamb. By its light shall all the nations walk, and the kings of the earth shall bring their glory into it . . . (Apoc. 21:2-27).

In spite of her unrestrained ambition, never could the earthly Jerusalem have dreamed of so exhilarating a reality. How true it is that God is able "to do far more abundantly than all that we ask or think" (Eph. 3:20). Glorious things had been spoken of God's city, they have all come true through Jesus Christ in whom all the promises of God find their Yes (2 Cor. 1:20).

## D. SAINT MATTHEW

The venerable Gospel according to St. Matthew has always been highly esteemed in the Church for its close relationship to the Palestinian milieu into which Jesus came and for its admirable syntheses of Jesus' teaching. Its author, Matthew (or Levi), was an apostle and an eye-witness, who according to Papias (ca. 140 A. D.) "set in order the sayings of the Lord in the Hebrew (i.e., Aramaic) tongue, which each one translated, each as best he could."

Since the Aramaic work of St. Matthew is no longer extant, it is impossible to discover in what way it "set in order the sayings of the Lord." The canonical Gospel we now have was written in Greek seemingly at a later date and by an author acquainted with the Hellenistic milieu of the Church of Asia Minor. He makes extensive use of materials known in the early Church as didaché, or instruction.

The Gospel of St. Matthew preserves its essentially Jewish character by emphasizing the theme of fulfillment. More than any other evangelist it quotes Old Testament prophecy and applies it to incidents of Jesus' life. The genealogy going back to Abraham, the stress on Jesus as the Messianic king and lawgiver, who is at the same time the "suffering servant of Yahweh," shows that to this evangelist the keynote of Christian teaching is that Jesus was the one foretold by Moses and the prophets.

The evangelist takes for granted an institutional development of the Church and a Hellenistic as well as Jewish background, indicating a period of development when the center of the Church was no longer Jerusalem but Antioch. If the canonical Gospel was written there, it would be within the realm of a Hellenistic as well as a Semitic culture.

The author of St. Matthew's Gospel is a literary artist who has long reflected upon the Christian teaching and its formulations in the early Church. He includes examples of Christian exegesis and homiletics, as well as norms for Christian conduct. Early liturgical formulations are present, as in the great commission in 28:18-20, which was probably a baptismal formula. The version of the Lord's prayer in 6:7-13 (which differs from the Lucan version, 11:2-4) seems to reflect the current worship of the Church.

St. Matthew's Gospel is above all the Gospel of the Kingdom, in its parables, in the preaching of Jesus, in the consciousness of the condition of the redeemed people of God living in the midst of an unredeemed world. There is a strong current of apocalyptic eschatology (especially in chapters 24 and 25) in which, by symbol and parable, St. Matthew exhorts Christians to prepare for the definitive coming of the heavenly Kingdom by diligent use of their talents and by love of neighbor: "As long as you did it for one of these, the least of my brethren, you did it for me" (25:40).

# THE GOSPEL ACCORDING TO MATTHEW

*Gerard S. Sloyan*

Martin Buber, the eminent Jewish thinker of our day, writes in *Two Types of Faith* that Christianity as such begins when the summons issued by Jesus to enter into the "Reign of God" which has come near begins to be understood as an invitation to conversion. This, in his view, is the moment of unfaithfulness to the religion of ancient Israel.

He considers the supposition that some special gift of God has been given to man, "salvation" in Jesus Christ who now must be "believed in," to be both a betrayal of the true meaning of Jesus (who in his original preaching never asked that men have faith in him), and an abrupt departure from Jewish tradition. "To the man needing salvation in the despondent hour, salvation is offered only if he will believe that it has happened and has happened in this way. This is not a matter of persisting-in but its opposite, facing-about."[1]

Essential to Buber's argument is the notion of the gradual overtaking in the early Church of the thoroughly Jewish teaching of Jesus by an alien spirit of Greek thought: that tragic time when Paul's hellenized concept of faith ("a holding henceforth that so-and-so is true by a kind of mental leap") dislodged the sounder Hebrew conception of faith as a trust and active fidelity which results from an intimate relation to the godhead.

For Buber, the Christian is required to believe (if he has been a Jew) "that which he is not able to believe as a continuation of his former beliefs." He has broken with the Judaism into which he was born and joined the new people of God. Persevering no longer in a trust in the Lord who has made covenant with His people, he enters into the forecourt of his new faith by its one gate: "holding true what has hitherto been considered not true, indeed quite absurd."

Christianity, in other words, is not an evolvement and a perfection of what had gone before. It is a wrench and a departure.

This view of faith in Jesus Christ is surely not that of the gospel according to Matthew. The first in order of the four canonical accounts assumes throughout that faith in God and membership in the Israel of His love is made perfect by active fidelity to Him through His "anointed one." Buber says that Jesus never makes himself the object of faith, that only Paul and the hellenizers did that.

To sustain his thesis he must dismember Matthew's gospel and declare passages by the score, "certainly unhistorical." A text which has been called "the fourth gospel in a nutshell," Matthew 11:27, would be one of these: "Everything has been entrusted to me by my Father; and no one knows the Son but

Published originally in *Worship*, 32 (1958), 342-51. Reprinted by permission of the publisher.

[1] Martin Buber, *Two Types of Faith* (New York: Macmillan, 1952), p. 10.

the Father, and no one knows the Father but the Son and those to whom the
Son may choose to reveal him." As it comes to us, Matthew's gospel is a book
which says on every page to the Jew for whom it was written: "Behold, the
Lord whom you so long awaited."

Matthew is, by elimination, to be identified with Levi the tax-gatherer of
Mark's (2:14) and Luke's (5:27) accounts, though the gospel that bears the
name of Matthew speaks of a Matthew only (9:9; 10:3). The name is a con-
traction of Mattathiah. He could not have been a thoroughly admirable sort.
Extortion of exorbitant sums from one's fellow nationals while in the even indirect employ of a foreign power does not attract the best types.

The "son of Alphaeus" (Mark 2:14) was doubtless well able to afford the
banquet that he gave to celebrate his new discipleship (Luke 5:29). Whatever
that steady gaze over the neatly piled coins had done to him, he had left all.
And when he heard himself defended by the new Rabbi as sick and a sinner,
one who needed a physician (Luke 5:30f), health and holiness must have already begun to take hold in him.

Did Matthew write the gospel attributed to him? An unbroken tradition
going back to the second century says that he did. What is the force of the tradition? At times, the sayings of the Lord come from this evangelist's pen as if
he had heard it all and relished every last maxim, every riposte against the un-
friendly rabbis who drew the noose tighter about Him. Yet there are times
when the phrases are so stiff that no eye-witness could have composed them.

There is abundant evidence that Matthew's gospel as we now have it is an
artfully compiled work from several written sources, Mark's gospel and a collection of "sayings of Jesus" originally in Hebrew or Aramaic being the chief
two candidates. What tradition assures us of is the priority of composition of
*some* account of the Master's life attributable to St. Matthew or the Matthean preaching in a Palestinian milieu, for there is scarcely any New Testament manuscript extant in Greek, Latin, or Syriac which does not place Matthew first.

We would know a lot more about the question if the five books of *Explana-
nations of the Sayings* [*Logíōn*] *of the Lord* written by Papias, bishop of Hierapolis (in ancient Phrygia, modern Turkey) around 125 A.D. were still to be
had. As it is we have to depend on the historian Eusebius (d. *ca.* 340), who
tells us that Matthew "set in order the sayings of the Lord in the Hebrew
tongue, which individuals then translated, each as best he could."[2] About three-
fifths of Matthew is devoted to our Lord's speech, which, coupled with its priority, accounts for the outstanding favor it enjoyed in the early Church.

It would probably be a mistake to conceive the word *logia* in the narrow, literal sense of "sayings" only. A collection of aphorisms of Jesus the primitive
Matthew may have been, but it is much more likely that the word meant things
done as well as said, and that it was the skeleton of our canonical Matthew
in its narrative portions as well as its didactic.

The original gospel in its Semitic tongue, written somewhere between 50-65

---

[2] Eusebius, *Ecclesiastical History*, III, 39, 16.

A.D., probably began with the ministry of the Baptist — the present chapter three — and ended with the traditional passion-resurrection account. In between, it seems to have been divided into five sections or books which were based on five great discourses of our Lord. It is hard to escape the latter conclusion, not simply because He who is presented as the new Moses should fittingly have had His career enshrined in a new "Pentateuch," but because the internal arrangement of illustrative narrative, sermon, and identical concluding phrase is so evident in each of five cases in the inspired gospel that has reached us.

The *first sermon* is that delivered on the mountain (5:1). Chapters 5, 6, and 7 comprise it. It is led up to by the call of disciples and a truncated version of the numerous lakeshore healings and exorcisms. Jesus calls on the aid of associates in proclaiming that God's rule (*basileía*, "kingdom" but more properly "reign") has arrived. He gives proof of it. Then in the discourse He expounds the conditions for life under His Father's gentle reign. With the editorial device, "When Jesus had finished this discourse . . . (7:28), we know that the "book" is at an end.

The instructions given to His disciples before Jesus sent them out on mission is the *second discourse* (10:5-42). The twelve go armed with power to exorcise and to heal, just as they had seen their Master do in the triple series of three miracles each which precedes this section, of which three are cases of demonic possession. "When Jesus had finished giving his twelve disciples their instructions, he left that place and began to teach and preach in the neighboring towns" (11:1).

The narrative sections in chapters 11 and 12 tell of opposition to the new reign of God on the part of the Baptist's captors, of the wicked cities Chorazin and Bethsaida, and the Pharisee mentality. They prepare for chapter 13, the *third discourse*, which is a collection of seven parables illustrative of the "reign of the heavens," both in its growth and in the opposition it will experience. Departure from that place followed, says v. 53, "when Jesus had finished these parables."

The duties of disciples not to scandalize, to seek peace in agreement, and to forgive without limit, form the burden of the *fourth collection* of sayings (chapter 18). Four chapters describing the formation of the disciples — including the promise of the keys to Peter, the transfiguration, and the prediction of the passion — have led up to it.

The *fifth sermon* is usually identified as our Lord's prophetic utterances about Jerusalem's destruction and the parables of watchfulness for the days when the kingdom shall be established in power (chapters 24 and 25), although the entire twenty-third chapter is likewise a spoken discourse — the seven blistering "Woes!" to the hypocritical scribes and Pharisees. In any case, 26:1 presents us with the familiar, "When Jesus had finished this discourse," just as chapters 19 through 23 had been a varied narrative describing mounting opposition to Jesus' mission.

Not all scholars are agreed on this five-book order of canonical Matthew as its internal principle of composition. L. Vaganay is its chief exponent. Some

say the more discernible division is into three sections 3:1–4:22; 4:23–11:
20; 12:1–25:46, of which the first and third parallel the order in Mark 1:
1-20 and 2:23–13:37, while the second has the author organizing his material completely on his own.

X. Léon-Dufour, S.J., thinks that Matthew is chiefly divided into two parts:
the restatement of Jesus' teaching as a guide to community behavior up to
Peter's confession at Caesarea Philippi, and the proclamation of salvation
(*kerygma*) under the sign of the coming passion and concern for the "last
days," after it.

What is undeniable, however, is the utter Jewishness of this book which
on every page is meant to be a "gospel of fulfillment" (5:17-20). Our Lord
is sent only to the lost sheep of the house of Israel, in Matthew's report of Him
(15:24). He is the savior of *his people* from their sins (1:21). Matthew, the
"Christian rabbi," has it as his sole purpose to issue his fellow Jews an invitation to enter the kingdom that has been promised them and on which all their
hopes are pinned.

He makes clear to a people that has confused and conflicting views on God's
anointed one that this Son of David, this "Nazoree" of an unidentified prophecy, was he (2:23). That the royal dignity belongs to Jesus by right is the point
of the early genealogy in the first chapter. This is "a table of descent [*gené-
seōs*] of Jesus Christ, son of David, son of Abraham" (v. 1). The infancy
narrative in Matthew has a distinct apologetic purpose. He whom the angel
announces to Joseph, whom the magi look upon, whose life Herod seeks to
take, is the infant king of the Jews.

When it comes to a selection of arguments to establish the truth of Christ's
claims, Matthew does not satisfy himself with miracles culminating in the bodily resurrection. They are there, but like most incidents in his gospel they are
at a minimum.

He presents Jesus as a *didáskalos* (rabbi, master 23:8; 26:18) who employs the Scriptures with an effortless ease, while the evangelist himself combs
the Hebrew writings for prophecy which the career of Jesus fulfilled. Mark
and Luke content themselves largely with messianic prophecy cited by Jesus
on His own behalf; Matthew goes far afield to produce any text which is in the
least applicable to events in the Lord's career. The theory can not be lightly
dismissed that he used a book of "testimonies," a kind of preacher's handbook
of Old Testament quotations. This would explain how Isaiah 62:11 and Zechariah 9:9 run together in 21:5; Zechariah 11:12f and Jeremiah 32:6ff in 27:10.

Sometimes his rabbinic use of texts is puzzling to our Western theological minds which want prophetic utterances to "prove" something in a way foreign to the thought of the first-century rabbi. Thus Matthew finds an Old Testament quotation to support the virginal conception of Jesus (1:23), his birth
in Bethlehem (2:6), the return from Egypt (2:15), the slaughter of the innocents (2:18), His preaching in Galilee (4:15f), preaching in parables (13:
15), the price of Judas' betrayal (27:10), and so on.

Some of these citations from the prophets and the psalms are prophecies in the proper sense, while others are such by analogy only. A few are the subtlest kind of accommodation — that illustrative use of a poetic passage in the Scriptures of the sort employed by the preacher or the catechist. Despite this major diffierence, the evangelist uses the one rubric throughout: "This was to fulfil what the Lord had declared through the prophet: . . ."

Yet the force of the roughly accommodated citation was far greater for Matthew's Jewish readers than it is for us. After all, their chief means to know what the Spirit of God was teaching them was a cumulative and allusive selection of texts which pointed tellingly in the direction of one Man. They knew no other mode of theological argumentation.

There was a time in the history of scholarship when the thoroughly Semitic character of Matthew's gospel was questioned, but that day is well past. The Greek is stiff and repetitive but generally correct. The author works with the Septuagint (Greek) Bible before him, but often enough the Scripture passages will be renditions into the Greek of Hebrew citations employed in what is presumed to be the original. They are not always from the received Hebrew text. Semitic turns of phrase are observable throughout, e.g., the participial construction "and smiting the servant of the high priest, he cut off his ear" (26:51). Matthew does not translate Hebrew words or explain customs when he comes to them. All this he can presume his Palestinian readers to be familiar with. As Grandmaison puts it:

> They know "what was said to the ancients"; they are more familiar with the whole gamut of rabbinical judgments, "of the tribunal, of the sanhedrim, and of gehenna", than the most learned modern exegete (5:19-22) . . . Nor are they ignorant of any of the ruses by which they can, under colour of piety, refuse to help their aged parents or swear without thereby committing themselves irretrievably (23:18-23). There is no need to explain to them what is meant by "an adulterous generation" (1239; cf. Is. 1:21; Jer. 3:9), a proselyte, or a "child of hell" (23:15).[3]

Semitic words and combinations abound in Matthew, e.g., "reign of the heavens," the latter word being a euphemistic substitution for the divine name (it occurs 32 times in Matthew, whereas Luke and Mark speak of the "reign of God" respectively 32 and 15 times), "the consummation of the world" (28: 18), "flesh and blood" meaning natural human powers (16:17), the "yoke" of doctrine (11:30), "binding and loosing" in the sense of a rabbinic declaration of moral requirement (16:19), and "gates of Hades" to designate either infernal powers or the power of death (16:18). The whole of Palestinian life and thought before the cataclysmic destruction of the holy city are epitomized in recurring phrases such as these.

When Matthew quotes our Lord he does it in recognizable forms of Aramaic poetry. There is the familiar device of antithesis in parallels: an affirmation matched by the denial of its opposite. There is the tendency to deal with a concept in successive spirals, the echoes from a former phrase providing some new and richer usage for a subsequent one.

[3] L. de Grandmaison, S.J., *Jesus Christ — His Person — His Message — His Credentials* (New York: Sheed and Ward, 1935), I, 61.

If this closely articulated style was the Master's own in oral discourse (and everything leads us to suppose so) we have an insight into His special gift as a preacher. Surely the grouping of sayings or deeds in threes, sevens, and tens is no accident but a familiar Oriental teaching device, reminding us that the lengthy oral catecheses of the apostolic period would require such memory aids. C. F. Burney in his book of over thirty years ago, *The Poetry of Our Lord* (Oxford: Clarendon Press, 1925), attempts to give the "Our Father" and the commission to Peter (16:17-19) in rhythmical Aramaic, as well as certain parables. The latter device, the *mashal* or storied comparison, must likewise have been current in Jesus' day, or so we deduce from its flowering in written rabbinic sources not long afterwards.

Our Lord has a single message for His own people, that the rule of Yahweh is established. It is *euaggélion*, the biblical "good news" hinted at often in ancient times but most effectively by that poet of the glorious return from exile, the "second-Isaiah." "And this gospel of the Kingdom will be proclaimed throughout the earth as a testimony to all nations," our Lord says (24:14), just as His prophetic predecessor had announced, "Go up onto a high mountain, / Zion, herald of glad tidings; Cry out at the top of your voice / . . Here comes with power / the Lord God, / who rules by his strong arm (Is. 40:9f.). "You are my servant, he said to me, / Israel, through whom I show my glory . . I will make you a light to the nations, that my salvation may reach to the end of the earth" (Is. 49:3, 6). No broader view of Israel's mission to the world was possible than that found in Isaiah, chapters 40–56.

The new people of God proclaimed by Jesus in Matthew, His *ekklesía* or divinely elected assembly (16:18; 18:17), is none other than the old people of promise and covenant. The central place of the chosen people is guaranteed, even while salvation is being proffered to the heathen. The latter will be incorporated into the sacred nation in the "new world" which Christ preaches. In that regeneration, however, the twelve who follow Him will "sit on twelve thrones as judges of the twelve tribes of Israel" (19:28). Nothing of peoplehood is lost except the spirit of isolation.

It must be clear to all Christians — surely it is to all Jews — that the interpretation of fulfillment provided by Matthew's gospel goes far beyond the Old Testament data. It would be strange if it did not. The Hebrew scriptures look to the future. They demand completion beyond themselves, not within themselves. No process of reworking their contents will suffice. Development of a massive kind was required in order that the hope of Malachi's time or even the period of the Maccabees should have palpable fulfillment.

The people longed for deliverance, for God with them, for a Davidic king anointed of God. They required a priestly personage to offer spotless sacrifice and the temple cleansed. All this they thought they had been promised. Matthew's contention is that it has all come to passing virtue of a direct divine intervention.

The person of Jesus Christ is Matthew's chief argument, not a congeries of probabilities from a mass of prophetic data. It is in no dazed spirit of self-discovery but with a sovereign certainty dating even to His boyhood that Jesus says: "I am he." In the same spirit the evangelist says: "This is the last age. The reign is come. He is the Son of God who calls Himself the Son of Man."

Because Matthew has come to believe in the kingdom's central figure he finds confirmation for His identity everywhere. Every line in Scripture has a myriad of possible meanings. Matthew, no matter where he looks, finds *this* meaning, for he has already come to believe that Jesus is the Christ. The point is not that Old Testament prophecy has no force in pointing to the Messiah, but that only once the Messiah has come can the full force of prophecy be discerned.

The Palestinian Christians before Jerusalem's fall in the year 70 were in a delicate position. They saw the Pharisees who had successfully opposed Jesus waxing as strong as ever. Naturally the latter's opposition to the Christians hardened. Convinced that they themselves were the legitimate heirs to the promise, they cultivated a spirit of Mosaic observance in whatever areas they thought it necessary or allowable (e.g., Acts 13:39).

It must have been a great temptation, though, to new believers in Christ to revert to the old ways. The scribes had as much learning as ever and their tassels were just as long. Temple worship was no less magnificent. Undoubtedly the lure of the synagogue was a strong one.

That is why St. Matthew never misses a chance to stiffen the spirits of his readers by his emphasis on the superiority of Jesus' teachings. He selects any texts calculated to tighten the bond between the new law and the Law and prophets. He presents a Master who quotes no authorities and who introduces no refined distinctions, but who has captured the spirit of *Torah* (the Law) at a level high above the pedagogic discipline of diet and ritual observance. Jesus is the rabbi and leader (23:10) who alone must be followed. His interpretation of what is merely human in religious traditions (15:1-20) and what is transient though divinely imposed (5:32; 19:9) is not only perfectly safe; it is the one way to salvation.

Cut off from the synagogue, the Christians become "Church-conscious" early, not unlike the community at Qumrân which was so painfully aware of its own corporate existence. The Greek word that has come to mean Church, *ekklēsía*, occurs only twice in the gospels, both times in Matthew. He is careful to underline the dignity of the Twelve, while Mark is busy pointing out their lack of comprehension. Only Matthew shows us Peter walking on the water (14:28ff), Peter paying the temple tax miraculously acquired (17:24ff), Peter described as the rock upon whom a visible edifice of believers is to rise (16:18).

J. Huby, S.J., in his little book posthumously augmented by his confrere Father Léon-Dufour, S.J., *Lévangile et les évangiles* (Paris: Beauchesne, 1954) describes St. Matthew's portrait of Christ as a masterful blending of opposing traits. In this gospel, Jewish traditionalism in a Palestinian framework is coupled with a spirit of "catholic universalism." The result is the emergence of a real person of His country and time, a soul "in whom Galilee's gardens are extended."[4]

This Teacher who belongs to no school of thought passes judgment on the

[4] Huby, p. 136, quoting Émile Clermont.

Law and completes it with the authority of a Master. "Thus said Yahweh . . . but I tell you" is a juxtaposition which could spring only from a "living personal voice bound to no commitments whatever."[5]

Matthew might have stopped at presenting Jesus as Israel's Messiah, that and no more, but he had loved Him as the Son of God. Without Christ's divinity, "the gospel is no more than the tomb of a dead man." [6] Matthew seeks, and finds, a living Christ not among the dead but the living.

# LITERARY GENRE OF THE INFANCY GOSPEL IN ST. MATTHEW

Salvador Muñoz Iglesias

To perceive the full meaning of any piece of writing the reader must first recognize what literary genre its author employed. Since, then, the aim of a biblical exegete is to find the theological content of the inspired writings of Sacred Scripture, his point of departure must be the literary structures that the sacred writers used. And when we examine the infancy gospels of St. Matthew and St. Luke we are led to suspect that they involve a more complex literary device than a simple, objective description of facts.

## Main motifs

But before forming a comprehensive view of the character of the work, an analysis of its various motifs is required. Unlike some years ago, today it is widely admitted that the literary motifs of the infancy gospels are inspired by Hebrew rather than pagan sources. The main motifs in Matthew's infancy gospel are: 1) Davidic origin of Jesus, 2) previous announcements in dreams, 3) slaughter of the Innocents, 4) the star of the Magi, 5) flight into Egypt, and 6) return to Nazareth.

Matthew's account begins with the genealogy, by which he affirms that Jesus was descended from King David. This is established in three ways: by the genealogy itself, by explicit testimonies quoted in the infancy account, and by the fact that Jesus was born in Bethlehem, "the town of David" (Luke 2:11).

Matthew's apologetic intent in presenting his genealogy is clear from the opening line, "The origin of Jesus Christ, son of David, the son of Abraham" (Matthew 1:1). Both Matthew and Luke attempted to establish the Davidic

[5] *Ibid.*, p. 128.
[6] *Ibid.*, p. 130.

Reprinted from *Theology Digest*, 9 (1961), 15-20. Originally published as "El genero literario del Evangelio de la Infancia en San Mateo," *Estudios Biblicos* 17, (1958), 243-273. Reprinted by permission of the publisher.

ancestry of Jesus by their genealogies and by explicit testimonies. In Matthew the angel calls Joseph "son of David" (1:20); in Luke the angel expressly tells Mary that Yahweh will give her son "the throne of David his father" (1:32).

Again, in Matthew, the chief priests and scribes knew of the prophecy of Micah which said the Messiah would be born in Bethlehem. When Herod is puzzled by the announcement of the Magi and consults the scribes, they quote him this prophecy.

It is frequently considered an axiom on the part of independent criticism that the primitive Christian community, to fortify its beliefs, invented facts for which they sought confirmatory proof in a previous prophecy. Thus Christ's birth at Bethlehem might have been invented to support the Christian belief in Jesus as the Messiah and then substantiated by recourse to the prophecy of Micah.

The Synoptic Gospels as well as early Pauline preaching repeatedly testify to Jesus' descent from David. This belief of the Christian community appears as primitive as the belief in Jesus' messiahship. On the contrary, the birth of Christ in Bethlehem is not stated anywhere in the New Testament except in the infancy gospels. In fact, bystanders once argued "This is the Christ." Others rejoined, "Can the Christ come from Galilee? Doesn't the Scripture say that it is of the offspring of David, and from Bethlehem, the village where David lived, that the Christ is to come?" (John 7:40-42).

Again in verse 52, John records the answer of the priests to the objection presented by Nicodemus: "Search the Scriptures and you will see that out of Galilee arises no prophet." This conflicting opinion on the part of the people and of the priests presents a real difficulty. It supposes that all concerned were unaware of the birth of Jesus in Bethlehem.

## Birth at Bethlehem

Hence the shortage of testimonies keeps us from declaring with certainty the antiquity of the Christian belief in Christ's birth at Bethlehem. However, a glance at the various opinions of Jewish contemporaries regarding the place where the Messiah was to be born will convince us that there was no apologetic need for the first Christians to invent either the Davidic ancestry of Jesus or his birth in Bethlehem.

One tendency of contemporary Judaism, represented in the *Book of Jubilees,* was to hope that the Messiah would be a descendant of Levi, not of David. The most common thought about the place of his birth was that he would present himself in such a way that no one would know where he came from. That is why the crowds are surprised at the simple appearance of Jesus: "Yet we know where this man is from; but when the Christ comes, no one will know where he is from" (John 7:27).

Since opinions of the Jews varied, it would have served no useful apologetic purpose for the Christians to fabricate Jesus' Davidic origin or his birth at Beth-

lehem. It was not the faith that invented the facts, but rather the facts which
originated and imposed the faith.

The text of Micah adduced by St. Matthew in connection with the birth of
Christ in Bethlehem did not originate the belief in this event. But it is logical
that, given the historical fact, the text might be used to confirm it and to give
it that theological value which derives from a divine prediction in a prophetic
text. The meaning of the text itself (Micah 5:1) is rather obscure.

### Announcement in dreams

The next motif we discover in the infancy narrative is the pre-announcement
in dreams of the hero's birth and mission. Three times in the infancy gospel
an angel appears to Joseph in dreams: to announce the virginal conception,
to command the flight into Egypt, and to order the family's return to the land
of Israel. We would like to underline the parallel between Matthew's announcement of the birth by means of a dream and the midrashic legends concerning
the birth of Moses.

Exodus does not mention any previous announcement of the birth of Moses. But the legend that grew up around him is prolific in dreams announcing
his birth. Various legends say that his father Amram, his sister Miriam, and
even Pharaoh dreamed of Moses' birth.

We read in the *Sefer-Zikhronoth* that the spirit of God came over Miriam,
and she had a dream in the night. Later, she related to her parents what the
dream figure dressed in red had said: "Tell your father and your mother that
he who will be born of them during the night will be carried away and thrown
into the water, and that for him the waters will be bisected. And signs and
prodigies will be brought to pass through him. He will save my people of Israel
and he will be its guide."

Undoubtedly some of these legends, like the *Chronicle of Moses,* are of very
late origin, even as late as the tenth century A.D. Yet others, like those collected in the Pseudo-Philo and in Josephus, are certainly ancient, perhaps antedating Christianity. Even granting that the two accounts of Moses and of Jesus have no literary dependence, it is evident that the same motif pervades
them.

A second motif common to the infancy narratives of Jesus and Moses is
the royal decree to kill all the children of a certain region in order to reach
the hero of the account. This motif contains in the two narratives many circumstances that are the same. In both there is an announcement which disturbs
the peace of the king and his court: in Matthew, the inquiry of the Wise Men;
in the legends about Moses, the dream of Pharaoh or the prediction of a
scribe.

In both stories the king decrees the death of all the children of a locality: in
Matthew, the children born in Bethlehem during the last two years; in the
Mosaic legends, all the male children who were born of the Israelites in Egypt.
But the hero, in both cases, is saved by the intervention of God.

## Targum of Jerusalem

The *Targum of Jerusalem* concerning Exod. 1–15 recounts the dream of Pharaoh in this way: "Pharaoh while sleeping had a dream. Behold all of the land of Egypt was placed on the pan of a balance scale, and a lamb, the son of a sheep, on the other pan; and the pan which carried the lamb was heavier. He commanded that all the wise men of Egypt be called and that his dream be recounted to them. Immediately Yamens and Yimbres, the chiefs of the *wise men*, took up the word and said to Pharaoh, 'A son is going to be born in the community of Israel who will destroy all of Egypt.' "

For that reason Pharaoh, the king of Egypt, gave the Jewish midwives the order of extermination: Substantially the same legend is given in the *Chronicle of Moses* and by Josephus, though the latter ascribes Pharaoh's order to the prediction of a scribe.

## Similar episodes

We must note, however, that similar episodes regarding many infants are found in the histories of all peoples and in the legends of all literatures. The basis for all these legends is very simple: Every man who has power is afraid when he hears the announcement of a possible rival, and he attempts to rid himself of the rival. This has occurred repeatedly among all peoples of all times. The simple presence of these motifs in various stories neither refutes their historicity nor establishes literary dependence.

In St. Matthew the order for the massacre is occasioned by the report of the Wise Men who say they have seen a star in the East which has announced the birth of the king of the Jews. This star, however, has no literary connection with the theme of light shining in the room where the hero is born. It is probably not related, therefore, with the rays that illuminated the house where Moses was born, nor with the increase by forty-eight which the light of the sun acquired on the day of the birth of Isaac, nor with the luminous phenomena which usually accompany the angelic apparitions and theophanies.

However, a resemblance to Matthew's account of the star is found in the midrashic legend about the birth of Abraham. Harowitz gives us this version: "When our father Abraham was born, the astrologers said to their king Nimrod, 'A son has been born to Terach; get hold of him and give him all that he desires.' Nimrod asks, 'Why do you say this?' They answered, 'We have seen that on the day he was born a star rose and devoured four stars in the heavens; and this means to us that he will make himself master of two worlds.' "

The intent of Nimrod to do away with Abraham clearly appears in a later legend discovered by Nestle. In this version Nimrod is told, "Certainly a child has been born who is destined to conquer this world and the one to come. So give his parents all the money which they ask of you for the child, and then kill it." Terach, however, saved his son by hiding him in a cave for three years. However, the impossibility of assigning a date to these legends prior to the time Matthew wrote reduces the probability that he was dependent on them. Daniel Völter, for whom the account of Matthew is founded on the *Vita Augusti* of Suetonius and on the visit of Tiridates to Nero, likewise finds Old Testament parallels for the entire passage of the Magi. He tries, for instance, to connect the motif of the star with the prophecy of Balaam: "A star has come forth from Jacob, a comet has risen from Israel; and has shattered the temples of Moab, and the skull of all the sons of Seth" (Num. 24:17).

## Motif of light

As a matter of fact, the Messianic motif of light, which fills the entire Old Testament literature, does play an important role in the two Gospel narratives of the infancy of Christ. But it is always identified with the Messiah himself. The star of Jacob prophesied by Balaam is a personification. It is never an atmospheric phenomenon, like the star in the story of the Magi.

We believe that in this case Matthew, whether he is relating a real historical fact or describing a symbolic episode, is moving in a literary environment perfectly consonant with the Persian origin of the Magi.

Another episode found only in Matthew's account of the infancy gospel is the flight into Egypt. The flight is completely logical, given the decree to slaughter the Innocents. Even on the hypothesis that it were a simple literary motif, it would not be more than an episodic variant within the more comprehensive motif of the persecution of the hero.

Völter would look for an independent literary basis in the obscure verse of Micah (4:9). But his claim seems too forced and to have little foundation in contemporary Messianic beliefs. It is certain that rabbinic tradition talked of a disappearance and a hiding of a Messiah for a very long period of time. But this was not a flight from his enemies, and his mother did not have to accompany him. Either the Gospel did not consider the parallel of Micah, or fidelity to history forced Matthew to separate himself completely from the model. Rather, the evangelist had in mind the case of Moses who twice escaped the persecution of the Pharaoh. This is suggested by the final motif which is considered next.

The infancy gospel of St. Matthew closes with the passage about the return to Nazareth. The angel tells Joseph: "Those who sought the child's life are dead" (Matthew 2:20). Almost the same words are found in Exodus when God inspires Moses to return from Midian to Egypt.

The literary dependence on Exodus extends to the detailed description of the trip. "So Moses took his wife and children, with his ass to carry them, and returned to Egypt" (Exod. 4:20). And the parallel in Matthew: "So he arose, and took the child and his mother with him, and came into the land of Israel" (Matthew 2:21).

The evangelist has undoubtedly seen in this flight of Jesus into Egypt and his return to Nazareth a parallel with the flight of Moses to Midian and his return to Egypt to free the people of Israel. Perhaps the thought that Jesus is the true Son of God, typically symbolized in the people of Israel who were rescued out of Egypt, also influenced Matthew.

If we prescind for the moment from the genealogy (which is a kind of introduction), we see that the infancy gospel of St. Matthew consists of five episodes, each of which is said to fulfill an Old Testament prophecy. The virginal conception of Christ is connected with prophecy in Is. 7:14; the adoration of the Magi recalls Micah 5:1-3; the flight into Egypt is a fulfillment of Hosea 11:1; the slaughter of the Innocents is related to Jeremiah 31:15; and the return to Nazareth fulfills the words attributed to the prophets: "He shall be called a Nazarene."

## Predilection for five

This five-part structure is surprising if we consider that the general framework of Matthew's entire Gospel also comprises five parts — the five famous discourses. Some suspect that Matthew's predilection for the number five reveals a deliberate intention to imitate the author of the Pentateuch. Matthew may have wanted to reveal the historical parallelism between Christ and Moses. At any rate, a mere glance at Matthew's infancy gospel manifests an unusual similarity between the infancy of Jesus and that of Moses, as the latter is narrated in Exodus and midrash literature.

Thus, the births of the two "saviors of Israel" are previously announced through a dream or a prophecy. At the announcement of Jesus' birth Herod and his court tremble, just as Pharaoh and his people trembled at the announcement of Moses' birth. And just as Herod consults the scribes, Pharaoh consults his astrologers. Both tyrants decree a murder of children, from which the heroes are miraculously saved. In both cases the future savior, persecuted and away from his people, receives a heavenly admonition to return because "those who were plotting against his life are dead" (Matthew 2:20 and Exod. 4:20).

These parallels make very probable the hypothesis that Matthew was imitating the account of Moses' infancy. Matthew's account also contains frequent allusions to Abraham's life and to Old Testament Messianic expectations. This evidence and the literary structure of the five episodes are certain proof that Matthew wrote in the genre of haggadic midrash.

## Not pure fancy

The haggadic construction used by St. Matthew is not necessarily synonymous with pure fancy. It is simply a free way of narrating history by adding picturesque details in order to highlight the theological teaching, which is taken from real historical facts. The prevailing religious and didactic character of all of Sacred Scripture makes possible the use of this literary genre.

The theological teaching of Matthew in these two chapters is substantially the same anyway, whether it is a moderate haggadic construction or an objective historical account. We say "*a moderate* haggadic construction," because the historicity of the central facts is certain. The names of the people (Jesus, Joseph, Mary, Herod), the Davidic ancestry of Jesus and most probably the birth in Bethlehem, the virginal conception, and the residence in Nazareth are beyond question.

We admit with Lagrange that higher criticism could consider some of these facts as legends without denying the supernatural character of the work of Christ. But, like Lagrange, we do not consider necessary either the hypothesis of a pure literary invention with symbolistic meaning or that of a folklore production emanating from a preliterary tradition. We even consider both hypotheses gratuitous and unfounded.

From the kernel of the facts which really took place, Matthew could legitimately deduce his theology: Christ fulfilled the Messianic prophecies; he is the son of David, born of a virgin in Bethlehem; his kingdom is universal, but the object of a fearsome hostility, over which finally he would emerge victorious.

"In this perspective," we can conclude with Jean Racette that "it goes without saying that St. Matthew has not believed nor wished to make others believe that everything which he states corresponds necessarily to actual events. It is possible that he has included in his narrative one or other detail, not because he considered it rigorously historical, but simply because he believed it peculiarly suited to throw into relief some aspect of the fundamentally historical event: the appearance of the Immanuel, who was born of a virgin at Bethlehem of Juda, the Savior Messiah, Light of the nations and the King of Israel, persecuted by evil, but finally the victor over both death and evil."

# ORAL TECHNIQUES IN
# MATTHEW'S GOSPEL

Charles H. Lohr, S.J.

Our written Gospels complete what began with oral tradition. Hence they are best considered in the light of known techniques of oral composition and transmission.

We may distinguish three phases in the process by which the Synoptic Gospels reached their final form: 1) the origin and growth of the materials themselves (Formgeschichte), 2) the formation of restricted unities within the available material (Traditionsgeschichte), and 3) the actual composition of the Gospels (Redaktionsgeschichte).

My object is to point out certain techniques proper to an oral style of com-

Reprinted from *Theology Digest*, 12 (1964), 92-98. Originally published as "Oral Techniques in the Gospel of Matthew," *The Catholic Biblical Quarterly* 23, (1961), 403-435. Reprinted by permission of the publisher.

position in various oral literatures which seem to have played a part in Matthew's attempt to bring together his materials into a unified and artistic whole.

In folk-literature strict unity is a basic law of composition, and such definite techniques as prologue and epilogue, recurring lines, foreshadowings, retrospections, themes, and overall structures unify the work and organize its parts.

I suggest that analogous devices were as important in the third phase of the formation of Matthew as groupings of subject matter and catch words were in the second phase. The evangelist has to bring some unity out of the multiplicity of sayings and stories. For this purpose there are available to him devices similar to those used by the early classical authors, of equally great antiquity among the Semites, with which the early Jewish-Christian community is familiar and which they expect him to use.

Matthew reveals his concern for the continuity and interconnection of his materials by 1) his adaptation of his sources to the stereotyped style of tradition, 2) his use of various formulaic devices for the elaboration of unifying themes, and 3) his structural arrangements.

## Use of formulae

Matthew reflects the technique of the scribes and poets of oral tradition in his repetition of formulae and his recasting and abbreviation of the Marcan narratives. In contrast to Luke, Matthew uses an apt expression repeatedly. Short sentences and noun-adjective combinations are frequently repeated in Matthew: word-collections like "the Prophets and the Law," "heirs to the Kingdom," "the lost sheep of Israel's house," and concluding formulae like "Let him who has ears to hear listen," and introductory and transitional formulae like "At that same time," or "When Jesus had finished this discourse."

Matthew tends to omit or condense Mark's subsidiary and pleonastic details as found especially in his picturesque accounts of the miracles. In the double narrative of the healing of the issue of blood and the raising of Jairus's daughter (Matthew 9:18-26; Mark 5:21-43), Matthew not only omits Mark's realistic touches about the woman's distress, but he refers to Jairus simply as "an official," and introduces him with a standard formula, "and coming up, he bowed low before them, saying" (cf. 8:2; 15:25; 20:20; 28:9). Moreover, Matthew's tendency to shorten the narrative bears particularly on those parts not directly connected with the sayings of Jesus, so that many of the miracle-stories become in effect pronouncement-stories.

Another aspect of this process may be seen in Matthew's occasional substantive changes of the Marcan account; he introduces small modifications, such as the popular motif of narrative style which involves the number *two*. The Gadarene demoniacs appear as two (8:28-34), instead of one as in Mark (5:1-20). Similarly, one blind man in Mark (10:46-52) becomes two in Matthew (20:29-34). Finally, the several false witnesses of Mark 14:57 appear as two in Matthew 26:60.

Matthew also uses repeated formulae for the elaboration of unifying themes. The principal devices of this type are *inclusio*, refrain, foreshadowing, and retrospection. These serve two main functions: 1) to indicate the divisions of the work, and 2) to build up a thematic structure to focus the various elements of the tradition on the central interest.

## Inclusio

In the first device, known in Semitic stylistics as *inclusio* and among classical scholars as ring composition, a word or phrase occurring at the beginning of a poem is repeated at its close. Ring composition forces the attention of the audience back from the conclusion of a passage to its beginning and thus unites the parts of a story. Its function is to provide a frame which will link more or less self-contained passages to the web of the narrative.

Matthew is very fond of this device. But the use he makes of it in interconnecting materials has not been observed. The conception of Jesus and his redemptive work dominates his Gospel. His characteristic title for Jesus is Immanuel — a name foretold by Isaiah (7:14) and interpreted by Matthew at the outset of his Gospel as meaning "God with us" (1:23). At the end of his Gospel, Matthew records the promise of the glorified Christ: "I will be with you always . . ." (28:29). This instance of ring composition gives the spirit of the whole work. It also binds independent units to the narrative. For example, a traditional expression, "But many who are first now will be last then, and many who are now last will be first," which in Mark 10:31 is tacked onto the saying about the reward of those who have given up mother and father, is used by Matthew to incorporate the parable of the laborers in the vineyard (19:30; 20:16). Similarly in Matthew 12:39, 45 "a wicked generation," 15:2, 20 "unwashed hands," 16:6, 11 "Be on your guard against the yeast of the Pharisees and Sadducees."

## Refrain

Very similar to ring composition is the refrain which is used to group together a number of verses connected by some unity of thought. A refrain placed where the thought comes to a natural pause marks the close.

There are traces in Matthew of a use of refrains to mark strophes; e.g., in the repeated phrases in the Sermon on the Mount, "and the rain fell, and the rivers rose . . ." (7:24-27), and "You have heard . . . but I tell you . . ." (5:17-48). But the most important use is organizational. The most obvious example is Matthew's use of the phrase, "When Jesus had finished his discourse" (7:28; 11:1; 13:53; 19:1; 26:1) to group his sayings material in five sermons. Another example may be found in cc. 8-9 where Matthew has collected a number of Jesus' "mighty deeds" into three sets of three miracles separated by the interpolation of two blocks of material dealing with discipleship. In the third set the first two accounts end with the formula "and the news of this spread all over that part of the country" (9:26-31). The last miracle concludes: "And the crowds were amazed and said, 'Nothing like this was ever seen in Israel!' " (9:33). Here not a word but an idea is repeated.

## Refrain in miracles

These refrains are the climax of gradually mounting reactions to Jesus' wonderful works. For the first group of miracles no reactions are noted. The first miracle of the second group is the calming of the storm. The disciples said, "What kind of a man is this? For the very winds and sea obey him!" (8:27). At the cure of the demoniacs the people begged Jesus to leave their district (8:34). And when the crowd saw the healing of a man sick of the palsy, "they were filled with awe and praised God for giving such power to men" (9:8). At the end of the second and third groups, other reactions to Jesus' signs are noted. The scribes said, "This man is talking blasphemy" (9:3); and the Pharisees' reaction foreshadows the opposition which is to be the theme of the next section (11–12): "It is by the aid of the prince of the demons that he drives them out" (9:34).

The audience of an oral piece of literature is very sensitive to such echoing intimations, so that, while these refrains help to bind the parts of the story together, they involve the hearers at the same time in the strong undercurrent which demands their own reaction and response. It is, therefore, not by chance that the interpolated matter which divides the groups of miracles has to do with the implications of discipleship.

## Foreshadowing

A third form of repetition involves anticipation, the tendency in oral literature to prepare the reader for the incidents that he is to expect during the course of the work. This pervasive presence of foreshadowing in Matthew is another indication of his indebtedness to oral technique. The very first verse announces the evangelist's theme: "Jesus the Messiah, the son of David, the son of Abraham." The genealogy presents Christ as the completion of Israel's history. He is the beginning of the seventh seven (1:17). There follows the quotation from Isaiah which gives us his name, Immanuel, "God with us" (1:23). The title "Son of David" recurs very frequently (9:27; 12:23; 15:22; 20:30, 31; 21:9, 15; 22:43), and there is an underlying theme of "new sons to Abraham," which is connected with the Baptist (3:9) and recurs in the miracles of the centurion and the Canaanite Woman (8:11; 15:26).

Similarly Matthew often employs dreams (the expression *kat' onar* occurs six times; whereas, dreams are mentioned elsewhere in the NT only twice). Five of the six dreams which occur are found in the first two chapters (1:20; 2:12, 13, 19, 22) and put the beginning of Jesus' career in an atmosphere of destiny in which powers more than human are engaged. The first of the dreams is Joseph's, in which Jesus is given the name which signifies his mission and foreshadows his death: "For it is he who is to save his people from their sins" (1:21). The last of the dreams, that of Pilate's wife (27:19), carries us back to the context in which we began and suggests again the presence of suprahuman forces. Another type of foreshadowing may be found in the prologue to Jesus' public life (4:23-25). One further type of foreshadowing is the use of a little scene to forecast what is to come. At the end of the third set of miracles in the "mighty works" section, a scene (9:33ff) is sketched which foreshadows the opposition of the pharisees, the main theme of the next narrative section (Matthew 11–12).

## Use of retrospection

In a fourth device, known as retrospection, the later stages of a narrative are related to what has gone before in various forms; e.g., summaries for recapitulation and repeated words and phrases used for characterization. Thus the author builds up themes which help to impose on the materials of the second stage of the tradition the unity so necessary in folk-literature. This device can also artistically highlight the significance of the present by projecting the ongoing life of the past into the action.

Retrospection is very common in the First Gospel; e.g., the summary placed between the two miracles of the loaves (Matthew 15:30-31). The summary not only keeps the power of Jesus in the foreground, but the reference enables the compiler to insure the interconnection of episodes which naturally tend to fragmentation. This summary, however, is only one of a network of such references, by which our attention is constantly drawn back to the figure of Jesus as *iatros*, whose wonderful works are seen as signs meant to open the eyes of Israel to the salvation effected by the suffering of the servant of Yahweh.

The oral style readily lends itself to a process of thematic development, because all of its devices are essentially repetitive. Its repeated formulae, used as refrains, foreshadowing, and retrospection, easily become familiar and assume a fulness and richness of signification as motifs in the narrative. The formulae interanimate one another and are of the greatest importance in what we have distinguished as the third stage of a tradition.

In Matthew the development of themes by formulaic repetition is an important feature of his effort to bring together the materials of the tradition in a unified whole, e.g., the theme of the "the kingdom of heaven."

## Foreshadows Resurrection

One theme which runs through the whole Gospel and involves the use of foreshadowing illustrates the importance of such development. Jesus' death and subsequent Resurrection with its promise of immortality for the believer is the main theme of all the Gospels. Matthew foreshadows this theme in the motif of the Son of Man, which makes its appearance first in the collection of miracles. From the very outset a basic paradox is stated: The Son of Man has the power to forgive sins (9:6), but no place to rest his head (8:20). This bipolar image of humility and power increases in depth with each repetition, as Matthew draws on an ever-widening context: The Lord of the Sabbath (12:8) is regarded as a glutton and a drinker (11:19); the one who is to come (10:23; cf. 11:3) — who will send his angels into the harvest (13:41) — has come not to be waited on, but to wait on others (20:28). Toward the end of the first half of the Gospel a new and important motivation enters into this theme:

The figure of Jonah with which the Son of Man is connected in 12:39-41. The story of Jonah and the fish evokes notions of rebirth and immortality and may actually reflect an established allegory symbolizing the resurrection of the dead. This passage is probably meant to foreshadow the resurrection account, but its position in the development of the Son of Man motif suggests that Matthew intends the earlier references to that motif to culminate in the notion of immortality, so that the later references to the passion may be seen in that light.

In the second half of the Gospel, after the lines have been clearly drawn by Peter's confession (16:13), there occurs the first direct statement of Jesus' imminent passion and death (16:21). From this point on, the prophecies of the passion are clearer and more frequent. But the Son of Man motif balances the references to the passion. The predictions of the passion and the allusions to the humiliation and glorification of the Son of Man from this point on foreshadow the events which end the Gospel and refer back to the promise of immortality in the figure of Jonah. The passion account itself looks back to the significance thus built up for it by the many-sided contextual associations of the formula, "the Son of Man."

## Overall unity

We can now look at the Gospel as a series of sections established by the alternation of narrative and discourse material and observe how these sections are related to each other.

The strict unity so essential in the overall development of an oral composition is also necessary within the separate sections of such a work. Because oral literature is directed to a listening audience, the composer has to choose a subject which is at once simple and attractive, omitting details and concentrating on a single mood or effect. Among the various means at the disposal of the author for the creation of the unique effect, the two methods most common in the Hebraic tradition are grouping like materials and developing a leading idea by stressing key words.

The habit of grouping together like materials is most obvious in Matthew's collection of the sayings of the Lord into five extensive sermons. These discourses have not simply grown, but have been built up by design, and stamped each with a character of its own, determined by its place in Matthew's outline.

The same desire to bring home a single point in each section is found in Matthew's groupings of narrative material; e.g., Jesus' "mighty works" (Matthew 8–9), in which the central idea is the power of Jesus and the invitation to follow him.

## Unity from key words

A second method of unifying the individual sections of a composition is the development of a leading idea by putting stress on certain salient words; e.g., the controversy section (Matthew 11–12). Here the types of material are highly diverse: discourse material, pronouncement-stories, miracles, etc. Matthew has therefore made much use of the repetition of key words to bind these elements together. The central idea of the section is the rejection of the Son of Man by "this generation" and the judgment which is impending because of their failure to recognize his mighty works. Matthew established this notion by the iteration of several important words in different contexts of the section, especially *genea* (11:16; 12:39, 41, 42, 45), *dynameis* (11:20, 21, 23), *semeion* (12:38, 39 ter), *krisis* (11:22, 24; 12:18, 20, 36).

The importance of this method of repeating key words for the correct interpretation of a passage is clear in the next narrative section (12:53-17:27). Here the most significant key words are *artos* (loaf of bread — 14:17, 19; 15:2, 26, 33, 34, 36; 16:5, 7–12), *phagein* (to eat — 14:16, 20; 15:20, 32, 37), *esthien* (to eat — 15:2, 27), *chortazein* (to feed — 14:20; 15:33, 37), *zyme* (yeast — 16:6, 11, 12). Their repetition is obviously connected with the two great miracles of the section. The inclusion of so many pericopes in which the ideas of bread and nourishment are central shows how Matthew makes his material provide its own interpretation by the repetition in different contexts of that aspect of his subject necessary to a correct understanding. Such repetition has enabled Matthew to suggest the deeper meaning of these central miracles and to impart to the idea of bread a symbolic value and significance.

## Symmetrical structure

One of the various structural devices available to a compiler in the task of interrelating his different materials is that of arrangement according to concentric symmetry, that is, according to the pattern a b c x c b a. In this scheme the elements are arranged so that one section — the most prominent — forms the center about which the rest are grouped in carefully balanced blocks. On either side of the central pivot, groups of incidents match. In a more developed form, each section within this general plan may have its own structure in which the individual elements are arranged in concentric patterns. A related method of composition seems to have been used by Matthew.

The Gospel taken as a whole can be regarded as one great symmetrical structure. The division of the Gospel would appear as follows:

| | | |
|---|---|---|
| A | 1–4 | Narrative: Birth and beginnings |
| I | 5-7 | SERMON: BLESSINGS, ENTERING KINGDOM |
| B | 8-9 | Narrative: Authority and invitation |
| II | 10 | SERMON: MISSION DISCOURSE |
| C | 11-12 | Narrative: Rejection by this generation |
| X | 13 | SERMON: PARABLES OF THE KINGDOM |
| C | 14-17 | Narrative: Acknowledgment by disciples |
| II | 18 | SERMON: COMMUNITY DISCOURSE |
| B | 19-22 | Narrative: Authority and invitation |
| I | 23-25 | SERMON: WOES, COMING KINGDOM |
| A | 26-28 | Narrative: Death and rebirth |

There are considerable advantages in regarding the structure of the Gospel in this way. It shows first of all the old question of the relation of the sermons to the narration to be a false problem. The Gospel cannot be divided into five books each of which is made up of sermon plus narrative, or vice versa, because whichever way it is taken, there is one narrative section left over. Secondly, it provides a motive for Matthew's rearrangements of Marcan and other materials in 4:23–13:58. Thirdly, an understanding of this structure supplies us with a key to the meaning of the Gospel as Matthew himself saw it. The discourse containing the parables of the Kingdom is the central pivot about which the other sayings and doings of Jesus revolve.

## Concentric patterns

There are at least two ways of establishing concentric patterns: 1) by the use of disparate matter as central points, and 2) by the symmetrical repetition of key words.

In order to achieve certain arrangements, Semitic authors inserted a different type of material between two groups of homogeneous matter. Because of the difference in content, such insertions serve a formal function by marking the divisions of a section or of a whole work.

In Matthew this method is fundamental. The whole Gospel is structured by the alternation of sermons and narratives, but this technique is also found within the individual sections. For example, the "mighty works" section (8–9) is composed of three sets of three miracles separated by the interpolation of two blocks of two pericopes each on discipleship. In the central miracle of the central set Jesus is called "Son of God" (8:29). The sermon containing the parables of the Kingdom (13) exhibits a similar structure. Three groups of parables are divided by the insertion of two explanations of the purpose of parables (13:10-23, 34-43). This literary principle seems to be behind the arrangement of materials in cc. 19–22. In outline the section would appear in this way:

| | |
|---|---|
| 19, 1-30 | Four questions |
| 20, 1-16 | Parable of laborers in vineyard |
| 17-19 | Prediction of passion |
| 20-28 | Question of the mother of the two sons of Zebedee |
| 29-34 | Miracle: cure of two blind men |
| 21, 1-17 | Entry into Jerusalem and cleansing of Temple |
| 18-22 | Miracle: the withered fig-tree |
| 23-32 | Question about authority answered by question about two sons |
| 33-46 | Parable of the wicked husbandmen |
| 22, 1-14 | Parable of the marriage feast |
| 15-46 | Four questions |

The other method of establishing concentric patterns is by the symmetrical repetition of key words, a recognized device in Hebrew poetry. Matthew seems to have made use of this method in cc. 11–12. The key words noted above seem to fall into a pattern centering about the title "Son of David."

We have seen how Matthew made a skillful use of the devices of oral style to assure the continuity and interconnection of his materials. He has made them serve a single purpose easily appreciated by a community familiar with such techniques. Papias tells us that Mark did not make "any special arrangement of the Lord's sayings"; but he justifies the Marcan style on the ground that, as the "interpreter of Peter," he wished to "omit nothing." Papias' statement reflects the community's dissatisfaction with the Marcan style. The community knew that the function of the wise man was to arrange sayings and proverbs (Qoh. 12:9). The evangelist creating our Gospels leads and is led. He brings together the materials of the tradition, but the community demands that he adjust them to the traditional style and structures. They are as familiar with the material as he is himself; they realize that they are themselves a part of the tradition and are able to cooperate with the evangelist in his presentation by entering into the narrative and supplying the connections hinted at by him. But for this he must employ the techniques with which they are familiar.

# ST. PETER'S DOUBLE CONFESSION IN MATTHEW 16:16-19

Edmund F. Sutcliffe, S.J.

In the last few decades not a few scholars have pointed out that the passage Matthew 16:17-19 does not fit well into its context. Two of the latest studies of this subject are those of O. Cullmann and A. Vögtle.[1] Both give sound reasons to demonstrate the genuineness of the commission promised by Christ to Peter and it is not proposed to repeat them here. Both agree further that Peter is promised authority over the whole Church, but Cullmann limits this authority to the brief period during which he was head of the Church at Jerusalem.[2] This, he holds, came to an end when he set out on missionary activity.

Published originally in *The Heythrop Journal*, 3 (1962), 31-41. Reprinted by permission of the publisher.

[1] O. Cullmann, *Peter, Disciple, Apostle, Martyr: an Historical and Theological Study*. Translated from the German by Floyd V. Filson (London, 1953), pp. 155-238, and A. Vögtle, *Das öffentliche Wirken Jesu auf dem Hintergrund der Qumranbewegung*. (Freiburger Universitätsreden. Neue Folge, Heft 27, Freiburg im Breisgau, 1958). Also, 'Messiasbekenntnis und Petrusverheissung' in BZ, N.F. 1 (1957), pp. 252-72; 2 (1958), pp. 85-103. In this he limits the verses from a post-Resurrection context to Matthew 16:18-19, excluding any part of Peter's confession and our Lord's reference to it. This article contains abundant bibliographical references as also Cullmann's book.

[2] Cf. Cullmann, *Peter* . . . , p. 226.

Both agree also that the passage, 16:17-19, does not harmonize well with the context. In St. Mark's account of Peter's confession Christ makes no commendation of it, 8:27-30. He merely charges the Apostles not to tell anyone about Him; and this must mean not to spread the tidings that He is the Messiah. The reason appears at once in what follows. Peter and the other Apostles recognized Him to be the Messiah but they still entertained the current national and political conception of the messianic office. To correct this mistaken notion, as Mark continues, Christ began to tell them of the sufferings He was to undergo and of the death to which He was to be condemned. Peter thereupon rebuked Him, as such a future was far from his thoughts. Christ then in turn gave a sharp rebuke to Peter in the sight, and surely also in the hearing, of the others, Mark 8:31-33. This incident explains why Christ had neither accepted nor rejected Peter's confession. He could not deny — Peter had confessed the truth — but to accept the confession would have seemed to imply an acceptance also of the conception of the Messiah that accompanied it. This important sequence is lost in Matthew's account where Christ gives the most explicit assent to Peter's words.

As regards the original setting of the momentous promise to Peter, Cullmann finds the most suitable occasion at the Last Supper, Luke 22:31ff, when Christ commissioned Peter to confirm his brethren. Vögtle rightly thinks an occasion after the Resurrection more appropriate.

What follows is concerned only with the conflation of two confessions, the confession of Christ's messiahship and the confession of His divinity. Mark and Luke report only the first. Mark 8:29, gives as Peter's reply only "Thou art the Christ" and Luke 9:20, only "the Christ of God." Matthew has the addition "the Son of the Living God" Cullmann considers that "this expansion appears rather a weakening of the Marcan text," p. 172. His reason is that the simple words of Mark's form "are more powerful in their simplicity." Vögtle too leaves this Matthaean addition as part of the first confession made at Caesarea Philippi, and as referring only to the messiahship. On the contrary, it may be urged that the words are a solemn heightening of that confession and it is here proposed that they belong to a second confession in which Peter professed his belief in Christ's divinity.

But before discussing the question of two confessions in Matthew 16:13-20 it may be well to recall how well conflation in that text would agree with Matthew's habit of joining matters of similar import to the disregard of chronological order.

## Matthew's attitude to time and place

The first Gospel attaches little importance to circumstances of time and place. The emphasis is all on the historical fact that certain events occurred and certain pronouncements were made and little interest is shown in their local and temporal setting. Hence the author tends to group his material not chronologically but according to subject-matter. This is not to overlook the general scheme which begins with the Birth of Christ and ends with the Passion and Resurrection, but within the limits of the public ministry it is often impossible to assign chronological sequence. This habit of logical grouping can be misleading for the reader who, like most modern students, would like to know the circumstances of all the actions of our Lord's life. To interpret correctly it is requisite to note carefully whether the evangelist does in fact mention a time and place referring to the particular event or discourse in question. If he does, we have of course the information required in regard to that particular event or discourse. But he may, and this is where the difficulty of correct understanding lies, he may join with the event or discourse to which the notes of time and place do belong, other actions and sayings called to mind by mental association but without the addition of a warning that the action took place or the words were spoken elsewhere or at a different time. Failure to note this has been the cause of many misunderstandings. Especially was this the case with the older exegetes whose attitude may be described as an acceptance of the apparent implication of the evangelist's words as a true indication of his mind and therefore to be received on his authority.

How then, it may be asked, are we to distinguish such cases? Help is sometimes forthcoming from the narrative of the other evangelists who give a different order or another setting. Sometimes Matthew's own text when carefully considered reveals hints that his order is logical only and not chronological. A simple example of divergent order is given in the narrative of our Lord's temptations in the wilderness. Matthew's second and third temptations (4:5, 8) are the suggestion that He should throw Himself down from the pinnacle of the Temple and the vision of the glory of the kingdoms of the world. Luke 4:5, 9, narrates these two in the reverse order. Another example which is universally recognized is the date of the anointing at Bethany. Matthew 26:6; Mark 14:2; and John 12:1, all agree as to the place. But whereas St. John (12:1) makes it plain that it took place six days before the Passover, the two former evangelists mention it after having arrived at two days before that feast (Matthew 26:2 and Mark 14:1). They do not say that it occurred at that date but that is the temporal setting in which they give their account of it; and no doubt, had we not the fourth Gospel to help us, many would suppose that we knew the date from the two synoptists. In this case it is not difficult to see the reason for the position chosen in their narratives. They were beginning the history of the Passion to which this anointing was a suitable prelude as our Lord Himself said it had been done in view of His burial (Matthew 26:12; Mark 14:8). A connexion between the supposed waste of precious ointment and Judas's determination to betray His Master is possible but not so obvious.

Opinions are not unanimous on the question whether our Lord purged the Temple precincts of illegal traffic on one or on two occasions. St. John, who has a chronological scheme of feasts, describes such a cleansing at the time of the first Passover of the public ministry (2:13-20). The three Synoptists mention a cleansing in connexion with the triumphal entry into Jerusalem. The example of the anointing at Bethany prepares us for the possibility that they are speaking of the same event as St. John though in a different setting. That they are not assigning a definite date becomes probable when it is noticed that Matthew's account (21:12-13) falls within his narrative of the triumphal entry (21:7-16), whereas Mark's account (11:15-17) comes after the entry (11:1-11) and after he has spoken of the following day (11:12). Thus Matthew apparently puts the cleansing on Palm Sunday, Mark apparently on the next day. Luke's account (19:45-46) follows the triumphal entry (19:35-44) and the connexion of the two events is not so clear as in the first Gospel. The probability becomes a practical certainty when we notice that the synoptist account is almost identical with John's. Mark adds to Matthew that Christ would not allow anyone to carry a tool or vessel through the temple (11:16) so making of the sacred place a convenient short cut. But no one considers that this additional information differentiates the two accounts. And there is similarly no reason for thinking that the Synoptists have in mind an event other than that described in John because they quote our Lord's words about the merchants making a den of thieves the place that by rights should have been a house of prayer. John did not necessarily say all he might have said. On the contrary his plan was to supplement the earlier writers and not to repeat what they had clearly put on record. The same remarks apply to the insignificant detail that Matthew and Mark mention Christ's overturning the tables of the money-changers and the chairs of the dove-sellers whereas John records the former only. And our conviction becomes a certainty in view of the lack of chronological interest that is here discussed. The identity is accepted by modern writers such as Lagrange, Staab and Buzy among others.[3] It remains to explain the reason that led the Synoptists to put their account of the event in its actual position in their narrative. This seems to have been that they give no account of the early Judean ministry and make no mention of a previous visit to Jerusalem. So their scheme offered no suitable place earlier in their narrative.

To these examples of disregarded chronological order should now be added instances of Matthew's habit of grouping his material by subject matter. A series of miracles of varying character are gathered in chapters 8 and 9. Chapter 12 gives instances of the opposition of the Pharisees and chapter 13 collects a number of parables. In the same way many hold that in the Sermon on the Mount elements have been introduced spoken by Christ on other occasions.[4] And no doubt this is so though difficult to prove in detail.

[3] M.-J. Lagrange, O.P., *Évangile selon Saint Jean* (*Études Bibliques*) (Paris, 1925²), p. 64; K. Staab, *Das Evangelium nach Matthäus* (Echter Bibel, Würzburg, 1951), p. 112; D. Buzy, S.C.J., *Évangiles de S. Matthieu et de S. Marc* (La Sainte Bible, Pirot-Clamer, Tome IX, Paris, 1935), p. 273.

[4] Lagrange, *Évangile selon Saint Matthieu* (Paris, 1923²), pp. 77-9; Staab (see note 3), p. 29; Buzy (see note 3), p. 48 f. J. Maldonatus (1533-83) writes as follows on Matthew 7:1: "Ego iam monui non esse anxie quaerendam in Evangelistis sententiarum connexionem, quia res non eo ordine scribere voluerunt, quo factae a Christo, vel dictae sunt. Quod praecipue in eius concionibus observatur, in quibus nec omnia, quae dixit, nec eo, quo dixit, ordine recensent, contenti praecipua eius doctrinae capita commemorare" (*Commentarii in Quauor Evangelistas*, I [Mainz 1611], p. 158.

Certainly much in the discourse is given in other contexts in Luke. But it must be borne in mind that in the course of His ministry Christ will have had to repeat the same lessons many times when addressing different audiences.

The combination of two separate discourses is more obvious in Matthew's chapter 10. After choosing His twelve Apostles our Lord sends them on their first mission to preach the near advent of the Kingdom of Heaven and gives them instructions suitable for this work (10:5-15). These instructions expressly exclude any missionary activity among either Gentiles or Samaritans and no opposition is envisaged beyond a refusal to receive them or listen to their preaching. Then immediately following this text come further instructions (10:16-42 if the whole is a unity). Here persecution is foretold from both Jews and pagans and missionary activity is foreseen outside the limits of Palestine. Such preaching and persecutions took place after our Lord's Ascension and instructions for this future work would hardly have been given when the Apostles were setting out on their first work among their fellow-countrymen. The recognition of this neglect of temporal perspective helps to explain the utterance of Christ during His last discourse in John 16:4, "These things I did not tell you from the beginning because I was with you"; and now He was about to leave them. What He has just been saying was that they would be driven from the synagogues and that men would think that they were doing a service to God by putting them to death. These words gave considerable trouble to St. Augustine and the older exegetes as they seemed to be in contradiction to the similar predictions in Matthew 10.[5] Actually these words of Christ are an additional argument to show that Matthew has anticipated the actual occasion when these instructions were given. Similar predictions, partly in the same words as in Matthew 10, are found in the eschatological discourse of Matthew 24:9-10; Mark 13:9-13; and Luke 21:12-19; and it may well be that we have there the historical occasion of the instructions.

Finally it should be noticed that Matthew's indications of time are sometimes no more than literary links with a following passage. Thus at the end of the Sermon on the Mount he adds: "And when Jesus had finished speaking, the crowds were in admiration at His doctrine" (7:28). But he certainly did not wish us to believe that their admiration was reserved for the end of the discourse. Quite in the same style he tells us that when Christ had fasted for forty days and forty nights "afterwards he was hungry" (4:1). This makes a convenient transition to the devil's first suggestion that He should turn stones into bread.

## The temporal and local setting in Matthew 16:16b-19

The words of Christ here in question are those in which He gave His unqualified approval to Peter's words, and declared His intention to build His Church on the Rock which is Peter, and His promise to confer on him the full authority for its due administration and government which is symbolized by the possession of the keys. It is not within the scope of this article to

---

[5] Augustine, Tract. in *Ioannis ev.*, XCIV, 1 (PL 35, 1868); F. Toletus, S.J., *In S. Ioannis Ev. Comm.* II (Rome, 1588), pp. 227-30.

show the strongly semitic character of the passage nor to analyse its meaning. This has been done, and excellently done, elsewhere.[6]

For our present purpose it is required only to stress the fact that St. Peter's confession as recorded in Matthew was a recognition of Christ's divine nature. He did not speak of Christ merely as a Son of God. This title was used of men raised by God to adoptive sonship, as of Solomon in 2 Sam. 7:14. Peter acknowledges that He is "the Son of the living God." This implies an entirely unique relationship to God possessed by no other. The epithet "living" adds solemnity to the phrase but does not alter the sense. It comes from Ps. 41 (42) 3 where it distinguishes the one true God from dumb and lifeless deities. The phrase (without the epithet) occurs again in the account of the trial before the Sanhedrin given in Luke 22:70. Christ was asked officially: "Art thou the Son of God?"[7] His agreement that He was the Son of God was at once pronounced to be sufficient ground for His condemnation. Further witnesses were not required. This report by the third evangelist shows that the condemnation was based not on the claim to be the Messiah but on the claim to be "the Son of God." That was the ground for the charge of blasphemy (Matthew 26:65; Mark 14:64).

Here we must take note of the assertion made in Strack-Billerbeck's well-known and universally appreciated commentary (I, p. 1006) that "son of God" is a title of the Messiah. It will be remarked that the definite article is absent from the statement. For proof reference is made to the commentary on Romans 1:3. There also (III, p. 17) there is no reference to the presence or absence of the article. The only "proof" attempted is based on Luke 4:41. Here the evil spirits cry out "Thou are the Son of God," but, says the commentary, "with the addition 'because they knew him to be the Christ,' whereby the equivalence of 'the Son of God' and 'the Christ' is confirmed." This may appear conclusive, but in fact gives an erroneous report of the text. The text does not say, as the comment suggests, that the spirits called Him the Son of God because they knew Him to be the Christ. What it does

---

[6] For instance by Lagrange (see note 4), pp. 319-29; Buzy (see note 3), pp. 213-23. The discovery of the Qumran documents has revealed a striking parallel in the Hymns, which on internal evidence can hardly be the work of another than the Authorized Teacher. In 1 QH 7:8 f in an enumeration of God's benefits he includes the following: "Thou hast set me as a strong tower, as a lofty rampart, and hast established my edifice on a rock and lasting foundations for my Community and all my walls for a tested rampart that cannot be shaken." The parallelism of "edifice" and "Community" manifests the metaphorical use of the former word. It occurs in 1 QS 11:8 with the same meaning.

[7] J. Klausner (*Jesus of Nazareth, His Life, Times, and Teaching*. Translated from the original Hebrew by H. Danby [London, 1929], p. 342) objects that 'the words "Son of God" . . . from the mouth of a Jewish High Priest, and particularly from a Sadducee, are inconceivable'. This statement requires qualification. It is, no doubt, correct in the sense that the high-priest would not have used the expression spontaneously or, in any case, have used it with approval. But the court was determined to find cause, adequate in its own judgement, for a condemnation. In these circumstances it is perfectly credible that the high-priest as a last resort should use words he knew or suspected to be admitted by the prisoner in order to obtain, as he did in fact obtain, an admission from his mouth that could be condemned as blasphemy.

say is that Christ rebuked the spirits and "would not allow them to speak because they knew him to be the Christ [or: the Messiah]." It was in the spread of a report that He was the Messiah that lay the danger of a wave of enthusiasm among the people based on purely national and patriotic sentiment with the peril of political upheaval, consequent reaction of the Roman power, and grave hindrance to Christ's true work. The passage does not confirm the alleged equivalence.

The same standpoint is found in Strack-Billerbeck's explanation of Christ's condemnation by the Sanhedrin. And here it presented a problem how to explain in what Jesus was judged to have blasphemed. They state (Is. p. 1017) that it was not blasphemy to claim to be the Messiah. It would even be the duty of the Messiah to do so when he came. They explain further that "to sit on the right hand of God or on the throne of God was a feature, based on Ps. 109 (110) 1, of the Jewish representation of the glory belonging to the Messiah." But, they say, "it was expected that the enthronement of the Messiah would take place visibly before all eyes in this world and at the command of God." It could not, we may add, be blasphemy to transfer the enthronement from this world to the next. This would seem more consonant with the dignity and majesty of God. Neither could the omission of a reference to the command of God be reckoned blasphemous. Where then was the blasphemy found by the court? It was, we read, in that "Jesus appeared of his own authority and without divine authorization to be taking the place belonging to him at the right hand of God in the invisible world, and from there above (this) world, coming on the clouds of heaven, to exercise his rule as Messiah — that is what seemed to the high-priest to be an offence against the divine majesty." This is not convincing. It is admitted that the Messiah could lawfully claim to be the Messiah. It is admitted that the honour of sitting at the right hand of God would be his. And as it was considered to be an honour destined for the Messiah by divine authority, any claim to that honour necessarily included implicitly an acknowledgment of that authority. This explanation does not succeed in establishing an element of blasphemy in Christ's words.

That Peter's words were in fact an acknowledgement of Christ's divinity is shown by Christ's own reply. When Peter declared "Thou art the Christ the Son of the living God," Christ in His turn declared that Peter had not come to this belief except by revelation from His Father in heaven. But for the recognition of the messianic character of Jesus such a revelation was not required. Men familiar with the text of the Old Testament who saw its predictions fulfilled under their eyes in the words, actions, and character of Jesus of Nazareth could themselves arrive at the knowledge that here was the promised Messiah in their midst. The basis of this recognition of the messianic character of Jesus was certainly the revelation contained in the Old Testament. This was available to all and no special revelation was required to recognize its fulfillment. This is well illustrated by the reply made by Jesus to the question sent by John the Baptist through his disciples (Matthew

11:2-6; Luke 7:18-23). John's question was: "Art thou he who is to come or are we to look for another?" Jesus did not give a direct answer. Instead He then and there healed many of various afflictions and disease, drove out evil spirits, and gave sight to the blind. He then bade John's disciples report what they had heard and seen and so left St. John to draw his own conclusion as to whether He was the Messiah or no. For this a revelation from heaven was not necessary. John had not desired an answer for his own sake. He wished to detach his disciples from himself to become the followers of one he knew to be greater than he. Even the crowds were able to draw the right conclusion from what they heard and saw. And their belief was manifested by the messianic title "Son of David" used of Jesus.[8]

This confession of the divinity of Jesus is not found in the parallel accounts of Mark and Luke (Mark 8:27-30; Luke 9:18-21). In both the confession is limited to an explicit acknowledgement that Jesus is the Messiah. And if the text of Matthew with the omission of verses 17-19 and the words "Son of the Living God" is compared with theirs, it is found to be identical in substance. There are numerous verbal variants which do not affect the sense. Matthew's text would read with Mark's "Thou art the Christ" where Luke's has "the Christ of God." And all three end with a prohibition given by our Lord to make Him known. In Matthew it is "to tell no man that he is the Christ"; in Mark "to speak to no man concerning him"; in Luke "to tell this to no man." It is remarkable that Matthew after the confession of the divinity has the clearest wording to show that what is not to be spoken of is our Lord's messiahship. With the false ideas current among the people concerning the true character and function of the Messiah there was real danger of a tumultuous popular movement. The messianic character of Jesus could not be proclaimed by Himself or His disciples until it became recognized that His mission had no temporal ambitions and was not aiming at an earthly kingdom.

This conclusion of Matthew's account with the prohibition to make it known that He was the Messiah, so agreeing exactly with the accounts of the other two Synoptists, itself suggests that he has combined two separate occasions. And this suggestion is confirmed by other considerations.

As the text stands in Matthew Christ appears to have promised to Peter at Caesarea Philippi supreme authority in His Church. To him personally were the keys to be confided and whatever he himself bound or loosed on earth would be bound or loosed in heaven. Heaven would ratify all his acts of authority in the Church. And this honorific promise was, as the text stands, made not to Peter privately but in the presence and hearing of the other Apostles. Yet the subsequent narrative contains no hint that they were aware of this. On the contrary they appear to be completely ignorant of any precedence accorded to Peter. In 18:1 the disciples come to Jesus to ask "Who is greater in the kingdom of heaven?" And the parallel texts of Mark 9:34 and Luke 9:46 make it plain that the question reflected personal ambition for they had been discussing which of them would be the chief (literally: great-

---

[8] Matthew 9:27; 15:22, 20:30f.; 21:9, 15; cf. 12:23.

er). Then James and John even went so far as boldly to ask Jesus through their mother for the two chief posts in His kingdom, the one to sit on His right and the other on His left (Matthew 20:20-21; Mark 10:35-37). And as late as the Last Supper the spirit of rivalry led to a dispute which of them was to be considered the most important (Luke 22:24).

Then it may be asked whether a recognition of Christ's divinity at Caesarea Philippi fits well into the Gospel story as a whole. It was only after the Resurrection that the Apostle Thomas acknowledged Christ to be God (John 20:28). It seems clear that previously he had not had that faith. And the evangelical narrative does not manifest a consciousness on the part of the Apostles that they were living in the daily visible presence of God. If Peter already had faith in the divinity of Jesus, would he, so soon after his profession of this faith, have had the temerity "to rebuke him" as he did when he heard our Lord foretell His sufferings at the hands of the Jewish authorities to be followed by His death (Matthew 16:22). Even such a simple desire as to wish to draw Christ's attention to the splendour of the Temple buildings seems to indicate an absence of any thought that they were speaking to the omniscient God (Matthew 24:1). Who would wish to give information to a person he believed to be divine? Then we know that when the Second Person of the Trinity took to Himself human nature, He wished to make Himself one of the human family, to share human experience, to be treated as a fellow-man. Are we perhaps justified in concluding that even with His Apostles He did not wish the full truth as to His nature to be known till after the Resurrection when the period of His earthly life was over?

Thus it may well be that St. Matthew has antedated a confession of Christ's divinity made after the Resurrection and combined it with the solemn recognition of His messiahship pronounced by Peter at Caesarea Philippi. One more possibility presents itself. In antedating the episode has he accommodated the wording of Peter's second confession to the circumstances of the first? In place of the explicit form used by St. Thomas has he substituted words of similar import but lacking the same clarity? His addition to the confession, an addition lacking in the other Synoptists, is, as will be remembered, "Son of the Living God." What would be the reason for such an accommodation? Before the Apostles separated from each other and left Jerusalem to preach the Gospel it is safe to say that they consulted together as to the wisest method of procedure. Should the whole truth be told at once? Or should they adopt a progressive method adapting the content of their preaching to what their auditors and readers would be able to receive? Christ Himself by His injunction not to cast pearls before swine (Matthew 7:6) had given a warning that more harm than good would come from explaining sacred mysteries to people as yet incapable of receiving or appreciating them. St. Paul has told us that he was guided by such considerations. He told the Corinthians that he had given them only milk to drink but no solid food which they were as yet incapable of assimilating (1 Cor. 3:2). And the same principle was long adopted in the Church as is clear from the *disciplina arcani*.

We shall not be wrong in believing that the Apostles were equally prudent. And if a judgment may be formed after a scrutiny of the contents of the synoptic Gospels, it was decided that it would be inopportune to proclaim the divinity of Christ at the beginning of their preaching. First they must let the facts of His life and teaching show that He was a messenger sent by God, that He was the Messiah promised in the ancient prophecies, that He was charged with the office of proclaiming eternal truths for the benefit of all mankind. With this foundation of the good tidings firmly laid and adherence to the cause of Christ won it would be possible and prudent to proclaim also His divinity. Hence it is that the earlier Gospels are reticent about the divinity of Christ. These Gospels were not intended to be complete handbooks giving the whole of the Christian message. Their purpose was to serve as introductions to Christian doctrine and so to prepare the way for the reception of the whole truth. Towards the end of the first century Ebionites and other heretics had begun openly to deny the divinity of Christ and to proclaim that His existence began with His birth. To meet this false teaching the bishops of Asia Minor decided that the time was ripe for a clear and authoritative exposition of the truth. St. John acknowledged the wisdom of the proposal, composed his Gospel, and so provided the necessary supplement to the writings of his predecessors.[9]

These considerations help to explain the character of St. Matthew's Gospel. It is largely impersonal as it is not primarily a record of the Apostle's own knowledge and experience. It is based on a plan for the promulgation of Christianity prepared by the combined consultation of the Apostles. Its purpose is doctrinal. But the exposition of doctrine was not to be exhaustive. Only so much of the truth was to be included as could be appreciated by men with no previous knowledge of Christianity and would be likely to win their adherence to Christ's person and teaching. Once this foundation was truly laid, the edifice could be safely built upon it. The purpose of the Gospel was doctrinal but it was also historical. Christ had done and said and taught what is recorded of Him. And that is the essential basis of history. It records what actually happened. But as the evangelist's interest in history was entirely due to his interest in doctrine, it seemed to him to be of little importance precisely at what moment of time or what position in space some action was done or some teaching proposed. His work is both doctrinal and historical but the history is the handmaid of the doctrine.

[9] St. Jerome: 'Novissimus omnium scripsit evangelium, rogatus ab Asiae episcopis, adversus Cerinthum aliosque haereticos et maxine tunc Ebionitarum dogma consurgens, qui asserunt Christum ante Mariam non fuisse. Unde et compulsus est divinam eius divinitatem edicere', *De Viris Illustribus* 9 (PL 23, 623).

# JESUS AS THE "SUFFERING SERVANT"

*Benjamin Willaert*

It is in the Incarnation that the foundation of our redemption lies. Jesus is God come to dwell among men, God-become-man to redeem men. Thus it is God's salvific will that initiates all our redemption; it is God himself who comes forth to meet us as Redeemer in Jesus.

We do not mean that our redemption climaxed in an Incarnation that is abstracted from the further salvific deeds of Jesus' life. His Incarnation must not be thought of statically; an adequate notion of it must include all the salvific events of his life. To become man is not merely to take up a certain structure of being; it is to take on oneself a human lot. All the activities of Christ's life, including his suffering and death, are moments of his redeeming incarnation. Incarnation and crucifixion are not extrinsic to each other; Christ's death on the cross is really only a determined moment of the Incarnation.

## A redemptive life

The whole life of Jesus is redemptive, but we spontaneously and almost exclusively associate the idea of redemption with the final phase of Jesus' life. We have made great progress in recent years in coming to recognize, along with the redemptive value of the suffering and death of Christ, the life-giving power of his resurrection as well; but we ought not to forget that the preaching of Christ, too, is redemptive — that his words are words of life. The primitive Christian message of the crucifixion and resurrection did not fail to add our Lord's own preaching of the kingdom and of what that kingdom asks of its members. Genuine Christian *metanoia*, or renewal of life, must not be presented merely as a participation in the glorified life of the risen Lord through Church and sacraments, but also as a result of the acceptance in faith of the Christian teaching.

Still, the concept of redemption is specially linked with the passion and resurrection. Nor is this emphasis unjustified, provided it be not exclusive. Jesus himself closed his life of preaching with the revelation to his apostles that he is that Old Testament Son of Man who must fulfill the will of God, gaining his glorification through suffering and death. In Jesus' own view, his passion and resurrection were the culmination of his life. We can scarcely go wrong if we consider primary what he considered primary.

For Saint Paul the crucifixion's effects were mainly negative; his guiding interest is the resurrection. On the cross Christ conquered sin, death, and the devil — the obstacles to man's return to God; he redeemed us more positively in the resurrection, returning us to God in newness of life. Paul's attitude

Reprinted from *Theology Digest*, 10 (1962), 25-30. Originally published as "Jezus, de lijdénde dienaar Gods," *Collationes Brugenses et Gandavenses*, 6 (1960), 163-185. Reprinted by permission of the publisher.

here is characteristic of the very earliest days of the Christian witness, for the proper redemptive value of the death of Christ was not so keenly appreciated at the outset as it was somewhat later. At first the apostles began the Good News with the contrast between the shameful thing the Jews had done to Christ and what God had done in raising him. Their sole positive emphasis was on the resurrection (Act 3:13-15).

Only later did it come clear to them that Christ *must* suffer according to the Scriptures, and they brought this out by invoking various texts from the Old Testament, especially from the Fourth Song of the Suffering Servant in Isaiah. Saint Paul was clearly alluding to this when he wrote: "For I passed on to you as of first importance the account I had received, that Christ died for our sins according to the Scriptures" (1 Cor. 15:3). The Apostle wrote these lines between 55 and 57 A.D., so the Suffering Servant theme must have been current Christian theology quite early in the first century.

## Jesus' own teaching

But we have a further thesis. We hope to establish in these pages that the Jesus-Servant connection was the theological perspective of Jesus himself, clearly evinced in his own prophecies of his approaching passion. Such a conclusion will carry considerable theological relevance, since the doctrine of the redemptive value of our Lord's suffering and death is based mainly on the early Christian theology of the Servant of Yahweh. It will be very worthwhile to be able to find this theology on the lips of Christ himself.

First let us read carefully the most relevant verses of the Fourth Servant Song from Isaiah:

> Lo! My servant shall prosper, he shall be exalted, and lifted up, and shall be very high (52:13). He was despised, and avoided by men, a man of sorrows, and acquainted with pain; and like one from whom men hide their faces, he was despised, and we esteemed him not. Yet it was our pains that he bore, our sorrows that he carried; while we accounted him stricken, smitten by God, and afflicted. He was wounded for our transgressions, he was crushed for our iniquities; the chastisement of our welfare was upon him, and through his stripes we were healed. All we like sheep had gone astray, we had turned everyone to his own way; and the Lord made to light upon him the guilt of us all. . . . He was cut off from the land of the living, for our transgressions was stricken to death . . . although he had done no violence, nor was any deceit in his mouth. Yet the Lord saw fit to crush him with pain, so that, although he makes himself a guilt-offering, he shall see posterity, shall prolong his life, and the pleasure of the Lord shall prosper in his hand. The fruit of his suffering shall he see, in knowing himself righteous he shall be satisfied; my servant shall bring righteousness to many, and he shall himself bear their guilt. Therefore will I divide him a portion with the great, and with the strong shall he share the spoil; because he poured out his lifeblood to the utmost, and was numbered with the transgressors, and himself bore the sin of many, and made intercession for the transgressors (53:3-12).

"Of whom is the prophet speaking? Of himself or of someone else?" (Acts
8:34). The eunuch's challenge to Philip has remained the conundrum of the
exegete. For us, it is of less concern whether the Servant is a single individual,
or the whole people, or the faithful remnant of ideal Israel, or all simultaneously. Our interest is in the theology implicit in this Servant-concept,
and in its influence on Jesus' own notions. But before we examine Jesus' passion-prophecies, let us comment on our text from Isaiah.

The Servant's divine mission involves suffering, as is disclosed as early as
the Third Song (Is. 50). But especially in our Fourth Song that suffering
emerges as a special trait of the Servant. He suffers in place of the many, to
unite them with God. Utterly unique in the history of Hebrew thought is this
portrait of a man with a *mission to suffer*. Many a prophet must suffer incidentally, in consequence of his function to bear witness in favor of God against
the world. But the Servant of Yahweh suffers as his very function.

## Passion-prophecies

As we have said, no one questions the very early date of the Christian
teaching that the Isaian Suffering Servant is Jesus Christ. It is clear from Paul
and Acts, as well as from the Gospels, that the notion was a tool of the primitive kerygma and a weapon of apologetics almost from the very beginning.
But we hold that it is not primitive Christianity's theological elaboration. It
goes back to Jesus himself.

Liberalism and Bultmann ascribe the "redemptive death theory" to Paul.
The gospel-sayings of Jesus on the point are alleged to be post-factum adap-
tations of Jesus' teaching made in the light of Paul's. Catholic doctrine, of
course, defends the origin of the redemptive death notion in the preaching of
Christ himself, and the liberalist stand is condemned in the Holy office Decree
*Lamentabili* (1907).

Paul's theological elaboration of the redemptive death notion is based on
the nucleus propounded by Jesus. We will find this nucleus in the great Synoptic passion-prophecies, which, although probably stylized in redaction, owe
their origin to genuine logia (sayings) of Jesus himself:

(1) He had to go to Jerusalem and endure great suffering there at the hands
of the elders, high priests, and scribes, and be killed, and be raised to life on
the third day (Matthew 16:21; Mark 8:31; Luke 9:22). (2) The Son of
Man is going to be handed over to men, and they will kill him, but on the
third day he will be raised to life again (Matthew 17:23; Mark 9:31; Luke
9:44). (3) Everything written in the prophets about the Son of Man will be
fulfilled. For he will be handed over to the heathen, ridiculed and insulted
and spat upon, they will flog him and kill him, and on the third day he will
rise again (Luke 18:31-33; Matthew 20:18-19; Mark 10:33-34).

Hence we clearly find on the lips of Jesus the doctrine of his redemptive
death; but we will also find him claiming to be the Suffering Servant of Isaiah
53. In order to establish this, we do not have to show that these predictions

contain the "very words of Jesus." Too often the passion-prophecies are attacked with a false dilemma: *Either* they are "the very words of Jesus," uttered at the exact time and in the exact situation pictured in the gospel report,
*or* they are "interpolations after the event." Then the critics claim evidence of
later elaboration in some of the wording, and the genuinity of the prophecies
is discarded.

## Reflective history

The case is not that simple. The dilemma mutilates the problem in its very
posing. Recording speeches as a dictaphone would record them is not the only
way of writing their history. The redacted and stylized character of the passion prophecies as they appear in our Gospels may not constitute the ideal of
the twentieth-century newsman. But they serve clear notice nonetheless that
Jesus really did foretell his passion and resurrection. In fact, this redacted,
unjournalistic brand of history may be better history than if it were mechanical reporting, because it is reflective history. Are these "prophecies after the
event"? Speaking from a literary point of view, they probably are. They were
not very likely uttered in the exact wording and in the concrete biographical
situation in which later redaction placed them. But historically speaking the
prophecies are genuine. Throughout, the authors choose expressions which will
convey that Jesus really, at one or another time in his life, in one or another
manner, spoke out about his coming death and resurrection.

The passion-prophecies of the synoptics do indeed express the primitive
Christian tradition; but that tradition testifies that it was Jesus who originated
their content, really uttering prophecies of his coming passion. And the tradition is worthy of credit, inasmuch as its clear aim is to report things that
really happened. It is bad scholarship to cling to "the very words" in a given
text when a literary analysis tends in the other direction; but it is equally bad
scholarship to expurgate the text from our Gospels merely because it seems to
reflect the theology of the early Christian community.

## Lo! My servant shall prosper

If we now conduct an analysis of the Synoptic passion-prophecies, we will
find them replete with the influence of the Fourth Song of the Suffering Servant of Yahweh, Isaiah 53. At the very outset we are struck with the general
tenor of the passion-prophecies as compared with the Fourth Song. In both
portraits we are asked to contemplate a man who is handed over, must suffer much, is killed, yet attains his glory nonetheless.

But the similarity goes deeper than the general sweep of the outline. Jesus
is making a whole series of connections with Isaiah 53, circulating them
through the trigger words *paradidonai* (to hand over) and *polla pathein* (to
suffer much). Thrice in the Fourth Song the Servant is "handed over,"
(*paradidonai* — in v. 6 and twice in v. 12, in the Septuagint version). The
passion-prophecies use the same expression. Can this be mere coincidence?
Not in view of the word's special connotations, verified in both texts.

(1) In both texts "hand over" carries a *martyr-witness* connotation. At once one suspects that there is more than coincidence here. Then supporting evidence appears in the "handing over" of Paul (Acts 21:2; 28:17), John the Baptist (Matthew 4:12; Mark 1:14), the apostles (in Jesus' prophecy of their martyrdom, Matthew 10:17; cf. Mark 13:9; Acts 8:3), and Jesus himself (Mark 3:19; 14:10; 15:1; 15:15 and parallels; also Luke 24:20; Acts 3:13). Finally, the word was also current in the contemporary Jewish martyr-theology.

(2) In both texts, *paradidonai* connotes a handing over *by God*. In Isaiah, as we have seen, the connection is explicit. In the passion-prophecies of the New Testament, it is implicit: "The Son of Man is going to be handed over to men" — clearly, by Someone other than men. The human agents — Judas, Pilate, and the Jews — are presented as instruments in the hands of the One who really does the handing over.

(3) Jesus asserts his "handing over" to be the fulfillment of the Old Testament. In Matthew 26:24 and Mark 14:21 he says, "as it is written of him." In Luke he says "written by the prophets" (18: 31); or "according to that which is determined" (22:22); or "must be delivered" (24:7), using for "must" a word that Luke regularly employs (*dei*) to express a necessity deriving from the will of God as predetermined in the Old Testament.

This conspectus of comparisons demonstrates that "hand over" in the Synoptic prophecies is intended to convey more than mere matter-of-fact human activity, and that it seems to derive from the Old Testament. And we have found in the passion-prophecies strong indications that the source of "hand over" is Isaiah 53. Now let us seek confirmatory evidence for this outside the texts of the passion-prophecies, elsewhere in the Gospels and in the rest of the New Testament.

Compare, "The Son of Man will be delivered into the hands of sinners" (Matthew 26:45 and parallels) with the Septuagint reading of Isaiah 53:6: "And the Lord delivered him for their sins." The exact sense is not the same, but the ring is the same. Again, the line, "The Son of Man is come not to be served, but to serve, and to give his life as a ransom for the many" (Matthew 20:28; cf. Mark 10:45) is reminiscent of the Septuagint: "serving many well," and "his soul was delivered for the sins of the many" (Is 53:11-12). We could also cite Matthew 26:28; Mark 14:24; Luke 22:19. The overwhelming impression is one of a conscious tapping of Isaiah 53 as known in the Greek tradition.

There is further support in Paul and in Acts for our analysis of *paradidonai*. Both authors resume Jesus *paradidonai* with clear intent to link it with the Fourth Song: "The God of Abraham, Isaac, and Jacob, the God of our fathers, has glorified his Servant, whom you *handed over*" (Acts 3:13). The Vulgate renders *paida* erroneously as "Son," but Luke wants us to think of Jesus as the handed-over "Servant" known so well to Peter's hearers from the Fourth Song. See also Acts 3:14-15 (compare with Septuagint), Rom. 4: 24-25; 8:32; 1 Cor. 11:23; Gal. 1:4; 2:20.

The second of the two expressions that merit our close examination is the *pathein* (to suffer) of the passion-prophecies. We will see that when Jesus speaks of his approaching "suffering" there is good evidence that he is drawing the idea from Isaiah 53.

Throughout the New Testament, Jesus' "suffering" denotes, reasonably enough, all the elements of his passion, crucifixion, and death, undifferentiated. Consequently, our attention is arrested sharply by a curious use of the word in the first passion-prophecy: "The Son of Man *must suffer much,* and be *rejected* . . . and be *killed*, and . . . *rise* again" (Mark 8:31). *Pathein* (to suffer) is listed in a chronological series of particular sufferings. Why this redundant usage? The reason seems to be that "suffer much" was a standard expression in frequent use at the time of Jesus. As such, it was used in our text with another unit (the list of particular sufferings) without much thought for logic. "Suffer much" must have been a familiar formula. Where did it come from?

## Servant of Yahweh

It has come from the Old Testament. The Son of Man *must* suffer much. We hear "must" or "it is written" fully six times in the New Testament to qualify Jesus' "suffering" in general or his particular suffering. We think that the source is Isaiah 53, notwithstanding the fact that the word *pathein* is not found there. Our reason is that the *elements* of Christ's passion, found throughout the New Testament in the same breath with *pathein*, are the same elements as the Servant must undergo in Isaiah 53. We will give two samples.

Look at 1 Peter 2:21-25: "For Christ himself *suffered* (Is. 53:12). . . . He committed no sin, and deceit was never on his lips (cf. 53:9). . . . He carried the burden of our sins in his own body on the tree (cf. 53:12). . . . By his bruises you have been healed (cf. 53:5) . . . for you were astray like sheep (cf. 53:6)." All this in explicitation of "suffered."

Again, 1 Peter 1:11 seems to find in the same Fourth Song the "sufferings that are in Christ": The prophets searched "what time or circumstances the Spirit of Christ in them did signify when it foretold those sufferings that are in Christ and the glories that were to follow." But where can the Christ's sufferings-followed-by-glory be found if not in Isaiah 53?

We submit that the investigations of this article yield the following conclusion: In the latter part of his life Jesus looked toward his passion very consciously as an integral part of his task as Son of Man. His suffering is that of the Servant of Yahweh, a suffering for the sins of many, through which he must come into his glory.

A connected dogmatic question remains. *How* can this suffering and death benefit the many? What might lies hidden here that can invest a death with the power of life? We wish to touch this problem in a postscript:

Our redemption is ultimately a mystery of God's salvific love. Only God can redeem man. Whatever means and concrete instruments he may employ, it is his will that works the Redemption. When we look upon the life of Jesus, including his suffering and death, as a concrete human expression of

God's love, intended by God to heal the disobedience of man's sin with the obedience of Christ's love, then we are laying the emphasis where it belongs. When, on the other hand, we insist too much on the physical reality of the suffering and death, and look on the passion in its purely human reality, then we encounter difficulties, and we run the risk of endowing the passion with a sort of magical power. God does not choose to redeem us by a passion on account of any virtue proper to suffering, as if suffering and death contained in themselves gladness and life! Only Life can wake us to life.

But only Love can wake us to love. God wished to express his love for man in human shape. He meant His love to find expression in the love of Jesus. Jesus obeyed. He poured out his own love in an obedience to his Father and a desire to serve his fellow men, which went the limit of generosity, synthesizing the whole meaning of his life on earth in the only gift of love that can make no reservations. No man has greater love than the Man that gives his life for his friends.

# 5 SAINT JOHN

The Gospel according to John introduces new themes and new approaches to the apostolic preaching. Although as C. H. Dodd remarks, the fourth Gospel is still within the framework of the kerygma,[1] the perspective, the milieu of a well-developed Christianity, and the frequent blending of incidents in the life of Jesus with spiritual reflections show that a deeper understanding of God's revelation in Christ has taken place.

Disputes about the origin and sources of St. John's Gospel have led to numerous controversies over every aspect of the Gospel — its authorship, authenticity, the sources of its thought.[2] After more than a half-century of controversy, scholars generally concede that the work is essentially that of the apostle St. John, perhaps edited by his disciples, dating probably from the end of the first century A.D. The sources of St. John's theology seem to be the Jewish sapiential tradition, Hellenistic thought and contact with the speculations of devout Jews such as the Qumran community. But much of the Gospel is original with St. John and embodies more than a half-century of spiritual reflection.

St. John is concerned with the meaning of the person and mission of Jesus. From the opening sublime prologue to the epilogue, he declares that the humanity of Jesus is the revelation of the Father's glory (1:14), shown through Christ's words and actions, but especially through his "hour" — His death, resurrection and ascension, which mark the definitive revelation of divine love and the full outpouring of salvation through His glorification and sending of the Spirit.

[1] *The Interpretation of the Fourth Gospel* (Cambridge: University Press, 1960), p. 6.
[2] See Thomas A. Collins, "Changing Styles in Johannine Studies," in *The Bible in Current Catholic Thought*, pp. 202-25.

The fourth Gospel is a deeply spiritual document, full of the dualism of light and darkness, of symbolism, of the miracles as "signs" of the mission of Jesus,[3] of discourses and mystical insights. The articles in this section point out some of the spiritual meaning, the insight into glory, which was the contribution of the "disciple whom Jesus loved." But every study leads to further insights, and one returns from reading about the Gospel of St. John to the reading of the Gospel, with the conviction that here, of all parts of the New Testament, one is looking deepest into the mystery of God's love and glimpsing through it the "glory" of eternity.[4]

[3] See Raymond E. Brown, "The Gospel Miracles," in *The Bible in Current Catholic Thought*, pp. 184-201.

[4] See also Willem Grossouw, *Revelation and Redemption* (Westminster: Newman, 1955). M. E. Boismard, *St. John's Prologue* (Newman, 1957).

# THE WORD BECAME FLESH

Thomas Barrosse, C.S.C.

"The Word became flesh and dwelt among us." For many people these are the most familiar words of the entire New Testament, excepting perhaps the petitions of the Our Father. This Gospel statement expresses the fundamental Christian doctrine of the Incarnation: Jesus Christ has both a human nature and a divine nature — in Christ the Second Person of the Blessed Trinity has become man.

The evangelist's words do contain this truth. But "person," "human nature," and "divine nature" are terms employed to express the doctrine only long years after St. John's Gospel appeared. "Word" is not simply the equivalent of the "second divine Person," nor is "flesh" precisely the same as "human nature." The Gospel statement is much richer in meaning than the rather technical theological proposition, "The second Person of the Trinity assumed a human nature." To appreciate this wealth of meaning, we should try to understand what each of the words the evangelist used meant to him and to the first-century Christians for whom he wrote.

## The creative word

The very first expression in his statement has a meaning that only those familiar with the Old Testament will grasp fully. For us today, a word is only a passing sound or a written symbol to which we have somewhat arbitrarily attached a meaning. For men of the Old Testament, a word was a dynamic reality, especially if it were a word of promise or threat. Perhaps we can gain some appreciation of this attitude from the instinctive fear many people feel today when they hear others talk of an accident just before they begin a journey. It is as though merely speaking about an accident could cause one.

One or another Old Testament passage will illustrate this. When the blind Isaac mistakenly pronounced over Jacob the blessing he meant for his elder son Esau, it could not be retracted. In Genesis 27:33 he told his first-born regretfully, "I . . . blessed him; and he shall be blessed." Once God has spoken a word of promise, it effectively accomplishes the divine design without any possibility of failure. In Isaiah 55:10-11 God insists,

> For just as from the heavens the rain and snow come down
> And do not return there till they have watered the earth, making it fertile and fruitful,
> Giving seed to him who sows and bread to him who eats,
> So shall my word be that goes forth from my mouth;
> It shall not return to me void, but shall do my will, achieving the end for which I sent it.

Published originally in *The Bible Today*, 1 (1963), 590-95. Reprinted by permission of the publisher.

For us, a man's words express his ideas. For people of the Old Testament, by his words a man expressed himself. Of course, we still have something of this outlook. We are well aware that a man's words can reveal his learning, his ignorance, his virtue, or his sinfulness. We easily understand Ben Sirach when he explains that "through his lips the sinner is ensnared" (Sir. 20:12). By His words God too expresses Himself.

In the Old Testament we meet the divine word on the very first page of Genesis: "God said, 'Let there be light,'" and there was light . . ." (1:3). This divine word is a dynamic, effective reality. It calls all things into existence. It also reveals something of God. What this creative word brings into existence is magnificent, orderly, beautiful. By speaking this word God manifests His greatness, wisdom, and beauty. Indeed, He communicates something of these divine attributes to the creatures He calls into being. Something of Him can be recognized in them.

The author of the book of Wisdom is amazed that his pagan contemporaries worship creatures, not recognizing "how far more excellent is the Lord than these. . . . For from the greatness and the beauty of created things their original author, by analogy, is seen" (Wis. 13:3-5).

The prologue to the fourth Gospel (John 1:18) notes the same sad phenomenon. God's creative Word, the first divine self-manifestation, "was in the world." Indeed, "the world had come into being through" the divine Word. "But the world did not know" — did not recognize or acknowledge — the God who thus revealed Himself (John 1:3, 10). The fourth Gospel sometimes employs this term, "the world," to designate the contemporary pagan Roman society that had crucified Jesus and was persecuting His Church. But pagan Rome stands for the whole mass of idolatrous mankind who refuse to accept God's self-revelation. God's first self-communication, then, was rejected, or rather, not even recognized, by men.

## The prophetic word

The Old Testament speaks not only of God's creative Word but also of another divine word — the word spoken by the prophets and written in the Mosaic Law. The prophets acted as Yahweh's spokesmen; they delivered oracles in His name and declared that they were "Yahweh's word." These oracles usually leveled threats or offered promises that men could not disregard with impunity. What Yahweh threatened or promised infallibly came to pass. By this effective prophetic word of His, He controlled the destinies of nations and so revealed Himself as almighty Lord of history. What He threatened was punishment for evil, what He promised was reward for good. By His prophetic word He manifested Himself as a righteous and good Lord.

The Mosaic Law outlined a way of life. It contained God's own prescriptions for "following in His ways" and enjoying His intimacy. In short, it contained Yahweh's own indication of how to live near Him and like Him. It was an effective word: by observance of His prescriptions a man could "find life" (Lev. 18:5). It was a revealing word, manifesting something of His own inner life to be shared in by men — indeed, it communicated a share in His intimacy to those who observed it.

This second stage in God's self-revelation met the same rebuff as the first. The prologue to the fourth Gospel explains: God's Word came to "His own." God's prophetic and written word came to His chosen people. God revealed Himself more fully to them than He had by His creative Word to the world at large. But "His own" did not accept this divine self-revelation (John 1:11). "The Jews," as the fourth Gospel usually designates the officials of the first-century Judaism that formally rejected and condemned Christ, had not really understood or wholeheartedly submitted to God's self-revelation through Moses and the prophets. Jesus tells them this in so many words in John 5:46-47, "If you believe Moses, you would believe me. . . . If you do not believe his writings, how will you believe my words?" This second fuller divine self-communication, like the first, was refused by men.

## The image of the invisible God

Then came God's final and full self-revelation: the Word became flesh. "Flesh" in biblical usage does not have the carnal overtones it so easily carries for us. It regularly stands in opposition to "spirit." This latter word does not mean "immaterial" or "non-physical," but rather mysterious, uncontrollable force. The wind, a sudden movement of anger, a prophet's impulse to prophesy — all these are "spirit" in the Old Testament sense of the word. Indeed, the mighty, transcendent God Himself is "spirit." In contrast to Him, man is "flesh," that is, weak, perishable creature. To say, "The Word became flesh," is to make the amazing assertion: "The mighty God's self-revelation took weak human form."

Gerard Manley Hopkins in his poem, "The Blessed Virgin compared to the Air we breathe," notes how the earth's atmosphere softens the sun's intense brightness, refracting, diffusing, and adapting it so that we can see. Mary, he continues, plays a similar role in providing the transcendent God with a human nature in which He can move among us:

> Through her we may see Him
> Made sweeter, not made dim,
> And her hand leaves His light
> Sifted to suit our sight.

By taking human form, God's self-revelation becomes more understandable to us. In Jesus His Son, therefore, God reveals Himself to men. St. Paul calls Christ the "image of the invisible God" (Col. 1:15). In St. John's Gospel (14:9) Jesus says of Himself, "He who has seen me has seen the Father." Expressions like this could never have been used of the earlier forms of God's self-manifestation – His creative or His written word. Men could never have grasped Him so fully as they can in Jesus.

In Jesus, then, God's Word, His self-revelation, became flesh – took human form, became most fully understandable to men – and dwelt among us

Better than "dwelt among us" would be the rendering, "tented in our midst." It would express clearly the Old Testament resonances with which the statement is charged. During Israel's desert days God traveled in the midst of His wandering people in the tent, or "tabernacle," which housed the ark of the covenant. Later, when Solomon transferred the ark to the temple he had built, the protective divine presence was localized in the Jerusalem sanctuary. The rabbis designated this divine presence as the *shekinah* (literally, "dwelling"), and Greek-speaking Jews spoke of God's "tenting" (the Greek word for "tent" is *skene*) among His people. After the destruction of Jerusalem by the Babylonians, the divine presence departed from the temple; but the prophet Ezekiel assured his exiled people that God would later reestablish His covenant with Israel and would take up His dwelling with them once again. The Lord spoke:

> I will take the Israelites from among the nations to which they have come, and gather them from all sides to bring them back to their land . . . I will make with them a covenant of peace; it shall be an everlasting covenant with them, and I will multiply them, and put my sanctuary among them forever. *My dwelling shall be with them* (in the Greek Old Testament: My tenting shall be in their midst); I will be their God, and they shall be my people (Ez. 37:21, 26-27).

The evangelist in all likelihood alludes to the italicized words in saying that the Word-become-flesh "tented in our midst." In this way he presents Jesus as the new and definitive divine presence among men promised by the prophet centuries earlier.

## The glory of the Lord

"We gazed upon His glory," the evangelist continues, still speaking in Old Testament terms. Old Testament writers frequently use the word *glory* to designate the visible or audible manifestations of the saving divine presence. In Psalm 29, seeing the life-giving rain sent by God to men, the members of the heavenly court cry out in awe and praise: "Glory!" According to Exodus 24:15-17, Yahweh's "glory" descended upon the cloud-covered, quaking Mount Sinai when the Lord came down to covenant with Israel. According to Exodus 40:34-35 and 1 Kings 8:10-11, the thick cloud that rested upon the recently erected desert-tent and upon the newly completed Solomonic temple was a sign of the occupation of these sanctuaries by Yahweh's "glory": "Yahweh's glory filled the dwelling" (in the Greek: the "tent"); "Yahweh's glory filled Yahweh's house." Yahweh had come down to take up His residence in His people's midst. If in Jesus we have the definitive divine dwelling among men, in Him we would naturally expect to be able to gaze upon God's glory.

The fourth Gospel speaks frequently of Jesus' "glory." At the wedding feast of Cana, for example, by changing an immense quantity of water into wine He "manifested His glory" (John 2:11). But it is above all in His passion and resurrection that His glory appears. In fact, the evangelist calls this climactic event of Jesus' life quite simply His "glorification" (cf. John 12:23).

Men respond to this manifestation of glory with faith. At Cana He "manifested His glory, and His disciples believed in Him" (John 2:11). But especially after He has been glorified by His resurrection, His disciples remember His words and believe (cf. John 2:22). Faith for St. John means accepting Jesus for what He is. Men can accept Him only to the degree that He makes known His identity — only to the degree that He manifests His glory. But He is an altogether unique revelation of God, the revelation of God's hidden, trinitarian life. Therefore, the "glory" which He manifests and upon which men gaze is a unique glory: "glory which He has as Only-begotten from the Father."

The apostles, who lived with Jesus throughout His public ministry and saw Him after His resurrection, "gazed upon" this glory. During His ministry they heard Him speak of God as His Father. They saw Him work "signs," as the fourth Gospel calls them, which in symbol revealed Him to be in possession of the power that only a true Son of God could have: giving a bread that would nourish to life everlasting in John 6, opening the eyes of those born in the blindness of sin in John 9, raising the dead to the life of the age to come, in John 11. They saw Him after His victory over death in full possession of God's Holy Spirit and able to bestow that Spirit as He chose (John 20:22). How else but by faith in His divine Sonship could they respond to His manifestation of the unique "glory which He has as Only-begotten from the Father?" Thomas voiced the faith of them all with the words, "My Lord and my God" (John 20:28). In the same way all of us who read the evangelist's testimony to these things "believe that Jesus is the Christ, the Son of God, and through this faith have life in His name" (20:31).

## Full of grace and truth

The evangelist completes his brief description of the Incarnation by presenting the Word-become-flesh as "full of grace and truth." Commentators generally agree that here too he is employing Old Testament ideas. In the Old Testament the two great attributes of the God of the covenant are loyal attachment, *the* covenant virtue, and fidelity, or reliability. Greek-speaking Jews referred rather to His "mercy and truth," or, as one of the last-written Old Testament books shows, to His "grace and mercy." In the last centuries of the pre-Christian period Judaism had become acutely aware of the gratuitous character of the covenant God had made with His people. As they grasped this fact ever more clearly, they tended to interpret His great attribute less as loyalty to the covenant and more as mercy, favor, or grace. In the last centuries that preceded the birth of Christ Judaism had also become profoundly convinced of the inanity — the non-existence or falsity — of other gods and the reality of their own. In some quarters, at least, God's "truth" may have been understood less as His being true to His covenant than as His being real in contrast to the idols or even to the perishable world of men.

In any case, in St. John's Gospel, "truth" refers to the divine order — the order to which Jesus, His Father, and the Spirit belong and to which He has come to raise the men who will accept Him.

When the evangelist writes that the Word-become-flesh was "full of grace and truth," he means that the divine attributes of the God of Moses are to be found in Jesus. Only a few verses later (John 1:17) he explains that while the Law, God's written word, "was given through Moses, through Jesus Christ grace and truth came to be" — that is, in Him they took on concrete human form. God's promises and fidelity, God's favor, God's reality are tangibly among us in Him.

"So the Word became flesh and tented in our midst": the transcendent God's self-revelation took human form in Jesus, in whom we have God's full and definitive communication of Himself to men. "We gazed upon His glory, glory which He has as Only-begotten from the Father." The apostles, and through their testimony all the faithful, have witnessed this manifestation of God's hidden, trinitarian life in Jesus. He is "full of grace and truth" because the attributes of the God of Israel have taken tangible human form in Him. By our faith we have accepted Jesus for what He has shown Himself to be. We have accepted Him not merely by an intellectual assent but by effectively submitting ourselves to Him as God-become-man to communicate God's life to us. In this way we share in His Sonship. As the evangelist himself puts it: "To as many as receive Him He gave power to become children of God — that is, to those who believe in His name" (John 1:12).


# THE SPIRIT OF TRUTH AND OF LIFE IN JOHN'S GOSPEL

William A. Barry, S.J.

John's gospel, which is so rich thematically, is also the most unified of the four. Themes crisscross one another to such an extent that following out one of them eventually leads to all the others and yields a fairly complete synthesis of John's theological reflection on the Christian reality. In studying the theme of spirit in John, one is struck immediately by its relationship to the fecund biblical themes of knowledge and life, both of which receive so much attention in John. For him, knowing the truth means possessing eternal life: "Now this is everlasting life, that they may know thee, the only true God, and him whom thou hast sent, Jesus Christ" (John 17:3). Light and life are constantly coupled throughout the gospel. Jesus is the "light of life" (8:12), in whom "was life, and the life was the light of men" (1:4). Jesus is "the way,

Published originally in *The Bible Today*, 1 (1963), 601-8. Reprinted by permission of the publisher.

the truth, and the life" (14:6), the source of "living water" (4:10) which becomes "a fountain of water, springing up unto life everlasting" (4:14).

The notion of living water reminds us of John's later explanation of a similar saying of Jesus: "He said this, however, of the Spirit whom they who believed in him were to receive; for the Spirit had not yet been given, since Jesus had not yet been glorified" (7:39). For "it is the spirit that gives life; the flesh profits nothing. The words that I have spoken to you are spirit and life" (6:64). Thus in this brief concatenation of texts three great biblical themes have been brought into conjunction: knowledge of God, life and spirit.

In the Old Testament the *ruah Yahweh*, the spirit of Yahweh, has two predominant functions; it is the prophetic spirit and it is the life-giving breath of Yahweh. John interweaves and unites these two strands of Old Testament thought. For him the Spirit who teaches all truth by that very activity also gives life and vice-versa. We shall attempt to demonstrate this by juxtaposing these themes in order to note convergences and identities.

## The spirit of truth

In His final and moving discourse Jesus thrice calls the Counselor the Spirit of truth. "If you love me, keep my commandments. And I will ask the Father, and he will give you another Advocate to dwell with you forever, the Spirit of truth . . ." (14:15-17, who "will teach you all the truth" (16:13). Evidently this is the prophetic Spirit promised in Joel 3:1 for the messianic times:

> Then afterward I will pour out my spirit upon all mankind.
> Your sons and daughters shall prophesy,
> > your old men shall dream dreams,
> > your young men shall see visions.

This Spirit "will teach you all things, and bring to your mind whatever I have said to you" (14:26). What are all these "things"? What is "all the truth"? Are they dogmatic truths, formulations of the revelation of God to men? What does John mean by truth?

As a first approximation of the meaning of truth we can take what Jesus says about the Spirit in the last discourse. Here the truth embraces all that Jesus has told His apostles during their three years together. Not only that, but the Spirit will add to Jesus' words those things which the apostles "cannot bear now" (16:12), although He "will not speak on his own authority . . . but will receive of what is mine and declare it to you"(16:13-14). Moreover, Jesus identifies this "what is mine" with what the Father has. "All things that the Father has are mine. That is why I have said that he (the Spirit) will receive of what is mine, and will declare it to you" (16:15). Thus the Father and the Son together possess "all the truth" into which the Spirit of truth will guide them.

To this truth which He has heard from the Father (8:26, 40) Jesus comes "to bear witness" (18:37). He tells the Jews the truth and demands belief. "If I speak the truth, why do you not believe me?" (8:46). He even says that the Jews do not believe Him because He tells the truth (8:45). The reason for this anomaly is their parentage: "The father from whom you are is the devil . . . a liar and the father of lies" (8:44). The converse is also true: "He who is of God hears the words of God" (8:47). And the words of God are Jesus' own words as is evident from the context.

Plainly, a man's position relative to these words reveals his true parentage. The son of God believes Jesus and thus possesses the truth, for God's "word is truth" (17:17); the son of the devil refuses to believe Jesus and thus, like the devil, "has not stood in the truth" (8:44). Moreover, one must become a disciple of Jesus in order to know the truth. "If you abide in my word, you shall be my disciples indeed, and you shall know the truth, and the truth shall make you free" (8:31-32). This freedom is freedom from sin as we find out when Jesus adds: ". . . every one who commits sin is a slave of sin. But the slave does not abide in the house forever; the son abides there forever. If therefore the Son makes you free, you will be free indeed" (8: 34-36).

Now let us take our bearings by noting the identities established so far. God's word means Jesus' word, what the Spirit will declare to you, the truth. To be of God means to know the truth, to believe Jesus, to be Jesus' disciple, to be free of sin. If we include the saying: "If God were your Father, you would surely love me" (8:42), we have another identity to add: to be of God means to love Jesus. John's concept of knowing means loving-knowing. Finally, since it is the Spirit of truth who will guide the disciple into all truth, to know the truth means to possess the Spirit, "for he will dwell with you, and be in you" (14:17).

We have still not answered our initial question. We have been circling around the notion of truth, noting identities and convergences, but we have yet to confront it directly with the question: *what is truth?* What is the content of the message which the Father sends the Son to reveal to men and which the Spirit will make known by being with the disciples forever? The answer to this question is both simple and complex: simple, because Jesus said: "I am the truth" (14:6); complex, because this statement covers the whole Johannine view of Christian life and revelation. Let us examine more closely the message of Jesus as John records it.

In the texts which we have already seen there is an indication of the identity of the truth and the person of Jesus. *"The Truth shall make you* free . . . If therefore *the Son* makes you free, you will be free indeed" (8:32, 36). In addition we can compare: "Thy word (*logos*) is truth" (17:17) with "in the beginning was the Word (*logos*), and the Word was with God, and the Word was God. . .And the Word was made flesh and dwelt among us. . . full of grace and truth" (1:1, 14). We do not wish to press this comparison too much, for the *logos* of 17:17 may not refer back to the *logos* of the prologue. However, the juxtaposition of these two affirmations does indicate the lines of convergence between Jesus and the truth culminating in the identification: "I am the truth" (14:6).

Why is Jesus the truth? Let us begin by asking what the purpose of Jesus' mission was. Jesus Himself says: "I came that they may have life, and have it more abundantly" (10:10). But "this is everlasting life, that they may know thee, the only true God, and him whom thou hast sent, Jesus Christ" (17:3). Yet "no one has at any time seen God. The only-begotten Son, who is in the bosom of the Father, he has revealed him" (1:18; cf. 6:46).

The first impression could be that Jesus makes the Father known merely by telling men of Him. Undoubtedly this is true, but far more profoundly than by words Jesus reveals the Father by what He is, a theme that runs through the whole Gospel. "You know neither me nor my Father. If you knew me, you would then know my Father also" (8:19). "If I do not perform the works of my Father, do not believe me. But if I do perform them, and if you are not willing to believe me, believe the works, that you may know and believe that the Father is in me and I in the Father" (10:37-38). "He who believes in me, believes not in me but in him who sent me. And he who sees me, sees him who sent me" (12:44-45).

In the passage where He asserts that He is the way, the truth and the life, Jesus continues: "No one comes to the Father but through me. If you had known me, you would also have known my Father. And henceforth you do know him, and you have seen him" (14:6-7). Then in answer to Philip's importunate demand to be shown the Father, Jesus complains: "Have I been so long a time with you, and you have not known me? Philip, he who sees me sees also the Father. How canst thou say, 'Show us the Father'? Dost thou not believe that I am in the Father and the Father in me? . . . Otherwise believe because of the works themselves" (14:9-12). At its deepest level the revelation of the Father is not through words, but is the Word made flesh, Jesus Christ, the truth incarnate.

Hence Jesus is the "light of the world" (8:12; 9:5), "the light of life" (8:12). "In him was life, and the life was the light of men" (1:4). Without knowing Jesus we do not know the Father, and we walk in darkness. "He who walks in darkness does not know where he goes" (12:35). Without Him we are like the man born blind, groping our way in the blackness of night. Nor is it enough to see Jesus in the flesh; Judas saw and lived with Him for three years, but when he went out, "it was night" (13:30). The light had shone in his darkness, but he refused to walk in the light, preferring to "walk in darkness" (8:12), in a world absurd and incomprehensible unless illumined by Christ. "I have come a light into the world, that whoever believes in me may not remain in the darkness" (12:46).

Thus Jesus is the truth because He is in His person the revelation of the Father. To believe in Jesus is to know the Father, to become a "son of light" (12:36) because "I and the Father are one" (10:30). To know Jesus, therefore, is to possess eternal life because eternal life is identical with knowing the Father and the Son. But this knowing is hardly distinct from love in John. True enough, knowing Jesus fulfills in eminent fashion the usual definition of truth — knowledge of reality. If we know Jesus, we know the real world, in a sense the only real world, a universe shot through with the love of the Father.

However, in John this knowing also means a mutual presence of one to the other, a presence of the beloved to the lover. This presence of the disciple to his Master, of the friend to his friend (15:15), Christ compares to His relationship with the Father. "I know mine and mine know me, even as the Father knows me and I know the Father" (10:14-15). "I and the Father are one" (10:30). So Jesus prays "that they may be one, even as we are one; I in them and thou in me; that they may be perfected in unity, and that the world may know that thou hast sent me, and that thou has loved them even as thou hast loved me" (17:22-23).

Knowing Jesus, therefore, means to be at one with Him, with the Father, and with one another. And this threefold at-one-ment is an ontological unit, three facets of the same reality. It is not as if we first love Christ, then through this love become one in love with the Father in order finally to love our neighbor. No, to know Christ means to know the Father and at the same time to know one another, where "to know" has the pregnant Johannine sense of "know-love," or perfect at-one-ment.

It may seem that we have strayed far from our original concern with John's conception of the role of the Spirit. However, we have only been exploring the rich vein in the meaning of the truth into which the Spirit of truth is sent to lead us. It might appear from the development of the theme of truth that there is no role left for the Spirit since knowing Jesus is our at-one-ment. Curiously enough, however, in the last discourse Jesus constantly switches from the present to the future when speaking of knowing the Father in the Son. "And henceforth you do know him and have seen him" (14:7); "Yet a little while and the world no longer sees me. But you see me, for I live and you shall live. *In that day* you will know that I am in my Father, and you in me, and I in you" (14:19-20). "All things that I have heard from my Father, I have made known to you" (15:15); yet "I have many things to say to you, but you cannot bear them now. But when he, the Spirit of truth, has come, he will teach you all the truth" (16:12-13).

So the apostles have the truth and do not have it; they know the Father and do not; they have believed that Jesus has come from the Father (16:27), and do not (15:8-11). Jesus can berate them for not seeing the Father in Him; yet He can also implicitly excuse them: "The hour is coming when I will no longer speak to you in parables, but will speak to you plainly of the Father" (16:25).

When the apostles profess their belief in Him, Jesus can ask with gentle irony: "Do you now believe? Behold, the hour is coming, and has already come, for you to be scattered, each one to his own house, and to leave me alone" (16:31-32).

The apostles did not know Jesus until the death and resurrection because "the Spirit had not yet been given, since Jesus had not yet been glorified" (7:39). Jesus tells the apostles: "But I speak the truth to you; it is expedient for you that I depart. For if I do not go, the Advocate will not come to you; but if I go, I will send him to you" (16:7). Indeed only when the Spirit comes will they know "all the truth" (16:13), i.e., that Jesus is in the Father and the Father in Him and that all who know Jesus are one with Him and with the Father. Then only do we experience this at-one-ment deep within our own spirits.

Before we move on to the theme of life, one further point should be insisted on. To know Jesus is to know the Father, as we have said repeatedly. But we must also affirm: to know Christians is to know Jesus and the Father. Christian unity is a means of knowing Jesus and the Father. For Jesus prays "that all may be one, even as thou, Father, in me, and I in thee; that they also may be one in us, that the world may believe that thou has sent me. . . and that thou has loved them even as thou hast loved me" (17:21-23). The love of Christians for one another is only possible because of their at-one-ment with Christ and of His with the Father. Thus this love can be the sign by which men may come to believe in Christ and know the Father (13:35). The Spirit is the one who fuses Christians into this at-one-ment which bears witness to Christ.

## The life-giving Spirit

It should be a relatively easy task now to connect the theme of life with the themes of truth and spirit. We have already seen that eternal life consists in knowing the one true God and Jesus Christ whom He has sent (17:3). Since knowing Jesus is identical with knowing the Father, knowing Jesus means having eternal life. Hence Jesus is not just the light, but the "light of life" the life which is "the light of men" (1:4). Indeed "this is the will of my Father . . . that whoever beholds the Son, and believes in him, shall have everlasting life, and I will raise him up on the last day" (6:40). "Amen, Amen, I say to you, he who believes in me has everlasting life. I am the bread of life . . . If anyone eats of this bread, he shall live forever" (6:47-52).

Evidently knowing the truth and having eternal life are synonymous. Just as Jesus is the truth, so He is the life (14:6). Just as He has come to witness to the truth, so He has come "that they may have life, and have it more abundantly" (10:10). Just as the disciples do not know the truth until after the death and glorification of Christ, so too "must the Son of Man be lifted up, that those who believe in him . . . may have life everlasting" (3:14-15).

Just as the disciple knows the Father by knowing Jesus, so too he lives with the Father's life by living with the Son's life. "For as the Father has life in himself, even so he has given to the Son also to have life in himself" (5:26). "As the living Father has sent me, and as I live because of the Father, so he who eats me, he also shall live because of me" (6:58). The life we lead in Christ is identically the life of the Father. To know Jesus is to live with the life of the Father and Son in a perfect union of love. (Recall the overpowering statement of 1 John 4:8: "God is love.") To know means to live and to love, perfect at-one-ment.

We could logically and without reference to texts advance from these identities to the role of the Spirit in the life-giving process. The Spirit gives us the power to know the truth; since truth is life, the Spirit must by the same token be the Spirit of life. We need not, however, content ourselves with logical implication. John knows the Old Testament tradition linking the Spirit with life. "It is the spirit that gives life; the flesh profits nothing. The words that I have spoken to you are spirit and life" (6:64). "If anyone thirst, let him come to me and drink. He who believes in me, as the Scripture says, 'From within him there shall flow rivers of living water' " (7:37-38).

As we noted earlier, John explains this saying as a reference to the gift of the Spirit. Again just as we must be born to live, so too "unless a man be born again of water and the Spirit, he cannot enter into the kingdom of God. That which is born of the flesh is flesh; and that which is born of the Spirit is spirit" (3:5-6). And Christ is come to baptize "with the Holy Spirit" (1:33) and thus introduce us into the kingdom which is life.

In order to understand the full meaning of John's thought, we should study these Spirit texts against their Old Testament background. In the Old Testament Yahweh is a living God, life *par excellence,* and it is His life or breath which is the source of all created life. On the day of creation God breathed into man the breath of life (Gen. 2:7). He also announced: "My spirit (or breath) shall not remain in man forever, since he is flesh" (Gen. 6:3). Yahweh's breath, therefore, gives life to the flesh. John would also recall the opposition between flesh and spirit, man and God, which Isaiah expressed in berating the Israelites for trusting in foreign alliances:

> The Egyptians are men, not God;
> their horses are flesh, not spirit (Is. 31:3).

The impotence of man and flesh are here opposed to the creative power of God and His Spirit. To this theme of spirit as the source of natural life, the prophecies add the note of a new creation, a new outpouring of God's Spirit in messianic times, first on the Messiah himself (Is. 11: 1-3; 42:1), then on the whole people of God (Joel 3:1). Certainly the majestic promises in Ezekiel must have flashed through John's mind as he remembered Christ's words about the living water:

> I will sprinkle clean water upon you to cleanse you from all your impurities, and from all your idols I will cleanse you. I will give you a new heart and place a new spirit within you, taking from your bodies your stony hearts and giving you natural hearts. I will put my spirit within you and make you live by my statutes, careful to observe my decrees (Ez. 36:25-27).

The vivifying breath of Yahweh gives life to the dry bones in the famous vision of Ez. 37, and this vision is explained as the reaction of the people of Israel who are dead and without hope. "I will put my Spirit within you that you may live" (Ez. 37:14).

With this background the profound meaning of John's use of Spirit becomes clearer. Jesus is the Messiah, for the Baptist saw the Spirit descend and remain upon Him (John 1:32). Jesus has the Spirit beyond measure (3:34) and thus is the life, the spring whence all must drink in order to live (4:10-15; 7:39). From Him the Spirit is breathed out on all who believe in Him, but only after His glorification (7:39).

Now we can understand the immense significance of the scene in the upper room on the day of the resurrection. Just as God breathed to give life at the first creation, so Jesus inaugurates a new creation by breathing forth the Spirit. "As the Father has sent me, I also send you" (20:21). Christ's public career had begun with the descent of the Holy Spirit (1:33); so too will the apostles' mission begin. "When he had said this, he *breathed* upon them, and said to them, 'Receive the Holy Spirit'" (20:22). And these men became "living beings," living the very life of God.

To fulfill the prophecy of Ezekiel this new life of the Spirit is linked to the forgiveness of sins: "whose sins you shall forgive, they are forgiven them; and whose sins you shall retain, they are retained" (20:23). We are reminded of the earlier statement: "The truth will make you free" of sin (8:32), and once more the identity of truth and life is indicated.

Christ's death and resurrection have unlocked the springs of divine life, and that divine life is breathed out through Christ's glorified humanity on all flesh. "God is spirit, and they who worship him must worship in spirit and in truth" (4:24). The symbolic gesture of breathing signifies what our words cannot fully express: the gift of the life of God which is the Holy Spirit. And the worship in spirit and truth is the worship of the Father in the Son by the Holy Spirit dwelling in us.

## Conclusion

The biblical themes of spirit, life and truth converge for John on the person of Jesus Christ. He is the way, the truth and the life, but only after His death and resurrection. The glorified God-man is the center of Christian life and worship, the true vine whose life-force is identically the life-force of the branches (15:1-11). This life-force is the Spirit which Jesus enjoys beyond measure and which He communicates to His friends that they may live the same life that He lives with the Father. But this life is also knowledge of the truth.

In living this life we experience through faith the unity of the Father and the Son and the unity of one another in the Son and with the Father. The ground of this union of knowledge and love is the Spirit. It does seem that the Spirit-life theme emphasizes the ontological reality of the at-one-ment, while the Spirit-truth theme stresses the awareness we have of this at-one-ment, an awareness which is the peace that the world cannot give. For John the Spirit both grounds our union with the Father through Jesus and by that very fact gives us a belief which issues in the interior joy and peace of knowing that we are at one.

# THE THEOLOGY OF THE INCARNATION IN ST. JOHN

Raymond E. Brown, S.S.

Since "incarnation" means literally "entering or becoming flesh," when we think of the Incarnation in St. John, we naturally think of John 1:14: "The Word became flesh." In another article in this issue, Fr. Barrosse gives a thorough commentary on this verse; and so in our treatment of the Johannine theology of the Incarnation we shall be able to go into the wider implications of the Word's becoming flesh.

## The fact of the Incarnation

The fact of the Incarnation is very important in the Johannine writings (for our present purposes we use this term to refer to the Gospel and Epistles; unless otherwise indicated, all references are to the Gospel). Particularly in 1 John we find a determined insistence on the fact that Jesus Christ came in the flesh. Early heresies may account for such stress. The Docetists were teaching that the humanity of Christ was but an appearance, a phantasm through which God dealt with man. Cerinthus held that Christ, a spiritual being, descended upon Jesus, a normal man, at the baptism in the Jordan and remained with Jesus until just before the passion. Thus he divided Jesus and the Christ and denied that the Christ had ever suffered or shed blood.

Against such denials of the Incarnation, 1 John 4:2-3 stresses: "Every spirit that acknowledges Jesus Christ *come in the flesh* belongs to God." And 1 John 5:6 emphasizes that Jesus Christ came in water and in blood, not in water alone — a poetic way of stating that Jesus was the Christ not only at the baptism (water), but all through His life and at His death (blood). This same interest in assuring us of the reality of the Incarnation seems to govern some parts of the Gospel too, for instance 6:51ff, where there is such insistence on the flesh and blood of the Son of Man. In particular, 19:34-35, which solemnly testifies that blood, as well as water, came from the side of the pierced corpse, may have been directed against Docetist theories.

Thus while the Johannine writings emphasize the divinity of Jesus Christ (perhaps with greater precision than the rest of the New Testament), they are also very insistent on the true humanity of Jesus.

## The implications of the Incarnation

But St. John was too great a theologian to stop at proclaiming the fact of the Incarnation; his main purpose was not apologetics. Rather, he wished primarily to spell out for his Christian readers what this fact meant for them.

Published originally in *The Bible Today*, 1 (1963), 586-89. Reprinted by permission of the publisher.

If we give full force to the Greek of John 20:31, he was writing to those who already believed in Jesus Christ ("that you may continue to have faith"). And if we accept the usual date for the final *writing* of the Gospel (the last years of the first century A.D.), the work was addressed to a community that had believed for many years.

In many ways the problems of these Christians would not be unfamiliar to us. They had baptism and the Eucharist, the chief sacramental sources of grace. But what did this have to do with Jesus who walked in Galilee? True, the most ancient preaching of the Church enshrined in the synoptic Gospels tells us that Jesus had ordered the disciples to baptize in the divine name and to commemorate His death through the Eucharist. But why? It is in John's Gospel that we come closest to an answer, even though John tells us neither of the command to baptize nor of the institution of the Eucharist at the Last Supper. He takes the existence of these two sacraments for granted and seeks to show how they are rooted in Jesus' ministry and in the Incarnation.

The fact that Word became flesh means more than the taking on of a human nature. It means that in His whole method of dealing with men the Son of God will act as Son of Man and work through the things of the flesh. Today, in some circles, it has become fashionable to deprecate as hopelessly abstruse the strenuous debates of the early Christian centuries about the person and natures of Jesus Christ. But these debates show that instinctively Christians realized how important it was that nothing be allowed to obscure the true divinity and true humanity of Jesus. In recent times, in the face of liberal onslaught, orthodox Christians have been so busy insisting that Jesus was nothing less than God that there has been a danger of obscuring the fact that He was truly man in every way except sin. Even today, as the current theological debate about the limitations of the human knowledge of Christ shows, theologians have not worked out all the implications of the humanity of Christ.

St. John brings that humanity clearly before his Christian audience by showing that Christ, by continuing to operate in His Church through baptism and the Eucharist, is only continuing what He did on earth during His ministry. If the Son came down from heaven to lift men up (3:13-16), He does so through the things of this earth. When Jesus spoke to the Samaritan woman (4:13-14), He insisted that water would be the source of life for men. God had creatively begotten man in the beginning by breathing on him and giving man His spirit or breath (Gen. 2:7). Now, through Jesus, God was breathing His Holy Spirit upon men (John 20:22) and begetting them from above (3:3). But He would not do so in a purely invisible, intangible way. Jesus the Man would use the water of this world to cleanse men and communicate the Spirit. As 3:5 states, this begetting from above is of water, as well as of Spirit. Indeed, the Spirit would not be given (or if we stick close to the best Greek text of 7:39, the Spirit would not even be a reality for man) until Jesus was raised up on the Cross, and *water* and blood flowed from His side. It was then (19:30) that He handed over the Spirit.

Again, it was through such material things as bread and wine that Jesus would give to men the food of eternal life. Jesus insists that His flesh and blood are really food and drink (6:56) and that man cannot have life without them (6:54). They are a food more real than the barley bread and fishes He had multiplied.

Thus, when John tell us that the Word became flesh, he means more than the fact of the Incarnation. The whole of God's message, in the full sense of "Word," inextricably bound itself to the sphere of the flesh. John shows this by stressing that Jesus communicated His greatest gift, *life*, through the things of this world. Baptism and Eucharist, which are the lifeblood of Christian existence in the Church, are merely the explication of the implications of the Incarnation.

## Application of this theology

As the Lutheran theologian Dietrich Bonhoeffer has pointed out, one of the greatest defeats religion has suffered in modern times is its acceptance of a role which allots to it only the fringes of human existence. "There are no atheists in foxholes" is an axiom symptomatic of a world view that only danger, suffering, need and death evoke the presence of God. And, to some extent, religion has tacitly acquiesced by publicly proclaiming its purpose as the salvation of souls, as if that were its only goal. But does not the catechism teach us that the reason for human existence is twofold: to know, love and serve God *in this world*, and to be happy with Him forever in the next?

Yes, *in this world*! Religion has to be worldly, in the best sense of the word. "God *loved the world* so much that He actually gave His only Son" (3:16; also 1 John 4:9). And Jesus never forgot that He came as the light *of the world* (8:12). Whether we phrase the purpose of His mission in terms of the coming of the kingdom into time (synoptic Gospels) or of the gift of life to men (John), it is a mission to this world. He speaks of heaven and hell, but rarely and without detail. His concern is the knowing and loving and serving God in this life — the things we can do. He leaves to His Father the mysterious allotment of gifts in the next life. The Son became incarnate to teach men how to live a life in this world and not primarily to unveil the secrets of the next.

It is true that Jesus had some harsh things to say about the world that refused to believe in Him (7:7), but He kept trying to penetrate it with His love (14:31). His purpose was to save the world (3:17; 12:47) — a purpose so characteristic that He was called the Savior of the world (4:42; 1 4:14). That is why He sought to overthrow the prince of this world (12:31; 14:30), that He might claim it as His own. The disciples whom Jesus sent forth did not belong to this world as if they were its possession (17:14, 16), but their task was to continue Jesus' mission to the world (17:23). Their faith would overcome the world (1 John 5:4).

The Incarnation, then, means that the Church, which is the Body of Christ, is just as inextricably bound to this world as was its Master. Once the Word became flesh, a purely spiritual religion, or one with its vision too farsightedly fixed on the next world, became impossible. No one can find Christ outside the world; nor can one find the real world outside Christ, because the Incarnation has changed the nature of the world. The reality of the world, as Bonhoeffer insists, involves the God who has become manifest in Jesus Christ. And today perhaps more than at any time since the Incarnation, the Church must fight to prove the place of Christ in this world. The Church must open the eyes of the world to see that it is the world of Christ. If the Church is where Jesus reigns over the world, the Church cannot turn its back on this world. And indeed the only way the Church can defend its place in the world is not by settling for an existence on the fringes of life, but by assuring Christ's place in all of life and in the whole world.

And so we cannot settle for the salvation of souls. This life is too important a part of human existence to be written off as merely a trial. If this were not true, the Word would not have become flesh and God would not have loved the world. The salvation of the soul is a transition from a *rich life* based on acceptance of God through Jesus and service in His name. The next world does not constitute a refuge from this world, but involves a continuation of the Christian life begun here below. That is why John assures us that he who believes already possesses eternal life and has passed from death to life (5:24). The salvation of the soul cannot in any sense be looked upon as a consolation prize dangled before those neurotically incapable of facing the demands of this life. It is because this life and the next life constitute a continuum that John can emphasize the here and now aspect of judgment (3:18-19). Men must be brought to praise God in this world as in the next. God's will must come about on this earth as well as in heaven.

The Johannine theology of the Incarnation contains in nucleus a very important lesson for the Church of all time: a docetic spirituality or a docetic conception of the apostolate is not true to a Jesus Christ who came in water and blood (1 John 5:6).

# THE JUDGE OF ALL THE EARTH[1]

### John L. McKenzie, S.J.

It is a curious accident of language that Hebrew has no single word which can be translated as "justice". Like other accidents of language, this defect in the Hebrew vocabulary reveals a deep difference between the mind of the

[1] Gen. 18:25.

Published originally in *The Way* (31 Farm Street, London W.1), Vol. 2, #3 (July, 1962), 209-18. Reprinted by permission of the publisher.

Israelites who wrote the Old Testament and our own ways of thinking. We have inherited our ideas of law and justice from Greece and even more from Rome; these two ancient civilizations have given us the ideas and words. In our political thinking justice is the supreme virtue of civil society from which all other virtues flow; and a government which fails to render justice to its citizens is so corrupt that it ceases to be a legitimate government which can claim the allegiance of its citizens. Hebrew has several words for law, perhaps none of which correspond in meaning and use to our English word law; one of the most commonly used words we translate literally "judgment", the verdict of the judge. If we wish to translate "justice" into Hebrew, we shall do it best by combining two words. Where we think of justice, the Israelite thought of "righteous judgment". The phrase does not imply juridical positivism, as a modern reader could easily infer. It does imply the absence of an abstract idea of justice. Justice was produced by the verdict of the judge, who is the source and defender of justice. There is no "higher justice" above the law and the judge to which the Israelites would think of appealing. Nothing is just until it is judicially declared. For justice had no reality for the Israelites unless it was, as we should say, effectively realized; and only the declaration of the judge could give to justice concrete reality.

In spite of the intense activity of our courts, most of the citizens of our country have never had a personal encounter with the majesty of the law incarnated in the person of the judge on the bench. The novel, the theatre, and the cinema have made us all familiar with the most awesome judicial action of English law; the judge puts on the black cap and pronounces the words which terminate the earthly life of a human person. This is total justice, and we can conceive of no greater judicial power. The judge is merely the officer of society; but when he pronounces the sentence of death, many feel that he assumes an attribute of God. It is not, I fear, for this reason that so many are convinced that neither society nor its officers have the right to pronounce this sentence. But this is our idea of the judge; behind the judge who imposes a fine for a traffic violation stands the hangman. Nothing keeps the judge from summoning the hangman for the traffic violation except abstract justice, embodied in written law.

When we join ourselves to the prayer of the priest with which the sacrifice of the Mass begins, we take a phrase from the Psalms and ask God to judge us. Most of us feel that this is an extremely bold approach; we hope that he will not take our prayer seriously. In our ways of thinking the good citizen is one who never has any occasion to encounter a judge; to invite the judge to pronounce a verdict is to invite the officer whose minister is the hangman. But this prayer was not written by a citizen of England or the United States, and it means something altogether different. Where the judge is the source and defender of justice, he is the saviour and the deliverer. To render judgment is to vindicate a claim. In the primitive thought and speech of early Israel a claim is righteous when it is mine; and the judge renders righteous judgment when he delivers a verdict in my favour. In the oldest conceptions of God judgment is an attribute of salvation.

This is evidently a rather primitive idea of justice, and we shall see that the growth of Israel in its faith and its knowledge demanded a growth likewise in its conception of justice. But in Psalm 7:7; 9:5; 42:1 and other prayers, the Israelite candidly asks God to judge him where it is clear that he is asking God to defend him. The judgment of God is the attribute by which he redeems Zion from the attacks of its enemies.[2] Because God is a God of judgment Israel can await in confidence the works of his grace and pity.[3] Because of the sins of Israel judgment is remote,[4] judgment here is evidently deliverance, for we would say that sins bring judgment near. The man who announced the defeat and death of Absalom declared that God had "judged" David from his enemies.[5] Solomon's prayer at the dedication of the temple appeals to the judgment of God to forgive the sins of His people — surely a paradoxical expression.[6] In this quality of judge God is frequently called the defender of the judgment of the poor, the orphan and the widow.[7]

Where the judge is conceived as one who is on your own side, he is evidently not on the side of your enemies. To the enemies of Israel God is the vindictive judge. He is the judge of the world and of nations; in his appointed judgment he rises in anger against the enemies of Israel.[8] The judgment which he passes on the world in righteousness and on peoples in equity is a condemnation.[9] When he judges nations he shatters kings on the day of his anger.[10]

Why is God the judge-defender-avenger of Israel and the judge-adversary of the nations? Simply because he is united to Israel by a covenant of his own election and establishment. Between God and Israel, in the unsophisticated thinking of early Israel, a relationship arose like the relations of the members of the family and clan. These groups preserved themselves from extinction by solidarity against all other groups; the individual demanded and received from the group the protection of his person and his claims, as he accepted the responsibility of defending the persons and claims of others. God is the "judge" of Israel because he is the kinsman and the avenger.

The prophetic revolution of the eighth and seventh centuries B.C. in Israel raised the question of this relationship. What happens if one of the parties is unfaithful to the obligations of the covenant? The relationship is like the relationships of family and clan, but it is also unlike them. Israel can release God from his promises by failing to fulfil its own. If it loses its fidelity, its only claim to the "judgments" of God, it must expect the judgment which he renders to the nations. By the time of Ezekiel, the early sixth century B.C., it was established in prophetic speech that the judgments of God upon

[2] Is. 1:27.
[3] Is. 30:18.
[4] Is. 59:9.
[5] 2 Sam 18:31.
[6] 1 Kings 8:49.
[7] Deut. 10:18; Ps. 75:10; 81:3; 103:6; 139:13; Job 36:6.
[8] Ps. 7:7.
[9] Ps. 9:8; 95:13.
[10] Ps. 109:6.

Israel were not his saving acts but his punishments. In these as in his saving acts God exhibited the righteousness which is the essential quality of the judge. It is not righteous for him to treat virtue and sin equally. When this was perceived, Israel was educated in the concept of justice. Like all men, Israel also stands under judgment at all times.

It is not characteristic of Old Testament thought to conceive the judgment of God upon mankind in terms of a vast assizes to which all humanity is summoned, although the image is used in Joel[11] and Daniel[12] The Old Testament regularly sees the judgments of God in the events of history or the catastrophes of nature. Judgment is not deferred to a far off eschatological event, but is executed here and now. The Israelite prophets reject any suggestion that the events of history and the catastrophes of nature are merely casual, needing no explanation other than the concurrence of various opposing forces. These vindicate the judgment of God on men and nations.

The idea of judgment passes from the Old Testament into the New Testament, and, like so many theological ideas, experiences a transformation. If one consults the concordance of the New Testament, it is at once evident that the words "judge" and "judgment" and compounds of these words occur much less frequently in the Synoptic Gospels than they do in the Pauline and Johannine writings. The content of the Gospels bears out the statistics of the concordance; judgment is not a really dominant theme in the Synoptic Gospels. This does not imply that it is absent. Judgment is that which inevitably follows sin.[13] The judgment is usually mentioned without further details, and the interpreter wonders whether it refers to a judgment of this world or the next — in modern theological terms, whether the judgment is historical or eschatological. This question is of more importance than one might think; and we shall return to it later in this article.

Paul is much more conscious of the judgment than the authors of the Synoptic Gospels, so conscious indeed that it is troublesome for the interpreter who attempts to synthesize his thought. There is a past judgment, a sentence of condemnation which has fallen upon all men. This is the judgment passed upon all men in their ancestor,[14] who by his act brought all of humanity into a state of guilt. From his origin upon the earth man is under judgment. It is this thought of Paul which was the occasion of Augustine's famous and harsh phrase for unredeemed man, *massa damnata*. The saving act of Jesus Christ is an annulment of the judgment.[15] The judgment is a judgment of death; Jesus by his death restores life to the condemned.

But there is also a future judgment in Paul, and the future judgment is more prominent in his writings than the past judgment. This is the judgment which the sinner cannot escape.[16] It is a judgment accomplished on the day

[11] Joel 4:9-16.
[12] Dan. 7:9-12.
[13] Matthew 5:21-25; 12:40-42; 23:13, 33; Mark 12:40; Luke 10:14; 11:31-32; 12:58.
[14] Rom. 5:16, 18.
[15] Rom. 8:1, 3.
[16] Rom. 2:1-3.

of wrath,[17] a day when God will judge the world,[18] the living and the dead.[19] One of his readers might have asked Paul whether a race condemned in its origin is capable of further judgment. But since neither his readers nor Paul himself placed the question, we must answer it ourselves, or find a reason why the question should not be asked. The answer here as so often in the theology of Paul lies in the versatility — one might say the mercurial quality — of Paul's thought. And the key here is perhaps that the judgment of all men in Adam is original with Paul, while the future judgment was an existing commonplace which Paul accepted. Here it is necessary to supply some information from extrabiblical sources.

The idea of judgment in the Old Testament sketched above experienced remarkable development in Jewish apocalyptic literature of the first century or two before the Christian era. In many of these writings the judgment of God on the nations was dramatized into a vast assizes to which all men are summoned. Not infrequently this dramatic scene is painted in vivid and gruesome colours. The interest in apocalyptic literature (as the name of the literature indicates) lay in alleged revelations concerning the world catastrophe, the great act by which God overturns the world and vindicates His supremacy and His justice. This is the final victory of God over evil.

It is important to notice that the biblical belief in the final victory of God over evil is not of necessity linked with any particular dramatic or metaphorical expression. The last judgment scene which is depicted over so many cathedral doors and so many high altars has become in popular belief an article of faith scarcely less sacred than the Trinity of persons, and one accepts certain risks if one points out that an article of faith does not include purely artistic features. In the Synoptic Gospels the last judgment scene is reflected only in Matthew,[20] not paralleled in the other Gospels. Nor is it certainly reflected even there. The scene is not called a judgment, it does not resemble a judgment scene, nor are any legal terms employed. One may appear to be playing with words to dwell upon this, but legal terminology was available to the New Testament writers when they wished to use it, and they frequently did. If we call the scene in Matthew the last judgment, we are using a term which Matthew did not use.

With these reservations, one must still say that the apocalyptic judgment of Jewish belief is most probably what is implied in the judgment mentioned in the synoptic Gospels and in the future judgment of Paul. Sound method demands that when we take this as an acceptance of the belief in a final "judgment" in the biblical sense, we are not compelled to a literal acceptance of the apocalyptic imagery in which this belief is sometimes expressed. Man is under a judgment from which he can escape, if he accepts the saving act of Jesus Christ; there awaits a judgment from which no deliverance can be expected. The terms of this judgment are man's response to his encounter with

[17] Rom. 3:5.
[18] Rom. 3:6.
[19] 2 Tim. 4:1.
[20] Matthew 25:31-46.

God in Jesus Christ; it is altogether fitting that the judgment of man's decision in this crisis should be committed to him who is the focus of the decision, the Lord Jesus Christ who comes to judge the living and the dead.

The judgment is a dominant theme in the Gospel of John; and it is presented in what appears at first sight to be a complex of paradoxes. Jesus came into the world not to judge the world but to save the world;[21] yet Jesus has come into the world for judgment.[22] The Father judges no one;[23] yet it must be the Father who seeks the glory of Jesus and who judges.[24] The Father judges no one because he has given all judgment to the Son[25] and Jesus says that he judges justly[26] and truthfully.[27] Yet Jesus says he does not judge.[28]

The unity of thought which underlies these paradoxes is the entirely distinctive concept of the judgment presented by John. There is a judgment of the last day in John[29] and a resurrection of judgment which is contrasted with the resurrection of life.[30] But when one assembles the passages in which the judgment occurs in John, it is clear that the judgment is not past or future; it is present, it occurs now. The unbeliever is already judged.[31] The judge of the unbeliever on the last day is the word which Jesus has spoken.[32] The spirit proves that there is judgment by showing that the prince of the world is already judged.[33] The judgment of the world occurs *now*, when the decisive hour of the rejection of Jesus by his own people is near.[34]

What is this judgment which is eternally present, which is not the work of the Father but is committed to the Son? John has transformed the judgment from an act of God to an act of man; it is man who pronounces judgment upon himself. Jesus is judge in the sense that he is the object of decision; in this sense the Father judges no one but commits all judgment to the Son. In the same sense Jesus comes not to judge the world but to save the world; the decision is judgment or salvation to the man who makes it. In John the judgment is unbelief, refusal to accept Jesus as the Son. This judgment is pronounced when one encounters Jesus.

Effectively, then, John tells Christians that it is nonsense to await the judgment; the judgment is an accomplished fact, accomplished by the personal decision of each one. The "world", which in John's language means those who do not believe in Jesus, is judged by his very coming. Apocalyptic ex-

[21] John 3:17; 12:46.
[22] John 9:39.
[23] John 5:22.
[24] John 8:50.
[25] John 5:22, 27.
[26] John 5:30.
[27] John 8:16.
[28] John 8:12; 12:47.
[29] John 12:48.
[30] John 5:29.
[31] John 3:18; 5:24
[32] John 12:48.
[33] John 16:11.
[34] John 12:31.

pectations can degenerate into an unreal dreamworld which has little reference to present reality; more than once in the history of Christianity they have been a refuge for those who felt defeated by the world. By recalling that the judgment is accomplished now by the personal decision of each man, John recalls Christians to a sense of their own responsibility and to the immediate effects of their decisions.

If these be the implications of the judgment as it is presented by John, they must have certain repercussions in the personal life of the individual Christian which are not always felt clearly. Christian humility is explained in such a way that the Christian learns to have a low esteem of his personal importance and value; and as a corrective of the pride and vanity which is natural to man the lessons are not to be dismissed. But humility, like all the virtues except love, becomes a distortion of the Christian ideal unless it is taken as part of a larger whole. The Christian who has become so humble that he believes his own personal decisions are important to no one, even to himself, is fleeing from Christian virtue, not pursuing it. What St. Paul meant when he said that the saints will judge the world[35] was clearer to him than it is to us. But it is not impossible that an element of the Johannine judgment crept into his language here, and that he meant that the lives of the saints will prove that the world which rejects Jesus Christ is wrong. Effectively the judgment of God in the present world is expressed in the lives of those who believe in him. And it is terribly important that those who believe in him should vindicate his judgment in what they say and do.

There is a judgment of God in history; and history is the actions of man in society. Just as history is a complex and protracted process and not a single action, so the judgment of God in history is not a single event. The Bible is calmly assured that the history which is dominated by the saving acts and judgments of God is none the less written by the men whose decisions determine the events. The celebrated problem of the reconciliation of the sovereignty of God and the freedom of man is not a genuine problem in the books of the Bible. One may say that this is due either to a more profound insight in the biblical writers or to their incapacity for the type of philosophical reflection which presents the problem. For one reason or the other, the Bible affirms each of these truths without losing its grasp on the other. And therefore John can present the judgment as both the action of God and the action of man. Surely one who knows that he shares in the formation of the judgment of God can scarcely think of his own personal decisions as unimportant. History is woven of these personal decisions, so closely interlocked between man and man and in the course of the personal life of each man that no one can set a limit to the consequences of his decisions. Each of us writes history each day, and when we write history we write God's judgment.

The personal decision which is judgment is never made by each man in the permanent and final form which makes further judgment impossible and unnecessary until each man is himself removed from history. The "now" of

[35] 1 Cor. 6:2.

the judgment is not an instant; it is the "now" of the present life, of all the
days and years in which we encounter Jesus Christ the incarnate Word. And
indeed the word "encounter", so popular in modern theological writing, is
not the perfect word to denote the unique experience of the personal meeting between God and man which occurs when the Word is made flesh and
dwells among us. The reality of Jesus Christ is too immense to be apprehended
in a single instant and in a single decision. Neither total acceptance of
him nor total rejection of him is a decision easily and quickly made. In either
case one learns anew each day of one's life what the reality is which one
has accepted or rejected. And the magnitude of the decision, as well as its
incalculable consequences, are not seen by us in their fullness. One decision
leads infallibly to another, and the more one advances in the chain of decisions
the more difficult it becomes to reverse the series. At what point does one
really make a final and irreversible decision? The Church tells us that our
judgment is not determined until we have passed from the land of the living. The Church as well as experience also tells us that men rarely aban-
don the decisions which have made them to be one thing rather than another.
Each of these personal decisions is a factor forming the judgment which is
not reversed.

In the thought of St. John, Jesus judges the world by his very coming and
presence. I have paraphrased his thought by saying that Jesus is the judge
by being the object of decision rather than its agent. It is a recurrent theme
in St. John that the Jews who encountered Jesus did not recognize their judgment in him, and that their failure to recognize him is no excuse. The transparent reality of God in Christ can be concealed only by those who wish
to conceal it. That transparent reality is the risen Jesus Christ living in his
Church. St. John tells us that men judge themselves; and the entire New
Testament, with one accord, tells Christians with more severity than usual
that the judgment of other men does not belong to the Christian. The Christian can ask himself and not others whether the transparent reality of the risen
Jesus living in His Church is dimmed and obscured to the world by himself; for each of us is the Church in his own time and place. He can ask himself whether in him the world sees the Church as essentially and primarily
a community of love and not as something else. He can ask himself whether
men will encounter Christ in the Church if they think, for reasons which are
not entirely spurious, that the Church is a power society whose officers seem
more interested in total control than in total dedication. He can ask himself
whether men encounter Christ in a community where words like due submission to properly constituted authority are heard far more frequently than
such words as "A new commandment I give you, that you love one another",
and "Let him who would be first among you be the slave of others". He can
ask himself whether the fullness of Christ has ever been revealed in the exis-
tent reality of the Church, and he will conclude that it has not because the
members of the Church have not received the fullness of Christ — because
they did not choose to receive it. And he must admit that the reality of Christ

can be most effectively concealed by those whose responsibility in the Church is the greatest.

It is not ours to judge any except ourselves; but we know that what dulls the encounter between the world and Christ in his Church is one thing here and now, another thing there and then. Can the Christian honestly take refuge from responsibility, which is his own judgment, because he thinks that leadership has failed him? Is he genuinely responsible if he shows a great readiness to do what is right as long as everyone else has done it before him? Can he take real comfort in the thought that if what he is doing is, as he fears, wrong, at least he is doing wrong under clerical leadership? At one time in English history a layman, Thomas More, took a position in which he was supported by only one of the English bishops. We sometimes seek in the Church and her leadership a security which the Church does not promise: the security which is felt in blindly following directions which we know are not good, the assurance that we can safely let someone else do our personal thinking and make our personal decisions. This is a flight from judgment. That more men have not faced their own crisis as Thomas More faced his is due simply to the fact that few of us are aware of our responsibility as Thomas More was. In him and those who like him made their own decision, and only in them, could one see Christ in His Church in the England of his time. It would be a mistake to think that this situation is unique.

One final aspect of the judgment as John conceives it may further enlarge our understanding of judgment. John returns to the primitive biblical conception of judgment in this respect, that it is the coming of Jesus as saviour that places man under judgment. Jesus judges by his saving act and saves by his judgment. Judgment becomes again deliverance in a more profound sense. When we combine this with another aspect of the Johannine thought in which judgment is transformed from an act of God to an act of man, it appears that we have the saving act also transformed from an act of God to an act of man; and this is a heresy which the Church has repudiated vigorously and often. Like all heresies, this one is a distortion of a truth. John, like Paul, has no doubt that God alone saves and that man is incapable of saving himself. The act by which man judges and saves is the creation of God's saving and judging will within him. Man himself must make the decision; but he could not make it if God had not empowered him to make it. He is saved when he is judged, when he encounters Jesus Christ, the object of decision.

For the Christian the judgment is an object of hope rather than an object of fear. When we attribute judgment to God, we use a human term which can be misinterpreted if the analogy is pushed too hard. The judgment of God is not an act of law, for law is above the judge. God alone can pronounce a judgment which is a deliverance. The human judgment which we know cannot be exercised unless the judge lays aside love and mercy. The judgment of God is a judgment of love and mercy; were it anything else, it would not be the judgment of God.

# THE QUENCHING OF THIRST:
# REFLECTIONS ON THE UTTERANCE
# IN THE TEMPLE,   JOHN 7:37-39

J. Blenkinsopp

The invitation of Christ to come and drink, as recorded in John 7:37-39, is the most direct appeal possible, and yet to judge by the numerous and often contradictory comments made on it, beset by difficulties: must we put a full-stop after "let him come to me and drink"? from whom do the rivers of living water flow? what exactly is the "scripture-text" referred to? — and others. All these questions must be answered as far as it is possible to answer them, but perhaps in trying to do so we neglect to see the text in a larger field of vision. The object of these brief reflections is to attempt to show one or two ways of doing just that — in particular by concentrating not on these individual problems but on the literary form of the passage and the motif which it contains.

Even a superficial reading of St. John's Gospel would suffice to bring to our notice the recurrence of some short phrases which were evidently meant to serve as notes explanatory of more difficult or obscure points in the gospel, or to emphasise sayings or actions which were seen to be of special significance. Some are merely topographical, mentioning the place where certain words were spoken or some miracle performed. Thus, at the end of John the Baptist's witness to Christ, we are told: "These things took place in Bethany beyond the Jordan where John was baptising" (1:28), and so for the miracle at Cana, the eucharistic discourse in the synagoguge at Capernaum and elsewhere. Others have as their object to clear up obscurities for such as were not familiar with the Palestinian scene or to introduce some new *dramatis persona* and establish his or her identity, as with the sister of Martha who was the same as the woman in the incident in the house of Simon the Leper (11:2). Others again, and the greatest number, were inserted to explain the sense of words spoken by the actors in the drama; the parents of the man born blind (9:22-23), the high-priest who makes his mysterious prophecy (11:51-52), Judas who complains of the wasted ointment (12:6) and even the words of the prophet with which John ends the "Book of Signs." [1] More important than all these, however, was comment required after the great utterances of Christ which this gospel records, and we notice how often recurs the theme of the non-comprehension of his words by the hearers. In some cases this is mentioned only in passing, but elsewhere the explanation takes on a definite and recognisable physiognomy. The saying about the Temple (2:21-22), the prophetic gesture of the messianic ride into the city (12:16) and the invitation to drink (7:37) all have reference to an action

Published originally in *Scripture*, 12 (1960), 39-48. Reprinted by permission of the publisher.
[1] The term is used of the first part of the gospel up to the Passion by C. H. Dodd, *The Interpretation of the Fourth Gospel*, 1955.

which communicates, in the language of symbol, the living truth of the messianic presence of Jesus. In the first two cases it is Jesus himself who acts, at the feast of Booths. His words were spoken at the time of and very probably with reference to the joyful and meaningful liturgy of the Water Libation.[2] In all three cases the symbolism of the act is given depth by the quoting of a scripture text, and it is stated that the hearers did not understand at the time but that the meaning only went home with the coming of the illuminating presence of the Spirit, itself dependent on Jesus being glorified. In these texts, then, we find a definite pattern which consists of prophetic sign or saying, scripture text and interpretative comment. This gives us the cue for reading our text in the following way:

> On the last day — the Great Day — of the feast, Jesus stood up (or perhaps, was standing) and cried out:
> *Saying*: If anyone thirst, let him come to me and drink (that is, the believer in me).
> *Text*: As the Scripture text says: Rivers of living water shall flow from his midst.
> *Interpretation*: This He said of the Spirit which the believers in him were going to receive, for as yet the Spirit had not been given, since Jesus had not been glorified.

Read in this way, it is seen as an example of a literary pattern which in its turn reflects the basic thematic structure of the work as a whole; and is very revealing of the theology which dictated what that structure should be like. Thus we can readily understand that the giving of the Spirit is, theologically speaking, the watershed of the Fourth Gospel; on the one side, incomprehension, on the other, the illumination which is not denied to the believer, to him who "comes to" Christ.[3] That is why the first part of the gospel, the signs and sayings which are spoken "in figures" (John 16:25-29), ends on the sombre note of the quotation from Isaiah which was, as we know from the Synoptics, the *locus classicus* for the scandal and mystery of the rejection of the Christ; after that point the author goes at once into the account of the Passion or "glorification" which culminates in the giving of the Spirit in accordance with a promise often repeated.

Coming back to the saying which we have seen to be central in the passage, we note that it is prefaced by the statement that Jesus stood up and cried out. The author here uses the solemn verb *krazo* to denote an enunciation of special importance as is the case elsewhere. In Rom. 9:27, for instance, we find it used of a declaration from Isaiah which is given special importance, and also in the Fourth Gospel itself where it introduces a series

[2] Lev. 23:33-35 has caused some difficulty in regard to the chronology of the feast; some writers have placed the last of the water-libations on an eighth and even a ninth day; see G. F. Moore, *Judaism in the First Centuries of the Christian Era*, 1946, p. 43. It is, however, more generally accepted that this liturgy took place only up to a seventh day, the 'Great Day.'

[3] To 'come to' Christ in St. John is synonymous for 'to believe.' cf. 6:35; 3:20 (to come to the Light); 5:40.

of sayings on messianic faith and rejection, strongly reminiscent of similar sayings in St. Matthew, while both have strong points of contact with some expressions in the Wisdom literature, especially Proverbs.[4] This provides a valuable clue to the literary milieu of the utterance we are considering and is confirmed by another consideration, namely, that the invitation formula, found likewise in John and Matthew, introduces many expressions in the sapiential books. Thus, in Prov. 1:20:

> Wisdom cries aloud in the street;
> In the markets she raises her voice

and further on, she takes up her stand (using the same verb as in (John 7:37) and calls out (Prov. 8:6). We find an invitation even closer in form to that in our text in the next chapter of Proverbs where Wisdom "has sent her maids to call from the highest places in the town: Whoever is simple, let him turn in here!" — all of which suggests that standing up and crying out was a common literary convention applied to Wisdom personified.

It is striking in reading these texts how often literary formula and pattern go hand in hand with motif, taking this latter in the sense of a concrete, non-conceptual figure (e.g. making a feast, drinking living water) which, like a motif in music, is significant because it tends to recur in a given context. Thus, to take an example mentioned already, we find that when Wisdom cries aloud this saying is put on her lips: "They will seek me diligently but they will not find me," which we have practically in the same words from the mouth of Jesus, in a saying placed very near to that uttered at the feast of Booths (John 7:34). With this we can also compare the little collection of sayings on prayer in Matthew 7:7-11, transcribed presumably from an earlier source to which St. Luke also had access, and note in particular the recurrence of the verb "to seek" (zeîtein) and the motif of the quest which is classic in the sapiential books and the literature which has been, directly or indirectly, inspired by them.[5] We find another example of motif recurrence in Prov. 9, where Wisdom is a king issuing his invitation to a banquet, and in the parable of the king (or, a certain man in Luke) who made a marriage feast. Indeed the evangelical *masal* develops motifs, many if not most of which are prominent throughout the Wisdom literature. There are, in fact, apart from the full-length *mesalim* or parables, several shorter specimens introduced by the formula: "To what shall I compare?. . ." reminiscent on the one hand of rabbinical didactic methods and on the other of Wisdom for-

---

[4] John 12:44-45 and Matthew 10:40-41, which latter follows three sayings on discipleship which use expressions echoing strongly sapiential sayings. Thus, the verb *philein* (to love) for the relationship between Jesus and his disciples and the adjective *haxios* (worthy) with gen. of person; cf. Wis. 8:2 and Prov. 8:17. On this point see remarks of A. Feuillet in *Biblica* 1958, pp. 295-6. It should be noted, however, that *philein* in the sense given, though unusual, is not quite *hapax* in the New Testament. In Cor. 16:22 it is used of Christ and also in John 16:27, due perhaps to the earlier 'the Father loves (*philei*) you.' There is also the curious interchange between the verbs *philein* and *agapān* in the threefold affirmation of love on the part of Peter in John 21:15-17.

[5] e.g. Wis. 1:1-2; 6:12; Prov. 1:28; 8:17.

mulas.[6] This brings us back to the text on the quenching of thirst which illustrates and is illustrated by this tendency. The use of the figure: "living water" or "fountains of water" or water *tout court* for Wisdom was a commonplace in the literature of all that long epoch in which the sapiential genre was current — right through from the sapiential Psalms and Proverbs to the allegorical exegetes of the Alexandrian school. It often spilled over into other genres in use at that time, and is found more than once in the apochryphal gospels and apocalypses. In reference to secret gnosis or doctrines communicated, Jesus, in the recently published coptic book of Sayings, is made to say to Didymos Thomas the *mustîs* or initiate: "I am not thy master, because thou hast drunk, thou hast become drunk from the bubbling spring which I have measured out." In Ben Sirach (Ecclesiasticus) the God-fearer, in the same way, is said to drink the waters of Wisdom (Sir. 15:3) and in the well-known twenty-fourth chapter of the same book it is said of the Torah — personified as Wisdom in accordance with the religious and philosophical propaganda of diaspora Judaism:

> They who eat of me will yet hunger,
> And they who drink of me will yet thirst.

words which are strongly reminiscent of *logia* in John and are not without bearing on our text as we shall see. In fact in the same chapter there is a passage which I suggest is of some significance for the study of the invitation to drink in John 7:37. The author — in keeping with a type of midrashic homily common in that literature, compares Wisdom (the Law) to the life-giving river which in old biblical tradition flowed out of Eden forming four other tributary rivers, and he makes the wise man say:

> I am like a water course coming from the river and like a waterway leading into paradise . . . and lo, my water course has become a river and the river has turned into a sea.

The similarity of these words to the Johannine text which speaks of living water, striking though it is in terms of literary comparison, is even more so in the light of the thought-world — the *Gedankengang* — of the gospel as a whole. In fact, what Ben Sirach, an Alexandrian Jew, says of the Torah, John predicates of Christ; both are considered as hypostases or personifications of Wisdom, and it is surely not an accident that John should have made one of the basic themes of his gospel the antithesis between Christ and the Torah, as he has enunciated in the prologue:

> The Torah was given through Moses,
> Grace and Truth through Jesus Christ (John 1:17)

The same idea underlies many of the "signs" or miracles: the water for the rites of purification, the wine that is given by Christ, the well of "our

[6] cf. Matthew 11:16-9 with Prv 1:24 and Ben Sirach 4:11. In the Lukan parallel (7:31ff). the saying is referred explicitly to Wisdom. Other themes treated in this way are: the rich fool, the great feast, hidden treasure, calculations for war — all of which can be easily illustrated from both the Synoptics and the Wisdom books.

father, Jacob" contrasted with the living water promised to the Samaritan woman, and others. We know, in fact, that in the thought-world in which the gospel was written and to which it contributed, two tendencies were at work which can be at least indirectly illustrated from the gospel itself, and throw some light upon its major themes. In the first place, under the influence of Greek speculative thought and Stoic ideas in particular, Wisdom as an hypostasis or person tended to merge with the Logos, the divine principle at work in the creation and ordering of the world. In Philo, Wisdom and Logos are practically identical and in the Christian Alexandrians the identification is complete. This tendency could be illustrated further from other literary currents which emerged in the inter-testamentary period. In the Book of Henoch, for example, Wisdom is seen as having her place in heaven, coming to earth only to be rejected, and returning whence she came to be poured out in the latter days as water from which all who are thirsty may drink their fill.[7] We have already seen that the quenching of thirst with the water that makes wise is thematic in the Apocryphal writings and among those who attempted a synthesis between the words of Christ and the currents and cross-currents of thought which we refer to summarily and inclusively as Gnosticism.

At the same time another tendency was at work, this time within normative Judaism, which aimed at resisting the dangers inherent in this process of hypostasising abstract qualities — the old danger of polytheistic superstition in particular, so that the Torah came to be regarded as the only legitimate and adequate object of which Wisdom could be predicated. All this was doubtless a reaction against what was going on in the enemy camp after the schism of the Christian or Nazarene sect. In this context of contemporary history and against this background John's concept of Christ becomes more fully intelligible. We know in fact from early tradition that he wrote the gospel as a counter-blast to the gnostic heretic Cerinthus, and it is not unnatural that in doing so he should fight his opponent with the latter's own weapons. In this light the saying on living water would illustrate admirably John's doctrine of spiritual, Christian gnosis — which, for St. John, is the same as eternal life (John 17:3). In this connection we can note that Origen who, more perhaps than any other commentator on this gospel, brings us near to the inner world of ideas in which it was written, goes not to the many parallel passages in the prophets for the source of the quotation, but to the Wisdom books. He quotes, for example, from Prov. 5:15 and 9:4 where "Wisdom which, according to hypostasis is the same as the Word (Logos) of God" stands up and cries out.[8] He found ample material in these writings to justify and expand his teaching that the Christian himself must become a source of knowledge and therefore of life for others. Such texts as the following from Prov. 5:15-16 were read by him with this meaning:

[7] Henoch 84:3; 94:5; 98:1; 99:1.
[8] Homily on Ps. 2:5 in *Opera* ed. Delargue, 11, p. 550.

> Drink water from your own cistern,
> Flowing water from your own well,
> Should your streams be scattered abroad,
> Streams of water in the streets?

This served him as an illustration for the Christian gnosis which begins as a well, overflows and becomes a stream, and then grows into a mighty river. The idiom which he speaks here is not essentially different, it seems, from that in John 7:37-39.

The *logion* of Christ at the feast of Booths is therefore sapiential both in form and in content — with reference, that is, to the sapiential motifs of living water which is poured out and the quenching of thirst. There is also, as we have seen, evidence for supposing that what we have here is a text, which represents Jesus as hypostatic Wisdom hidden indeed in his real identity from the eyes and the understanding of those who heard that cry in the Temple on that day, but revealed through the ministry of the Spirit which enlightens the baptised intelligence. A corollary to this would be that we have here a valuable point of contact with the Synoptic Gospels going beyond the text referred to as the Johannine Logion (Matthew 11:25-30 par.) and this could raise the question whether both they and John were able to draw upon, to a greater or lesser extent, some earlier collection or collections of *Logia Kuriaka* or Sayings of Our Lord which had already, in the early years of the bitter polemic between Church and Synagogue, presented him to the contemporary world as not only greater than Solomon (Matthew 12:41 and Luke 11:31) but — in opposition to the false claims of the Torah — as Christ, the Wisdom of God (1 Cor. 1:24).

We saw at the beginning how the structure of this passage illustrates a typical process in the Fourth Gospel. It presents some facet of the mysterious identity of the Protagonist by means of a symbolic action or utterance, accompanied by a Scripture quotation and interpretative comment. Here there is the specific difference that the prophetic action is not performed by Jesus himself, but was witnessed by him and his hearers in the course of the liturgy of the last day of the feast of Tabernacles. Coming in the month of Tishri — the end of September and the beginning of October — it corresponded to the time of year when expectation of the winter rains was at its highest. From the regulations which governed the observance of the feast and its liturgy (Lev. 22; Num. 29:12-39) we can get some idea of what it meant to the faithful who took part in it. It had been originally superimposed upon a harvest festival, the rain-making character of which was explicit, and this aspect was never really lost sight of, as later writers testify. In the rabbinical tractate *Roš ha-Šanah* (New Year's Day) we read: "Why does the Torah say: Make a libation of water at the feast? The Holy One (blessed is He!) says: Make a libation of water before me at the feast that the rains of the year may be blessed to you." The bearing of the Lulab in one hand and the Ethrog in the other — three water plants bound together and an orange or lemon respectively — the waving of these three times to the four

points of the compass and the procession seven times round the altar seem
to have had, originally at least, the same significance. As for the libation of
water itself, it took place on each day of the celebrations but climactically on
the last, the Great Day. It consisted in a procession of the priests to the pool
of Siloam whose waters were fed from the spring of the Virgin by means of
Ezekiel's tunnel. Here a gold jug was filled with water; then they returned by
the Water Gate where their coming was announced to the crowd by three
blasts on a trumpet, and finally there was the seven-fold procession round
the altar. Then one of the priests mounted the ramp at the side of the altar
and raising his hands on high so that all could see them,[9] poured the water
into a silver funnel whence it flowed into the ground. All this was to the
overwhelming applause and joy of the worshippers present who, as Josephus
and the rabbis give us to understand, followed every detail of the ceremony
with passionate interest. This joy was, to the onlooker, the most spectacular
thing of all and was the climax of all the religious enthusiasm which the great
feasts always occasioned. We are told: "He that has never seen the joy of
the *Beth ha-She'ubah* has never in his life seen joy." [10]

This ceremony was moreover accompanied by the singing of the whole or
a part of the Hallel-psalms 113–118 and especially Psalm 118 in which occurs
the phrase:

> This is the day which the Lord has made;
> Let us rejoice and be glad in it.
> Save us, we beseech Thee, O Lord!
> O Lord, we beseech Thee, give us success!

This invocation was repeated many times. It has been pointed out too that
the first of the psalms of this collection contains the reference to the giving
of the water from the rock in the desert (Ps. 113:8), a text associated in its
turn with that of Isaiah 12:3: "With joy you will draw water from the
wells of salvation" — which good rabbinical tradition has associated with
the water libation at the feast. In view of the other examples of images or
"types" occurring in this Gospel and which can be traced to the Exodus —
the Brazen Serpent and the Manna in particular — it is possible that the
author had the incident of the rock in mind but this would not, of course,
prejudice the question of the literary form of the saying which is, as we have
tried to demonstrate, sapiential.

If, as it seems, this was in fact the actual historical context in which Our
Lord made this invitation to drink and quench the thirst, we see how the
symbolism achieves deeper resonance and a new dimension. In his comment
the author has referred the outpouring to the Spirit which was to be given,
and it is significant that a constant theme of rabbinical tradition has connected the water-libation of the feast with the outpouring of the Spirit in the

[9] Admonished by the example of Alexander Jannaeus who poured it over his feet and
was pelted by the crowd and almost lynched! See Josephus, *Ant.* XIII, 13, 51 and the rabbinical tract *Sukkah* 4, 9.
[10] *Sukkah* 4, 9. The Hebrew phrase means 'the place of the drawing' (of water).

Age of the Messiah. According to Rabbi bar-Kahana (c. A.D. 130) the feast holds within itself the promise of the Messiah, and a vague expectation that he would appear in the month of Tishri persisted long after the days of Jesus Christ. Again, the tractate on this feast in the Jerusalem Talmud explains the name of the ceremony by referring to the Isaian text quoted above, explaining the name "Place of Drawing" from the fact that it was "from there that they drew the Holy Spirit."[11] This is very close to the quotation which St. Peter made from Joel on the day of Pentecost to account for the ecstatic phenomena which took place at that time.

In the Quenching of Thirst passage, then, we have a combination of symbolic action and sapiential saying which refers to the action, accompanied by a word of explanation making the spiritual context plain for the Christian reader. The whole is symbolical in the sense of being a sign (not, however, in the strict Johannine sense of sign as synonym for miracle) pointing to the ultimately mysterious identity of the central figure. It speaks in a language at once more complex and more direct than that of definition, namely, in the idiom of symbolism, in the way that Jung has defined a sign or symbol as "the best possible expression of a relatively unknown thing."[12] In this sense the quenching of thirst is, for the man open to the persuasive force of this idiom, that deep and lasting satisfaction and utter self-fulfilment that comes through the knowledge of and association with the living God. Not that it was understood so at the time, as the comment makes clear, but addressed to the baptised Christian it would be fully comprehensible. This too was part of the sapiential tradition — the necessity of initiation for gnosis and comprehension of the Christian mysteries, and it is natural that just as Christ was represented vividly to early Christians as the element into which they were baptised and, in point of fact, "living water" was prescribed for baptism where possible,[13] he himself should be referred to as the Living Water.[14] Though St. John nowhere speaks explicitly of the two great Christian sacraments in the gospel — probably due to the discipline of the secret then considered binding — no Christian would have missed the strong sacramental associations of this and other sayings and signs strewn about the gospel. In this way, as we saw at the beginning, the text speaks on two levels: to those who having ears could not or would not hear, and on the other hand to the baptised intelligence of those who have received the Spirit; and the need of the Christian of today to quench his thirst at the mystery of Christ participated through the sacramental life of the Church is no less great than that of John's Christians at Ephesus.

[11] *Sukkah 55a.*
[12] In the chapter on Definitions in *Psychological Types*, trans. H. G. Baynes, 1938.
[13] *Didache* 7, 1; Hippolytus 5, 14; *Acts of Thomas* 52, etc.
[14] We might mention here a curious ascription to Thymoteus, one of the early Manichaeans, 'About baptism he spoke in the same way, namely, that the Lord Jesus Christ was himself the Baptism and that there was no other, in accordance as it is written: I am the Living Water.' This is found in Petrus Siculus, *Historia Manichaeorum*, PG 104, 1284; where it was written must remain a matter for speculation.

# THE HOLY EUCHARIST: SYMBOL
# OF THE PASSION

Carroll Stuhlmueller, C.P.

The holy Eucharist is the bread of life, but inscribed very clearly upon it is a sign of death. Unfortunately, it is easy to forget that the bread received at the altar is sacrificial food. When the sacred Host is exposed in the monstrance for adoration only a handful of people are aware that they are worshipping a sacrificial Victim.

The Romans referred to an animal slaughtered in sacred ceremonies as *hostia*. The word "host" can be traced to the Latin *hostia*. Jesus in the Blessed Sacrament is king, friend and spouse of our souls, but more than anything else He is the sacrificial Victim of Calvary. At Benediction the Church proclaims that ancient faith when she sings *O Salutaris Hostia:* "O Saving Victim."

Even though the first Christians had no crucifix, they found in the Eucharist the most graphic representation of the sacrifice of Calvary. This Blessed Sacrament was their sacred symbol of the passion. The crucifix receives a definitive artistic form only in the sixth century, yet the first Christians were not for a moment robbed of the memory of our Lord's sufferings, for given into their keeping was the holy Eucharist.

The holy Eucharist also symbolizes the glorious resurrection of our Lord. The Church joyfully acclaims the Blessed Sacrament as the pledge and foretaste here on earth of future glory. This present article, however, directs its attention to the death symbolism. A subsequent article will consider the Eucharist under the aspect of joy and victory.

For a personal appreciation of the doctrine that the Bread of Life is necessarily sacrificial food, attention must be directed first of all to the scriptural theme of death and life. This biblical thought-pattern helps to explain the constant concern of the Church to associate closely the lifegiving bread of holy Communion with Christ's sacramental death in the Mass. This union of Communion with the Mass emerges all the more strikingly from a study of the paschal symbolism of the most Blessed Sacrament. Our investigations, however, are limited to the scriptural level.

## Dying, behold we live

The biblical theme of life and death is difficult to grasp, but the notion is essential to the doctrine of the Eucharist. There is not an exact time sequence that life comes first and then death, or that a person must die before he can live, although some scriptural texts may give this impression. "He who

Published originally in *Worship*, 34 (1960), 196-205. Reprinted by permission of the publisher.

loses his life for my sake, will find it." "If we are buried with him . . ., so we also may walk in the newness of life."

Actually, both death and life exist together, like soldiers in mortal combat. When a person is succumbing to the blows of death, life is bursting forth. St. Paul writes: "I die daily." Yet, each "death" gives the Apostle greater right to exclaim: "I live, now, no, not I, but Christ lives in me."

There is always a war of elements when light strikes darkness, when hot air blasts against a pocket of cold air, when goodness confronts evil. Could anything different, therefore, take place when the light of God's Word appeared in this shadow of death? How could the darkness comprehend It?

Christ's entire life was carried forward under the momentum to execute the will of His heavenly Father. The divine will was His life-giving food, but not to be eaten in peace. Jesus is pitted against men who do the works of their father, the devil. What happens when a Man so selfless that He has nowhere to lay His head is sent into a world governed by materialistic Sadducees?

Can a religion of spirit and truth, which finds its greatness in interior virtue rather than in the first places at banquet tables, remain unmolested when it meets the Pharisee, the self-canonized fraud? How long will He survive who practises heroic love of enemies, when those enemies hate with a deadly hate?

To die — Christ solemnly explained — that is why I came! Struggle must ensue, when life meets the darkness of death. No other outcome is possible, once the eternal life of Christ is pledged to come upon this earth and to destroy the power of death in sin. The eternal vocation of the divine Word was to take the flesh of the Virgin Mary and to dwell amongst men as Lord and Savior. This meant that He was the sacrificial Lamb, slain from the foundation of the earth.

Yet, death did not destroy life but made it possible for this life to emerge more active and glorious. At no moment was Jesus more alive than when He was dying. His cry from the cross that "It is finished" was a triumphant declaration that here is the perfect and consummate expression of obedience, of courage, and, most of all, of charity. Yes, to die is to live.

This scriptural law of life and death must regulate the gift of life in the Eucharist. The fulness of life can come only through a death-inflicting sacrifice. To symbolize life the Eucharist must bear the sign of Christ's death, for it was through and in the sacrifice of Calvary that Jesus was lifted up to the Glory of heavenly life.

The Eucharist must bring to mind that moment when Christ hung dying upon the cross, for then He was most alive in his vigorous attack upon sin and in His heroic obedience to His heavenly Father's will. At death began His mission of sending the Spirit of life to His followers. As the sacred symbol of the passion, the Eucharist plants in human hearts the cross of Jesus, in order that dying with Christ each one may participate in His heavenly life.

Attentive to how closely Scripture associates life with death, we are ready to understand better the New Testament's manner of linking the eucharistic Bread of Life with the death-inflicting sacrifice of the cross.

## My flesh laid down in sacrifice

In clear and forceful words Jesus Christ announces: "I am the bread of life." In almost the same breath he adds that the Eucharist is the bread of death — the most striking sign or symbol of His passion and death. "Unless you eat the flesh of the Son of Man and drink his blood, you shall not have life in you." How can anyone eat flesh and drink blood, unless what they are eating and drinking has first been killed?

The picture is disturbing, but our Lord insists that it is true. When He says plainly that this bread is "my flesh for the life of the world," His words carry the deeper meaning: here is my flesh *laid down in sacrifice* for the salvation of all mankind. The Blessed Sacrament is a mystery of faith. This bread will be a picture, a sign, a symbol and a mystic renewal of something in face of which we stand in awe.

Christ gives a further explanation when He fulfills this promise of the Bread of Life. As He sits with His apostles at the Last Supper, the night on which He is to be betrayed, He makes His life-giving death an ever present reality for all ages. Time with its past and future becomes an eternal present. Jesus is involved in the very act of delivering His body over to death and of shedding His blood in sacrifice. "This is my body which is being given for you, . . . my blood which is being shed."

The earliest account of the institution of the Bread of Life is the most explicit of all in stressing the sacrificial character of the bread. Writing little more than twenty years after the first Holy Thursday, St. Paul told the Corinthians: "As often as you eat this bread and drink the cup, you proclaim the death of the Lord until he comes." The Eucharist places each Christian upon Calvary. Dying with Christ, the worshipper puts to death sin. That death is an heroic affirmation of life in all its fulness. Like Christ, the Christian is never more alive than when he dies at the moment of holy Communion that Christ may live in him.

## Food from the sacrificial altar

In the first three centuries of Christianity, everyone present at the renewal of the sacrifice of the cross partakes of the sacrificial food. The practice of many communities directs each worshipper to approach the altar of sacrifice and receive the sacrificial food in outstretched hands. After eating part of the consecrated Bread the faithful are allowed to take home with them whatever remains. However, even this privilege of private Communion at home does not rob the sacrament of its sacrificial character. The Eucharist remains the sign of the cross, for this sacred food is the Christian's abiding remembrance of Christ's death and a repeated participation in His sacrifice.

The pagan neighbors had a similar practice which transformed their family meal into an act of religion. Meat purchased at the market was considered sacrificial food. Before the animals were sacrificed, certain ritualistic observances dedicated the animal to the pagan gods. St. Paul faces this situation in 1 Corinthians 10:23-30. To eat such meat even at home is to become partakers "of the table of the devils." St. Paul asks: "Are not they who eat of the sacrifices partakers of the altar?" However, "we have an altar from which they have no right to eat" (Heb. 13:10). From the altar of immolation the Christians received their sacred food. The Bread of Life was Jesus' body and blood, laid down in sacrifice.

If the pagans felt united with the gods at their sacred meal, the Christian was caught up into something far superior — the death of Christ. To the extent that sinful desires are crucified and destroyed, the heavenly life of Christ is imparted to the Christian by the holy Eucharist.

## Preserving the memorial of the passion

Church laws, which regulate the care of the Eucharist, rest solidly upon this divine tradition uniting sacrifice and sacrament. For instance, a priest is absolutely forbidden to consecrate bread alone, even if a dying person must pass into eternity without holy Viaticum. One reason is this: the separate consecration of only one element would not symbolize that moment when the body of Christ hung upon the cross and spilled out the blood upon the ground.

Another example is the prescription of the new Holy Week ritual that holy Communion be received only during or immediately after the Mass of the Lord's Supper. At first, this restriction may strike one as very unreasonable, since formerly holy Communion was distributed at frequent intervals before the morning Mass. For some there was less danger of being prevented from fulfilling the wish of Christ to "take and eat" on the anniversary of the institution. Yet, especially during Holy Week, the Church wants her children to be just as conscious of the sign of the cross upon the eucharistic Food as Christ was on the first Holy Thursday. As Christians gather at night in their own "upper room" for the liturgical reenactment of the Last Supper, they are to have one heart with the suffering heart of Jesus. With Christ they are reliving His last moments on earth.

Pope Pius XII was repeating this same divine and apostolic tradition when he wrote in his encyclical *Mediator Dei*: "Holy Communion pertains to the integrity of the Mass." "By feasting upon the Bread of Angels we can by a sacramental communion . . . become partakers of the sacrifice." True, "the integrity of the sacrifice requires only that the priest partake of the heavenly food." However, the Pope frequently exhorts all the faithful to "approach the holy table . . . [and] to partake fervently and frequently of the richest treasure of our religion."

He makes his own the exhortation of Pope Benedict XIV, in praising those celebrants who allow the faithful to communicate from Hosts consecrated at the very Mass which is then being offered. In this way "all their actions at the altar manifest more clearly the living unity of the Mystical Body." To partake of the sacrifice is much more than an external action. The Bread of Life stirs up a strong desire "to become as like as possible to Christ in His grievous sufferings." "We become a victim, as it were, along with Christ."

### Sacrificial banquet of the Pasch

In order to understand better the actions and the words of Christ in giving us the Eucharist as sacrificial food, we must turn to the Old Testament. The Old Testament is "our tutor in Christ." The ritual of the Jewish temple prepared for the Christian liturgy, since "the first tabernacle is a figure of the present time." We ask if there is anything in the Old Testament heritage which makes it very unlikely that Christ would have established a mere Communion service?

Limitations of space restrict us to one Old Testament rite, the paschal lamb, and only to one element of its observance, the sacrificial aspect of the banquet. The Pasch is certainly a type of Christ's death on the cross and of the Eucharist. It may be difficult to decide whether the typical sense is verified in each detail of the paschal meal.

Yet, the New Testament tradition consistently inserts the account of the holy Eucharist into the general context of the Pasch. Such an association of ideas is like the accompanying notes of an organ. Repeated allusions to the Pasch provide a greater richness to our understanding of the eucharistic mystery.

In the days of Christ the words Passover, Pasch and Unleavened Bread were used without distinction. The three synoptic Gospels begin their account of the Eucharist with a reference to the feast of Unleavened Bread. We read in St. Luke: "Now the day of the Unleavened Bread came, on which the Passover had to be sacrificed. . . ." St. John opens the public life of Christ with John the Baptist's announcement: "Behold the lamb of God, who takes away the sins of the world."

St. John again deftly touches upon the memory of the paschal ceremony before relating the miracle of the multiplication of the five barley loaves and the two fishes and the subsequent eucharistic discourse: "Now the Passover, the feast of the Jews, was near." Since the word "Jew" in St. John's Gospel indicates someone opposed to Christ, the phrase "the feast of the Jews" implies that near and close at hand is another Passover — the true Christian Pasch which will provide the real Unleavened Bread of immortality: Jesus, our Lamb of God and our Bread of Life.

The account of the Last Supper is introduced in St. John's Gospel with a brief but significant remark: "Before the feast of the Passover, Jesus, knowing that his hour had come to pass out of this world. . . ." St. John concludes his passion narrative with another reference to the Paschal Lamb:

"For all these things came to pass that the Scripture might be fulfilled, 'Not a bone of him shall you break.' "

## This holiest of nights

A passing reference to the fire at Our Lady of Angels School in Chicago, December 1958, flashes across our mind a succession of pictures of horror, sorrow and heroism: the horror of violent death; the sorrow of losing one's beloved; the heroism of dying for a friend. Likewise, the mere mention of the Pasch should remind us, as it did the early Christians, of all the particulars of this holiest of nights.

At the beginning of the paschal meal one of the children at table asks the father: "What does this rite of yours mean?" Each holy Communion should draw forth a similar question from the Christian, since the Bread of Life is received in the midst of a paschal sacrifice. The Mosaic law prescribed the order of ceremony for this "night of vigil for the Lord." Its details can teach Christians the deeper meaning of their paschal meal.

> A lamb . . . a year-old male lamb without blemish, . . . shall be slaughtered during the evening twilight. They shall take some of its blood and apply it to the two doorposts and the lintel of every house in which they partake of the lamb. That same night they shall eat its roasted flesh with unleavened bread and bitter herbs . . . It is the Passover of the Lord. For on this same night I will go through Egypt, striking down every first-born of the land, both man and beast, and executing judgment on all the gods of Egypt — I, the Lord! But the blood will mark the houses where you are. Seeing the blood, I will pass over you; thus, when I strike the land of Egypt, no destructive blow will come upon you (Exod. 12:5-13).

## Jesus, our paschal Lamb

This association with the paschal celebration reveals the full meaning of our ceremony. Jesus is the Lamb of God, acclaimed as such by John the Baptist and by the Baptist's disciple, John the Evangelist, who refers twenty-eight times to the Lamb in the Apocalypse. Also in Hebrews and in First Peter we are told that Christ, our paschal Lamb, "through the Holy Spirit offered himself unblemished unto God," for "you were redeemed . . . not with perishable things, with silver or gold, but with the precious blood of Christ, as of a lamb without blemish and without spot."

The angel of death destroys the life of Christ in punishment and expiation for sin. We are saved because the blood of this Lamb has traced a sentence of forgiveness across the lintel of our hearts. Seeing this precious blood sprinkled upon our souls, this same angel of death will pass over us, as he did over the houses of the Israelites in Egypt. We become "holy and without blemish in his [God's] sight . . . through Jesus Christ. . . . In him we have redemption through his blood." Our Egypt of sin and oppression is dead and past. Like the Israelites we begin a new life, as we eat the Bread of Life.

## The table of the Lord

After the slaughter of the paschal lamb and the sprinkling of its blood, the Jewish family prepared for the sacrificial banquet. The lamb was roasted and served with unleavened bread, wine, bitter herbs and wild lettuce. The family takes part as though ready to set out on a journey: with their long oriental robes tucked up, with sandals on their feet and with staff in hand. The bitter herbs are a final farewell to the heavy misery and dark discouragement of the Egyptian slavery. They are about to set out on the journey towards the promised land of Palestine.

Christians sit down at the "table of the Lord" to eat their sacrificial meal. Their Lamb too has been slaughtered, and its precious blood has been sprinkled across the lintels of their hearts. As the Christians look at the table set before them, the cry of John the Baptist echoes in their hearts, with tones of sorrowing, grateful love: "Behold the lamb of God, who takes away the sins of the world!" This Victim, whom they are about to consume, is "Christ Jesus, whom God has set forth as a propitiation by his blood."

Not only is Christ their paschal lamb; He is likewise their bitter herbs. The Christians could never completely forget the bitter taste of sin and its crushing burden of discouragement, even though Christ had taken all this bitterness upon Himself. "For our sakes he [God] made him to be sin." Engraved across their paschal meal is the sign of the cross. The Jews had been told: "This shall be a memorial feast for you." The Christians were commemorating the memorial of the passion and death, the price of their liberation from the "Egyptian slavery" of sin.

Christians eat this sacrificial food, as St. Peter declared, "having girded up the loins of your understanding." Christ is food for the long, wearisome journey, traveled "in darkness and in the shadow of death." Like Elijah in the desert of Sinai, Christians must rise from the table and march "in the strength of this food" to a promised land where in joy eternal they will celebrate "the marriage supper of the lamb."

From the Bread of Life they will absorb the stamina to withstand the sorrows of life and the burning heat of their "Sinai desert." They must die daily to sin and imperfection and rise to newness of life in Jesus Christ. The Bread of Life, therefore, is really the bread of death to every form of sin and human weakness. The Eucharist inscribes the sign of the cross upon the soul of the Christian, so that he is entitled to exclaim: "I bear the marks of the Lord Jesus in my body."

## A holy nation

Many liturgical laws carefully guarded the Jewish paschal banquet from the least profanation. Only members of the chosen people may be present.

And lest the meal degenerate into a perfunctory act of mere externalism, the father shall always explain the meaning of the rite to his family. Finally, the lamb must be completely consumed. "Whatever is left over in the morning shall be burned." These regulations are carefully fulfilled in the Mass.

The Christian family, gathered around the sacrificial banquet, "is a chosen race, a royal priesthood, a holy nation, a purchased people." "As the One who called you is also holy," St. Peter wrote in a context redolent of the paschal ceremony,"be you also holy in all your behavior." This holy people is sanctified by the spirit of charity. "Because the bread is one, we, though many, are one body, all of us who partake of the one bread."

Again we see the sign of the cross by which we have come to know His great love and by which we are united in one Mystical Body. The four corners of the cross bring together the four ends of the earth in the pierced heart of Jesus.

This "lamb standing as if slain" before the eyes of those "who pierced him" by their sins, must be wholly consumed. The sacrifice will continue until the last fragment has been eaten. Every holy Communion, therefore, is marked with the sign of the cross, for each is a continuation of the paschal sacrifice.

The New Testament places the sign of the cross upon the eucharistic meal, announcing that sacrificial food is received at the table of the Lord. "When your children ask you, 'What does this rite of yours mean?' you shall reply 'This is the Passover sacrifice of the Lord.' " This same solemn proclamation is made by the priest when he lifts the sacred Victim before the eyes of the communicants and says: "Behold the Lamb of God; behold Him who takes away the sins of the world." The Bread of Life is the food of love because the sign of redemptive death is engraved upon it.

# THE HOLY EUCHARIST: SYMBOL OF CHRIST'S GLORY

Carroll Stuhlmueller, C.P.

The Holy Eucharist is the sacred symbol of the passion and death of Jesus Christ. Although the first Christians did not place a crucifix above their altar, in the Eucharist they recognized the supreme sign of the cross. They

Published originally in *Worship*, 34 (1960), 259-69. Reprinted by permission of the publisher.

lived the words of St. Paul: "As often as you shall eat this bread and drink the cup, you proclaim the death of the Lord until he comes."

Pope Piux XII in *Mediator Dei* expressed this sentiment of the apostolic days: "The eucharistic species . . . Jesus Christ is symbolically shown by separate symbols to be in a state of victimhood." The Pope thus expressed in technical language what the Church had been singing through the centuries: "O holy banquet, in which Christ is received, the memory of His passion is renewed. . . ."

## Joyful sorrow

On Easter morning the sacred body of Jesus, marked with the scars of the nails and lance, rose triumphantly from the dead. The light of this glorious resurrection formed a halo of joy, peace and victory around the eucharistic sign of the cross. The silence, born of Good Friday's sorrow, is quickly driven out by the bells of Easter Sunday morning. That the mourning over Christ's death be cut this short, never made the early Christians feel ill at ease. St. Paul had written: "Christ, our passover, has been sacrificed. Therefore let us keep festival!"

In this same spirit of joyful sorrow and sorrowing joy an Old Testament prophet, named Zechariah, had announced the "day of the Lord." At first, his words reverberate with the echo of victorious bells, tumultuously ringing out their news: *Haec dies* — "that day which the Lord has made." Zechariah repeatedly proclaims the triumph of God "in that day." However, the peal of bells stops without warning, and there begins the toll of single, mournful strokes: "In that day I will pour out . . . a spirit of favor and of prayer; and they shall look at him whom they have pierced; and they shall mourn for him like the mourning for an only child." Then, just as suddenly a change is rung, as this sorrow turns into joy: Jerusalem becomes the center of God's paradise on earth: "In that day living waters shall go forth from Jerusalem" (Zech. 12:14).

This theme of sorrow and joy, of death and life, meets us on almost every page of the Bible. The quick interchange of darkness and light in biblical thought leads us to a fuller understanding of the mystery of the Eucharist. God "is not the God of the dead, but of the living, for all are alive to him."

The institution of the Eucharist, as related in St. Luke's passion-resurrection narrative, begins with the darkness of the agony in the garden but closes with the light of the words: "He parted from them and was carried up into heaven. And they worshipped him, and returned to Jerusalem with great joy." Time slows down to a dead halt, but at once eternity speeds forward: "The author of life you killed, whom God has raised up from the dead."

## Lifted up to glory

To be "lifted up" or "raised up" is a phrase often used of Christ's ascent to the cross. The words technically mean to be swept up to victory and glory. "Even so must the Son of Man be lifted up, that those who believe in him may have life everlasting." "The hour has come for the Son of Man to be glorified. . . . And I, if I be lifted up from the earth, will draw all things to myself."

The cross provides a means of journeying upward to heavenly glory. The darkness of Calvary is only for a moment. In quick succession St. John writes: "Now it was *night*. When, therefore, he [Judas] had gone out, Jesus said, 'Now has the Son of Man been *glorified*, and God has been glorified in him.'" Since the Eucharist draws our thoughts upward to Jesus upon the cross, it is consequently lifting us up to the heavenly triumph of the Son of Man.

From all eternity the cross was surrounded with the glory of heaven. St. John writes that Jesus is "the Lamb who has been slain before the foundation of the world." "At the first, before the earth" the angels dwelt with awe and wonder on the vocation of the divine Word, who was destined "in that day" to become "obedient unto death." St. Peter confessed: "Into these things angels desire to look."

When "that day" was over, heavenly glory joyfully received back again His scarred, crucified, but triumphant body. Next to the throne of God is the "Lamb, standing as if slain," whom thousands praise with a loud voice: "Worthy is the Lamb who was slain to receive power and divinity and wisdom and strength and honor and glory and blessing." The angels sing this same song around His eucharistic throne.

The glorious triumph of the Lamb was foreseen by Christ as He sat with His disciples in the upper room and instituted the holy Eucharist as a memorial of His passion. The contrast of death and life, of darkness and light, appears in His final discourse. It was "on the night in which he was betrayed," that Christ celebrated the feast "of the Unleavened Bread . . . not with perishable things, with silver or gold, but with the precious blood of Christ, as of a lamb without blemish and without spot."

At this sacred repast Christ announced that hereafter He Himself was to be the passover lamb, killed and eaten. St. Peter wrote later: "You were redeemed . . . not with perishable things, with silver or gold, but with the precious blood of Christ, as of a lamb without blemish and without spot."

Yet, Christ was a lamb, not only doomed to death, but also destined for exaltation. In death Christ manifested His life of love and obedience towards His heavenly Father. Life was conquering when it seemed to be dying. The heroic sacrifice of self freed Christ of all human and earthly restrictions.

In the moment of dying He was actually affirming the power of His love and thereby was rising to heavenly glory. "Now," Christ said of the hours of His passion, "is the Son of Man glorified."

## Memorial of joy

During the Last Supper, a mysterious glow of joy and peace pervades the room. The Eucharist will be a memorial, not only of sorrow and death, but also of joy and life. Listen once again as Christ says to His disciples:

> If you loved me, you would indeed rejoice. . . . These things I have spoken to you that my joy may be in you. . . . But because I have spoken to you these things, sadness has filled your heart. But I speak the truth to you; it is expedient for you that I depart. . . . You therefore have sorrow now; but I will see you again, and your heart shall rejoice. . . . But now I am coming to you; and these things I speak in the world, in order that they may have my joy made full in themselves.

Years later when St. John was composing his Gospel, that "now" was a present reality. Christ had come! Through the gift of the Spirit, St. John tasted the joy unspeakable of the paschal mystery in each Mass and Communion. The joy of the resurrection has cast a glorious splendor over the entire fourth Gospel; each event of Christ's life, but especially His sacrifice on the cross and its memorial in the Eucharist, is seen transfigured with glory.

Jesus Himself also looked upon the Last Supper as the foretaste of a heavenly banquet. Each synoptic Gospel echoes these words of Christ: "I will eat of it no more, until it has been fulfilled in the kingdom of God . . . for I say to you that I will not drink of the fruit of the vine, until the kingdom of God comes." A study of the Jewish paschal meal helps to unravel the mystery of joy contained in the memorial of the passion.

## The joyful Paschal meal

For the Jews the feast of the pasch celebrated freedom from hardship and oppression; it pointed ahead with hope to a new life of enduring happiness. The greatest of these joys came from an anticipated union with God in peace and holiness.

Fittingly enough, therefore, the Jews interrupted their paschal meal with the singing of the Hallel or Praise (Pss. 112–117). In the time of our Lord, Psalms 112–113A were chanted before the repast, Psalms 113B–117 after it. The Last Supper began as the usual Jewish paschal meal. Earlier in the day Jesus had "sent Peter and John, saying 'Go and prepare for the passover that we may eat it.' "

The first pasch in Jewish history was the day centuries before Christ when God fulfilled His promise: "I will rescue you by my outstretched arm and with mighty acts of judgment. I will take you as my own people, and you shall have me as your God . . . I will free you from the labor of the Egyptians." Since Egypt had become a synonym for the state of sin, that day marked the beginning of Israelite independence from sin and its evil oppression.

A new life, therefore, lay before the nation. "The Lord said to Moses and Aaron in the land of Egypt, 'This month shall stand at the head of your calendar; you shall reckon it the first month of the year.' " The slave-labor camps of Egypt were throwing wide their doors, and hearts were free to sing "this song to the Lord," composed by Moses and Miriam:

> "Who is like you among the gods, O Lord?
> Who is like you, magnificent in holiness?

> O terrible in renown, worker of wonders, . . .
> In your mercy you led the people you redeemed."

"This day of the Lord" signaled the beginning of a journey towards "a good and spacious land, a land flowing with milk and honey." At the end of this exodus there awaited the Israelites the reward of life with God in the promised land of Palestine. The pasch was intended to provide the people with strength for this journey. They were instructed: "This is how you are to eat it: with your loins girt, sandals on your feet and your staff in hand, you shall eat like those *who are in flight*." Stretching out before them was the triumphant "way of the Lord."

Each subsequent paschal meal vibrated with the spirit of the first pasch. The participants chanted these words: "This is the day the Lord has made." In the strength of the food eaten at the meal they were to rise up and march towards the fulfilment of all God's promises.

Wondrous deeds of God would accompany this new exodus from sin, which led towards the revelation of the glory of God. Reclining at the Last Supper, the apostles sang about "this highway for our God in the desert." It was the melody flowing rhythmically from the heart of every Jew as he partook of the paschal lamb:

> "The sea beheld and fled;
> the Jordan turned back.
> The mountains skipped like rams,
> the hills like the lambs of the flock."

## A journey to happiness

The Last Supper was the last paschal meal ever to be celebrated under the Mosaic law and the first under the new dispensation. As our Lord reclined with His disciples in the upper room, the mystery of the passion-resurrection began to be enacted. Christ could announce the inauguration of a "new covenant," since the promises and hopes of the "old covenant" were now being accomplished. Here was truly the beginning of a new era. "This," He solemnly declared, "is my blood of the new covenant."

The words of Christ sounded a trumpet, summoning His followers to leave the oppression of sin and to march with Him towards the promised land of heaven. As men *in flight* from sin, they must follow "the way of the Lord" which they find in the footsteps of Him who is "the way, the truth and the life."

With good reason Christ wanted the apostles to rejoice. This paschal meal was more than a commemorating of a past event — the exodus of their forefathers out of Egypt. They themselves were setting out on a journey. This was a day of independence, the start of a new life. Christ was telling His disciples: "I go away and I am coming to you. If you loved me, you would indeed rejoice that I am going to the Father." "And if I go and prepare a place for you, I am coming again, and I will take you to myself; that where I am, there you also may be. And where I go you know, and the way you know."

When St. John recorded this discourse of our Lord, the apostles understood the meaning of this mystery of joy, hidden in the words of Christ. The pentecostal Spirit had revealed where Christ had gone in order to "prepare a place for you." For Jesus, the "exodus" or journey led along the way of the cross. Wondrous acts of God attended this last earthly journey of Christ. As He was being "lifted up" upon the cross, He was rising to heavenly glory.

"I am coming again, and I will take you to myself." Each Mass celebrated by the apostles was a partial fulfilment of this promise of Christ. It signaled the beginning of a new journey, along the way pointed out by Jesus in His way of the cross. As the early Christians celebrated their paschal meal, God was saying once again: "You shall eat like those who are in flight." "This is the day of the Lord." Rise, take up your cross and follow in the blood-stained footsteps of Jesus Christ.

This journey was possible, since the Bread of Life infused within their hearts Christ's life of heroic obedience and self-sacrificing charity. The Eucharist struck a blow of death in the souls of the apostles, and it continues to be the bread of death to all their followers. Christ's presence in the Eucharist can tolerate neither sin nor the least imperfection. The warmth of His charity breaks the cold of selfishness. His obedience sweeps away the forces of disobedience. The poverty of Christ destroys every desire except the one concern to love God.

The journey is not yet over. The cross is not the goal. It is simply a sign post. The Israelites rose from their paschal meal not simply to lose themselves in a desert of heat and thirst. Their intention was to pass through the desolate waste of the Sinai desert to reach the promised land.

But in the desolate desert the revelation of God took place. God was present for a blinding moment atop the majestic peaks of Mount Sinai, and the memory of His glory urged them to push forward till they arrived at the land of God in Palestine.

The Christian's promised land is heaven. Though still on earth, the breaking of the Bread of Life lifts him up upon the cross, and through the cross he participates in Christ's heavenly glory. For a moment he is swept upward in joy, for never before has he felt so close to the presence of God. The cross is his Mount Sinai, and the earth shakes at the revelation of God's glory.

He must never lose the cross, for in the cross is life. Life and death, happiness and sorrow, can and actually do exist together for the man of faith who realizes the meaning of the Mass. Although the Christian remains in this vale of tears and death, his soul shares the joy of eternal life with each Mass and holy Communion.

The way of the cross leads the Christian to union with Christ, who is marked with the scars of crucifixion but at the same time glorified in the promised land of heaven. Eating the Bread of Life, which is their paschal Lamb, Christians joyously sing: "Let us be glad and rejoice, and give glory to him; for the marriage of the Lamb has come." This marriage is the union of Christ with all Christians.

## The glory of heavenly peace

There are still other features of the Jewish paschal meal which imparted a spirit of joy to the Eucharist, the Christian's passover sacrifice. The Mosaic law prescribed that the entire household gather at the banquet table, with the father at the head. There was to be peace, unity and contentment as all broke the same bread, drank from the same goblet of wine and mingled their voices in the great song of praise.

Outsiders who participated became as members of the family. "If a family is too small for a whole lamb, it shall join the nearest household in procuring one and shall share in the lamb." Unity was part of the pasch.

It was natural that Christ should pray for a spirit of unity at His final paschal supper on earth:

> That all may be one, even as thou, Father, in me and I in thee, that they also may be one in us, that the world may believe that thou hast sent me. And *the glory* that thou hast given me, I have given to them, that they may be one. . . . Father, I will that where I am, they also whom thou hast given me may be with me; *in order that they may behold my glory*.

To eat the Christian pasch, we must belong to the household of which Christ is the head. We must experience a bond of familial love with every other member of our household. No one seated at this table can be as a stranger or a foreigner. All are united like branches of the same vine, as we drink from the one cup of Christ's blood. "Many will come," Christ had prophesied, "from the east and from the west, and will feast with Abraham and Isaac and Jacob in the kingdom of heaven."

Here in the eucharistic brotherhood "there is neither east nor west, border nor breed nor birth." The *pax christiana* reigns everywhere among men of good will. Such peace of all men with one another is a sharing in heavenly glory. Seated at "the table of the Lord," "the members of God's household" are able by faith to behold Christ in glory, as He had promised.

## United by blood

To be present at this agape or love-feast, one's garments must be washed in the blood of the Lamb. The forgiveness of Christ must have removed all stains of hate, jealousy, selfishness and sensuality. This redemption from sin has come through the blood of Christ.

St. John is very conscious of the role of blood in the paschal liturgy. Since the Jewish pasch gave a prominent place to the "blood ritual," it is not surprising that the importance of blood is stressed in the New Testament passover. As the blood of the paschal lamb had once brought deliverance from Egypt and salvation from death in the days of Moses, the blood of Christ brings glory and union with God.

The Israelites gathered to eat the pasch in a home whose door posts had been sprinkled with blood of the lamb. God had given this order: "They

shall take some of the blood and apply it to the doorposts and the lintels
of every house in which they partake of the lamb. . . . Seeing the blood,
I will pass over you, thus, when I strike the land of Egypt, no destructive
blow will come upon you."

The full meaning of this blood-ritual comes to our mind when we recol-
lect that for the Jew blood symbolized life. "The life of the living body,"
Leviticus declares, "is in the blood." Blood belongs to God in a particular
way, for the reason that life is God's special property. Whatever is consecrated by blood is solemnly dedicated to God. The blood of the paschal
lamb, sprinkled upon the doorposts of the Israelite homes, sets apart the
occupants of that home. Their life belongs to God.

God calls His chosen people "a kingdom of priests, a holy nation," "my
special possession, dearer to me than all other people." They are destined
to be consecrated again by blood at the foot of Mount Sinai. On this second
occasion we read that Moses "took the blood," half of which had already
been "splashed upon the altar," "and sprinkled it on the people, saying:
'This is the blood of the covenant which the Lord has made with you.'"

Just as the blood flowing between the members of one's body unites every
part in the pulse of one life, so also the blood, sprinkled upon the altar,
representing God, and upon the people, unites God and man in a new, mysterious bond of life.

## United by the blood of Christ

The Christians celebrate their paschal sacrifice, the Eucharist, with the
realization that the days of shadow and prefiguration are past. Through the
gift of faith God had "commanded light to shine out of darkness" and has
granted "enlightenment concerning the knowledge of the glory of God, shining on the face of Christ Jesus." The Christian is totally consecrated and
united to God, not by "the blood of goats and bulls" but by the blood of
Jesus Christ. St. Peter writes: "You were redeemed . . . with the precious
blood of Christ, as of a lamb without blemish and without spot." "How
much more will the blood of Christ, who through the spirit offered himself
unblemished unto God, cleanse your conscience from dead works to serve
the living God!"

As the early Christians gather in a family circle for their paschal meal,
their mind recalls the ancient rubric to sprinkle the blood of the lamb upon
the doorposts. Unbelievable as it may seem, Christ is their paschal lamb,
while their own bodies and souls are the doorposts sprinkled with His blood.
"He who eats my flesh and drinks my blood has life everlasting." Holy Communion consecrates the life of each Christian as "my special possession, dearer to me than all other people." "He abides in me and I in him."

Sorrow again intermingles with joy, death with life. The paschal lamb of
the Christian pasch must be first put to death, before its blood can be drunk
and mystically sprinkled upon the doorposts of the human heart. Yet, as
Jesus was "lifted up" for sacrifice upon the cross and for the spilling of His

blood, He was also being elevated to heavenly glory. The blood of Christ unites the worshipper with the triumphant Christ of Easter Sunday morning.

## Joyful shout of victory

The joyful significance of the Eucharist, the Christian pasch, cannot be adequately understood without allusion to many Jewish ceremonies. The New Testament writers, and especially St. John, reveal such a richness of thought, that they pass quickly from one Old Testament rite to another. "For all the promises of God find their 'Yes' in him." All of the Jewish liturgical acts were "a shadow of things to come, but the body [casting that shadow] is of Christ." Nonetheless, the apostles looked upon the Eucharist primarily as a paschal sacrifice.

The Eucharist "lifts up" the Christian to the mystery of the cross. The bells toll the death of "him whom they have pierced; and they shall mourn for him like the mourning for an only child." Quickly but not unexpectedly the bells ring out a joyous *Alleluia*. "He has risen." The way of the cross is an elevation to glory. The Christian can begin and end his eucharistic sacrifice with the words of our Lord: "Father, the hour has come! Glorify thy Son . . . that to all thou hast given him he may give everlasting life."

The sign of the cross appears upon the eucharistic, sacrificial meal. This is a sign of sorrow and mourning; the Lamb of God has been slain. Yet, this divine sorrow does not exclude joy; instead, it gives a foretaste of a glorious banquet of heavenly joys. The Christian pasch is not so much the descent of heaven upon the earth but rather the earthly is lifted up to the heavenly. "For Christ, our passover, has been sacrificed. Therefore, let us keep festival!" The *eschaton* or final day has arrived — at least for a moment. The glorified Christ is in our midst.

The Consecration and Communion bells sound the notes of the angels' trumpets, announcing the *parousia* or triumphant presence of Jesus. He who went into a distant country to obtain a kingdom has returned. "When Christ, your life, shall appear," St. Paul writes, "then you too will appear with him in glory." At each Mass Jesus is summoning His followers: "Come, rise from the dead. This is the day which the Lord has made."

Forming one family with all Christians and looking to the risen Christ at the head of the table, the worshipper begins a new, heavenly life with each eucharistic repast. Consecrated with the blood of the Lamb, he sings the triumphant *Hallel* of praise, sung by his forefathers:

> The joyful shout of victory. . .
> "The right hand of the Lord has struck with power. . . ."
> I shall not die, but live,
> and declare the works of the Lord. . . .
> This is the day the Lord has made;
> let us be glad and rejoice in it. . . .
> Blessed is he who comes in the name of the Lord. . . .
> The Lord is God, and he has given us light.

# THE PASSION
# ACCORDING TO JOHN

David M. Stanley, S.J.

It is characteristic of the Fourth Gospel that Jesus' passion is conceived as the beginning of His exaltation and glorification, as the supreme revelation to the world of His universal kingship and His divinity. Three aspects of Christ's redemptive work, which have impressed themselves upon the mind of St. John, give rise to this, at first sight, extraordinary viewpoint.

## *"Lifted up" to the Father*

In the first place, John regards Jesus' mission in human history as culminating in His "passing from this world to the Father" (John 13:1). The evangelist tells us in his account of the Last Supper that Jesus was "conscious that the Father had put sovereign power into his hands, and that he had come forth from God and was going home to the Father" (John 13:3).

This statement is, of course, merely a summary of the Prologue (John 1: 1-18), which described the coming of the Word as a cyclic movement, beginning in the heart of the Trinity, descending into man's world in creation, in the Mosaic Covenant, and in the Incarnation; and then returning to the bosom of the Father after revealing to us the "God whom no man has ever seen," after granting to those who found faith in Him the divine "power to become God's children."

For John then, the first stage in Jesus' journey home to God is accomplished by mounting the cross. "Just as Moses lifted up the serpent in the desert, so the Son of Man must be lifted up, in order that each one who believes in him may possess eternal life" (John 3:14-15). Thus, as Jesus had promised His disciples, this lifting-up or exaltation would not only involve Himself, but all His disciples. "And when I, for my part, am lifted up from the earth, I will draw all men to myself" (John 12:33).

And the sacred writer goes on to explain this saying of the Master, for fear its meaning might escape his reader. "He said this to point out the kind of death he was going to die" (John 12:34).

Later, after he has told the story of the crucifixion, John recalls the prophecy found in Zechariah 12:10: "They shall look upon him whom they have pierced" (John 19:37), exemplifying this attraction exercised by the Crucified through the approach and loving service of Joseph of Arimathea and Nicodemus, whom fear had previously kept from publishing their discipleship. It is therefore by being "lifted up" that Jesus has, on John's view, accomplished His work as redeemer.

But the evangelist also points out that this "lifting up" is calculated to fulfill the other principal function of the Word become man: His role as

Published originally in *Worship*, 33 (1959), 210-30. Reprinted by permission of the publisher.

revealer of divine truth. "When you have lifted up the Son of Man, then at last you will realize that I AM" (John 8:28).

The mysterious "I AM," which will recur throughout this Gospel, appears to be a conscious reference to Moses' first encounter with Yahweh at the burning bush (Exod. 3:1ff). "But," Moses said to God, "suppose I go to the Israelites, and say to them, 'The God of your fathers has sent me to you,' and they say to me, 'What is his name?', what am I to say to them?" "I am who am," God said to Moses. Then He added, "This is what you shall say to the Israelites, 'I AM has sent me to you'" (Exod. 3:13-14).

Accordingly, in the passage we have cited from the Fourth Gospel, the crucifixion-exaltation of Jesus is the moment of His definitive self-revelation to men. In that "hour," the divinity of the Word become man begins to be manifested to the world.

## Passion and glory

This brings us to the second aspect of the passion of Christ which John wishes to underscore: it is His "glory." This theme dominates the discourse after the Last Supper, when, as Jesus knows, the hour of His passion is upon Him. "At last the Son of Man is glorified, and in him God is glorified. Since God is glorified in him, God will, in turn, glorify him in himself. And he will glorify him without delay" (John 14:31-32).

Since it is only through the operation of "the other Paraclete," the Holy Spirit, that the disciples are to come into possession "of the full truth" of Jesus' divinity, the Holy Spirit is also said to glorify Jesus. "He will glorify me, because he will take what is mine and announce it to you" (John 16:14). And as Jesus begins His last solemn prayer to the Father, He declares,

> Father, the hour is come. Glorify your Son, that your Son may glorify you. You have given him authority over all humanity, in order that he may give eternal life to all you have given him. This is eternal life: that they may know you, the only God worthy of the name, and Jesus Christ, whom you have sent (John 17:1-3).

This conception of the revelation of Jesus' divinity as "glory" is, doubtless, adapted from the Old Testament theme of the divine *kabōd*, or glory, which had there become a technical term for the sensible manifestations of God's protective presence among His people. In the theophany at the burning bush, as in the miracles of the exodus out of Egypt, it was the divine glory which had made itself felt by Moses and the chosen people.

Just as Yahweh's self-revelation in the Old Testament had been termed His glory, so Jesus' self-revelation through His cross and passion is called His glory by St. John.

We have a striking exemplification of this in chapter 12, where John remarks that "although he had given such strong proofs of his claims under their very eyes, they refused to believe in him" (John 12:37). But this is only what Isaiah had foretold would happen, because, as that prophet had also remarked, their eyes had been blinded, their hearts hardened. Then John adds, "Isaiah said this because he had seen his glory and had spoken of him" (John 12:41).

Isaiah had indeed spoken of Christ and of His passion and exaltation in the fifty-third chapter of the book attributed to him, where we have such a precious prophecy of Jesus' work as the suffering and glorified Servant of God.

But when had Isaiah seen His glory? John is probably thinking of the prophet's inaugural vision, described in the sixth chapter of Isaiah. "The year of the death of king Uzziah, I saw the Lord seated upon a throne, raised aloft, and the hem of his garment filled the temple. Seraphim stood before him . . . and they cried one to another, 'Holy, holy, holy is Yahweh of hosts: all the earth is full of his glory' " (Is. 6:1-3).

Thus the whole passion story, as it comes from the pen of St. John, is glory-filled: both in the sense that it is the medium through which Jesus' divinity is revealed to the believer, and in the sense that it is a glorious, triumphant act of the Word become man, through which He prepares for His return to the Father, through which also He assures the triumph of God's kingdom or divine sovereignty over the "powers of darkness," that is, over Satan.

## Passion and kingship

This brings us to a third theme, which is scarcely less prominent in John's passion than the first two: the passion is the final revelation of Jesus' divine kingship.

One thinks immediately perhaps of the episode of the title proclaiming Christ's royalty that was nailed to the top of His cross, a trilingual (and consequently, universal) pronouncement before the whole world that the Crucified is, in very fact, a king. Pilate's round refusal to change the inscription, at the request of the Jews, who wish to make it read like an unfounded claim on Jesus' part, is proof of this truth in John's eyes.

The theme of Jesus' kingship is however brought out even more strikingly in the narrative of the trial before Pilate, which the evangelist has, with great care, set in the place of honor at the very centre of his passion narrative. The hearing before the highpriest and Sanhedrin is passed over in order that the reader may devote all his attention to the dialogue between Christ and Pilate, which, as we shall see, is arranged with consummate art and deep theological insight. It is the disclosure of Jesus' kingly character which dominates this whole episode.

In order to illustrate this theme of royalty, John introduces another motif into his account of the passion: the characterization of Jesus as the new or second Adam.

It is as summing up in Himself the entire human race, John says equivalently, that Jesus undergoes suffering and death, in order that, through His glorification as Lord of the new creation, humanity may also attain its exaltation. As the inspired author will declare in the Apocalypse, "He has made us a kingdom, priests for God his Father" (Apoc. 1:6).

The author of the letter to the Hebrews, who owes so much of his own theological viewpoint to the school of John, has epitomized this Johannine view of Christ's passion in a masterly exegetical exposition of the messianic significance of Psalm 8.

> It was not to angels that he subjected the world to come, of which we are speaking. But, as someone has somewhere testified,
>> "What is Man that you remember him,
>> or Son of Man that you consider him?
>> You have, for a little while, made him less than angels:
>> with glory and honor have you crowned him;
>> you have subjected everything under his feet."
>
> In the "subjection of everything to him," he has left nothing unsubjected to him. Now, however, we do not yet see that "everything has been subjected." But we behold him, who "for a little while was made less than angels," Jesus, "crowned with glory and honor" because of his suffering of death, in order that, by God's favor, he might experience death for the sake of all men. It was indeed fitting for him, for whom and by whom all things exist, when bringing many sons to glory, to render perfect through his passion the author of their salvation. For the Sanctifier and the sanctified spring from one [Father] (Heb. 2:5-11).

In this magnificent passage, we have a striking summary of the whole of John's passion-account. Jesus Christ, Son of Man, the second Adam, who was "for a little while" (during His earthly career) set below the angels, is seen "crowned with glory and honor because of his suffering and death."

Actually, the author of Hebrews develops John's theme in his own personal way. On his view, Jesus was "made perfect" as author of men's salvation by means of His passion. The writer sees in Christ's awful torments a means of perfecting His human nature. "Son of God, though he was, he learned obedience in the school of suffering; and being thus made perfect, he has become, for all who hearken to him, the cause of eternal salvation" (Heb. 5:9).

This conception is a bold one: a man is not completely human until he has suffered deeply, and the incarnate Son designed to seek no exemption from this stern rule of human psychology.

John tells the story of the passion of Christ in chapters 18–19 of his Gospel, and his account falls naturally into three sections: the scene in the Garden, which sets the tone for the whole narrative and presents Jesus as the second Adam; the conversations with Pilate, in which Jesus' royalty is highlighted; and the events upon Calvary, which combine the themes of kingship and of the second Adam, and introduce the role of the Mother of Jesus (and of the Church) as the second Eve.

## I. The glory of the second Adam

From the first, the sacred author strikes a note of triumph, of glory. This is "the hour" of Jesus' self-manifestation as Son of God, to which the whole Gospel has been looking forward since its beginning. It is the hour of victory, as John promised in the Prologue.

> "And that Light keeps shining in the darkness:
> for the darkness has never put it out" (John 1:5).

As Jesus leaves the Cenacle upon Mount Zion to keep the rendezvous which is to inaugurate this drama, He walks backward through Old Testament history. "He went out," John informs us, "to a place beyond the torrent Kidron" — a reference that recalls David's flight from his rebellious son Absalom (2 Sam. 15:23). It was this very route that David had taken in his hour of trial, when his own royal power was at stake. Jesus, for John, is the new David, who marches out to vindicate His kingship.

The evangelist has already made use of the Davidic typology in his account of the Last Supper, where he recorded Jesus' announcement of Judas' treachery by means of a citation from Psalm 41:9: "The man who eats my bread has lifted up his heel against me" (John 13:18). The rabbis had long understood this remark of the psalmist as an allusion to Ahithophel, who had conspired with Absalom against King David. Judas is the new Ahithophel who betrays the new David.

When Jesus reaches Gethsemane, however, He assumes another, more ancient and more fundamental role. "He went out to a place. . .where there was a Garden."

John does not, like the other evangelists, tell us the name of this villa, Gethsemane, the olive-press, which is such an apt name for what, in the synoptic tradition, is the scene of the Master's terrible mental anguish. For John, it is quite simply "a Garden," for Jesus has reached the new Eden, the place of His confrontation, as new Adam, with "the old serpent," with Satan.

It is the first time, in the Fourth Gospel, that Jesus is characterized as the second Adam. His adversary is mentioned immediately. "Judas, his betrayer, was also acquainted with the place." The evangelist has carefully prepared his reader for this episode by telling him earlier of Judas' close association with the devil. "The devil had already planted the idea of betraying him in the mind of Judas Iscariot, Simon's son" (John 13:2).

This association ripens into a kind of diabolical possession, in the course of the Last Supper, as Judas hardens his heart against Jesus' last efforts to save him. After he receives the bit of bread dipped in sauce, "Satan took full possession of him" (John 13:27).

Accordingly, it is "in a Garden" that the two ancient foes prepare to meet each other: the Man, Jesus, the new Adam, and Satan in the person of the traitor Judas.

## Jesus' majesty

John employs all his genius to direct his reader's attention to this dramatic overture of the passion. Jesus is always in complete control of the situation. His divine foreknowledge extends to every least detail of the struggle that faces Him: Jesus knew "perfectly all that lay ahead of him." He stands, as the Light of the world, awaiting the approach of "the darkness."

John insinuates this by his mention (a detail omitted by the other evangelists) of the lanterns carried by Jesus' enemies. Twice before in his story, John has quoted a proverb which describes the present moment admirably. "As long as a man walks during the daytime, he does not stumble, because he sees the Light of this world. But when a man walks at night, he stumbles, because the Light is not in him" (John 11: 9-10). "Walk while you have the Light, for fear the darkness put out your light. The man who walks around in the darkness does not know where he is going. While you have the Light, keep your faith in the Light, in order that you may come under the influence of the Light" (John 12:35-36).

The present episode will depict Judas and his accomplices, minions of the darkness, as "not knowing where they are going," and will call attention to their "stumbling."

As the new Adam, Jesus displays a sense of solidarity with His own, in keeping with His role. At the moment of His arrest, He will command His captors, "Let these men go unmolested." And the evangelist points out that this physical safety of the disciples is a symbol of their eternal salvation, which Jesus had promised His Father to safeguard: "Of those you have given me, I have not lost a single one" (John 17:12).

In order that the majesty of the new Adam should command this whole scene, John has omitted the terrible anguish of mind and the bloody sweat associated by the other Gospels with Gethsemane. We catch only a brief echo of Jesus' agonizing prayer to His Father in His remark to Peter, "Am I not to drink the cup which the Father has presented to me?"

As a matter of fact, in order to leave the drama in the Garden free of any hint of Jesus' struggle there (His "agony," as Luke calls it) John has, characteristically, anticipated this part of the passion by insinuating it into the scene in an earlier chapter (John 12:20-36), where Jesus meets the "Greeks," Greek-speaking Jews of the diaspora on pilgrimage in Jerusalem for the Passover. When Philip tells of the desire of these strangers for an interview, Jesus is represented as experiencing, in this approach of the Jews of the dispersion, a presentiment of His death.

Several expressions employed here by John remind us of the synoptic accounts of Jesus' struggle or agony in Gethsemane. "Now my heart is in a turmoil (cf. Matthew 26:38, "My heart is near breaking with sorrow"), and what shall I say? 'Father, deliver me from this hour.' No; for this very purpose I have come to this hour. (cf. Matthew 26:39, "O my Father, if it is possible, have this cup removed from me. Still, it must be as you wish, not as I wish"). "Father, glorify your name" (cf. Matthew 26:42, "O my Father, if this cannot be removed from me without my drinking it, may your will be carried out"). On this occasion, when the heavenly voice replies to Christ, some of the crowd think that an angel has spoken to him, a detail reminiscent of the angel mentioned in Luke 22:43.

Of all this, in the Garden, nothing is mentioned by John. He wishes to convey one single impression: the majesty of the second Adam whose final victory over Satan is assured.

At the approach of Judas and the guard, "Jesus, knowing perfectly all that lay ahead of him, came forward. And he says to them, 'Whom are you seeking?' They replied, 'Jesus the Nazarene.' Jesus says to them, 'I AM.' Now Judas his betrayer was also among them. But when he said to them, 'I AM,' they backed away and fell to the ground."

It is Christ's personality which dominates the whole scene. The sacred writer suggests that this awkward stumbling of Judas and his collaborators, who trip over one another as they draw back in fear in such an undignified manner, is the result of the impact of the hidden divinity of Jesus Christ. This dramatic effect is due to the pronouncing of the divine name, "I AM." And John allows us a glimpse of the victorious outcome of this last struggle between Satan and the new Adam which is only now beginning.

The forces of the darkness cannot work their will upon the Son of God until He permits. "So once again, he asked them, 'Whom are you seeking?' They said, 'Jesus the Nazarene.' Jesus replied, 'I have told you that I AM. If you are looking for me, let these men go unmolested.' "

To His would-be captors, Christ issues orders as if they were His own servants. He will of course allow them to capture Him, to crucify Him, because this is the Father's plan for His own glorification as well as for the salvation of humanity. "This is why the Father loves me: because I surrender my life to receive it back again. No man takes it from me: I myself surrender it of my own accord. I possess the authority to surrender it: I possess the authority to receive it back again. Such is the injunction I have received from my Father" (John 10:17-18).

To the Father alone it belongs to decree the hour for Jesus' exaltation. No worldly force, not even Satan's preternatural power, can prove effectual in the face of this eternal design.

## The role of Peter

Indeed, as Peter himself now illustrates, Jesus' own disciples are powerless when, acting according to their very human viewpoint, they attempt to interfere with God's loving plans for the world's redemption. Simon Peter's efforts to strike the first blow for the kingdom by cutting off Malchus' ear may be well-intentioned.

Such zeal however is misguided, because it stems from a complete lack of insight into the real meaning of the Master's passion. "Sheathe your sword. Am I not to drink this cup which my Father has presented to me?" As we have remarked, John here recalls the saying which, according to Matthew (26:39, 43), Jesus had repeated during His struggle in Gethsemane. But John gives it His own personal interpretation. Jesus does not merely accept the cup of suffering out of deference to His Father's will. He rebuffs any attempt, even from His own, to defraud Him of it.

John will mention a second incident in which Peter plays the leading part, but which is much less to his credit. He twice denies he is one of Jesus' followers, and a third time even refuses to admit he was in the Garden with Him. Peter thus, on John's view, cuts himself off from the saving solidarity with the second Adam.

The significance John has seen in this painful incident may be grasped from the dialogue recorded in the Epilogue to this Gospel, where the risen Christ questions Peter three times about his love for Him before bestowing on him supreme power over His Church (John 21:15-17). Peter's threefold protestation of devotion to his Master is necessary to atone for his sinful denials during the passion and to gain readmission into the solidarity with the glorified second Adam.

## Jesus and the leaders of Judaism

The evangelist mentions two hearings conducted by Jewish authorities after Jesus' arrest: one, during the night, an unofficial questioning by Annas, the deposed high priest; the second, a formal trial (presumably during the daytime, although John does not say so), conducted by Caiaphas, the actual highpriest, as president of the supreme tribunal of Israel, the Sanhedrin.

These data, provided by John, throw considerable light upon the anomalous tradition, recorded by Matthew and Mark, about two "trials" before the Sanhedrin, which fails to provide any plausible reason why a second meeting, following so rapidly upon the first, should have been held at all.

Our evangelist not only makes it clear that the first session, held unofficially by the ex-pontiff Annas, was not a trial in the proper sense, but also explains the confusion that had arisen in the oral tradition behind the Matthean and Markan accounts, a confusion probably due to the equivocal use of the term "highpriest" to designate both Annas and Caiaphas. The somewhat obscure memory of two meetings, each presided over by "the highpriest" (actually Annas, in the first instance, Caiaphas, in the second) led to the impression that both sessions had been attended by the whole Sanhedrin.

A curious feature of John's story of these two meetings is that, while he devotes some space to that held before Annas, he passes over the legal Jewish trial in utter silence.

At the interrogation conducted by Annas, the impression of Jesus' majestic serenity and utter self-composure is considerably heightened. He refuses to answer the questions put to Him; and, when struck on the face by a guard, protests against the injustice, while insisting upon His right to answer as He did. Since the religious authorities of Jerusalem have already heard and rejected what He has taught, there is no point in making any defense before this curious, insincere old man who has no business questioning Jesus.

The omission of any description of the formal hearing before the Sanhedrin is due, in the last analysis, to the fact that the issue has already, in this Gospel, been settled on that occasion when Jesus declared that these faithless judges, as tools of Satan, have been themselves indicted and condemned.

"Now is the judgment of this world. Now the ruler of this world will be expelled" (John 12:31).

Moreover, the task of making the issue clear, as John is well aware, falls to the Spirit of Truth, the Paraclete or defense-counsel, who vindicates, for the Christian, the justice of Jesus' claims.

> And when he comes, he will convict the world on three counts: [their] sin, the justice [of my claims], and judgment: [their] sin, because they have no faith in me; the justice [of my claims] because I am returning to my Father and you will no longer behold me; judgment, because the ruler of this world has had sentence passed upon him (John 16:8-10).

## II. The kingly character of Jesus Christ

As Père Boismard has pointed out, the episode connected with Pilate is arranged by John with great artistry. The first half of the narrative recounts how the Jews demand Jesus' death from the governor (John 18:28-32), Pilate holds his first conversation with Jesus (33-38a), and then proclaims Jesus' innocence to the Jews (38b-40). The account of Jesus' scourging and crowning with thorns forms the centre of the whole sequence and underscores its fundamental meaning (19:1-3).

In the second half, three sections correspond closely with those in the first part: Pilate again proclaims Jesus to be innocent (4-8), speaks with Jesus a second time (9-11), while in the end, the Jews succeed in obtaining Jesus' death from the governor (12-16).

However admirable the arrangement of this récit, it is its doctrinal significance which interests us principally: the evangelist's teaching regarding the kingly character of Christ. To this may be added a subordinate aim of John's: to show the reader that it is Jesus' claim to be Son of God which is the basic reason for His death.

Pilate's opening question to the Jews, "What charge do you bring against this man?", is not meant to imply that the procurator has not already been given some specious pretext by the Jews for arraigning Jesus before the imperial tribunal. We know in fact, from Luke, that they had already declared, "We have detected this fellow trying to incite our nation to revolt and attempting to prevent the payment of taxes to Caesar, and declaring himself the Messiah — a king" (Luke 23:2).

Pilate's purpose is to get at the Jews' real motive in having recourse to him. When they refuse to answer his question, Pilate humiliates them by suggesting they try their prisoner in their own courts (which under Roman law were no longer empowered to pass sentence of death), and so forces them to admit their true aim. "We have no power to execute anyone."

Pilate begins his interrogation of his Prisoner by asking, "Are you king of the Jews?" As it stands, the question is dangerously ambiguous; and Jesus must have the issue clarified before replying. It would seem that the Jews had cunningly twisted the expression, "King of Israel," a religious title, assumed frequently by Yahweh in the Old Testament and regarded by John as messianic (John 1:49), into a profane and political formula, which suggested that Jesus was trying to subvert Roman domination in Palestine.

In the mouth of a Roman official, "King of the Jews" might be an inaccurate reference to Jesus' true messianic title, "King of Israel," or it might be an echo of the false accusation of the Jews.

Accordingly, Jesus asks the governor, "Are you asking this on your own, or have others been talking to you about me?" When Pilate, somewhat nettled, demands to know the facts of the case, Jesus explains to him that "My kingdom does not have its origin in this world," and advances a proof that even Pilate can assess. Were Jesus a mere king like others known in the world, the country would now be torn by civil war, with His subjects rising to His defense.

Still, as Pilate realizes, Jesus does not renounce His claims to royalty, "Yet you are a king?" "You are right in asserting that I am a king," Jesus replies. "To this was I born."

Here we are given a new insight into the purpose of the Incarnation. It provides the grounds, ultimately, for Jesus' royal character and his office as King of the universe. This kingship is also intimately connected with Jesus' mission of explaining to men the "God no man has ever seen," or, "testifying to Truth."

This royal testimony however can only be grasped by the man whose mind is open to truth, whose heart loves truth. Such profound theology is beyond the practical Roman man of affairs. "What does truth mean?" Pilate asks, half bewildered, half contemptuous. And before his question can be answered, he beats a hasty retreat to the Jews outside, whose pragmatic opportunism he still thinks he can cope with.

Pilate's "What does truth mean?" sums up the whole issue in the Fourth Gospel. In a very real sense, it might be said that John has written his whole book simply to provide an answer to this question. For John, as Sir Edwyn Hoskyns has pointed out, there is a marked difference between Pilate and Israel's religious leaders. They are simply Satan's tools in the story of the passion, while the Roman governor symbolizes the world, half-conscious of its need of salvation. The rest of this episode will only complete the contrast between Pilate and the Jews.

## The scourging and crowning with thorns

On the one hand, John does not delay over the painful details of the outrageous treatment of Christ planned by Pilate to give the Jews' blood-lust some satisfaction. On the other hand, he has set the incident in a place of prominence, since it symbolizes the royal character of Jesus.

It is to be noted that Pilate shows Jesus to the crowd wearing the insignia of royalty, the crown of thorns and the purple cloak. The gesture permits Pilate to show his contempt of the Jews: it permits John to imply that the governor admits Jesus' claims to kingship. The effect upon the priests and their followers is to force them to disclose their true motive in demanding

crucifixion. "We have a law, and according to that law he has to die, because he has declared himself God's Son."

## Second dialogue between Christ and Pilate

John uses a curious expression to describe Pilate's reaction: "When Pilate
heard this kind of language, he became still more alarmed" (John 19:8).
Until now, no mention of Pilate's fear has been made. The evangelist wishes us to understand that it was this emotion which had been governing Pilate's actions during the early part of the trial.

It explains why he has appeared almost to plead Jesus' cause. Pilate's next
question is also to be understood in this context. "Where do you come
from?" The query, to which Jesus refuses a reply, has a more profound significance here than in Luke's Gospel when Pilate "asked whether the man were
a Galilean" (Luke 23:6). For John, the Roman procurator seeks information about Jesus' origin, which (as the reader already knows) is divine. Pilate
however does not deserve an answer: the question does not fall within his
competence as governor, and he has already displayed indifference to supernatural values with his rhetorical question, "What does truth mean?"

Jesus does reply to Pilate's claim to have power of life and death over Him.
"You have no authority whatsoever over me, except what has been accorded you from above. Consequently, he who hands me over to you is guilty of
a greater sin." This rather cryptic remark makes Pilate all the more anxious
to release the Prisoner.

What does Jesus mean? He distinguishes clearly the governor's part in His
own death from that of His real enemies. Pilate is God's unwitting instrument
in the divine plan of the world's salvation (a role, however, which does not
excuse him from a grave sin against justice). His action appears in a very
different light from that of him "who hands me over to you." Who is this
betrayer?

It is certainly Caiaphas who, with the Sanhedrin's connivance, handed Jesus to the Romans. It is Judas who delivered his Master into the power of the
Jews. But, in the last analysis, it is most truly the person described in this
Gospel as "the darkness," Satan, whose work cannot be considered good in
any sense.

The Jews finally win the battle of wits with Pilate by insinuating that
they will indict him for treason in the imperial courts of Rome. Once again
we find the kingship of Christ in question. "If you release this fellow, you are
no friend of Caesar's. Anyone who declares himself a king is in opposition
to Caesar."

## Pilate passes the death sentence

Pilate's fear of this Jewish threat outweighs his fear for himself and his fear
of committing an injustice. He prepares to pass the sentence of death by having the Prisoner led before the bench.

There is an obscurity in the Gospel text here, which may be intentional on John's part. He probably means that Pilate "took his seat on the bench." The expression employed however could mean that Pilate seated Jesus on the bench. In a very real sense, it is Jesus who is judge in this court, and it is actually He Himself who freely accepts His own death out of love for His Father's will and for mankind's redemption (John 10:17-18).

John's purpose is to stress the theological truth which is illustrated by this solemn moment. Accordingly, he does not bother to record the official death-sentence expressed by the formula, *Ibis ad crucem*: "You shall go to the cross." Instead he draws attention to the date and the time of day when sentence is passed." It was the day of the preparation of the Paschal Lamb; the time was around noon" (John 19:14).

It was the very hour when, in the temple enclosure, the priests began to sacrifice the lambs used at the Passover. John's time-signature enables him to point to Jesus as the new Paschal Lamb, offered in sacrifice to "bear the world's sin," and thus terminate the old Passover commemoration, bringing to completion the whole of the Mosaic cult and code.

This is the moment also for Israel's final apostasy. When Pilate asks whether he is to crucify their king, the religious leaders of Israel cry, "We have no king but Caesar." In this terrible hour, the Jews renounce, not merely Jesus as their messiah, but almighty God Himself, who had always been regarded through Jewish history, even during the regnal period, as sole king of Israel. Their denial of Jesus' kingship involves them in a denial of faith in Yahweh.

This, for John, is only as it should be, since to deny that Christ is king, is equivalently to deny His divinity. Had not Jesus asserted, during this very trial, that the revelation of His kingship was part of the purpose of the incarnation of the Son of God?

## III. The events upon Calvary

When John describes Jesus as "carrying his own cross" on the way to Calvary, he is recalling for his reader that Jesus is the new Isaac, who carries on His own back the wood for His own sacrifice (Gen. 22:6).

Thus we are once more reminded by the evangelist (cf. John 3:16) of the tenderness and pathetic character of the Father's love for His only-begotten Son. Abraham himself carried the fire and the knife on the journey up the mountain, for fear any harm should come to his little son, whom he was ready to kill at God's command. Accordingly, we see how in this, the final stage of the passion, the Father's love accompanies Jesus.

Christ's crucifixion between the two bandits fulfills another Old Testament type, the Suffering Servant of Yahweh (Is. 53:12; cf. Luke 22:37). Still, He dies an acknowledged king, as the inscription Pilate affixes to His cross proves. This title was written in Aramaic (Jesus' own native tongue and that of His people), in Latin (the official language of imperial Rome), and in Greek (the common language of the ancient Near East).

Thus the universality of Christ's kingship is admitted by the Roman con-

querors and published to the whole world. The Jews' objection to the way
the inscription reads, which fails to move Pilate, only serves to underline this
universal sovereignty of the Crucified.

Jesus then dies as king. He also dies as highpriest of the New Covenant.
"His tunic was without seam, woven from top to bottom in one piece" (John
19:23). According to the Jewish historian Josephus, the robe of the Jewish
highpriest was a seamless one, described by Ben Sira as a "glorious robe"
(Sir. 50:11). Our author's reference to the seamless robe of Jesus would appear to suggest the priestly character of Christ upon the cross.

In his Apocalypse, John will recall this double office of Christ, at once
priest and king, in the opening vision of his revelation of the risen Lord,
"robed in a tunic reaching to his feet and girded about the breast with a
golden belt" (Apoc. 1:13).

This description of Christ's garments concludes with a citation of Psalm
22. Here once more we have an interesting example of the most personal
way John makes use of the data furnished by the apostolic tradition.

Matthew and Mark also cite this psalm in their descriptions of the crucifixion. In their accounts, Jesus intones the terrible words with which the
poem opens, "My God, my God, why have you abandoned me?" (Matthew
27:46; Mark 15:34). John, for whom Jesus' passion is primarily the beginning of His glory, omits this seeming cry of desperation, and instead, points
out the fulfilment of those other words in the same psalm,

> "They divided up my clothes among them,
> and for my garment they rolled dice" (John 19:24).

## The new Eve: Mary

Now that "his hour" is at last come, the Mother of Jesus again makes her
appearance in the Fourth Gospel. This was the crisis to which her Son had
referred at Cana, when he refused to accept her cooperation in performing
the miracle of the water made wine. On that occasion, He had implied that
when His hour would come, His Mother would have her role to play in the
redemption of mankind. John's account of this scene on Calvary contains
several echoes of the Cana story.

Here, as there, our Lady is simply "his mother." Here, as there, Jesus addresses her by the strange title, "Woman." Here, as there, John mentions
"the hour": "that very hour, the disciple took her into his own home" (John
19:27). This last phrase is reminiscent of the lines in the Prologue describing
the coming of the Word "to his own home" or "his own land":

> He came to his own land;
> Yet his own folk would not have him.
> But as for those who did accept him,
> He gave them power to become God's children . . .

By employing the same phrases to describe the disciple's reception of the
Mother of Jesus, the evangelist points out that Mary is also involved in the

Christian's adoptive filiation. One cannot become a child of God without becoming an adoptive son of the Mother of Jesus.

What meaning does John see in this important episode which took place at the cross of Jesus? Mary is most accurately described as "his mother" because here, even more than at Cana, her motherhood is at stake.

At Cana, Mary's Son had asked her to relinquish her mother's claim upon His miraculous powers. Here, He asks her to relinquish her natural, maternal affection for Himself, exchanging it for a completely supernatural love, by assuming the motherhood of "the disciple he loved," representative of all Jesus' faithful followers. "Woman, there is your son," Christ says, indicating John. "There is your mother," he tells the disciple.

These words, the sacred writer never forgets, are those of the Word, by whom "all things came to be" in the creation of the universe. Accordingly, we are witnessing a new creation. We have arrived at the heart of Calvary's mystery, the redemption. Jesus addresses His Mother as "Woman" to recall the divine prophecy concerning her role as co-redemptrix, recorded in Gen. 3:15. Accordingly, by these words of the Word, "his mother" becomes the new Eve, "mother of all the living." Jesus asks His Mother's consent to the enlarging of her divine maternity to include the Father's adoptive children.

One might even say that, in the Father's plan, it was not enough for her to be Mother of Jesus: she must also become Mother of all the disciples whom Jesus loves. Upon Calvary, Mary, Mother of Jesus "according to the flesh" becomes Mother of the whole Christ "according to the Spirit." She declares, with Paul, "even if we knew Christ according to the flesh, still that is now no longer the way we know him" (2 Cor. 5:17). The new Eve, she now knows the new Adam through the operation of the Spirit.

This perhaps accounts for the strange expression used here to describe the death of Jesus, "And having bowed his head, he handed over the Spirit" (John 19:30). For John, Jesus' last breath, breathed upon the heads of His Mother and the disciple He loved, is a symbol of that Holy Spirit whose sending is inaugurated by the death of Christ. Earlier, John could state, "The Spirit was not yet given, because Jesus was not yet glorified" (John 7:39).

In this hour, the beginning of Jesus' glorification, the mission of the Spirit, proceeding from the Son as from the Father, has commenced. The new creation has occurred, the work of the new Adam assisted by the new Eve.

## The new Eve: the Church

The piercing of Jesus' side is of paramount importance in the theology of John. This is shown by the affidavit our author appends to his description of the scene, affirming the truth of the eye-witness testimony which he records (John 19:35).

The first Johannine epistle also makes much of it. "Thus there are three that witness, the Spirit, the water, and the blood" (1 John 5:8). It is upon this "testimony of God . . . about his Son" that the whole structure of the Christian faith reposes.

What is the symbolic significance of this last episode upon Calvary? In the issuing of the blood and water from the side of the dead Christ, the evangelist contemplates the creation of the Church as the new Eve. Long ago, in Eden, God had cast a deep sleep upon Adam, had opened his side, and taken a rib which He fashioned into woman, a partner for the first man (Gen. 2:21-22).

Likewise, once the new Adam has fallen asleep in death, His sacred side is opened to permit the two miraculous elements, water and blood, to flow out. In John's Gospel, flowing or "living" water is a symbol of the Spirit, a sacramental symbol: baptism. Blood, as we learn from Cana and from the eucharistic discourse at Capharnaum, stands for the Eucharist, the sacrament by which the Christian life of the Church is nourished.

St. Augustine has remarked that from the side of Jesus, there "flowed forth blood and water, in which we see the sacraments, by which the Church is built up."

The reader who is familiar with John's writings should not be astonished to find both the Church and the Mother of Jesus represented on Calvary as the new Eve. The mystery of Cana has already revealed Mary as a symbol of the Christian Church; and the glorious picture of the Apocalypse of "the woman clothed with the sun" represents at once the Mother of Christ and the Church (Apoc. 12:1-12).

It remains to point out the composite picture of the Redeemer, which John again refers to by means of two Old Testament citations. Jesus is "God's lamb" because He fulfils the typology of the Passover lamb, eaten at the annual commemoration of Israel's redemption from Egypt, and of the Suffering Servant, described as a "lamb led to the slaughter" (Is. 53:7).

The evangelist, at the beginning of his Gospel, had put this double typology in the mouth of John the Baptist: "There is God's lamb, who carries the world's sin" (John 1:29). Here he cites the words, "Not a bone of his shall be broken," a text composed of two Old Testament verses: one, from the rubrics concerning the Passover supper (Exod. 12:46); the other, the psalmist's description of the Suffering Servant of Yahweh (Ps. 33:21).

Finally, by means of a text from Zechariah, "They will look upon him whom they have pierced" (Zech. 12:10), John points out the glory of the Crucified, as he does in the opening vision of his Apocalypse. "See, he is coming amid the clouds, and every eye will see him, even those who pierced him" (Apoc. 1:7).

## IV. Epilogue: the burial of Jesus

Joseph of Arimathea obtains Pilate's permission to take Jesus' body down from the cross. Nicodemus brings a very large quantity of spices, thus providing a truly royal burial for his Master. John carefully notes (and the point is of considerable importance in his eyes) that they prepared the body "in accordance with the Jewish custom of embalming."

The Egyptian custom of embalming, the process known as mummification, involved the removal of the brain and entrails. The sacred body of the dead Christ, which was to rise "the third day" (that is, according to Jewish opinion, before corruption set in) did not suffer any such mutilation. Its integrity was not violated at its burial.

With superb artistry, John ends his story of the passion where it began — in a Garden. "Now there was a garden in the locality where Jesus had been crucified; and in the garden, a new tomb in which no one had been laid to rest. It was there, accordingly, out of respect for the Jewish day of preparation, that they laid Jesus, since the tomb was nearby." From his labor of redemption which had begun in a Garden, the new Adam finds rest in a Garden.

It is however not the same Garden. The first Garden reminded us of Eden, the earthly paradise. This second Garden, with its new tomb, is a symbol of the celestial paradise, which, according to Luke, Jesus had promised to share with the good thief, "This very day you will be with me in Paradise" (Luke 23:43).

# ST. JOHN AND THE PASCHAL MYSTERY

David Michael Stanley, S.J.

The twentieth chapter of the Fourth Gospel was intended originally to form its conclusion, and the sacred author has put a good deal of thought into its composition as well as into the selection of incidents from the risen life of Jesus, in order to deepen his reader's faith in the paschal mystery.

Not that there was any dearth of materials provided by apostolic tradition. Indeed, John tells us that "Jesus also performed many other signs before his disciples' eyes which are not written in this book. These have been written in order that you may persevere in your belief that Jesus is the Messiah, the Son of God, and that, by perseverance in your belief, you may possess life in his name" (John 20:30-31).

From the abundance of evangelical treasure which lay to hand, John has carefully chosen four incidents: the astonishing experience of Peter and another disciple at the tomb of Jesus on Easter morning; the commission by

Published originally in *Worship*, 33 (1959), 293-301. Reprinted by permission of the publisher.

the risen Lord to Mary Magdalene of the Good News of His resurrection and
ascension; Christ's gift of the Holy Spirit to His disciples on Easter Sunday
evening; and the profession of faith made by the incredulous Thomas one
week later.

These narratives sum up, in John's eyes, the paschal experience of the disciples; and he has arranged them in such a way that they form a coherent
unity.

We must, accordingly, examine each of these four episodes in turn, if we
wish to arrive at our evangelist's understanding of the paschal mystery.

### The Easter faith of the disciples

John, who until this point in his Gospel has followed the Jewish liturgical
calendar, now abandons it. He dates his narrative of Jesus' glorified life from
"the first day of the week," the Christian Sunday, the day commemorative
of the resurrection.

Mary Magdalene, having discovered the empty tomb, hurries to tell the
tragic news to Peter and "the other disciple whom Jesus dearly loved" (tradition identifies him as John): "They took the Lord out of the tomb, and
we do not know where they put him" (John 20:2).

Mary's "we do not know" is very meaningful for the evangelist. Her ignorance (and that of her women companions) has a profoundly religious
significance for John. Like her later failure to recognize the risen Christ (John
20:14), it is a symbol of her lack of real faith. The Magdalene is represented as still without belief in her Master's resurrection.

Neither, as yet, do the two disciples believe, as they in turn begin to run
to the sepulchre. Out of respect for Peter, whom Jesus had at Caesarea Philippi made head of His future Church, John, first to arrive, waits outside the
tomb, after taking a quick look inside. The sacred author is well aware that,
in the divine plan, Peter must be the first to receive the grace of paschal
faith.

Upon entering the tomb, Peter "takes a long look at the cloths on the
ground and at the shroud which had covered his head, not on the ground
with the cloths but unrolled in a different spot" (John 20:6-7). It is, John
insinuates, the contour of these cloths, in which Jesus' dead body had been
wrapped, that gives Peter the first inkling of what has happened.

Since the evangelist preserves such a discreet silence about this "testimony
of the senses," we can only conjecture what it was that struck Peter's observant eye. The shape and position of these now useless garments made it clear
to the apostle that the body of the Master had not been stolen. He begins
to suspect that it had emerged from the grave-clothes without disturbing
them in any way, with the result that they still retained, in their collapsed
state, something of the shape of that sacred body, which they had taken on
when they had been tightly wrapped around it.

In short, Peter's eyes told him that Jesus' corpse had *apparently* vanished
into thin air. But the grace of Christian faith which Peter received at this

very instant assured him that Jesus had risen from death, as He Himself had long ago predicted.

"Now after that, the other disciple, who had arrived first at the tomb, also entered: and he looked — and he believed" (John 20:8). These last four words describe one of the most momentous happenings in the history of mankind: the birth of Christian faith in the mystery of the resurrection.

And immediately, as if to forestall the charge that would be made centuries later by all the world's rationalists, John assures us that this new belief was not the result of any self-hypnotism on the part of these two disciples. He rules out the possibility of a delusion produced by wishful thinking, the fruit of brooding over the Old Testament prophecies which described the exaltation of the Suffering Servant (cf. Is. 52:13; 53:10,12).

That was precisely what could not have happened, John tells us soberly, because "they had not as yet understood the Scriptures, which had declared that he must rise from death" (John 20:9).

Indeed, John's next remark shows how far this pair was from anything like the irrational enthusiasm or auto-suggestion which a later sophisticated but faithless age was to attribute to them. "Then the disciples went off home," says John.

Even twenty centuries later, this bald remark cannot fail to astonish the reader. Peter and John do not run now, as they had on their approach: they simply "go home," as if things were what they had anticipated. Nothing however was to be the same again for these two. The New Creation had been ushered in: the Lord Jesus had risen from death to a new life with God.

## The Magdalene and the risen Lord

Peter and John had received the gift of paschal faith: Mary Magdalene was still without it. She lingered, in tears, near the entrance to the tomb which had been robbed of its precious treasure. Without faith in Christ's resurrection, Mary remains utterly disconsolate.

Even the sight of two divine messengers, seated "one at the head, the other at the foot" of the place where Jesus' dead body had lain, fails to distract her from her grief. To them she can only plaintively repeat her despairing message, "They took my Lord away, and I do not know where they put him" (John 20:13).

With that, she turns her back upon the angelic vision, and finds herself face to face with One who she mistakenly thinks is the caretaker of this garden in which Christ's sepulchre stood.

The risen Christ's query re-echoes that of the angels. "Woman, why are you crying? who is it you are looking for?"

No reader of John's account can fail to sense the drama in this poignant situation. Mary's lack of faith and her tears of misery have blinded her, and she fails to recognize the very Person she seeks so helplessly. "Sir, if *you* removed him, tell me where you put him; and I will take him away" (John 20:15).

The irony of the last spoken phrase in Greek is impossible to reproduce in English. It could mean, "I will raise him up." In her desperate love for her dead Master, John seems to suggest, Mary would attempt to do what God's omnipotence has by now already done.

One word from Jesus is sufficient to transform Mary's grief into Christian joy, "Mariam." The sacred writer keeps the name in its Aramaic form, as if to convey to us the very accents of that beloved voice which Mary does not fail to recognize. He has preserved too the native word with which Mary expresses her new faith, "Rabboni." This term, more solemn than the customary "Rabbi", was also used by the Jews in addressing God Himself.

The laconic record of this dialogue is characteristic of John's reticence. He hesitates to intrude into the privacy of this wonderful recognition-scene, leaving the rest to his reader's imagination.

After some moments, Jesus makes a rather puzzling remark to Mary. "Do not go on clinging to me: because I have not yet ascended to the Father" (John 20:17a). In her delight, the Magdalene had evidently thrown herself at the knees of Jesus and had grasped them in a tight embrace. Jesus forbids this veneration of His sacred humanity at this juncture.

A week later, He will insist that Thomas touch His body. Momentarily however, He seems, almost unfeelingly, to deny this same favor to the adoring Mary.

What is the reason for this? "Because I have not yet ascended to the Father." The glorification of Jesus' human nature has, assuredly, been begun by His resurrection from the tomb. It is still, however, incomplete, because He has yet to take His place at the right hand of the Father.

Until that occurs, the work of His glorification is unfinished, and it is only when He is ascended into the glory of His Father that His sacred humanity will become the centre of Christian worship, the New Temple He had spoken of during His public life (John 2:19-21).

Still, if He at this point rejects Mary's adoration, Jesus confides to her an important commission. She is to be the first evangelist of the *praeconium paschale*, the Good News that His glorification is to be completed without delay. "Now, go to my brothers, and tell them, 'I am ascending to my Father and your Father, to my God and your God'" (John 20:17b).

And John describes Mary as the first herald of the Gospel. "Mary Magdalene goes off to make the announcement to the disciples, 'I have seen the Lord, and this is what he told me'" (John 20:18).

The Johannine tradition that Jesus' resurrection was closely followed by His ascension is markedly different from that preserved elsewhere in the New Testament. It does not, however, contradict the Lucan datum that Jesus ascended into heaven some forty days after Easter (Acts 1:3-9). Rather, it supplements it. Luke describes Christ's *final* departure at the close of the period during which He appeared at intervals to His own: John insinuates that, during the times when He was not with His disciples, Christ's glorified humanity was in heaven, enjoying the full glory of the Father.

## The gift of the Holy Spirit

"In the late evening, the same first day of the week, with the doors of the room, where the disciples had gathered out of fear of the Jews, locked tight, Jesus entered and stood before them. And he said to them, 'Peace be to you.' "

It is now the turn of the whole group of Jesus' chosen followers to share in the joy of His glorification. The evangelist notes that Christ gives them concrete proof of the reality of His resurrection; for the disciples are to be official witnesses to this supremely important event.

If, as John is very much aware, the essential element in their testimony is their supernatural paschal faith, still this other element, their role as eye-witnesses, is not to be neglected.

With the reality of Christ's physical presence among them established beyond any reasonable doubt, the disciples are ready to receive a new grace, the Gift *par excellence* of the risen Master, that "other Advocate" whom He had promised to them:

"Then Jesus said, 'Peace be to you,' once more. 'Just as the Father has sent me, I, in my turn, am sending you.' And with this remark, he breathed into them. And he says to them, 'Receive a Holy Spirit. If you remit anyone's sins, they will be remitted for them. If you retain anyone's sins, they will be retained' " (John 20:21-23).

Once again, the Fourth Gospel refines upon the tradition recorded by St. Luke in the Acts of the Apostles. That author has picked out Pentecost as the day when the "promised Spirit" descended upon the apostolic community, forming them into the New Israel, the Church. John indicates (without, of course, denying the significance of Pentecost for the coming-to-be of the Church) that Christ's bestowal of the Holy Spirit had been begun even earlier.

Indeed, he would appear to suggest that Jesus had, in the very act of dying, "handed over the Spirit" to His Mother and the beloved disciple as they stood beneath the cross, upon which He had begun the work of the New Creation (John 19:30).

Now, on Easter evening, He continues this work of the New Creation by "breathing into" the little group of frightened disciples that Holy Spirit who is source of supernatural life.

Here again, the expression "breathe into," employed by the evangelist, is to be noted. It is the same as that used in the Greek Bible for the creation of the first man: "And God molded the Man out of clay dug up from the earth; and he *breathed* the life-breath *into* its face, and the Man became a living being" (Gen. 2:7).

The infusion of the Spirit here described has a special significance: by His presence, the Spirit brings to the disciples the power to forgive men's sins. Or, more exactly, the Spirit's presence gives to the disciples full control over the sins of men, i.e., they are formally given a share of that office of judge, which John earlier pointed out as a characteristic of the Second Adam, the Son of Man.

It will be recalled that in the previous passage John had associated God's role as the giver of life with that of judge; and he had stated that the Father had bestowed both of them upon the Son. In the present scene, the risen Christ exercises this twofold function by imparting the Holy Spirit to His disciples. Christ "breathes into" them, as did the Creator in the beginning, and thus gives them a share in His judiciary activity: the forgiveness of sin.

> Just as the Father possesses life by himself,
> so too he gave life to the Son
> to possess by himself.
> And he communicated to him
> the power of passing judgment,
> because he is Son of Man . . . (John 5:26-27).

The absolutely universal scope of this newly communicated life-giving power, exercised in the sacrament of penance, is described by John through two expressions current amongst the rabbinical writers, "remit" and "retain," signifying full exercise of jurisdiction.

### Thomas' profession of faith in Christ's divinity

We come to the fourth episode through which John expresses the meaning of the paschal mystery, as it has appealed to him.

It appears that the apostle Thomas was absent on Easter Sunday evening from the group of disciples to whom the risen Christ had appeared. When informed of what had happened, Thomas rejects their testimony, and lays down the conditions under which he will believe in Jesus' resurrection: "Unless I see in his hands the mark of the nails and stick my finger into the place where the nails were, and stick my hand into his side, I am not going to believe" (John 20:25).

It is on another Sunday that the risen Christ appears to His disciples in the same room and with the same greeting, "Peace." This time, however, Thomas is in the group, and the Lord addresses the doubter: "Give me your finger here, and see my hands. Now give me your hand, and stick it into my side. And do not go on being a doubter: become a believer" (John 20:27).

John insists, almost crudely, upon the details of this dialogue, because he knows how necessary it is to the Christian faith that there were eye-witnesses to the reality of Jesus' risen body.

Still, John has a deeper purpose. Jesus is as insistent here that Thomas should touch His body, as He was insistent earlier with Mary Magdalene, that she should stop touching Him. In the interval between Easter Sunday morning and this evening a week later, Jesus' humanity has been completely glorified, and so has become the centre of Christian cult and Christian belief.

This is borne out by Thomas' response, "My Lord and my God" (John 20:28). Here we have one of the rare instances in the New Testament where the title, God, is given to Jesus Christ. For the evangelist is fully conscious that, as a result of Jesus' resurrection and ascension and of His gift of the Holy Spirit, the divinity of Christ has been revealed to the disciples.

## The "ninth" beatitude

The incident with Thomas terminates in a saying of Jesus which John has deliberately chosen as the climax of his whole Gospel. He has brought out the necessary function, on the part of the apostolic college, of eye-witnessing. He has still one last lesson to impart to succeeding generations of Christians, who will read his book until the end of time.

This lesson is contained in Jesus' final remark to Thomas: "Is it because you have seen me that you have come to believe? Happy those who, though they did not see, yet become believers" (John 20:29).

Since this remark is meant for us, who live many centuries after Jesus' earthly career ended, it is imperative that we grasp its full import.

Often one hears Christians wishing that they had had the grace of living in Palestine while Jesus was there. How easy, they say, it would have been, to believe in His teaching, to become His disciples. It is precisely to those of us who have felt or expressed this desire, that this "ninth" beatitude is addressed.

John knows, because Jesus has said it (and the example of Thomas is there to prove it), that, important as seeing is, it is *not* believing. Our Gospels testify to the fact that many saw Jesus without finding faith in Him.

John, for his part, knows that it is necessary "to see the Son" in Jesus, and so "believe in him" (John 6:40). John also knows that this cannot be done without the assistance of Him who is Spirit of Truth, whose role is to lead men into "the full truth" (John 16:13). Finally, John knows that, until the time of Jesus' glorification, "the Spirit was not yet" (John 7:39). That is why it was not yet possible, during Jesus' earthly life, for men to learn the "full truth" about Him, to find complete Christian, paschal faith in Him.

But for us who live in the "last days" of the New Creation, such faith is possible, because the risen Christ has given the Holy Spirit to us.

And so, John's last message to us takes the form of a beatitude, which does not apply to the apostolic eye-witnesses, but only to us of later Christian generations. You are the happy ones, because you inherit the faith through the light of the Spirit. Your Christian lives are a perpetual Easter, when Christ lives once more after His death and the Spirit has been given, "that you may persevere in your belief that Jesus is the Messiah, the Son of God, and that, by perseverance in your belief, you may possess life in his name" (John 20:30-31).

# 6 SAINT PAUL

In God's providential design Saul the Pharisee became Paul the Apostle through the direct intervention of the risen and glorified Christ. St. Paul's conversion, dating from a few years after Christ's Ascension, and his apostolic career of about thirty years, coincide with the formative years of the Christian community, as well as the formation of its oral and written message. In fact, the earliest Christian writings are the epistles of St. Paul.

So comprehensive are St. Paul's epistles, so pervaded with both Jewish and Hellinistic thought, so deep and thorough in their grasp of the cosmic implications of the Christian message, that rationalist scholars have doubted that one man could have written them all. Father Barnabas Mary Ahern discusses this problem in the first article of this section.

But the man who was a "Hebrew of Hebrews, as regards the Law, a Pharisee" (Phil. 3:5), and at the same time the Apostle of the Gentiles, who became all things to all men that he might save all (1 Cor. 9:22) convinces by the fiery intensity of his message, by the coherence and apostolic authenticity of his doctrine, that he was the divinely appointed witness to the Gentiles, that he did in three decades herald the good news of salvation from one end of the Mediterranean world to the other.

No problem of an individual was too small to merit his attention; no doctrinal problem too large for him to show how it is subsumed in the all-embracing "plan of the mystery hidden from eternity in God" but now "revealed through his apostles and prophets" (Eph. 3:9, 5). Although St. Paul speaks of "my gospel" (Rom. 2:16;16:25), it is clear that what he preaches is the gospel "which I also re-

351

ceived" (1 Cor. 15:3), that is, the teaching of the church of Jerusalem (Gal. 1:18-19). Yet the primitive apostolic preaching received in St. Paul's epistles a depth and flexibility which adapted it to the demands of a complex Greco-Roman world.

Although St. Paul does not dwell on the incidents of Christ's life and earthly ministry, he shows an intense awareness of what His life, death, and glorious resurrection mean to the individual, to the community of Christians, to the whole human race, to Jew as well as Gentile, to angelic and demonic powers, even to inanimate nature. He is truly the first great theologian of the Church.

The writings of St. Paul, with their subtlety and intensity, as well as their difficulty, have given rise to innumerable controversies, but they also have brought in every century new insights into the relevance of the Christian message for that age. In our own day innumerable studies, scholarly and popular,[1] have drawn from the writings of St. Paul a new understanding of the Church, the Christian message, and the redemption of the whole universe. The following articles present a few of the fruits of scholarly investigations, and they indicate what a harvest our age is reaping from the study of St. Paul.

[1] See David M. Stanley, *Christ's Resurrection in Pauline Soteriology* (Rome: Pontifical Biblical Institute, 1961). Amédée Brunot, *Saint Paul and His Message* (New York: Hawthorn Books, 1959). Lucien Cerfaux, *Christ in the Theology of Saint Paul* and *The Church in the Theology of Saint Paul* (New York: Herder and Herder, 1959). Francois Amiot, *The Key Concepts of Saint Paul* (New York: Herder and Herder, 1962).

# WHO WROTE
# THE PAULINE EPISTLES?

Barnabas M. Ahern, C.P.

A short time ago the international press carried the news story of an interesting venture. An English minister had used an I.B.M. machine to determine how many letters ascribed to St. Paul were actually written by him. Feeding epistle after epistle into the mechanical device, the investigator computed with mathematical exactness the similarities and differences of vocabulary, the recurrence of words and word groupings.

The results were both interesting and valuable. This exact measurement of the Pauline vocabulary provides a mechanically flawless analysis of the epistles' verbal content which will prove of service to all future scholars. For the investigator himself the results of his study à la I.B.M. were definitive — he found in this exact computation convincing proof that Paul was the actual author of very few of the epistles bearing his name.

## Deficiencies of mechanical computation

Though this ingenious research caused a flurry in the press, it passed almost unnoticed by scholars. Denial of Pauline authenticity is never a cause for surprise. From the very beginning, men doubted that the Apostle had written the Epistle to the Hebrews. In the nineteenth century the Tübingen school denied his authorship of all letters except the Great Epistles (Romans, Galatians, 1 and 2 Corinthians). In our own day, though there has been a swing back from the radical thesis of Baur and the scholars of Tübingen, many are still reluctant to list the Epistle to the Ephesians and the pastoral epistles among Paul's authentic epistles.

The debate will continue. We have emerged from the tensions of the early twentieth century when the Biblical Commission had to view the literary authorship of the New Testament writings as a doctrinal question. Provided a New Testament book is recognized as truly inspired by God and is accepted as a genuine emergent of first-century Christianity, its actual authorship is a matter of free debate according to the norms of improved methods of criticism, historical, literary and textual. The attitude of modern scholars to the question of biblical authorship is that of St. Augustine: "It matters not who wrote the book of Job, so long as we recognize that God is its author."

There is another reason why the results of the I.B.M. study caused little stir in scholarly circles. It is obvious that conclusions based merely on a mechanical study of vocabulary cannot be definitive. A machine cannot think. It cannot take into account the many factors which must be kept in mind in dealing with the delicate question of an ancient book's provenance. Multiple

Published originally in *The Bible Today*, 1 (1964), 754-60. Reprinted by permission of the publisher.

elements in the book's composition would radically alter its literary style and would thus effectively counterbalance the results of verbal computation. The use of secretaries, the incorporation of previously written or oral material, changing historical situations, psychological and doctrinal development in the writer himself, new problems and a new milieu, association with writers and speakers using a hitherto unfamiliar style — all these factors show how precipitate is a definitive conclusion based on verbal study alone.

### Definition of Pauline authorship

The investigation of literary authorship is, therefore, a complex problem, so complex that some feel it is an idle pursuit. The fact is, however, that an author's identification, though adding nothing to the inspiration of a sacred book, is of inestimable help in the historical study of early Christianity. Hence it is worthwhile to know the norms which students of St. Paul generally use to ascertain the number of epistles actually written by him.

First of all, we must define the meaning of literary authorship. This does not require that Paul should have written the letter with his own pen. As explained in an earlier number of *The* BIBLE *Today*, scribal composition in ancient times was the task of an amanuensis. Instinctively one conjures up the image of impetuous Paul pacing a room and pouring out a flood of words which his secretary faithfully copies. Some of these copyists, like the more able secretaries of our own day, would have handled the dictation with a certain liberty, correcting and rewording it to produce a more fluent and readable manuscript. The fact that Paul used a scribe is proven by the common practice of his day and by evidence in the epistles themselves (cf. Rom. 16: 22; 1 Cor. 16:21; Col. 4:18; 2 Thess. 3:17). Whether these scribes were mere copyists or careful editors of Paul's dictation, he himself is to be considered the true literary author of the emergent letter.

Such literary authorship cannot be ascribed to him in those other instances which could and probably did occur. In our own day an expert secretary, acting as executive assistant, may write a whole letter from the few thoughts suggested by his or her employer. Reading what has been written, the employer finds his own thoughts expressed far better than he himself could have expressed them; he signs the letter and sends it out as his own. Paul was free to do the same; the striking differences in the literary composition of Colossians and Ephesians suggest to some that he actually used this liberty. The approval of such a letter, however, would not suffice to make Paul the literary author of the composition.

Another distinct possibility is the phenomenon which appears already in the book of Isaiah. A later disciple familiar with the thoughts of the great Apostle might set these forth in a letter written in the literary style and thought-patterns of his own making. Most scholars think that the Epistle to the Hebrews is a work of this kind. Because this letter draws inspiration from the Apostle's themes, it was long considered a unit of the Pauline corpus, just as the composition of Isaiah's disciples (Is. 40-66) was included as part of the prophecy of Isaiah. In this case, however, Paul is not the literary author of the epistle.

When, therefore, scholars study the question of scriptural authorship, they understand the term in its restricted sense. They seek to discover what epistles are the authentic literary composition of Paul, the transcript of his dictation, whether slavishly copied by an amanuensis or freely edited by a competent secretary. Their aim is to sort out the letters in which Paul himself speaks and the letters in which a ghost writer or a later disciple develops in personal composition the themes which were dear to the Apostle.[1]

## Norms for investigating authorship

Today it is obvious that there is no external norm to guide this investigation. The long-standing tradition that Paul is the author of all fourteen epistles has no dogmatic value; it is merely a historical tradition which labors under the weakness of its origin. In the early ages of Christianity, when the world knew nothing of modern scientific precision, the term "author" was ambiguous. It could refer both to the man who actually wrote a book and also to the one who merely sponsored it. Moreover, pseudonymous writing was in vogue. To gain acceptance for his work, a literary author found it convenient to inscribe his book with the name of a more famous man, especially when its themes were closely associated with the great man's fame. With such circumstances surrounding its origin, our historical tradition on the Pauline authorship of the fourteen epistles is an uncertain guide in solving the modern question of strictly literary authorship.

Scholars are forced, therefore, to study the internal structure of the epistles in order to ascertain whether Paul himself wrote them. His name in the superscription of all the epistles except Hebrews is the first indication that he himself authored these letters. The accompanying names of co-workers strengthen this indication, since there would be no need for this insertion if the letters were merely pseudonymous. The fact is, however, that the names of co-workers are omitted both in the suspect pastoral letters and Ephesians and also in the widely accepted letters to the Romans and Galatians. We may say, then, that Paul's name in the superscription is an invitation to begin investigation. It is like a bare mound in the land of Palestine which piques the curiosity of the archeologist and fires him with hope that excavation will uncover the tell of an ancient biblical site.

## Doctrinal content as a test of authorship

The doctrine of an epistle is always its best part. In the question of authorship, however, doctrine is only of secondary importance. The divergent doctrinal emphases which separate 1–2 Thessalonians from Colossians are not

---

[1] The limitation of space does not permit the discussion in this article of the allied question of integrity, i.e., whether each epistle was written as a unified draft or is a collocation of several distinct letters. Many scholars think that Romans, 1-2 Corinthians, and Philippians are a collation of separate letters.

a real argument for diverse authorship. The differences are just as easily explained by the development of Paul's insights. The fact must also be taken into account that in each of his letters he treated those doctrines which best suited the needs of his readers. On the other hand, similarity in doctrine, as in Ephesians and Colossians or in Romans and Galatians, can never be regarded as final proof of identical authorship. A disciple could easily have shared Paul's thoughts and expressed them with the very emphases which the Apostle himself employed. The argument from doctrine, therefore, is valid only when authenticity is supported by other reasons.

When, however, the doctrine of an epistle deals with a situation outside the time and milieu of the Apostle, who died in 67 A. D., this factor creates real doubts about Pauline authorship. Some scholars, therefore, have denied that Paul wrote the pastoral letters on the score that these letters deal with Church institutions which they think arose only after Paul's death.

## Identity tags

It is really the less important elements of an epistle which provide the best clues in solving the problem of authenticity. First among these are revealing details which would hardly find place in a letter unless Paul himself put them there. A pseudonymous writer of Romans would hardly have wasted almost an entire chapter of his epistle (ch. 16) in listing "all the uncles, and the cousins, and the aunts," with pithy greetings to each. This long list of salutations would be meaningful only to those for whom a loving Paul intended this personal remembrance. So, too, the unprecedented inclusion of "bishops and deacons" in the opening salutation of Philippians is difficult to explain except as Paul's graceful way of saying "thank you" to those leaders of the church at Philippi who had authorized the gifts which he greatly appreciated (Phil. 4:16-19). There is also the signature in Paul's own hand at the close of 2 Thessalonians, with the word of warning, "Thus I write" (3:6). This safeguard against forged letters (repeated in 1 Corinthians 16:21) would hardly find place in a letter written by someone else.

## Historical content as a norm

The numerous historical allusions in the Pauline letters are invaluable arguments for proving the Apostle's authorship. The pointedness of these references gives to his letters a historical verisimilitude which would be difficult for anyone but himself to inject. Though it is true that the incidents described or mentioned do not always fit four-square into the historical framework of the Acts of the Apostles, this divergence is easily explained. Luke, as a historian, has a broad canvas to cover; as a sacred historian developing the theme of Christian progress, he writes with a tendentious style and with a freedom to abbreviate and telescope. Paul, on the other hand, uses historical fact as a personal memory to sharpen the doctrinal or apologetic theme which he develops. Hence he is not bound by the perspectives of historical context; if he cites facts or recalls memories he marshals them in line with the theme of his own letter. The divergence between the Lucan narrative in Acts and the corresponding material in Galatians is simply the difference which will always exist between accounts written from a different point of view.

The fact is that history as narrated in Paul's letters is handled so personally by the author that only he who played an intimate role in this history and who now utilizes it for his personal purposes could have composed these portions of the Pauline epistles. This is especially true in the heated argumentation and uniquely personal polemic of Galatians and 2 Corinthians. These letters have their only *raison d'être* as a *moi et toi* dialogue between the founder of a church and his wayward converts. The historical facts with which the author lashes the Galatians are presented with such practical, personal pointedness that they stand out as incidents which only one man could have used in this way — Paul, the founder of the Galatian church, who must now defend his apostleship and his doctrine. In 2 Corinthians it is the same. The writer has his eye on his immediate audience; they have questioned the sincerity and authority of the man who taught them the faith. His epistle to them is so patently a direct answer of a father to the criticisms of his children that the letter loses meaning unless it is seen as a response of the founder of the church at Corinth to the difficulties which had arisen there.

The very framework of 1 Corinthians is built around a series of problems in the Corinthian church: its breakdown in Christian spirit, its moral lapses, its doctrinal queries. Whatever unity is to be found in the letter comes from the author's intention to right a general situation which threatened to go wrong. Only Paul, the founder and father of the church at Corinth, could have dealt so directly, so personally and so authoritatively with these problems. No executive secretary, acting as a ghost writer, could have composed an epistle which evidences such complete familiarity with the soul of Paul, the status of his converts, and their mutual relations. The allusions to historical incidents and situations, and the directness with which the author handles these in this epistle, as also in Galatians, 2 Corinthians, 1–2 Thessalonians, Philippians, and Colossians, are difficult to explain except as the authentic cachet of Pauline authorship.

## Literary style as a norm: its weaknesses

This historical verisimilitude provides the best argument for the authenticity of most of the letters ascribed to Paul. Because of the force of this argument no one has seriously questioned the Pauline authorship of Galatians or 1–2 Corinthians. Many scholars are convinced that the same reason guarantees the authenticity of 1–2 Thessalonians, Philippians, and Colossians. These conclusions, however, must be tested by yet another norm, the literary criterion. Once a man is identified as the author of several epistles, it is to be expected that each of his compositions should show signs of the same literary style.

Some scholars rank this norm as first in importance. Our English investigator, in fact, would reach definitive conclusions solely from his I.B.M. computation of words and word groupings. This preference of the literary criteria to the historical is not warranted. The style and vocabulary of the separate epistles may be the only determinant of authorship in epistles like Ephesians, which shows no historical identity tag. But in letters where the author is involved in a revealing historical situation, the argument from style of writing remains secondary. The argument may corroborate conclusions drawn from history or it may raise doubts. In this latter case, however, the burden of proof rests on the literary critic who would question results based on the historical content of the text.

The reason for this secondary importance of literary norms is obvious. The treatment of different situations and doctrines will inevitably alter an author's vocabulary. Paul, in dealing with the doubts and fears of the Thessalonians about the parousia, will use different words and concepts than when he deals with the problem of nascent Jewish Gnosticism in his letter to the Colossians. The influence of a secretary also has to be taken into account, since he probably was free to correct the language of Paul's dictation and to rephrase it. There is the further fact that every writer, with new experiences and new contacts, tends to change his style, forsaking old ways of expression and old forms of argumentation for new ones. Hence, a mere change of vocabulary and literary style does not conclusively prove that someone besides Paul originally dictated the letter ascribed to him.

## Literary style as a norm: its strength

The literary argument, however, can throw strong doubts on Pauline authorship, especially when the letter itself shows no compelling historical reason why it must be attributed to Paul. The fact that the vocabulary of the pastoral epistles differs greatly from the vocabulary of the generally accepted Pauline letters strengthens the doubts which have already arisen in the minds of some who identify the historical milieu of these letters as late in the first century. So, too, the vocabulary and style of Ephesians are for some a weighty argument against Pauline authorship, since this encyclical letter lacks the counter-balance of significant historical allusion.

On the other hand, the literary argument has strong corroborative value when used to strengthen positions already stabilized by historical reasons. In the generally accepted Pauline letters (1–2 Thessalonians, Galatians, Romans, 1–2 Corinthians, Philippians, Colossians, Philemon) commentators consistently point out elements of literary style which they characterize as typical of Paul. It may be of interest to note some of these.

1. *Paul's use of Scripture.* The Apostle shows a great liberty in his use of the Old Testament. Most often he cites no more than a single verse verbatim. If he delays over scriptural teaching, as in his study of Abraham (Rom. 4), he freely reconstructs the biblical background to drive home his own point of doctrine. In Galatians 4:21-28 he allegorizes the theme of Sarah and Hagar. Such extensive use of Scripture, however, is rare. One of the strongest arguments, therefore, against Paul's authorship of Hebrews is its strikingly diverse use of Scripture.

2. *Imagery in Paul.* Almost all of Paul's comparisons and figures are drawn from the milieu of a city-dweller. He does speak of the "seed" of resurrec-

tion (cf. 1 Cor. 15:35-44) and introduces the olive tree theme in Romans 11:16-24; but his other comparisons are almost all taken from urban life.

3. *Sentence structure.* Time and again the Pauline epistles show the abruptness of oral style. Sentences are left half-finished and are often marred by grammatical error. In such anacolutha, the errors of extemporaneous style, the impetuous flow of oral dictation breaks through.

4. *Thought structure.* This same oral character of the Pauline letters accounts for a certain looseness of construction in developing themes and in tying thoughts together. Paul often interjects a question or formulates an objection to anticipate the mind of his readers. This severs the coherent flow of thought, even though it helps to move the theme forward. Paul writes as one would speak, thus providing another proof that the letters ascribed to him were a transcript of his dictation.

5. *Thought-binders.* The epistles often show, especially in their doctrinal portions, a device of style which Père Lyonnet has called *"pierres d'attente"* (foundation stones for later building). In the earlier part of an epistle Paul anticipates with a phrase or sentence the theme which he will later develop at length. These elements bind the whole treatment into unity and show that the author knew from the beginning of his letter the general course of its development.

6. *Recurring phrases.* The authentic epistles of Paul are also marked by phrases which are often repeated. Some are merely literary expressions, like his *mé genoito* ("far from it!"). Others are richly doctrinal, like his phrase "in Christ Jesus."

## Conclusion

For these reasons the majority of scholars are now convinced that the greater number of epistles attributed to Paul were actually written by him. Few hold the authenticity of Hebrews; the authorship of Ephesians and the pastoral letters is still under debate. Likely the debate will continue for a long time.

# THE BLOOD OF CHRIST IN ST. PAUL'S SOTERIOLOGY

Edward F. Siegman, C.Pp.,S.

When we trace the process of redemption in theology today, we begin with the role of Christ (objective redemption), especially His passion and death.

Published originally in *Proceedings of the Second Precious Blood Study Week* (Rensselaer, Indiana: St. Joseph's College, 1960), pp. 11-35. For full documentation see the original article. The author wishes to express his indebtedness to the studies and class lectures of Father Stanislas Lyonnet, S.J., of the Pontifical Biblical Institute, which are listed in the original publication. Reprinted by permission of the publisher.

Only in recent decades have we begun to take into consideration the Savior's resurrection as an integral part of the redemptive work. Even today thought habits of long standing may account for our passing immediately from the death of Christ to its efficacy in the individual (subjective redemption) through the use of the channels of grace by the individual. To appreciate what St. Paul writes about the saving work of Christ, we must be careful to insert the resurrection into the framework of objective redemption and faith into subjective redemption. Moreover, if we advert to the chronological succession of these aspects of the mystery in the Apostle's awareness (and, to a certain extent, in the consciousness of the primitive Church) we can more readily explain his emphasis upon Christ's resurrection. This, in turn, is necessary to evaluate the role that he assigns to the Blood of the Redeemer in effecting our salvation.

## The Resurrection of Christ

St. Paul's first contact with Jesus was not, like the other Apostles', with the meek and humble Galilean teacher who went about heralding the reign of God and healing men's ills; with the Master who ate and drank with His disciples, who became tired and needed rest and sleep; in short, with the Christ who was like us in all things, sin excepted. It was the glorified Savior on the road to Damascus, the "Son of God in power" (Rom. 1:4), who made the unwilling Paul experience "the power of His resurrection" (Phil. 3:10). So shattering was this power that it made Paul not only a Christian, but also an Apostle, who, though "born out of due time" (1 Cor. 15:8), labored more than the rest because the impelling love of Christ for him left him no alternative (2 Cor. 5:14).

When he wrote 1 Cor. two decades later, he asserted with unmistakable force the salvific power of Christ's resurrection; no resurrection, no redemption, he insists. "If Christ has not risen, then our preaching has been baseless, and your faith also is baseless . . . if Christ has not risen, your faith is ineffectual, you are still in your sins" (15:14, 17). Edgar J. Goodspeed, in the American Translation published by the Chicago University Press, brings out the incisive vigor of the Apostle's statement thus: ". . . if Christ was not raised, there is nothing to our message; there is nothing to our faith either, . . . your faith is a delusion." In Rom. 4:24, 25 he borrows the language of an early baptismal profession of faith when he ascribes redemption to Jesus' death and resurrection as to a single integral action: "(Jesus) . . . was delivered up for our sins, and rose again for our justification." The Angelic Doctor caught the implications of the Hebrew parallelism and explained: "The passion and the resurrection of Christ are the cause of our justification in both its aspects," i.e., remission of sins (negative aspect) as well as infusion of grace (positive aspect) (ST III, q. 56, a. 2, ad 4). Occasionally only the resurrection is mentioned, e.g., in 1 Thess. 1:10, when he reminds his converts of the basic points of doctrine in which he had instructed them:

they "await from heaven Jesus, his (the Father's) Son, whom he raised from the dead, our deliverer from the wrath to come."

This was Paul's faith as it grew out of his initial total surrender to the risen Lord. Obedient to the command to continue on into the city of Damascus where further instructions would be given him, the blinded "chosen instrument" was led by the hand to Ananias for baptism. Ananias explained how this sacrament would enable Paul to die with Christ and rise again, sharing in the Savior's glorious divine life; how by immersion in the baptismal waters he would be cleansed of sin and by emerging from them participate in the life of grace, as we now call it, so that henceforth he would be "in Christ." In Rom. 6:2-5 Paul reminded the Christians of the capital of the Empire of this great experience in words that he must have repeated again and again to his thousands of converts: "How can we who are dead with respect to sin live in sin any longer? You know well enough that all we who have been baptized into Christ Jesus have been baptized into his death. We were, in fact, buried with him by means of baptism into death, in order that just as Christ has risen from the dead to mediate the Father's glory to us, so we also must live and act in the newness that is (divine) life. Since we have been united with him in the likeness of his death, we must remain united with him also in the likeness of his resurrection."

## The Diaspora Jew and the Greek Old Testament

This was Paul's experience of justification, as he often called the process of redemption, especially in its subjective aspect. But the Damascus vision, the instruction received from Ananias, and his baptism were only the beginning. Soon after baptism he must have assisted at the liturgical meeting of the Christians of Damascus and partaken of the Lord's Supper. On this and subsequent occasions when he participated in the liturgy, he listened to the Scriptures being read. How familiar the words were! Paul knew them practically by heart, but the very first time he listened to them in the Christian *ekklesia* and heard them explained in the light of their fulfillment in Christ, he realized that all his life, as a Jewish student and later as a rabbi candidate, he had not really understood them. His condition was that which he described of his countrymen in 2 Cor. 3:14: ". . . their minds were darkened; for to this day, when the Old Testament is read, this same veil remains, for it is only Christ who can remove it." Various charismatics were present, i.e., Christians endowed with special gifts of the Holy Spirit, especially prophets and teachers, who preached, explained the Old Testament christologically, and catechized. Disciples who had listened to Our Lord and witnessed His miracles held the assembled Christians spellbound with their recital of all that they recalled. Especially would the story of Our Lord's passion and death as it followed the institution of the Eucharist move the hearers and inspire them, though most of them had heard it over and over again. By this time it had become stereotyped and had the form that we find in the synoptic gospels. No one, however, listened more attentively and with greater love and

fervor than the former persecutor, the young rabbi who had sat at the feet
of the famous Gamaliel, the Pharisee who had been a fanatic before he became the slave of Christ.

Until now the *Torah*, the Law (the Pentateuch as explained by the rabbis)
had been his very life. By it he had hoped to obtain his salvation. More than
once he must have had serious doubts about the sufficiency of this Law; that
may account for the fierceness with which he tried to destroy those who said
openly that the Law was now fulfilled in Christ and no longer had binding
force. But now that he had been vanquished by the despised Galilean, now
that he understood the profound mystery of Christ's death and resurrection,
now that he had made these mysteries his own by baptism, his life was no
longer the Law, but Christ. The vision of Christ on the cross was a picture
that would never be effaced, it was his daily meditation, his hourly preoccupation: "With Christ I am nailed to the cross. It is now no longer I that
live, but Christ lives in me. And the life that I now live in the flesh, I live by
faith in the Son of God, who loved me and gave himself up for me" (Gal. 2:
20). Once having seen this by faith, Paul could not understand how anyone could still regard the Mosaic Law as necessary for salvation and minimize
the efficacy of Christ's sacrifice, as long as he had the same experience of
union with Christ that he had; only some species of black magic could therefore account for the deplorable return of the Galatian Christians to Jewish
practices: "O senseless Galatians! who has bewitched you, before whose eyes
Jesus Christ has been depicted crucified? . . . For if justice is by the Law,
then Christ died in vain" (Gal. 3:1; 2:21).

During his long retreat in the Syro-Arabian desert, east of Damascus, Paul
had ample time to meditate upon all that he had experienced and heard
about the crucified Messiah whom he had seen in glory.[1] Paul wrote his letters in Greek, because he was above all the Apostle of the Gentiles. The
Jewish members of the churches he established — all in the Diaspora —
likewise knew Greek far better than Hebrew, if they knew Hebrew at all.
We have no way of knowing to what extent Paul had been formally educated
in Hellenistic culture. From his epistles a number of scholars are inclined
to conclude that his formal non-Jewish education was minimal. Whatever
Greek background that is found in his letters a man as alert and intelligent
as Paul could easily have assimilated from his environment and numerous
contacts.

In any case, Paul was a Jew. His book was the Old Testament, which he
knew thoroughly in Hebrew as well as in the Greek translation used in the
Diaspora, the Septuagint. His rabbinic training made him conversant with

---

[1] Gal. 1:17-18 states that Paul retired to Arabia shortly after his conversion, returned
to Damascus, and then "after three years" went to Jerusalem. It is generally thought that
by Arabia the Apostle meant the Nabatean Kingdom east and south of Palestine. Perhaps
he lived in the Syro-Arabian Desert, or in some city like Petra. Three years, according to
Hebrew calculation, could be three full years, or as little as one full year and parts of the
preceding and following years. Paul's conversion took place c. 34-36 A.D. (few scholars
place it earlier), the first visit to Jerusalem after his conversion, c. 37-39.

the oral traditions of Israel's teachers and with their method of interpreting Scripture. As Paul reflected upon the truths which he had recently learned, especially as he pondered deeply over the deeds of Our Lord, most of all His passion, death, and resurrection, he spontaneously, yet with ever deeper penetration, saw them as the fulfillment and perfection of what Yahweh had said and done through His prophets and other faithful mediators in the Old Testament. In other words, he constructed, step by step, his theology in the terms and thought-categories of the Bible. When he expressed this theology and explained it in Greek — generally piecemeal, as he dealt with particular situations, and not as a continuous development — he used the words as they were used in the Septuagint, and not, ordinarily, with the specific meaning that these terms might have in current writers with Greek background and culture.

Elementary as this principle is, its neglect has accounted for many a false interpretation of Paul's statements. To cite a few obvious examples relevant to the present topic: the Greek verb that we translate "justify" is often used by contemporary writers in a forensic sense of a sentence of acquittal, the external pronouncement that the person is innocent of the crime of which he is accused. Had St. Paul used the term in this way, he would mean by justification little more than an external imputation of innocence. The noun in Greek translated "justice" means the familiar virtue that prompts us to give everyone his due. If this is what Paul meant when he states that the justice of God was manifested in the redemptive death of Christ (Rom. 3:21, 25-26), then those exegetes are right who understand the Apostle to mean that God exacted condign satisfaction for sin. But in his theology of justice, Paul by-passed both his rabbinic theology, which seemed to regard virtuous deeds as practically obliging God toward the doer, and Greek conceptions, and went back to the OT, especially Deutero-Isaiah, for whom justice is preeminently God's *saving* justice, a justice that guaranteed all the blessings He promised Israel in virtue of the covenant. Similarly, the verb "justify" "make just" means to give victory over enemies, to make pleasing to God, hence, to cause one to pass from the condition of enmity to friendship with God, hence a real change in the justified person's internal state.

To us "redemption" suggests paying a ransom price; in this we are in line with the meaning of the Greek verb that "redeem" or "redemption" ordinarily translates. This Greek verb is derived from a noun meaning "ransom," the price paid to buy freedom for a slave or captive. But the Hebrew term which the Septuagint translated with this verb and related terms does not necessarily imply the payment of a purchase price. Its basic meaning is the intervention of Yahweh in carrying out the duties of the *go'el*, the nearest of kin, who, in Hebrew law, had obligations toward the persons and property of his relatives, such as blood vengeance, or securing their freedom if they were enslaved, or purchasing property which poverty may have forced the relatives to sell, in order that this endangered property might remain within the clan. The Hebrew was conscious of Yahweh's being his nearest relative,

his blood-brother, his *go'el*, as a result of the Sinai Covenant. But when Yahweh intervened as *go'el*, he did so simply by an exercise of His irresistible
power. Inconceivable that He should pay a ransom price to Pharoah or to
the King of Babylon!

The Greek noun which is often rendered "propitiation," e.g., by our CCD
revision, suggests, when it is used of God, the pagan notion of placating an
angered god by sacrifice or votive offerings. The Hebrew terms translated in
the Septuagint by this Greek noun and related verb never have God as their
object. The context makes clear in practically every case that there is simply
question of removing disability, especially sin, by purification and thus making fit for reunion with God. Accordingly, in Rom. 3:25, when Paul states
that God has "set forth Christ as a propitiation by his blood," he means that
Christ's Blood was the means God used to purify us from sin and reunite
us to Himself. There is no reason to believe that Paul thought of God's being
appeased or placated by the Blood of His Son; *at-one-ment* in its etymological
sense reproduces what Paul means far better than the word propitiation.

## The life is (in) the blood

When Paul reflected that Jesus changed the wine into His own Blood at the
Last Supper, that He shed it first when He was circumcised, and that beginning with the bloody sweat and continuing through the buffeting, the horrible
scourging and crowning, the inhuman crucifixion, until finally the thrust of
the soldier's spear drained it to the last drop, the Apostle recognized without
difficulty the sacrificial value of the Blood, its power to purify from sin as
well as to reconcile mankind to God. "There is no atonement except by
blood," was a rabbinic axiom with which he was familiar. This rabbinic
axiom developed the principle of Lev. 17:11: "Since the life of a living body
is in its blood, I have made you put it on the altar, so that atonement may
thereby be made for your own lives, because it is the blood, as the seat of
life, that makes atonement." Paul could easily argue that the Blood of the
God-Man is divine, infinite life, and hence when Christ poured it on the altar of the cross to give it to His Father, He effected what the blood of the
OT sacrifices could only foreshadow: He purified mankind from sin and put
them once more "at-one" with His Father from whom they had been wholly
estranged.

At this point it must be emphasized that for the Hebrew blood did not signify death, but rather life. There is, moreover, no teaching in the OT that
would have us regard the sacrificial victims as a substitute for the offerer,
who might by vicarious substitution cause the victim to give its life for the
life of the offerer, who had forfeited his life by sin. "I take no pleasure in
the death of the wicked," Yahweh said through Ezekiel (33:11), "but rather
in this, that the wicked man convert from his way and live." Similarly, the
author of Wis. assures us that "God did not make death, nor does he rejoice
in the destruction of the living" (1:13). The scapegoat, upon which the sins
of the Israelites were laid through confession and imposition of the high

priest's hands, is no exception, since the goat was not sacrificed, it was sent into the desert, the supposed dwelling-place of demons, "to carry off their iniquities to an isolated region" (Lev. 16:22).

Preservation from harm in the case of the blood of the paschal lamb, purification from defilement in the case of most of the OT sacrifices, union with Yahweh by means of sharing in life in the case of practically all the sacrifices, especially the Covenant sacrifice of Sinai (Exod. 24:8) and the so called "peace offerings" ("communion sacrifices" is the more descriptive rendition), these were the functions of blood with which Paul was familiar, thanks to his OT and rabbinic background.

But how could the sacrificial shedding of the Savior's Blood be beneficial to us, if He was not our substitute, if vicarious satisfaction was not essential to the sacrificial theology of the OT? We may answer: not substitution, but a form of *identification* made possible the redemption of mankind by the sacrifice of Christ. The OT conception of *corporate personality* facilitated for the Hebrew theologian the transition from the act of Christ to its efficacy for the individual. The OT calls the father of the human race *Adam*, which means mankind, because he was mankind *in germine*. When Gn. speaks of Israel, or Moab, or Edom, it is not always easy to decide whether the individual is meant or the clan that took its name from the respective eponymous ancestor. Again, the king is a corporate personality. In the desert, at the Sinai Covenant, the Hebrew people became Yahweh's special possession, a relationship so close that Yahweh calls the nation His son (Exod. 4:22; 19:5). Later on, when the tribes chose a king to rule and lead them in battle, the king was the corporate personality of the people, and as such he is called Yahweh's son, begotten, as it were, on the day of his enthronement (Ps. 2:7). Both the OT prophetic characters with whom Our Lord identified Himself in order gradually to reveal His messianic kingship, the Son of Man in Dan. 7, and the Suffering Servant of Yahweh (Is. 42:1-9; 49:1-6; 50:4-11; 52:13–53:12), were corporate personalities, i.e., both were individuals (the Messiah), yet described in such a way as to suggest that each stands for the people of God. Accordingly, Paul would reflect that when Christ suffered and died, when He shed His Blood in release of divine life, when He rose from the dead to return to the Father, we suffered and died with Him; we rose from the dead to return to the Father. This truth he formulates in so many words: "The love of Christ (for us) urges us on (in our apostolic labors), because we have come to the conclusion that, since One died for all, therefore all died; further, that Christ died for all, in order that they who are alive may live no longer for themselves, but for Him who died for them and rose again" (2 Cor. 5:14-15). Our oneness with Christ in His resurrection, implicit in the text just quoted, is spelled out in Eph. 2:4-6: "God, who is rich in mercy, by reason of His immense love for us, even when we were dead because of our sins, brought us to life together with Christ . . . and raised us up together, and seated us together in heaven in Christ Jesus. . . ."

What the OT worshipper expressed, therefore, when he placed his hand on the sacrificial victim in order to identify himself with it, so that he might be one with the blood given to Yahweh, and further — in the case of the holocaust — ascend with the victim reduced to smoke even to the throne of Yahweh, this will-act of religion was finally "fulfilled," "accomplished," brought to full perfection and realization in the sacrifice of Christ. This conclusion underlies Paul's references to the redemptive death of the Savior. The Son of God took on our human condition; He became solidary with us, so that He might return us to God, when He himself returned to the Father through the port of entry, death, which had become such ever since the first Adam's sin. Mankind had to be returned to God because sin had estranged all men and made them enemies of God: the sin inherited from Adam, ratified by the personal sins of the individual (Rom. 5:12-14). But since sin is formally in the will, since it is rebellion against God and therefore aversion or hatred, Christ reversed this estrangement by perfect obedience and infinite love, expressed in His willingness to accept that which was most human in us, i.e., death, and further, a death unsurpassed in Jewish eyes for degradation and pain, crucifixion. In Christ, then, we like the Prodigal Son or the Lost Sheep were returned to the Father: we achieved what the OT worshipper could only vaguely desire, identification with his sacrifice as it was given to God.

These are the salient points in the rich theological background of Paul which will enable us to understand better his references to the Blood of the Savior in his epistles.

## The Eucharist

St. Paul teaches that the Eucharist is the one supreme sacrifice of the New Covenant which fulfilled what the OT sacrifices prepared for; that it inaugurated the New Covenant by means of Christ's Blood; and finally that it was a vivid foretaste of the heavenly banquet of beatific vision and union with Christ to be enjoyed at the Savior's second coming. This does not mean that the Apostle's comments on the Eucharist are his personal development, at least *in toto*. His allusions and references to this teaching are quite incidental and assume that the doctrine of the Eucharist is well-known and can serve as illustration for other points of doctrine; it is the sacred tradition handed down from the very beginning through the Apostles.

When he warned the Christians of Corinth against possible contamination by partaking of foods that had been offered in pagan temples (whenever this eating would really appear to be sacrificial), he appealed to the analogy of the Christian sacrifice in which is truly realized union with our God, Who is Christ: something which the pagan by his sacrifices hoped to attain, but all in vain, since his gods did not exist; instead, since the devils foster this worship, whatever union is effected is effected with the devils: "The cup of blessing that we consecrate, is it not the sharing of the blood of Christ? And the bread that we break, is it not the partaking of the body of the Lord? Consider Israel according to the flesh: are not they who eat of the sacrifices partakers of the altar? I do not mean to imply that what is sacrificed to idols is anything, or that an idol is anything. I say that what the Gentiles sacrifice, 'they sacrifice to devils and not to God'; and I would not have you become associates of devils" (1 Cor. 10:16-20; cf. Deut. 32:17). How much more privileged than the Israelite is the Christian who may actually drink of the Blood of Christ, and thus be united with the Lord in intimacy undreamed of by the OT worshipper who (through the priest) poured the blood on the altar, or, at best, was sprinkled with it. This sacrifice is the New Passover, as the Apostle suggests when he calls the cup to be consecrated the "cup of blessing," the name given in the Passover ritual to the third cup of wine drunk at the Paschal Supper, the cup most probably over which Our Lord pronounced the words of consecration.

Later on in the same epistle, in order to impress upon his readers the unseemliness of their conduct at the agape, the common meal which early Christians took before the celebration of the Eucharist in order to foster charity, Paul reminded them of the close connection between the two. Unbecoming and selfish behavior at the agape is an affront to Christ Himself, because it disregards the real presence and even more loses sight of the fact that the Eucharist is the re-enactment of His supreme sacrifice of love. Accordingly, Paul recalled the moving scene of the institution as he had received it from the sacred tradition which went back to Christ and as he in turn handed it on to the Corinthians when he first prepared them for participation in it: " . . . how the Lord Jesus, on the very night in which he was betrayed, took bread, and giving thanks, broke it and said:'This is my body which is (offered sacrificially) on your behalf; do this in remembrance of me.' So also the cup, after he had eaten the (Paschal) supper, saying, 'This cup is the new covenant in my blood; as often as you drink it, do this in remembrance of me. For as often as you shall eat this bread and drink the cup, you proclaim the death of the Lord, until he comes.' Therefore whoever eats this bread or drinks the cup of the Lord unworthily will be guilty of (an offense against) the body and the blood of the Lord" (1 Cor. 11:25-27).

Which formula of institution comes closer to that actually used by Our Lord, that given by St. Paul and St. Luke on the one hand, or that given by St. Mark? Mark's wording is simpler, "This is my blood of the covenant" (14:24), and so there is a strong presumption for its originality. Some scholars, however, believe that the tradition given by Mark represents a simplification of what Our Lord said. In any case, both reproduce liturgical wordings as used in different parts of the early Church, and both express the identical thought. It is certain that Our Lord referred by his mention of covenant to the words of Moses, as he sprinkled the sacrificial blood on the people and the altar to seal the covenant that made Yahweh and Israel blood brothers: "This is the blood of the covenant which Yahweh has made with you" (Exod. 24:8). Both Paul's and Mark's formulae mean: "Just as the Old Covenant was inaugurated by the shedding of blood which brought about or symbolized union of life, so also My Blood, shed mystically here in the Cenacle, shed really on Calvary, seals the New Covenant which enables all partakers to become my blood brothers and sisters, to be united with me in this sacrament and sacrifice, a prelude to perfect union in the next life."

### Bought with a price, 1 Cor. 6:19-20; 7:22-23

Two other texts in 1 Cor. refer to Christ's Blood as the instrument by which we have been made His own in the New Covenant. In a warning against the degradation of the vice of impurity, the Apostle asks: "Do you not realize that your members are the temple of the Holy Spirit, who is in you, whom you have from God, and that you are not your own? For you have been bought with a great price" (6:19-20). Certainly the "great price" is the Blood of Christ. In the next chapter, the same motivation is given for not permitting ourselves to be enslaved in any way by human masters: "A slave who has been called in the Lord is a freedman of the Lord; just as a freedman who has been called is a slave of Christ. You have been bought with a price; do not become the slaves of men" (7:22-23).

The terminology seems to be that of a contract of sale: Christ bought us for himself by paying a high price, His own Blood, for our souls which had been enslaved by Satan. But since the price could not have been paid to Satan, some scholars think that Paul may allude to a practice of his time, sacred manumission, a device by which a slave might buy his freedom by depositing in a sanctuary the price demanded. The priests of the sanctuary arranged for the devotee's purchase and technically he became the property of the god to which the sanctuary was dedicated. It is quite possible that some of the Christians at Corinth had obtained their freedom in this way before their conversion. But they might well have regarded the analogy as far fetched, had they suspected the allusion. In their own case, they would have recalled, it was they who painfully had to scrape together the ransom price. Moreover, despite the religious fiction involved, the price eventually was paid to their master.

At least to a Jew, the allusion that would have spontaneously come to mind by a reference in a religious context to freedom from slavery would be the Passover redemption of Yahweh. David Daube (*The NT and Rabbinic Judaism*, p. 282) has an instructive chapter on the notion of redemption in the OT and in rabbinic literature, in which he shows how this Pauline notion of "change of master" is rooted in the language of the liberation from Egypt and the transfer of masters: slaves of Pharaoh hitherto, henceforth they are slaves of Yahweh. But Yahweh redeemed them by His omnipotent power, not by paying a price. In 1 Cor. the price is mentioned by analogy: bought suggests price. But just as in the OT no price was paid except the deploying of Yahweh's mighty right arm, so in the New Covenant the only price in question is the life-Blood of the Son of God, infinite in value and power. But again, the price does not mean a contract of sale; it points to an intervention as gratuitous as that of Yahweh "redeeming" His people from Egypt and from Babylon.

The well-known hymn of Ap confirms this interpretation of Paul's language: "Worthy art thou to take the scroll and to open its seals, for thou wast slain, and has *bought* (CCD has "redeemed," based on the Vg *redemisti*, which correctly interprets the Greek) us for God with thy blood, out of every tribe and tongue and people and nation, and made them for our God a kingdom and priests, and they shall reign over the earth" (5:9-10). The verb is the same as in 1 Cor. 6:20; 7:23, "bought." In Ap, however, the references to the covenant are clear, and to the two-fold aspect of Yahweh's redemption: negative, liberation from Egypt; and positive, making Israel His special people, a kingdom of priests. "You have seen for yourselves how I treated the Egyptians and how I bore you up on eagle wings and brought you here to myself. Therefore, if you hearken to my voice and keep my covenant, you shall be my special possession, dearer to me than all other people, though all the earth is mine. You shall be a kingdom of priests, a holy nation" (Exod. 19:4-6). Since the Ap text, even though it uses the term "bought," must be understood in the light of the OT, there is a strong presumption that Paul's passing references have the same meaning. Hence, he would be thinking in Covenant terms: Yahweh by His great intervention as *go'el* transferred Israel from his master Pharaoh to the master Yahweh, and made them His own, His blood-brothers through the Covenant sacrifices. This action is brought to its ultimate perfection in the redemption wrought by the Blood of Christ, through which we are transferred from the slavery of sin and Satan to the sweet servitude of Christ.

A parallel to these texts is found in the Apostle's admonition to the clergy of Ephesus, as recorded in Acts 20:28. Paul reminds them that the presbyters have been placed over the Church by the Holy Spirit, the "church of God (the Father) which He has acquired for Himself (*peripoiesato*) by the blood of His Own (Son)." The thought is the same as the Ap text, since "church of God" is an alternate phrase for "kingdom of priests" and "holy nation" in the OT to designate Israel as the Covenant people (see Deut. 4:9-13; 23:1-8; 9:10; 18:16; 31:30; Exod. 12:16; Lev. 23:2-44; Num. 28:25) (according to the Greek). In this text as in the others, it is the Blood of Christ that frees from the bondage of sin and makes the Christian the special possession of God, either as an individual or as a member of the Church.

## At-one-ment, Rom. 3:21-26; 5:9

If there is any text that may be regarded as the Apostle's thesis on redemption by the Blood of Christ, it is Rom. 3:21-26. The pericope is the transition from the first to the second section of the epistle. In 1:16-17 Paul had stated his purpose, namely, to show that the Gospel, the good news of salvation brought by Christ, is not simply a body of truths to be accepted intellectually or a theoretical system of ethics; it is the very "power of God destined to bring salvation to everyone who believes, to Jew first and then to Greek." In this Gospel the "(salvific) justice of God is revealed," i.e., made known in the Hebrew sense of an existential experience, "from faith to faith," i.e., wholly by faith, or, as Dodd translates, "faith first and last," the faith

which means a total commitment of oneself to this gospel. Opposed to and
partially contemporary with this revelation of God's salvific justice, however,
is another "revelation": ". . . the wrath of God is revealed from heaven
against all ungodliness . . . ." This means that a process or reprobation is
also at work, among both Gentiles who have the natural law, and among Jews
who have the revealed law. "All have sinned and have need of the glory of
God" (3:23) summarizes this condition of mankind; it occurs in the midst
of the transitional paragraph, which tells how justification can be and is obtained.

> But now the (salvific) justice of God has been made manifest independ-
> ently of the Law, although it is attested by the Law and the Prophets
> (since both speak of justification by faith, cf. Gen. 17:5ff; Heb. 2:4); (I
> mean) the (salvific) justice of God (received) by faith by all who believe.
> There is no distinction (between Jews and Gentiles in this matter), as all
> have sinned and have need of the glory of God (i.e., His presence and pow-
> er, which banish sin and restore friendship with Him). They are justified
> freely by his grace (i.e., transferred from the condition of sin to friendship
> with God, thanks to his bounteous, gratuitous mercy) through the redemp-
> tion (effected by, and when accepted, resulting in incorporation) in Christ
> Jesus, whom God has set forth as a (means of) at-one-ment by his blood
> (release of divine life that brings men back to God, if applied) through
> faith. (This results in the) manifesting of the (salvific) justice of God, who
> (formerly) in his patient forbearance (partially, and by way of type or
> figure) remitted sins (through sacrifices and other OT rites). (Thus He
> prepared) to (fully) manifest his (salvific) justice at the present time, so
> that (all realize that) He himself is just and makes just everyone who has
> faith in Jesus" (Rom. 3:21-26).

The Greek term here translated by "at-one-ment" was used by the Greek
translators of the Hebrew OT (Septuagint) to render *kapporet*, the gold cov-
ering of the ark of the covenant (translated "propitiatory" in the CCD OT).
From Exod. 25:22 it is clear that here Yahweh was particularly close to His
people: since the ark was His footstool, the *kapporet* must have been His
throne: "There I will meet you, and there, from above the propitiatory (*kapporet*), between the two cherubim on the Ark of the Commandments, I will
tell you all the commands that I wish to give the Israelites."

Blood played an important role in purifying the *kapporet* on the Day of
Atonement (*Yom Kippurim*). Even the sanctuary and the holy of holies and
their furniture needed purification, because, according to Hebrew conceptions, people were solidary with the land on which they lived and everything in the land. Hence, the people's sins contaminated not only themselves
personally, but everything with which they had contact. If, then, the very
place where Yahweh was closest to His people was defiled, it would stand
most in need of purification so that contact with Him might be re-established.
On Yom Kippurim the high priest had to sacrifice a bullock as a sin offering
for himself and his family. Among other ceremonies, he was to take some of
its blood and "sprinkle it with his finger on the fore part of the propitiatory
(*kapporet*) and likewise sprinkle some of the blood with his finger seven

times in front of the propitiatory" (Lev. 16:14). Similarly, he sacrificed a goat as a sin offering for the people, sprinkling its blood also on the fore part and in front of the *kapporet*. The rubrics conclude: "Thus he shall make atonement for the sanctuary because of all the sinful defilements and faults of the Israelites" (16:16). After like rites prescribed for the Meeting Tent, the same explanation is given: "Thus he shall render it clean and holy, purged of the defilements of the Israelites" (16:19). Evidently, these sprinklings with blood had for their purpose to purify thoroughly this place where the people had most intimate access to Yahweh through their high priest.

In Rom. 3:21-26, therefore, Paul's reference to the *kapporet* conveys this thought: mankind is closest to God in the person of Christ. He is our means of at-one-ment with the Father. But sin stood in the way; it separated us from God and estranged us from Him. This sin patently could not defile the Incarnate Son of God, although the Apostle states that the Father sent "his Son in the likeness of the flesh, (the instrument) of sin as a sin offering, and thus condemned sin in the flesh" (Rom. 8:3). And how was this sin to be removed? "There is no remission except by blood!" was an axiom that needed no proof for a Jewish theologian. But what blood? Paul knew since his conversion that the blood of the OT victims was only preparatory, it effected only an imperfect, token remission. But the Blood of Christ is divine, since it is the Blood of God's Son; it is divine life released, and so its powers of cleansing are in no wise restricted. Thus Paul teaches that what the rites of Yom Kippurim could only foreshadow was realized by Christ, our at-one-ment, and that by His own Blood.

The Apostle refers back to this pericope in Rom. 5:9. The intervening chapter developed the thesis that we apply the efficacy of the divine Blood to ourselves by faith. This justification is, it is true, not yet the perfection of salvation, which will come only at the parousia, the second coming of Christ (and, *positis ponendis*, with the death of each individual). But if God has done so much for us while we were still sinners, enemies of His, now that we are His friends, reconciled to Him, have we not reason to be confident that He will carry through our justification to the fullness of salvation: "But God proves his love for us, because when as yet we were sinners, Christ died for us. Much more now that we are justified by his blood, shall we be saved through him from the wrath," i.e., from final reprobation (5:8-9). The implication is that the Blood of the Savior not only brings us to first justification (as theologians now distinguish our first reception of sanctifying grace), but it also effects second justification, and accounts for what the Council of Trent calls "the great gift of perseverance" (*magnum illud usque in finem perseverantiae donum: DB* 826).

## Universal efficacy of the Blood, Col. 1:20; Eph. 1:7;2:11-14

The efficacy of the Savior's Blood is not restricted to men. Paul knows of no limitation: all creation is affected by the redemption through the divine Blood, including even the angels. In the magnificent hymn which celebrates the universal headship of Christ, Paul makes this extension for the first time:

"It has pleased God the Father that in him (Christ) all his fullness (i.e., the fullness of divinity, but in a dynamic sense: the divinity which Christ receives to communicate to men) should dwell, and that through him he (the Father) should reconcile to himself all things, whether on the earth or in the heavens, making peace through the blood of his cross" (Col. 1:20).

This hymn has interesting points of contact with the Jewish liturgy for the Feast of Tents, with which are closely associated the New Year and Yom Kippurim. Allusions to creation and to the last judgment in the liturgical texts of the three feasts suggest the background for the Apostle's development. Especially significant is the designation of Yahweh as the peacemaker "on high, Who makes peace upon us and upon all Israel." What the Jew prayed for on the Great Day of Atonement, therefore, has actually been effected by the Blood of Christ and that in absolute universality.

Eph. 1:7 recalls in passing, that "in him (Christ) we have redemption through his blood," specifying by mentioning the negative aspect of redemption, "the remission of sin." In c. 2 Paul, when explaining that the Gentiles have been included in God's plan of salvation, identified the Blood as the instrument whereby they have been brought to God. The pericope is parallel to Col. 1:20 in part: "Bear in mind that formerly you, Gentiles in flesh, who are called 'uncircumcision' with respect to the so-called 'circumcision' in flesh made by human hand — bear in mind that you were at that time without Christ, excluded as aliens from the community of Israel and strangers to the covenants (full) of promise; without hope, and without God in the world. But now you are in Christ Jesus, you who were once afar off, having been brought near (cf. Is. 57:19) through the blood of Christ. For he himself is our peace, he it is who has made both (i.e., the heavenly and the earthly spheres) one, and has broken down the barrier formed by the dividing wall, the enmity, in his flesh" (Eph. 2:11-14).

Not all points in these passages are explained uniformly by exegetes; they are still the object of study which results in differing interpretations. How Paul can speak of the angels' being reconciled to God through Christ has especially puzzled theologians. From our present state of knowledge, it seems that Paul's language is influenced by his intention to counteract the excessive role attached to their mediation by some Judaizing teachers. Probably his polemic against the Law, which Judaism spoke of as given through angels (Gal. 3:19), accounts for his speaking as if the angels were hostile. His thought might be paraphrased as follows: If you say that the Law must be observed because it is given by angels, I reply that the Law has been abrogated, their mediation done away with, and so they are brought into the Christian scheme of things!

What must be emphasized, however, is that in Paul's thought Christ is the very center of union of the entire universe, human and angelic, rational and irrational. He is first in God's plan, and all things are to return to God through Christ, just as they have come into being through Christ: ". . . there is only one God, the Father, from whom are all things, and we (are to return) to him; and one Lord, Jesus Christ, through whom are all things, and we through him (return to the Father)" (1 Cor. 8:6). Sin disturbed the original harmony of the universe, and while it affected only men and angels directly, it indirectly wrought havoc on all creation (Rom. 8:19-22). In the incarnation Christ breaks through the barriers that separate men from God — however you wish to picture those barriers with concrete images — and through the human nature He assumed became solidary with mankind. As our corporate personality He offered the sacrifice, the essential aspect of which is the shedding of Blood, which blotted out sin and reinstated us with God. The reconciliation thus effected will be perfect only at the end of time, and patiently implies a change in man, not in God.

## Summary and conclusion

St. Paul understood the function of Christ's Blood in the one supreme sacrifice of the New Law in the light of OT thought patterns. In the OT sacrifices blood signified life released and effected purification and union with God. So also the Blood of Christ, which fulfills and perfectly actualizes what the OT sacrifices could only foreshadow.

*Negatively*, we have seen that there is little, if any, basis in the Bible for a theology of redemption based on a theory of juridical compensation, vicarious substitution, meritorious causality, or propitiation. Not that speculation along these lines is condemned or rejected. Revelation is something living; while it contains mysteries that defy our adequate comprehension, they can grow in clarity in the light of the Church's reflection and experience and the study of theologians in categories other than the biblical. We should not, however, attribute to St. Paul, or the inspired authors of the Bible in general, reconstructions like the following: Sin is an infinite offense against God. He could have arranged for its expiation in various ways, or freely condoned it. However, He chose to demand strict justice and required infinite compensation, which only a divine person could make. And so Christ as man suffered vicariously for us and paid the Father the infinite price of His own Blood. Or again, the Father could only condemn mankind for all eternity because of sin. But Christ offered the Father expiation of infinite value, and thus appeased His Father who accepted this more than adequate reparation.

*Positively*, we have seen that for St. Paul blood is life released and must always be given to God. The smoke of the burnt offerings, especially the holocaust, by which the volatilized offering seemed to ascend totally to God, symbolized return to God, since the offerer by the imposition of the hand identified himself with the victim. Among the Hebrews, however, blood was the essential element. Others might immolate the victim — and this function was ordinarily entrusted to subordinate ministers — but the splashing of the blood on the altar, i.e., giving it to Yahweh, was reserved to the officiating priests. It did not symbolize death, even though this release of life which it did symbolize was conditioned upon the death of the victim.

The Blood of Christ also presupposed His death. But this death was the expression of infinite love and obedience, which could find its terminus only in reunion with the beloved. The complete sacrifice of Christ, then, in which we are solidary with Him, is death and resurrection. Essential to both is the Blood, which is poured forth in death and as life ascends to God to Whom alone it belongs.

# REDEMPTION THROUGH DEATH AND RESURRECTION

Stanislas Lyonnet, S.J.

St. Paul could not conceive of Christ as savior and redeemer independently of the resurrection. If proof of this be needed, it may be found in chapter 15 of the first epistle to the Corinthians: "If Christ has not risen, your faith is vain" (v. 17). Paul does not say merely that if Christ had not risen the Corinthians would lack sufficient motive to believe in Him. He affirms rather that without the resurrection faith would lack a real object.

The very adjective he uses indicates that such faith would be worse than merely empty; it would be *mataia* — deceitful and illusory. That is why Paul adds, "In that case you are still in your sins" (v. 17). Père Spicq's comment on St. Paul's thought is directly to the point:

> If Christ has not risen, faith is sterile, and the faithful are still in their sins. In other words there has been no redemption or eternal salvation. The Gospel message is empty of all content . . . Redemption and resurrection are intrinsically united. We cannot emphasize too much this central doctrine of Pauline theory.

This bond between redemption and resurrection is more clearly affirmed in v. 45 of the same chapter of First Corinthians, where St. Paul declares that through resurrection Christ, the new Adam, has become "a life-giving spirit." Certainly this does not mean that the second person of the Blessed Trinity has become the third person. It means rather that through resurrection the humanity of Christ has passed from a carnal state to a spiritual state — a heavenly state, indeed, in which He can confer life upon all men by communicating to them His Holy Spirit.

This doctrine appears to find decisive confirmation in the well-known text with which Paul opens the epistle to the Romans. He announces that his gospel centers in the Son of God "who came from the line of David according to human origin and who by His resurrection was constituted Son of God

Published originally in *Worship*, 35 (1961), 281-87. Reprinted by permission of the publisher.

with all the power which belongs to Him as a sanctifying Spirit" (Rom. 1: 3-4). These words take on special importance from the fact that they are drawn from a very early creed or confession of faith. Such derivation makes the formula a convincing credential to guarantee Paul's person and doctrine before the Church of Rome.

In this text St. Paul declares that Christ, the Son of God from all eternity, has become one of us through His birth as a son of David. But what a contrast there is between His piteous lot as a human being and the glory that will be His after the resurrection. Then it is that He will be enthroned as the messianic Son of God to carry out His work as savior. For this He has been endowed with power through the very resurrection which made Him a "life-giving spirit."

An authentic commentary on these verses, so rich with doctrine, is found in a sermon which St. Luke places on the lips of St. Paul in chapter 13 of Acts. After recalling noteworthy events in Jesus' life, the author underlines the importance of the resurrection. He sees in it the fulfilment of the messianic prophecy, "You are my son; this day I have begotten thee" (Ps. 2:7).

Christ, therefore, is "constituted Son of God" by His resurrection. This statement does not imply that now for the first time Christ becomes "Son of God" in the depths of His being. He was always God's Son in that sense (cf. Rom. 1:3). The meaning is rather that Christ's sonship is now seen in relation to us; through resurrection He becomes capable of sharing His sonship with us. This is the meaning which the Fathers have found in this text. St. Cyril of Alexandria writes, "He is the Son through whom we also become sons and through whose Spirit we can cry out, 'Abba, Father!' "

Affirmations like these are easily adapted to any system in which resurrection is assigned an all-important role among the redeeming acts of God (objective redemption). Such, for instance, is the system of St. Thomas who treats the humanity of Christ as an instrument of the divinity both in death and in glory.

St. Paul, however, was not familiar with the philosophic concept of instrumental cause. If therefore we wish to represent his concept of the redemptive work of Christ, I think we can safely do so with the help of the following image which is completely based on scriptural concepts which were familiar to him.

St. Paul appears to us to represent the redemptive work of Christ as the return of humanity to God from whom sin has separated it. In dying and rising again Christ was the first to achieve this return as the representative of all men (cf. 1 Cor. 15:20); this is *objective* redemption. Each Christian follows in turn, dying and rising with Christ in baptism (cf. Rom. 6:3-4); this is *subjective* redemption.

The sin of Adam had separated mankind forever from God its Father. As time went on, this gap was bound to widen more and more. To express this absolute separation between God and man, the Bible speaks metaphorically of man lying under the "wrath of God." This "wrath" will be fully revealed at the last judgment when man becomes fixed in his rebellion. But even in this life the "wrath" appears in the rift which widens with the multiplication of sin (cf. Rom. 1:18ff).

Prompted by supreme love God decides to save mankind and to lead it back to Himself. Of all possible means He chooses the way which testifies best to His great love and respect for man. He desires that, in a certain sense, man should save himself by returning personally to the Father. God, therefore, sends His own Son to become one of us. Without assuming the guilt of our sins, He takes on Himself our condition as sinners. Like us, He becomes a prodigal son and a lost sheep, in order that He may be the first one to return to the Father. This Pauline theme is expressed by St. John with a play on the word "Passover": "He passes from this world to the Father" (John 13:1).

Man's return to God is not accomplished by legal make-believe, nor by reparation in the merely moral order. Instead, Christ physically assumes weak flesh which is fully subject to suffering and the penalty of sin, though He in no way becomes personally sinful (Rom. 8:3). He dies to this fleshly body in order to arise with a glorious body and to become a "life-giving spirit" (1 Cor. 15:45). From the sphere of sin to which He belongs as being part of sinful humanity He passes to the divine sphere to which He belongs forever as a result of His resurrection (Rom. 6:9). His death is thus a death to sin once for all; His life is now entirely unto God (Rom. 6:10).

Christ was not merely the first one to return to His Father; in a certain sense He has brought all of us with Him. The share which each Christian gains by baptism in the death and resurrection of Christ presupposes that the dying and rising Christ bore in Himself all those who would be called to participate in this mystery. This has always been the teaching of the Fathers.

Numerous Pauline texts suggest or suppose this inclusion of all humanity in Christ. There is no need, moreover, to attribute this concept of Paul to a Platonic philosophy which he did not profess. Jewish thought patterns could easily provide the form for his presentation. This is especially true of the notion of "first fruits" which he himself applies to the resurrection: "Christ has risen from the dead, the first fruits of those who have fallen asleep" (1 Cor. 15:20). The first fruits were understood to contain the whole harvest, so that in the Jewish ritual the offering of first fruits was equivalent to the offering of the entire yield.

All men, therefore, have in a certain sense returned to God in Christ. Something more, however, is required. As a free creature each Christian must ratify this return by his own choice. He in his turn must die and rise again. He must experience that personal return to God, and this is accomplished by faith and baptism, the sacrament of faith. It is in this way that each one passes from the world of flesh to the world of spirit, from the city of evil built by self-love to the city of God built by love of God.

This presentation enables us to distinguish clearly between what is objective and what is subjective in redemption: the return of all men to God in and through Christ is *objective* redemption; the ratification of this return by the free choice of each Christian is *subjective* redemption.

All this, however, leads to an objection which we welcome, since it provides opportunity to explain our thought more clearly. In what way do sacred Scripture and St. Paul in particular attribute to the resurrection of Christ a power to save?

To center attention too exclusively on the resurrection may lead some to think that this return of humanity to God in and through Christ takes place in a manner wholly biological. In St. John's Gospel Christ uses a comparison which might occasion this error; for He likens Himself to the seed which must fall into the ground and die in order to bear fruit.

This, however, is only a figure. For St. John as for St. Paul it is only through a free act of loving obedience that Christ Himself has "passed" and has made us "pass" with Him to the Father. What is more, the death of Christ also would lack all redemptive value if it were merely a process of the biological order. It is endowed with power to save precisely because it is the supreme expression of Christ's love and obedience.

St. Thomas never ceases to repeat this truth. In commenting, for instance, on Rom. 5:10 he observes: "It was not Christ's death, simply as death, which so pleased the Father that it reconciled man to Him. God does not rejoice in the death of the living (Wis. 1:13)." The aspect of Christ's death which merited our salvation was rather the fact that it proceeded "from the will of Christ; for Christ willed to die out of obedience to the Father (Phil. 2:8) and out of love for men (Eph. 5:2)."

His death, in other words, was redemptive precisely because it was the greatest act of love possible for man: "Greater love than this no man has than that a man lay down his life for his friends" (John 15:13).

Viewed in this light, death and resurrection do not stand in opposition to one another but are instead intimately united. Such a death already implies resurrection. The very love with which Christ freely accepted death is an expression of divine life. Such love is bound to be sovereignly efficacious, essentially life-giving, communicating life, first of all, to the concrete human nature of Christ Himself, body and soul, and then to all human nature.

Human conditions, it is true, made it necessary for an interval of time to intervene between Christ's death and His bodily resurrection. Otherwise His death would not be looked upon as true death; much less could it be certified. Such a death, however, was necessarily and perfectly conjoined with resurrection. The love which prompted it was bound to bring both death and resurrection.

In reality, it is a question of two aspects of one and the same unique mystery. It is something like the bond between remission of sin and the infusion of divine life, as St. Paul suggests in Rom. 4:25. This indissoluble unity of Christ's death and resurrection is strongly emphasized in the New Testament. St. Luke, for example, describes Jesus' long journey to suffering and death in the language of an ascent to heaven (Luke 9:51); on the other hand, he seems unable to narrate the glorious life of Christ without cease-lessly recalling the memory of His passion and death (Luke 25:7, 26, 39, 46).

Similarly, even when St. Paul seems to speak only of Christ's death, he is in reality thinking always of Christ's risen life. This is clear from his constant allusions to "life" which he cannot conceive of except as a share in the risen life of Christ.

St. John, for his part, designedly employs a unique term to designate at once the passion and the glorification of Christ. He borrowed this expression — "to glorify" or "to exalt" — from early Church use of the Suffering Serv-ant passages of the Old Testament. Father Hermann Schmidt has pointed out this same element in the teaching of the paschal liturgy. In the passion and death there shines forth gloriously the victory of the resurrection, and in the risen Christ there remain the scars of His suffering.

Tradition, therefore, emphasizes the truth that Christ by His death re-unites us to the Father. But always it considers death as a supreme act of love and therefore essentially as a victory over death "God has ruled from the wood." If, however, we abstract from the resurrection the death of Christ no longer appears to be a victory but only the payment of a debt.

This is why sacred Scripture, the Fathers, and St. Thomas have avoided constructing their synthesis of redemption on the exclusive foundation of mer-itorious casualty. St. Thomas has arranged his system around the efficient in-strumental causality of the humanity of Christ. Sacred Scripture presents a more figurative theme — the picture of man returning to God. In both cases, however, the death and glorification of Christ remain closely united. It is easy, therefore, to understand Paul's summing up of all his doctrine: "Christ was delivered up for our sins and rose again for our justification" (Rom. 4:25).


# PAUL'S TEACHING ON BEING AND BECOMING IN CHRIST

George T. Montague, S.M.


In an age profoundly influenced by the philosophy of existence and likewise titillated by the sweeping vistas of a philosophy of becoming such as Teilhard de Chardin throws open to the imagination, one naturally wonders what exist-ence, on the one hand, and becoming, on the other, mean for the Christian.

Published originally in *The Bible Today*, 1 (1962), 79-85. Reprinted by permission of the publisher.

More specifically, what is the being and the becoming of the Christian life? To answer the question, one naturally turns to St. Paul, not merely because he was the first to elaborate a theology of the Christian life, but because these two dimensions, being and becoming, weave through his writings as constant themes.

## The Christian a new being

For St. Paul, there is no doubt that the Christian has entered a new existence. The Christian life is defined as existing in Christ Jesus (1 Cor. 1:30; Col. 2:10). The stress in these passages is not on a moral demand but on the sheer fact of existing, of having being, less perhaps in the Aristotelian sense of existence, than in the Semitic sense of the fullness of goods, including peace, security and stable well-being, founded in faithful attachment to God. It is, in fact, precisely this sense that the text of Colossians reveals: "In him (Christ) dwells the fullness of the Godhead bodily — and you exist in him as men that have been filled" (Col. 2:9-10). And the same thought is found substantially in the text from Corinthians: "To his (God's) gift you owe your existence in Christ Jesus, who has become for us God-given wisdom, and justice, and sanctification, and redemption" (1 Cor. 1:30).

What is stated here explicitly is implied repeatedly in that basic common denominator to which St. Paul reduces all his theological insights, "in Christ Jesus," or similar formulas, of which A. Deissmann has counted 164 in the epistles, excluding Ephesians, Colossians and the Pastorals. In Christ Christians have entered into the possession of the fullness of being.

Our modern ear, accustomed to such commonplaces as "in the army" or "in the high income bracket," has difficulty in appreciating the impact which the formula, "in Christ," must have produced in Paul's listeners. He is not thinking of merely entering a state that would be the accretion of a new layer of dignity or responsibility. It is not even an investiture, although the apostle does say that the baptized have "put on Christ" (Gal. 3:27). The depth of its meaning is given when Paul says: "If anyone is in Christ, he is a *new creature*" (2 Cor. 5:17).

In Gal. 6:15 he explicitly rejects reliance on anything short of an absolute beginning in the Christian life: "In Christ Jesus neither circumcision nor uncircumcision is of any account, but only *a new creation*." Quite simply, the new life is so new and its effects so profound that it can be compared only to the act of creation: In Christ Jesus Christians have been created (Eph. 4:24; cf. 2:10).

## Christian life a definitive state

It is the conviction of this profound metamorphosis effected in baptism that explains why all the great themes by which Paul describes the Christian life appear primarily as illustrations of a *fait accompli*. Thus not only did Christ save the elect (Titus 3:5; 2 Tim. 1:9), but the latter bear henceforth the title "saved men" (Eph. 2:5, 8). Christians are not only "saints" but "the sanctified" — the perfect participle indicating a definitively acquired state (1 Cor. 1:2; 6:11); and the image of the temple, which Christians are, recalls that theirs is a holiness of being (1 Cor. 3:16; 2 Cor. 6:16). They once were darkness but now are light in the Lord (Eph. 5:8; 1 Thess. 5:5). Once sinners, they have now in Christ become the very "justice of God" (2 Cor. 5:21). Stated in terms of Paul's favorite antithesis of life and death, the same truth is brought home when he says that Christians have already died with Christ (Rom. 6:8; Col. 2:20; 3:3), they are dead to sin (Rom. 6:11); they have risen with Him (Col. 2:12; 3:1) and are henceforth alive to God in Christ (Rom. 6:11), and God has already seated them in heaven with Him (Eph. 2:6).

In the wake of such a gospel, it is not perhaps surprising that the Thessalonians should conclude that there was nothing more to do but to await the parousia, and Paul agrees with them when he equates the eschatological service of God with awaiting the return of His Son (1 Thess. 1:9f). He simply clarified for them what it means to await Christ. It means to prepare to appear with Him in a state of holiness which has been tempered by an ever-abounding charity. "May the Lord make you abound and overflow in charity towards one another and towards all men, just as we do towards you, in order to strengthen your hearts blameless in holiness in the presence of God our Father, when our Lord Jesus comes with all his saints" (1 Thess. 3:10-13). This means that the Christian's existence now in the end-time does not entitle him to passivity but necessarily fires him to action because "the time is short" (1 Cor. 7:29).

## Action follows being

But in addition to the parousia motive, Paul appeals time and again to the nature of Christian being as possessed here and now. Rudolf Schnackenburg, Alfred Wikenhauser and others have called attention to what they term "indicative-imperative" contrasts in the great Pauline themes. To practically every theme describing what Christians now are (in virtue of what has already taken place), there is a corresponding parenetic injunction that they should act in accordance with their new being.

Thus, if they are holy, they must "finish off their holiness" (2 Cor. 7:1). If by baptism they have "put on Christ" (Gal. 3:27), they must therefore put Him on (Rom. 13:14; Eph. 4:24). If they are a new creature, they must walk in newness of life (Rom. 6:4). If they are children of the light and of the day (1 Thess. 5:5; Eph. 5:8), they must now cast off the works of darkness and put on the armor of light, or walk as children of the light (Rom. 13:2; Eph. 5:8-11). Since they have died with Christ, they must put to death the passions which belong to earth (Col. 3:5). Because they have risen with Christ, they must walk in newness of life (Rom. 6:4, 11).

Most specific of these texts is that of 1 Cor. 5:7, where Paul tells the Corinthians: "Cast out the old leaven, that you may be fresh dough, as indeed you are without leaven." His point is that they have no longer any reason for acting immorally or for countenancing immorality in the community, for they are now truly new and different in their very being. They must purify themselves from *all* corruptive remains of their former pagan existence; they are to cast out the old leaven, since or *as* they are not leaven. The new conduct is not only demanded by their state but is in the exact line of it (the Greek *kathōs*). Hence J. Lilly translates, "Clean out the old yeast, that you may be fresh dough (as, of course, you really are)."

## True meaning of indicative-imperative

Thus the categorical imperative for the Christian is to act because of what he is. Yet the terms indicative-imperative, though valid, are far from exhausting Paul's thought on the relationship between Christian being and becoming. They could, in fact, lead to a misinterpretation. Taken alone, the contrasts might lead one to believe that Paul thought of the initial entry into the life, the state of "new creature," as simply a God-given state to which the Christian, in consideration of this noble dignity, should bring his own effort to bear. This would be a serious limitation of the apostle's horizon on three counts: first, man's effort is never something he *adds* to God's (at least not according to the teaching of St. Paul). Second, Christian growth is not just a repetition of acts. Third, God's "creative" act, the gift of the Spirit, is so dynamic that it pursues its work through the progressive stage to consummation.

The indicative-imperative contrast must, therefore, be broadened to express the two dimensions on which God's action (and man's acceptance and entry into it) work: one, the *constitutive* dimension by which God consecrates the Christian or "creates" him in Christ, the act by which the Christian begins to "be"; the other, the *progressive* dimension by which *the same action* is continued and deepened through the interim separating the Christian from final reunion with Christ.

To illustrate, it will suffice to look at texts which develop the "constitutive" dimension of Paul's themes into the "progressive." Thus Christians are not only "saved men" but they "are in the process of being saved" (1 Cor. 1:18, 15:2; 2 Cor. 2:15). In the same letter in which Paul says that God saved us (2 Tim. 1:9) he says that he himself suffers for the elect that they may attain salvation (2:10).

Christians are "the sanctified," but Paul asks God to sanctify them through and through (1 Thess. 5:23); the process continues (1 Thess. 4:3) till they are blameless in holiness (1 Thess. 3:13). Christians who are a temple in 1 Cor. 3:16 and 2 Cor. 6:16, *grow into* a temple in Eph. 2:21. In the same breath Paul says that they have been *built* (Eph. 2:20), yet they are in the process of *being built* (Eph. 2:22). Although God has already glorified Christians (Rom. 8:30), they are being transformed from glory to glory (2 Cor. 3:18); their present light affliction is producing an eternal weight of glory (2 Cor. 4:17).

Christ has all fullness (Col. 1:19; 2:9), yet He is being filled by the Church

(Eph. 2:21). In the same sense, Christians are filled men (Col. 1:10), yet Paul prays that they be filled (Eph. 3:19). They are all one in Jesus Christ (Gal. 3:28), yet they must attain the unity of the faith and become one perfect man (Eph. 4:13). Christ is already in the faithful (Rom. 8:10; Col. 1: 27), but Paul prays that Christ find a dwelling-place in their hearts (Eph. 3:17).

Finally, the great themes of death and life likewise reveal a dimension that is progressive as well as imperative. Paul himself aspires to an ever greater conforming to Christ's death (Phil. 3:10). Life is at work in Christians now (2 Cor. 4:12), this new life of salvation which progresses "from life to life" (2 Cor. 2:16).

## Theology of tense-antithesis

The shock of this tense–antithesis common to all the great themes of Paul invites further study. To understand the underlying theology, it will help to examine in particular the Pauline theme of newness and renewal, of which the "constitutive" dimension has already been discussed. The Christian by baptism is indeed "created in Christ Jesus" (Eph. 2:10), "he is a *new* creature" (2 Cor. 5:17), which is the only thing that counts (Gal. 5:15). But this newness is now the principle of a progressive transformation: the inward man is being renewed day by day, that is, he grows newer and newer (2 Cor. 4:16).

Far from being mere passivity, however, this process of renovation, which is the work of the Holy Spirit (Titus 3:5), demands the Christian's cooperation. His mind now has the principle of newness in the spirit that animates it, so that Paul's simple injunction that we must now walk in newness of life (Rom. 6:4) is made clearer by the injunctions, "Be transformed by the renewal of your mind" (Rom. 12:2) and "Be renewed in the spirit of your mind and put on the new man" (Eph. 4:23f), who, according to Col. 3:10, "is being renewed unto knowledge according to the image of his Creator," that is, the renewal leads to a more lucid knowledge of the mystery of God and Christ, to a restoration of the divine image and likeness (cf. Gen. 1:26f; 3:5), progressively regained by transformation into Christ (2 Cor. 3:18).

The key text on renewal is Titus 3:5, where Paul says: "He saved us through the bath of *regeneration* and the *renewal* of the Holy Spirit." The first thing to note about this text is that it clearly distinguishes two terms: *paliggenesia* (regeneration) and *anakainōsis* (renewal). The first term is borrowed from the realm of nature, the second from that of art; yet they are both bound closely together and associated with the rite of baptism (the bath), in such a way that the second is the follow-up, the consequence, the consummation of the first.

The *paliggenesia* refers to that free act of God by which He transfers the sinner from the kingdom of darkness to that of light, from death to life. It is the rebirth of which Jesus speaks in John 3:3: "Unless a man be born again . . ." (cf. the "being born of God" in John 1:13; 1 John 5:4). It is the absolute beginning, the constitutive aspect, in which the subject is wholly passive, even as the child has nothing to do with his own birth. The introduction of *renewal* brings an additional nuance of considerable importance: this is the gradual conforming of the Christian to that new spiritual world in which he now lives and moves, the restoration of the divine image, like that of a work of art. In it the subject cooperates with the Holy Spirit who dwells in him (Rom. 8:11) and impels him to live as befits his new state of divine sonship (Rom. 8:14).

The theme of renewal as descriptive of the progressive transformation of the Christian is most properly Pauline. Already used in the Septuagint for the renewal of nature by the spirit of Yahweh (Ps. 103:30), the verb in the passive, "to be renewed," is used of Christians only by St. Paul, and the noun *anakainōsis*, "renewal," unquotable anywhere in Greek before Paul, was apparently his own coining.

There are other themes in Paul which develop the theme of progress: the Christian life is a walking, a way of life, a path, a race, a combat, a pursuit. It grows, increases, abounds, bears fruit, becomes strong and stable. It calls for completion, finishing off, sanctification, increasing worthiness. It is a building process, a formation, a transformation, a glorification. But beyond all these themes, that of renewal seems to express best and in a way most characteristically Paul's, the relation between the Christian's being and his becoming. Whereas the natural man is born and then grows older, the Christian is reborn and then under the influence of the spirit grows newer and newer.

## Reasons for progress

The question may still be asked: "Why is the Christian life necessarily a life of continual progress?" One answer might be that the end-time given by God is the time of great opportunity (*kairos*), the time to prepare by interior holiness and growing charity for the return of the Lord. The thought is certainly Pauline, from the first Epistle to the Thessalonians to the Epistle to the Ephesians: "that we should be holy and blameless in his sight in love" (1:4).

But there is, I think, in the very heart of Paul's dominant formula, *in Christ*, the key to the imperiousness of Christian growth. In 2 Cor. 3:18, St. Paul says: "We all, with face unveiled, reflecting as in a mirror the glory of the Lord, are being transformed into that very image, from one degree of glory to another, as by the Lord, who is spirit." There is some dispute as to how to translate certain elements of this verse, particularly the final *apo kyriou pneumatos*, which some would render, "by the spirit of the Lord," others "by the Lord, who is the spirit." The context, however, which is one of contrasting the clear knowledge of Christ now available to us with the veiled knowledge of Him in the Old Law, makes it clear that "Lord" here means Christ, its ordinary meaning in Paul, and "spirit" does not refer directly to the Holy Spirit but is an appositive of "the Lord." He is transforming us because He is spirit — that is, He possesses now the power of divine influence by which He can bring His members into transforming union with Himself.

This is made possible because Christ's members are united through faith and baptism to His glorious body. To be "in Christ" means to be baptized into His body. "You have been baptized into one body" in 1 Cor. 12:13 does not mean that as a result of their baptism all Christians form a body, but rather (with Cerfaux), baptism effects a dynamic union with the physical body of Christ now glorious in heaven. As our present text makes clear, this contact with the "spiritual body" of Christ means being under the influence of its dynamic and transforming power, so that it is impossible to be truly "in Christ" without being continually open to the effects of this progressive transformation by Him. The Christian moves even now from flesh (*sarx* — mere humanness) to spirit (*pneuma* — a spirit-guided life) because he is united to the body of Christ, who is spirit.

### Being and becoming in Christ

"Being" in Christ, therefore, necessarily involves "becoming" in Him. It is not a question of acting *as if*, but of acting *because;* that is, Paul's theology of Christian becoming is rooted in Christian being. If Christians are under the progressive influence of Christ who is spirit, it is because they are already somehow one spirit with Him (1 Cor. 6:17). "Become what you are!"

Yet in the becoming, Christian action is not semi-Pelagian, as if man's efforts added something to those of God. Man's conscious response is actively engaged, but the Lord Himself has taken first responsibility for the progress of His members by making them one with Himself, the unfailing source of the transforming influence. His continuing action is guaranteed: "He who has begun this work in you will continue to perfect it until the day of Christ" (Phil. 1:6). It goes without saying, therefore, that the growth of Christians must be continual. To be in Christ is necessarily to become in Him.


# ST. PAUL AND THE JUSTIFICATION OF ABRAHAM

Myles M. Bourke


If one were to judge St. Paul's estimate of Abraham by the number of times he speaks of him in his epistles, one would conclude that, for Paul, the father

Published originally in *The Bible Today*, 1 (1964), 643-49. Reprinted by permission of the publisher.

of Israel was not a very important figure. Apart from a theologically insignificant mention in 2 Corinthians 11:22, the patriarch appears only in a few
texts of Romans and Galatians. Yet Paul assigns to Abraham a role which is
unique in salvation-history. He is pre-eminently the man of faith, whose complete acceptance of God's word makes him the prototype of all who believe
in Christ; he exemplifies the fact that men are justified not by what they do,
but by faith; the justification of the Gentiles is the fulfillment of the promise
made to him: "In thee shall all the nations be blessed" (Gal. 3:8; cf. Gen.
12:3). In him, the continuity of the two Testaments becomes vividly clear,
for if one cannot be a true descendant of Abraham unless he believes in
Christ, conversely, those who believe in Christ, whether they be Jew or Gentile, are true descendants of Abraham. He is the father of all believers (cf.
Rom. 4:11-12), and "if you belong to Christ, you are the offspring of Abraham, heirs according to the promise" (Gal. 3:29).

## Christ, the key to understanding the Old Testament

Before we discuss what Paul has to say about Abraham's justification by
faith, some observations should be made about his use of the Old Testament in general. Evidently, Paul had not become a Christian because of having read the Old Testament and realizing that it had been fulfilled in Jesus. He
had been changed from a persecutor of the Church to the most effective of
all the apostles because in his vision on the way to Damascus he had had an
experience which left no room for doubt that Jesus of Nazareth was the Messiah of Israel, and that He whom the Jews had crucified had been made
Lord and Christ by the Father.

Like every religious Jew, Paul had been convinced that the scriptures of
the Old Testament were the very word of God, and when he became a disciple of Christ he realized that since Jesus of Nazareth was the Messiah,
those scriptures must have pointed to Him and been a preparation for His
coming. The sacred history and the institutions of Israel could not have been
without meaning. The fact that most of Paul's Jewish brethren had not accepted the Messiah, a source of profound sorrow and continual distress for
him (cf. Rom. 9:1-3), could not mean that God's providential designs
had failed or that His election of Israel had been in vain. The promises made
to Abraham and his descendants held good; the prophecies about the salvation which Yahweh would send to His people could not be mistaken. Jesus
was no phenomenon outside of, and unrelated to, the nation which was
God's very own; the greatest glory of the Hebrews was that "the Christ
according to the flesh" was one of them (Rom. 9:5). And if it was impossible to understand Jesus apart from the Old Testament scriptures, it was also
impossible to understand them apart from Him. They could be grasped in
their full meaning only when seen in the light which streamed on them from
the risen Christ.

Hans Joachim Schoeps, a Jewish scholar quite sympathetic to Jesus, though
not to Paul, has said of the Apostle: "The retrospective way of thought is

the real axis of his argument. Not the meaning of Scripture, but Christ is the *a priori* for his judgment of the law." We would say, rather, that for Paul the full meaning of Scripture, and his judgment about the Law and every other institution of Israel, were derived from his faith in Jesus as Messiah and Son of God. But Schoeps is surely right in saying that Christ was the *a priori* for Paul's interpretation of Scripture. The question is simply whether that *a priori* was right. Those who, like Paul, believe that it was, cannot but accept the general trend of his interpretation of the Old Testament.

## Justification, works, faith

When we speak of someone as "just," we usually mean that he gives others what is due to them. That meaning of the word is found also in the Bible, but the biblical concept of justice is more inclusive (the just man is the opposite of the wicked; cf. Gen. 18:25), and in some respects quite different (God's justice is His saving activity on behalf of His people; cf. Is. 46:13). We shall not discuss here the probably insoluble problem of the basic meaning of the Hebrew root from which the various words belonging to the vocabulary of justice are derived. So far as biblical *usage* is concerned, there are two principal currents of meaning, depending on whether the words are used in connection with a judgment, or in connection with God's salvific and merciful acts.

The verb "to justify" and the words related to it such as "justice," "just," "justification," belong originally to the language of the law court. The judge "justifies" a man by declaring him innocent. He is a just judge if his verdict corresponds in fact with the guilt or innocence of the defendant. Perversion of the judicial function was one of the crimes denounced by the prophets, and the Mosaic Law warned: "Thou shalt not justify the guilty" (Exod. 23:7). When the judicial process was transferred from the human scene and used to describe God's dealing with man, the result was the crushing realization that because of man's sinfulness no verdict was possible but that which pronounced him guilty: "Before you no living man is just" (Ps. 142:2). And since God, "the judge of all the earth" (Gen. 18:25), cannot but act justly, man's situation seems desperate, for he can expect from God only a sentence of condemnation. Hence the foolishness of believing that one can be declared righteous (i.e., "be justified") by God on the basis of one's deeds, on the fulfillment of the Mosaic Law. Realizing this, the psalmist had pleaded: "Enter not into judgment with your servant" (Ps. 142:2). The law was holy and "spiritual" (cf. Rom. 7:12, 14) but it could only tell men what they should do; it did not give them the power to fulfill its commands. Only God's mercy could save them.

But man has not been left to himself. God can "create a clean heart" for him (Ps. 50:12), and the message of the Scripture is that He has done so. Strangely enough, the vocabulary of justice is used in the Bible to describe this merciful acting of God, a fact which has obscured its meaning for those who do not recognize the transfer from the area of the legal and judicial. The juridical terms have taken on a new meaning: God's justice is His mercy whereby, faithful to His covenant promises, He saves men. The many Old Testament texts in which God's justice is made parallel to His mercy, kindness, and salvation are the sources which indicate this new meaning; of all of these, perhaps the clearest is Psalm 84, in which God's justice is contrasted with His wrath. Although Israel has sinned and deserves punishment, the psalmist, conscious that God has forgiven His people, can sing: "You have withdrawn all your wrath; you have revoked your burning anger. . . . Kindness and truth shall meet; justice and peace shall kiss . . . . Justice shall walk before him, and salvation, along the way of his steps" (Ps. 84:4, 11, 14). Our familiar justice-mercy contrast disappears here. What we usually call God's "justice" is here called His wrath, and His justice is a synonym for His mercy.

There is a change also in the meaning of the verb "to justify." In the Fourth Servant Song, the verb no longer means the act of pronouncing a person innocent, but rather an act conferring forgiveness of sin and true interior righteousness. The Suffering Servant of the Lord "shall justify" many because His sufferings are the means whereby God will forgive men their sins: "Through his suffering, my servant shall justify many, and their guilt he shall bear . . . he shall take away the sins of many, and win pardon for their offenses" (Is. 53:11-12).

### *"What Israel was seeking . . ." (Rom. 11:7)*

Paul bears witness to the passionate desire of his people for justice, that is, for a right relationship with God (cf. Rom. 10:2-3). But he saw that they could not achieve what they desired as long as they continued to look for it where it could not be found. They believed that fidelity to the Mosaic Law was what made a man just, and so interpreted such statements as that of the psalmist: "The Lord rewarded me according to my justice . . . for I kept the ways of the Lord. . . . His statutes I put not from me" (Ps. 17:21-23). The ambition of the pious Jew was to observe perfectly the commandments of the Law (cf. Ps. 118:112). Paul, on the contrary, argued that the Law could not be the source of man's justice, for it places a curse on all who do not keep every one of its precepts, and since no one keeps it perfectly, all fall under that curse (Gal. 3:10-12).

George Foot Moore, the Christian author of a classical and sympathetic work on Judaism, wrote: "Paul's definition of righteousness as perfect conformity with the law of God would never have been conceded by a Jewish opponent." We may admit that the perfect fulfillment of the Law was an ideal which every Jew knew man could not achieve, and that in Galatians 3:10-12, Paul was pressing his point very hard — in the rabbinic manner! Yet, to a considerable extent observance of the Law was possible, and it is in the area of that attainable element of the goal that the root defect of the Jewish piety of Paul's time lay. It is hard to think that even the most observant Pharisee imagined that he could achieve perfect obedience to the entire

Law; his error lay, rather, in thinking that what he had achieved was, in the last analysis, achieved by his own powers. As an example of that belief, we may take a verse of the *Psalms of Solomon*, a Pharisaic composition of the first century B.C.: "Our works are subject to our own choice and power; to do right or wrong is the work of our hands" (Ps. Sol. 9:4). The correlative of that belief was that God, the just judge, must recognize the righteousness of those who kept the Law, and recognize it precisely as their own work. Keeping the Law by their unaided powers, men would, in a sense, put God in their debt and establish a claim against Him: He must recognize their justice and reward it.

This does not mean that Paul's Jewish contemporaries did not realize their deficiencies and their need for forgiveness of their sins. But, for them, nothing but their own free choice was necessary for the performance of good works. Their attitude may be summed up by the later Talmudic statement: "All is in the hands of God, save the fear of God." It is there that Paul found himself in complete disagreement with Jewish theology. And he pointed out that that theology was in disagreement with the Old Testament itself, for there one read that Abraham, the father of Israel, had been justified, not by works, but by faith: "Abraham believed God, and it was credited to him as justice" (Rom. 4:3; Gal. 3:6; cf. Gen. 15:6).

## Abraham justified by faith

That man is justified by faith is a truth which came to Paul as a consequence of his insight into the mystery of Christ. "For if justice is by the Law, then Christ died in vain" (Gal. 2:21). But Jesus' resurrection proved that He had not died in vain; on the contrary, "God was in Christ, reconciling the world to himself " (2 Cor. 5:19). The way in which that reconciliation had been brought about showed that man cannot be in right relation with God unless God takes the initiative; justification cannot be a reward for works which man has done. But on reading the Old Testament in the light of his knowledge of what God had done in Christ, Paul saw that in the matter of justification God had always dealt with men in the same way: justification had always come through faith, as the case of Abraham showed.

Paul speaks of Abraham's justification in both Galatians 3 and Romans 4. The former epistle was written in a context of fiery polemic; the latter is calmer in tone and carefully constructed. But each has as its background Paul's controversy with those Jewish Christians who insisted that the Gentile converts to Christianity must observe the Mosaic Law, or, at least, its capital prescription of circumcision. Only so, they argued, could the Gentiles be saved. For them, Christianity was a sect of Judaism, distinguished from the parent religion only by the belief that Jesus was the Messiah. For Paul, the demand that the Gentile Christians keep the Law of Moses revealed complete misunderstanding of the work of Christ; it exalted what man does rather than what God has done for him, and it was actually unfaithful to the profound intentions of the Old Testament.

By showing that Abraham had been justified by faith, Paul made it clear that his teaching on justification was in agreement with the religion of the Old Testament, rightly understood (cf. Rom. 3:31); and he set himself in opposition to the current view of late Judaism that God's election of Abraham was a reward for his keeping the precepts of God and for his loyalty at the time of his great testing, when he received the command to sacrifice Isaac. (According to the rabbinic tradition, the precepts observed by Abraham were those of the Mosaic Law, which had been revealed to him.) The view that Abraham's observance of commandment and fidelity under testing were the reason why God chose him and promised him that in his descendants all the nations of the earth would be blessed, was the result of a reading of the Genesis texts under the influence of that over-estimation of law which characterized late Judaism. What was central to its own spiritual life became the norm by which it interpreted the past.

But Paul asks: "What does the Scripture say?" In answer, he quotes Genesis 15:6: "Abraham believed God and it was credited to him as justice" (Rom. 4:3). Before the Mosaic Law existed, before Abraham himself had been circumcised, the childless patriarch was promised by God that his descendants would be as numerous as the stars; he believed the promise, and his faith was "credited to him as justice" (cf. Gen. 15:2-6). Abraham *did* nothing but believe. His circumcision, received later, was simply the sign which confirmed the fact that he had already been justified by his faith (cf. Rom. 4:11).

## Paul's use of Genesis 15:6

It is frequently said that Paul read into Genesis 15:6 a meaning which it does not have. The Jewish scholar Benno Jacob represents that opinion when he states that the text has nothing to do with the explanation given to it by "Christian exegetes who base their Christian faith on it," and he claims that the Hebrew verb translated "to believe" does not express what Christians mean by faith, nor does the Hebrew noun translated "justice" mean what Jacob calls "Pauline justification." Let us examine that opinion.

It cannot be denied that at times Paul uses rabbinic exegetical techniques, taking a verse out of its context and giving it a meaning which has little or nothing to do with its true sense. But that does not seem to be the case in his interpretation of Genesis 15:6. In the first place, he does not take it out of its context. The verse refers to an incident which took place before God made His covenant with Abraham and before Abraham was circumcised. So far as the sequence of events is concerned, Paul has respected the lines of the Genesis narrative.

Is it true, as Jacob claims, that the belief of Abraham was not faith in the Christian sense of that word? On the contrary — the Old Testament concept of faith and that of the New Testament are fundamentally the same. The agreement of the two is evident when one realizes that generally in the New Testament, faith is understood not simply as an act of intellectual assent, but as the total response of man to the word of God. Rudolf Bultmann's statement, "Paul understands faith primarily as obedience," is certainly right, provided one sees that the obedience of faith means the readiness to submit oneself entirely to God and accept His word. The obedience includes an intellectual element, viz., one's acceptance of the revelation that God has manifested Himself in the redemptive act of Christ, and that through that act He has made possible man's passage from the realm of sin and death into that of spirit and life, with and in Christ. But if the acceptance of that truth remains merely on the level of intellectual assent, there is no faith in the Pauline sense, for the faith of which Paul speaks is that which "acts through love" (Gal. 5:6).

We must admit, however, that the question of the relationship between Abraham's faith being "credited to him as justice" and the Christian's faith being similarly credited (cf. Rom. 4:24) is more complicated. To discuss it adequately would involve going into matters which cannot be dealt with here. But if we may accept the view that when Paul says that Abraham's faith was credited to him as justice, he means that by his act of faith in God's promise Abraham entered into a situation of right relationship with God (cf. Lucien Cerfaux: "God sees faith and grants justice; He creates justice in man"), we must grant that Paul has gone beyond the meaning of Genesis 15:6. For, most probably, in that verse "justice" means a righteous *act*, as in Isaiah 56:1 and 64:5, where the Hebrew word translated in the Confraternity version as "what is just" and "good deeds," respectively, is the same as that translated "justice" in Genesis 15:6. It is hardly conceivable that the author of Genesis 15:6 wished to say that Abraham was put into a situation of right relationship with God by his act of faith. If that were his meaning, one would have to draw the conclusion that previously Abraham had not been in God's favor — an impossible view, considering the way in which he is described from the time of his call by God (Gen. 12:1-3).

At the same time, it seems that Paul's understanding of Genesis 15:6 is a legitimate extension of its meaning, an extension justified by the total portrayal of Abraham in Genesis. Abraham was put into a condition of friendship with God (cf. Is. 41:8) by his first response to the call and promise of God narrated in Genesis 12:1-3. His justification, then, took place at the time that God first manifested Himself to him, when he immediately accepted and obeyed the word of God (cf. Gen. 12:4), before he had done anything but put his faith in Him who called him. In so far as that is so, there is identity between Abraham's justification and that of the Christian. In using Genesis 15:6 as he did, Paul went beyond the original meaning of the verse, but he did so in a way which was faithful to the tenor of the *Genesis* descriptions of Abraham. The text served as a suitable means for Paul to express, in summary form, Abraham's response to the word of God and the gift which that response brought him.

# ISRAEL'S MISSTEP AND HER RISE —
## The Dialectic of God's Saving Design in Romans 9–11

John M. Oesterreicher

In his Epistle to the Romans, St. Paul proclaims the mysteriousness of God's design in these words: "God has shut up all in unbelief that he may have mercy upon all" (11:32). There is no other term by which to characterize this staggering truth than "dialectic" — that interplay of real or seeming opposites which serves to give the world of senses as well as the world of grace their rich texture. God "making" Jews and Gentiles the prisoners of their disobedience so that He might prepare their freedom — this is a dialectic supreme.

### Israel's honors

Between the beginning of chapter nine and the conclusion of chapter eight of St. Paul's letter to the *Romans*, there is a typical Pauline tension that some exegetes find perplexing:

> I speak the truth in Christ, I do not lie, my conscience bearing me witness in the Holy Spirit, that I have great sadness and continuous sorrow in my heart (Rom 9:1-2).

Chapter eight, however, ends on the assurance that nothing could separate the Apostle "from the love of God which is in Christ Jesus our Lord" (Rom. 8:39).

There is, indeed, a sudden, unexpected switch from the last verse of chapter eight to the first of chapter nine, from a hymn of victory to a cry of anguish. Yet, there is no real change of mood. Dialectically, the two emotions — the Apostle's boundless confidence and his deep sorrow — are one. They are held together by the same love; in fact, they spring from the same passion: St. Paul's ardor is not unlike that of his Master, who thought nothing of "emptying Himself" of His divine glory in order to become a slave for our sake (Phil. 2:5-7). Paul's desire to be an outcast from Christ for the sake of those of his brethren who are divorced from the same Christ is no relapse into Jewish narrowness or national sensibility, as some would have it. Quite the opposite, the Apostle's *deepest* bond to his people is not blood but providence; his tie is more than biological — it is salvific, *heilsgeschichtlich*. The only triumph he seeks is God's.

In saying this, we do not wish to deny St. Paul's intimate sense of solidarity with his kinsmen who do not believe in Christ. Still, in Romans 9:1-5, Paul speaks not as a "Jew" but as an apostle whose love is not bounded but encompasses the Church *and* Israel. Both — his kinsmen "according to the

Published originally in *The Bible Today*, 1 (1964), 768-74. Reprinted by permission of the publisher.

SAINT PAUL

spirit" and those "according to the flesh" — he calls "brethren," though evidently not in the same sense. It would be quite inadequate, however, to say that the latter are his natural, and the former his supernatural, brethren. For his affection, anguish, and care are of the order of grace. Not as a "Jew," then, but as an apostle does he speak of what are generally called Israel's unique privileges:

> They are Israelites; they have been adopted as God's sons; theirs is the glory [of the divine presence], theirs are the covenants, the law, the worship [of the living God] as well as the promises. The patriarchs are theirs, and from them is the Christ, according to [his] humanity [literally: according to the flesh], he who is God above all, praised throughout the ages. Amen (Rom. 9:4-5).

"Privileges" or "prerogatives" can be misleading terms; they seem to contradict the Church's role as the new people of God. This apparent contradiction has led some exegetes to misinterpret the meaning of the passage. One, for instance, asks why St. Paul sets forth all the "advantages of Israel," only to say that they make the mystery of her rejection "truly great and inconceivable." Great and inconceivable as the disbelief of many in Israel is to St. Paul, the three chapters we are examining here were certainly not written to proclaim "Israel's rejection" by God. Another commentator holds that these privileges belong, not to the Israel of history, but to the "ideal" people fulfilling God's plan. Yet, in Romans 9:3-4 the Apostle's concern is obviously not with an ideal people but with the people around him; he gives the title "Israelites," not to the holy remnant that believes, but to those of his kinsmen who are blind to the wonder of Christ. He speaks of their sonship, of the glory, the covenants, the promises, the worship and the Law, not as marvels that graced his people only in the past, but as marvels *still present*. Theirs they are, as *is* "the Christ according to the flesh" (Rom. 9:5).

Any difficulty that might be felt in giving such honor to the Israel exiled from Christ disappears if, rather than speaking of Israel's "prerogatives," we call the marvels of Jewish history what they are: gifts freely given; manifestations of God's saving will granted to the Jews for no merit of their own; favors bestowed on them, not for their own sake but for that of the whole world. Because the marvels of sacred history are all this, they cannot simply disappear. Even in her aloofness from Christ, exiled Israel is still "honored" by them, for they are the honor of God, of the God of Israel whose gracious gifts are irrevocable (Rom. 11:29).

Such are the surprising ways of the Apostle, however, that no sooner has he bestowed the glorious name "Israelites" on his separated brethren than he goes on to declare: "They are not all Israelites who are sprung from Israel" (Rom. 9:6). The Hebrew genius likes to disclose the meaning of reality by conflicting, antithetical expressions. By using, side by side, expressions that are extreme and absolute, expressions that disregard nuance and thus lack the shadings that Western thought delights in, the Hebrew mind seeks to reveal the complexity and fullness of the world, even of the world of grace.

In his attempt to unfold the mysteriousness of God's saving design, St. Paul is not content with expressing the polarity of Jewish existence: they [the Jews] *are* Israelites; they are *not* Israelites. Many in Israel stumbled (Rom. 9:32), he argues further, yet God has not rejected His people (Rom. 11:1), having preserved a remnant in which grace has free rein and faith full thrust (Rom. 11:5-6). Again, the stumbling of the many was — marvelous to say — the signal for the awakening of Gentiles; the decrease of the first brought about the wealth of the latter (Rom. 11:11-12). As if this were not enough, the small remnant will in the end expand to untold numbers: "All Israel shall be saved" (Rom. 11:26). There is, then, in the scheme of salvation, and hence in St. Paul's three chapters, a movement running from heights to depths and to heights again. It is this upward-downward-upward movement that gives redemptive history its dialectical character.

## Israel's stumbling

Like others before and after him, Luther searched the Epistle to the Romans for an answer to the piercing problem of his life: "How do I find a gracious God?" In Romans 9–11, however, St. Paul is not concerned with the destiny of individuals, their predestination or reprobation, but with the fate and salvific function of the two great communities, Israel and the nations. His question is rather: "How does God's redemptive will accomplish its purpose? How will creation be soaked in His glory?"

As the Apostle asks this question, he sees that part of the Jewish people which refused to move with the great messianic current as temporarily suspended or inactivated, but not as rejected. He emphatically denies that God has spewn out His own; gladly he declares: "God has not cast off his people whom He foreknew" (Rom. 11:2). It is not human softness but his wish to have God's truth acknowledged that makes him so insistent. How foreign softness is to him he proves when he unhesitatingly challenges, indeed, wounds, his kinsmen. What could pain them more than a comparison of their present role with those of Esau and Pharaoh, their early foes and the hinderers of God's plan (Rom. 9:6-29)? If he hurts, however, it is in order to heal; if he provokes his "unbelieving" brethren to anger, it is in order to press them toward a new beginning.

Still, it is not St. Paul's main purpose in chapters nine and ten to expose the guilt of the people of Israel. As a matter of fact, nowhere in our trilogy is Israel's lack of response to the Christ expressly called "guilt." Though St. Paul leaves no doubt that Israel's failure is *her* failure, he shows a restraint not always discerned. Even an expression like "*Israel's* failure" requires Pauline qualification. Though the Apostle is saddened that those in Israel who accept the Good News are but few, "the chosen part," he is unimpressed by the number of those who have remained blind to the messianic Presence, and simply calls them "the others," "the rest."

What does the Apostle actually say about these, his "schismatic" kinsmen? That they have run against the stumbling-block set up by God in Zion and have struck themselves (Rom. 9:32); that their *zeal* for God is indisputable but that it lacks insight (Rom. 10:2); that, obtuse to the justice God works in us, they have strained themselves to be just in His eyes through their own efforts (Rom. 10:3). Again, that they have not believed that Jesus is the risen One, the King of glory, the Lord (Rom. 10:9); that they have not responded to the Good News and that, in contrast to many of the once heedless pagans, they have rebuffed God's embrace that is Christ (Rom. 10:16, 20-21); that they have been blinded, put to sleep, so that the message of the apostles has been no clearer to them than a sealed or hidden scroll.

There is force in these descriptions; St. Paul himself calls one of them "bold" (Rom. 10:20). They are all based on a psalm and on the books of Isaiah and Deuteronomy. Hence, whatever severity there is in them comes down from the Old Testament, a severity, however, that forever remains one of the glories of the Ancient Dispensation. Never has there been a people in whose midst men, inspired and intrepid, dared to castigate the sins of prince, priest, and people alike. Israel may have paid little heed to her prophets; but were the like ever born, ever active, elsewhere?

Though the Apostle plainly continues the stern prophetic tradition, he will not speak of Israel's failure without adding a word of mitigation. The prophets, too, were men of compassion; severe *and* mild, they not only accused but also brought God's comfort to their people. Thus St. Paul will not mention the discernment so sadly lacking in his unbelieving kinsmen without testifying to their *zeal* for God (Rom. 10:2-3). He will not declare: "Israel did not obey the gospel." Because love or, if you wish, truth — the two are one — demands a more discreet expression, he prefers to say: "*Not all* have surrendered to the gospel" (Rom. 10:16). Again, in looking at the many who are severed from communion with the Lord Jesus, he gently states: "*Some* of the branches have been broken off" (Rom. 11:17). This is not mere caution. By faith, he sees the "little flock" (Luke 12:32) as a mighty army and the small remnant as the Israel to whom the wide world has been joined. The few who believe, the infant Church, he recognizes as the core of all mankind redeemed.

Sure of God's saving purpose, St. Paul cannot but speak lovingly. Nowhere is this more manifest than in Romans 11:11-12. If anyone had reason to feel bitter toward his dissident brethren, it was he. Previously he had called them "hostile to all men" because they sought to prevent him and his fellow apostles from proclaiming the way of salvation to the Gentiles (1 Thess. 2:16). But in writing to the Romans he calls their failure a "faux pas," a "false step," a "blunder"; "they tripped," he adds, "they caught their feet," "they stumbled."

Those who are inclined to consider "misstep" an understatement that has no explanation other than a momentary weakness of the Apostle, a partiality toward his own flesh and blood, must find even more surprising his positive view of Israel's "No." Many, far too many, have stumbled, yet their stumbling is a means, not an end, in the hands of God. Israel's lapse has become an instrument of reconciliation. Compressed into a brief sentence, St. Paul's dialectical argument is this: Israel fell in order to rise. A paradox altogether divine!

## Israel's salvation

When the Lord brought Gentiles who once worshipped gods that were "nothings" into the Church, He made branches that had grown in the barren wilderness fruitful, the Apostle tells us. If He has done this, that is to say, if He was willing to transplant branches against their own "nature," how much more will He make fruitful those who are taken from the garden He Himself planted? St. Paul exclaims: "It is in God's power to graft them back" (Rom. 11:23). He who was willing to make mute pagans respond to His word cannot be less willing to make the people He addressed so often — who, it is true, alternated between response and contradiction but never remained dumb — say "Amen," and say it with such vigor that their response will reverberate throughout the cosmos.

For a moment, for a long moment, however, the road on which God takes the world to its salvation bypasses the majority in Israel in favor of her remnant and of generations of Gentiles. For the time being, Israel as a people is outside the Church. Still, it is not forsaken. God's word endures, His choice stands, His gifts and calling will not be revoked nor will they fail (Rom. 11:29). In spite of the present disbelief in Jesus as the Christ, the Jews remain destined for God, ordained for His saving purpose. Willing or not, they belong to Him; they cannot cease to be the people of His predilection, for He loves them because He is good and His mercy everlasting (Ps. 135 [136]).

Among the wonders that keep the unsubmissive Israel bound to God is the biblical principle of solidarity. "If the first handful of dough is holy, so is the whole lump; if the root is holy, so are the branches" (Rom. 11:16). As the first cake from the year's harvest hallows all the bread in the land when offered to God, so do the first fruits of Christ's as well as of the apostles' preaching foreshadow an outpouring of God's grace on the whole people. Again, as a root determines the growth, indeed, the character of a tree, so do the patriarchs, particularly Abraham, give direction to the lives of their descendants. The holy remnant is a pledge of the salvation of all Israel; Abraham, the recipient of God's promise, is himself a promise that the now aloof Israel will in the end turn to Christ.

This joyous assurance is the dialectical counterpart to the sorrow with which the Apostle begins chapter nine. At the same time, it is closely linked to the stern words with which he warns Rome's Gentile Christians not to gloat over the lapsed Israel, not to attribute to themselves what they owe to God's abundant mercy and to the richness of the olive stem that bears them. Together with the candid confession that by his untiring work among the Gentiles he ultimately seeks the reconciliation of his own kinsmen (Rom.

11:13-14), together with his exhortation that those chosen from among the Gentiles remain part of the life-giving tree by clinging to God's goodness (Rom. 11:17-24), his hopeful vision of Israel's history, which sees patriarch and remnant as tokens of a future of grace for his people (Rom. 11:16), seems to interrupt the mighty movement that leads from verse 11 to verse 32.

If these passages must be considered parenthetical, then they must be thought of as interludes necessary to heighten, rather than lessen, the crescendo of chapter eleven. They are necessary to strengthen St. Paul's message that without Israel's ingathering the world cannot attain its ultimate perfection, and that without accomplishing her salvific instrumentality for the world, Israel is not her true and full self. So vital is the link between Israel and the world that the people of Israel has been called the Alpha and Omega of the entire history of salvation.

Leaving the parenthetical verses behind, we would like to set down St. Paul's Good News in a translation of our own. As at the Easter Vigil the deacon sings, in an ever higher key, *Lumen Christi*, "Light of Christ," so the Apostle goes from joy to joy until he bursts into a jubilant shout: "If their misstep has enriched the world, if their smaller number has enriched the nations, what will their full tale not accomplish?" (Rom. 11:12). He rejoices further: "If their exclusion meant a world reconciled [to God], what will their inclusion mean if not life from the dead?" (Rom. 11:15). Finally, he exclaims: "Lest you trust your own mind [and invent your own solutions to Israel's future], I shall not leave you unaware of this mystery: A part of Israel has become hardened [and this, its insensibility, will last] until the totality of Gentiles has entered. [When this has happened], all Israel will be saved, as is written:

> Out of Zion will come the Deliverer;
>     he will banish all godlessness from Jacob.
> And this is what I shall do for them:
>     I shall take away their sins" (Rom. 11:25-27).

## The wholeness of God's saving design

This, then, is the working of God's saving design: though Israel's ingathering will be God's doing, God's plan for the world will not be accomplished without Israel. By itself, to be Abraham's offspring is nothing; indeed, it is wrong for a Jew (as it is for any man) to put his trust in his ancestry rather than in God's mercy. Such is the teaching of the Gospels as it is that of St. Paul (cf. Gal. 5:6). Yet he also teaches the complementary truth that there is much good in being a Jew: in looking at a Jew, God remembers the words He entrusted to Abraham and his sons (Rom. 3:1-2). Again, the Apostle writes that where there is a new birth "there is neither Jew nor Greek . . . All are one in Christ Jesus" (Gal. 3:28). But this proclamation of oneness must be seen in the light of the message in the Epistle to the Romans that Jews and Gentiles somehow need one another to become ready for Christ's offer of salvation and that the world needs both — the unity of both — to obtain the fullness of His peace. How could it be otherwise? What love is intent upon giving, only love can receive.

To one outstanding biblical scholar, the special importance that St. Paul assigned to the Jews and their ultimate turning to Christ seems artificial. He goes on to say that if the promise means future blessedness for "Israel," then the heir of this promise is *either* the historic Israel *or* the New Israel, the Body of Christ, in which no people holds a special place. St. Paul, he feels, tries to have it both ways. In a manner of speaking, this great exegete is right. St. Paul does love "both ways": ultimate blessedness for the Israel according to the flesh, not apart from, but in and through, union with the Israel according to the spirit. Instead of a sad *aut — aut*, "either — or," he preaches the jubilant *et — et*, "as well as," "not only — but also" which is the mark of the whole of Catholic doctrine.

To other exegetes, too, a promise that Israel as a people will be saved seems to be in conflict with the promises fulfilled in the Church; it seems to impair her unique place, as though abundance of grace could ever be determined. Not a few of the early Fathers, inclined as they were to allegorization, understood St. Paul's prophecy "All Israel shall be saved" as referring to the spiritual Israel, and so did some of the reformers.

If I may use resolute language, any interpretation of this kind emasculates St. Paul's message, which is that of the majesty of God, of His fearlessness, of a God unafraid, as it were, of astounding His critics as well as His followers. In any case, the overwhelming majority of exegetes throughout the ages give full force to St. Paul's prophecy of Israel's final return. Though we can but conjecture on its pattern and consequences, on its manner of unfolding and on its immediate fruit, this uncertainty in no way undoes the certainty of the hope itself. A divine promise, an apostolic legacy, Israel's eschatological conciliation with the Church is part of her unfailing expectation.


# THE CHRISTIAN'S UNION WITH THE BODY OF CHRIST IN CORINTHIANS, GALATIANS, ROMANS

Barnabas Mary Ahern, C.P.

Today there is a growing trend towards strong realism in explaining St. Paul's theme of the body of Christ.[1] Far from interpreting it as a mere meta-

Published originally in *The Catholic Biblical Quarterly*, 23, (1961), 199-209. Reprinted by permission of the publisher.

[1] Besides the authors mentioned in this article the following writers are also to be noted:

phor signifying the collectivity of Christians as an organization, many Pauline
scholars explain it as a literal designation of the risen Christ in all his concrete reality. This contemporary insight into Paul's thought has led J. A. T.
Robinson [2] to complain, "One could heartily wish that the misleading and un-
biblical phrase the 'mystical' body had never been invented."

A biblist, however, may never forget that other norms besides Scripture
determine the formulation of doctrine. The fact is that the encyclical *Mystici Corporis* [3] presents cogent reasons to show how aptly this phrase expresses
the full theological content of the Church's teaching. However, the absence
of this expression from Scripture plus the fact that contemporary formulae do
not always square with Pauline thought patterns urges a reinvestigation of the
scriptural source of our present doctrine. As Pope Pius XII [4] pointed out
in *Divino Afflante Spiritu,* much is to be gained for understanding a dogma
by pressing the sources of revelation for their precise literal contribution.

The following pages present a summary review of pertinent allusions to
the body of Christ in 1 Cor., Gal., and Rom. It is in these epistles that this
concept first receives explicit expression; here too we find the principles which
underlie all later development of this theme in Col. and Eph.

## Exponents of realism

Much work has already been done to demonstrate the dynamic realism
of Paul's thought. Canon Cerfaux [5] has affirmed time and again that in using
the words "Christ" and "body of Christ" Paul never speaks of a pneumatic
or mystical Christ but always of the real historic person who rose from the
tomb and ascended into heaven. Departing from the earlier position of authors like Prat [6] and Allo [7] he insists that Christians do not form a mystical
Christ but rather belong to the real organism of his risen person. [8] Père Benoit, [9] after several shifts of view, has also endorsed this thesis, asserting

E. Percy, *Der Leib Christi in den paulinischen Homologoumena und Antilegomena* (Lund:
Gleerup-Harrassowitz, 1942); P. L. Malevez, "L'Eglise, Corps du Christ. Sens et provenance de l'expression chez saint Paul," *RSR* 32 (1944) 27-94; W. Goosens, *L'Église, Corps
du Christ d'après saint Paul* (Paris: Gabalda, 1949); L. S. Thornton, *The Common Life in
the Body of Christ* (2d ed.; Westminster, 1944).

[2] *The Body: A Study in Pauline Theology* (Chicago: Regnery, 1952) 52 n. 1.

[3] *AAS* 35 (1943) 221-222.

[4] *AAS* 35 (1943) 310.

[5] *Christ in the Theology of St. Paul,* tr. G. Webb-A. Walker (New York: Herder,
1959) 324-343; *The Church in the Theology of St. Paul,* tr. G. Webb-A. Walker (New
York: Herder, 1959) 262-281.

[6] *Theology of St. Paul,* tr. J. L. Stoddard (Westminster, Md.: Newman, 1927) II, 258.

[7] *Première Epître aux Corinthiens* (EB; Paris: Gabalda, 1934) 328f.

[8] *The Church in the Theology of St. Paul,* 269.

[9] "Corps, Tête et Plérôme dans les epîtres de la Capitivité," *RB* 63 (1956) 7, 9-10.
In this article, on p. 6, B. retracts the earlier view expressed in his review of A. Wikenhauser's *Die Kirche als der Mystische Leib,* in *RB* 45 (1938) 118. According to this view
he conceded that the body theme in Rom. and 1 Cor. is only a metaphor, borrowed from
the Stoics, to express the union of Christians. He now says of this: "Cette manière de voir
ne me parait plus soutenable."

that the body of Christ is not a supra-personal collectivity but the full organism of the animated body-person who now reigns gloriously in heaven. It is, above all, the monograph study of J. A. T. Robinson, *The Body: A Study in Pauline Theology*, which presents a fully rounded coverage of this theme.[10] In this slender volume Robinson proceeds from a careful study of Hebrew monistic anthropology to its influence on the Pauline theme of the body of Christ "as the physical complement and extension of the one and the same Person and Life."[11] Needless to say, this realistic thesis has not won universal acceptance; but opposition to it is generally due to the influence of a philosophic postulate (cf. Bultmann[12] and Dibelius[13]) or to a misunderstanding of the thought patterns involved (cf. Zapelena[14]).

## Directive principles of Pauline thought

This fresh approach to St. Paul's thought rests its case on two principles which consistently govern his treatment. (1) As a Hebrew writing on religious themes, he speaks of the body not as a neutral element in the body-soul composite of Greek anthropology but rather as an animated and corporeal person whose thoughts and desires are contained and revealed under the sensible aspect of somatic experience.[15] Though it is an exaggeration to say that the Hebrew mentality knew nothing of the body in a restricted and neutral sense,[16] it is quite correct to say that a Hebrew using the word body in a religious context includes in that term the whole person with emphasis on what is sensible and somatic. This Semitic thought pattern is also our own; for though in abstract speculation we divide man into component parts, still in practical life we are always aware of man's unity, of the inseparable bond between psychic experience and somatic reaction. We deal with one another as corporeal persons; love and hate, hope and fear involve an automatic somatic experience and inevitably seek sensible expression.

(2) As an Israelite Paul thinks of Christ as a corporate personality.[17] This

[10] This book should be read with the reservations noted by P. Benoit in his review of it in *RB* 64 (1957) 581-3.
[11] J. A. T. Robinson, *op. cit.*, 51.
[12] *Theology of the New Testament*, tr. K. Grobel (New York: Scribners, 1951) I, 299, 310-11.
[13] *An die Thessalonicher 1-2, an die Philipper* (3d ed., *HNT*; Tübingen: Mohr-Siebeck, 1937) 85-93.
[14] "Vos estis corpus Christi (1 Cor 12:17)," *VD* 37 (1959) 78-95, 162-170.
[15] J. A. T. Robinson, *The Body*, 26-28 and *passim*; W. Gutbrod, *Die paulinische Anthropologie* (Stuttgart: Kohlhammer, 1934) 32ff. H. Mehl-Köhnlein, *L'homme selon l'apôtre Paul* (Neuchâtel: Delachaux-Niestlé, 1951) 9ff.
[16] Because Robinson seems to imply that the Hebrews always used the word body as referring to the whole person and never in the restricted and neutral sense, Benoit counters in *RB* 64 (1957) 582, by asking the pointed question, "L'Hébreu ne se pensait-il vraiment et toujours que dans ses rapports avec Dieu? Je crains qu'en évitant de faire de lui un philosophe, on en fasse un théologien."
[17] Cf. H. Wheeler Robinson, "The Hebrew Conception of Corporate Personality," *Werden und Wesen des Alten Testaments* (*BZAW* 66, 1936) 46ff.; T. W. Manson, *The Servant-Messiah* (Cambridge: University Press, 1953) 74 with bibliography.

concept, which probably stems from the role of the chief in Israel's tribal and national life, is found frequently in the OT and must be kept in mind if one is to understand the eponymic character of its history, the continuity of God's favor recorded in its sacred literature, the existence and permanence of its messianic hope. This concept is equally important for understanding Paul's presentation of Christ as the new Adam[18] and his teaching on the efficacy of sacramental contact with Christ. Because he is a corporate personality the Savior died and rose again with vicarious efficacy: "Since one died for all, therefore all died" (2 Cor. 5:14).[19] Herein lies his power to share with others the salvific effects of his death and resurrection.

These two notions of the body as a person and of Christ as a corporate personality are essential for correct and full understanding of Paul's teaching on the meaning and efficacy of the body of Christ.

## The body theme in 1 Cor. 6:14-17

His first allusion to this theme introduces it not so much as a master principle of his system but as the emergent of a particular context. He writes of it because he chooses to challenge an ugly problem on the level of its own realism.

Christians of Corinth had fallen back into fornication, into the commingling of body with body not merely as a physical experience but as a full personal and psychic interchange of thought and affection. Paul opposes the sin by appealing to another bond which the Christian has already contracted, the well-known bond between his *sôma* and the *sôma* of the glorified Christ, which is as real as the union between a man and a harlot: "Do you not know that your bodies are members of Christ? Shall I then take the members of Christ and make them members of a harlot" (1 Cor. 6:15)? In both cases the full person is involved. *Sôma* is not merely the physical element in the body-soul composite; for Paul the Hebrew it is the whole self as an animated body vital with the fullness of personality.

It is true, the union between a man and a harlot has in it only the weakness and earthiness of *sarx*: "He who cleaves to a harlot becomes one body with her. 'For the two,' it says, 'shall be in one flesh.' " On the other hand, the union between the Christian and the glorified Christ is vital with the strength and holiness of *pneuma*: "He who cleaves to the Lord is one spirit with him" (1 Cor. 6:17). Nevertheless, whether the union be in "flesh" or in "spirit" (in the Pauline sense of apart from God or in God), it is always the full body-person that is involved.[20] It is significant that the

[18] The "New Adam" theme is developed by S. Hanson, *The Unity of the Church in the New Testament, Colossians and Ephesians* (Uppsala: Almquist and Wiksells, 1946) 65-73; E. Percy, *Der Leib Christi*, 38-42; F. Prat, *Theology of St. Paul* II, 446-7; L. Cerfaux, *Christ in the Theology of St. Paul*, 230-43.

[19] A. Feuillet, "Mort du Christ et mort du chrétien d' après les épîtres pauliniennes," *RB* 66 (1959) 483-7.

[20] P. Benoit, "Corps, Tête et Plérôme," 13, n. 5: "C'est par opposition au *sôma* uni à

"cleaving" of the Christian to Christ in this text is the *kollasthai* of man cleaving to his wife in God's decree of permanence in marriage (Gen. 2:24: LXX).

## The body theme in Rom. 7:4

Again in Rom. 7:4 it is obviously the course of context which leads Paul to speak of Christians belonging to the risen body of the Savior in language which is uncompromisingly physical. In treating of the Christian's relation to the law and to Christ he has introduced the example of a woman free to marry another after the death of her husband. On the basis of this example he goes on to describe the Christian's new relation to Christ as physically real and personal as that of man and wife: "We have been made to die to the law, so as to belong to another who has risen from the dead, in order that we may bring forth fruit unto God" (Rom. 7:4).

These first allusions to the body of Christ are thus incidental, the emergent of a given context. Yet they have a validity all their own because they express so aptly the realism of the Christian's union with Christ as Paul sees it and as he, or his disciple, will express it later in the consummate synthesis of his thought in Eph. 5:25-32 where he likens the union of Christ and his church to the bond between a devoted husband and his wife. No union could be more intimate, because no dependence could be more complete. All that the Christian has as a Christian he receives in the total surrender of his body-person to the body-person of Christ: "You are in Christ Jesus, who has become for us God-given wisdom, and justice, and sanctification, and redemption" (1 Cor. 1:30-31).[21]

## Incorporation through baptism

This union begins at baptism, as Paul indicates in Gal. 3:27-28. Though shifting his thought pattern he maintains the dynamic realism of the Christian experience: "All you who have been baptized into Christ have put on Christ." The analogy is drawn from the action of putting on a garment; but, as G. Duncan[22] points out, "In Scripture it denotes that the wearer becomes in a subtle way identified with what he puts on." Thus God is clothed with majesty (Ps. 92:1); the arm of the Lord puts on strength (Is. 51:9); the wicked are clothed with shame and disgrace (Ps. 34:26); Job puts on justice (Job 29:14). The same use of *endyesthai* is found also, though rarely, in classical Greek where it signifies similarly entering into another's disposi-

---

la courtisane sous son aspect de *sarx* que Paul écrit ici *pneuma*; il songe en réalité au *sôma pneumatikon* du Christ ressuscité, dont le chrétien est un membre." Cf. E. Percy, *Der Leib Christi*, 14f.

[21] This text probably expresses better than any other the Christian's subjective participation in the mediation of Christ. W. L. Knox, *St. Paul and the Church of the Gentiles* (Cambridge: University Press, 1939) 115, n. 1, has called attention to its importance.

[22] *The Epistle of St. Paul to the Galatians* (Moffat NTC; Hodder and Stoughton: London, 1934) 123.

tions.[23] Paul employs this figure fifteen times. The present text shows how intimate is the identification which it evokes.[24] For he goes on to affirm that in the psycho-somatic rite of baptism the body-person of the Christian is so totally surrendered to Christ that whatever is merely *sarx* disappears, so that "There is neither Jew nor Greek; there is neither slave nor freeman; there is neither male nor female. For you are all one ('*eis* — masculine) in Christ Jesus" (Gal. 3:28).[25]

In speaking of the Apostle's conversion, Wikenhauser[26] has posed the question whether it was his faith at the Damascus theophany or his baptism a few days later that made him one with Christ. Probably it never occurred to Paul to differentiate the two moments, since in his mind both elements formed but one experience. For the Jew man acts always as a body-person, with an ambit of activity which necessarily includes a physical and sensible aspect.[27] Hence faith in Christ involves, by inherent necessity, the concomitant resolution to join one's whole self to the whole self (*sôma*) of Christ in the physical rite of baptism. Paul's inward experience on the road to Damascus had a radical exigency to be consummated in baptism that his whole self might be engaged in full union with the body-person of Christ. Through baptism the surrender of faith which he had elicited previously found expression in the psycho-somatic rite which completed the surrender of his whole self (*sôma*) to the body-person of the Savior.

Paul therefore teaches clearly that Christian life involves a real and personal union between the individual *sôma* of the Christian and the individual *sôma* of the glorified Christ, a union so intimate that the body-person of the Savior alone functions as the directive spiritual force. If they are two in one spirit, there is no doubt to whom the spirit belongs: "I live, now not I, but Christ lives in me" (Gal. 2:20).

## Body union through the Eucharist

This same realism prevails when Paul comes to speak of Christians as a collectivity in his discussion of the Eucharist. Once more the point of departure for his memorable statement is a particular problem, the danger of syncretism arising from sharing in the banquets of pagan worship. He declares that such conduct is incompatible with the celebration of the Christian sup-

[23] Dionysius Halicarn., *Antiquitates Romanae* 11, 5: *ton Tarkynion endyesthai;* Libanius, *Epistulae,* 1048, 2: *ripsas straitōtēn enedy ton sophistēn.* Cf. A. Oepke, *ThWNT* 2, 319-20.

[24] St. John Chrys., commenting on Gal. 3:28 (*PG* 61:656), observes that St. Paul has exhausted every means of expressing the intimacy of this union until finally he describes the Christian as manifesting Christ in himself (*en autō deiknys ton Christon*).

[25] W. D. Davies, *Paul and Rabbinic Judaism* (London: SPCK, 1958) 57, refers this text to the Rabbinic doctrine of the unity of man in Adam: "The 'body' of Adam included all mankind. Was it not natural, then, that Paul when he thought of the new humanity being incorporated 'in Christ' should have conceived of it as the 'body' of the second Adam, where there was neither Jew nor Greek, male nor female, bond nor free."

[26] *Die Christusmystik des Apostels Paulus* (2nd ed.; Freiburg im B.: Herder, 1956) 90ff.

[27] A. Schweitzer, *Die Mystik des Apostels Paulus* (Tübingen: Mohr-Siebeck, 1930) 110-40.

per which joins the Christian to Christ: "The bread that we break, is it not the sharing (*koinōnia*) of the body of the Lord" (1 Cor. 10:16)?

As proof of this real presence of Christ in the Eucharist Paul appeals to a fact which carried a barbed thrust to the disunited Corinthians. He recalls the truth which was recognized from the beginning (Acts 2:42):[28] the remarkable *koinōnia* of Christian fellowship — the unity of many with one another — has its total cause in the *koinōnia* of each individual with Christ in the breaking of the bread: "Because the bread is one, we though many, are one body, we who partake of the one bread" (1 Cor. 10:17). In this text the "one body" is still the individual body-person of the risen Christ. There is nothing here to urge that Paul is beginning to use the Stoic analogue as a metaphor for the social organization of the church.[29] The "many" are "one body" because communion makes each one con-corporeal with Christ. In the realism of Paul's thought, both baptism and communion enable the risen Savior to become "all in all" (cf. 1 Cor. 12:13). Indeed, Dr. Rawlinson[30] is on firm ground when he emphasizes the importance of the Eucharist as a prime element in shaping Paul's doctrine on the church as the body of Christ.

## Body theme in 1 Cor. 12 and Rom. 12

Here one is more tempted to find a metaphorical sense in Paul's extended discussion of the body of Christ. Familiar as he was with the expressions and thought patterns of the Stoa[31] he could have used their classic body theme as a metaphor to describe the unity in diversity which characterized the church as a social body with its distinct functions and members.[32]

But several reasons militate against this. First of all, F. de Visscher[33] has shown that the Greek noun *sôma* never denoted a collectivity or social group, but always a real physical body. If, therefore, Paul identifies Christians as the body of Christ, he cannot mean that Christians are merely an organization.

[28] S. Lyonnet, "La 'Koinōnia' de l'Église primitive et la sainte Eucharistie," *Actas del XXXV Congreso Eucaristico Internacional, Barcelona 1952*, Sesiones de Estudio 1,5111-15; M. Fraeyman, "Fractio panis in communitate primitiva," *Collationes Brugenses et Gandavenses* (1955) 370-3.

[29] L. Cerfaux, *The Church in the Theology of St. Paul*, 278-9.

[30] "Corpus Christi," *Mysterium Christi*, ed. G. K. Bell and A. Deissmann (Berlin 1931) 275-296.

[31] A. Fridrichsen, "Zum Thema 'Paulus und die Stoa,'" *Coniect. neotestam.* 9 (1944) 27-31; J. Nelis, "Les antithèses littéraires dans les Épitres de saint Paul," *NRT* 70 (1948), 360-387.

[32] The Stoa instructed the true man to regard himself as a member of the body-universe; cf. Seneca, *Ep.* 92,30; 95,52; Epictetus, *Dissert.* 2,5,24; 2,5,26; 2,10,31. A number of pertinent texts from the Stoa are presented by A. Wikenhauser, *Die Kirche als der Mystische Leib nach dem Apostel Paulus* (Münster in West.: Aschendorff, 1937) 130-43; cf. J. Dupont, *Gnosis. La connaissance religieuse dans les épîtres de saint Paul* (Louvain: Nauwelaerts, 1949) 435-8.

[33] The suggestion of T. W. Manson, "A Parallel to a New Testament Use of *sôma*," *JTS* 37 (1935) 835, has been effectively challenged by F. de Visscher, *Les édits d'Auguste décourverts à Cryène* (Louvain: Bibl. de 'Université, 1940) 91: "En dépit de nos récherches (dans la littérature contemporaine), il nous a été impossible de découvrir un seul exemple où ce mot servirait à désigner une collectivité."

Secondly, and more important, throughout this chapter Paul rests his argument not on the diversity which was obvious and provocative but on the unity which is "the first conviction of his faith and theology." [34] There is only one body, one Spirit, one Christ: for Paul this is the perfect answer to the problem. Though he describes the diversity at length (and here he may be following the language of the Stoa), still he constantly brings back the thoughts of his readers to the fundamental fact that each one is *syssōmos* with Christ: baptized into his body-person, they are constantly preserved in union with him by drinking of one Spirit in the Eucharist (v. 13).[35] If, then, like any real body, the body of Christ must be differentiated into many members, this only corroborates the truth that all Christians together are really the body of Christ, member for member, ruled and vivified by his Spirit.

The question immediately arises, "Is Paul then speaking of the risen body of the personal Christ, or is he speaking of a body apart from Christ yet vivified by him? *Tertium non datur*." But even today this type of question is fair and valid only when both the questioner and the one giving answer are both thinking in the same thought patterns. It would not be right to press Paul with this query for the simple reason that his thought here rises eminently above our thought and includes formalities which our thought patterns tend to differentiate. He knows and he has said clearly that every Christian is united really and corporally to the risen body of Christ. Concentrating on this thought of the allness and uniqueness of Christ, he has nothing left to say except that all Christians together must be the body of Christ. How this is possible is not his concern at this point. Canon Cerfaux [36] is content to translate Paul's words with the non-committal, "You are a body, a body which is that of Christ." It will be the later controversy with the Colossians which will render his expression precise in describing the nature of the bond as the relation of head and members.[37] At the stage of 1 Cor., his thought is moving at a level of eminence and realism which is all-inclusive.

## The body theme in Romans

In this epistle Paul simply presumes that his readers are familiar with the truth that Christian life has united them — body-person to body-person — with Christ. In developing his thought he is much more concerned to show the dynamic involvements of this union. In becoming a member of Christ's body one lives by his life and shares in all the salvific activity of him who died

[34] P. Benoit, "Corps, Tête et Plérôme," 14.

[35] E. Percy, *Der Leib Christi*, 17 and R. Schnackenburg, *Das Heilsgeschehen bei der Taufe nach dem Apostel Paulus*, 78-80, interpret the whole passage (v. 13) as referring to baptism, so that both members form a synonymous parallelism. However, in view of a previous reference to baptism as distinct from nourishment: food-drink (1 Cor. 10:2-4), it seems more likely that the "drinking of the Spirit" is a reference to the Christian sacrament of nourishment, the Eucharist. This is the concluson of E. Käsemann, *Leib und Leib Christi* (*Beiträge zur historischen Theologie*; Tübingen, 1933) 176; P. Benoit, "Corps, Tête et Plérôme," 15.

[36] *The Church in the Theology of St. Paul*, 277.

[37] P. Benoit, "Corps, Tête et Plérôme," 18ff.

and rose again as the corporate person par excellence. In the first part of this epistle Christ is seen at work in his task of dying and rising for men. In the second part the Christian shares dynamically in all that Christ is and has. So intimately is he united to the body-person of the Savior that his whole spiritual life becomes the death-life of Christ (Rom. 6:3-11) through the activity of the Spirt who vivifies and glorifies the whole body (Rom. 8).[38] In a word, life *in Christ* is inseparably connected with and provides foundation for life *with Christ*.

This conclusion emerges clearly from the inadequacy of P. Bonnard's recent effort [39] to present a definitive explanation of Paul's *syn*-phrases on the score of merely forensic justification. After reviewing and pointing out the weaknesses of various explanations of this Pauline expression (pp. 105–110), he makes his own suggestion that Paul has borrowed the use of *syn* from the Hellenistic liturgies, even though B. must admit that there is nothing so far discovered in the literature of the mysteries to substantiate his claim (p. 110). As for the reality contained in the *syn*-phrase it consists totally in the mere assent of the individual, living in the present, to the unique and definitive fact of Christ's death and resurrection (pp. 111-112).

This proposal, however, carries the sign of its own weakness. The very fact that Bonnard traces the Pauline *syn*-phrase to the mystery literature (though confessedly without actual verification) shows his awareness that in the Pauline corpus this phrase is essentially dependent upon the believer's real and present share in the life of the Savior, an element which is common to the teaching of Paul and the liturgy of the mystery cult.

Moreover, unless Paul's teaching on life *with Christ* is founded upon the realism of life *in Christ*, then Christian experience, as described in the Pauline epistles, is merely the human psychological effort of Jewish striving for justice. Indeed, the salvific event of Calvary is no more effective in the life of the individual than the divine intervention at Sinai unless the believer shares by real participation in the action of the Savior. In ruling out this real contact and in explaining Rom. 6:3-11 as descriptive of a mere mental attitude on the part of the believer, Bonnard is forced to reduce the baptismal liturgy to the commemorative value of the Pesach regulations in Exod. 13. This is precisely what he does (pp. 111-112; cf. p. 109).

The actual words of Paul, on the other hand, (especially *ebaptisthomen eis Christon* in v. 3[40] and *symphytoi* in v. 5)[41] plus the whole background

---

[38] Cf. A. Feuillet, "Le Mystère Pascal et la Résurrection des chrétiens d'après les Épîtres pauliniennes," *NRT* 79 (1957) 343: "Dans l'Épitre aux Romains, il est certain que les deux tableaux des chapitres VI (délivrance par le Christ dans le baptême) et VIII (délivrance par l'Ésprit Saint) se correspondent et se complètent."

[39] "Mourir et vivre avec Jésus-Christ selon saint Paul," *RHPhilRel* 36 (1956) 101-12. The page references in the text are all taken from this article.

[40] A. Oepke, *ThWNT* 1, 538-9.

[41] P. Gächter, "Zur Exegese von Rom. 6:5," *ZKT* 54 (1930) 88-92. All will not accept the author's conclusion that this verse involves an anacoluthon. However, his review of all proposed interpretations focuses attention on the general agreement that *symphytoi* involves the concept of real union.

of Pauline doctrine make clear that he teaches a true and intimate union between the Christian and the risen Christ, in virtue of which the baptized actually shares all that Christ has accomplished as his representative. This truth is succinctly stated by S. Lyonnet:[42]

> Strictly speaking, the Christ to whom St. Paul declares us united is always the glorious Christ; but, since he is a Christ who died and rose again, we, by the very fact of our union with him, share in the effects of his death and resurrection. It is in this sense that we are plunged into his death, are crucified and rise with him.

## Conclusion

The teaching of Paul on the body of Christ is eminently simple. For him all union is the surrender of the body of the Christian in the Semitic sense of self to the body-self of the risen Savior, thus forming with him only one body. The conclusion is inescapable. This union is an existential contact and a dynamic identification between the faithful and the body charged with power; especially is this true in baptism (Rom. 6:3-11; Gal. 4:27-28) and in the Eucharist (1 Cor. 10:16-17; 11:24-30). The life that is in the body becomes the life of those who are its members. Whether in the first moment of union or in the moment of Parousia consummation, both the Christian and Christ are inseparably united: "We know that Christ, having risen from the dead . . . lives unto God. Thus do you consider yourselves also as alive to God in Christ Jesus" (Rom. 6:10-11).

Seen in this light Paul's doctrine in the great epistles gives strength and meaning to contemporary doctrine on the mystical body. By placing emphasis on the realism of the union between the individual Christian and Christ he contributes a clear insight into the nature of the bond which unites all Christians to one another. Because each one has his all in Christ and because Christ is all in all in each one, therefore the bond which unites one to the other is the dynamic presence of Christ himself. For if Paul's words have any meaning at all, they affirm that between the sôma-person of Christ and the sôma-person of the Christian there exists a bond so real that the Savior could say to Paul in the moment of his conversion the very words which sum up all his doctrine on the body of Christ: "Saul, why dost thou persecute me? . . I am Jesus whom thou art persecuting."

[42] Note on Rom. 6:4 in J. Huby-S. Lyonnet, Saint Paul, Épître aux Romains (VS 10; Paris: Beauchesne, 1957) 590.

# PAUL'S VISION OF THE CHURCH IN 'EPHESIANS'

Christopher F. Mooney, S.J.

Today the trend toward a strong realism in explaining Paul's theme of the Church as the Body of Christ seems to have gained a very wide acceptance among exegetes, Catholic and Protestant alike. Far from interpreting it as a mere metaphor signifying the collectivity of Christians as an organisation, Pauline scholars explain it as a literal designation of the risen Christ in all his concrete reality. Mgr Cerfaux affirms again and again that for Paul Christians do not form a "moral body," a "mystical Christ," but rather belong to the real organism of his risen person.[1] And Professor Robinson, in his fully rounded coverage of this theme, emphasises that Paul's "underlying conception is not of a supra-personal collective, but of a specific personal organism." The Church for Paul "is in fact no other than the glorified body of the risen and ascended Christ."[2]

The position of the Dominican scholar, Pierre Benoit, is essentially that of Robinson and Cerfaux: the Body of Christ for Paul is not a supra-personal collectivity but the full organism of the real historical body-person who rose from the tomb and now reigns gloriously in heaven.[3] In fact, the only objection today to this realistic thesis seems to be from those who argue not from exegesis but from the apparent lack of harmony between such an understanding of Paul and the fuller theological development found in the Fathers and especially in the encyclical *Mystici Corporis*. These objections, however, seem to be merely an example of what has already occurred frequently enough: a simple misunderstanding on the part of theologians of thought patterns discovered by the exegetes.[4]

Along with this wide agreement regarding the realism of Paul's theme of the Body of Christ, there is also general acceptance of the fact that the Epistle to the Ephesians represents the deepest and most profound development of Paul's thought on the Church. It is this development of Paul's thought and its implications for our own outlook which we wish to examine in this article.

Published originally in *Scripture*, 15 (1963), 33-43. Reprinted by permission of the publisher.

[1] Lucien Cerfaux, *La Théologie de l'Église suivant saint Paul*, 2e éd., Paris 1948, pp. 206, 209, 210, 212, 254, 259.

[2] J. A. T. Robinson, *The Body*, London 1952, p. 51.

[3] Pierre Benoit, 'Corps, Tête et Plérôme dans les Épîtres de la Captivité,' *Revue Biblique*, LXIII (1956), pp. 7-12, 20-1.

[4] For example, Th. Zapelena, 'Vos Estis Corpus Christi,' *Verbum Domini*, XXVII (1959), pp. 78-95, 162-70. A clear reply to Zapelena as well as an excellent statement of the reationship between Paul and *Mystici Corporis* has been given by J. Havet, 'La Doctrine Paulinienne du "Corps du Christ", Essai de Mise au Point,' *Litérature et Théologie Pauliniennes*, Louvain 1960, pp. 186-216.

At the end of the major epistles, says Cerfaux, the thought of Paul is that all Christians as a group, in so far as they are a spiritual organism, are mystically identified with the Body of Christ. It would be to go beyond the bounds of Paul's thought in these letters, he continues, either to identify this organism with the Person of Christ or to speak of a "Mystical Body" of Christ as a collective person which forms the Church.[5] This is also the conclusion of Benoit.[6] In the key texts of 1 Cor. 12 and Rom. 12 Paul concentrates on the fact that every Christian is united really and corporally to the risen Body of Christ. Within this limited thought pattern Paul can only say that all Christians together must be the Body of Christ. How this is possible is simply not his concern at this point. In the captivity epistles, however, there appears quite suddenly a totally new dimension. To appreciate fully what this new dimension is and its effects on Paul's conception of the Church, it would be well firstly to review the two sources of Paul's thinking on the Body of Christ, and secondly to indicate some of the events in Paul's own life which most likely contributed to the development and precision of his thought.

With Professor Robinson and Fr. Benoit we can discern two ideas constantly governing Paul's treatment of the Body theme. First of all, because he is a Hebrew writing on religious themes, Paul uses the word "body" not as a neutral element in the body-soul composite of Greek anthropology, but rather as an animated and corporeal person, whose thoughts and desires are contained and revealed under the sensible aspect of bodily experience.[7] Or to look at it from another viewpoint, because Paul is a Hebrew "he cannot imagine a man without his body, and therefore associates the body with the whole work of man's ultimate salvation."[8] Using the word "body" in a religious context, the Hebrew mentality includes in that term the whole person, with emphasis on what is sensible and somatic.

The second concept influencing Paul's thought, one quite familiar to the Old Testament, is that of the corporate personality. According to this theory the Semites conceived their nation or community, including its past, present and future members, as a single individual, who could be represented in turn by any one member of the nation. As a result there was frequently a natural oscillation in speech between group and individual, as can be seen for example in the Servant Songs of Deutero-Isaiah. Originating most probably from the role of the chief in Israel's tribal life, this concept is most important for understanding Paul's presentation of Christ as the new Adam who died and rose again with vicarious efficacy.[9]

[5] Cerfaux, op. cit. p. 215. See also the excellent study of the major epistles by Barnabas Mary Ahern, 'The Christian's Union with the Body of Christ in Cor., Gal. and Rom.' *Catholic Biblical Quarterly* XXIII (1961), pp. 199-209.

[6] Benoit, art. cit., pp. 13-18.

[7] J. A. T. Robinson, op. cit., pp. 26-8; Ahern, art. cit., p. 200.

[8] Benoit, art. cit., p. 18.

[9] H. W. Robinson, 'The Hebrew Concept of the Corporate Personality,' *Werden und Wesen des Alten Testaments*, ed. by J. Hempel, Berlin 1936, pp. 58ff. Also A. Feuillet, Mort du Christ et mort du Chrétien d'après les épîtres paulimennes,' *Revue Biblique* IXVI (1959), pp. 483-7.

These two concepts are quite sufficient for understanding Paul's teaching, nor is it necessary to think of the Body theme as ambiguous or, as some have done, to search for its source in the Persian myth of celestial man.[10] This is not to say that there was no influence on Paul's thought from the doctrine of the Eucharistic Body of Christ. On the contrary, in 1 Cor. 10:17 Paul himself directly grounds the unity of the Church on the Eucharist: "The one bread makes us one body, though we are many in number; the same bread is shared by all." Such an emphasis, moreover, highlights again the intense realism of Paul's consent of "Body of Christ;" in so far as the Christian community feeds on the body and blood of Christ, it actually becomes the glorified body of the risen and ascended Christ. But as Robinson points out, there is a jump here from "feeding on" to "becoming" which is taken by no other New Testament writer, all of whom must have been as familiar with the words of institution as Paul himself. The Eucharist, therefore, however significant it may have been for Paul's theology of the Body, is in no sense a full explanation of its development. Some prior experience is necessary to explain the jump in thought just indicated, and this experience Robinson places on the Damascus road. "The appearance on which Paul's whole faith and apostleship was founded was the revelation of the resurrection Body of Christ, not as an individual but as the Christian community."[11]

With these two main sources of Paul's thought in mind, we may now look briefly at the experiences which Paul himself underwent between the time he wrote Romans, probably in the winter of A.D. 57-58 and his arrival in Rome in the spring of 61, where he was to write the captivity epistles. In the first place, during these years Paul must have been impressed with the phenomenon of the Church, successfully organised in many places under its own hierarchy, yet very consciously united with the mother-church in Jerusalem.[12] Moreover, these were years of suffering and danger and finally imprisonment for Paul. His life was threatened by the Jews at Corinth, Jerusalem and during his more than two years' captivity in Caesarea.[13] The long journey to Rome, lasting all winter, brought shipwreck off Malta and three months there in hardship and danger.[14] He finally sailed to Puteoli, where there was a Christian community, and came eventually to Rome where he was met and welcomed by the Roman Christians. Such experiences must have impressed on the Apostle the solidarity of all "in Christ" as well as the universality of the Church.

Secondly, judging from Luke's account, Paul's mystical experience must have increased considerably during the whole period which led up to the

[10] Alfred Wikenhauser, *Die Kirche als der mystische Lieb Christi nach dem Apostel Paulus*, Münster 1940, pp. 232-40. cf. Cerfaux, op. cit. p. 281.
[11] J. A. T. Robinson, op. cit., p. 58. This is one of Robinson's most interesting hypotheses.
[12] Acts, chapters 20-28, gives us a picture of well-established communities in many places. In an unpublished text David M. Stanley, S.J., has developed at length the influence of these experiences on the captivity epistles.
[13] Acts 20:3; 21:27ff; 23:12-21; 25:27.
[14] Acts 28:11.

Roman captivity: he seems to live more continually under the guidance of the Holy Spirit. He goes to Jerusalem on the last journey from Greece "under compulsion by the Spirit" and "in every city the Holy Spirit assures me that imprisonment and persecution are awaiting me."[15] In Jerusalem even some of the scribes and Pharisees sense Paul's intense spiritual life, and in prison he is comforted by a vision of Christ himself.[16] Finally, on the journey to Rome, he prophesies, receives the vision of an angel, prophesies again.[17] All this seems to indicate how deep was Paul's spiritual growth during these years, a growth which, to judge by the captivity letters, had for its object the contemplation of Christ present in his Church.

Paul's thought on the Church in Ephesians is best put in perspective with a word on Colossians, since the two letters are linked so closely. While Paul was captive in Rome, the Church at Colossae began to be threatened by dangerous speculations on the heavenly powers, basically Jewish in origin but highly coloured by Hellenistic philosophy. So much importance was being attributed to these "powers" in their control of the universe and the course of events that the supremacy of Christ would seem to be compromised. The reaction of Paul was instantaneous, almost belligerent. His letter to Colossae asserted with vigour the supremacy of Christ as *Kyrios* over the whole universe. In the famous two-strophied hymn of Col. 1:15-20 Paul went back to the pre-existence of Christ with the Father, in whose image he is the source as well as the instrument and final end of creation. The Incarnation, crowned by the triumph of the Redemption, was seen as placing the human nature of Christ at the head not only of the whole human race but also of the entire created universe, the latter indirectly concerned in the salvation of man as it had been in his fall.[18]

It will be noted that the movement of Paul's thought here was the result of a situation which was imposed upon him. He himself did not choose the heavenly spheres as a terrain on which to do battle. Yet in accepting the terms of the contest at Colossae he placed himself on a psychological plane which was to have enormous consequences. For it was on this "celestial" level of thinking that he was soon to compose Ephesians, there to elaborate the full vision of the Church barely hinted at in Colossians.[19]

It is surprising that Mgr Cerfaux sees nothing essentially new added to the idea of the Church in Ephesians.[20] This is true only in the sense that the full flowering of the thought adds nothing essential to the seed of the idea. For throughout Colossians the perspective is clearly christological. Paul's whole energy is brought to bear on the supremacy of Christ over the heavenly powers. The concept of the Church, on the other hand, is kept well in the background and indeed, in the key text of Col. 1:18, seems to be added only

[15] Acts 20:22-23.
[16] Acts 23:9-11.
[17] Acts 27:1-34.
[18] Benoit, art. cit., pp. 34, 40.
[19] Pierre Benoit, 'L'Horizon Paulinien de l'Épître aux Éphésiens,' *Revue Biblique* XLVI (1937), p. 508.
[20] Cerfaux, op. cit., pp. 221-222.

as an afterthought, forced upon Paul by the very vastness of the canvas he is painting. The idea dominating Colossians therefore is one of subordination, with the idea of identification touched upon but left undeveloped. In Ephesians, however, it is precisely this latter notion of identification between Christ and his Church which is rethought under the full light of Paul's spiritual and intellectual maturity.[21] The perspective now becomes ecclesiological, and one senses immediately an atmosphere of serenity and calm reflection quite absent from the previous letter — as on the field of battle after victory has been won.

But what is of capital importance to recognise is that this ecclesiological perspective of Ephesians is itself situated within a new angle of vision, an angle defined by Benoit in Paul's own phrase: "in the spaces above the earth."[22] The errors at Colossae had forced Paul to turn his gaze toward the "powers" that ruled the heavens, and to affirm with full vigour that over them Christ was supreme. Forced by circumstances to think for the first time in these terms and sustained undoubtedly by his own growing mystical experience, Paul's attention focused more and more on heaven and away from earth. When his gaze had finally adjusted itself and he looked back again to the Church on earth from this new point of view, he found that he saw her under a completely new light. Her role in the plan of salvation had obviously not changed, but Paul's angle of vision had. Viewed from heaven, the drama being played out on the vast stage of the cosmos did not look the same as it did when viewed from earth. The scenery was indeed still the same; the lighting was quite different.

It is this change of lighting which must be taken into account. To read Ephesians from the perspective of the major epistles, without allowing for this new angle of vision, tends to produce the odd sensation that the book one is studying is slightly out of focus and that one is somehow seeing double. Initially this can be rather disconcerting and has itself been enough to make many serious exegetes doubt Paul's authorship, but this is another and more complex question. The point being made here is that when Paul looks back from heaven to earth on the members of the Church working out their salvation, he sees them now with a physiognomy quite different from that sketched in his earlier letters. They now appear more clearly distinct from Christ himself and more strongly united among themselves. That which strikes Paul most is the Church's collective unity, and this he begins to vest more and more in the attributes of a living person. The Church is now seen in process of growing and building up *toward* Christ who watches and directs this growth from his triumphant seat "in the heavens."[23]

Does this mean that Paul now wishes to assert a *separation* between Christ and his Church? Quite the contrary. What he is trying to do in Ephesians is

[21] Benoit, 'L'Horizon Paulinien . . .,' pp. 523-524.
[22] Ibid., pp. 511, 513; Eph. 6:12. Also Eph. 1:3; 1:20; 2:6; 3:10. These expressions do not appear in Colossians.
[23] Paul had already hinted at this development in Col. 1:18 and 24; 2:19; 3:1-4.

precisely to preserve that intimate and vital union between Christ and the individual Christian which so dominated his earlier thought, and at one and the same time to express what he now sees from the new angle of vision forced upon him by the Colossian controversy. This is no easy task, and he accomplishes it by a skilful if sometimes laborious deployment of three images, the very ones he had earlier used to emphasise union: those of Body, Temple and Bride. In Ephesians these images play a double role; they emphasise the collective unity of the Church, personified as it were and distinct from the person of Christ, and they serve as well to recall and underline the Church's lack of autonomy, her intimate union with Christ and total dependence upon him for her very being and life.[24] Let us see how each of these images accomplishes this double purpose.

Paul first perfects the image of the Body until it is able to express the new physiognomy of the Church which he has discovered. To appreciate what he does, it is important to realise that until now the word "Church" had served almost always as a designation for local communities.[25] In the major epistles it had almost never appeared in the ecumenical meaning we take for granted today, that of universal Church, the entire assembly of Christians.[26] Originally linked in Paul's mind with the Old Testament concept of "God's People," the term "Church of God" had gradually been applied by him to the individual Churches he had founded. Not until Col. 1:18 did it suddenly take on a strong ecumenical sense, and it did so there as a result of a synthesis of the themes of Head and Body that seem hitherto to have undergone separate developments in Paul's mind.

The Head theme, for example, when it appeared in 1 Cor. 11:2-4, was used to express not the union of Christians with or in Christ but a certain hierarchy of subordination: "head" in the sense of "superior." Thus in 1 Cor. 12:21 the "head" is simply a member of the body and is not identified with Christ at all. The Body theme, on the other hand, had always been used to express the idea of unity which was central to Paul's concept of salvation.[27] Through physical contact with the physical Body-Person of Christ through Baptism and the Eucharist, the Christian received as through a channel the life of the Spirit, and so in a very real sense became Christ, his members, his Body. The linking of these two themes of Head and Body, therefore, was natural enough when it occurred for the first time in Col. 1:18. Paul was emphasising the superiority of Christ as Head of the heavenly powers, and there was an easy passage from the use of "head" in the sense of "superior" to its use in the physical sense as Christ himself, Head of his body the Church. The word "head," moreover, when applied to the body, already contained the idea of vital principle and source of nourishment.[28]

[24] Benoit, 'L'Horizon Paulinien . . .,' pp. 515-517.
[25] Cerfaux, op. cit., pp. 143-157, gives a full treatment of texts.
[26] Ibid., p. 241. Benoit ('Corps, Tête . . .,' p. 22) finds the ecumenical meaning weakly asserted in three or four early texts, especially 1 Cor. 12:27ff.
[27] Cf. 1 Cor. 6:15; 10:17; 12:7-11; Rom. 12:6-8.
[28] Benoit, 'Corps, Tête . . .,' pp. 23-29. For quite another interpretation see J. Λ. T. Robinson, pp. 65-67, and Benoit's answer in Revue Biblique LXIV (1957), p. 585.

It is in the fourth chapter of Ephesians, however, that one finds the full implications of this linking of the three concepts of Head, Body and Church. At the start of the chapter Paul affirms the collective unity of Christians along with their organic diversity (vv. 3-11), followed by an emphasis on the new idea that the Body of Christ grows and perfects itself. What enables Paul to assert this is precisely his identifying Christ not with the Body but with the Head. The Head does not grow, yet it is from the fullness of perfection already present in him that there comes the vital energy responsible for the Body's growth (vv. 12-16). This distinction between Christ as Head and his Church as Body had never before been made so strongly by Paul, and it illustrates in a most striking way the preoccupation of his thought in Ephesians.[29]

This is not to say that the intense realism of the Pauline conception of the Body of Christ is in any way lessened. He can still affirm without hesitation that the universal Church is identified with the physical Body of Christ in heaven.[30] This he can do because, as Cerfaux points out, the ontological distinction seen from his new angle of vision in no way excludes a "mystical" identification at one and the same time. The physical Body of Christ pours out its life on Christians and these become his Body in the sense that the mystically present cause is attributed to the effect.[31] The Church quite literally is Christ's Body because she is composed of all Christians who in their material personality are united to the risen Body-Person of Christ and receive through him the new life of the Spirit. It would be vain, says Benoit, even false, to force Paul's terminology here to mean exclusively either Christ's physical Body and Spirit, or his Body the Church, which is his Spirit communicated to men. In Ephesians Paul means both together, indissolubly united: the individual Body of Christ grown to include all Christians united to him in their own bodies through faith and Baptism, with the fullness of the Spirit flowing from the Head down through all the members.[32]

What has just been said may be seen more clearly, perhaps, in the perfecting of the second of Paul's images of the Church, that of Temple of God. Never does Paul use this metaphor to describe the Christian's relationship to Christ, but always to God and to the Spirit, and in the earlier letters its chief function was to bring home intimacy of union.[33] In Ephesians, however, it is rather distinction and growth which the image emphasises, both key aspects of Paul's new angle of vision. In chapter two, for example, Christ is already enthroned "above the heavens" and all Christians on earth are

[29] Again, there is a hint but no development of this idea in Col. 2:19. Cf. Benoit, 'L'Horizon Paulinien . . .,' pp. 359-360.
[30] Eph. 1:23 is explicit, while Eph. 5:23 is implicit from the use of 'Church' and 'Body' in a parallelism.
[31] Cerfaux, op. cit., p. 259. 'To say that the Church is the Body of Christ because the life of grace and the life of Christ are alike is not enough. To say that there is an identity of life and therefore an identity of the Church and the Body is too much.' (ibid., p. 258, n. 4.)
[32] Benoit, 'Corps, Tête . . .,' p. 21.
[33] 1 Cor. 3:16; 6:19; 2 Cor. 6:16.

mounting up little by little toward him, all the while receiving support from Christ's representatives on earth (vv. 6 and 19-22). On the other hand in chapter four (vv. 12 and 16), where, as we have seen, Paul develops anew the themes of Body and Head, Christ is seen as the key-stone of the Temple, toward which it is slowly rising. Head and key-stone are thus made to correspond in position as well as function, since both give strength and unity while yet remaining distinct from the whole.[34]

It is interesting to note how this second image of the Church is linked in chapter two with Paul's preoccupation with unity and his effort to underscore the collective aspect of salvation. His earlier synthesis, achieved with such anguish in Romans, is now rethought and fitted into a larger horizon. The mental and visual adjustment necessary from the vantage-point of Ephesians has enabled Paul to see Jew and Gentile united at last and integrated into the heavenly Temple mounting up toward Christ the key-stone. The hateful division existing between them in the past has been blotted out by Christ's blood, which, by reconciling them to each other, has reconciled them to God (vv. 1-19). Salvation for both Jew and Gentile remains, as always for Paul, essentially human and moral, but now it becomes part of a much vaster setting. In Colossians Paul had insisted on a cosmic conception of Christ and the salvation he wrought, and this enables him now to see the Church too on a cosmic plane. Always limited to a group of human beings, she appears nonetheless to guard within herself the destiny of the whole cosmos. It is in this way that the Church, as the risen Body of Christ, becomes extended, as it were, or swelled in Paul's mind to the dimensions of the new universe, "the fullness of him who is filled all in all." [35]

But Paul has not yet said his last word on the Church. In chapter five, through the moving image of the Bride, he brings to a focus all the disparate rays of his thought and presents us with a synthesis, a fusion of the themes of Head and Body and, implicitly, that of heavenly Temple. This remarkable text on marriage gives an extraordinary expression to the new angle of vision from which Paul views the Church in Ephesians. There is present, first of all, the fundamental idea of "Body of Christ" of which Christians are now "members," and which Christ has incorporated into himself by the purifying action of Baptism (vv. 26 and 30). But this baptismal action and salvation are presented in a collective fashion which gives to the group of Christians a personal quality: it is the "body" which Christ has saved (v. 23) and it is the "Church" which he has baptised (v. 26).

And yet though so clearly attached to Christ as his Body, the Church is nevertheless distinguished from him as "Head." Subject to him always, she becomes the model of that obedience which every wife owes her husband (vv. 23-24). This image of "head" as "superior," however, has a divisive connotation and Paul does not wish to insist upon it. For Christ is also the Sav-

[34] Cerfaux, op. cit., p. 260.
[35] Eph. 1:23, following Benoit, 'Corps, Tête . . .,' pp. 40-44. For a different interpretation see J. A. T. Robinson, pp. 67-70. Cf. also A. Feuillet, 'L'Église plérôme du Christ d'après *Eph*,' *Nouvelle Revue Théologique* LXXVIII (1956), pp. 446-472, 593-610.

iour, who "loved the Church and gave himself up for her," dying in the place of sinners so that he could make them pure and holy by his sacrifice. At this point we should expect Paul to insist once more on the other meaning of "head" as vital principle. But no, he finds this too impersonal to express the closeness of the union, too weak to bear the weight of this gift of love. And so he employs a more striking image, one already found in the Old Testament, that of marriage, and we now see sketched in Paul's richest lines the theme of the Bride of Christ.[36]

This particular theme, so intimately bound up with that of the Body, had occurred explicitly only once before, though Paul had already twice used the metaphor of sexual union at least implicitly.[37] Moreover there is a chance, as Cerfaux says, that the virgin-Church of Ephesians is a personification of the heavenly Temple and the heavenly Jerusalem. Christ delivered himself up for the Church and purified and washed her, just as Yahweh purified Jerusalem and washed away its sins. He loved the Church as Yahweh loved His people in the Old Testament. He desires her to be glorious and holy and without flaw, just as Yahweh wished Jerusalem to be rescued and renewed.[38] This image of the Bride is thus far stronger than that of Head-Body, since it contains, in addition to an intimate physical union, a union of hearts which can demand the total gift of oneself. The husband is not only the "head" whom the wife must obey, he is also, and above all, the intimate associate who loves his wife as his own flesh and sacrifices himself for her. This is what Christ has done for the Church which is his Bride (vv. 25-29). In this union, model of all human marriages, there is fully realised and definitively clarified the "mystery" seen by Paul to be present in the opening chapters of Genesis (vv. 31-32).

In these final lines we may be allowed to see the ultimate flowering of Paul's thought on the Church as the Body of Christ. This thought, we have found, underwent a profound development between the period of the major epistles and the writing of Ephesians. One key to this development is very likely Paul's growing mystical experience. Yet this alone might never have sufficed were it not for the new angle of vision forced upon him by the Colossian controversy. It is this which enabled him to look down from "the spaces above the earth" and to see the Church at one and the same time identified with the risen Body of Christ yet clearly distinct from him. This new vision he communicates to his readers by a skilful transformation of three images in such a way that he preserves intact his prior vision of intimate union.

With Benoit we may summarise Paul's deployment of these images by picturing a diptych, the two panels of which are heaven and earth, the two personages, Christ and his Church.[39] On the one side is Christ, seated triumphantly in heaven as Head of the Church, communicating to his Body the

[36] Benoit, "Corps, Tête . . .," p. 28.
[37] 2 Cor. 11:12 is explicit; 1 Cor. 6:16-17 and Rom. 7:4 are implicit.
[38] Cerfaux, op. cit., pp. 263-264.
[39] Benoit, 'L'Horizon Paulinien . . .,' pp. 517-518.

life of the Spirit necessary for its growth. From here he constructs the heavenly Temple of God, of which he is the keystone. More than that, he loves and cherishes the Church as a man does his wife, delivers himself up for her at the time of their marriage and thus saves and purifies her and renders her immaculate.

On the other panel is the Church saved by his blood, a single Body with him, subject to him as a wife to her husband. Yet all the while the Church herself is in process of growth and development, as a body nourished by its head, as a spiritual edifice rising up toward heaven, to become at last "the fullness of Him who is filled all in all." It should be noted that each of these three images is linked in turn not only with the word "Church" used in an ecumenical sense, but also with the Person of Christ, thus showing the degree to which Paul's theology of the Church is simply an extension of his christology. The images are likewise imposed one upon the other, a veil being lifted each time, as it were, revealing a new depth in the total mystery. And at every step too there are those expressions of wonder and love, so characteristic of mystical experience, which culminate at last in the image of the Bride, the ultimate development of Paul's thought on the relationship between Christ and his Church.

# THE MYSTERY REVEALED TO PAUL IN 'EPHESIANS' 3:1-13

Mother Kathryn Sullivan, R.S.C.J.

Solemnity and reverence mark the first half of the Epistle to the Ephesians. According to the fine custom of his day, Paul opens his letter with a few words of gratitude for the welfare of his readers. Here, however, the introductory prayer is expanded to provide the framework for the first three chapters. It begins with a heartfelt hymn of thanksgiving (1:3-14) and closes with a doxology acknowledging God's infinite power (3:20-21).

Throughout this section Paul never forgets that he is offering a prayer to God, yet three times he pauses to develop more fully a thought that has occurred to him. These parentheses overflow with adoring gratitude to God and are woven into the prayer in such a way as to make them integral but distinct parts. The passage we are considering is one of these parentheses (1:19 –2:10; 2:11-22; 3:1-13). To it may be applied words that are true of the whole epistle: It is "a meditation on wisdom as found in the mystery of Christ" (Schlier).

Published originally in *The Bible Today*, 1 (1963), 247-254. Reprinted by permission of the publisher.

Having recalled in chapter 2 that this wisdom is expressed in the magnificence of Christ's work and the splendor of the Church, Paul resumes his prayer in the first verse of our passage, but it immediately occurs to him that his readers may wonder why he now champions a cause he once persecuted and how he can claim special insight into doctrines that were once anathema to him. So he stops to explain that this mystery was revealed to him in a special manner (3:1-6) and that he was chosen expressly to carry it to the Gentiles (3:14-21). Let us now examine the digression.

> For this reason I, Paul, the prisoner of Christ Jesus for the sake of you, the Gentiles . . . (3:1).

The sentence is left unfinished until verse 14. Paul apparently is about to tell his readers that he is "bowed in prayer" that they may more fully appreciate the graces offered them in the Church, but he interrupts his thought to justify his right to preach this mystery to them. Surely, he argues, his imprisonment gives him this privilege, for it was incurred because of this mystery. This was literally true; he was in chains because of his apostolate to the Gentiles and the consequent riot in the Jerusalem Temple (Acts 21:28). Had he restricted his labors to his own people, they might have rejected him, but they would not have treated him so shamefully that at this moment he would be imprisoned in Rome and on trial for his life. There is, however, another level on which we can understand his words. He calls himself "the prisoner of Christ Jesus."

Is this an allusion to the moment when Christ made him His captive and gave him the grace of conversion as the persecutor of Christians journeyed along the road to Damascus? Paul once told the Philippians that he had not yet attained his ideal and was far from perfect, but that he was still seeking to capture this goal, just as he himself had been captured by Jesus Christ (Phil. 3:12).

Or is he disregarding the role played by human agents in bringing about his imprisonment and looking higher? In this perspective he sees that he is the prisoner of Christ, the Anointed One of Israel, the prisoner of Jesus the Savior of the world. It is by the Lord's will and for the Lord's cause that he is in bonds, and he accepts all his sufferings for the sake of the Gentiles. Does this not entitle him to speak to them? Moreover, he assumes that they have been told the story of his conversion —

> For I suppose you have heard of the dispensation of the grace of God that was given to me in your regard (3:2).

There are two ways of considering the first few words of this verse. Scholars who believe that the epistle was written to Ephesian Christians well known to Paul as a result of his three-year stay in their midst find in his "I suppose" a politely rhetorical way of alluding to what he knows they already know. Yet the impersonal tone of the whole letter, the absence of personal allusions, the presence of other hints that he is addressing strangers (cf. 1:15; 4:21), suggest that this is a doctrinal treatise presented in an open letter and that the words "to the saints in Ephesus" were later added to the introductory salutation. According to this theory, he here refers to himself as one known to his readers only by reputation, saying equivalently: "No doubt when the message of the gospel was brought to you, you learned of the great responsibility that was entrusted to me to administer the divine grace for your best interests."

Paul uses a significant word in this sentence, "dispensation" or "administration." Actually, *oikonomia* (a word dear to Polybius) is composed of two parts: *oikos*, "house," and *nomos*, "management." It appears in English as "economy," i.e., the policy or system or mode of operation for the direction of something to an end. More specifically it refers to God's plan for the government of the world. Here Paul is thinking in terms of its original meaning: the management of a house. Just as a wise master assigns different tasks to his servants, so God is thought to distribute His grace in such a way that each one can best carry out his charge.

There is a passage in another epistle that throws light on this verse. In First Corinthians 12, Paul describes how the spirit gives each member of the Church a separate gift. Some of these gifts are more spectacular than others, but all come from God and all enable their recipients to serve the community. The gift given to one is for the benefit of all. It is in this light that he looks upon his vocation to carry the message of salvation to the Gentiles. Like the steward in Jesus' parable (Luke 12:42ff), Paul has been allotted this responsibility in the Church of God. He then explains how this was done.

> By revelation was made known to me the mystery, as I have written above in brief (3:3).

For this mission to the Gentiles, he declares he was well prepared by God, who revealed this divine secret to him. When, we may ask, was this revelation made? Was it at the moment of his conversion? In his epistles Paul makes four allusions to this great grace, and there are three accounts in Acts describing this turning-point in his life. One of the thoughts frequently stressed in these passages is that his call to the faith brought with it the call to be an apostle (cf. Rom. 1:1) and that he is meant to carry "the Name" to the Gentiles (Acts 26:15).

What is the "mystery" that was revealed to Paul? In the Church this word has acquired a liturgical and cultic value. In the New Testament it is a technical theological term with messianic and eschatological overtones. In the Old Testament it is found (with its synonyms) only in the late books (Tobit, Judith, Daniel) of the Greek Bible. There it corresponds to the Aramaic word for "something secret" (*raz*) or to the Hebrew word (*sod*) for the "heavenly assembly" or the "decisions reached at the assembly." This word was also used at Qumran and by the Gnostics and devotees of the mystery religions of Paul's day. A few verses later he is going to explain the exact value he attaches to this chameleon-like word, but here he merely refers his readers to what he has already written on this subject.

In his letter to the Romans he equated the "mystery" with the gospel, which he calls "the good news which heralds Jesus the Messiah" (16:25). To the Corinthians he wrote that this message is a "stumbling-block" to the Jews, an "absurdity" to the Gentiles, but to those who believe, both Jews and Gentiles, the "power and wisdom of God" (1 Cor. 1:23f). Only to the spiritually mature (3:1) can Paul, the "steward of God's mysteries" (cf. 4:1), convey something of this revelation, long hidden (Col. 1:26), now revealed (Eph. 1:9).

Paul wishes his readers to examine the evidence his own epistles afford so that they will realize that anyone who has understood so much about God's hidden plans must surely be inspired and therefore conclude that he, Paul, is qualified to preach to them. He then thinks of another way in which they can convince themselves.

> . . . and by reading you can perceive how well versed I am in the mystery of Christ (3:4).

If they read with care what he has written, they will surely see that he is not merely repeating formulas and handing them on to his disciples. In fact, if they continue this "reading" and go to the Bible, they will find the background for a fuller understanding of "mystery."

The prophets had familiarized the people with the idea of God's secrets, especially those connected with the divine plan for the government of the world: "Indeed, Yahweh-God does nothing without revealing his plan to his servants the prophets" (Amos 3:7). The Deutero-Isaiah taught that the history of Israel is the fulfillment in time of a divine plan that was to be completed hereafter (Is. 41:21-28).

One of the valuable lessons of the book of Daniel is that "there is a God in heaven who reveals secrets . . . and he who reveals secrets makes known to you what shall be" (2:27-29). The prophet is not only given a vision, but an explanation of the future of the history of the world is also provided. In this way the words of Amos are fulfilled and the secrets of the heavenly council are brought to men.

The books of Wisdom continue and develop this theme (Sir. 48:24-25; Wis. 6:22). Their authors seem well aware of the existence of mysteries in pagan cults and had no doubt read some of the apocryphal apocalypses, e.g., Enoch, Ezra, Baruch, etc. Jews of the first century before Christ could have found further references to mystery in the literature of Qumran, but present evidence suggests that to the sectarians the understanding of mystery was reserved to "the perfect" and consisted largely of knowledge of the mysteries of good and evil, the divine plan for Israel and the nature of the Law.

All this would provide ample Semitic background-reading for Paul's disciples. To understand all the resonances of the word "mystery," there would have been no need for them to seek parallels in the Greek mystery religions of the day.

The word, therefore, was one they knew well. Paul now goes on to clarify its meaning according to the revelation given to him:

> . . . that mystery which in other ages was not known to the sons of men, as now it has been revealed to this holy apostles and prophets in the spirit (3:5).

Some find this reference to the "holy apostles and prophets" disturbing. Is this not proof, they ask, that Paul never wrote the epistle? Surely he would never have made so flattering an allusion to a group of which he was a member. This objection loses its force when we recall that in his day the adjective lacked the moral connotation it now enjoys. "Holy" then meant consecration rather than the possession of heroic virtue.

Another misunderstanding has arisen in regard to the allusion to the prophets. These could well denote first-generation Christians who enjoyed charismatic gifts. Like the apostles, they received the revelation of the divine plan, became the foundation-stones of the Church (Eph. 2:20), and heralded the good news of salvation (Rom. 12:6: 1 Cor. 12:28). Might there not also be a reference to the Old Testament prophets? Isaiah, we were told, foresaw secret things and mysteries "that are to come to pass at last" (Sir. 48:25-27), and Daniel's experience with mysteries was quite extensive.

In fact, Paul restates this truth in the great doxology that is the crown and close of Romans (16:25-27). With majestic gravity he sums up the special aspect of the gospel that he has made the theme of the epistle: the life of Jesus and His salvific work are the revelation of God's mysterious plan hidden from the beginning, confided to and proclaimed by prophets and apostles, who thus fulfill God's merciful will. The revelation of Jesus certainly was new, yet "eyes enlightened by faith" (Eph. 1:18) can trace its pattern in prophetic Old Testament passages.

This verse marks an interesting advance in Paul's use of the word "mystery." In Second Thessalonians and First Corinthians he had identified it with "something secret" and God's "hidden wisdom"; in Romans he equates it with Christ. This provides the necessary foundation for the deeper meaning of mystery which he now gives.

> . . . namely that the Gentiles are joint heirs, fellow-members of the same body and joint partakers of the promise in Christ Jesus through the gospel (3:6).

This then, is the revelation of God's eternal purpose: the Gentiles are now co-heirs (*synkleronomos*) of an inheritance to which they had no claim by birth, co-members (*syssomos*) with the Jews in the living unity of the Body of Christ, co-sharers (*symmetochos*) of the covenant-promises from which they had once been excluded (Eph. 2:12). These three words compounded with the prefix *syn-* show that the Gentiles are incorporated into the new Israel and are grafted to the olive tree so as to make the mystery visible in the Church. All this has been realized in Jesus and announced in the gospel.

These words acquire their full value when seen in the light of the theme of the epistle. Jesus came to restore unity to a disunited world by reuniting all things to Himself. He began this work of reconciliation by destroying the division that long separated Jew and Gentile, and by establishing the Church, through which this work of reconciliation can extend through space and continue through time. Here is the key to the divine plan of unity.

The reference to the gospel reminds Paul of the grandeur and limits of his ministry. He continues:

> Of that gospel I was made a minister by the gift of God's grace, which was given to me in accordance with the working of his power (3:7).

As before, he stresses the help God has given him. His ministry was determined in two ways: by the original gift of divine grace and by the continuous support of divine power. Others may have received greater gifts and rendered greater services, but he has tried to be faithful to his own stewardship of the mystery. There is here an interesting allusion to the resurrection: the divine power by which Christ was raised from the dead (Eph. 1: 19-23) is the same power that enables the Apostle to accomplish God's will for the Gentiles:

> Yes, to me, the very least of all the saints, there was given this grace, to announce among the Gentiles the good tidings of the unfathomable riches of Christ (3:8).

The thought of the magnitude of the mystery that he is called to proclaim and of the limitless wealth of Christ's redemptive grace reminds Paul of his own inadequacy and unworthiness. To the Corinthians he acknowledged that he was the least of the apostles (1 Cor. 15:9); to Timothy he admits that he is, of all sinners, the chief (1 Tim. 1:15); here he uses (perhaps coins) a double superlative or a comparative grafted on a superlative, which may perhaps be a pun on his own name (*paullus*, little), and with characteristic humility declares that he is "less than the least" of all those dedicated to God's service.

It is instructive to watch this double effect of apostolic experience on Paul. Preaching the gospel has convinced him more and more of his own unworthiness and disclosed to him the ever-widening dimensions of the gospel's power, centered in and emanating from the Person and work of Christ (Col. 1:27; 2:2). When writing to the Romans he used the same adjective to describe the unsearchable, inexhaustible wonder of the ways of God with Jew and Gentile (11:33). The use of the word here is appropriate and reminds him of his obligation

> to enlighten all men as to what is the dispensation of the mystery which has been hidden from all eternity in God who created all things (3:9).

Paul recalls that God created all things as a unity, that this unity was disrupted by sin, then further corrupted by the idolatry and immorality of men who were aided and abetted in their wickedness by the forces of evil. Then, according to Paul, who again employs the word which means literally the "management of a house" and here has the value of "wise purposefulness," God's hidden plan began to take shape. The course of history has been so ordered that this plan will be accomplished by Christ. As Canon Cerfaux has succinctly said in *Christ in the Theology of Saint Paul* (p. 423): "Christ's

work will consist in restoring this primitive unity, in establishing once again
what had been in the beginning. This new-found unity will be ecumenical
(Jew and pagan again will be reunited), cosmic (the Powers will be stripped
of their dominion over the cosmos and over men), and eschatological (the
re-establishment of this unity will mark the birth of the new world). There
is parallelism, but not equivalence, between the restored unity and the primordial unity, for the primordial unity belongs to the old world and came
from Christ who created it. The second unity belongs to the new and definitive world and comes from the risen Christ who is our Saviour."

St. Ireneus explored this mystery of re-establishment or recapitulation. He
saw it as the mystery of salvation foreseen by the Father, accomplished by
the Son during His incarnation and to be perfected by Him at the parousia:
When (the Son of God) became incarnate and was made man, He summed
up in Himself the long line of men, and gave us salvation instantly and com-
prehensively, so that what we had lost in Adam (namely, to be according to
the image and likeness of God) we might recover in Christ Jesus (*Adv.
Haer.* 3, 18, 1).

It is from the risen Jesus that this fullness of power will reach all creation, and He who enjoys the primacy and is the origin of the visible and invisible world will unify all that is and all that will be. This is the meaning
of Christ's incarnation. The father sent the Son to the world

> in order that through the Church there be made known to the Principalities
> and Powers in the heavens the manifold wisdom of God according to the
> eternal purpose which he accomplished in Christ Jesus our Lord (3:10-11).

From these verses we see that Paul's apostolate means more than the exposition of the universality of the mystery, more than the winning of new
converts; it also means that as the Church grows through his efforts, God's
wisdom will be more and more manifest — even to the demons in the skies.
The allusion to these members of the demonic hordes gives a glimpse of
another world and serves as a corrective to our inveterate centripetal and
myopic tendencies.

The hiddenness of divine mysteries is a recurrent theme in Jewish apocalyptic texts and the importance of spirits in Semitic thought has been confirmed by the many references to spirit forces in the Qumran texts. To the
angels, it was generally believed, not everything had been revealed. The fallen angels seem to have been unaware of the divine plan. The good angels
could watch with wonder the unfolding in time of the mystery that all things
are summed up in Christ. To describe this divine wisdom, Paul uses a rare
and poetical adjective, *polypoikilos*, "many-colored," "richly wrought,"
"dappled," "multiple-dimensioned." It is difficult to find any words that are
able to convey the variety, the many-faceted beauty of the manifestation in
the world of nature and in the history of men of the infinite wisdom of God
who is the center and circumference of all that is and whose plan for the
world is fulfilled in Christ. This means, Paul goes on to say, that

> in him we have assurance and confident access through faith in him (3:12).

Paul never loses sight of the needs of souls, so he returns from thoughts of the working of divine wisdom in time and space to the comforting realization of all that faith in Christ can mean for him and for his readers. Complete trust placed in our risen Savior means that we can enjoy the full liberty of a free and fearless approach to God. *Parrhesia* usually denotes frank and forthright speech. It is the privilege of fully expressing one's own mind that was vigorously defended by the citizens of the Greek city-states. It is perfect communion between man and the Creator, between man and creation. Adam conversing familiarly with God in the garden of paradise enables us to see the friendly intimacy which should characterize our dialogue with life and Life. It is the incommunicable experience in which we are linked with Love and with all that Love loves.

This grasp of reality has enabled Paul to accept with joy the personal inconveniences of his apostolate to the Gentiles and it is the fullness of this consolation that he wishes his readers to share.

> Therefore I pray you not to be disheartened at my tribulations for you, for they are your glory (3:13).

Paul began this long digression with an allusion to his imprisonment; before resuming his interrupted prayer, he again speaks as "a prisoner of Christ." True, his apostolate has brought him suffering, but this is no indication that God does not love him. On the contrary. Paul rejoices that his imprisonment is a means of exercising another form of ministry for his readers. As he had written to the Colossians, his sufferings enable him "to fill up what is wanting to the tribulations of Christ" (1:24). To describe Christ's sufferings and his own, he here uses the same word. That the sufferings of Christ's people are the sufferings of the Messiah, Paul had been told on the road to Damascus; now it is his privilege to share in these sufferings. Is there not ample reason for his readers to glory?

Turning from thoughts of the scope and nature of his mission, he recalls the wonderful opportunities offered to his readers. He knows that their own experience will afford them new insights into the mystery of the wisdom that is Christ. This he makes the theme of the conclusion of his long-interrupted prayer.

# THE REDEMPTION OF THE UNIVERSE

Stanislas Lyonnet, S.J.

Redemption as the term is used by St. Paul, implies above all the redemption of man. As a matter of fact, it implies almost exclusively the redemption of man. At times, however, Paul's redemptive horizon broadens to embrace the

Reprinted from *The Church: Readings in Theology* (New York: P. J. Kenedy & Sons, 1963), pp. 136-156. Reprinted by permission of the author.

whole of creation, the classic instance of which is chapter eight of the epistle to the Romans.

It is this passage which we would like to examine here, and we are the first to admit the difficulties involved. The chief problem is the obscurity of the Apostle's expression, giving rise for centuries now to variant exegetical interpretations. Even today agreement is far from universal. Yet such difficulties should not keep us from the truths which the Apostle clearly intended to expound to the Romans, and which he would undoubtedly apply to the twentieth century Christian — especially since Paul's teaching of a cosmic redemption is more pertinent today than at any other moment in history.

Paul begins his eighth chapter in Romans with a reference to the fifth. He restates his doctrine of the Christian life whose vital principle is the working of the Holy Spirit in us: a life of peace as befits those already reconciled with him and certain of a definitive salvation already possessed in hope. Yet though reconciled, humanity is not exempt from suffering and death. Far from establishing an obstacle to our hope, suffering and death are rather, in the words of the Apostle, "*conditiones optimae*" (5:3-4), and to such a degree that in chapter eight he draws from them a new motive for hope (8:17ff).

Taking a closer look at the passage, we find that Paul says that if "we suffer with Christ we shall also be glorified with him." He continues: "For I think that the sufferings of the present time are not to be compared to the glory which is to be revealed in us. Indeed, creation, filled with expectation, awaits the revelation of the sons of God: if creation was made subject to vanity — and not by its own choice but because of him who made it subject — it is with the hope that creation itself be liberated from the servitude of corruption to enter into the freedom of the glory of the children of God. For we know that all creation groans in the pains of childbirth until today. And not only it; we ourselves who possess the first fruits of the Spirit, we groan within ourselves in the expectation of the redemption of our body." [1]

[1] Among the recent studies devoted to this passage of the epistle to the Romans, see in particular A. Viard, "Expectatio creaturae" in *Revue Biblique*, 69 (1952), pp. 337-354, and A. M. Dubarle, "Le gemissement des creatures dans l'ordre du Cosmos" in *Revue des Sciences phil. et theol.*, 38 (1954), pp. 445-465.

With regard to the timeliness and importance of the problem, permit us to cite this reflection of M. Blondel which is taken from the *Correspondance M. Blondel-A. Valensin*, vol. 1, p. 47: "The problem of the Incarnation seems to me . . . (perhaps antecedent to any other philosophical question) to be the touchstone for a true cosmology in an integral metaphysics . . . I share the ideas and sentiments of P. Teilhard de Chardin with regard to the problems of Christology. Before horizons enlarged by the natural and human sciences, one cannot, without a betrayal of Catholicism, be content with mediocre explanations and limited viewpoints which make a historical accident of Christ, which isolate him in the cosmos as an unrelated incident and which seem to make of him an intruder, not one at home, in the overwhelming and hostile immensity of the universe. Long before Loisyism . . . I recognized with intense clarity the alternative: either fall back on a dead symbolism, or advance toward an integral realism which would put Christian metaphysics in accord with the mysticism lived by the saints and the faithful themselves . . . We are drawn towards the "*instauratio tota in Christo*" . . . Let us advance then without hesitation, in that direction in which as we grow in our appreciation of man and the world,

Confronted by language so profound, the hearer might protest that the Apostle's creative imagination has carried him away, that he has forsaken the solid ground of dogma and theology to indulge in exalted but illusory dreams of poetic fancy. In the case of Paul such a hypothesis is, a priori, hardly tenable. Rather, is not the hearer at fault? Possibly he lacks the insight to understand the metaphorical element of Paul's language.

We shall answer this question in the second section of our paper by examining the objective context of the Apostle's affirmation. But first it would be well to place Paul's statements in their proper context, the biblical context. And then it will remain for us to show briefly in a third section how the Christian future, far from turning Christians away from their present task, both justifies and transfigures it.

# I

In refutation to the reproach of poetic flight, Paul could repeat what he previously had said to the procurator Portius Festus, who had been scandalized to hear a man of good judgment such as Paul preaching the resurrection of Christ in the presence of King Agrippa: "I am not mad, excellent Festus, but I speak words of truth and sound sense" (Acts 26:25).

Then Paul appealed to the King himself. Though strange and incomprehensible to the ears of a pagan like Festus, Paul's statements could not surprise a Jew like King Agrippa, who was at home with the Scriptures. "For the king knows about these things and to him I speak with complete confidence" (v. 26). "Do you believe the prophets, King Agrippa? I know that you do!" (v. 27). To modern readers the Apostle poses the same question: "Do you believe in the prophets?" If so: "Reread what they have proclaimed and my teaching will cease to seem an enigma to you."

In our specific problem, in fact in regard to all of Pauline theology, it is important never to lose sight of the fact that Paul was a Jew for whom the Old Testament was and remained the Book par excellence. The Apostle spoke excellent Greek, but he thought essentially in the categories of the Jews of his day.

A Jew brought up on the Scriptures would always be acutely aware of the unity of the redemptive plan. The history of salvation which the Bible recounts is not presented to the Jew as a series of distinct and separate episodes, but rather as the realization of a single plan of love. True, the plan unfolds itself in history and progressively so; but it is of one piece. The unity of this plan can be demonstrated by the fact that the Bible sums up its successive stages in a single word: alliance, *berit*, which the Greek Septuagint translates

so much more will Christ grow in our minds and hearts." Blondel remarks further in the same work (p. 48) that it is indispensable "to indicate clearly and with increased force the absolute transcendence of the divine gift, the inevitably supernatural character of the deifying design, and as a consequence the moral transformation and the spiritual expansion which grace permits and which it must accomplish," On this *Correspondance*, see J. Levie in *Nouvelle revue theologique*, 91 (1959), pp. 1073-1081.

as *diatheke*, "the Testament" — undoubtedly to lay the accent upon the divine initiative.

In the Old Testament the alliance between God and Israel was not a treaty between two equals, but rather and above all the gift of God to a people whom he had freely singled out, not through any merit on their part, but as Deuteronomy recalls, "out of love for them and to keep the oath made to their fathers" (Deut. 7:8). More significant yet, the oath made to Abraham, which was the basis for the alliance of Sinai, was itself called an "alliance," a "testament." This alliance was irrevocable, as would be the messianic alliance made on behalf of David, according to Psalm 88: "Forever will I continue my kindness to him, and my alliance shall stand firm with him. . . . I will not violate my alliance nor change the utterance of my lips. Once have I sworn by my holiness: I will never lie to David" (vv. 29-36).

Finally, the definitive realization of God's salvific plan in the "last times" is also referred to as an "alliance," or a "testament." The book of Isaiah in the second and third parts makes more than one allusion to it. Jeremiah described it explicitly as a "new alliance" (31:33), and Christ was to use this term at the Last Supper to proclaim formally the continuity and the unity of the "Two Testaments."

Further, the Bible speaks of an alliance prior to Abraham — a universal alliance established by God with mankind in the person of Noah after the whole of humanity had been re-created in the cataclysm of the deluge. This alliance extended beyond the human world and in some way embraced the material universe as well.

We read in chapters eight and nine of Genesis: "I will no more curse the earth because of man . . . never again will I destroy living things as I have done. So long as the earth lasts, seedtime and harvest, cold and heat, summer and winter, night and day, shall not cease" (Gen. 8:21-22). "Behold I have established my alliance with you, and with your descendants; and with every living being among you, all that has come forth out of the ark, all the living things of the earth. I have established my alliance with you: never again will all flesh be destroyed by the waters of the flood, nor shall there be from henceforth a flood to lay waste to the earth" (Gen. 9:9-11).

The sign of this alliance was not inscribed in the flesh of man by circumcision, as was the case with Abraham, but rather in the universe, in the broad heavens, so as to signify that the alliance with Noah was not limited to any one part of the created world, but embraced its totality. "This is the sign of the alliance which I place between me and you and all living beings among you from generation unto generation: I set my bow in the cloud, and it shall be the sign of alliance between me and the earth" (Gen. 9:12-13).

Thus after the cataclysm of the deluge, the punishment for man's sin, the physical universe regained its equilibrium, its harmony, its rhythm — precisely that of which the creation narrative spoke. Certainly the solemn declaration of Gen. 8:22: "So long as the earth lasts . . . summer and winter, night and day, shall not cease" evokes the words of Gen. 1:3-5: "God divided the light and the darkness. And there was evening and there was morning . . ." Similarly the promise of Gen. 8:21: "I will no more curse the earth because of man" recalls the words of Gen. 3:17: "Cursed is the earth because of you."

Confronted by this spectacle of the harmony of the *kosmos*, the Greek was struck above all by a beauty which delighted his eyes as well as his mind, while the Israelite, "instructed by the Scriptures," first encountered the sign of a God faithful to his plan of love. Jeremiah, for instance, expressly compared the alliance with David to the alliance with heaven and earth (Jer. 33: 20, 25). Perhaps this was also what the Psalmist was thinking of when he proclaimed that "the heavens declare the glory of God" and devoted the second half of his psalm to praising the gift of the Law: *"Lex Domini immaculata."* It is, in any event, the image Paul created for the pagan peasants of Lystra by reminding them that "God has not failed to give witness to himself by his kindnesses, giving you rains and fruitful seasons from heaven, filling your hearts with food and gladness" (Acts 14:16-17; cf. Ps. 103).

Moreover, for the Israelite, the history of salvation did not begin only with Abraham or Noah, nor even with Adam. It began with creation itself. This was its first act. Thus, to cite but one example, in Psalm 135, recounting this "history of salvation" in the form of "litanies" with the refrain "for his great love is without end," the Psalmist began with the work of creation: "He alone spread out the earth upon the waters . . . He made the great lights . . . the sun to rule over the day . . . the moon and the stars to rule over the night. . . ." Then, without any transition, follow the "historical" benefits on behalf of Israel which the Bible terms precisely the "unspeakable works" of God: "He smote Egypt in her first-born . . . brought forth Israel from her midst . . . He divided the sea of rushes into two parts . . ." (v. 4-13).

In this regard, the extra-canonical Jewish tradition outdid the biblical tradition itself, if one may so express it, and in its attempt to emphasize still more the unity of the history of salvation it intentionally fixed its various stages on the same calendar day. So, according to the book of Jubilees, the sacrifice of Isaac was set on the 15th of Nisan, the same day on which the Pasch would later be celebrated. I will cite only one particularly significant example of this typical process. It deals fittingly with the feast of the Pasch.

According to Exodus, the Pasch commemorates a single event: "the night during which Jahweh had watched over his people to bring them forth from the land of Egypt" (Exod. 12:42). The Palestinian Targum, the more or less paraphrastic translation of the Hebrew text into the current Aramaic, offers an extremely informative gloss on this section. It is not just a single night which this feast celebrates. Rather it is four nights which sum up, as we shall see, the whole history of salvation.

The first night is that on which the Word of God appeared in order to create the world. (For us Christians the anniversary of the creation of the world is Sunday, the first day of the week, that day on which Christ rose, as the breviary hymn has it: *Primo die quo Trinitas Beata mundum condidit, vel quo resurgens Conditor nos, morte victa, liberat.*) The second night commemorates the time when the Word of God made an alliance with Abraham and promised him the birth of a son in whom all the nations of the earth would be blessed; another tradition of the Targum even adds the commemoration of the sacrifice of Isaac, that is, his "spiritual birth," which, in fact, according to the book of Jubilees, took place on the 15th of Nisan. The third night is that during which the Word of the Lord, striking the first-born of the Egyptians, delivered Israel from bondage in order to constitute Israel the first-born son of God. The fourth night is not of the past, but of the future, when the messianic king will come on the clouds to preside at the definitive redemption of Israel.

Four nights, four births: birth of the universe, birth of Israel, birth of the new world, birth of the "new heavens" and the "new earth," according to the expression of Isaiah (65:17) taken up again in the Apocalypse (21:1) and the second epistle of St. Peter (3:13).

One can readily see how, for a Jew "instructed in the Scriptures," the history of the universe was a part of the history of salvation. Created for man, the universe in some way shares his destiny. Just as the execution of the first alliance with Noah had cosmic implications so the eschatological alliance will necessarily have its impact on the whole of creation.

But what were as yet only more or less vague suggestions — differently interpreted by the Jewish doctors themselves — was to become in Paul a clearly defined doctrine. The resurrection of Christ would bring together bits of truth until then dispersed throughout the Old Testament. On the road to Damascus Saul the Jew, disciple of Gamaliel, encountered the risen Christ. His eyes opened under the guidance of the Spirit, the Apostle saw written, as it were, in the splendor of Christ's glorified body, the destiny to which God invited not only every human person but even the entire universe.

This we will now show by determining in as precise a manner as possible, the exact meaning of the Apostle's teachings in Rom. 8:17-23.

## II

It seems possible to disengage from these verses at least a threefold doctrine, which, for clarity's sake, can be formulated in the following propositions: (1) The redemption of the universe is only a consequence of the redemption of man; (2) It is, more precisely, a consequence of the redemption of man's body; (3) Yet the universe is not simply an instrument of man's redemption — it is itself an object of redemption.

### 1. The redemption of the universe, a consequence of the redemption of man

Without a shadow of doubt this affirmation emerges from the whole of the Apostle's argumentation in the present passage: the redemption of the universe can only be conceived in connection with the redemption of man. The latter is primary from any point of view. Unlike some more or less gnostic representations of contemporaries who thought man would be freed from matter because God would transport him to a new universe, for Paul, as for the Bible, it is precisely because man is saved that he can draw the whole universe after him into this salvation. Already in the Old Testament man is at the center of the universe; all the more is this true of the New Testament since we know that God has deigned to take up residence among us.

The bold proclamation of this fundamental doctrine by the new religion was the more commendable since it directly contradicted some of the most profound tendencies of Greek philosophy. One recalls the jeers of Celsus which Origen has preserved for us in his *Contra Celsum*. Celsus compares Christians "to moths swarming about at night, to ants filing out from their hill, or to frogs leaving their pond and saying: 'We are those to whom God has foretold everything and revealed all things to come; and overlooking the whole cosmos and the course of the stars, neglecting even this immense earth, he communicates his designs for the world to us, and us alone. To us alone has he sent his heralds, and sends them even now, solicitous as he is of uniting us to him eternally.'"

"Truly," gibes Celsus, "we are like little grub worms who cry out: 'God exists, and of a sudden we have become completely like God. To us he has subjected everything — the earth, water, air, stars. Everything exists for us and has received the command to serve us. And, because some have sinned, God will come or will send his Son to consume the impious in flames, and to lead us, the others, into eternal life with him.'" "Such language," adds Celsus, "would be somewhat more tolerable on the part of worms or frogs than on the part of Jews and Christians" (Origen, *Contra Celsum*, 4, 23; *PG* 11, 1060).

Such words are not to be taken as said simply in jest. Rather we are here confronted by one of the most typical reactions of the Greek spirit to the central dogma of Christianity. One hundred and fifty years later, the philosopher Plotinus expressed himself with no less vigor, and a Plotinist like E. Bréhier does not hesitate to describe this declamation as "one of the most beautiful and haughty reactions of Hellenic rationalism to the religious individualism which was overrunning the Greco-Roman world during this epoch." Here Bréhier is certainly referring to Christianity, in particular to the central place it allots the human person. He continues: "Plotinus does not attack the details of Christian belief — this he leaves to two of his dearest disciples, Amelius and Porphyry; he himself goes straight to its principle, i.e., the exaltation of the believer who relates everything to his own salvation. In opposition to this Plotinus upholds the ancient Hellenic tradition according to which the true end of man consists in understanding his place in the system of realities and not in assigning the first place to himself." [2]

Bréhier has in mind here the treatise of Plotinus *Against the Gnostics* (II, ch. 9). It is clear enough that Plotinus is alluding to Christians: those "sense-

---

[2] *Plotin-Ennéades*, texte átabli et traduit par E. Bréhier, vol. IV, pp. 107-10.

less men who let themselves be persuaded when they hear words such as these: You will be superior to all things, above men as well as gods (i.e., stellar deities). How great is presumption among men! Once they were humble, modest, and simple people of the world; now they give heed to the words: You are a son of God; the others whom you admired so much are not sons of God — not even the stars to whom tradition bids us offer homage. You have become without effort superior to heaven itself!" (II, 9,9).

"These men pretend," says Plotinus elsewhere, "that Providence works uniquely in their favor . . . But Providence watches over the All rather than over the parts, and the soul of the All receives this guidance much more than the parts . . . Who of these senseless ones who think themselves to be above wisdom, enjoys the wondrous order and wisdom of the universe?" (II, 9, 16). Plotinus then invites them to contemplate "the beauties of the visible world, its proportions, its harmony and the spectacle which the stars offer in spite of their distance" (ibid.).

Yet, even at the risk of giving scandal to cultured Hellenistic minds, Paul makes no allowance for such a conception. If he speaks of a redemption of the universe, he conceives of it only in dependence on that of man.

## 2. The redemption of the universe as a consequence of the redemption of man's body

The redemption of the universe is in Paul's thought essentially a corollary of the resurrection of the body and consequently is based, like it, on the fact of the resurrection of Christ.

At the beginning of this chapter Paul explains that Christ, in virtue of his death and resurrection, communicates to human nature and to each Christian in particular a new principle which is none other than the Holy Spirit, the third person of the Holy Trinity. The Christian is defined as one animated by the Holy Spirit. Now in verse 11 the Apostle adds that this new principle not only exercises its influence on the soul, but is equally the source of life for the Christian's body, as it was for Christ's body: "If the Spirit of him who raised Jesus from the dead dwells in you . . . He will give life to your mortal bodies too, by his spirit who dwells in you."

Paul introduces our passage, in verses 17 and 18, by referring to the resurrection of the body: he speaks of the "glorification" which awaits those who are conjoined to the passion of Christ, and of the "glory" which, as a result, must be revealed in them. Here, as in the entire epistle, Paul has in mind salvation in its fullness which is completed only with the resurrection of the body at the Parousia.

Again, verse 23, concluding our passage, leaves no room for doubt: after referring to the expectation of the universe, Paul mentions the expectation of the Christian which he defines with unmistakable clarity as the expectation of "the redemption of our body"; certainly not in the sense that the Christian awaits an emancipation from the body! He awaits with firm hope the liberation of his body itself, as well as his soul, from the carnal condition. In other words, it will partake of the same condition as the risen body of Christ.

## 3. *The universe, object of the redemption*

The Christian expects, too, with an equally firm hope that this new condition will become — in a manner impossible for us to imagine — the lot of the entire universe.

Here (v. 19) Paul adds to the clear statements concerning the present and future of the world an allusion to the past whose exact meaning is not certain and upon which not all exegetes are in agreement. On this point the Apostle seems to be taking up — without going beyond — the affirmation of Genesis (3:17) in which God, speaking to our first parents after their sin, says to Adam: "Cursed be the earth because of you . . . thorns and thistles shall it bring forth for you." There are evidently several ways of understanding such an affirmation. For St. Thomas, for example, thorns and thistles would have grown on the earth even if man had not sinned; but in this case their growth would not have been *"in poenam hominis"* (II-II, q. 164, art. 2, ad 1).

We will not delay over this problem which St. Paul did not intend to treat *ex professo*. The past of the universe certainly interests him much less than its present and its future. In regard to the present and future his thought does not present the same obscurity. Whatever may have been the primitive state of the universe before sin, its present state is not the definitive one. Like the human universe, the material universe itself is in expectation of a future state.

Paul, in describing this expectation, does not hesitate to make use of imagery. He portrays the whole of creation awaiting its deliverance as a person who, head thrust forward (*apokaradokia*, v. 19), fixes his eyes on the horizon, whence, with the return of Christ, the new day will finally dawn for mankind in full possession of the glory destined for the children of God.

The universe will not be content merely to look on from the outside at this triumph of redeemed humanity, as an impressed spectator delighting in a magnificent panorama. The material universe is called to share in the future state of the children of God. "It will be freed," says Paul, from what in its present state is "vanity, servitude and corruption," in order to share in "the freedom of the glory of the children of God." It will leave, then, its present condition to enter this new one which the Apostle does not hesitate to call a "freedom" — in fact, a freedom that is quite the same as that belonging to the glory of the children of God: and not merely, as it is often translated, "the glorious freedom of the children of God," but "the freedom of the glory of the children of God."

In Paul's mind the term "glory," especially in this eschatological context, signifies a very precise reality — the active and visible presence of God himself which is communicated to the humanity of Christ glorified in his resurrection and ascension; it is through Christ's glorified humanity that this presence will be communicated to our humanity in its fullness at the general resurrection of the body.

According to the Apostle, this assertion itself rests on a certitude of faith. For "we know" from the Scriptures, continues Paul, that the present universe "is in labor" toward a better state — *odinei*, is in the pains of childbirth: the Apostle does not shrink from the deeply human and richly expressive biblical metaphor of the pains of childbirth (v. 22). From a purely human point of view that is incapable of going beyond appearances, the universe, true enough, seems at times to be floundering under the weight of torturing evil. Faith teaches us, however, that this is not the sign of agony, but rather the presage of birth.

Such an article of faith was most likely part of the very first *Credo* of the Church. St. Peter, from the start of his preaching on the day of Pentecost, referred to this "universal restoration" of which God had spoken through the mouth of his holy prophets (Acts 3:21). Moreover, Paul mentions it not only in this passage of the epistle to the Romans, but also in the epistles to the Colossians and Ephesians. The Apostle is careful not to limit his horizon to the human world alone. If he is thinking here above all of the angelic world (because of the adversaries he must combat, especially in the letter to the Colossians), he nevertheless affirms with particular emphasis that Christ — the Christ made flesh, according to what seems to me the correct opinion of a number of modern exegetes — is the very center of the entire creation.

The absolute dependence of the entire universe on Christ is mirrored in the use of the prepositions *en, eis,* and *dia.* "Everything was created by him and for him; everything subsists in him." As Huby clearly and precisely explains: "In him all things have been created as in the supreme center of unity, harmony and cohesion, which gives the world its meaning, its value and thereby its reality, or, to use another metaphor, the nucleus, the meeting point (Lightfoot) where all the threads, all the forces of the universe converge and are co-ordinated. Were one to have an instantaneous view of the whole universe, past, present and future, he would see every being as ontologically dependent on Christ and as definitively intelligible only through him" (*Epîtres de la captivité*, p. 40).

In its turn, the epistle to the Ephesians describes explicitly the salvific plan of God as the recapitulation of all things in Christ — not just all men, but all things; so much so that nothing that exists should escape the vital influence of Christ. Each, of course, comes under this influence in a way proper to its own condition, but nothing is deprived of its rebirth. In short, God has created nothing for death, but rather only for life.

Finally, this authentically biblical doctrine was taken into the entire Catholic tradition without exception. The Greek Fathers were not alone in taking delight in the unity of the creative and redemptive plan, the fact that the entire universe shares the destiny of the human nature assumed by the Son of God. The hymns of victory of a St. John Chrysostom found their Latin echo in a St. Ambrose, who saw in the resurrection of Christ the resurrection of the entire universe and not just that of man: *"Resurrexit in eo mundus, resurrexit in eo caelum, resurrexit in eo terra. Erat enim caelum novum et terra nova"* (*De fide resurrectionis*. Second Nocturn of the Fifth Sunday after Easter).

But even if we skip over all other examples, St. Thomas' magnificent conclusion to the *Summa Contra Gentiles* sums up this Latin tradition superbly. "Because all corporal beings," explains the Angelic Doctor, "exist in some way for man, it is fitting that at that time (after the last judgment) the state of the entire corporal universe will be transformed, so that it may be in harmony with what will then be the state of man. And since men will then be incorruptible, the present state of corruptibility will be removed from the corporal universe. This is what the Apostle teaches (Rom. 8:21). Thus, since the material universe will finally be adapted to the state of man, and since men will not only be freed from corruption, but clothed in glory, the material universe must also acquire in its way *quamdam claritatis gloriam*. This is the teaching of Apocalypse 21:1: '*Vidi caelum novum*'; and Isaiah 65:17: 'Behold I create new heavens and a new earth and the former things shall not be in remembrance . . . But you will rejoice and be glad forever. Amen.'" With this citation and with this hymn of triumph the work of the Angelic Doctor ends.

In Paul's day Jewish thought, it seems, was divided. Certain doctors represented the end of the world as an annihilation, a sort of general conflagration, in the manner of the Stoic *ekpurosis*; others saw it as a transformation. For Paul and for Christianity, there is no possible doubt. The universe is not destined to be destroyed, but to be transformed, to be, as the human body, "glorified" in its own way.

Of course, revelation teaches us nothing about the "how" of this transformation — revelation does not furnish us with any information of a properly "cosmological" order. Its teaching is of the religious order, not the "scientific." But it teaches us with certitude, that however this transformation may come about, it will lead to life and not to death.

In the same way, the dogma of the resurrection of the body cannot supply the biologist with a new datum; yet it teaches the Christian a truth far more important, though of another order. It teaches him that, appearances to the contrary, this body, in which he may already detect the ravages of sickness, which he knows is going to decompose and turn to dust, is nevertheless promised a share in the glory of the risen Christ.

But by this very fact, i.e., precisely because we have to deal with an essentially religious doctrine and not one of a purely scientific nature, the dogma of the redemption of the universe has not been revealed to us only, nor even principally, to render our intellectual world-synthesis more sweeping and more unified. Before all else this doctrine is intended to direct our lives and shape our attitudes, or — in the words of St. Paul — it should permit us to "walk in a manner worthy of the Lord" (Col. 1:10). This is the point we wish to elaborate in our final section.

## III

Three lessons — three important consequences — seem to flow directly from the Pauline doctrine we have just expounded.

1. From the fact that the goal of Christian hope is placed in the redemption of the body and of the universe, it follows that the Christian conception of "salvation" is essentially a collective conception. For the bodily resurrection is characterized by the fact that, with the exception of Christ and his mother, it will take place for all at the same time, at the end of time, at that moment of "time" which the New Testament calls the Parousia.

Admittedly, this great hope has ceased little by little to be the true expectation of most Christians. We are accustomed to think only of what we call "the salvation of our soul," forgetting that this salvation is itself only a part of a whole. Moreover, a number of exegetes have thought it necessary to contrast in Paul two conceptions of salvation. They maintain that the first, whereby salvation is obtained by the resurrection of the body, is a relic of his Judaism which he later abandoned, replacing it by the Greek conception. In the Greek conception the resurrection no longer plays any real role and salvation is obtained immediately after death in the union of the soul, finally emancipated from the bonds of the body, with the divinity.

Nothing could be more inaccurate. To the end of his life, Paul never ceased to await the resurrection and the return of Christ at the Parousia — the redemption of the universe — all the while believing that at his death he would rejoin Christ in God. He never saw the slightest contradiction between these two aspects, as if it would be necessary to adopt the one and reject the other. However, the second aspect was basically individualistic; the first, on the contrary, was essentially collective and complemented the hope of Paul as well as of all early Christians.

For them, even if a Christian was definitively united to God in what was later termed the "beatific vision," his salvation was not yet complete. He would be fully "saved" only on taking possession of his glorious body, which means when all the elect were saved along with him or, to use a Pauline formula, when the body of Christ attained its perfect state. *"Irrequietum est cor meum donec requiescat in Te"*; or better yet, to avoid any ambiguity: *"Donec requiescamus omnes in Te!"*

2. From the fact that the redemption of the body extends to the whole universe, it follows that the work of man — his efforts to master the material universe, to draw out its secrets, to domesticate and utilize it, to transform brute matter into instruments of greater and greater perfection right up to "electronic brains" capable of operations defying the intelligence even of the man who made them — all such human work acquires a value for eternity.

Of course, matter offers man a resistance which can only be overcome by painful efforts. This is the painful, "laborious" character of human work which the Bible affirms as a penalty of original sin. But it never insinuates that without sin man would not have had to work. It even says explicitly that Adam before his sin was placed in the earthly Paradise "to cultivate it."

For the sinner, work, by reasons of its inherent painfulness, is a means of expiation or purification, the means par excellence. "You shall eat your bread in the sweat of your brow" (Gen. 3:19). But let us be careful not to restrict the value of work to this single aspect or even to consider it simply as a means of earning a living. Work has another, perhaps less familiar, aspect which springs immediately from the dogma of the redemption of the universe.

God has not created this universe to destine it to death. He has placed in our hands an unfinished universe, entrusting to us the glorious mission of perfecting his work. Because of sin, man is incapable of fulfilling this mission without painful effort, but God, in deciding to redeem man and in promising him a Redeemer, has entrusted this task to him once again, so to speak, and has enabled him to bring it to completion.

For the God of the Bible is exactly the opposite of Zeus who was jealous of man's happiness and who reserved to himself the secrets of nature, condemning Prometheus for having loved men too much in bringing them fire. For us Christians every new advance in the harnessing of nature by man, every new conquest of itself enters into the divine plan. It continues creation. It enables material creation to tend toward the end for which it was created. Such advances prepare in a certain, though enigmatic, way for the future redemption of the universe. In similar fashion, each time the spirit takes a greater hold on the human body, rendering it a more docile servant of the soul, it prepares in a real, but nonetheless enigmatic, manner for the future resurrection of the body.

3. Finally, from this there comes a third, equally important lesson. We have seen that Paul and the Bible conceived the redemption of the universe only as dependent upon the redemption of man himself. Without the redemption of man there could be neither redemption of the body nor, consequently, redemption of the universe. It follows that any effort to prepare for a redemption of the universe through human labor alone, without regard for the redemption of man, is a total delusion. By the same token, every so-called asceticism that tends to submit the body to the soul without looking toward the redemption of this soul can lead only to tragic failure. The body would then rise only to imprison the soul completely. Believing that he was working toward his salvation, man would be working in fact toward the loss of his soul as well as his body.

Gnostics may consider matter itself evil. But for Paul, as for the Bible, evil exists only in man — more precisely in the spirit of the man who, instead of ordering himself to God and others, seeks to order others and even God to himself. It follows then of necessity that every conquest of the universe which is not ordered toward establishing in man the reign of love serves to strengthen in him the tyranny of egoism; far from preparing the redemption of the universe, it can only contribute to its ruin. On the other hand, each time that man strives by his work — even if without apparent success — to place the universe at the service of love, it must be said that he is mysteriously but efficaciously preparing the world for redemption.

In this way one may see how authentic Christian hope in a future world — far from luring the Christian from concern for the world, far from turning him aside from enriching the universe through dedicated labor — makes just such effort one of his most pressing duties. For, if what we have said is correct, if a "redeemed" universe can in the final analysis only be a universe placed entirely at the service of love, who then but the Christian — I mean the man authentically inspired by the love of Christ (for there is no other, whether he bears officially the name of Christian or whether he is one in fact without knowing it) — who then but such a man is capable of placing the universe at the service of love and thus contributing, modestly but efficaciously, to the redemption of the universe, the object of his hope?

# 7 THE APOCALYPSE

The preaching of the message of salvation of all men in Christ burst upon the world with the descent of the Holy Spirit at Pentecost. The difficulty of bearing witness to Christ was soon experienced by the apostles and especially by the first witness unto death — Stephen. Persecution of the Church grew in extent and violence through the first three centuries of her history, until to be a Christian became synonymous with a vocation to martyrdom.

The Apocalypse of St. John was written to encourage the Christians of the first century to stand firm in their witness. In the difficult symbolic language of apocalyptic literature, St. John shows the history and fate of governments which war against God's plan of salvation in Christ. He shows Christ, as Lord of history, present in His Church, encouraging His suffering members and leading them to the marriage of the Lamb in glory.

Although the Apocalypse may be a difficult book, it has been fruitfully studied according to its own literary type.[1] The articles in this section give a valuable introduction to modern commentaries. Yet, in spite of the complexity of its language and symbolism, the Apocalypse is a consoling book, not only because of its promise of future glory, but also because it clearly states that Christ is with His suffering Church and with every Christian now: "Behold, I stand at the door and knock; if anyone hears my voice and opens the door, I will come in and eat with him, and he with me" (Apoc. 3:20).

[1]William Heidt, The Apocalypse. New Testament Reading Guide (Collegeville: The Liturgical Press, 1962). Henry Barclay Swete, The Apocalypse of St. John (London: MacMillan and Co., 1907). William Barclay, The Revelation of St. John (Edinburgh: The Saint Andrew Press, 1959).

# INTRODUCTION TO APOCALYPTIC

Michael J. Cantley

If a "popularity contest" were to be conducted of the various books of the Bible, it is more than likely that such books as Leviticus and Numbers would be found not far from the bottom of the list. Not only is much of their material unintelligible to the modern reader, but he is inclined to think that little of it is meaningful. Without taking time to refute the latter contention (and no biblical theologian would deny that it can be refuted), we might say that this conviction has discouraged the enthusiastic amateur. Quite simply, there are few amateurs who have written about the books in question.

It is a different matter when it comes to the apocalyptic books of the Bible, notably the books of Daniel and the Apocalypse of St. John. Despite their obscurity, they have always retained their popularity. Many reasons, ranging from morbid curiosity about symbolic language to an innate religious appreciation of their essential message, could be given for this interest. But whatever the reason, the interest is there and has produced at times, as anyone who has listened to the "elucidations" of the self-made Bible scholar can attest, an array of interpretations that would baffle the original composers themselves. It has been said that anyone can "prove" almost anything from the Bible. The statement, intended in irony, might well be restricted to apocalytic literature.

It is far from our purpose here to give a detailed interpretation of Daniel or of St. John's Apocalypse. Rather, our purpose is to provide an introduction to this peculiar literary form, an introduction that will, it is hoped, serve to prepare the reader for a more fruitful, because more intelligent, approach to such literature. Apocalyptic is the child of a special mentality, a special age and a special need. Without an understanding of these there can be no true appreciation of apocalyptic.

## General description

The word itself, if we restrict ourselves to etymology, means "unfolding," or "revelation," the latter being the name actually given, and quite properly, to this inspired work of St. John in most Protestant Bibles. While the word does give some indication of the content (although even this must not be understood wholly in the sense of a revelation of truths utterly unknown and unknowable), it can be more misleading than instructive. In fact, it has led many to think that the sacred authors are giving detailed information on events that are to take place in the far distant future and has produced many of the "elucidations" referred to above. Instead of trying to define this

Published originally in *The Bible Today*, 1 (1963), 500-504. Reprinted by permission of the publisher.

particular literature through its commonly accepted name, therefore, we would do better to attempt to describe it by some of its dominant characteristics.

Above all we can say that apocalyptic is *crisis literature, written generally in time of persecution to bring consolation to its readers.* Moreover, it interprets the difficulties of the present in terms of the past and looks forward to a definitive redemption in the future. It is characterized by a fondness for systematic presentation of its point of view, by outbursts of imaginative language and by an unalterable faith and invincible confidence in the authority of the inspired literature of Judaism.

## The age of apocalyptic

Although it reached its golden age between the second century B.C. and the second century A.D., there are clear traces of the apocalyptic genre from very early times. It is more frequently found in prophetic works, but appears unexpectedly in other places also. For example, in Deuteronomy 28:60-68 we find a series of maledictions, in apocalyptic style, inspired by the remembrance of the plagues of Egypt. Many of the Psalms are written in the form of apocalypse, and concentrate the burden of their message on the eschatological expectations of the nation (e.g., Pss. 11; 73; 97; 98). The same tendency can also be discovered in the wisdom literature (Prov. 1:20-33; Job 18:5-21; 20:22-29; 27:19-23; Wis. 5:20-23; 11:15-19; 17–19). These texts all depict a state of suffering and evidence confidence in the glorious intervention of God and His will to reestablish right order and give peace and profit to the just.

With a theme of suffering and hope for divine intervention to alleviate that suffering, we might expect that this form of literature would develop most fully in the postexilic age, when the nation was most distressed and discouragement most widespread. The postexilic age was also the post-prophetic age, and it was only natural for man to begin to scrutinize the ancient texts more carefully in order to find in them the answer to present difficulties. It is precisely for these reasons that this age is the age of the apocalypse. These writings undertake to convince souls that the ancient promises are still worthy of belief. Under cover of symbols, the nation's story unrolls by successive stages, presenting an outline of history in which very clear figures are intermingled with others that are arbitrarily vague. The reader is invited to see that God has dominated the stage of history in a manner perfectly consistent with His promises. It remains now for the faithful soul to wait confidently for the realization of the final step in man's history, the last judgment and unending happiness.

This gives us an insight into some further characteristics of apocalyptic: pseudonymity, since a fictitious author can, at times, provide another clue to the message contained; a teaching that is esoteric in character, accessible only to the initiated; a deterministic view of history wherein the succession of events, determined by the infallible and omnipotent divine will, inevitably moves the nation to its destiny; frequent intervention of angels as emissaries of God and of His message; and a universalism of sorts.

## Historical background of Old Testament apocalyptic

The principal sources of Old Testament apocalyptic are to be found in the books of Isaiah, Ezekiel and Daniel. The age that gave rise to the apocalyptic sections of these books was one of political upheaval. We will describe the age in very general terms.

In 587 B.C., Nebuchadnezzar destroyed the city of Jerusalem and transported the Jewish people to Babylon, where they were kept in bondage for about fifty years. Then, in 538 B.C., Cyrus, King of the Persians, permitted the Jews to return home, but as subjects of a foreign power. The Greek empire of Alexander followed some two hundred years later. His united world of one language, culture and religion militated against the Jewish religion. The books of Maccabees, Sirach and Wisdom indicate that many Jews succumbed to the pagan influence and fell away from the true worship of Yahweh. Those who remained faithful tended to become isolated from the mainstream of life and to live in a spiritual ghetto.

When Alexander died in 322 B.C., his Asian holdings were seized by Seleucus (358-280 B.C.), founder of the Seleucid Empire. In 168 B.C. the Greco-Syrian (Seleucid) Empire, under Antiochus IV Epiphanes, brought the issue with the Jews to a head. He converted the Jerusalem temple into a pagan shrine for Zeus, and under penalty of death forbade all observance of the Jewish law. These events touched off the Maccabean rebellion. But independence was shortlived, and towards its end was even more bitter than former subjection. The Hasmonean dynasty, successor to the Maccabees, was cruel and irreligious, even to the point of usurping the office of the High Priest. In 63 B.C. the Romans annexed Judea without opposition and thus it continued until 70 A.D. when Titus put down a serious revolt. An uneasy state of affairs led to a final revolt in 135 A.D., which, as a result of its failure, saw the end of the Jewish state and left Jerusalem, for the first time, a pagan city.

It was against the background of the Maccabean Wars that the principal apocalyptic composition of the Old Testament, the book of *Daniel*, was written. The author ascribed his work to a sixth-century B.C. figure in order to bring out the special view of history mentioned above; in other words, God had foreseen all of this from the beginning, long before it actually transpired. The message is presented within the framework of a succession of four kingdoms: the Babylonian, the Median (which the author, for his schematic purposes, describes as succeeding the Babylonian kingdom, but which actually was contemporary with it), the Persian, and the Greco-Syrian. These kingdoms are presented in symbolic figures (a huge statue in *ch.* 2; four beasts in *ch.* 7) which could be identified with little difficulty by the second-century B.C. readers. Succeeding these four is the kingdom of the Messiah, the Son of Man, which would bring consolation to the saints who are now suffering.

## Historical background of New Testament apocalyptic

The political situation in the early days of the Church, leading to the composition of the great Apocalypse of St. John, is not unlike that of the Jewish nation. The Gospels and Epistles bear constant witness to the fact that the Church was born to persecution. But most of the early opposition to the Church came from Jewish factions. The Roman government took no official stand on the matter, and even St. Paul was released from his first Roman imprisonment in 63 A.D. Shortly after this, however, the official situation changed. Nero (37-68) became emperor, fired Rome and made the Christian community the scapegoat for his insane action. Paul suffered martyrdom in 67 A.D. The troubles continued under Vespasian (69-79), Titus (79-81) and Domitian (81-96). All this was a new experience for the Christians and they were unprepared for it.

It was at this time, around 96 A.D., that the vision came to St. John on Patmos. He writes about it in the Apocalypse. His message was a "revelation" — a document attesting to the triumph of Christ. As Christ had overcome the world in His passion and resurrection, so would His Church triumph in a world gone mad. This is the whole message and purpose of John's book. Some have tried to see in the Apocalypse a revelation of the total course of history. It was not written to satisfy idle curiosity about the future, nor to provide a blueprint by which a person of ingenuity could plot the course and destiny of peoples and nations down to our present day.

## Reading the apocalyptic literature

The strange literary form of these books is the result of two factors. First of all, the author is an Oriental, given to imaginative and symbolic modes of expression. Secondly, his intention was to console and strengthen the faith of his readers and, at the same time, to keep his message safe from hostile eyes. To accomplish this end, he used symbolic language that could be understood only by the initiated. We might compare this to the *disciplina arcani* of the early Church, the process whereby Christians recognized one another by the use of certain symbols and kept themselves and their teachings safe from their pagan persecutors.

An attempt to read and understand the apocalyptic genre can be a rather disconcerting experience because we lack familiarity with the metaphorical language which is its stock in trade. The same complaint, but in varying degrees, has been voiced about many of the other books of the Bible.

While the difficulties are not to be minimized, neither are they to be made an excuse for ignoring the Sacred Scriptures, which are of paramount importance to our spiritual lives. This we have on the testimony of St. Jerome, who says, "To ignore the Scriptures is to ignore Christ," and of Pope Piux XII, who brings his remarks in *Divino Afflante Spiritu* to a close with the recommendation to read the Scriptures because: "There those who are wearied and oppressed by adversities and afflictions will find true consolation and divine strength to suffer and bear with patience; there — that is, in the Holy

Gospel — Christ, the highest and greatest example of justice, charity, and mercy, is present to all; and to the lacerated and trembling human race are laid open the fountains of that divine grace without which both peoples and their rulers can never arrive at, never establish, peace in the state and unity of heart; there in fine will all learn Christ, 'who is the head of all principality and power' and 'who of God is made unto us wisdom and justice and sanctification and redemption.' "

No one who approaches the Scripture with an open heart and a mind attuned by the discipline of the Church to the message of Christ will come away empty. Those who study the text of the Bible, and humbly seek aid from the wonderful sources at their command, in books and periodicals, will find God's Word a library to fill every human need and spiritual aspiration.

# THE APOCALYPSE

Patrick Fannon, S.M.M.

No book of the Bible can claim to have received such a poor press in the past as that accorded the Apocalypse. Some of the early Greek Fathers — Cyril of Jerusalem, Gregory Nazianzen, John Chrysostom, Theodoret — shared hesitations about its inspired character. Heretics and near-heretics gave it their dubious support. It provoked the *irrisus infidelium*. The underworld sects of the Middle Ages borrowed their slogans from its pages. Luther shied away from it: "my spirit cannot acquiesce in this book," while Zwingli forthrightly denounced it: "It is not a book of the Bible." A leading divine, some three hundred years ago, described it as a book "which either finds a man cracked or leaves him so." More recent oracles have been content to pronounce it pure fantasy, the ravings of a crank from the lunatic fringe.

Even sympathetic readers, not given to lampooning the Word of God, have admitted themselves utterly baffled by the studied obscurities in the text. They have found themselves on the shore of a Sargasso Sea of symbols, or mesmerised by a cabbalism of numbers, or gazing with uncomprehending wonder at the ceremonial of the liturgy of heaven. Little cause for amazement, then, if the Apocalypse has not won the respect we might have expected for the final flourish of revelation.

Modern studies, however, have been trying to make compensation and have done much to make intelligible this most difficult book. Our chief obstacle to understanding a great part of the Bible lies not so much in the actual text as in the mentality of its authors. The Semites did not think as we do,

Published originally in *Scripture*, 14 (1962), 33-43. Reprinted by permission of the publisher.

our thought-patterns are as distant as east from west. Hence, some appreciation of Hebrew modes of thinking is going to offer an important key to unlocking the message of the Apocalypse. But that is not all. The growing awareness that the prophets of the Old Testament wrote from the standpoint of their own times has led scholars to see that the starting-point of this New Testament work (which tradition has always recognized as manifesting prophetic traits) was the author's contemporary situation. In this attempt to unravel the complicated snarl of problems tied up in the Apocalypse, we must let ourselves be guided by those two threads.

In the years following the return of the Jews from their Exile, despite the preaching of such late prophets as Haggai, Zechariah, Joel and Malachi, it became apparent that the previous vehicle for divine revelation, prophecy, was receding before a new expression: apocalyptic. This was a fusion of the ancient eschatological oracle (concerned with the coming era and the awful "Day of Yahweh") with the prophetic vision (of the "new times"), and consisted in the revelation ("apocalypse") of divine secrets manifested in dreams and symbolic visions. This new art-form arose from the seeking of fervent souls, in those bitterly disappointing post-Exilic years, for an understanding of their present disillusionment in a future realization of God's plan for them. A new world was brought in to redress the balance of the old.

If we try to define the characteristics of the literary form of apocalyptic, we shall find that three main trends may be listed. There is first of all an overweaning delight in symbols and visions. We are introduced to a weird symbolism of numbers, beasts, names in a *décor* that Impressionism itself could never have conjured up. It should have been (but not always was) obvious even to the most literal-minded expositor that these marvels were not to be taken at their face value. They stood for something else. A second facet of apocalyptic is that its absorbing interest in the ultimate issues of God's plan for the world includes an almost vindictive and savage gloating over the downfall of the enemies of God and of the nation. Even the whole order of nature is involved in what has been (recently) termed a "cosmic break-up": the stars fall from their places, the sun no longer gives its light, the moon is turned into blood, the sea gives up its dead. Finally, amid such luxuriant splendour can be discerned the relics of prophecy whose ghost had not yet been completely laid. The apocalypses in Ezekiel, Zechariah and Daniel were followed by numerous non-canonical successors (like the Qumrân *War of the Sons of Light with the Sons of Darkness*), but while there are undoubtedly family resemblances among all this *genre*, the vagaries traceable in the non-canonical apocalypses are mercifully absent from those included in the Bible. Similar passports may be produced by all, but an attentive scrutiny will linger over the special particularities.

If we turn to the one apocalypse which the New Testament has retained in its Canon, that of St. John, we may expect to find in it some of these notes of apocalyptic. In the first place, we encounter symbols and visions. For purposes of convenience, we may distinguish a triple catalogue of symbols and offer what many believe to be their correct deciphering. After the seven letters to the Churches of Asia Minor, we are shown a heavenly *liturgy*. The long robe and golden cincture worn by the Son of Man (an image borrowed from the book of Daniel) signify the priesthood and royalty of Christ; his white hair, burning eyes, feet of bronze tell us of his eternity, divine knowledge and lasting stability; the two-edged sword which issued from his mouth symbolizes the pronouncement of death-dealing decrees which will effect the destruction of the persecutors of God's Church. Among the numerous assistants at the Throne are the twenty-four elders who thus link up the present scene with the orders of priests classified in 1 Chronicles (and recalled to us in Luke 1:5, where we read that Zechariah was performing the duties of the sanctuary in his *turn* — that of Abijah). The "seven spirits" are reminiscent of the book of Tobit where Raphael declares himself to be one of the seven who stand in the presence of God. The four living creatures — the *Hayim* of Ezekiel — lion, bull, man and eagle, represent that which is noble, strong, intelligent and agile in creation. (We are accustomed to designate the Evangelists by these symbols.) The crowns worn by the angels tell of their governing role over the world, and the horns and eyes of the Lamb attribute power and knowledge to It. The incense burnt here as elsewhere in the Apocalypse denotes the prayers offered before the throne of God.

A second chapter of symbols describes the *destruction* to be meted out to the godless in three series of disasters: seven seals broken — the divine decrees are to become effective; seven trumpets — the processional heralding God's destroying entry; seven bowls smashed — God's anger is to be poured out over the world. The four horsemen who emerge after the breaking of the first seal in a scenario which is nothing if not prismatic conjure up the Parthian cavalry which contributed so greatly to the fall of Rome. It will be noted by close readers of the Apocalypse that the opening of the seventh seal introduces us to the series of trumpets — we are working, as it were, in ever-widening circles. The cosmic upheaval and the seven plagues visited on the nations all belong to the same destructive symbolism promising final vindication.

A third group of symbols is found in the *dramatis personae* and the *numbers* which are sprinkled over the pages of the Apocalypse. The divinity connoted by "Alpha and Omega" is more obvious than the unusual "Amen" given to God. "Abaddon" and its Greek equivalent "Apollyon" signify "destruction" and the Plain of Megiddo, the time-honored battlefield for supremacy in the Palestinian Corridor, becomes the scene of eschatological disaster — "Armageddon." "Gog and Magog" are terms co-opted from Ezekiel to designate the pagan nations assembled against the Church. But it is perhaps against Rome and her rulers that invective is most generously hurled through with a nice economy of terms. She is "Babylon," the "great harlot," her empire the "Beast" (also said of Nero), her emperor-worship "Satan's throne." As to those cryptic numbers, we are told that "four" is the symbolic number for the cosmos, that "seven" denotes perfection, that "one hundred and forty-four thousand" is the sacred number (twelve) squared and multiplied by a thousand to show mass. "Seven thousand" covers people of all social classes ("seven") within the great number ("thousand"). The term "foursquare," oc-curring in chapter 21:16, we may easily decipher as meaning "fully perfect." The quaint "a time, and times, and half a time" is taken to mean three and a half years — the forty-two months of 11:2 — the duration-type of all perse-cutions which derives from Daniel. Lastly, "six hundred and sixty-six" dis-creetly indicate Nero by representing the sum of the numerical values the letters of his name possessed in Hebrew.

To those who have inquired "Why did not John give us a plain tale instead of this cryptogram to be decoded almost term by term" it has been answered that a "disguise" was expedient in view of his troubled times — his intended read-ers would possess the key to the puzzle where unauthorized aliens would be completely at a loss. That this was in fact what could happen nobody can deny, and its utility in this respect should not be overlooked. But the literary form of apocalyptic was not devised simply to hoodwink the authorities; it derives from a greater need. Besides being an escape-valve of fantasy for the repressions of a bitterly suffering people, apocalyptic (in its better examples) demanded an adventure of faith and trust into an unknown world. It af-firmed that history, too, came under the providence of God and its final issues lie in the unseen but directing hand of God. And its very inadequacy to nullify present suffering turned eyes towards the future, to the future life. The very mystery of God's providence suggested a use of symbols in any striving to express that mystery, caught only in tantalizing glimpses and beyond the normal means of expression. Let us attempt to sketch God's glory in heaven, His plan of history, the role of the cosmic Christ, the final beauty of the Church — and we shall resort to symbols of contemporary design which a later generation will need to demythologise.

The second characteristic we have noted in this highly specialized art-form of apocalyptic is its inclination to delight in the coming destruction of the national persecutors. We shall find, however, in the Apocalypse of St. John that while the approaching doom of the nations is emphasized, it is seen as no more than a just punishment for the wrongs they have committed. They are to be punished qua evil-doers — not qua opponents to Jewish sovereignty, a trait which marks non-canonical apocalyptic. In other words, John's Apoc-alypse has in mind the just vindication of the rights of God and the Church — a thesis we will rashly impugn. Further, opportunities for a repentance which will avert total disaster are offered but rejected. As in the case of Pharaoh, the seven plagues serve only to harden oppression. And John does not scruple to point out the real cause of the troubles afflicting the Church. The imperial despotism was no mere police action; behind it lay supreme malice — the malice of Satan.

We have noted earlier that apocalyptic was an outgrowth of prophetism, and in the New Testament Apocalypse the element of prophecy is strong. While employing the style, imagery and procedure of Jewish apocalyptic, it remains faithful to the great tradition of the ancient prophets. Like the prophets, the author has a passion for the salvation of souls (as the seven opening letters will show) and wishes to reply to the most vexatious problems of his time. This prophetic core in the Apocalypse has always been recognized in tradition, but an oblique view of the nature of prophecy had the unfortunate effect of seeing the contents of the Apocalypse as a detailed blue-print of events to be pursued during the history of the Church. For many, the Book was little more than a sop to their curiosity — it was made to reveal secrets it never concealed. But not only is the Apocalypse firmly embedded in the prophetic tradition; it has no hesitations in borrowing from Ezekiel, Zechariah and Daniel to an extent which is nothing short of plagirising. We can even go further. John has exploited the Old Testament in such a way that no less than five hundred Old Testament allusions decorate his work. Have we, then, nothing more than a thinly disguised compilation, a "resultant text" offering the best readings from past Jewish literature? On the contrary. While John has pressed into service the Old Testament he has done so within a Christian perspective. The late date of the Apocalypse ensures that period of reflection necessary to the appreciation of how the Old Testament was being fulfilled in the New, of how the ancient themes were now being interwoven to form the full picture. We have here a Christian mind which has re-thought the *data* of the past in terms of the present Christian dispensation. The language we are listening to, however, still retains its Jewish accent.

Even when we have investigated the literary form of apocalyptic, with its symbolism, vindication and prophetism, and seen what light this can shed on the meaning of our Apocalypse, we are still a far throw from grasping the message bequeathed to us. We have already observed that the author's own standpoint must be our starting-point for the interpretation of his message (as in the case for the Old Testament prophetical writings,) but (like, once more, those same ancient writings) this message does not stop there. Its sights are set on more distant targets also. How, then, are we to approach this question of the interpretation of the Apocalypse, how define its objectives? Scholars are not agreed on a solution, differing like star from star. Yet, each proposal has its own helpful contribution to make to illumine the problem. We may, with Père Feuillet, distinguish no less than seven different approaches to the interpretation of the Apocalypse.

In the first instance there is *Millenarianism* which is based on Apoc. 20: 1-6 and which, in varying ways, proposes a thousand-year reign of Christ before his Parousia. We may summarily dismiss the crass literalism of certain medieval interpreters and their modern followers who see in this text a pre-Parousia coming of Christ down to earth, followed by such a reign. Einar Molland, in his *Christendom* (a recent ecumenical survey of the sects found within Christianity), tells us that a fabulous building has been erected in America containing even more fabulous apartments designed to accommodate the *entourage* of Christ during the millennium. (One has the uneasy suspicion that the present — but only temporary — occupants will enjoy an undisturbed tenure.) There are other considerable authorities, however, who suggest a spiritual and symbolic interpretation of the same text. Augustine, after the precedent of Irenaeus, Justin, Hippolytus and Tertullian, thinks that the thousand years is contemporary with the whole earthly phase of the Kingdom of God, from the Resurrection and Ascension onwards. But it is difficult to reconcile this view of the millennium — which supposes precisely that Satan is enchained — with the evidence provided by John that he is still provoking the terrible crises which bring such intense suffering to the Church. It is John's care to show that *after* the persecutions of Rome, there will be relief. Hence, Fr. Boismard advances the view (already gaining wide acceptance) that the "thousand years" corresponds to the earthly phase of the Church from the end of the persecutions fomented by Rome until the end of time. And so the return of Christ described in Apoc. 19:11ff must be understood in a symbolic sense) or may even form a doublet, a repetition, of 20: 7-11). Although the Church has never condemned Millenarianism, a decree of the Holy Office (21 July 1944) states *tuto doceri non posse*. What is attacked in this decree is the idea that Christ will return visibly upon the earth before the Parousia. Those who hold (like Feret) that a flowering of Christian civilization will grace the world before its consummation are at liberty to do so.

A second method of interpretation of the Apocalypse, which claims names like Allo, Bonsirven and Cerfaux in support, is that which attempts to see in this Book a series of *recapitulations* — the successive cycles of visions (seven seals, seven trumpets, seven bowls) are merely presentations of the same disasters, complementary signs, parallel to one another, which herald the last things. This opinion, which so admirably simplifies matters, has also in its favor the fact that we cannot discover in the relevant parts of the Apocalypse any constant chronological progression. But in this debate of recapitulation *v.* continuous narrative, authors like R. H. Charles (whose great knowledge of apocalyptic has proved immensely valuable to the last generation) and Ernst Lohmeyer have voted for continuous narrative: successive events do follow a strict sequence; their case seems to be strengthened by such a verse as 15:1, "seven angels with seven plagues, which are the *last,* for with them the wrath of God *is ended.*"

A third approach tends to see in the Apocalypse a detailed forecast of the whole run of history — the method of *universal history*. This interpretation of the episodes in the Apocalypse, which had a resounding success in the Middle Ages, gives rise to the notion of the seven ages of the world. Each period of history, however, in this view was colored by the hopes of its commentator: his times were "hard" and consequently accommodated to those critical times of the Apocalypse which were to usher in the end. Now while it is evidently too much to expect the Apocalyptist to plot minutely the future unrolling of the Church's history, so satisfying to our curiosity, still it remains true that certain capital stages of the religious history of humanity are envisaged by him. What is revealed is less the successive events of history taken in themselves, but more their true bearing in relation to God's Kingdom. While the future is not announced in detail, it is prophesied that the oppression suffered by the Church must end in a total check; God will have the last word.

This Christian philosophy of history, affirming that *de jure* sovereignty belongs to God, which sovereignty will be asserted *de facto* in God's own time when He will pass judgment on all evil and recognize true merit, must, however, derive from an examination of the *data* presented by John. The method of *contemporary history*, situating the Apocalypse within the framework of John's contemporary situation offers, therefore, a welcome corrective to the previous approach. The realization that his eye was primarily on his own time delivers us from the need to scour history books to detect his characters and their roles. But while this interpretation is such a corrective, its weakness lies in confining the message of the Apocalypse to John's period. He had more to offer than that.

A fifth thesis is concerned to limit that message to the end of time. Dealing neither with the past nor the present, the Apocalypse is orientated towards describing the end of the world and the signs which will precede it — and all these things were at hand. Now while it is doubtlessly true that the Apocalypse does envisage the Parousia and the completion of history, it is forcing the texts to attempt to prove that the author was inculcating the naïve conviction that the Parousia was chronologically at hand. The *eschatological* interpretation fails to take sufficient notice of John's emphasis on the victorious Christ, Lord of History, exercising a real but hidden mastery over the forces of evil which are so utterly opposed to him. Their end is near in that the plan of God for the world is on the point of being realized completely. The end is in sight, the final age has arrived.

The question: Whence did John draw the materials for his work? has given rise to a further method of interpretation — the method of *literary analysis*. That much came to him in visions, as he claims, cannot be overlooked, and we have already noted the part played by the Old Testament in John's thought-pattern. However, this is a far cry from the efforts of scholars at the close of the last century who saw in the Apocalypse a compilation of older apocalyptic material. Vischer of Germany asserted that the bulk of the book was a previous Jewish apocalypse made Christian by the addition of a prologue and an epilogue with a few interpolations within the body of the work. The Christian element was no more than an ingredient, a spice. Modern scholars, however, on the whole are becoming less favorable to such hardy hypotheses which turn the Apocalypse into a casual compilation of diverse sources; the unity of inspiration and of style are opposed to it. Still, the book is not a simple account of visions, Old Testament allusions and Christian ideas shaped by a master-mind. It results from a work of reflection and composition which must have used pre-existing elements, and it is legitimate to attempt to define the pre-history of the text. We may, with Boismard, distinguish two primitive texts written by the same author at different times, then fused into one text — our Apocalypse — by another hand. Using this hypothesis much can be done to explain the doublets, ruptures in the series of visions, passages apparently out of context. To take one example, the "New Jerusalem" of chapters 21–22 — is it one "city" or two? We can discern two descriptions: one which presents it as the messianic city, the

Church on earth, in chapters 21:9–22:15, and another which has rather in mind the eternal city, the Church glorious and triumphant when time has passed away, in chapter 21:1-8. Fr Boismard suggests that a "Text I" offered the "messianic Jerusalem" and a "Text II" the "heavenly Jerusalem." One would expect the "messianic Jerusalem" to precede the heavenly one since it prefigures it. Nevertheless, we might refrain from exposing ourselves to the Seer's curse (22:19) by rearranging those chapters.

Finally, there is the *comparative* method of interpretation with its two departments for home affairs (examining the contents of the Apocalypse in the light of traditional Christian material and biblical sources, an aspect we have already discussed) and foreign affairs. This latter attempts to disentangle *motifs* from pagan mythology — for example, the evil Angro-mainyu in conflict with the good Ahura-mazda, the Zoroastrian *fravashis* or "folk angels" — which have been laid under contribution for a Christian syncretist religion. While the last generation of scholars has tended to recoil from such hazardous parallels in Comparative Religion, we can still remark the occasional unfashionable reminiscence of such hypotheses. The background to John's Christian thought is biblical, not pagan, and the Old Testament it is that must clarify his references since his Apocalypse is to a certain point the re-reading of the Old in the light of the New. The hands held out to us may be the hands of Esau, but the voice is the voice of Jacob.

We have observed that these methods of interpretation offer some help towards understanding the Apocalypse, and we have tried to single out that contribution in each case. We may now move on to consider the Apocalypse in those perspectives.

A specific time of crisis gave rise to the writing of the Apocalypse. Whether the John who wrote it (1:1) is St. John the Evangelist or another John (variously referred to as "John the Elder" or "John the Seer") attached to his circle of influence need not detain us. "It seems," Kiddle remarks, "that the authorship of *Revelation* may prove the one mystery of the book which will never be revealed in this world." What is important is that it was written to fortify the Christian morale during a time of such persecution that the question must have risen unbidden to many lips: How can this be our fate when *He* has said "Fear not, I have conquered the world?" Nero, or *Nero redivivus*, Domitian, is indicated as the perpetrator of this early "final solution" which discredited the closing years of the first century.

John accepts the challenge and, to realize his aim, takes up the two great themes of traditional prophetism favored by apocalyptic writers: the "great Day of Yahweh," full of impending doom, and the "new times" of peace and happiness in the established Kingdom of God. The Church, the new People of God, decimated by a ferocious persecution, would be vindicated and merit an eternal recompense.

After the Letters to the seven Churches of Asia Minor (whose historical geography has been so well made known to us by Ramsay and others), an opening vision in chapter four portrays the majesty of God in heaven, absolute master of human destiny. Into this liturgical scene enters the Lamb of

God to whom is made over the book containing the decrees of extermination of the oppressors which begin to take shape, in chapter six, with the invasion of the barbarian Parthians who set in motion the usual *cortège* of war, pest and famine. We catch a glimpse of the faithful, preserved from these evils while awaiting their definitive happiness in heaven. Strangely enough, a similar mercy is shown the persecutors: a series of plagues can be the occasion of their conversion, but, as in the case of the Egyptians, this overture evokes no such response. God will destroy these impious corruptors who would divert the world to the Roman emperor-worship, and a lament on Rome is sung only to be echoed by songs of triumph in heaven. A further vision takes up this theme of the destruction of Rome — but the destruction this time is effected by Christ.

The perspective of the "new times" begins to govern the Apocalypse from chapter twenty — there is a period of prosperity for the Church which is terminated, however, by a renewed attack of Satan who is overthrown. We are then faced with the resurrection of the dead and the judgment. With death itself no more, chapter twenty-one opens up the vista of the Church in glory; a retrospective vision, recalling the perfection of that same Church, the new Jerusalem, during its reign on earth, closes the book.

But John's message of consolation and encouragement was not confined to those of his own time. We have already observed that he offers us a philosophy of history: the whole sweep of the historical process is under God's control and the life, death and resurrection of Christ, the Lamb of God of both the Fourth Gospel and the Apocalypse, have a direct bearing on everything, the Church in particular. The basic structure of the Apocalypse of the struggle of the sons of darkness against the sons of light (a theme common also to the Fourth Gospel) transcends any particular phase of history, but behind that struggle lies the permanent vision of faith recorded in chapters four and five of the Apocalypse: God maintains a controlling interest over earthly catastrophes, subordinating them to His divine plan. In fact, they are part of that same plan. There may be a "pause," as it were, in the divine economy to enable Christians to stabilize their relationship to Him, a challenge that demands the response of faith, but the reward is certain.

And why? Because (often enough despite appearances) God is with His people. The *Shekinah*, His Presence, transitory in the Old Testament, is here to stay. God has taken up a permanent dwelling with His people, the Church. One great hope of the Old Dispensation has been fulfilled. But the figure of the Son of Man in the midst of the vision of heaven tells us that still another ancient expectation is being realized — the ascent of humanity to God. The closing chapters of the Apocalypse show that state finally attained: the Church is clothed at last in the glory that was hers from the beginning. The Bride is sharing in the privileges of the Bridegroom, Paradise has been regained.

If we were to try and seek what role John would have us play during this interval before the last act of the drama of redemption, we shall find it is that of witness: witness to the work of Christ as a past event, a present experience and a future hope. This may entail some suffering — it is not without interest that we find the Greek word *martyria* ("bearing witness") hardening, in the Apocalypse, into our "martyrdom." Yet that great Victory Hymn of the persecuted Church still echoes its epic of Christian hope, and its rewarding and consolatory promise is held out to us.

# THE ERA OF THE CHURCH
# IN SAINT JOHN

André Feuillet, S.S.

The history of the Judeo-Christian religion is a history of salvation, a history that progresses through three phases or "ages." There is the Old Testament age of preparation, the age of Christ's sojourn on earth, and the age of the Church — the time from Christ's ascension till the parousia.

Each of these eras is distinguished by its own particular characteristics. A man who is Christian finds himself in religious surroundings very different from those of a Jew living under the Old Covenant or from those of a disciple hurrying after Jesus on the roads of Galilee or Judea. The age of the Christian is the age of the Church, which was born in the redemptive drama of Good Friday and the victory of Easter morning. The following pages attempt to define the characteristics of this third age in salvation history.

The synoptic Gospels show us a Church, a messianic community, inseparable from the conviction of Jesus that he was the promised Messiah. The Gospel of John is richer even than Matthew in ecclesiology in proportion as it is Christological, showing the Incarnate Son of God revealing to men the mysterious treasures of divine life. John is the only one of the evangelists to emphasize the connection between Jesus and the Church. John's whole theme is the "Hour of Jesus," which is also the hour of the Church and of the sacraments. Christ's ministry, his preaching, his miracles are seen as more than a mere anticipation of a distant future. "The hour is coming and now is here" (4:23; 5:25).

## Apocalypse a complement

Difficult though it is, the Apocalypse is an almost indispensable complement to the fourth Gospel — not because it offers any entirely new insights but because more clearly than the Gospel it expresses certain concrete aspects of the age of the Church. More than that, the Apocalypse locates the Chris-

Reprinted from *Theology Digest*, 11 (1963), 3-10. Originally published as "Le temps de l'Église d'après le quatrième Évangile et l'Apocalypse," *LaMaison-Dieu*, 65 (1961), 60-79. Reprinted by permission of the publisher.

tian community within the context of the history of the world. It can be seen as a kind of continuation of the prophets, of 1 and 2 Isaiah especially; it is a kind of Christian Book of Daniel. That is why we plan to give the Apocalypse a supporting role in our presentation, which we will conclude by a consideration of the magnificent figure of the Woman — the people of God — a symbol which recapitulates what John teaches us about the age of the Church.

We proceed then directly to the heart of the fourth Gospel where we find — in the Last Supper discourse — Christ's teaching about what his disciples are to be after he has left them. This teaching is completed and illustrated by chapters nineteen to twenty-one, where details of the death and resurrection awaken us to a realization of what it is Jesus has promised his followers.

Man's greatness is focused by the Bible on the fact that he can enter into dialogue with God, as contrasted with the Greek stress upon his abstract reflection on what God is in himself. The dialogue of the Christian with the divine persons is typfied in three points of the fourteenth and sixteenth chapters of John's Gospel: 1) Jesus will go away but will return, to be more closely than ever united with his disciples; 2) the Father will care for them with special solicitude from the time of Christ's departure to the time of the parousia; 3) the Father and Son will send the Holy Spirit to enlighten and fortify the disciples.

We would like first to examine what the Gospel says about the hour of the Church in reference to man's relationship with each of these three Persons. Later we shall briefly discuss the era of the Church from the viewpoint of the disciples' interrelationships.

## Christ with men

The efficacious presence of the risen Christ is the outstanding characteristic of the age of the Church according to John 14–16. Disturbed by the prospect of Christ's departure, the apostles are reassured that they will not be left orphans (14:18). It is true that the unbelieving world will think Jesus has disappeared forever, that he has faded away into history. But the disciples will know that his saddening departure is to be followed immediately by his return — and by a joy at his return like the joy of a mother who has brought a new human being into existence (14:18f; 16:19f). Though he will be yet invisible to the world, the Savior will make himself visible to his own: "Yet a little while and the world no longer sees me; but you see me, for I live and you shall live" (14:19).

These promises are made not only to the Twelve but to all believers of all times, according to the measure of their faith in him. Their assurance of the presence beside them of the glorious Christ will fill them with a joy which "no one shall take away" (16:22) because it will be in his divine victory that they will be made joyful (17:13). He will come as a friend and, together with his Father, will dwell with them (14:23), that they may be led to the many heavenly abodes prepared for them (14:2-3). The only condition for these remarkable benefactions is total fidelity to the word of Jesus, the Word spoken by the Father.

Two episodes from John 20 and 21 illustrate what we have been saying. Mary Magdalene is forbidden to touch the Savior for, as he says, "I have not yet ascended to my Father" (20:17). The most profound contact we can have with Christ is not the physical contact that the crowds experienced along the roads he walked during his public ministry; paradoxically it is only when he has returned to his Father that we will really "touch" him, through faith and the sacraments.

The other episode, the symbolic catch of fish (21:1, 13), shows us how Christ comes to the assistance of his followers in their apostolic ministry. This is not just another miracle of Christ; it is an act of the Church, accomplished with the all-powerful aid of its Founder.

Both episodes follow the passion, in which the apparent victory of the forces of darkness has in reality marked their defeat. No other evangelist shows as well as John that Calvary is a kind of epiphany of Christ the King, that it means the beginning of his kingship — a kingship not of this world but nonetheless completely victorious over earthly powers. Thus it is that the Easter appearances of Christ found in John are much more than perceptible testimonials to the fact of his resurrection. The appearances both proclaim and symbolize the permanent presence and action of the Son of God, a presence and action which are to characterize the Church from the ascension to the parousia. And the joy and peace of those present at the appearances of the risen Christ are a foretaste of the joy and peace promised in the Last Discourse and offered through the Church to all Christians of all times.

### Father with men

The action and the being of the Son are inseparable from the action and being of the Father. If Christ must maintain the tie with his own after he leaves, the Father too will look after them. When faith encounters the Son, it will simultaneously find the Father (14:9-11). Keeping the word of Jesus will assure the disciples of the love of the Father and of his presence in them together with the Son (14:23). The Father will protect them because of the love they show for his glorified Son (16:26-28). The prayers of those commissioned to continue Christ's work will unfailingly be heard (cf. 14:13-14) and will result in their doing things greater than what Christ worked during his earthly life (14:12), on a par with the powers given to him in his resurrection. They will be invested with the power given the Son so that they can work effectively for the establishment of the Kingdom.

When the risen Christ says to Mary Magdalene, "Go to my brothers and say to them, 'I ascend to my Father and your Father, to my God and your God' " (20:17), he is really saying that the cross and resurrection have established a new covenant, extending to all believers the privilege of divine sonship. Christ has become our brother and his Father ours. The "my brothers" is very likely an allusion to Ps. 22:23: "I will proclaim your name to my brothers"; and it has an excellent parallel in Hebrews (2:9-12): "Made a little lower than the angels . . . crowned with glory and honor . . . [Christ] is not ashamed to call them brothers, saying, 'I will declare thy name to my brothers; in the midst of the church I will praise thee.'" Catherinet has indicated, moreover, the similarity between John 20:17 and the words of Ruth when she proposed that Naomi return to Moab: "Wherever you go I will go, wherever you lodge I will lodge, your people shall be my people and your God my God" (1:16). The "I ascend to my Father" shows that, under the covenant of grace, both Father and Son will be much closer to the disciples than they were before.

### Spirit with men

The fourth Gospel insists often that the departure and glorification of Jesus coincide with the giving of the Spirit. The role to be played in the future Church by this intercessor or advocate — this Paraclete — is explained in chapters fourteen to sixteen. Not only will the Spirit put carnal man in touch with supernatural reality; he will give him a deeper understanding of the Son of God made flesh, of his heavenly Father and of Christ his brother, forming with man a family. The Spirit will give witness of Christ to Christians living in an unbelieving world; and he will show them that Christ's apparent defeat is really glorious victory, the pattern and foreshadowing of their own triumph-in-defeat through persecution.

The apostles are the first to benefit by the promises made at the farewell discourse (14:16-17, 26; 15:26; 16:7-15); yet these promises hold true for all Christians of all times. It is like the passion narrative, where Jesus is described as "giving up his spirit"; the words are very probably ambivalent. He does not merely *yield up* his spirit. He gives his Spirit to all the world — founds the Church with its sacraments in the blood and water that flow from his side. It is here we see his death as a victory, a victory to which (as John tells us in a closely parallel passage) "There are three that bear witness in heaven: the Spirit, and the water, and the blood — and these three are one"(1 John 5:7).

### Man with men

Just as Christians are joined to the Trinity through a faith and love manifested in the keeping of the commandments, they are joined to one another by observance of the new commandment of fraternal love. There is a convergence of the many different works of Jesus upon his one supreme work — the redemption and founding of the Church. We can find the same sort of convergence of the many different commandments given Christians upon the single overriding commandment of love; it corresponds in turn to the Father's command to the Son that he give his life for the world. Thus Calvary specifies the content of the command to love: What we must give for our brothers is our own lives.

The synoptics put the stress on the universal love we ought to display for our fellowmen, enemies included. John instead emphasizes the reciprocal love which ought to unite the disciples of Christ — a communion only to be found among God's people, possibly in function of a Eucharistic communion. Not that John envisions a ghetto; rather, he points to a basis in reality for the new love which is to be characteristic of this new people during the age of their separation from Christ: "Little children, yet a little while I am with you. . . . . Where I go you cannot come. A new commandment I give you, that as I have loved you, you also love one another" (13:33-34). The underlying concrete reality is a sharing in the bond of love which unites the Father and the Son: "That the love with which thou hast loved me may be in them, and I in them" (17:26). Far from making Christianity a closed society, this love is to be the principal means of its expansion. This love will be the mark by which the world will recognize in the Church the presence of Christ as envoy and Son of the Father. Unity and fraternal charity are built into the structure of the Church, and they also assure her development.

To understand the religious message of the author of the Apocalypse, it is extremely important to recall the burning issues to which he sought to offer a solution. These problems were two: one concerning the Christian-Jewish relationships, the other concerning the Christian-pagan conflict. Only the second will concern us here.

### Christian vs. pagan

In those days the pagan world for all practical purposes mean the Roman empire, since it was in this vast empire that Christians of that epoch had to live their lives. At first the Roman authorities were not unfavorable to Christianity; historically Rome had always been tolerant of religion. There was some little change with the burning of Rome in 64 A.D.; Christians were held responsible and so persecuted by Nero. But the definitive clash came only with Domitian's edict that divine honors be paid him during his lifetime.

This new cult met little resistance among the general population. What was one god more or one god less in those polytheistic times? The Jews had relatively little trouble adjusting; they easily got a dispensation from cultic observances contrary to their beliefs. For Christians, however, the situation was entirely different. They saw Domitian's edict as an act directly hostile to the religion of Christ, in fact an aping of it. Here was a simple mortal man acting as though he were, like Christ, an incarnation of the divinity, a Saviour to be worshipped by all men regardless of race or class. Christians reacted vigorously against this satanic notion. A constantly growing supranational religious body like the Christians could expect no such exemption as favored the Jews. So there immediately ensued a bloody persecution which with interruptions was to last a very long time.

It was toward the end of the reign of Domitian, when this persecution was at its height, that the Apocalypse was written. It laid down the line of conduct to be followed in the crisis: inviolable fidelity to Christ, true king of the world, resistance to the point of martyrdom against the totalitarian state which claimed to set itself up in place of God. The Apocalypse description of the fall of Babylon (pagan Rome) may not have been verified in every detail; but it certainly has held true in its general outline: A handful of Christians prevailed over the mighty empire of Rome. Today, when totalitarian states, armed with instruments of terrible destruction, threaten anew a frail and unarmed Church of Christ, there is no New Testament book so timely as the Apocalypse. It is in this context of imminent and tragic crisis that we must understand the author's conception of the age of the Church.

## Christ Lord of history

The age of the Church signifies principally and primarily *the presence in history* of the risen Christ. Unlike the wholly future-oriented Jewish apocalypses, John's book sees the parousia of Christ only in relation to his first coming. It insists that the summit of the world's religious history has already been reached, that salvation and victory over the powers of evil have already in principle been achieved. Christ, who has overcome by his blood all hostile powers, is an actual fact the risen and glorious king of the universe — the real and sovereign Lord of history. To sustain the Christians through persecution, the author emphasizes that it is not totalitarian despots who will decide the destiny of mankind. Only the victorious Christ holds the divine book of the elect; only he can open it.

## Christ the king

We have already seen in John's narrative of the passion a kind of epiphany of Christ the King. Jesus reminded Pilate that political power is limited by and subject to a higher transcendent sovereignty and power. If political power remains neutral, like Pilate, it invites its own destruction. The same points are made by the author of the Apocalypse; but his tone is, in the context of crisis and persecution, much more aggressive.

Scholars have remarked how similar in style are the letters at the beginning of the Apocalypse and the edicts of Domitian. A heavenly emperor is spoken of. He sends messages through ambassadors accredited to the Churches fighting for him on earth. There are the solemn imperial titles pointedly bestowed on Christ; sovereign among the kings of the earth (1:5), King of kings, Lord of lords (17:14; 19:16). We have the solemn description of the Lamb's enthronement and the extraordinary prominence given the royalty of Christ. Schutz has noted the almost exact correspondence between the titles applied to Christ in the Apocalypse and those applied to Domitian in Martial.

Essentially a manual of combat, the Apocalypse presents the age of the Church as a *time of terrible war between Christ and Antichrist.* Though the bitterest assault against the Church will not be unleashed until just before the parousia (20:7-10), the battle is already raging. True, the Serpent was mortally wounded when Christ vanquished him (cf. ch. 12), but he is still able to wield his unholy flail. This flail is described under the two symbols of the beast which rises from the sea and the beast which rises from the land.

## Symbols of paganism

The beast which rises from the sea (the West), of which the divinized emperor of the times was only a partial incarnation, is presented as a mockery of the Lamb. Its wounding and healing are a caricature of the passion and resurrection of Christ (13:3; cf. 5:6). Its enthronement by the dragon is a ridiculous parody of the enthronement of the Lamb. Its adorers are marked with a sign just as are the adorers of Christ and God (cf. 13:4, 16-17; 5:8-9; 7:2; 14:1). The beast which rises from the land (Asia) has a prophetical office; it puts its religious power at the service of the first beast. This symbol was doubtless conceived by John as an incarnation of contemporary philosophico-religious paganism, which accepted and advanced the cult of divinized despots. This second beast gives the tyrannical state its ideology and spirit; and there are good reasons to see in it, as Rissi does, a caricature of the Holy Spirit, who makes known the teaching and person of Christ the King. A third symbol (17–18) is the Babylon of the prophets, described as a courtesan of unheard-of power and riches, who leads nations astray by her wiles and seduces men with an illusion of eternal happiness: "I sit a queen, I am no widow, and I shall not see mourning"(18:7).

It should be noted that John, obviously describing the pagan Rome of his time, is in no sense driven by blind fanaticism. He appreciates and even in a certain fashion glorifies the grandeur of Rome. But he sees what no one else of his time saw — that Rome in all her splendor was headed for ruin. Christians needed his convincing presentation of Rome's imminent downfall to strengthen them in their terrible trials. He in fact anticipated all the other similar crises which would plague the Church throughout her future existence, supplying a corrective to naïve and infantile faith in a kind of automatic and continual progress. He foretold that the satanic beast would slaughter Christians, but at the same time he taught that it was by their immolation, not by military arms, that the martyrs of Christ would, as Christ did, vanquish the devil and his forces.

The philosopher of history studies the present *in reference to the past*. The author of the Apocalypse like the prophets of Israel explains his own times *in reference to the future*. He is well aware that present happenings can be properly understood only in the light of their eventual outcome. The prophet of Patmos showed how the contemporary trials of the Church — colliding with an omnipotent totalitarian state — fitted into a larger and divine plan. The terrible assaults of the ancient dragon were only the death throes of a creature already defeated and mortally wounded.

## Liturgy celebrates sonship

This second part of our study should include one final remark. Commentators have underlined the profound inter-relationships between the teaching of the fourth Gospel and the sacramental life of the Church. But the Apocalypse presents a liturgical character even more sharply defined. We have pointed out in an article in *Revue Biblique* (65 [1958] 5–32) how the twenty-four ancients or presbyters surrounding the divine throne are a kind of celestial prototype of the hierarchy of the Church. It is clear that the doxologies, acclamations, and hymns sprinkled throughout the Apocalypse are an echo of the liturgical Christian chants. It is *primarily in the liturgy* that the Christian expresses and celebrates his sonship of God and the permanent presence and action in him of the risen Christ and the Holy Spirit. It is in the liturgy that he becomes certain of his victory over the forces of evil. The first chapters of the book contain many of these wonderful promises: "Him who overcomes I will permit to eat of the tree of life . . . . To him who overcomes I will give the hidden manna" (2:7, 17; cf. John 6). "Behold, I stand at the door and knock. If any man listens to my voice and opens the door to me, I will come into him and will sup with him, and he with me"(3:20).

## The woman: Church or Mary?

Before concluding this sketchy study, we would like to say something of the symbol of the woman used in the fourth Gospel and the Apocalypse to represent the Church and to characterize the conditions of its present-day existence. In recent times much has been written about the woman in Apoc. 12. Some authors like to think that this symbol represents primarily or even exclusively the Virgin Mary. The references to the Old Testament (the Isaian texts on the glorified Zion giving birth: 66:7-8; 26:17-18; cf. Canticles 6:10) show clearly, however, that the woman of this wonderfully enchanting vision is the ideal Zion of the prophets who, once she has given Christ to the world, becomes the Christian Church. Like the people of the old covenant, she lives in the desert, protected and fed by God while awaiting the parousia (6:14).

If the Virgin Mary is seen here secondarily (and we think she ought to be, at least in the first verses of the chapter) this can be only as an incarnation of the people of God; in fact it is through her that the Church has given the Messiah to the world. As Mother of the Messiah, Mary is simultaneously the image of the Christian Church through which her Son is daily given to souls through preaching and the sacraments. Considering the woman as both militant and victorious, we cannot help thinking that it is chiefly through Mary that the Church is already triumphant in heaven. But while such a secondary Marian interpretation of the text is legitimate, we must be careful not to substitute our modern, anachronistic, individual conceptions of Marian piety for the essentially salvation-history point of view of the sacred author.

The fourth Gospel's narrations of the passion and the Easter Christophanies have as their main point that the Church is both the fruit of Christ's messianic work and the privileged setting of his subsequent saving action.

The scene (19:25-27) where Christ bids farewell to his mother is no exception. Even a Protestant like Hoskyns, however, does not hesitate to admit that here Mary stands for the Church, in perfect keeping with the spirit of Apoc. 12. Deprived of the sensible presence of Jesus, Christians will be loved by God as by the most gentle of mothers — and this because of the Church which Mary represents and which prolongs on earth the saving work of Christ.

The two Gospel texts — 20:17 (Magdalene) and 19:25-27 (Mary) — are fundamentally in harmony. They reinforce and complete one another in giving us a full picture of this decisive stage in the history of salvation which is called the age of the Church. We learn on the one hand that after the departure of Jesus the disciples will have as their Father the heavenly Father himself; on the other hand that they will have a mother while they remain on earth. This is the privileged life of Christians here below from the time of the ascension to the parousia.

# 8 THE NEW TESTAMENT AND THE MODERN WORLD

The great danger of modern religious studies—Biblical, liturgical, and dogmatic—is not that they are not sound, but that to most people, they are merely irrelevant. Father Charles Davis says: "When I read the recent work of the biblicists, the liturgists, the patristic scholars and dogmatic theologians, I am filled with wonder and delight at all they have to offer. But when I rush down the steps of the cultural museum in which they are found and enter the arena of the modern world, what they say seems curiously remote and sometimes pathetically irrelevant."[1]

This anthology of New Testament studies includes some articles of considerable length and difficulty, demanding effort from readers to understand what the Biblical scholar is saying. There is no way of eliminating this effort since such Scriptural concepts as the day of the Lord, body-person, redemption and being "in Christ," are fundamental to the renewal of our minds which enables them to receive the full impact of God's revelation in Christ.

But when all the effort has been made, we might ask with T. S. Eliot, will it have been worth while? Will we only have learned a new "Biblical" language which we cannot communicate to others? Father Davis states emphatically: "Biblical Theology, understood as the assembling and ordering of biblical data, cannot stand by itself. The biblical movement is not enough. It is a mistaken optimism in the modern world to suppose that it is."[2]

Beyond study, even beyond prayer and reflection, comes the work of inter-

[1] Charles Davis, *Theology for Today* (New York: Sheed and Ward, 1962), pp. 13-14.
[2] Ibid., p. 19.

preting the Christian message to an increasingly non-religious world. Some of the articles in previous sections of this anthology go beyond Biblical scholarship into the task of interpretation, of re-thinking the Word of God in terms of an age of science and technology, of political and social upheaval.

The final section continues the task of interpretation with two brief but important articles. For the message of Christ is a message of a Divine Person to human beings, and demands of them a personal relationship, not only of God to man, but of man to man. The word of God came to John the Baptist in the desert. It comes to us in our homes, offices, schools, factories, churches. "The word of God is living and efficient and keener than any two-edged sword, and extending even to the division of soul and spirit, of joints also and of marrow" (Heb. 4:12). It confronts us with divine power and with the divine vocation of being witnesses to Christ. But it also reassures us as we turn from the study of the word of God, to the work of the apostolate of His love: "I am with you all days, even unto the consummation of the world" (Mt. 28:20).

# ROLE OF WITNESS IN TRANSMITTING THE MESSAGE

Alfonso Nebreda, S.J.

## Introduction

The New Testament expresses the Lord's missionary command in three diverse ways. According to Mark, Christ said: "Preach the gospel to every creature" (Mark 16:16). Matthew expresses the command in the following words: "Go, therefore, and make disciples of all nations" (Matthew 28:19). Luke offers another formula: "You shall be witnesses for me" (Acts 1:8). Despite three modes of expression these texts are complementary. Christ's command is to announce a message (Mark) which aims at making disciples (Matthew) and which consists in bearing witness (Luke).

If we analyze the best record of primitive evangelization, the Acts of the Apostles, we will immediately detect how witness remains at the core of the transmission of the message. The Acts of the Apostles forcefully presents two types of witness: the direct witness of the apostles and indirect witness of the community and of individual Christians..The apostles witnessed by *word* under the strength and guidance of the Spirit:

> And when they had prayed, the place where they had assembled was shaken, and they were all filled with the Holy Spirit, and spoke of God with boldness (Acts 4:31; cf. 1:8; 4:19-20; 10:33).

In addition they witnessed by *signs* which confirmed the words:

> Now by the hands of the apostles many signs and wonders were done among the people. And with one accord they all would meet in Solomon's portice (Acts 5:12; cf. 2:43).

The persecutions accompanying such catechizing and especially the joy in accepting these trials belong intimately within this direct witnessing of the apostles.

> So they departed from the presence of the Sanhedrin, rejoicing that they had been counted worthy to suffer disgrace for the name of Jesus (Acts 5:41).

The indirect witness of the community, namely of those who obey the Spirit (cf. Acts 5:32) centers around the holy life, full of joy and charity, of the first Christians.

> And they continued steadfastly in the teaching of the apostles and in the communion of the breaking of the bread and in the prayers. And fear came upon every soul; many wonders also and signs were done by means of the apostles in Jerusalem, and great fear came upon all. And all who believed

Reprinted from *Pastoral Catechetics*, Johannes Hofinger and Theodore Stone, eds. (New York: Herder and Herder, 1964), pp. 67-84. Reprinted by permission of the publisher.

were together and held all things in common, and would sell their possessions and goods and distribute them among all according as anyone had
need. And continuing daily with one accord in the temple, and breaking
bread in their houses, they took their food with gladness and simplicity of
heart, praising God and being in favor with all the people. And day by day
the Lord added to their company such as were to be saved (Acts 2:42-47;
cf. 4:32-35; 5:12-16).

This is the way the message was transmitted. The apostles preached the life-
giving message and by it they were transformed. And the life of the Christian community confirmed this transformation by showing in action the meaning and power of the gospel.

Why is Christianity transmitted by witness? In order to understand the importance and implications of witness in today's transmission of the message,
we propose to look at the problem from the three major points of view
which constitute the frame of this book, namely *revelation*: God meeting
man; *faith*: man meeting God; and thirdly, the problem of *transmission*.

Being a missionary the author might be permitted to present the role of
witness mainly in terms of missionary approach. Today we seem to be at the
crossroads of a new missionary conception. The idea of missions is no longer
restricted to foreign and home missions. Instead the whole Church is looked
upon as being in the state of mission, in that she is to bear witness to Christ
everywhere among those who do not believe. So understood it is evident that
the mission of the Church does not limit itself to so-called missionary countries, but covers the whole field of pastoral activity in the world. Concentrating on a richer concept of Christian faith which goes beyond mere holding of certain truths of revelation to a personal commitment involving the
whole man, we are led to reexamine our pastoral methods among the many
Christians who, although baptized, have never been led to make such a personal commitment. The recovery of this personal characteristic of faith, of
which the Church becomes again more and more conscious through her missionary activity, is a constant reminder for pastors and catechists that special
attention must be given to preparing the ground for the message, taking into
account both the human elements for the faithful transmission of the divine
message and the concrete situation of man in his response to God. This will
be therefore the perspective from which we intend to examine the role of witness in the transmission of the message. Even in the case of *catechesis proper*,[1] which presupposes a personal global conversion, the main concern remains to stress the approach and ways of proceeding which help deepen that
conversion. Conversion, after all, must be a permanent dimension of Christian existence.

[1] Three stages can be distinguished in the process of faith. The following terms used in
this article and elsewhere in the book refer to these stages: *Pre-evangelization:* that stage
in the process of faith which prepares the ground for conversion. *Evangelization:* that
stage in the process of faith in which the kerygma is proclaimed. The person, already disposed, is challenged to accept Christ as the Lord and Savior. *Catechesis proper:* that stage
in the process of faith which presupposes conversion and belief. Religious education for
members of the Church commonly falls in this category.

## 1. Revelation: God meeting man

"Persons can be known only by revelation. We have no access to personal intimacy except through the free witness of the person. And persons do not witness of themselves but under the inspiration of love."[2]

It is against this background that we wish to explore the meaning of Christian revelation. God's revelation is not intended as cold information on a series of abstract truths. It is essentially the self-manifestation of his intimacy — the opening of his heart. Everything in Christian revelation can be summed up as follows: God reveals himself as the Father who in his Son through his Spirit invites us to share in his divine life. This is precisely what the theology of the New Testament, especially St. Paul, calls the mystery of Christ. The word mystery here does not mean a problem or a puzzle which baffles the intellect, stimulates and mortifies curiosity. It is a warm welcome inviting one to catch a glimpse of the intimacy of a *Person*.

More than by what we say do we reveal ourselves in our way of looking, in our tone of voice, in a gesture, in our whole behavior. The same applies to God. More than by his words he speaks to us through his wonderful deeds (mirabilia Dei), which culminate in his Word-Made-Flesh for us and for our salvation. Words have only a subsidiary role: explaining the sense of those deeds and especially the Person of his Son. In fact the content of revelation is but God's providential plan of salvation in Christ. And it is above all in realizing this plan that God reveals to us who he is and the communion to which he calls us.

Christianity then, centered and summed up in the mystery of Christ, is not a system, an objective interpretation of nature, a philosophy of life. It is essentially a message of salvation, the proclamation of the good tidings of God coming to us in Christ. No wonder that it can never be transmitted by mere words. Values cannot be taught: they must be shown as operative in an incarnate witness. Christianity in its ultimate analysis is a Person — Christ. We do not enter into contact with a Person through words or arguments but by a phenomenon of communion.[3]

This insight shows already the importance of Christian witness in the transmission of the message. Witness, involving the whole personality, places man on the level of personal relations. It forces the modern positivistic mentality, which tends to reject speculation on ultimate origins, to confront Christianity as a fact. It leads him to discover the radical difference between the realm of things and the world of human beings, giving him a sense of the person which will bring him to face God as Someone rather than as a Something. This thought introduces us to a discussion of faith as man's personal answer to God's call.

[2] R. Latourelle S.J.: "La revelation comme parole, temoignage et recontre," *Gregorianum* (1962), 48-49.

[3] This point as well as the personal structure of the act of faith has been masterly studied by J. Mouroux, *I Believe*, New York 1959. See also from the same author *From Baptism to the Act of Faith*, Boston 1963.

## 2. Faith: man meeting God

The following recounts one of the most interesting experiences of my eight-year stay in Japan. For several hours one day I had been discussing religious ideas with an old Buddhist bonze[4] of a Zen monastery not far from Tokyo, when I asked him: "How do you manage to convey to your novices your spiritual ideas?" The venerable old monk smiled. "Thus far," he said in a typically polite Japanese way, "I have been admiring the excellence of your Japanese. If I were blind, it would have been difficult for me to tell that you were not Japanese. And yet this question of yours, even if I had been blind, would have immediately told me that you were a westerner. How can you transmit a religious experience in words? Only by a spiritual contact, by 'rubbing,' so to say, two persons with each other, will the disciple perceive the message . . ."

Never have I been given closer insight into the biblical meaning of the word knowledge. Only by purifying our western intellectualist conception of knowledge can we grasp the all-embracing humanism of biblical anthropology.[5] Eastern psychology, in which the different faculties in man are not so sharply distinguished but merged and blended in a more global and inclusive operation, is certainly closer to the concept of Old Testament "knowing." It casts a remarkable light on the words of our Lord recorded by St. John: "Now this is everlasting life, that they may know thee, the only true God, and him whom thou has sent, Jesus Christ" (John 17:3).

As far as pastoral theology is concerned, the emphasis on a richer conception of Christian faith is perhaps the most significant result of recent research.[6] Also in the field of catechetics the awareness of this deeper concept of faith has brought about definite progress: this emphasis moves from the object (what to believe) to the subject (how faith affects the believer both in mentality and behavior), finally concentrating on interpersonal communion between the believer and God.[7]

These three levels belong essentially to the knowledge of faith. Faith must be objective since it is concerned with the facts and truths which constitute divine revelation. This is why catechetics implies a task of *instruction* or information. Faith demands acceptance of a new hierarchy of values. For this reason catechetics also involves the role of *formation* — shaping a man's mentality and behavior into a Christian personality. But faith is above all an entering into that personal communion with God to which divine revelation invites man. This last definition points to the highest task of catechetics: *initiation* into the mystery of God who acts in man and makes himself known in Christ living in his Church.

[4] Bonze: a Buddhist monk of the far east.

[5] Biblical anthropology refers to culture, customs, physical and mental characteristics, etc.

[6] See the works of F. X. Arnold, especially *Dienst am Glauben*, Frieburg 1948, and "Faith as Assent and Commitment," *Lumen Vitae* 2 (1956), 571-582.

[7] See M. van Caster S.J., "Teaching, Formation and Initiation," *Lumen Vitae* 9 (1956), 612-617.

The catechetical evolution during the twentieth century could give the impression that the above chronological order is the logical way of proceeding, as if information was the point of departure leading to formation, and finally blossoming into initiation or communion with God in Christ. And yet, as Father van Caster stresses, the reverse is more accurate. Contact with God is not to be found at the end of an impersonal instruction and an anthropocentric formation. There is not first a revelation of abstract ideas; on the contrary the "ideas are the result of reflection on the living knowledge accorded by God in a contact with Him . . . . As soon as the catechist really presents a sign of God, it is God making Himself known in this sign and introducing man into a dialogue with Him."[8]

The growing insistence on personalistic lines in present-day philosophies casts a significant light on the point we are discussing. There is a radical difference between knowing an object and knowing a person; and one of the saddest consequences of our technical civilization seems to be the blurring of this distinction and the tendency to objectify all our knowledge of persons. We are keenly aware and jealous of the unique characteristics of our personal indentity. And yet we feel the fundamental inadequacy of words and concepts to express this identity.

Words, being the common heritage of a given culture, become worn out by usage. Having to rely on words for our self-expression, we feel imprisoned in the tight and rigid enclosure which they force on us. If we were to describe adequately our personal feelings we would almost have to invent new words and expressions. This is why in moments of privileged self-consciousness or of deep personal emotions, words fail and we have to recede into silence.

The same inadequacy applies to concepts. We are justly proud of our power to reason and to build up universal concepts. This power constitutes the basic difference between man's way of knowing and the way inferior creatures know. And yet it is precisely here that our limitations appear. To know by abstraction is to siphon from unique concrete things common features which can then be applied to any individual, yet without being able to represent any of them in their striking originality. It is like the biologist wanting to analyze life by dissecting it. If this inadequacy holds true of any existing reality, how much more does it hold true of the most wonderous being — a person?

A person can never reveal himself or be known in mere words or concepts. Words and concepts will at most help in knowing about him, but "to know about a person" and "to know a person" are things basically different. We may have heard or read thousands of things about someone. But unless we meet this person we will not know him. A simple example may illustrate this point. Imagine a well known personality in the field of literature or science. Among his many students there is a brilliant young man who had studied under him for long years and has even written books on the

[8] Ibid. 613-614.

achievements of his master. Who knows better the thinker as a man: this brilliant student who possesses such a wide and deep amount of knowledge about his master, or the learned man's wife? And yet, if we ask the wife about her husband, she will most likely come out with a series of clichés and platitudes, and eventually be at a loss of what to say. But the fact remains that she knows her husband as no one else. Many years of intimate communion have given her an insight so deep and unique that it cannot be conveyed in words. In confronting human situations she will, by intuition, judge correctly about her husband's personality.

Meeting a person *as a person* thus implies an involvement wherein all the faculties of a man are opened in an effort to look at the other and understand the other as the other. Such involvement, which we might call "sympathy," "communion," "encounter," enkindles in man his latent powers of intuition and opens in him unused eyes which are essentially eyes of love. This is why, in dealing with persons, it is not accurate to say that knowledge brings about love. The reverse is more correct. It is love which brings about knowledge. And this is not only true of the person seeking to know, but also and especially of the person who is to be known. As we have stressed before, persons can be known only by revelation — through their free witness. But persons do not witness of themselves except under the inspiration of love. If a person is to be known as he is, he must feel that we approach him with an attitude of understanding. Otherwise he will instinctively refuse to show himself as he is, and we will be left with a picture of him which is, perforce, a caricature.

It is hardly necessary to stress how all this applies to the knowledge of God. One of the great intuitions of Cardinal Newman was the decisive role of the moral attitude of the seeker in the process of faith. We cannot understand justice unless we love justice; we cannot understand peace unless we love peace; we cannot understand a person unless we love the person. Father de la Taille has presented this truth in a beautiful way: "The light of faith, although residing in the mind, does not enter man through the mind but through the heart. There is its door of entry, there is the passage through which God pours it more or less abundantly, more or less alive, according as love itself lives in us beyond any other affection or, on the contrary, according as self-love dominates over or oppresses love of God."[9]

Now we perceive more clearly why we cannot attain even the level of true instruction (information) in catechetics unless the task of initiation is duly performed: stressing from the beginning the need of a spiritual openness which is to lead to true encounter with God. It is precisely here that the role of witness reveals its importance. Showing beyond words and concepts how faith affects and transforms a living man, witness focuses attention on the realm of persons. It invites, almost compels others to see this faith-in-action as an interpersonal relation between the witness and God. By its power of radiation it gently involves others in an atmosphere of religious con-

[9] M. de la Taille S.J., "L'oraison contemplative," *Recherches de Science Religieuse* 9 (1919), 279.

tagion where God is more deeply grasped as the Father who invites us to share his friendship and his life in Christ.

### 3. Witness: meeting point of man and God

God meeting man in revelation and man meeting God in faith are the two predominant mysterious lines which converge in Christian existence. And yet these two lines need a meeting point where Christian faith takes its birth. God could have provided otherwise; but he who has lovingly decided to need man decreed to make use of human mediation. St. Paul proclaims this fact: "Faith depends on hearing" (Rom. 10:17).

God adapts man from within so that he might welcome the word of salvation presented to him in historical mediations. His interior grace, "enlightening every man that comes into this world" (John 1:9), receives in scripture different names. It is called revelation (Matthew 11:25), attraction of the Father (John 6:44-46, 66), enlightening of the heart (2 Cor. 4:6), witness (1 John 5:10). But together with this interior witness there is a divine message presented in human words, expressing from without the call which the Spirit utters within man's heart. In Christ, the great Witness, the basic law governing the transmission of Christianity was promulgated. It is the law of the incarnation. In his Son-Made-Flesh God made clear again and this time in unique fashion how seriously he took mankind. Christ is as truly man as he is truly God. St. Paul has stressed the full implication of this guiding principle of Christianity: "Jesus, who though he was by nature God, did not consider being equal to God a thing to be clung to, but emptied himself, taking the nature of a slave and being made like unto men" (Phil. 2:6-7). The same law applies in the prolongation of the incarnation, by which the Word of God becomes flesh in a son of man to make him a Son of God. If God accepts the human word as channel of transmission, this means, by the same token, that he accepts the condition and dynamism of words: that they be truly human, that is, meaningful. This condition implies that we speak to man, not simply at him. This is the root of the transcendent importance of the work of pre-evangelization, bridging as it does the gaps in and preparing the ground for a truly human dialogue.[10] But the word alone, even if duly purified, is insufficient. Never before, perhaps, has man been made so painfully aware of the pitfalls of human words as he is now. We are confronted daily with a flood of words whose main purpose seems not communication between man and man but a distortion of what man actually thinks. The finest words have been abused to convey the most hideous realities. No wonder that modern man is incurably suspicious of ideologies and words.

But there is a total existential word, a word full of truth and free of ambiguities. It is the living word of the man — his whole life, his attitude toward things and persons. It is here that witness takes root and shows its de-

[10] See our *Distinguishing the Different Stages in Missionary Preaching*, Rome 1962, 23-26.

cisive importance, especially since that which is to be transmitted is not a theory of abstract and impersonal truths but a message of life, an ensemble of values all centered upon a Person and addressed to persons.

Within the trinitarian life — fountainhead of all Christian existence — we know the identity of the divine persons by the testimony each one gives of the other. We know the Father by the Son:

> The hour is coming when I will no longer speak to you in parables, but will speak to you plainly of the Father (John 16:25; see 3:11; 3:32-34).

Jesus is shown to us as the Son by the testimony which his Father gives to us:

> A bright cloud overshadowed them, and behold, a voice out of the cloud said, "This is my beloved Son, in whom I am well pleased; hear him" (Matthew 17:5; see Matthew 3:17; John 12:28).

The Holy Spirit is known by the testimony of the Son:

> But when the Advocate has come, whom I will send you from the Father, the Spirit of truth who proceeds from the Father, he will bear witness concerning me (John 15:26).

Christ stresses again and again that he is the witness of his Father:

> For I have not spoken on my own authority, but he who sent me, the Father, has commanded what I should say, and what I should declare. . . . The things, therefore, that I speak, I speak as the Father has bidden me (John 12:49-50).

The witness of Christ consisted in transmitting to man the truths which he has contemplated in the bosom of the Father:

> No one has at any time seen God. The only-begotten Son, who is in the bosom of the Father, he has revealed him (John 1:18).

This is the witness which must be prolonged by the Church. As Christ transmits to her what he saw and heard from his Father, so she in turn is to transmit what she saw and heard from her Lord:

> Even as you have sent me into the world, so also I have sent them into the world (John 17:18; see 20:21).

But the force of Christ's preaching resides in his works and in his whole personality more than in his words. The same applies to the Church. There are two ways by which she transmits her message: by her words (*verbal* evangelization) and by the witness of her life (*factual* evangelization). In both ways the same core of the message is proclaimed: the paschal mystery of the Lord — dead, risen and living forever. This mystery, as St. Augustine explains, can be considered either in the Head (Christ), as the apostles presented it, or in the body (the Church). The apostles saw Christ and believed in the Church. We see the Church and believe in Christ. The history of conversions shows that they start very often from experience of the paschal mystery in the encounter either with a true Christian or with a fervent community. Thus it is the factual evangelization (witness) which confronts man with the risen Christ.

Then and only then will the verbal evangelization have a meaningful impact on the mind and the heart.

According to Vatican Council I the Church is "the sign raised up to the nations." [11] And yet the image of the historical Church appears so distorted in the eyes of the unbeliever that one wonders whether it is a sign or a countersign. Looking as he does from the outside through spectacles colored with all sorts of prejudices, is it not only to be expected that the nonbeliever feels repelled by the facade of an institution which, at best, belongs to the past and very often is associated with dark and oppressive memories? For him only the small sign of a Christian making present and accessible at his own level the true meaning of the living Church will work the miracle. This is the power and tremendous responsibility of Christian witness: to prolong and actualize the witness of Christ in his Church.

Christ, the great witness of God, has within him the two essential ingredients of witnessing. He is both transcendent and immanent to his milieu. He belongs essentially to his people: he is a true Jew of his time; he thinks like a Jew, he speaks like a Jew, he eats like a Jew; he is a Jew. And yet he cannot be reduced to his milieu. There is something in him which points to his heavenly origin. He is a living reminder of God's greatness and goodness, the embodiment of the kingdom of God.[12]

The same ingredients hold true for the Christian witness. He must belong to his environment, be a true citizen of his nation and his time, love his people, love his times. Nobody should be able to denounce him as a stranger to any truly human enterprise. And yet, being in Christ, he will be a beacon revealing to his distracted fellowmen the reality and value of the true life hidden in the heart of the Father.

## 4. Witness in catechesis proper

If the main role of the catechist is to foster a true communion with God — to introduce God to man and man to God — it is obvious that the indispensable requirement for such a task is that the catechist know God and also be sufficiently acquainted with the man whom he wants to introduce. In catechesis proper everything should rest upon the global faith and conversion which was attained at the stage of evangelization. In the catechesis proper everything should be directed to a development of this same personal faith. More than a time for convincing or arguing, catechesis proper is the time for a truly religious atmosphere, breathing the pure, happy air of the Christian community. The tone of the instructions should be more akin to that of a good spiritual retreat than to that of a classroom. In a truly religious environment the student should begin to feel himself at home as he progressively takes part in the worship of the Christian community. In instructions the main emphasis should not concern an exhaustive treatment of every detail of the

[11] Denz., 1794.

[12] Yves de Montcheuil S.J. in his *Problemes de la vie spirituelle*, Paris 1945, 21-47, explains this concept beautifully.

creed and all precepts of moral observance; one should try, rather, to build up the Christian personality, that sense of Christ which the apostle extols.

Catechesis proper should indeed make full use of the biblical and liturgical signs. The word of God, incarnated in the bible, not only communicates divine revelation but also puts man in contact with the saving actions and power of God. However the saving actions of God, handed over in the bible to the Church, are not merely records of sacred history; they are made present and actualized in our midst through the sacramental signs of liturgy. It is in this context that the sign of witness should be incorporated and fully stressed. A subtle yet forceful use of the lives of saints, an intelligent use of the growing literature of conversion, will help personalize and interiorize the Christian message in a fashion perfectly adapted to the psychology of the students. Yet, the all inclusive immediate witness will be the religion teacher himself. The religion teacher will show what it means to be a true Christian in today's world by what he is more than by what he says.

To be a Christian is not just to keep a series of laws — to go to Mass on Sunday, or to refrain from meat on Friday — so that one will be "in line." A Christian is not "in line," he is *in Christ*. In the Son of God he has become a new creature; he has entered a new life — a life of faith, hope and charity. He is one who cries with St. Paul: "I live in the faith of the Son of God who loved me and gave himself up for me" (Gal. 2:20). In everything the Christian tries to see the hand of God.

The Christian knows and confesses himself to be a sinner because, as St. John so forcefully declares: "If we say that we have no sin, we deceive ourselves, and the truth is not in us . . . . If we say we have not sinned, we make him a liar, and his word is not in us" (1 John 1:8-9). But he remains basically a man of hope, who acknowledges in deep gratitude that he has been saved by the merciful power of God in the blood of his Son (see 1 John 1:7).

The Christian is above all someone who knows God, one who loves him with his whole heart, and with his whole soul, and with his whole strength, and with his whole mind, and his neighbor as himself (see Luke 10:27), because "he who does not love does not know God; for God is love" (1 John 4:8). He is the man who sees God in everybody and everybody in God.

Finally the Christian is one who knows himself to be a living cell of the wonderful organism the body of Christ, and who feels himself involved in the responsibility of collaborating to make it healthier and to grow into "the mature measure of the fullness of Christ" (Eph. 4:13).

If such is the catechist, then everything which he has to say will carry the weight of his Christian witness. His students might forget what he says, but the image of what he is will accompany and guide them in their journey through life.

## 5. Witness and the nonbeliever

If witness is so important at the stage of catechesis proper, in a sense its role is even more decisive in the first approach to the nonbeliever. Witness is truly the core of pre-evangelization. It will be worth remembering that many of our baptized youngsters and adults, so far as their commitment in faith is concerned, are at a level where they require a thorough pre-evangelization before they can be led to a real conversion which will turn their notional assent into a real adherence to God in a personal communion.

When we consider therefore that the difficulties which hinder the dialogue with the nonbeliever are not so much merely intellectual problems, but rather total, existential prejudices which set us as persons in a doubtful light and a suspect position, we realize that what we are, or seem to be, counts for much more than what we merely say. Against such prejudices there is no power in mere words. The nonbeliever's opinion is anchored to his prejudices; our words will not budge it. If *we* are a doubtful quantity, anything that comes from us will be equally suspect. There is no other way to communicate with the nonbeliever than to wait patiently until our witness, that is, the weight of our whole personality, shines through our deeds and words warmly enough to melt away the prejudices.

Collective witness must surely be used whenever possible. But this supposes the existence of a Christian community so radiant that it touches the life nerve of the nonbeliever. If the community witness is not strong or bright or wide enough to reach sufficiently into the lives of those who approach us for the first time, then we ourselves must be the incarnation of the witness of Christ. If we were to describe the basic character of Christian witness, we would say that it results from the sense of God, the sense of the mystery of man and the sense of our own misery, these senses all blended into a conscious religious attitude.

## Sense of God

God is not an object but a most personal Being who constantly obliges man to break the mold of his tiny conceptions, for God does not let himself be imprisoned in any category. Reverence for the mystery of God must shine through every glance, every gesture, every word of the Christian who wants to welcome the nonbeliever in truth. His whole personality must radiate a permeating sense of the divine majesty, the transcendence of grace and God's mysterious working within him. Moreover he must be a sincere and admiring ambassador of divine discretion which respects the sanctuary of a conscience created free by the Almighty:

> Behold, I stand at the door and knock. If any man listens to my voice and opens the door to me, I will come in to him and will sup with him, and he with me (Apoc 3:20).

Even from a psychological, human point of view, who can tell the beneficial effect of such reverence in the dialogue with a man who in the darkness gropes for the passage leading to a mystery as yet dimly perceived? When such a reverence does not remain merely at the level of human relations, but is the spontaneous fruit of a deeply religious sense of God, it can constitute the first spark which suggests something beyond this world, unsettling man and attracting him to the mystery of God.

## Sense of Mystery of Man

This sense of mystery is a logical consequence of the sense of God. No man is an island closed upon himself. Rather he is a sponge, little by little impregnated by God — a creature of God's love, carrying in his every cell the image and likeness of his Father who makes him capable of knowing and loving in order to beatify him with his own happiness, to make man his son in his Son. The mystery of human liberty demands a special meditation on the part of the Christian witness. The mystery of liberty, hallowed, accepted and contemplated in the mystery of God who wants man to be free and who communicates with him in utter delicacy and discretion, is the natural complement of the mystery of divine grace at work in the depth of human conscience. Mystery of grace, mystery of conscience — these words suggest what reverence and respect should constitute the climate of a true Christian witness.

God does not ignore the history of a man, his past, his social, psychological conditioning, his culture, his environment. It is precisely here that God wants to incarnate his word as a living and actualized prolongation of his substantial Word who once "was made flesh and dwelt among us" (John 1:14). Amid the bafflement and indecisiveness of a man's life, the Lord works in him with a constancy and patience which reveals infinite love, so that he may finally take possession of this heart immersed in its human conditions.

## Consciousness of one's own misery

In an authentic religious experience, awareness of one's own misery is the very reverse of the sense of God. This is a precious indispensable element, one belonging to the attitude of a true Christian witness. Even though a man knows himself as messenger of God he understands that he will never be God's plenipotentiary. God is too jealous to yield his prerogatives to anyone. But if God, being as he is the Creator and Almighty, respects to such an extent the free will of his creature, what should be said of him who remains a poor servant and a sinner? The humble image of John the Baptist, true ambassador, comes to mind: "He must increase, but I must decrease" (John 3:30). If Christ the Lord calls himself and willingly behaves as "servant of Yahweh" how much more must be the Christian who is conscious of his poverty and sins?

As a corollary to our reflections on the mystery of the sense of God, it would be good to remind ourselves that we do not *possess* truth, since truth is God and God is not a thing to be possessed, but a Person. It is more true to say that we are *possessed* by Truth, to the extent that we go out of ourselves to make room for Love — to the extent that we enter into communion with God and "practice the truth in love" (Eph. 4:15). The well known biblical attitude of the "poor" (*'anawim*), growing from a deep sense of the grandeur of God and an awareness of one's own lowliness, could serve as the best description of a true Christian witness.

A man habitually breathing the air of the three elements described above will not find it overly difficult to find the correct approach in his dialogue with the nonbeliever.

## Sympathy and understanding

The problem here, more than one of merely suggesting practical rules or techniques for the dialogue with nonbelievers, is above all one of sensibility, of spiritual insight so that we might establish harmony in our relations with another soul. At the outset the primary task of witness is not to impart knowledge or to correct erroneous consciences. Rather it is a time to allow another to discover in the warmth of a sympathy full of respect and veneration something of God's love which will be a seed of the greater revelation of God's goodness and kindness. Thus, existentially, witness develops its proper dynamism and begins to take root. The secret is to attain in depth a spiritual agreement of hearts. In the atmosphere built up by the sense of God and the sense of the mystery of man, such a communion will spring spontaneously. This will lead the witness first to *accept* everything good which is to be found in the other's situation, not only what appears on the surface but even what lies hidden to the other's consciousness. The first response to sympathy on the other's part will come through of itself when he feels well wishing eyes and a loving regard being directed toward him in an honest effort to do him justice — when we accept without ambiguity or paternalism whatever is good and noble in the man's life. It is this desire of justifying others from within as far as possible which best characterizes the approach of the Christian witness to the nonbeliever. "Justify from within" means a sincere effort to put oneself in the other's place, to try to see things through his eyes, to feel with the other's heart. Here also we must remember an elementary fact of human psychology: if we love it is not primarily because we understand; but we understand because we love. This understanding, indispensable climate of a welcoming witness, issues only from a sympathy which is already the fruit of love. This is why we have to purify continuously our own witness and try to look at man through the eyes and heart of God the Father. Only by loving as God loves will we succeed in discovering, even in someone aggressive and hostile, the amiable features of a person who was made by Love to love.

Although we may justify the other beyond what the actual situation would allow, positive fruits will accrue, fruits of truth, loyalty and softening of attitude. Now is not the time to discuss, much less to refute or correct; it is not even time to teach. It is rather the time to bear witness to the Love of God and the basic goodness of man. As for things which cannot be justified an understanding and discreet silence will suffice.

Thus when the other sees himself welcomed, and finds in us an echo full of goodness and openness, he will feel in turn a gentle but imperative invitation to understand us. The circle of mutual understanding is now complete. From its center, more existentially experienced than intellectually perceived, will blossom forth the promise-filled discovery: God is good and invites man to open his heart to love.

# THE CHARITY OF CHRIST

Barnabas M. Ahern, C.P.

We were a group of eight seated at a dinner table, seven close friends and myself. The scene was a beautiful home in the white section of a typical northern American city. Eventually conversation turned to the mushroom growth of negro housing, that inevitable theme of conversation wherever white people gather together. This time, as almost always, views and judgments were sharpened by personal experience of displacement from old homes and flight to new safe areas. Every word threw sparks and spread fire. The heat of hatred was oppressive.

All my companions were well-trained, practising Catholics, people who had always counted charity a duty, who had given regularly to worthy causes, and who had probably regretted and confessed words and deeds against charity. The new negro problem, however, seemed to them completely outside the ambit of charity as they understood it.

For them, as for many modern Catholics, charity is a practice, one virtue of many which a christian must exercise. Too many have forgotten that charity is the whole meaning of christian life, "the fulfilment of the law." [1] Since Christ's words required love for one another as a sign of discipleship, we need to study again the meaning of his charity, and to see how completely it inspired his whole earthly life. Only then will we understand that the love which he requires of his disciples is the very spirit in which he himself lived, the life which his chosen must share.

## Christ, brother of all men

Perhaps the root of misunderstanding lies in the catechism answer to the question: Who is Christ? The ordinary Catholic answers immediately with the timeless response, He is God, the second person of the Trinity, who became man to save us from our sins and to lead us to heaven. This answer is correct; but it is still far from the whole truth. Christ became man, it is true, but not a person with a vague, general and abstract manhood. Rather he became a very definite man like ourselves, so truly one of us that the complete definition of the incarnate Word must present him as God who became the man Jesus, our brother.

Pubished originally in *The Way* (31 Farm Street, London W.1), Vol. 4, #2 (April, 1964), 100-109. Reprinted by permission of the publisher.
[1] Rom 13:8.

It is always in this way that he appears in the living language of sacred scripture. One of the most revealing words he ever uttered was his command to Mary Magdalene after his resurrection: "Go to my brothers and say to them." [2] Paul, on the way to Damascus, heard Christ identify himself with every christian, "Saul, Saul, why do you persecute me? . . . I am Jesus whom you are persecuting." [3] For the apostle, Jesus is the elder brother of the whole christian family, "the firstborn among many brothers." [4] It is, above all, the author of the epistle to the Hebrews who loves to linger over the bond of flesh and blood which makes the God-man a real member of the whole human family. [5] Pondering the intimate union of Christ with all men, the sacred author thrills with love and pride as he cries out, "He is not ashamed to call them brothers." [6] All the love and solicitude and compassion which an elder brother feels for the younger children of the family are but a faint image of the charity which Christ feels toward us.

His whole being reflected as perfectly as a human heart can the boundless expanse of the heavenly Father's love for us. The tender yearning and infinite care which God manifested for his people in the days of the old covenant found its perfect human expression in the heart of Christ, the God-man, our brother. In him, St. Paul writes, "the goodness and kindness of God our Savior appeared." [7] Because "God is love," [8] his Son, on entering the human family as our brother, pledged his whole existence to the fulfilment of that simple will which governs all God's dealings with us: love. For the first word of Jesus in becoming incarnate was the heartfelt cry, "Behold, I come . . . to do thy will, O God." [9]

At that moment the Son of God became a brother to every human being; and from that moment he carried them all in his human heart. He would fulfil God's promise in a way surpassing all Isaiah had dreamed of: "Even to your old age I am the same, even when your hair is grey I will bear you." [10]

The conviction of what incarnation meant for him was with him from the beginning of his earthly life. He who was God assumed flesh and blood to live as a brother to all men, and to die that he might take them with himself to the bosom of the heavenly Father. This Father was the very one who sent his divine Word into the world to reveal by word and deed the height and depth of God's love. "By sending his Son in the likeness of sinful flesh," [11] God made Jesus like a prodigal son, living in the "far country" of wayward men, that in and through him, all prodigals might one day return to the Father's house.

## The inaugural vision

Christ's intuitive knowledge of his mission was transformed into a totally human experience on the day when baptism inaugurated his public ministry.

[2] John 20:17.
[3] Acts 9:4-5.
[4] Rom. 8:29.
[5] Heb. 2:9-18; 3:6; 4:14-16; 5:13.
[6] Heb. 2:11.
[7] Tit. 3:4.
[8] 1 John 4:8.
[9] Heb. 10:7.
[10] Is. 46:4.
[11] Rom. 8:3.

Coming up out of the waters of the Jordan, he received a vision which fired his whole human consciousness with an awareness of all that life upon earth involved. "The Holy Spirit descended upon him in bodily form as a dove, and a voice came down from heaven, Thou art my beloved Son, in thee I am well pleased." [12]

For those who know the Old Testament, every word of this description is alight with revelation. Men of the old covenant looked forward to the messianic days when the creative Spirit of God would pour out his best gifts to form a new Israel, beloved of God. Those days had now come; the Spirit, "descending and abiding" upon Jesus, would enable him to bestow the best of all God's gifts, to baptize all men with the Holy Spirit. [13]

Even more, he himself would be the new Israel, incorporating in his humanity and enfolding in his love all those who, through faith in him, would become true Israelites. Though a distinct person like every man, Jesus was also, in some way, one person with all men; scholars call this rich mystery of his being "corporate personality." Through his God-given love for men and his divine power to save them, he embodies every man in himself, and is bound to them with a tie which no power in heaven or on earth can sever: "Who shall separate us from the love of Christ?" [14] At the Jordan, then, God speaks to his Son in the very words which he once addressed to the ideal Israel, his perfect servant: "Thou art my beloved Son, in thee I am well pleased." [15]

This inaugural vision pervades the whole earthly life of Jesus. Isaiah's vision of the all-holy Yahweh in the temple dominated every prophecy he uttered; Jeremiah's first contact with a merciful God intimately touching his lips fills the whole message of his prophecy with tenderness; Catherine of Siena's early vision of Christ the high priest inspired her with lifelong love of the pope, *"il dolce Cristo in terra,"* the sweet Christ on earth. So, too, the first vision of Jesus struck the keynote of his whole ministry. Ever after he would move among men with full awareness of his intimate bond with them. As brother with brother, he would make them the new Israel by sharing the fullness of his own beloved sonship: "To as many as received him, he gave the power of becoming sons of God." [16] For this he had come: to love all men as brothers and to unite them to himself, that in him and through him, the new Israel, they too might live as beloved sons of the Father.

Later, at the time of his transfiguration, the vision was repeated. Here, however, a new emphasis was added. There was to be no limit to his love, no bounds to his labour and efforts for men. Having loved his own who were in the world, he must love them even to the end. [17] Therefore, when the baptismal vision came again, a new note appears. Now Moses and Elijah were with him; and they "spoke of his death, which he was about to accomplish in Jerusalem." [18] Jesus, as the perfect servant of Yahweh, must fulfil the prophecy of Isaiah that the one who represents and embodies all Israel

[12] Luke 3:22.
[13] John 1:33.
[14] Rom. 8:35.
[15] Luke, 3:22; cf. Is. 42:1.
[16] John 1:12.
[17] Cf. John 13:1.
[18] Luke 9:31.

shall himself die, in order that his brothers may live. Only in this way will God's saving love find fulfilment: "The will of the Lord shall be accomplished through him . . . Through his sufferings, my servant shall justify many, and their guilt he shall bear." [19]

## The spontaneity of Christ's charity

Brotherly love: strong, solicitous, selfless; this was truly the inspiration of all that Christ did and said. This charity was vitally active, always taking the initiative to enter intimately the lives of all whom he met. Constantly aware of the bond between himself and every man, this loving brother forged new friendships with spontaneous interest and affection. In our own day, Mother Marie Thérèse de Lescure, who died as Superior General of the Society of the Sacred Heart, surprised the religious whose houses she visited by her overflowing joy in meeting people whom she had never seen before. Asked for an explanation of this instant reaction, she smiled and answered, "Do we not bear within us the love which the Sacred Heart has for them?" These words were but a modern translation of the cry of St. Paul, "The love of Christ impels us." [20]

Christ's charity, the very source of his followers' zeal, was alive with this spontaneity of love. He it was who took the initiative in calling his first disciples. The opening chapter of St. John's gospel [21] describes his first meeting with John and Andrew, Peter, Philip and Nathanael. His bearing and his smile and his seemingly artless question, "What is it you seek?," prompted in John and Andrew the query which Jesus knew would lead to lifelong friendship, "Rabbi, where do you live?" [22] With Peter the forthright, Christ's initiative was more direct. Here Jesus spoke the first word to master instantly the strong fisherman, "You are Simon, the son of John; you shall be called Cephas." [23] He takes the same initiative with reluctant Nathanael, breaking down all reserve by revealing his deep insight into the young man's whole soul: "Before Philip called you, when you were under the fig tree, I saw you." [24]

All during the days of his public ministry, Christ's charity led him constantly to take the first step in winning new loyalties. The widow of Nain was not even aware of his presence. Knowing that grief and gratitude would prepare both mother and son to love God in fellowship with him, he came out of the shadows and spoke a single word. At once hearts were opened to the light of a new faith in God and in himself. To the mother he spoke kindly: "Do not weep," and to the son, commandingly: "Young man, I say to thee, arise." [25] Their lives would never be the same again. This abrupt encounter with the spontaneous charity of the God-man brought them to know him and his Father in a new way, to anticipate with living awareness the definition of God which John would formulate later: "God is love." [26]

[19] Is. 53:10-11.
[20] 2 Cor. 5:14.
[21] John 1:35-51.
[22] John 1:38.
[23] John 1:42.
[24] John 1:48.
[25] Luke 7:13-14.
[26] 1 John 4:8.

This spontaneity of Christ's charity is the whole meaning of the recurring *cliché*, "Jesus, having compassion." Especially in the gospel of Mark this phrase is frequently inserted as the single reason for his deeds of mercy. Before men were even aware of his presence, he saw their need and, moved by pity, came forward to help them. His initiative is shaped to the character of each person he meets. When men like Zaccheaus felt stirrings of desire for his friendship, he acted instantly to speak the word of invitation: "Zaccheaus, make haste and come down; for I must stay in thy house today." [27] At other times he would check his spontaneity in order to achieve his loving purpose. His conversation with the woman at the well of Samaria [28] reads like a stanza from Thompson's *Hound of Heaven*, with the hunter patiently pacing his quarry, until at last she is ready for true love.

The charity of Christ is always vital and spontaneous. He had entered the human family as a brother, to turn the hearts of his brethren to their heavenly Father. On every occasion and in every way, openly or secretly, he launched the initiative and took the first steps. For he had come to spread the fire of God's love upon earth, and his whole desire was to enkindle it.

## The completeness of Christ's charity

In this lifetime task he never lost sight of the fact that he was living on earth among men of flesh and blood. "For, of course, it is not angels that He is succouring; but He is succouring the offspring of Abraham." [29] When he dealt with men, therefore, he knew that his charity must deal with the whole man, a composite of body and spirit. There were occasions, it is true, when his work of charity was on the purely spiritual level. But preaching and instructing and forgiving sin were only part of his ministry. Quite as much of his time was taken up in feeding the hungry, in curing ills, and in ministering to bodily needs.

For Jesus, all this activity was an exercise of messianic mercy. He was a brother to human beings and loved each one in his wholeness. Christ, who is the God-creator of man, could never think of benefiting him with a cure which would touch only the body. Whatever he did for man physically was bound to change the whole man, bringing health to the body and new life to the soul. When he gave sight to the blind, he enabled them not only to see trees and men, but also to glimpse the goodness of God with new understanding. When he gave strength to withered limbs, he empowered men not only to walk upon earth but also to take new giant strides in serving God. When he raised men from the dead, he not only brought them back to life upon earth, but also vivified them with the life of a new love for the Father.

Jesus was not one to distinguish between spiritual and corporal works of mercy. The miraculous deeds of the divine Word were themselves words proclaiming to men that love of God which enfolds their whole being. In our own day devoted doctors and solicitous nurses, in bringing health to tired and wasted bodies, invigorate the whole man with new joy and peace. They are

---

[27] Luke 19:5.            [28] John 4:1-42.            [29] Heb. 2:16.

truly carrying on the messianic mission of Christ; and in their ministrations we can see how his miraculous activity was not merely a proof of who he was, but also a full manifestation of the messianic love with which he desired to fill the hearts of all his brothers. This is why St. Matthew sees in the cures of Jesus the perfect fulfilment of the salvation which the Messiah was to bring to the whole world. Having alluded to the miracles of the Master who "cured all who were sick," Matthew declares that Jesus worked these wonders "that there might be fulfilled what was spoken through Isaiah the prophet, who said, He himself took up our infirmities, and bore the burden of our ills.[30]

## The realism of Christ's charity

The "burden of our ills," however, was heavier than a merely physical weight. The burden of sin pressed down on every human life. The presence of the Son of God upon earth did not instantly lighten the burden; for, even after his coming, men would still subscribe to the words of St. John, "If we say that we have no sin, we deceive ourselves, and the truth is not in us." [31] Christ, therefore, found himself in the midst of prodigal sons; his was the superhuman task of bringing them back to his Father.

He took it for granted that the law of his life would be struggle, that his charity would often be thwarted and misunderstood. The failings of his brothers often wrung from the heart of Christ a cry of anguish, "O, you of little faith." But never did human failing or human sin surprise or shock him. Men of his own day could not understand the freedom with which he moved among publicans and sinners. Even in our own time men marvel that Christ, the all-holy, never registered shock in the presence of moral ugliness. He is constantly serene in the presence of men and women whose behaviour repels an ordinary good man. The simple truth is that he was the God of whom the psalmist wrote, "He knows how we are formed; he remembers that we are dust." [32] He dealt with men just as he found them. "As a father has compassion on his children," so this Lord had compassion on those he had come to save.[33]

This unruffled peace of true love made him free to use all the devices of charity which prudence put at his command. With a mind clear of prejudice and a soul untrammelled by the unruly emotions of human weakness, he was ingenious in all the exercises of charity. If kindness and encouragement would win the wayward, he would be kindness itself. No intemperate zeal ever led him to break a bruised reed or to extinguish a smoking wick.[34] If, on the other hand, a situation called for remonstrance and rebuke, Christ could lash the offender with words which laid bare faults that otherwise would fester in their hiddenness. No wrath could be so fearful as that of the gentle Lamb of God when sham and hypocrisy had to be unmasked. Even the evangelist whom Dante has called "the scribe of the meekness of Christ," like all the

[30] Matthew 8:16-17.
[31] 1 John 1:8.
[32] Ps. 102:14.
[33] Cf. Ps. 102:13.
[34] Cf. Matthew 12:20.

other evangelists, has reported in his narrative the vitriolic words which Christ spoke to the Pharisees.[35]

Christ, was truly "all things to all men." His love for them was the strong and realistic love of a devoted older brother. He worked with them just as he found them, shaping his every act of charity to suit their immediate needs.

## The hopefulness of Christ's charity

In his dealing with men, however, Christ always looked beyond what they were to what they could and should be. True love always has double vision. It sees the loved brother in his present condition; but it sees too all the good that life holds for him. Hence "charity believes all things, hopes all things," [36] and works constantly to achieve perfect fulfilment.

He had unshakeable confidence in the task of love which had been given to him. He had just as much confidence in the power of man, his brother and God's son, to respond to the Father's love. In the heart of everyone of them Christ knew that "hope springs eternal." Like Nicodemus, they might not see clearly what life could be; Christ would illumine them, tempering the light to their present weakness in order to strengthen it for new insights. Like Zaccheaus, they might seem outside the pale of God's acceptance; Christ would enter into the very intimacy of their lives to convince them how fully God could live there. Like the apostles they might walk the treadmill of their own half-heartedness; Christ would rebuke and encourage and constantly urge them on to the future which he knew was theirs for the asking. No matter how often he failed to make men advance, he ever remained confident that just around the corner in every man's life are those "good works which God has made ready beforehand that we may walk in them." [37]

No one ever had so much confidence in what man could be, because no one has known so well the riches of God's mercy which alone makes man all he should be. He who dwells in the bosom of the Father is always aware of that love without limit which can turn stones into children of Abraham.[38] Christ, as God and man, shared this love, so that he himself was all love, and all hope for every man whose simple "Yes, Father," would open his heart to the powerful love of God "with whom all things are possible."

## Charity unto the end

There were, then, no limits to the charity of Christ. Because he was so sure of his Father's love for men and because, as a devoted brother, he shared this love in the most perfect way a human being can, he was ready to do everything to bring them all, in and through himself, to their Father in heaven.

In a sense he failed; no matter how hard he tried, some men refused to say "yes." "He came unto his own, and his own received him not." [39] But love knows no thwarting; even death cannot quench it. His death, in fact, would spell love's ultimate triumph. He was so much one of us, so truly our brother,

---

[35] Luke 11:37-52.          [37] Eph. 2:10.          [39] John 1:11.
[36] 1 Cor. 13:7.            [38] Cf. Matthew 3:9.

that in his return to the Father he must bring all men with him. No matter what terrors death held for him, he saw clearly the certainty of this final triumph; "And I, if I be lifted up, will draw all things to myself." [40] Once safe in the bosom of the Father, our brother would be powerful to send into the world the very Spirit of God, thereby filling men's hearts with the love which he had laboured to put there. And so, "having loved His own who were in the world, He loved them unto the end," [41] not merely to the end of his human life but to the perfect fulfilment of love's ingenuity.

The story of his final sufferings, written in letters of blood, provide the world's most eloquent commentary on St. Paul's description of perfect love: "Charity is patient; . . . bears with all things . . . endures all things." [42] Love sealed his lips against recrimination; love prompted him to speak words of gratitude to the women of Jerusalem, words of pardon to the penitent thief, words of prayerful pleading for his brothers: "Father, forgive them for they know not what they do." [43] But it was in death itself that he accomplished his greatest act of love. At that moment, like the true Israel returning to the promised land, he left the desert of our world, bearing all men within himself to the heavenly country where his Father waited. Ever after, through the gift of his Holy Spirit, he would fill the heart of each prodigal son with his own love; and would lead him, as a beloved brother, through the experience of his own death and resurrection. "In this we have come to know his love, that he has laid down his life for us." [44]

## The impelling charity of Christ

"And we likewise ought to lay down our life for the brethren." [45] This is the only possible conclusion for one who knows the charity of Christ, not merely as a series of practices to be imitated, but as the very life which each christian receives through the gift of Christ's Spirit at baptism. Charity is a whole state of mind; it is a connatural movement expressive of Christ's life in us; it is the very fruit of the Holy Spirit dwelling in our souls as he dwells in the soul of Christ.

It is well to end where we began: in the dining room with friends and in the discussion of the negro problem. Problems like this one, problems with people and situations, problems with superiors and subjects, problems with persons poor in gifts and poor in virtue: all these have their only answer in the charity of Christ. His love for all men is a light which enables us to see each one as a brother. His love is a power which strengthens us to deal with each as someone who belongs to the family of God; who therefore has a right to love which is "patient and kind, thinks no evil, bears with all things, hopes all things, endures all things." [46]

The spontaneity, realism and completeness of Christ's charity in us makes life not only liveable but lovable. It turns every meeting into a family gathering; it makes every service and every deed of kindness the helping hand of a

[40] John 12:32.     [43] Luke 23:34.     [46] 1 Cor. 13:4-7.
[41] John 13:1.     [44] 1 John 3:16.
[42] 1 Cor. 13:4-7.     [45] 1 John 3:16.

brother assisting a brother along the way to God. Christian life thus becomes a warm and beautiful experience. The fervour of the first days of the Church lives again as men cry out, "See how these Christians love one another." Those who seek God spread peace and joy around them, for they know only one rule of life: "The Charity of Christ impels us." [47]

[47] 2 Cor. 5:14.

# INDEX

## A

Abraham 49, 51, 69, 96, 155, 191, 193, 197, 238, 241, 246, 249, 251, 274, 339, 384ff., 388f., 395, 426f.

Acts of the Apostles 16, 91, 94, 96, 100ff., 122, 185, 192, 195, 206, 235, 274, 347, 356, 463f.

Adam 51, 103f., 111, 193, 299, 365f., 375, 423, 434

Adam, new 330ff., 341, 347, 374ff., 400, 408

*Agape see* Charity

*'Anawim* 68ff., 207f., 474

Angels 60, 216, 321, 327, 333, 345, 371f., 422, 445ff.

Antioch 119, 190, 195, 196, 236, 238

Apocalypse 99, 109, 237, 317, 340, 342, 437ff.

Apocalyptic literature 102, 182, 299f., 307, 439ff.

Apocryphal books 55, 58ff., 247, 308f.

Apostles 66, 97f., 119ff., 124f., 127ff., 166, 172, 182, 264, 454

Apostolic preaching 91ff., 97, 99ff., 112, 127ff., 135, 153, 155f., 161, 166ff., 178ff., 198, 201, 241, 272, 277

Aramaic Matthew *see* Matthew

Archaeology 7f.

Augustine, St. 34, 175, 211, 264, 298, 342, 353, 447f., 470

## B

Babylonian captivity 49, 70, 93, 441

Baptism 15, 63, 88, 92, 97, 102, 104, 110f., 159, 172, 176, 293, 361, 375, 384, 401ff., 412, 478, 483

Beatitudes 123, 186, 211, 349

Bethlehem 48, 71, 194, 200ff., 233, 246ff.

Bible *see* Scripture

Biblical commission — *Instruction on Biblical Research*, (April 21, 1964) 128f., 353

Biblical criticism 21ff., 127, 139ff.

Biblical theology 5ff., 143, 200f., 461f.

Blood 84, 174f., 243, 293, 315, 323, 325ff., 341, 363f.; of Christ 163, 174f., 177, 315, 326f., 359ff., 454; of New Covenant 163, 175, 359ff.; of Old Covenant 84, 175, 359ff.

Body, Mystical *see* Mystical Body of Christ

Bride *see* Spouse

Buber, Martin 239

Bultmann, Rudolph 45, 104f., 131f., 140, 143ff., 272, 390, 399

## C

Cana 282f., 304, 340ff.

Catechesis 16, 27, 128, 466ff., 471f.

Chanaan 6f., 93

Charisms 33, 361, 420

Charity 87, 122ff., 218ff., 275f., 289, 294, 303, 313, 324, 365, 454, 456, 465, 474ff., 476ff.

Christ, divinity of 109f., 111ff., 116ff., 160f., 181f., 198, 246, 348ff., 372; glory of 42f., 76f., 110f., 116ff., 162ff., 169f., 172, 191, 199, 277, 282ff., 319ff., 329ff., 346, 431f., 453; Head of the Church 114, 118f., 412ff., 470; in prophecy 50ff., 102f., 107; king 53f., 100f., 190f., 226, 231ff., 330f., 336f., 457f.; life and light of the world 74, 284ff., 312ff., 333; the Lord 95, 100, 108f., 111ff., 121, 160, 162, 165, 233, 282, 385, 449ff., 457; the Prophet 188f., 220, 241, 255, 272; Savior 123, 332ff., 359ff., 374ff., 434ff.; Son of God 51, 53, 113, 115, 118f., 121f., 160, 161, 164, 181, 188, 191, 210, 228, 232, 233, 245, 250, 259, 261, 265, 293, 331, 349, 360, 375ff., 454, 476ff.; Son of Man 50f., 53ff., 64, 102, 107, 115, 160, 164, 169ff., 191, 245, 270, 274ff., 293, 312, 320, 328f., 331, 347, 441, 451; Wisdom of God 79, 83, 420; Word of God 80, 279ff., 286, 340

Christian community 66, 92, 96, 104, 131, 150, 206, 212, 247, 272, 352, 452f., 463f., 473

Christian life 379ff., 403ff., 424, 470ff.

Church 16, 18f., 36f., 38, 88f., 94, 111f., 118f., 125f., 135, 148, 152, 192, 199, 245, 294f., 303, 312, 407ff., 417, 452ff., 459f., 464, 471; and Gospels 16f., 134ff., 148, 150, 178; founded on Peter 125, 264, 267; new Israel 94, 111, 347, 478; primitive 16, 27, 91f., 94ff., 104ff., 119ff., 123ff., 131ff., 178, 180, 183f., 199, 236f., 238, 245, 442; spouse of Christ 38, 83, 237, 341ff., 414ff., 451f.

Colossians, epistle to 66, 185f., 355f., 371f., 411, 414, 423, 432ff.

Commandments 218, 222, 454f.

# J

Jerusalem 99, 102, 119, 182, 187, 188, 199, 202, 221, 224ff., 238, 249, 272, 320, 441
Jerusalem, destruction of 7, 54, 124, 224f., 234, 236, 241, 282; the new 235ff., 449ff.
Jesus *see* Christ
Job 11, 77
Joel, prophecy of, 100, 109, 117, 285, 298, 311
John the Apostle 63f., 277ff., 344ff., 442; epistles of 66f.; gospel of 17, 66f., 79, 80, 94, 102, 116, 122, 147f., 176f., 262, 277ff., 452ff., 479
John the Baptist 51, 58, 61, 63f., 71, 97, 120, 123, 180f., 189, 198, 200, 209, 225, 241, 266, 274, 304, 317, 318, 342, 474
Jonah 12, 23f., 257
Joseph (foster-father of Jesus) 200, 225, 251, 255
Josephus Flavius 54, 57, 59f., 310, 340
Judah 57, 224
Judaism 16, 45, 62, 85, 308, 370ff., 385ff., 391ff.
Judas Iscariot 94, 105, 304, 332ff.
Judgment 115, 245, 295ff.
Justice 67, 84, 123, 295ff., 363, 386ff.
Justification 67, 116, 385ff., 475

# K

*Kerygma see* Apostolic preaching
Kingdom of God 110, 118, 120, 123f., 152, 178, 210, 212, 224, 238, 241, 259, 448, 450
Kingship 9, 49, 191, 232, 330f., 337, 454

# L

La Grange, M. J. 252, 263n.
Lamb *see* Paschal Lamb
Law of Moses *see* Mosaic Law
Light-darkness dualism 62, 64, 67, 277f., 332ff.
Literary forms *see* Forms, literary
Liturgy 35ff., 74f., 135f., 163f., 177, 458f., 461
*Logia* 135f., 240, 307
Logos *see* Christ, Word of God
Lord *see* Christ
Love *see* Charity
Luke, gospel of 19, 94, 102, 134, 136, 178, 184ff., 213ff., 218ff., 223, 224ff., 227f., 306, 463

# M

Magdalene, Mary, 344ff., 348, 454, 477
Magi 246f., 250ff.
*Magnificat* 71
Mark, gospel of 97, 101f., 133ff., 151f., 153ff., 161ff., 166ff., 174ff., 186, 227, 232, 253, 261, 463
Mary, Blessed Virgin 71, 185, 187f., 199, 200, 252, 281, 340f., 459f.
Mass, Sacrific of *see* Eucharist
Matthew 240; Aramaic 180, 238, 240, 243; gospel of 24ff., 64, 101f., 134, 174f., 200f., 227, 230, 238ff. 246ff., 299, 463
Mediator *see* Christ
Melchisedech 24
Messiah 24f., 51ff., 60f., 64, 70, 95, 100, 107f., 111ff., 113, 115ff., 118f., 121, 166ff., 181f., 226, 233, 247, 250, 261, 265ff., 290, 337, 343, 349, 365, 385, 441, 452
Messianic kingdom 52ff., 71, 91, 118, 120ff., 232, 365
"Messianic secret" 153, 158f., 162, 178, 182
Midrash 24, 72ff., 148f., 248ff., 307
Miracles, in John 283, 307; in Synoptic gospels 114, 127, 135, 158, 166f., 170, 187, 241, 254ff.
Mosaic law 9, 69, 84, 86, 96, 195, 219, 245, 280, 307, 317, 322, 325, 362, 386, 389
Moses 8f., 43, 76, 93, 95, 188, 191, 227f., 248, 251, 322, 328
Mystical Body of Christ 88, 111, 118, 176, 294f., 397ff., 407ff.

# N

Near Eastern literature 8f., 244
Negeb 57

# O

Old Testament, background for New Testament 5ff., 43, 45, 47ff., 112f., 127, 193, 198, 201, 208, 224, 228f., 251, 279, 283, 290, 329, 415, 441, 450

# P

Papias 153, 155, 180, 238, 240, 260
Parables 11, 150ff., 156, 167, 181, 187, 213ff., 219ff., 232, 241, 259
Parousia *see* Second Coming of Christ
Paschal Lamb 102, 233, 316f., 321ff., 339, 342, 365, 451, 458, 481
Paschal Mystery 102, 270ff., 316ff., 343ff., 367ff., 374ff., 470
Passion of Christ 101, 103, 114, 122f., 162f., 170, 171, 182, 188, 226ff., 232, 234, 241, 257, 270, 272f., 305, 312ff., 319ff., 328ff., 343, 359, 454, 458
Passover 102, 194, 262, 316ff., 320, 333, 339, 342, 367ff., 376f.
Paul 35, 63, 67, 96f., 103, 106, 119f., 155, 175ff., 180, 184, 185, 193, 195f., 209, 236, 238, 247, 270f., 298f., 313, 351ff.,